THE

METHODIST CHURCH PROPERTY CASE.

Report of the Suit of

HENRY B. BASCOM, AND OTHERS,

vs.

GEORGE LANE, AND OTHERS,

HEARD BEFORE

THE HON. JUDGES NELSON AND BETTS, IN THE CIRCUIT COURT, UNITED STATES, FOR THE SOUTHERN DISTRICT OF NEW-YORK, MAY 17-29, 1851.

BY R. SUTTON,

SPECIAL AND CONGRESSIONAL REPORTER.

Richmond and Louisville:

PUBLISHED BY JOHN EARLY,

FOR THE METHODIST EPISCOPAL CHURCH, SOUTH.

1851.

ADVERTISEMENT.

This Report, which was agreed upon by both parties to the suit, is published, with their common sanction, by the Book Agents at New-York and Richmond.

CIRCUIT COURT, UNITED STATES.

FOR THE SOUTHERN DISTRICT OF NEW-YORK.

THE Hon. JUDGES NELSON and BETTS, Presiding.

HENRY B. BASCOM, and others,
vs.
GEORGE LANE, and others.
} *In Equity.*

Counsel for Plaintiffs,
Mr. D. LORD Hon. REVERDY JOHNSON, and Mr. JOHNSON, Jr.

Counsel for Defendants,
Hon. RUFUS CHOATE, Mr. GEORGE WOOD, and Mr. E. L. FANCHER.

FIRST DAY.—Monday, May 19, 1851.

Mr. Lord.—May it please your Honours,—In opening a case of this magnitude and importance, I feel that it is incumbent on me to give a brief detail before reading the papers, in order that these papers, and the whole subject, may be more easily understood. In our ordinary controversies we need no such preliminary; but we are now investigating the concerns of a religious denomination, and this controversy will relate to matters which are not of general information. The Court, therefore, will indulge me in the endeavour to state some of the general facts and circumstances out of which the controversy arises, particularly with the view of having an accurate definition of the subjects which will constantly recur in the reading of the papers.

The subject of this controversy is what is called, among gentlemen of this denomination, their "Book Concern." This is a fund which, upon the papers, appears to amount to some $750,000. The origin and history of it seem to be this:—Upon the earliest establishment of the Methodist denomination by Mr. Wesley, he called to his aid the press in the dissemination of religious truth; and when Methodism was first introduced into this country, books were provided from England, to supply the wants of its very few adherents in regard to religious literature. Upon the independence of this country, the Methodist denomination had become measurably numerous, though not large. When it was organized as a separate Church, in addition to the means of instruction afforded by preaching, it was very obvious that a great want was to be supplied in the furnishing of religious literature to its people; and one of their preachers organized a system of publishing books in this country. It was originally established in Philadelphia. This preacher, whose name I think was Cooper, lent a small sum of money to the object, and invested it in books. They were sold among the denomination; and out of the profits a small capital was gradually formed, which was employed in publishing books. This came to be a matter of some magnitude; and in the year 1836 it had been removed to this city, and become an extensive establishment. It had undergone considerable vicissitudes; but at that period it was emerging from its difficulties, and becoming a great establishment. It was then destroyed by fire. It was afterward reinvigorated, as everything in this city seems to have been by the fires of that period; and from that time to the present it has gone on with great prosperity, so that it has accumulated a capital of about $750,000.

The manner in which these books were circulated will perhaps be worthy of your Honours' attention in the history and consideration of this case. It was early provided that the preachers should see that their congregations were supplied with books. They took the books from the publishing establishment, and sold them: and in that way there was in fact a real, substantial, and beneficial monopoly in the furnishing of religious books, and all the preachers were agents in carrying it out. They were very faithful men—stimulated, not by the love of gain, but by the higher purpose of religious devotion. Of course, a fund thus constructed could not but become very considerable. Your Honours will have your attention called to the fact that it was really the result of the devotion and services of the preachers. It was not, like many charitable funds, a fund growing out of donations of wealthy men; but it was, in its main features, the earnings of this system. Its profits, after providing capital enough to carry on its business successfully, were devoted at an early period to one single purpose in two or three branches:—That purpose was, the making up of the deficiencies in the salaries of travelling preachers, and providing for the supernumerary, superannuated preachers, the wives and children of preachers, and the widows and orphans of deceased preachers. The number of these appear regularly on the Minutes of the General Conference of this society. That, therefore, was the destination of the profits of this fund; for it was no object to accumulate capital for the mere purposes of accumulation.

It is now necessary that I should introduce another subject—the conferences of the Methodist Episcopal Church—because they become very important, vitally important, to be understood in this controversy. The concerns of the Methodist Church are managed by what are called Annual and General Conferences. At the introduction of Methodism into this country, its preachers were not very numerous. Although the extent of country was great, there were in all but seven annual conferences. I ought, perhaps, to explain what the annual conferences are. Originally all the preachers of this denomination met every year, and disposed of that which was general in their concerns. The conferences consisted of travelling preachers, who served particular districts of country, somewhat analogous to the division of districts in our judicial system. Originally the whole of Methodism in the United States was but one conference, and consisted of but a small number of preachers. In 1784 that was the case. But it very soon became necessary to divide this conference. It was divided; but, although a division, in fact it was a multiplication also. At first the annual conference was in fact the General Conference of the Methodist Church; then the earliest formed from this were the Philadelphia and New-York Conferences. As the territory increased, these annual conferences were divided, and formed new bodies; until in 1844, which is the period at which we shall arrive, there were something like thirty-two or thirty-three annual conferences. These annual conferences had a general oversight of the Churches; they examined the character of the preachers, the working of the system, and reports were yearly made to them of the deficiencies of the funds raised in the districts to supply their preachers. Every two years preachers were changed from one congregation to another. Collections were taken up in these various congregations to supply the preachers. Their salaries were very small; the people, to a great extent, poor. Many of these districts could not quite pay their preachers. These deficiencies were reported to the annual conferences, and supplied out of their funds. That will show your Honours what we mean when we come to speak by-and-by of the "deficiencies" of the travelling preachers. That means the deficiencies in funds supplied by poorer congregations to pay their own preachers; for it is a part of the economy of this Church that the richer portions of the country should supply the wants of the poorer, and the clergy always be kept on a footing of absolute equality. Every four years these annual conferences met in a General Conference. This General Conference was the general legislative body of this Church, and all matters of general concern were there considered. They established articles of religion; they made changes in the religion and economy of the Church. Every year when they separated, they published a new book of discipline, which contained the doctrines of the Church, and that superseded everything which had gone before, and became the law of the Church as to organization, discipline, and doctrine. This was therefore the act of the Church in the most absolute sense. This was the state of things from the organization of Methodism in this country in 1784, up to 1808. In 1808 the body had become so numerous, and its power was so absolute, that the more conservative men in the Church were a little alarmed at the extent of it; because it will appear in its history that it was considered capable of changing the articles of religion, and it was considered dangerous that such a body, which might be attended by more members from nearer, and less from more distant conferences, should have such great powers. In 1808 a change was made in the organization of the General Conference. They resolved that the General Conference should consist of delegations from each annual conference. It was, therefore, the general body of the Methodist Church, met together in the form of its ministers, but only by committees. Instead of being a meeting of the whole absolutely, it was a meeting of the whole by delegations. At that period provision was made against the absolute power which this body possessed, and there were various "restrictive rules," so called, established to limit it. Those restrictions were to this effect; and the extent of the powers of that body, as it existed before, and, indeed, as we say, continued to exist, will appear by the character of these restrictions. Our view of the powers of that body is, that they were equally unlimited with those of previous General Conferences, except so far as these restrictions restrained them. One of the restrictions was, that they should not change the articles of religion; another that they should not change their hierarchy; another, that they should not change the degree of representation. That is, supposing the delegation be one out of every eight in the annual conferences, that ratio should not be changed by the General Conference. Another was, that they should not change what were called the rules of the United Societies. The United Societies are ecclesiastical organizations of the members of the Churches, with rules which govern them in their relations with one another, with the world, and in regard to religious observances. It was provided that the General Conference should not make a change with regard to the mode of trial of members and preachers; and the last, the sixth restrictive rule, (which is the one which will most come before your Honours' attention,) provided that they should never apply the profits of this Book Concern to any other purpose than that of supplying the deficiencies of the travelling, and providing for the supernumerary, superannuated preachers, their wives and children, and the widows and orphans of such as were deceased. There was one provision over-riding the whole—that upon the request of three-fourths of the annual conferences, sanctioned by a vote of the General Conference, these restrictive rules might be varied, but without this primary vote of the Church they could not be changed. That presents to your Honours the subject of the general and annual conferences; and a great question in this case will arise upon the character and power of the General Conference, and the instruction and effect of that sixth restrictive rule.

I now come to the particular controversy in this case. It is one in relation to which the excitement at this time and in this country is great. It grew out of the existence of slavery. Very early the Methodists, both on the subject of temperance and of slavery, took a ground, the highest and most exclusive; and one of the rules of the United Societies (which are the particular, and private, and domestic organizations of Churches composing the denomination) was, that no person should belong to them who bought men and women with the view of reducing them to slavery. As we suppose, that originally had reference to the slave-trade as a matter of commerce which was then carried on. But very soon it was evident that this Society viewed it in a larger aspect, and in one of the earlier conferences a rule of a very extreme character was adopted. It was at a conference which began at Baltimore in December, 1784, which is known as the "Christmas Conference." They adopted a rule quite exclusive on the subject of slavery, not merely as to the buying and selling of men and women, but in the most severe form and manner, compelling the manumission of slaves. That threatened to become so destructive to the Society, in its attempts to penetrate the Southern and Western parts of the country, which were considered the most open fields for the operation of the Methodist principles, that at the first meeting of the conference afterwards, the very next year, the rule was suspended, and in the next book of discipline it was omitted. From time to time rules were adopted in this Church, sometimes of a more stringent, and sometimes of a more lax character, on the subject of holding slaves. The Church, North and South, always considered slavery an evil; that is, that it would have been better if no such thing had ever existed. They, however, treated it as one of the evils among them, and conformed their religious discipline on the subject to the laws of the various States; so that it was declared that no person should hold any office in the Church who did not manumit his slaves, when the laws of his State permitted it. If the State did not permit it, the holding of slaves was not to be a subject of official or personal reproach. They provided also that their preachers should teach the members of their Churches to instruct their slaves; showing that they took the practical view of this as a thing to be dealt with as existing, and which it was not in the power of any man, or body of men, clerical or lay, by their wishes to destroy.

About the year 1836, the agitation, which has been called "abolitionism," began in this country. In 1840, it began seriously to disturb the peace of the Methodist Church. In that year a case arose from one of the Baltimore Conferences, which gave very serious concern and alarm to the conservative members of the General Conference; and the bishops and conference, in their action on it, gave it what I would call a "go-by." They avoided dealing with it in its strength, and expressed conservative and soothing opinions, recommending to all the avoiding of any agitation of so destructive and distressing a question. From that time until the meeting of the General Conference in 1844, this agitation raged among the Northern and North-Western conferences, and had, of course, produced a reaction at the South. In 1844, the thing became exceedingly rife, and presented itself in the General Conference of that year in a form which was decisive. And it will be one of the objects of the papers which we shall read, and the argument we shall present, to show that a state of things occurred which made necessary the separation of this Church into two parts.

It seems that the Baltimore Conference, which lies on a line between the North and the South, took ground with the more ultra persons in the North. There was a preacher named Harding, who, by marriage or inheritance, acquired one or two slaves which, by the laws of Maryland, he could not emancipate. This circumstance was brought very early to the attention of the General Conference of 1844, in connexion with a vast number of petitions from New-England, Western New-York, and other places, on the question of slavery. It came up in an appellate form. The Baltimore Conference had suspended this clergyman, degraded him, in fact, on account of this connexion with slavery. It was in vain urged that his connexion with the slaves was such that he could not manumit them.

Hon. Reverdy Johnson.—In fact they were not his.

Mr. Lord.—The Conference determined that they would degrade him for that connexion, though the slaves were not his. He appealed to the General Conference, and there the question was discussed with great animation and great ability, and the sentence of degradation was confirmed.

The matter, however, then took a still graver aspect. One of the bishops, a gentleman of Georgia, was in a somewhat similar position. He had one slave left him, on condition that he should liberate her and send her to Liberia, with her consent. But she would not go to Liberia, and the bishop remained her owner. She lived where she pleased, but still remained legally a slave; and, as it was said, she might have been sold for his debts, and he made liable for her support. He also, through inheritance from a former wife, had a slave whom he could not manumit. Also upon his second marriage, his lady had some slaves which he could not manumit; indeed they were secured to her by marriage settlement. This was his connexion with slavery. In every other respect he was blameless. Everything estimable was conceded to him. But the spirit of agitation was rife; it had been warmed up in the Conference by the debates on the Baltimore case; and nothing would do but that this bishop should be dealt with. But it was a matter of some delicacy to deal with the bishop. Should he be tried? for there was a provision for the trial of bishops; and if he should be tried and condemned, he would not only be degraded from the episcopacy, but expelled from the Church. They did not venture to go against this man in that way. A course was taken which, if this had not been a religious body, sincerely adherent to religious principles, (however, we may deem them mistaken,) would have been regarded as debasing. I will not characterize it otherwise than as a queer sort of proceeding. They resolved to request Bishop Andrew to desist from all action as a bishop, during the existence of his connexion with slavery; which was very much the same as if Congress, or any body that should assume to itself such an office, should say that one of your Honours venturing to take a little wine at dinner should be requested never to act as judge until you chose to abstain. In other words, without a crime which could be tried, on a matter of mere expediency they requested this bishop to cease to be a bishop. And it was followed up by several circumstances at that Conference, unintentional I am persuaded, which gave effect to this degradation, and which are rarely to be seen in such cases.

It seems that after every General Conference they republished their Discipline, Hymn Book, and some publications that were of a character to be renewed. It was put, as a question, What should become of the name of Bishop Andrew? Should it be put in the Hymn Book? The vote of the Conference was that it should; so that in every Methodist congregation there should appear to the children, while turning over the leaves of the Hymn Books as their parents were singing, the name of Bishop Andrew. The question would be, What is the matter with Bishop Andrew? In that way, unintentionally, this degradation was made in the most conspicuous manner in which I think it could be. At that period there was a new election of bishops, and when other Reverend gentlemen acted in the consecration, Bishop Andrew, who was on the spot,* a man of unblemished character, against whom no shadow of imputation rested, was excluded; at least, having been requested to suspend his duties, he could not with decency act.

This, as your Honours may see, was the declaration of a permanent purpose, which it was very evident to the gentlemen of the Southern Conference, prevented them from prosecuting in harmony the objects which the Church had in view—as they define it—the spreading of Christian holiness over these lands; for it was evident, these principles being assented to, that this Church must be extinct in the Southern States. The gentlemen from the Southern States made a declaration to the Conference of 1844, that such would be the effect of these measures being taken. They also made a protest, which will be presented and read, giving very fully their views on this subject. That protest was followed by a reply on the other side, which gave the views of the majority. That, I presume, will also be laid before the Court, and you will see whether or not there had not arisen a state of things in which, as the delegates of the South expressed it, the Church was already divided. This became apparent to some gentlemen of wisdom in that Conference; and it was moved to appoint a committee for the purpose of determining whether there could not be a division of the Church into two bodies, so that they might go on separate from each other, in pursuit of the same objects, with the same organization, only, as a Methodist writer, an English gentleman, expressed it, "Whereas this year it was the province of Canterbury, next year it might be the provinces of Canterbury and York." A plan of division was presented, underwent discussion, and was adopted by a large vote. It was in substance this:—That if the Southern conferences should find it necessary, they might organize themselves into a separate and independent Methodist Church at the South, and in that event commissioners were appointed to deal with regard to the distribution of the funds. That was made the occasion, in connexion with the constitutional scruples of some gentlemen, of the question, whether they would have a right to give to the Southern body of the Church their share of the Book Concern without an alteration of the restrictive articles. A provision was made that this fund should be divided, if the sixth restrictive article was changed, and a ratio of division was provided, and commissioners were appointed on the part of the Northern Church to act with commissioners from the Southern Church to carry this division into effect. They then separated. On the separation, the gentlemen from the Southern conferences immediately presented the subject in a general address to the Southern conferences, giving them the details of what had happened in the General Conference, and asking the Southern conferences to take up the question and say whether they found it necessary to form an independent body or not. The fifteen or sixteen Southern conferences—sixteen, I think, there were—all united in voting that it was impossible to go on with the Northern gentlemen in this state of things; that the only way of retaining the existence of the society in the South, was by establishing a separate organization. They elected delegates to meet at Louisville in 1845, by whom this measure should be considered in general council. The Convention of 1845 adopted a plan of a Southern organization, and appointed a General Conference of the Methodist Church, South, to be held in 1846. They adopted every article of religion, every article of doctrine,

* This was afterwards shown to be a misapprehension of the counsel as to this fact.

everything of discipline, and the organization of the Church, as held by the Northern Church. Indeed, they took the established Book of Discipline, and printed it anew, with the same mode of representation, and in every respect the two were identical, except that the General Conference, instead of being one, was now divided into two. They appointed commissioners to deal with commissioners from the Church, North, with respect to the division of the common fund. When these commissioners assembled, this state of things met them: the commissioners of the Northern Church had been overtaken by scruples as to the constitutionality of that thing, and refused to treat at all. The commissioners of the Southern Church deferred until their Conference of 1848 met, which determined, after the Mississippi style, that the Conference of 1844 had no power to enter into this plan, and that the Northern Church was the only Church; and that the plan of the Southern Church, which had really been formed at the invitation of the General Conference of 1844, was null and void, and that by that very organization they had all become seceders; that is to say, these fifteen or sixteen conferences had ceased to be members of the Methodist Episcopal Church at all. They adopted an additional rule, which, I confess, always seemed to be one which nothing could sanction, that the supernumerary and superannuated preachers, the orphans and widows of preachers, as well as travelling preachers of the Southern Church, should not partake of this fund which had been earned by their common services, and which was provided originally as a reward to those who could work no longer, for their past services. I can understand, and have often seen in these controversies, that when the connexion is broken, it would be a misappropriation of a fund, devoted to the spreading of certain religious truths, to apply it to the propagation of different principles, carried on by a different ecclesiastical organization; but I have not, to this moment, been able to understand how the orphans and widows of the preachers, the old men and supernumeraries of that Southern Church, should be excluded from participation in a fund which they, and their fathers, and husbands, had earned. I have not been able to see how it is possible that they can be shut out from it by that which has taken place, even if our friends on the other side should be right on the subject of secession.

We now claim in behalf of these Southern conferences, that this fund shall be divided as to the beneficiaries.

We also suppose it must be divided as to the trustees. But that is another question. It may remain in the hands of the same trustees and the beneficiaries in the Southern country be entitled to it; but I suppose that if we are right, your Honours will say, that the Southern Conference, under the circumstances, has an equal right with the North to appoint the trustees—the persons by whom it is to be distributed; that not only should they be entitled to the profits of the fund, but also to a division of the capital, and to appoint the trustees to manage the capital, or that they should be appointed by your Honors or nominated by the Southern conferences. This is the whole question before us. It is a grave question, undoubtedly, in its amount and interest, reaching not only to this fund, but, so far as I can see, to the stability and title of every Methodist parsonage or preaching-house in the Southern country, because, they all being established for the benefit of the Methodist Church, if this is secession, I do not see but that the Methodist Church is exterminated altogether in the Southern country.

If your Honours please, I will now call your attention to the Bill and the Defendants' Answer.

The bill is filed in the name of commissioners, who have been appointed by the Southern Church, and who are preachers entitled to be beneficiaries of this fund. One of these commissioners has died since his appointment, and we propose to render the proceedings perfect in respect to this demise by substituting, by assent, the name of another gentleman who has been duly appointed his successor.

The parties to the bill are "Henry B. Bascom, a citizen of Lexington, in the State of Kentucky; Alexander L. P. Green, a citizen of Nashville, in the State of Tennessee; Charles B. Parsons, a citizen of Louisville, in the State of Kentucky;"—these were travelling preachers, and they were entitled to a share of this fund; then there are "John Kelly, a citizen of Wilson County, in the State of Tennessee; James W. Allen, a citizen of Limestone County, in the State of Alabama."—these are supernumerary preachers—"and John Tevis, a citizen of Shelby County, in the State of Kentucky," who was a superannuated preacher. Your Honours will see, therefore, that we have all the classes of beneficiaries, except the widows and orphans.

The defendants are George Lane, Levi Scott, George Peck, and Nathan Bangs, citizens of the city of New-York, who are the persons that have in charge this "Book Concern," and it is due both to them and to ourselves that I should say that they have not participated in the heat to which this case has given rise, but have deemed it necessary to remain inactive, until their course shall be pointed out by the determination of this suit. Of their proceedings we cannot complain, nor can they be spoken of but with respect.

In their bill "the Complainants state and show to your Honourable Court, that before and on the 8th day of June, 1844, there existed in the United States of America, a voluntary Association, known as the Methodist Episcopal Church in the United States of America; not incorporated by any legal enactment, but composed of seven bishops, four thousand eight hundred and twenty-eight preachers belonging to the travelling connexion; and in bishops, ministers, and membership, about one million one hundred and nine thousand nine hundred and sixty,—then being in the United States, and territories of the United States, united and holden together in one organized body, by certain doctrines of faith and morals, and by certain rules of government and discipline.

"That the general government of the Methodist Episcopal Church was vested in one general body, called the General Conference, and in certain subordinate bodies, called annual conferences, and in bishops, and travelling ministers and preachers; and the great object of the said Methodist Episcopal Church was the diffusion of the principles of the Saviour of mankind—good morals, pure religion, piety, and holyness, among the people of the world. And the complainants allege, that the constitution, organization, form of government, and rules of discipline, as well as the articles of religion and doctrines of faith of the Methodist Episcopal Church, were of general knowledge and notoriety, nevertheless, for the more particular information of the Court, they refer to a printed volume, which will be produced on the trial of the cause, entitled 'The Doctrines and Discipline of the Methodist Episcopal Church.' And the complainants allege, that differences, and disagreements having sprung up in the Church, between what was called by the Church the Northern and Southern members, upon the administration of the Church government, with reference to the ownership of slaves by the ministry of the Church, of such a character, and attended with such consequences, as threatened fearfully to impair the usefulness of the Church, as well as permanently to disturb its harmony; and became and was with the members of the Church, a question of very grave and serious importance, whether a separation ought not to take place by some geographical boundary, with necessary and proper exceptions, so as that the Methodist Episcopal Church should thereafter constitute two separate and distinct Methodist Episcopal Churches. And thereupon the complainants allege, that at a General Conference of the Church, holden, according to usage and discipline, at New-York, on the 8th day of June, 1844, the following resolutions were duly and legally, and by a majority of over three-fourths of the entire body, passed; which resolutions are herewith copied, and prayed to be taken as part of this bill, which are in the words and figures, to wit:—

"'Resolved, by the delegates of the several annual conferences, in General Conference assembled, 1. That should the annual conferences in the slave-holding States find it necessary to unite in a distinct ecclesiastical connexion, the following rule shall be observed with regard to the Northern boundary of such connexion : All the societies, stations, and conferences adhering to the Church in the South, by a vote of a majority of the members of said societies, stations, and conferences, shall remain under the unmolested pastoral care of the Southern Church ; and the ministers of the Methodist Episcopal Church shall in no wise attempt to organize churches or societies within the limits of the Church, South, nor shall they attempt to exercise any pastorial oversight therein ; it being understood that the ministry of the South reciprocally observe the same rule in relation to stations, societies, and conferences, adhering by vote of a majority, to the Methodist Episcopal Church ; provided also, that this rule shall apply only to societies, stations, and conferences, bordering on the line of division, and not to interior charges, which shall, in all cases, be left to the care of that Church within whose territory they are situated.

" '2. That ministers, local and travelling, of every grade and office, in the Methodist Episcopal Church, may, as they prefer, remain in that Church, or, without blame, attach themselves to the Church, South.

" '3. Resolved, By the delegates of all the annual conferences, in General Conference assembled, That we recommend to all the annual conferences, at their first approaching sessions, to authorize a change of the sixth restrictive article, so that the first clause shall read thus, "They shall not appropriate the produce of the Book Concern, nor of the Chartered Fund, to any other purpose other than for the benefit of the travelling, supernumerary, superannuated, and worn-out preachers, their wives, widows, and children, and to such other purposes as may be determined upon by a vote of two-thirds of the members of the General Conference."

" '4. That whenever the annual conferences, by a vote of three-fourths of all their members voting on the third resolution, shall have concurred in the recommendation to alter the sixth restrictive article, the Agents at New-York and Cincinnati shall, and they are hereby authorized and directed to, deliver over to any authorized agent or appointee of the Church, South, should one be organized, all notes and book accounts against the ministers, church-members, or citizens, within its boundaries, with authority to collect the same for the sole use of the Southern Church, and that said agents also convey to aforesaid agent or appointee of the South, all the real estate, and assign to him all the property, including presses, stock, and all right and interest connected with the Printing Establishments at Charleston, Richmond, and Nashville, which now belong to the Methodist Episcopal Church.

" '5. That when the Annual Conferences shall have approved the aforesaid change in the sixth restrictive article, there shall be transferred to the above Agent for the Southern Church, so much of the capital and produce of the Methodist Book Concern, as will, with the notes, book accounts, presses, &c., mentioned in the last resolution, bear the same proportion to the whole property of said Concern, that the travelling preachers in the Southern Church shall bear to all the travelling ministers of the Methodist Episcopal Church. The division to be made on the basis of the number of travelling preachers in the forthcoming Minutes.

" '6. That the above transfer shall be in the form of annual payments of $25,000 per annum, and specifically in stock of the Book Concern, and in Southern notes and accounts due the establishment, and accruing after the first transfer mentioned above ; and until the payments are made, the Southern Church shall share in all the net profits of the Book Concern, in the proportion that the amount due them, or in arrears, bears to all the property of the Concern.

" '7. That Nathan Bangs, George Peck, and James B. Finley, be, and they are hereby appointed, commissioners, to act in concert with the same number of commissioners, appointed by the Southern organization, (should one be formed,) to estimate the amounts which will fall due to the South by the preceding rule, and to have full power to carry into effect the whole arrangements proposed with regard to the division of property, should the separation take place. And if by any means a vacancy occurs in this Board of Commissioners, the Book Committee at New-York shall fill said vacancy.

" '8. That whenever Agents of the Southern Church are clothed with legal authority or corporate power, to act in the premises, the Agents at New-York are hereby authorized and directed to act in concert with said Southern Agents, so as to give the provisions of these resolutions a legally binding force.

" '9. That all the property of the Methodist Episcopal Church, in meeting-houses, parsonages, colleges, schools, conference funds, cemeteries, and of every kind, within the limits of the Southern organization, shall be forever free from any claim set up on the part of the Methodist Episcopal Church, so far as this resolution can be of force in the premises.

"'10. That the Church so formed in the South shall have a common right to use all the copy-rights in possession of the Book-Concerns at New-York and Cincinnati, at the time of the settlement by the commissioners.

"'11. That the Book Agents at New-York be directed to make such compensation to the conferences South for their dividend from the Chartered Fund, as the commissioners above provided for shall agree upon.

"'12. That the Bishops be respectfully requested to lay that part of this report requiring the action of the annual conferences, before them as soon as possible, beginning with the New-York Conference.'

"And the complainants allege, that the said General Conference had full, competent, and lawful power and authority, to pass and adopt the said resolutions, and each and all of them, and that the same thereby became and were of binding force and validity.

"And the complainants further allege, that after the adoption of the foregoing resolutions, such proceedings were had in the several Annual Conferences of the Methodist Episcopal Church in the slave-holding States; that a full convention thereof, by delegates, elected on the basis of the resolutions of the General Conference of 1844, assembled at Louisville, in Kentucky, on the first day of May, 1845; and the said convention, after full and mature consideration, adopted the following resolutions, which they pray may be taken as part of this bill:—

"'Be it resolved by the delegates of the several annual conferences of the Methodist Episcopal Church in the slave-holding States, in general convention assembled, That it is right, expedient, and necessary, to erect the annual conferences represented in this convention into a distinct ecclesiastical connexion, separate from the jurisdiction of the General Conference of the Methodist Episcopal Church, as at present constituted; and accordingly we, the delegates of said annual conferences, acting under the provisional plan of separation adopted by the General Conference of 1844, do solemnly declare the jurisdiction hitherto exercised over said annual conferences, by the General Conference of the Methodist Episcopal Church, entirely dissolved; and that said annual conferences shall be, and they hereby are constituted, a separate ecclesiastical connexion, under the provisional plan of separation aforesaid, and based upon the Discipline of the Methodist Episcopal Church, comprehending the doctrines and entire moral, ecclesiastical, and economical rules and regulations of said Discipline, except only in so far as verbal alterations may be necessary to a distinct organization, and to be known by the style and title of the Methodist Episcopal Church, South.

"'Resolved, That we cannot abandon or compromise the principles of action upon which we proceed to a separate organization in the South; nevertheless, cherishing a sincere desire to maintain Christian union and fraternal intercourse with the Church, North, we shall always be ready, kindly and respectfully, to entertain, and duly and carefully consider, any proposition or plan, having for its object the union of the two great bodies in the North and South, whether such proposed union be jurisdictional or connexional.'

"And the complainants further allege, That afterwards, viz., on the second day of July, Anno Domini, 1845, a council of the bishops of the Methodist Episcopal Church met at New-York, (which council was composed of the Northern bishops alone,) and then and there unanimously adopted the following resolutions, which they pray may be taken as part of this bill:—

"'Resolved, That the plan reported by the select committee of nine, at the last General Conference, and adopted by that body, in regard to a distinct ecclesiastical connexion, should such a course be found necessary by the annual conferences in the slave-holding States, is regarded by us as of binding obligation in the premises, so far as our administration is concerned.

"'Resolved, That, in order to ascertain fairly the desire and purpose of those societies bordering on the line of division in regard to their adherence to the Church North or South, due notice should be given of the time, place, and object of the meeting for the above purpose, at which a chairman and secretary should be appointed, and the sense of all the members present be ascertained, and the same be forwarded to the bishop who may preside at the ensuing annual conferences; or forward to said presiding bishop a writen request to be recognised and have a preac[illegible]sent them, with the names of the majority appended thereto.'

"And the complainants allege, That by and in virtue of the foregoing proceedings, the Methodist Episcopal Church in the United States, as it had existed before the year 1844, became and was divided into two distinct Methodist Episcopal Churches, with distinct and independent powers and authority, composed of the several annual conferences, charges, stations, and societies, lying or being situated North and South of the afore-described line of division.

"And the complainants further allege, That by force of the foregoing proceedings, the Methodist Episcopal Church, South, became and was entitled to its proportion of all the property, real and personal, and all funds and effects, (said property and funds of the Methodist Episcopal Church, had been obtained and collected by voluntary contribution, in which contribution the members of the Church South contributed the largest portion of the same,) which, up to the time of the separation, had belonged to the Methodist Episcopal Church in the United States, and that the Methodist Episcopal Church, South, was, and is so entitled, without any change or alteration of the sixth restrictive article above mentioned; but the complainants allege, That, if the change in the sixth restrictive article were necessary in order that the Church, South, should obtain an equitable division of the Church property, a majority of three-fourths of all the members of the several annual conferences which voted directly on the question, in view of a division of the property, has been obtained.

"And the complainants further say, That before and on the said 8th day of June, 1844, the Methodist Episcopal Church in the United States owned and possessed large amounts of property in various parts of the United States, in addition to the meeting-houses, parsonages, and other estates of that description, and that said property, real and personal, was in the hands of the agents and trustees, being in some instances corporations, but more frequently in private and unincorporated individuals: That among other descriptions and claims of property, there belonged to the said Church, what was denominated the 'Book Concern,' in the city of New-York, consisting of houses, lots, machinery, printing-presses, book-bindery, books, paper, debts, cash, and other articles of property, amounting in all to about the sum of seven hundred thousand dollars, the whole of which lands and goods, property and effects, so situated, are now in the possession of the defendants, Lane and Scott, denominated hereinafter as Book Agents.

"And the complainants further say, That after the separation of the Methodist Episcopal Church into two distinct Churches, by virtue of the resolutions of the General Conference of 1844, and the action of the annual conferences in the South, as hereinbefore set forth, the Agents of the Book Concern at New-York, in pursuance of the provisions and terms of said resolutions, paid to the several annual conferences of the Methodist Episcopal Church, South, their proportion of profits and income of the Book Concern, as fixed and set apart by the said agents for the year 1845. But the complainants further allege, That since the year 1845, the said agents have utterly refused to pay to the said annual conferences, South, and to complainants, for and on behalf of them, their said just proportions of the profits and income of the said Book Concern, and still continue to withhold the same; to the manifest loss and injury of the said Church, South, and in plain violation of their rights. And the complainants further say, That the General Conference of the Church, South, holden at Petersburgh, Virginia, on the day of May, 1846, in pursuance of, and in compliance with, the aforesaid resolutions of the General Conference of 1844, proceeded to appoint the complainants, Bascom and Green, together with S. A. Latta, commissioners, to meet the commissioners appointed by the General Conference of the Methodist Episcopal Church of 1844, and settle and receive from said commissioners the just proportion of the property and effects due the South, according to the plan of separation, which resolutions are in the words and figures following, to wit, and prayed to be taken as part of this bill:—

"'1. Resolved, by the delegates of the several annual conferences of the Methodist Episcopal Church, South, in General Conference assembled, That three commissioners be appointed, in accordance with the "Plan of Separation," adopted by the General Conference of the Methodist Episcopal Church, in 1844, to act in concert with the commissioners appointed by the said Methodist Episcopal Church, to estimate the amount due to the South, according to the aforesaid "Plan of Separation," and to adjust and settle all matters pertaining to the division of the Church property and funds, as provided for in the said "Plan of Separation," with full powers to carry into effect the whole arrangement with regard to said division.

"'2. Resolved, That the Commissioners of the Methodist Episcopal Church, South, shall forthwith notify the commissioners and Book Agents of the Methodist Episcopal Church, of their appointment as aforesaid, and of their readiness to adjust and settle the matters aforesaid; and should no such settlement be effected before the session of the General Conference of the Methodist Episcopal Church, in 1848, said commissioners shall have power and authority, for and in behalf of this conference, to attend the General Conference of the Methodist Episcopal Church, to settle and adjust all questions involving property or funds, which may be pending between the Methodist Episcopal Church and the Methodist Episcopal Church, South.

"'3 Resolved, That should the commissioners appointed by this General Conference, after proper effort, fail to effect a settlement, as above, then, and in that case, they shall be, and they are hereby authorized to take such measures as may best secure the just and equitable claims of the Methodist Episcopal Church, South, to the property and funds aforesaid.'

"And thereupon, and under the authority of said last-recited resolutions, the said Bascom, Green, and Latta were duly appointed such commissioners, and their said appointment duly certified and made known to the commissioners appointed by the said resolutions of the General Conference of 1844. And the said complainants further say, that the said Bascom, Green, and Latta, immediately after their said appointments as such commissioners as aforesaid, applied to Nathan Bangs, George Peck, and James B. Finley, commissioners appointed by the seventh resolution of the said General Conference of 1844, and the said Book Agents at New-York, to act in concert with the commissioners appointed upon the part of the South, to settle and divide the property belonging to the Methodist Episcopal Church, between the Church North and the Church South, and requested them to proceed to the duty assigned them, by dividing the property, as contemplated and directed by said resolution; and that they, the complainants, Bascom and Green, together with the said Latta, have repeatedly called on them since for this purpose; but the defendants have wholly failed and refused to act in the premises, and complainants have not been enabled, although they have used all honourable and fair means, to get a settlement with them of this unpleasant question; nor have they been enabled to induce the said Book Agents of the Methodist Episcopal Church, nor the Church itself, nor the commissioners to pay to the Church South its proportionate share of said property and funds, as provided by said plan of separation.

"The complainants further show, that since the appointment of the said Samuel A. Latta, as one of the Commissioners, by the General Conference of the Methodist Episcopal Church, South, say on the   day of February, 1849, he, the said Latta, hath resigned his office as such commissioner; and that they, the said Bascom and Green, by virtue of and under the authority of the said General Conference of the Methodist Episcopal Church, South, have appointed their co-complainant, Parsons, to fill the vacancy of said Latta. And the complainants allege, that they are members of the Methodist Episcopal Church, South; that they are preachers—Kelly and Allen are supernumerary, and Tevis superannuated preachers, and belong to the travelling connexion of said Church, South, and that, as such, they have a personal interest in the real estate, personal property, debts, and funds, now holden by the Methodist Episcopal Church, through the said defendants, as agents and trustees appointed by the General Conference of the Methodist Episcopal Church. Complainants further allege, that there are about fifteen hundred preachers belonging to the travelling connexion of the Methodist Episcopal Church, South, each of whom has a direct and personal interest in the same right with your complainants to said property, as above described, situated and held as aforesaid; that the great number of persons interested as aforesaid, in the recovery sought by this bill, makes it inconvenient, indeed, impossible, to bring them all before the court as complainants; that they are citizens of other States than the State of New-York, and their interests in the property in question exceeds two thousand dollars.

"Complainants further allege, that the defendants are members of the Methodist Episcopal Church, are preachers belonging to the travelling connexion of that Church, and that each of them has a personal interest in the said property and funds, as above described; in addition to which, the said defendants, Lane and Scott, have the custody and control, by law, and by virtue of their appointment as Agents of the Book-Concern by the General Conference of the Methodist Episcopal Church, of all the said property and effects of said Book-Concern above described. That in addition to these defendants, there are nearly thirty-eight hundred preachers belonging to the travelling connexion of the Methodist Episcopal Church, each of whom has an interest in the said property in the same right, so that it will be impossible, in view of attaining a just decision of this controversy, to make all those interested, parties to this bill.

"Complainants further allege, that the entire membership of the Methodist Episcopal Church, South, is about four hundred and sixty thousand five hundred and fifty-three, and that the entire membership of the Methodist Episcopal Church is about six hundred and thirty-nine thousand and sixty-six; so that it will be at once seen by the Honourable Court, that it is utterly impracticable and impossible to bring all the parties in interest before the Court, in this bill, either as complainants or as defendants.

"And the complainants further say, that they bring this Bill by the authority and under the direction of the General and the annual Conferences of the Methodist Episcopal Church, South, and for the benefit and in behalf of the said Church, South, and the said General Conference, and for the benefit and in behalf of all the annual conferences in the said Church, South, and of themselves, and of all the preachers in the travelling connexion, and all other ministers and members of said Church, and all others having interest in the same right in its funds and property.

"To the end, therefore, and forasmuch as complainants, and those they represent, are greatly aggrieved and injured by the oppressive course pursued by the Methodist Episcopal Church, in their refusal to divide the said property according to equity, and in pursuance of the Plan of Separation, so as aforesaid set forth; and that complainants, so as aforesaid, are without relief, except in a Court of Equity, they pray your Honourable Court that they may be allowed to prosecute this bill in their own behalf, and in behalf of all those bodies and persons so interested, belonging to the Church, South, as above set forth; and that said defendants, by suitable process directed, &c., commanding, &c., be made defendants to this bill, for themselves and those they represent, as agents, trustees, and commissioners, and that, upon oath, they make full, true, and perfect answers to each allegation in this bill contained, setting forth their own rights, and the rights of those under whom they now act, and have heretofore acted, to the end that this Honourable Court may be enabled to ascertain the rights of all the parties, and decree accordingly.

"And the complainants particularly pray that defendants, Lane and Scott, may be required to produce a full, particular, and just account of all the real estate, personal estate, goods, debts, money, and effects of every sort or kind, now held by them, or either of them, as agent or agents, trustees, or members of the Methodist Episcopal Church in the United States; and that the said Bangs, Peck, and Finley, be required to answer upon oath, whether they were not appointed by the General Conference of the Methodist Episcopal Church of 1844, held at New-York, commissioners to act upon the part of the North, with the commissioners to be appointed on the part of the South, in case of a separate and distinct ecclesiastical connexion being formed by the South, in the division of the Church property, so called; and whether the complainants, Bascom, Green, and Parsons, and the said Samuel A. Latta, as commissioners, did not call upon them for a settlement, and to arrange the distribution of the Church property according to the Plan of Separation; and if they did not refuse so to act in the settlement and division of said Church property; and that they, all the said defendants, also be made to answer, all and singular, the allegations and matters in this bill set forth, as fully as though the same were repeated to them in the form of interrogatories, and they especially interrogated thereto."

And then a decree is prayed, which I need not read.

To the bill of the plaintiffs the defendants have put in an answer.

Mr. Johnson, Junior, and Mr. Fancher, read the answer, at the request of Mr. Lord, as follows:—

"These defendants now, and at all times hereafter, saving and reserving to themselves all, and all manner of, advantage and benefit of exception to the manifold errors, uncertainties, insufficiencies, and other imperfections, in the plaintiffs' said Bill of Complaint contained, for answer thereunto, or unto so much and such parts thereof as they are advised it is material or necessary for them to make answer—they answering, say:—

"That they admit, that before and on the 8th day of June, 1844, there existed, and, as these defendants say, there still exists, in the United States of America, a voluntary association, known as 'The Methodist Episcopal Church;' and, although not incorporated in one body by any legal enactment, yet the same was, and is, a duly organized evangelical Church. And these defendants further say, that although 'The Methodist Episcopal Church' is not a body politic and corporate at common law; yet, under the law of pious and charitable uses, as protected and enforced in courts of equity, it has an organization, and performs functions, and exercises and discharges powers and duties, analagous to institutions strictly and legally incorporated; and that the said Church is, in courts of equity, fully protected in the use and enjoyment of such functions, powers, and duties. And these defendants admit, that on the day above mentioned, the said Church was composed of the number of bishops stated by the plaintiffs; but these defendants say, that, according to their information and belief, the plaintiffs have not accurately stated the number of travelling preachers, ministers, or members belonging to the Church at that time: And the defendants further admit, that the said Church was united and holden together in one organized body, by certain doctrines of faith and morals, and by certain rules of government and discipline.

"These defendants further answering, say, that, exercised within the restrictions and constitutional powers contained in its Book of Discipline, the supreme government of the Methodist Episcopal Church, comprising the authority to make rules and regulations for the Church, limited by such restrictions and constitutional powers, was, and is, vested in a delegated body called the General Conference; and that there are within the system and polity of the Church, annual conferences, which, in some, but not in all respects, are bodies subordinate to the General Conference; also quarterly conferences, bishops, presiding elders, and travelling ministers, in whom, and in which conferences, respectively, are vested the powers and authority specified in the Book of Discipline; and, beyond the powers of government thus alluded to, these defendants deny the allegation of the plaintiffs' bill, that the general government of the said Church was or is vested as therein stated.

"And these defendants admit, that the plaintiffs have partially stated the great object of the said Methodist Episcopal Church; nevertheless, the defendants, more fully to set forth the design of the said Church, say, that it comprehends the exercise of its ecclesiastical government and discipline, involving the itinerancy of its bishops and ministers; the promulgation of the doctrines of the Gospel among all men; the due administration of Scriptural ordinances and the holy sacraments; the promotion of works of piety and benevolence; the revival and spread of Scriptural holiness, and the conversion of the world to the faith and practice of Christianity.

"And these defendants admit, that the constitution, organization, form of government, and rules of discipline, as well as the articles of religion and doctrines of faith, of the Methodist Episcopal Church, were, and are, of general knowledge and notoriety; and are contained in a printed volume, entitled, 'The Doctrines and Discipline of the Methodist Episcopal Church.' Yet these defendants say, that such printed volume—in this answer designated the 'Book of Discipline'—has been, according to the forms, and in the manner therein prescribed, and at various times since the organization of the said Church, altered, amended, and revised, in sundry particulars, a full and particular relation of which would be too extended to be here set forth; but, for an accurate account thereof, these defendants crave leave to produce, and refer to, a printed book, entitled 'Emory's History of the Discipline;' also the several editions of the said Book of Discipline, published by the agents for the Methodist Book Concern, in the city of New-York.

"And these defendants, in respect of the 'differences and disagreements' alleged by the plaintiffs to have 'sprung up in the Church between what were called the Northern and Southern members, upon the administration of the Church government with reference to the ownership of slaves by the ministry of the Church,'—answer and say, that, according to the best of their knowledge, information, and belief, no such differences or disagreements had sprung up in the Church between the Northern and Southern members, prior to the session of the General Conference held in the city of New-York, in 1844, attended with or seriously threatening the consequences alleged by the plaintiffs.

"And these defendants, according to their best knowledge, information, and belief, also deny that it ever, prior to that session of the General Conference, became, or was, a question of grave or serious importance with the members of the Church, or with any, except a few of them, whether a separation ought not to take place by geographical boundaries, or otherwise, so as that the Methodist Episcopal Church should thereafter constitute two separate and distinct Methodist Episcopal Churches; or, that it was 'thereupon,' as erroneously alleged by the plaintiffs, that the resolutions which they denominate the 'Plan of Separation,' and which are set forth in their bill, were passed at the General Conference of 1844, held in the city of New-York; and these defendants say, that then, and always hitherto, the greater portion of the Church have not thought there was any sufficient cause for a separation or division of the Church.

"And these defendants, further answering with respect to such differences and disagreements, say, that during, and subsequent to, the session of the General Conference of 1844, those differences and disagreements principally grew out of the voluntary connexion of a bishop with slavery, and out of the proceedings of that body in reference thereto, hereafter referred to; that the rules of the Book of Discipline, and the uniform action of the General Conference, have always been adverse to the system of human slavery, it being regarded as a great evil; and, prior to the session of the General Conference in 1844, the whole Church, by common consent, united in proper effort for the mitigation and final removal of the evil; that the ministers have never been allowed to hold slaves, except in instances under the laws of the slave-holding States deemed to be cases of necessity; that the Church never made, nor has its Book of Discipline ever contained, any law respecting the holding of slaves by a bishop of the Church; that the General Conference have always refused to elect a slave-holder to that office; that, at the session of the General Conference in 1844, held in the city of New-York, it became known that the Rev. James O. Andrew, one of the bishops of the Methodist Episcopal Church, had, since his election to that office, become an owner of slaves,—of one, by bequest; of another, by inheritance; and of others, by his intermarriage with a lady in the State of Georgia who held a number of slaves in her own right, which, by the laws of the State, became the property of her husband; that, as will appear by its printed Journal, (pp. 65–83,) such proceedings were had by that General Conference, upon the admitted facts contained in a statement in writing made by Bishop Andrew, and which was in due form brought before the Conference by one of its standing committees called the "Committee on the Episcopacy," whose duty it was to inquire into the conduct and administration of the bishops, and to make report to the Conference,—as that the following preamble and resolution were duly and legally adopted by that Conference, to wit:—

"'Whereas the Discipline of our Church forbids the doing anything calculated to destroy our itinerant general superintendency; and whereas Bishop Andrew has become connected with slavery by marriage and otherwise; and this act having drawn after it circumstances which, in the estimation of the General Conference, will greatly embarrass the exercise of his office as an itinerant general superintendent, if not in some places entirely prevent it; therefore,

"'Resolved, That it is the sense of this General Conference that he desist from the exercise of his office so long as this impediment remains.'

"And these defendants, upon their information and belief, further say, that the adoption of this resolution gave offence to a minority of the members of that General Conference, and who were delegates from annual conferences in the slave-holding States; and principally, if not wholly, induced those delegates to present a formal Protest against such action of the General Conference, which was admitted to record on its Journal, and, with the report in reference thereto of the committee appointed by the General Conference for that purpose, is appended to such Journal, (pp. 186–210,) to all which these defendants desire leave to refer; and which also induced such delegations from the annual conferences in the slave-holding States to present to said General Conference the declaration already referred to, which was read, and referred to a committee of nine, whose report thereon is the so-called 'Plan of Separation,' herein mentioned; which declaration is recorded on page 109 of the printed

Journal of the General Conference, and to which also the defendants crave leave to refer; and which resolution, in the case of Bishop Andrew, further induced such delegates, (although without the authority of the General Conference, and in no manner sanctioned by any action of that body,) immediately after the adjournment of such General Conference of 1844,—before the happening of the contingencies mentioned in the so-called 'Plan of Separation,' necessary to give the same effect, and before such delegates had departed from the city of New-York,—to address a circular to their constituents and the ministers and members of the Church in the slaveholding States, therein expressing their own opinion in favour of a separation from the jurisdiction of the General Conference, and advising the annual conferences within those States to elect from their own bodies, severally, delegates to a convention proposed by them to be held at Louisville, Kentucky, in May following, to consider and determine the matter; all which, finally led those annual conferences, or portions of them, at that convention,—to withdraw and separate from the Methodist Episcopal Church;—to renounce and declare themselves wholly absolved from its jurisdiction, government, and authority, and to institute a new and distinct ecclesiastical organization, separate from, and independent of, the General Conference of the Methodist Episcopal Church, under the denomination of 'The Methodist Episcopal Church, South,'—which is the same organization mentioned in said Bill of Complaint; and the plaintiffs, and all those whom they, professedly, represent, are adherents thereof, and are no longer attached to the Methodist Episcopal Church; and these defendants believe and submit, that these proceedings were, in no part, authorized by the rules of government, or the constitutional law of the Methodist Episcopal Church, as contained in its Book of Discipline, but were in palpable hostility thereto.

"These defendants, further answering, insist and submit, that the said resolution of the General Conference in the case of Bishop Andrew, instead of moving to a secession, called for due submission and respect from all the delegates to that conference, and all the ministers and members of the Church; and the defendants, upon their belief, say, that the same, and all the proceedings of that body leading thereto, were regular, constitutional and valid; that the voluntary connexion of Bishop Andrew with slavery was justly considered by a majority of said General Conference, and by most of the ministers and members of the Church, as 'improper conduct;' and that every bishop is, by a law of the Book of Discipline, amenable to the General Conference, who are thereby declared to 'have power to expel him for improper conduct, if they see it necessary;' and that such resolution and proceedings, in the case of Bishop Andrew, were in due accordance with the good government of the Church.

"And these defendants, further answering, admit, that the resolutions set forth by the plaintiffs, commencing at folio 7 of their bill, were, at a General Conference of the Church, holden, according to usage and discipline, at New-York, passed on the 8th day of June, 1844, by a majority of over three-fourths of the entire body; although, as these defendants state, such resolutions were, in respect of their operation or effect, provisional and contingent,—were occasioned by, and based upon, the said declaration of the Southern delegates, and were intended only to meet the future emergency predicted therein, should the same arise; and that such resolutions were connected with, and preceded by, the statement and preamble embodied in the report of the said committee of nine, appointed by the General Conference to consider and report on such declaration,—which report was adopted by the conference, as will appear by its printed journal, (pp. 130, 137,) and which statement and preamble are to be taken, in connexion with said resolutions, as a part of said report thus adopted, and to which the defendants crave leave to refer as a part of this answer. But these defendants are advised by counsel, that the said resolutions, embodied in such report of the committee of nine, called the 'Plan of Separation,' were not duly or legally passed; and that the General Conference of 1844 had no competent, nor any valid power or authority to pass or adopt the said resolutions called the 'Plan of Separation,' or any or either of them, except that portion thereof comprising the recommendation to the annual conferences to change the sixth restrictive rule: and these defendants are also advised by counsel, that the last-named resolutions, when adopted, were null and void, and without any binding force or validity, except in the matter of such recommendation merely; and these defendants therefore humbly submit these questions to this Honourable Court: and to show the extent of the constitutional power of the said General Conference in this respect, these defendants state,—

"That from the ordination and election of the first bishops of the Church, in 1784, to the year 1808, the General Conference was composed of all the preachers in the connexion who had travelled four years from the time they were received by an annual conference; but in the General Conference of 1808, on the recommendation of a majority of the annual conferences severally acting in their primary capacities, it was proposed to do away with such general assembly of ministers, and to organize a delegated General Conference, to consist of a delegated number, to be elected by the several annual conferences, according to a fixed ratio of representation; which proposition was agreed to in said general convention of 1808, upon the condition of adopting certain articles to restrict the powers of the future delegated General Conferences; whereupon a constitution for the government of the General Conference, embracing six restrictive articles, was accordingly established, defining who shall compose the General Conference, and what are the regulations and powers belonging to it; and the whole body of preachers, then assembled in general convention, adopted, by such constitution, the present plan for a delegated General Conference; transferring to them the powers of the whole body of preachers, with the express exceptions and limitations specified in such restrictive articles; which constitution and restrictive articles the defendants pray may be taken as a part of this answer, as if here set forth; and for the contents of the same, and for the particulars of these facts and allegations, these defendants crave leave to produce and refer to the said constitution and restrictive articles, contained in the Book of Discipline for 1808, pp. 14, 15; also the subsequent editions of the 'Discipline;' also 'Emory's History of the Discipline,' pp. 111–113; also 'Bangs' History of the Methodist Episcopal Church,' vol. ii, pp. 225–234:—

"That such constitution and restrictive rules, thus adopted,—containing a general grant of all powers to make rules and regulations for the government of the Church, under the restraints and within the limitations therein embodied,—constituted the paramount law of the Church; and have always been so considered, as well by the delegated General Conferences, whose legislative action they were intended to regulate, as by the annual conferences, the bishops, ministers, and members of the Church, whose rights and privileges were secured thereby; nor have the delegated General Conference ever had, or claimed, any power to alter or amend these restrictive articles except in the manner therein prescribed, in conjunction with the constitutional majority and action of the annual conferences; nor have any alterations thereof ever been made, except in conformity with the provisions contained therein for such alterations; and never without such constitutional majority and assent of the several annual conferences, voting thereon in their primary capacities:—

"That this constitution, embodying these restrictive articles, is still—and during the session of the General Conference of 1844, and at the time of the passage of the resolutions called the 'Plan of Separation,' was—the fundamental law of the Church, as will be seen on reference to the Book of Discipline, pp. 21–23, edition of 1844; that the General Conference is the representative body above mentioned with powers limited as aforesaid, to make rules and regulations for the government of the Church. And these defendants, as they are further advised by counsel, believe and submit, that these restrictive articles limit and restrain the exercise of the powers of the General Conference to the enactment of rules and regulations for the Church, to carry on throughout the whole work, the economy and purposes of its government, as already settled; prohibiting any change or alteration in any part or rule of such government, so as to do away episcopacy, or destroy the plan of the itinerant general superintendency of the Church; that they prohibit the exercise of any power by the General Conference to do away the privileges of the ministers, preachers, or members, of trial by a committee, or before the society, and of an appeal; and also prohibit the General Conference, without the consent of three-fourths of the whole body of ministers, to be expressed in their several annual conferences, from appropriating the produce of the Book Concern, or Chartered Fund, to any purpose other than for the benefit of the preachers belonging to the travelling connexion of the Church, their wives, widows, and children. And the defendants, therefore, further submit to this Honourable Court, whether the said resolutions, denominated the 'Plan of Separation,' are not, in each and every of these particulars, inconsistent with, and subversive of, said constitutional law of the

Church, and in contravention of the limitations contained in the aforesaid restrictive articles.

"And these defendants, further answering, submit, as further advised by counsel, that even had the so-called 'Plan of Separation' been constitutional, or valid, it merely provided a prospective plan, which, without the happening of certain future conditions, or on the failure of which conditions, or either of them, could never have, by its express terms, and, as defendants say, was never intended to have, any force or validity. And these defendants expressly aver that these conditions have not happened; and they therefore further insist and submit, that the said so-called 'Plan of Separation' has always been inoperative; has never had any force or validity; and is absolutely null and void.

"And these defendants, further answering, say, that the so-called 'Plan of Separation,' whether constitutional or not, was never ratified by the annual conferences therein named; and therefore gave the Southern annual conferences no authority to act in the premises; and hence, as the defendants submit and insist, the Southern annual conferences have, in all respects, as to the Church, South, acted on their own responsibility, without any authority from the General Conference of 1844.

"And these defendants, further answering, say, that they admit the resolutions set forth by the plaintiffs, commencing at folio 20 of their bill, were adopted at a convention of delegates from annual conferences in the slave-holding States, assembled at Louisville, in Kentucky, on the first day of May, 1845; but these defendants deny, that the delegates composing that convention were elected on the basis, or according to the authority, of said provisional 'Plan of Separation,' so called, or of any resolutions of the General Conference of 1844; and especially do these defendants deny, that said Louisville Convention, in adopting their said resolutions, or in any proceedings had therein, acted under the provisional 'Plan of Separation,' adopted by that General Conference, as is stated in one of such resolutions; but, on the contrary thereof, these defendants say, that said provisional plan did not confer any authority upon that convention to adopt their said resolutions—to organize the new ecclesiastical connexion therein mentioned—or to dismember the Methodist Episcopal Church; and, further, that the said convention was not convened by, or in pursuance of, any constitutional authority of that Church, or of its General Conference; and also, that the proceedings leading to, and the transactions of, the said Louisville Convention, and which resulted in the organization of the Methodist Episcopal Church, South, were occasioned and had, by such of the ministers and members of the annual conferences in the slave-holding States, as have attached themselves to the said Church, South, upon their own responsibility, and by their own unauthorized acts, whilst they repudiate the authority of the General Conference of the Methodist Episcopal Church—they refusing, and declaring their refusal, to submit to such authority; and that by revolutionary measures, tending to the dismemberment of the Methodist Episcopal Church, and by insubordinate proceedings, unwarranted by said 'Plan of Separation,' so called, or by any authority of the Methodist Episcopal Church, they did institute the said 'Methodist Episcopal Church, South,' as an independent ecclesiastical organization, separate from the jurisdiction of the General Conference of the Methodist Episcopal Church; and did solemnly declare such jurisdiction over them entirely dissolved. And, for some of the particulars of these facts and allegations, these defendants ask leave to refer to the aforesaid declaration, presented on the 5th June, 1844, to the General Conference of the Methodist Episcopal Church, at its session in New-York, signed by fifty-one of the delegates in that conference from slave-holding States, and who are now attached to said Church, South; which Declaration is recorded in the Journal of said General Conference, page 109; also to the 'Protest in the case of Bishop Andrew,' hereinbefore referred to, presented to said General Conference on the 6th day of said June, signed by such delegates and others, now attached to said Church, South; also to the address to their constituents, the resolutions and proceedings of such delegates at their meeting in the city of New-York, on the 11th June, 1844; also to the correspondence between Bishop Soule and Bishop Andrew, involving the request of the former to the latter, that he should resume his episcopal functions, and his acceptance of that request, notwithstanding the aforesaid resolution of the General Conference of 1844, in his case; also to the proceedings of said Louisville Convention; and also to the proceedings of the body assuming to be a General Conference composed of delegates from annual conferences attached to said Church, South, held at Petersburg, Va., in May, 1846.

Wherefore, these defendants insist and submit, that the 'Methodist Episcopal Church, South,' exists as a separate ecclesiastical communion, solely by the result, and in virtue, of the acts and doings of the individual bishops, ministers, and members attached to such Church, South, proceeding in the premises upon their own responsibility; and that such bishops, ministers, and members, have voluntarily withdrawn themselves from the Methodist Episcopal Church, and have renounced all their rights and privileges in her communion and under her government. And these defendants deny that the annual conferences represented in said Louisville Convention, were, as is erroneously stated in the first of the resolutions of the convention set forth by the plaintiffs, constituted a separate ecclesiastical connexion under the provisional 'Plan of Separation,' so called, aforesaid.

"And these defendants, further answering, admit, that at the time and place in that behalf mentioned by the plaintiffs, a council of bishops of the Methodist Episcopal Church, called by the plaintiffs 'Northern Bishops,' met and unanimously adopted the resolutions commencing at folio 24 of the said bill; but these defendants say, that the same were, as well by the express terms thereof, as by the extent of any authority possessed by such council, or bishops, limited in their application and effect to the administration of the said bishops; which administration was, at that time, interrupted, resisted and prevented, in the slave-holding States, by such portion of the revolutionary measures above alluded to as had then occurred, and by kindred measures of some of the present adherents of said Church, South. Moreover, these defendants further state, that said bishops were amenable to the General Conference, who have power to inquire into their administration, and expel them for "improper conduct," if they see it necessary; that the said provisional Plan was an act of the General Conference, to whom said bishops were amenable; and that the General Conference had not then declared the said provisional Plan null and void. But these defendants, with respect to those resolutions of the bishops, submit, that they can have no influence or effect whatever upon the question of the alleged division of the Church; nor can any effect or virtue be attached to their acts or resolutions, tending to divide or dismember the Church, or to warrant, in any sense, the allegation of the plaintiffs, that by, or in virtue of, such resolutions,—in conjunction with such other proceedings as are alleged by the plaintiffs, or otherwise,—the Methodist Episcopal Church ever became divided into two distinct Methodist Episcopal Churches.

And these defendants, further answering, deny, that, by or in virtue of the proceedings alleged in the said Bill of Complaint, or of any part thereof, or otherwise howsoever, 'the Methodist Episcopal Church' in the United States, as it had existed before the year 1844, or as it at any time existed, was lawfully divided into two distinct Methodist Episcopal Churches, in the manner alleged in said bill, or in any other manner whatever. And these defendants submit, that the separation and voluntary withdrawal from the Church of a portion of her bishops, ministers, and members, as herein mentioned, was an unauthorized separation from the Church.

"And these defendants, further answering, say, that the so-called 'Plan of Separation' was wholly prospective and contingent in its provisions; and that the General Conference of 1844 adopted the said provisional Plan in view of, and based the same entirely upon, the declaration of the delegates from the annual conferences in the slave-holding States hereinbefore mentioned, which alleged that certain acts of the General Conference therein referred to, especially the act in the case of Bishop Andrew, must produce a state of things in the South which would render a continuance of the jurisdiction of that General Conference over those conferences, inconsistent with the success of the ministry in the slave-holding States; and, therefore, the General Conference, by the said Plan, made provision for the adjustment of relations between the Methodist Episcopal Church and her separating ministers and members, to meet the emergency which might arise in the event of the contingency thus predicted in such declaration, when a separation should occur by the act and deed of the annual conferences in the slave-holding States, from the necessity of the case. And these defendants are informed and believe, and therefore state, that, independent of the aforesaid proceedings of the Southern delegates, which contributed to such separation, the acts of the General Conference alone, and which are thus complained of, did not produce a state of things in the South which rendered a continuance of the jurisdiction aforesaid 'inconsistent with the success of the ministry in the slave-holding States;' nor was the separation of the ministers and members now composing the Southern Church, occasioned solely because the annual conferences in the slave-holding States found it necessary to unite in a distinct ecclesiastical connexion; but the way for such separation was prepared, and the same was superinduced and consummated, by the revolutionary measures hereinbefore referred to, and which were begun at the seat, and nearly at the time, of the session of the said General Conference, before the predicted state of things in the South was, or possibly could be, produced by any acts of the General Conference.

"Also, that the General Conference, by said provisional Plan, proposed, in the event of the happening of the contingencies therein mentioned, regulations to be mutually observed by the Methodist Episcopal Church, on the one part, and the prospective new Church and the ministers and members thereof, on the other part, with respect to the 'Northern boundary' of such new Church, which required that such Northern boundary should be fixed at the Northern extremities of those 'societies, stations, and conferences,' a majority of whose members should, of their own free will and accord, vote to adhere to the said Southern Church; the due observance of which regulations was, as these defendants insist and submit, a fundamental condition of said provisional plan. And these defendants, as they are informed and believe, state, that in this respect the said provisional Plan has been violated by the said Church, South, and by the said separating bishops, ministers, and members now attached thereto, more particularly in the instances following:—The said bishops, Andrew and Soule, since said Southern organization, stationed preachers in Cincinnati, within the territory of the Ohio Annual Conference; and in Northampton county, Virginia, within the district of the Philadelphia Annual Conference; both which annual conferences have always remained attached to the Methodist Episcopal Church; and the aforesaid body, acting as the General Conference of the Church, South, sanctioned these doings of said bishops, and also authorized the Virginia Annual Conference, which is claimed as a member of the Church, South, to send ministers into the territory of the Baltimore Annual Conference, which is still attached to the Methodist Episcopal Church. And the said Methodist Episcopal Church, South, and the bishops, ministers, and members attached thereto, as thus stated, have violated and disregarded said so-called Plan.

"Also, that the General Conference of the Methodist Episcopal Church, at its session held at Pittsburgh, Pa., in May, 1848,—having, as these defendants submit, and as they, according to their judgment and belief, state, full power and rightful authority so to do,—did find and declare, that the fundamental conditions of said proposed Plan, so-called, had severally failed; that the failure of either of them, separately, was sufficient to render said so-called Plan null and void; and that the practical workings of said so-called Plan were incompatible with the great constitutional provisions contained in said Book of Discipline; and they, the said General Conference, did also find and declare, the whole and every part of said provisional Plan, so-called, to be null and void. And for the particulars hereof, these defendants desire leave to refer to the proceedings of, and reports adopted by, said General Conference of 1848; especially to its printed journal, pp. 73–85, 129, 130, and the Final Report of the Committee on the State of the Church, adopted by said Conference, and appended to its journal, pp. 154–164.

"Also, that the so-called 'Plan of Separation,' in no event authorized a division, or reorganization of the Methodist Episcopal Church into two separate Churches; but provided regulations to be observed, on the happening of the contingencies named in the so-called Plan, should the Southern annual conferences, on their own responsibility, withdraw from the Methodist Episcopal Church, and unite in a distinct confederation.

"Wherefore, these defendants further insist and submit, that—instead of the division of the Methodist Episcopal Church into two distinct Churches, under and in pursuance of said so-called Plan of Separation, as is alleged by the plaintiffs—all those bishops, ministers, and members, who have attached themselves, by their own act and deed, to the Methodist Episcopal Church, South, including the plaintiffs, and all those represented in or by them in said Bill of Complaint, have voluntarily withdrawn from the Methodist Episcopal Church, and separated themselves from its privileges and government; and have thereby renounced and forfeited all right and claim, at law or in equity, to any portion of the funds and property in question in this cause.

"And these defendants, further answering, deny that, by force of the proceedings alleged by the plaintiffs, or otherwise, the Methodist Episcopal Church, South, became, was, or is entitled, at law or in equity, to any proportion of all, or any of, the property, real or personal, or of all or any of the funds or effects, which, up to the time of the separation, or any other time, belonged to the Methodist Episcopal Church, in the United States, or elsewhere; and especially do these defendants deny, that the Methodist Episcopal Church, South, was, or is so entitled to any produce of the Book Concern or Chartered Fund, or any property or funds pertaining thereto, without any change or alteration of the sixth restrictive article above mentioned; or that, as erroneously alleged by the plaintiffs, a majority of three-fourths of all the members of the several annual conferences which voted directly on the question in view of a division of the property, has been obtained, infavour of any alteration of that article.

"And these defendants, with respect to the allegation of the plaintiffs, that 'said property and funds of the Methodist Episcopal Church had been obtained and collected by voluntary contribution, in which contribution the members of the Church, South, contributed the largest portion of the same,' deny, that, so far as the allegation has reference to the property and funds of the Book Concern, in the city of New-York, and its appendages, the same, or the greater portion thereof, have been obtained by voluntary contribution; and the defendants say, that the same were originally obtained as is hereinafter stated; but, in so far as the same were obtained by voluntary contributions, on the rebuilding of the Book Concern when damaged by fire, and in respect of any portion thereof contributed from the South, these defendants state, that all such contributions were made, intended, and given for the very object for which said Book Concern was then, and always had been, designed; that, on occasion of the contributions referred to, many others largely contributed, who have since left the Church; yet that any such separatists have never had, nor presumed to make, a claim for their quota of such contributions; nor, on that account, as these defendants submit, can they, or the plaintiffs, or those whom the plaintiffs represent, have or make any claim to recall the portion of donations they have severally made by such voluntary gifts and contributions.

"And these defendants, further answering, admit, that before and on the 8th day of June, 1844, with the qualification and exception hereinafter stated, relative to the Chartered Fund and the Book Concern in the city of New-York, the Methodist Episcopal Church owned and possessed large amounts of property in various parts of the United States; not, however, as the plaintiffs say, in addition to, but principally consisting of, meeting-houses, parsonages, and other estates of that description. But these defendants deny, that, among other or any descriptions or claims of property, there ever belonged to said Church, in the aggregate, or to its lay membership, what was and still is, denominated 'the Book Concern,' in the city of New-York; and these defendants say, that said Book Concern, with all houses, lots, machinery, printing-presses, book-bindery, books, paper, debts, cash, and other articles of property pertaining thereto, is now, and always has been, the property of the preachers belonging to the travelling connexion of the Methodist Episcopal Church, and their families; but if any of such preachers do not, during life, continue in such travelling connexion and in the communion, and subject to the government, of the Methodist Episcopal Church, they forfeit, for themselves and their families, all their ownership in, and all claim upon, said Book Concern, and the produce thereof. And further, that the property of the said Book Concern, consisting as aforesaid, amounts, in value, at the present time, to about the sum stated in the schedule hereto annexed, marked A, which schedule contains a general statement of all the assets and property pertaining to said Book Concern, and of the value thereof, on the first day of January, 1849, as accurately as the same could then, or can now be conveniently ascertained; and which schedule is hereby referred to, and made a part of this answer. And the defendants admit, that all said lands, property, and effects pertaining to said Book Concern, and enumerated in said schedule, are in the possession of the defendants, Lane and Scott, as agents for said Book Concern, who have been duly appointed as such agents by the General Conference of the Methodist Episcopal Church; and the defendants state, that such agents are enabled to hold said lands, and the buildings thereon and appurtenances, for the objects of said Book Concern and the purposes of such agency, by virtue of an act of the Legislature of the State of New-York, entitled, 'An Act relative to the Methodist Book Concern in the city of New York,' passed April 21, 1837, which has ever since been, and still is, a valid law of the State of New-York, and of which the following is a copy, to wit:—

"'An Act relative to the Methodist Book Concern, in the city of New-York, passed April 21, 1837.

"'§ 1. It shall be lawful for Thomas Mason and George Lane, Agents for the Methodist Book Concern, appointed by the General Conference of the Methodist Episcopal Church, and their successors, as such agents, to take and hold real estate, in trust for the purposes of such agency, and to demise and convey the same; but the value of such real estate so taken and held by them shall not exceed two hundred thousand dollars.

"'§ 2. The real estate heretofore conveyed to Thomas Mason and George Lane, as agents as aforesaid, shall be considered as part of the real estate to be held by them, and their successors, as such agents, in trust as aforesaid.'—*Session Laws of New-York, of* 1837; ch. 232, p. 220.

"And these defendants, further answering, state, that the said Book Concern was originally commenced and instituted by travelling ministers of the Methodist Episcopal Church, on their own capital, with the great design, in the first place, of circulating religious knowledge; by whom it was surrendered to the ownership of all the travelling preachers in full connexion, and made subject to the control of all the travelling preachers in their general convention, then called the General Conference; and it was agreed, from time to time, that the profits arising from the sale of the books should be applied to pious and charitable objects, but principally to the support of travelling ministers and their families, until, in the General Conference of 1796, it was determined that the said moneys should, in future, be applied wholly to the relief of travelling preachers, including such of them as were superannuated, and the widows and orphans of such as were deceased; one of the decisions of which General Conference in that year was, 'the produce of the sale of our books, after the book debts are paid, and a sufficient capital is provided for carrying on the business, shall be regularly paid into the Chartered Fund;' and the object of said fund was for 'the relief of distressed travelling preachers, for the families of travelling preachers, and for the superannuated and worn-out preachers, and the widows and orphans of preachers.' That, from that time to the General Conference of 1808, no other appropriation whatever was made of the proceeds of said Book Concern, but for the benefit of travelling preachers of the Methodist Episcopal Church, and their families; and that until, and in, the General Conference of that year, as is hereinbefore stated, all the travelling preachers in full connexion, who had travelled four years, belonging to the Church, had a seat in, and were members of, the General Conference; at which time, on the occasion of adopting the plan for a delegated General Conference, with constitutional powers limited by certain restrictions, as above detailed, the said General Conference of travelling preachers established a Constitution, as already stated, specifying who should compose, and defining the regulations and powers belonging to, such delegated General Conference, and therein and thereby providing that the General Conference should have full powers to make rules and regulations for the Church, under six specified limitations and restrictions, commonly called the Restrictive Articles, which are fully set out in the Book of Discipline—by means whereof, the said general convention of travelling preachers, as defendants submit they lawfully might do, committed the management of the said Book Concern to such delegated General Conference, as to agents, or trustees, under and subject to the limitation and restriction contained in the sixth of said restrictive articles, which the defendants crave leave to read and refer to as a part of this answer.

"And the defendants pray that said constitution and restrictive articles, especially the above-recited sixth restrictive article, may be taken as a part of this answer; and that they may have leave to read and refer to said constitution and restrictive articles, and to the proceedings of said general convention of travelling preachers, as a part also of this answer.

"And these defendants, further answering, say, that the recommendation of the General Conference of 1844, contained in the aforesaid resolution embodied in the so-called 'Plan of Separation,' to all the annual conferences, to authorize a change of the sixth restrictive article, so that the first clause should read as in said resolution specified, has not been concurred in by the constitutional majority of the members of such annual conferences; and that such recommendation has entirely failed: that such recommendation was duly laid before all the annual conferences; and that they all voted thereon; but, on canvassing the votes at the General Conference in

1848,—which body had full power to determine the number of votes by the annual conferences for altering such restrictive rule,—it was ascertained and declared, that the number of votes necessary to authorize such alteration had not been obtained; nor have the annual conferences at any time since authorized such change of said article.

"And these defendants, for the proceedings of said General Conference, and the particulars, in respect of such votes, crave leave to refer to the journal of that conference, page 56, and to the Report of the Committee on the State of the Church, being document L, recorded in the Journal of Reports of said General Conference.

"Wherefore, these defendants, as touching the allegations and claims in the plaintiffs' bill, with regard to the property denominated the 'Book-Concern,' and 'Chartered Fund,' and the moneys, effects, and credits pertaining thereto, insist and submit, that the Methodist Episcopal Church, South, is not entitled, at law or in equity, to have a division of such property made, as claimed by said bill; nor is such Church, South, thus entitled to any share or portion thereof; nor are any of the ministers, preachers, or members, attached to such Church, South, thus entitled to any portion of the same; and that they—being no longer travelling preachers belonging to the Methodist Episcopal Church—could not be so entitled, without a constitutional change in the said sixth restrictive article, which would authorize such division.

"And these defendants, further answering, deny, that at the time alleged by the plaintiffs, or at any other time, the agents of the Book Concern at New-York, in pursuance of the provisions or terms of said resolutions, called by the plaintiffs the 'Plan of Separation,' paid to the several annual conferences of the Methodist Episcopal Church, South, their proportion of the profits and income of the Book Concern, as fixed and set apart by the said agents for the year 1845; and, in respect of such allegation, these defendants say, that the portion of profits and income, alluded to by the plaintiffs, which said book-agents paid to such annual conferences, had accrued and been apportioned to such Southern conferences previous to the organization of the Methodist Episcopal Church, South, whilst such conferences were connected with the Methodist Episcopal Church; and that such payment was made without any reference whatever to the said so-called 'Plan of Separation.' And the defendants admit, that, since the year 1845, the said agents have refused to pay to the annual conferences, South, who have separated from the Methodist Episcopal Church, as aforesaid, anything further from the profits or income of said Book Concern—as, these defendants submit, in justice and right, and according to their duty, said agents ought to have done. And these defendants deny, that such annual conferences, South, are legally entitled to any portion or share of such profits or income; or that the withholding thereof from them, by said agents, is in violation of their rights.

"And these defendants, further answering, admit, that the body assuming to act as the General Conference of the Methodist Episcopal Church, South, holden at Petersburg, Va., in May, 1846, proceeded to appoint the commissioners as stated in said bill, and for the purposes therein stated; and the defendants also admit, that the body aforesaid adopted the resolutions commencing at folio 34 of the plaintiffs' bill; but these defendants submit and insist, that such resolutious are entirely nugatory in their effect upon the property and funds therein referred to, and the matters pertaining to the same.

"And the defendants admit that said commissioners have made the applications to these defendants and James B. Finley, and the requests of them, in the said bill stated; and that these defendants have refused to act in the premises; and they say, they have thus refused for the reasons and on the grounds herein set forth.

"The defendants also admit, that the plaintiffs have not been enabled to induce the said book-agents—nor the Methodist Episcopal Church—nor the commissioners named by the plaintiffs—to pay to the Church, South, any portion or share of said property and funds, except as aforesaid; but the defendants deny, that said Church, South, is lawfully entitled to any proportionate or other share of said property or funds, as provided by said 'Plan of Separation,' so-called, or otherwise.

"And the defendants admit, that the plaintiffs are members of the Methodist Episcopal Church, South, and that they are preachers belonging to the travelling connexion of said Church, South; but these defendants deny, that, as such, they, or any or either of them, have any personal interest in the real estate, personal property, debts or funds above-mentioned; or in any property, debts or funds, if any, now holden by the Methodist Episcopal Church, through these defendants, or any of them, as agents or trustees, appointed by the General Conference of the Methodist Episcopal Church, or otherwise.

"And these defendants, further answering, say, that they have not sufficient knowledge or information, either to admit or deny, whether the allegations in the plaintiffs' bill respecting the number of preachers belonging to the travelling connexion of the Methodist Episcopal Church, South, and the number in the membership of that Church,—are true or not; and the plaintiffs are, therefore, left to make such proof thereof as they may be able and advised to do; these defendants, however, according to their belief, say, that such numbers have been over-stated by the plaintiffs.

"And these defendants, further answering, deny, that the preachers belonging to the travelling connexion of the Methodist Episcopal Church, South, or any or either of them, have a direct and personal, or other legal or equitable interest, in the same right with the plaintiffs, or otherwise, in said property, situated and held as hereinbefore stated, or in any part or portion thereof, to any amount whatever. And the defendants utterly deny that the lay membership of the Church, South, whether in number as stated by the plaintiffs, or otherwise, are parties in interest in the subject-matter of the plaintiffs' bill, or have, or ever had, any pecuniary interest in the said funds or property.

"And these defendants, further answering, admit, that these defendants are members of the Methodist Episcopal Church, and are preachers belonging to the travelling connexion of that Church, and that each of them has a personal interest in the said property and funds; but these defendants state, that such interest is the same only as is held in common by all the preachers in the travelling connexion of the Methodist Episcopal Church, and depends upon the contingency of their remaining in that connexion. And these defendants admit that the defendants, Lane and Scott, have the custody and control by law, and by virtue of their appointment as agents of the Book Concern by the General Conference of the Methodist Episcopal Church, of all the said property and effects of the said Book Concern.

"And these defendants, further answering, say, that they have no certain knowledge thereof, but, according to their information and belief, they deny, that the plaintiffs have brought their said bill by the authority, and under the direction, of all the annual conferences and travelling preachers, or members, in said Church, South. And these defendants claim and insist upon the same benefit and advantage of this objection to the right of said plaintiffs to bring said bill, as if the same were interposed by plea, or demurrer, or in other proper manner.

"And these defendants, George Lane and Levi Scott, further answering, say, that the schedule hereto annexed, marked A, contains a full, particular and just account of all the real estate, personal estate, goods, debts, money and effects of every sort or kind, held by them, or either of them, as agent or agents, trustees, or members, of the Methodist Episcopal Church, so far as such account can, at the present time, be conveniently made up; and the same comprises all the assets and property pertaining to said Book Concern.

"And these defendants, Nathan Bangs and George Peck, admit, that, by the terms of the resolutions already referred to, they, together with James B. Finley, were appointed by the General Conference of the Methodist Episcopal Church, of 1844, held at New-York, commissioners, for the purposes stated in such resolutions, in the event aforesaid of their becoming operative; but say, that they have not received any other appointment or authority as commissioners, or otherwise, to act upon the part of said General Conference, or said Church, with any commissioners on the part of the South, in relation to any division, distribution, or settlement of the property herein referred to, or of any so-called 'Church property.' And these defendants, Bangs and Peck, further say, that inasmuch as the said resolutions, denominated the 'Plan of Separation,' have never had any validity, and have been declared null and void, in the manner hereinbefore stated—they admit they have refused to act, as such commissioners under those resolutions, in any settlement or division of any property.

"And the defendants submit that the plaintiffs are not entitled to the relief or decree prayed for in said Bill of Complaint, or to any other relief or decree against these defendants, touching the matters in said bill set forth.

"And these defendants, in answering, further say, that as they are advised by counsel and believe, and therefore submit, the claim of the Methodist Episcopal

Church, South, to a pro rata portion of the funds and property in question in this suit, is not clear, but on the contrary must be conceeded to be at least doubtful in law, and that these defendants cannot safely pay or deliver over the same to them, or their agents lawfully constituted, without their first having their rights therein and thereto established, and without the sanction and authority of a court of law; and they therefore pray, that, in any event, they may be protected from all injury in the premises; that their rights and duties therein may be established, and all proper costs, counsel fees, commissions, and expenses of every kind, may be allowed to them under the decree of this Honourable Court.

MR. LORD,—A replication has been filed to this answer which it is not necessary to read.

Since these proceedings began, we have had to lament the death of Dr. Bascom, one of the parties to this suit. Dr. William A. Smith has been substituted in the place of Bishop Bascom. I have the consent of my friends on the other side, dated the 14th of May, and if your Honours please I move that an order be made, making this substitution as of to-day.

THE COURT,—Take your order.

MR. LORD,—If your Honours please, in introducing these proofs I may say that they are mostly, if not altogether, documents to be introduced by consent. We have on each side consented that the Book of Discipline of the Methodist Episcopal Church, printed in 1840, which was the book in force at the time of the Conference of 1844, shall be considered in evidence. And we have printed those extracts which, on reading the book, we considered to bear upon the case, and which your Honours will find in the Book of Proofs, No. 1. If the gentlemen on the other side think there is any other part that is material to the case, they can read it to the Court. We also, in regard to such historical facts as may bear on this controversy, have on each side agreed to refer to Emory's History of the Discipline of the Church; and further, we have marked our extracts and printed them.

MR. CHOATE,—With the right reserved to both parties of looking beyond them, I suppose?

MR. LORD,—Yes, sir, with the same right reserved to both parties of looking beyond them. We also refer to the printed journals of the several General Conferences of the Church, for the years 1840 and 1844, which were Conferences common to the two Churches, and to the journals of the Conference of 1848; all of which we have agreed to admit in evidence. The Conference of 1848 of course bore a different relation, a very different relation, to the subject, we suppose, than those of 1840 and 1844. We also refer to the manuscript journals of the several General Conferences of the same Church, prior to 1840, which are accessible to both solicitors at the Methodist Book Concern, in the city of New-York, which shall be held and considered to be duly authenticated and verified by proof; and extracts from any part of them shall be admitted as evidence, and either party shall be at liberty to refer to and read them with the same effect as if the original had actually been produced in proof. In introducing this evidence to the Court, I shall not take the course of reading the book through, but I shall introduce each distinct portion as it bears upon the points of the case, as they are presented in our brief of the points of the argument. The first to which I shall refer are those in relation to the Book Concern. I shall refer your Honours to the pages, so that they may be marked as I proceed. I refer to page 30 of the Book of Proofs, No. 1, which are proofs common to both parties.

The Book of Proofs, No. 2, contains proceedings which we introduce in evidence to show the acts of the portion of the Church with which we are more especially connected. The stipulation in regard to the admission of that is in the preface to the book in these words :—

"The plaintiffs in this cause, by their solicitor, propose and consent to the following documents and papers, and the matters therein stated, as further evidence in this action.

"And the defendants, by their solicitor, consent that said documents and papers be read in evidence, to show the proceedings therein detailed of the various bodies and members thereof, and persons, as such proceedings are by those bodies, members, and persons, respectively for themselves reported.

"But the defendants, except as above, do not admit any statements of alleged matters of fact or of opinion, or any of the arguments in said documents or papers contained.

"The Discipline of the 'Methodist Episcopal Church, South,' may be referred to as containing the doctrines, and rules of government and discipline of said organization."

Turning to page 30 of Book of Proofs, No. 1, I read as follows. It is an extract from the Book of Discipline of 1840 :—

"*Of the Printing and Circulating of Books, and of the profits arising therefrom.*

"1. The principal establishment of the Book Concern shall be in the city of New-York; and there shall be such other establishments as the General Conference may deem expedient."—P. 198.

"28. The profits arising from the Book-Concern, after a sufficient capital to carry on the business is retained, shall be regularly applied to the support of the deficient travelling preachers and their families, the widows and orphans of preachers, &c. The general book-steward shall every year send forward to each annual conference an account of the dividend which the several annual conferences may draw that year; and each conference may draw for its proportionate part on any person who has book-money in hands, and the drafts, with the receipt of the conference thereon, shall be sent to the general book-steward, and be placed to the credit of the person who paid the same." Pp. 207, 208.

Now, if your Honours please, I turn to the history and origin of this Book Concern, as given in Dr. Emory's History of the Discipline. His History I would explain is in the form of annals. He gives the history of the alterations in the Discipline at each successive General Conference, or other authorized act of the Church. I quote from page 17 of the Book of Proofs, No. 1.

"*Of the printing and circulating of Books, and of the Profits arising therefrom.*

"1800. The form of questions and answers laid aside, and the whole section remodelled as follows:—

"1. Ezekiel Cooper is appointed the superintendent of the Book Concern, who shall have authority to regulate the publications, and all other parts of the business, according to the state of the finances from time to time. It shall be his duty to inform the annual conferences if any of the preachers or private members of the society neglect to make due payment. He may publish any books or tracts which, at any time, may be approved of or recommended by the majority of an annual conference, provided such books or tracts be also approved of by the book committee, which shall be appointed by the Philadelphia Annual Conference. He may reprint any book or tract which has once been approved and published by us, when, in his judgment, the same ought to be reprinted. Let his accounts and books be examined by the Philadelphia Conference at the time of the sitting of the said conference.

"2. It shall be the duty of every presiding elder, where no book-steward is appointed, to see that his district be fully supplied with books. He is to order such books as are wanted, and to give direction to whose care the same are to be sent; and he is to take the oversight of all our books sent into his district, and to account with the superintendent for the same. He is to have the books distributed among the several circuits in his district, and is to keep an account with each preacher who receives or sells the books; and is to receive the money, and to forward it to the superintendent. When a presiding elder is removed, he is to make a full settlement for all the books sold or remaining in his district; and is also to make a transfer to his successor of all the books and accounts left with the preachers in the district, the amount of which shall go to his credit, and pass to the debit of his successor.

"3. It shall be the duty of every preacher, who has the charge of a circuit, to see that his circuit be duly supplied with books, and to take charge of all the books which are sent to him, from time to time, or which may be in his circuit; and he is to account with the presiding elder for the same. When a preacher leaves his circuit, he must settle with the presiding elder for all the books he has disposed of; he is also to make out an inventory of all that are remaining unsold, which shall be collected at one place; the amount of which shall go to his credit, and be transferred to his successor, who is to take charge of the same. If the preacher who has the charge of the circuit be negligent in dispersing the books, the presiding elder shall commit the charge of the books to another.

"4. The superintendent of the book business may, from time to time, supply the preachers with books in those circuits which are adjacent or convenient to Philadelphia, and settle with them for the same: in such cases the regulations respecting the presiding elders are not to apply.

"5. In all cases where books are sent to distant places, the presiding elders or preachers shall be allowed to put a small additional price on such books as will best bear it, in order to pay the expense of freight or carriage; but the addition must not be more than what is necessary to defray such expenses.

"6. Every annual conference shall appoint a committee or committees to examine the accounts of the presiding elders, preachers, and book-stewards, in their respective districts or circuits. Every presiding elder, minister, and preacher, shall do everything in their power to recover all debts due to the Concern, and also all the books belonging to the Concern, which may remain in the hands of any person within their districts or circuits. If any preacher or member be indebted to the Book Concern, and refuse to make payment, or to come to a just settlement, let him be dealt with for a breach of trust, and such effectual measures be adopted for the recovery of such debts as shall be agreeable to the direction of the annual conferences respectively.

"7. There shall be no drafts made upon the Book Concern till its debts are discharged, and a sufficient capital provided for carrying on the business; after which, the profits arising from the books shall be regularly paid to the chartered fund, and be applied, with the annual income of the funded stock, to the support of the distressed travelling preachers and their families, the widows and orphans of preachers, &c.

"8. It shall be the duty of the preacher or preachers who travel with any of the bishops, if he or they be authorized by the superintendent of the Book Concern, to act as an agent in the settlement of accounts, collecting money, or in transacting any business belonging to the Book Concern."—Pp. 258–260.

In 1804, while the conference consisted of all the preachers, it was altered to read in this way,—pp. 19, 20, Book of proofs, No. 1.

"1804.—7. The profits arising from the Book Concern, after a sufficient capital to carry on the business is retained, shall be regularly applied to the support of the distressed travelling preachers and their families, the widows and orphans of preachers, &c. The general book-steward, shall every year send forward to each annual conference an account of the dividend which the several annual conferences may draw that year; and each conference may draw for their proportionate part, on any person who has book money in hand, and the drafts, with the receipt of the conference thereon, shall be sent to the general book-steward, and be placed to the credit of the person who paid the same. But each annual conference is authorized, at all events, to draw on the general book-steward for one hundred dollars."—Pp. 261, 262.

Your Honours will observe the change to be, that the profits were not to be paid into the Chartered Fund, but to be distributed by the agencies of the annual conferences; and it thus remained, in substance, until the rule was adopted as it now stands in the Discipline of 1840.

The next subject, extracts in relation to which I will read, is the Conferences, Annual and General; but in that connexion I will read extracts from the Book of Discipline of 1840, beginning on page 25 of the first of the proofs, on the subject of the Holy Scriptures, the Church, and its rites and ceremonies; for they bear upon this part of the case. The articles of religion are printed at large, and what I shall read are but extracts.

"ARTICLES OF RELIGION.

"V. *The Sufficiency of the Holy Scriptures for Salvation.*

"The Holy Scriptures contain all things necessary to salvation: so that whatsoever is not read therein, nor may be proved thereby, is not to be required of any man, that it should be believed as an article of faith, or be thought requisite or necessary to salvation."—P. 10.

"XIII. *Of the Church.*

"The visible Church of Christ is a congregation of faithful men, in which the pure word of God is preached, and the sacraments duly administered according to Christ's ordinance in all those things that of necessity are requisite to the same."—P. 14.

"XXII. *Of the Rites and Ceremonies of Churches.*

"It is not necessary that rites and ceremonies should in all places be the same, or exactly alike: for they have been always different, and may be changed according to the diversity of countries, times, and men's manners, so that nothing be ordained against God's word. Whosoever, through his private judgment, willingly and purposely doth openly break the rites and ceremonies of the Church to which he belongs, which are not repugnant to the word of God, and are ordained and approved by common authority, ought to be rebuked openly, that others may fear to do the like, as one that offendeth against the common order of the Church, and woundeth the consciences of weak brethren.

"Every particular Church may ordain, change, or abolish rites and ceremonies, so that all things may be done to edification."—Pp. 18, 19.

"XXIII. *Of the Rulers of the United States of America.*

"The president, the congress, the general assemblies, the governors, and the councils of state, *as the delegates of the people*, are the rulers of the United States of America, according to the division of power made to them by the Constitution of the United States, and by the Constitutions of their respective States. And the said States are a sovereign and independent nation, and ought not to be subject to any foreign jurisdiction."*

"*Of the General Conference.*

"*Quest.* 2. Who shall compose the General Conference, and what are the regulations and powers belonging to it?

"*Ans.* 1. The General Conference shall be composed of one member for every twenty-one members of each annual conference, to be appointed either by seniority or choice, at the discretion of such annual conference: yet so that such representatives shall have travelled at least four full calendar years from the time that they were received on trial by an annual conference, and are in full connexion at the time of holding the conference.

"2. The General Conference shall meet on the first day of May, in the year of our Lord 1812, in the city of New-York, and thenceforward on the first day of May

"* As far as it respects civil affairs, we believe it the duty of Christians, and especially all Christian ministers, to be subject to the supreme authority of the country where they may reside, and to use all laudable means to enjoin obedience to the powers that be; and therefore it is expected that all our preachers and people, who may be under the British, or any other government, will behave themselves as peaceable and orderly subjects."—P. 19.

once in four years perpetually, in such place or places as shall be fixed on by the General Conference from time to time: but the general superintendents, with or by the advice of all the annual conferences, or if there be no general superintendent, all the annual conferences respectively, shall have power to call a General Conference, if they judge it necessary at any time.

"3. At all times when the General Conference is met, it shall take two-thirds of the representatives of all the annual conferences to make a quorum for transacting business.

"4. One of the general superintendents shall preside in the General Conference; but in case no general superintendent be present, the General Conference shall choose a president pro tem.

"5. The General Conference shall have full powers to make rules and regulations for our Church, under the following limitations and restrictions, viz:—"

The six articles that I am going to read are known under the technical name of "Restrictive Articles." I may here also observe, that the designation "General Superintendents," in what I have read, is the name given to their bishops.

"1. The General Conference shall not revoke, alter, or change our articles of religion, nor establish any new standards or rules of doctrine contrary to our present existing and established standards of doctrine.

"2. They shall not allow of more than one representative for every fourteen members of the annual conference, nor allow of a less number than one for every thirty: provided, nevertheless, that when there shall be in any annual conference a fraction of two-thirds the number which shall be fixed for the ratio of representation, such annual conference shall be entitled to an additional delegate for such fraction; and provided, also, that no conference shall be denied the privilege of two delegates.

"3. They shall not change or alter any part or rule of our government, so as to do away episcopacy, or destroy the plan of our itinerant general superintendency.

"4. They shall not revoke or change the general rules of the United Societies.

"5. They shall not do away the privileges of our ministers or preachers of trial by a committee, and of an appeal; neither shall they do away the privileges of our members of trial before the society, or by a committee, and of an appeal.

"6. They shall not appropriate the produce of the Book-Concern, nor of the Charter Fund, to any purpose other than for the benefit of the travelling, supernumerary, superannuated and worn-out preachers, their wives, widows, and children. Provided, nevertheless, that upon the concurrent recommendation of three-fourths of all the members of the several annual conferences, who shall be present and vote on such recommendation, then a majority of two-thirds of the General Conference succeeding shall suffice to alter any of the above restrictions, excepting the first article: and also, whenever such alteration or alterations shall have been first recommended by two-thirds of the General Conference, so soon as three-fourths of the members of all the annual conferences shall have concurred as aforesaid, such alteration or alterations shall take effect."—Pp. 21–24.

"*Of the Annual Conferences.*

"*Quest.* 3. Who shall attend the yearly conferences?

"*Ans.* All the travelling preachers who are in full connexion, and those who are to be received into full connexion."—P. 24.

"*Of the Allowance to the Ministers and Preachers, and to their Wives, Widows, and Children.*

"1. The annual allowance of the married travelling, supernumerary, and superannuated preachers, and the bishops, shall be two hundred dollars, and their travelling expenses.

"2. The annual allowance of the unmarried travelling, supernumerary, and superannuated preachers, and bishops, shall be one hundred dollars, and their travelling expenses.

"3. Each child of a travelling preacher or bishop shall be allowed sixteen dollars annually, to the age of seven years, and twenty-four dollars annually from the age of seven to fourteen years; and those preachers whose wives are dead shall be allowed for each child annually a sum sufficient to pay the board of such child or children during the above term of years: *Nevertheless*, this rule shall not apply to the children of preachers whose families are provided for by other means in their circuits respectively.

"4. The annual allowance of the widows of travelling, superannuated, worn-out, and supernumerary preachers, and the bishops, shall be one hundred dollars.

"5. The orphans of travelling, supernumerary, superannuated, and worn-out preachers, and the bishops, shall be allowed by the annual conferences the same sums respectively which are allowed to the children of living preachers. And on the death of a preacher leaving a child or children without so much of worldly goods as should be necessary to his, her, or their support, the annual conference of which he was a member shall raise, in such a manner as may be deemed best, a yearly sum for the subsistence and education of such orphan child or children, until he, she, or they, shall have arrived at fourteen years of age. The amount of which yearly sum shall be fixed by a committee of the conference at each session in advance."—Pp. 181, 182.

Now, if your Honours please, I propose to read historical documents, to show how this power of the General Conferences has taken its shape from time to time; so that it may be seen what has been done, how it has arisen, and how it has grown up. I am about to read an extract from Emory's History of the Discipline. By "Discipline" is meant the book of that designation containing the articles of religion and everything relating to this Church.

"In our civil governments the statutes are scattered through the several volumes of laws, which have been published from time to time, and therefore these are all preserved. But, in the Methodist Episcopal Church, the Discipline, as revised at each General Conference, being in itself complete, supplants all that had gone before it, and the previous editions are cast aside, as of no further use. Thus it has continued, until now nearly sixty years have elapsed since the organization of the Church, and the Discipline has undergone about twenty distinct revisions"—P. 3.

For the present I pass over the questions which relate to slavery, as I propose to read all those parts which relate to that subject together, and distinct from other questions. I proceed, therefore, to page 3 of the first of the proofs:—

"The close of the year 1784 constituted a new and most important epoch in American Methodism. The independence of the United States having been confirmed by the peace of 1783, the authority of England over them, both civil and ecclesiastical, came to an end. The connexion with the Church of England being thus providentially *dissolved*, Mr. Wesley, who had always resisted a *separation* from it, took measures, on the application of the American societies, to organize them into a Church. In explanation of his views and wishes, he addressed to the brethren in America the following letter:—

"'Bristol, September 10, 1784.

"'*To Dr. Coke, Mr. Asbury, and our Brethren in North America*:—

"'1. By a very uncommon train of providences, many of the provinces of North America are totally disjoined from the British empire, and erected into independent States. The English government has no authority over them, either civil or ecclesiastical, any more than over the States of Holland. A civil authority is exercised over them, partly by the congress, partly by the state assemblies. But no one either exercises or claims any ecclesiastical authority at all. In this peculiar situation some thousands of the inhabitants of these States desire my advice; and in compliance with their desire I have drawn up a little sketch.

"'2. Lord King's account of the primitive Church convinced me, many years ago, that bishops and presbyters are the same order, and, consequently, have the same right to ordain. For many years I have been importuned, from time to time, to exercise this right, by ordaining part of our travelling preachers; but I have still refused, not only for peace' sake, but because I was determined as little as possible to violate the established order of the national Church to which I belonged.

"'3. But the case is widely different between England and North America. Here there are bishops who have a legal jurisdiction. In America there are none, and but few parish ministers; so that for some hundred miles together there is none either to baptize or to administer the Lord's Supper. Here, therefore, my scruples are at an end; and I conceive myself at full liberty, as I violate no order, and invade no man's right, by appointing and sending labourers into the harvest.

"'4. I have, accordingly, appointed Dr. Coke, and Mr. Francis Asbury to be joint *superintendents* over our brethren in North America; as also Richard Whatcoat and Thomas Vasey to act as *elders* among them, by baptizing and administering the Lord's Supper.

"'5. If any one will point out a more rational and Scriptural way of feeding and guiding those poor sheep in the wilderness, I will gladly embrace it. At present I cannot see any better method than that I have taken.

"'6. It has indeed been proposed to desire the English bishops to ordain part of our preachers for America. But to this I object: (1.) I desired the bishop of London to ordain one only, but could not prevail. (2.) If they consented, we know the slowness of their proceedings; but the matter admits of no delay. (3.) If they would ordain them *now*, they would likewise expect to govern them. And how grievously would this entangle us! (4.) As our American brethren are now totally disentangled both from the state and from the English hierarchy, we dare not entangle them again either with the one or the other. They are now at full liberty simply to follow the Scriptures and the primitive Church. And we judge it best that they should stand fast in that liberty wherewith God has so strangely made them free.—Pp. 22-24. John Wesley.'"

I continue to read on the 5th page of No. 1, of the Proofs, and our object in reading this is to show that the Methodist Episcopal Church had its origin in a separation, which did not involve them in any differences of doctrine, or a secession from their English brethren.

"To carry into effect the proposed organization, a General Conference of preachers was called, to meet in Baltimore at Christmas, 1784. Sixty out of the eighty-three preachers, then in the travelling connexion, attended at the appointed time. 'At this conference,' say the Annual Minutes for 1785, 'it was unanimously agreed that circumstances made it expedient for us to become a separate body, under the denomination of "The Methodist Episcopal Church."' And again they say, 'We formed ourselves into an independent Church; and following the counsel of Mr. John Wesley, who recommended the episcopal mode of Church government, we thought it best to become an episcopal Church, making the episcopal office elective, and the elected superintendent or bishop amenable to the body of ministers and preachers.' They adopted a Form of Discipline for the government of the Church. This was substantially the same with the Large Minutes, the principal alterations being only such as were necessary to adapt it to the state of things in America. As this was the first Discipline of the Methodist Episcopal Church, it is here republished entire, together with the portions of the Large Minutes which were left out or altered. Those parts of the Large Minutes which were left out of the Discipline of 1784, are here enclosed in brackets, and, when the passages are long, are printed in smaller type; while what was contained in the latter, and not in the former, is printed in italics. Where there has been merely a substitution of one passage for another, the language of the Large Minutes is given at the foot of the page. The figures in parentheses refer to the Large Minutes.

"'*Minutes of several Conversations between the Rev. Thomas Coke, LL.D., the Rev. Francis Asbury, and others, at a Conference, begun in Baltimore, in the State of Maryland, on Monday, the 27th of December, in the year* 1784.*

"'*Quest.* 2. *What can be done in order to the future union of the Methodists?*

"'*Ans. During the life of the Rev. Mr. Wesley, we acknowledge ourselves his sons*

* First Discipline of the Methodist Episcopal Church, as compared with Large Minutes.

in the gospel, ready, in matters belonging to Church government, to obey his commands. And we do engage, after his death, to do everything that we judge consistent with the cause of religion in America and the political interests of these States, to preserve and promote our union with the Methodists in Europe.

" '*Quest.* 3. *As the ecclesiastical as well as civil affairs of these United States have passed through a very considerable change by the Revolution, what plan of Church government shall we hereafter pursue?*

" '*Ans. We will form ourselves into an Episcopal Church, under the direction of superintendents, elders, deacons, and helpers, according to the forms of ordination annexed to our Liturgy, and the Form of Discipline set forth in these Minutes.*

" '*Quest.* 4. (3.) What may we reasonably believe to be God's design in raising up the preachers called Methodists?

" '*Ans.* [Not to form any new sect; but] to reform the *continent*, [particularly the Church;] and to spread Scriptural holiness over *these lands*.'—Pp. 25–27."

For the reasons before given, I pass over the passages on pp. 7, 8, and 9, which relate to slavery, and come to p. 10.

"1787.—In 1787 the Discipline underwent an entire change in its form. It will have been perceived, that the first and second editions consisted of a series of questions and answers, arranged with very little method. The book was now divided into sections, with appropriate heads.—P. 81.

" *Of the Origin of the Methodist Episcopal Church.*

"1789.—'Sec. 3. On the Nature and Constitution of our Church.

" 'We are thoroughly convinced that the Church of England, to which we have been united, is deficient in several of the most important parts of Christian discipline; and that (a few ministers and members excepted) it has lost the life and power of religion. We are not ignorant of the spirit and design it has ever discovered in Europe, of rising to pre-eminence and worldly dignities by virtue of a national establishment, and by the most servile devotion to the will of temporal governors: and we fear the same spirit will lead the same Church in these United States (though altered in its name) to similar designs and attempts, if the number and strength of its members will ever afford a probability of success; and particularly to obtain a national establishment, which we cordially abhor as the great bane of truth and holiness, and consequently a great impediment to the progress of vital Christianity.

" 'For these reasons we have thought it our duty to form ourselves into an independent Church. And as the most excellent mode of Church government, according to our maturest judgment, is that of a moderate episcopacy, and as we are persuaded that the uninterrupted succession of bishops from the apostles can be proved neither from Scripture nor antiquity, we therefore have constituted ourselves into an episcopal Church, under the direction of bishops, elders, deacons, and preachers, according to the forms of ordination annexed to our Prayer-book, and the regulations laid down in this form of Discipline.'

" 'Sec. 4. On constituting of bishops, and their duty.

" '*Quest.* 1. What is the proper origin of the episcopal authority in our Church?

" '*Ans.* In the year 1784 the Rev. John Wesley, who, under God, has been the father of the great revival of religion now extending over the earth by the means of the Methodists, determined, at the intercession of multitudes of his spiritual children on this continent, to ordain ministers for America, and for this purpose sent over three regularly-ordained clergy; but preferring the episcopal mode of Church government to any other, he solemnly set apart, by the imposition of his hands and prayer, one of them, namely, Thomas Coke, doctor of civil law, late of Jesus College, in the University of Oxford, for the episcopal office; and having delivered to him letters of episcopal orders, commissioned and directed him to set apart Francis Asbury, then general assistant of the Methodist Society in America, for the same episcopal office, he, the said Francis Asbury, being first ordained deacon and elder. In consequence of which, the said Francis Asbury was solemnly set apart for the said episcopal office by prayer and the imposition of the hands of the said Thomas

Coke, other regularly-ordained ministers assisting in the sacred ceremony. At which time the General Conference held at Baltimore did unanimously receive the said Thomas Coke and Francis Asbury as their bishops, being fully satisfied of the validity of their episcopal ordination.'—Pp. 93, 94.

" *Of the General and Annual Conferences.*

"Of the General Conference.

" Nothing appears on this subject, until 1792, when the first General Conference, after the organization of the Church, was held. We then find the following :—

" 1792. '*Quest.* 2. Who shall compose the General Conference ?

" '*Ans.* All the travelling preachers who shall be in full connexion at the time of holding the Conference.

" '*Quest.* 3. When and where shall the next General Conference be held ?

" '*Ans.* On the first day of November, in the year 1796, in the town of Baltimore.'

" 1796. Question 3, struck out.

" 1800. An additional qualification for membership was added, namely :—to 'have travelled four years.'

" 1804. It was provided that the 'four years' should date 'from the time that they were received on trial by an annual conference.'

" 1808. This was the last meeting of a General Conference, composed of all the preachers who had travelled four years. It was then resolved to have, in future, a delegated General Conference, and the following was adopted as its constitution, in lieu of the former :—

" '*Quest.* 2. Who shall compose the General Conference, and what are the regulations and powers belonging to it ?

" '*Ans.* 1. The General Conference shall be composed of one member for every five members of each annual conference, to be appointed either by seniority or choice, at the discretion of such annual conference ; yet so that such representatives shall shall have travelled at least four full calendar years from the time that they were received on trial by an annual conference, and are in full connexion at the time of holding the Conference.

" '2. The General Conference shall meet on the first day of May, in the year of our Lord 1812, in the city of New-York, and thenceforward on the first day of May, once in four years perpetually, in such place or places as shall be fixed on by the General Conference from time to time : but the general superintendents, with or by the advice of all the annual conferences, or if there be no general superintendent, all the annual conferences respectively, shall have power to call a General Conference, if they judge it necessary, at any time.

" '3. At all times when the General Conference is met, it shall take two-thirds of the representatives of all the annual conferences to make a quorum for transacting business.

" '4. One of the general superintendents shall preside in the General Conference ; but in case no general superintendent be present, the General Conference shall choose a president pro tem.

" '5. The General Conference shall have full powers to make rules and regulations for our Church, under the following limitations and restrictions, namely :—

" '1. The General Conference shall not revoke, alter, or change our Articles of Religion, nor establish any new standards or rules of doctrine contrary to our present existing and established standards of doctrine.

" '2. They shall not allow of more than one representative for every five members of the annual conference, nor allow of a less number than one for every seven.

" '3. They shall not change or alter any part or rule of our government, so as to do away episcopacy, or destroy the plan of our itinerant general superintendency.

" '4. They shall not revoke or change the general rules of the United Societies.

" '5. They shall not do away the privileges of our ministers or preachers of trial by a committee, and of an appeal : neither shall they do away the privileges of our members of trial before the society, or by a committee, and of an appeal.

" '6. They shall not appropriate the produce of the Book Concern, nor of the Chartered Fund, to any purpose other than for the benefit of the travelling, supernumerary, superannuated, and worn-out preachers, their wives, widows, and children.

" 'Provided, nevertheless, that upon the joint recommendation of all the annual conferences, then a majority of two-thirds of the General Conference succeeding shall suffice to alter any of the above restrictions.'

"1816. The ratio of representation, in Ans. 1., was altered to one for every seven.

"1832. The former proviso, at the close of the restrictive rules, was struck out, and the following substituted :—'Provided, nevertheless, that upon the concurrent recommendation of three-fourths of all the members of the several annual conferences, who shall be present and vote on such recommendation, then a majority of two-thirds of the General Conference succeeding shall suffice to alter any of the above restrictions excepting the first article; and also, whenever such alteration or alterations shall have been first recommended by two-thirds of the General Conference, so soon as three-fourths of the members of all the annual conferences shall have concurred as aforesaid, such alteration or alterations shall take effect.'

"1836. The ratio of representation was altered to one for every twenty-one; and to allow this, the second of the restrictive rules was changed to the following :—

"'2. They shall not allow of more than one representative for every fourteen members of the annual conference, nor allow of a less number than one for every thirty: provided, nevertheless, that when there shall be in any annual conference a fraction of two-thirds the number which shall be fixed for the ratio of representation, such annual conference shall be entitled to an additional delegate for such fraction; and provided, also, that no conference shall be denied the privilege of two delegates.' —Pp. 111–114.

"*Bishops and their Duty.*

"1792. '*Quest.* 3. What is the bishop's duty?

"'*Ans.* 1. To preside in our conferences.

"'2. To fix the appointments of the preachers for the several circuits.

"'3. In the intervals of the conferences to change, receive, or suspend preachers, as necessity may require.

"'4. To travel through the connexion at large.

"'5. To oversee the spiritual and temporal business of the societies.

"'6. To ordain bishops, elders, and deacons.

"'*Quest.* 4. To whom is the bishop amenable for his conduct?

"'*Ans.* To the General Conference, who have power to expel him for improper conduct, if they see it necessary.

"'*Quest.* 5. What provision shall be made for the trial of an immoral bishop, in the interval of the General Conference?

"'*Ans.* If a bishop be guilty of immorality, three travelling elders shall call upon him, and examine him on the subject: and if the three elders verily believe that the bishop is guilty of the crime, they shall call to their aid two presiding elders from two districts in the neighbourhood of that where the crime was committed, each of which presiding elders shall bring with him two elders, or an elder and a deacon. The above-mentioned nine persons shall form a conference, to examine into the charge brought against the bishop; and if two-thirds of them verily believe him to be guilty of the crime laid to his charge, they shall have authority to suspend the bishop till the ensuing General Conference, and the districts shall be regulated in the mean time as is provided in the case of the death of a bishop.'—Pp. 121, 122.

"1804. To the second of the bishop's duties (Question 3) is added this clause: 'Provided he shall not allow any preacher to remain in the same station more than two years successively; excepting the presiding elders, the editor and general book-steward, the assistant editor and general book-steward, the supernumerary, superannuated, and worn out preachers.' To the third is added, 'and as the Discipline directs.'

"In the answer to Question 5, the word 'guilty,' in the first line, is changed to 'accused,' and the following clause is added at the close :—'But no accusation shall be received against a bishop except it be delivered in writing, signed by those who are to prove the crime: and a copy of the accusation shall be given to the accused bishop.'—P. 122."

I will now read, if your Honours please, some extracts from the printed Journals and Documents of the General Conference in relation to the Canada Conference. It seems that the Canada Methodists separated from the Methodists of this country.

The action of the Methodist body on that subject we have thought to be material to notice. I will read, beginning on page 32.

"MAY 5, 1828.—A petition from the Canada Annual Conference was presented by William Ryerson, praying that they may be separated from the jurisdiction of the General Conference of the Methodist Episcopal Church in the United States; which was, on motion, referred to a special committee, to consist of seven members.

"THE PETITION.

"'*To the Bishops and Members of the General Conference of the Methodist Episcopal Church, assembled at Pittsburgh:*—

"'REVEREND FATHERS AND BRETHREN:—The Canada Conference having, after mature deliberation, deemed a separation expedient, most humbly pray that they may be set off a separate and independent Church in Canada.

"'Your petitioners are induced to present this their humble prayer for the following reasons:—

"'1st. Our political relations, and the political feelings of a great part of the community, are such that we labour under many very serious embarrassments on account of our union with the United States; from which embarrassments we would, in all probability, be relieved by a separation.

"'2d. The local circumstances of our societies in this province; the rapid increase and extension of the work, both among the white inhabitants and the Indians; the prospects of division among ourselves, if our present relation be continued—render it necessary for us to be under ecclesiastical regulations somewhat of a peculiar character, so as to suit our local circumstances. These circumstances, together with our being scattered over a large country, render it highly necessary to have a superintendent who may devote himself exclusively to the interests of the Church in this province. By this means he would be identified with us, would more sensibly feel our interests his own, and his influence would be proportionably greater in preserving us in the unity of the Spirit and the bond of peace.

"'3d. It is highly probable we shall obtain some important religious privileges by becoming a separate body.

"'4th. In the event of a war between the two nations, it would be altogether impracticable for a superintendent to discharge the duties of the office unless he be resident in this province.

"'5th. It is the general wish of our people in this province to become separate; nor will they, according to present appearances, be satisfied without such separation.

"'These, reverend fathers and brethren, are some of the principal reasons which induce us to pray for an independent ecclesiastical establishment in Upper Canada.

"'Your petitioners, likewise, most humbly and earnestly solicit that the General Conference may also be pleased,

"'1st. To maintain with the British Conference, as far as practicable, the main principles of the late arrangements with regard to Canada.

"'2d. That the General Conference will appoint such an individual for a superintendent of our societies in Canada as may be nominated by the delegates of the Canada Conference.

"'3d. That the Church in Canada may be embraced in the general and friendly principle recognised by the two connexions,—"The Wesleyan Methodists are the same in every part of the world."

"'4th. That the General Conference will, together with an independent establishment, be pleased to grant your petitioners a portion of the Book Concern, of the Chartered Fund, and a portion of the fund of the Missionary Society.

"'JAMES RICHARDSON,
Sec. Canada Conf.'

"'*September* 7, 1827.

"MAY 6, 1828.—The committee on the petition from Canada was announced by the chair, and consists of the following members, to wit:—

"N. Bangs, Isaac Bonny, Charles Pitman, Zachariah Paddock, Russel Bigalow, and Caleb Leach.

"*Report of the Committee on Canada Affairs.*

"'The Committee on Canada Affairs, to whom was referred the petition of the Canada Conference praying this General Conference to grant a separate establishment of that branch of the Methodist Episcopal Church situated in the Province of Upper Canada, under certain conditions expressed in said petition, beg leave to report:—

"'That, having heard the statements of the delegation from the Canada Conference explanatory of the situation of the Church in that Province, and of the necessity and expediency of the measure prayed for in the petition; and also considered the petition itself, together with the address of the Canada Conference to the several annual conferences in the United States, the committee are unanimously of the opinion, that, however peculiar may be the situation of our brethren in Canada, and however much we may sympathize with them in their present state of perplexity, this General Conference cannot consistently grant them a separate Church establishment, according to the prayer of the petitioners. The committee, therefore, recommend to the General Conference the adoption of the following resolutions:— .

"'1. That, inasmuch as the several annual conferences have not recommended it to the General Conference, it is unconstitutional, and also, under the circumstances, inexpedient, to grant the prayer of the petitioners for a separate Church establishment in Upper Canada.

"'2. That an affectionate circular address be prepared by this General Conference, stating the reasons why their request cannot be granted, and expressing the unabated attachment of this Conference for their brethren in Canada, and their earnest desire for their continuance with them in the fellowship of the Church.

"'All which is respectfully submitted.

"'PITTSBURGH, *May* 12, 1828. (Signed,) N. BANGS, *Chairman.*'

"MAY 17.—Rev. John Ryerson, one of the delegates from the Canada Conference, offered the following substitute for the report under consideration:—

"'Whereas the Canada Annual Conference, situated in the Province of Upper Canada, under a foreign government, have, in their memorial, presented to this Conference the disabilities under which they labour, in consequence of their union with a foreign ecclesiastical government, and setting forth their desire to be set off as a separate Church establishment; and whereas this General Conference disclaim all right to exercise ecclesiastical jurisdiction under such circumstances, except by mutual agreement:—

"'1. *Resolved*, therefore, by the delegates of the annual conferences in General Conference assembled, that the compact existing between the Canada Annual Conference and the Methodist Episcopal Church in the United States be, and hereby is, dissolved by mutual consent.

"'2. That our superintendents or superintendent be, and hereby are, respectfully advised and requested to ordain such person as may be elected by the Canada Conference a superintendent for the Canada connexion.

"'3. That we do hereby recommend to our brethren in Canada to adopt the form of government of the Methodist Episcopal Church in the United States, with such modifications as their particular relations shall render necessary.

"'4. That we do hereby express to our Canada brethren our sincere desire that the most friendly feeling may exist between them and the connexion of the Methodist Episcopal Church in the United States.

"'5. That the claims of the Canada Conference on our Book Concern and Chartered Fund, and any other claims they may suppose they justly have, shall be left open for future negotiation and adjustment between the two connexions.

G. R. JONES.
"'*May 17th.* MOSES CRUME.'

"The question on the first resolution was decided in the effirmative—104 for, and 43 against it. The other four resolutions were, on motion, referred to a special committee, to consist of five members. The president reported the names of the committee, which were as follows:—

"John Emory, Wilbur Fisk, G. R. Jones, Beverly Waugh, Robert Paine.

"The committee reported as follows:—

"'*Resolved* by the delegates of the annual conferences in General Conference assembled, that, whereas the jurisdiction of the Methodist Episcopal Church in the United States of America has heretofore been extended over the ministers and members in connexion with said Church in the Province of Upper Canada, by mutual agreement, and by the consent and desire of our brethren in that province; and whereas this General Conference is satisfactorily assured that our brethren in the said Province, under peculiar and pressing circumstances, do now desire to organize themselves into a distinct Methodist Episcopal Church, in friendly relations with the Methodist Episcopal Church in the United States, therefore be it resolved, and it is hereby resolved, by the delegates of the annual conferences in General Conference assembled:—

"'1. If the annual conference in Upper Canada, at its ensuing session, or any succeeding session previously to the next General Conference, shall definitely determine on this course, and elect a general superintendent of the Methodist Episcopal Church in that province, this General Conference does hereby authorize any one or more of the general superintendents of the Methodist Episcopal Church in the United States, with the assistance of any two or more elders, to ordain such general superintendent for the said Church in Upper Canada, provided always that nothing herein contained be contrary to, or inconsistent with, the laws existing in the said Province; and provided that no such general superintendent of the Methodist Episcopal Church in Upper Canada, or any of his successors in office, shall at any time exercise any ecclesiastical jurisdiction whatever in any part of the United States, or of the territories thereof; and provided also that this article shall be expressly ratified and agreed to by the said Canada Annual Conference, before any such ordination shall take place.

"'2. That the delegate who has been selected by this General Conference to attend the ensuing annual conference of the British Wesleyan Methodist Connexion, be, and hereby is, instructed to express to that body the earnest and affectionate desire of this General Conference, that the arrangement made with that Connexion in relation to the labours of their missionaries in Upper Canada may still be maintained and observed.

"'3. That our brethren and friends, ministers or others, in Upper Canada, shall at all times, at their request, be furnished with any of our books and periodical publications on the same terms with those by which our agents are regulated in furnishing them in the United States: and until there shall be an adjustment of any claims which the Canada Church may have on this connexion, the Book Agents shall divide to the said Canada Church an equal proportion of any annual dividend which may be made from the Book Concern to the several annual conferences respectively; provided, however, that the aforesaid dividend shall be apportioned to the Canada Church only as long as they may continue to support and patronize our Book Concern, as in time past.

"'Respectfully submitted. (Signed) W. Fisk, *Chairman.*

"'Pittsburgh, *May* 20, 1828.'

"Wednesday Morning, May 21.—It was, on motion, *Resolved*, That the subject of the petition from the Canada Conference be resumed: Whereupon, the resolutions, as reported by the last committee appointed on that subject, were read. It was then resolved, that the subject shall now be considered and acted on.

"Samuel H. Thompson moved, and it was seconded, that the resolutions as reported by the committee be adopted. The question being taken, it was decided in the affirmative—108 voting in favour of adoption, and 22 against it.

"May 23.—J. Emory moved, and it was seconded, that the resolution first adopted on the subject of the separation of the Canada Conference from the Connexion in the United States be re-considered; and the motion prevailed. It was then resolved, on motion, that this resolution be rescinded.

"May 4, 1832.—An address from the delegates of the Methodist Episcopal Church of Canada was presented and read, and, on motion, that part of it relating to the Book Concern was referred to the Committee on the Book Concern, and that part of it relating to Missions, referred to the Committee on Missions.

"May 18.—On motion, the report of the Committee on the Book Concern respecting the Canada business was called up. (The delegates, Messrs. William Case, Franklin Metcalf, and William Ryerson, having presented their certificates, which were accepted.) The report of the committee was then read, and seconded that it be adopted.

"May 19.—The report on the Canada business was called up, and, after some remarks on the subject, D. Ostrander moved an amendment, which was withdrawn.

"Brothers Emory, Ryerson, and others, addressed the Conference on the subject until the hour of adjournment.

"MAY 21.—On motion, the consideration of the report on the Canada business was resumed. The report was read. Brother Case, one of the delegates from Canada, requested that Brother Fisk might be permitted to address the Conference for him, and in his place, to give his views on the subject, which was granted,—and replies were made by Brothers Few, Ryerson, &c., when it was moved and seconded that the vote should be taken without further debate. The question on the first resolution in the report was then read, voted, and lost—75 to 130. On motion by J. Emory, seconded by W. Capers, to amend the report, such amendment, together with the remaining items in the report, were referred to a select committee of five, to examine and report thereon.

"In the afternoon session, the select committee on the Canada business was announced by the president, (Bishop Hedding,)—namely, D. Ostrander, G. Pickering, J. Emory, L. Clark, and Abner Chase.

"MAY 23.—The report on the Canada business was then read by the secretary, and the first resolution taken up for consideration. Brothers Case, Ostrander, Cox, Winans, Ryerson, Emory, and others, spoke on the subject. The previous question was called for. Bishop Soule requested leave, and stated some points. Brother Ostrander moved an amendment, which was adopted. The vote on the previous question was then taken and carried. It was then moved to adopt the resolution as amended, voted and carried—153 to 34. It was then moved to adopt the preamble to the report; an amendment was moved and withdrawn. N. Bangs moved to take the previous question—carried. The question on the adoption of the preamble was then taken and carried—103 to 63.

"On motion of A. Brunson, seconded by W. Arnold, an amendment was proposed, which was adopted. The whole report amended, read thus, viz :—

"The report of this committee was made and adopted May 23, as follows :—

"'The committee to whom was referred the business of the negotiation with the delegates of the Canada Conference on the subject of our Book Concern, having had the same under their serious consideration, are of opinion that, in consideration of their former relation to us, and the friendly feeling and brotherly affection which now exist between the two Connexions, as well as in view of the liberal and efficient support they have formerly given to the Concern, an apportionment of the property of the Concern ought to be made to them. But, as constitutional difficulties are believed to be in the way of such an appropriation by this Conference, because they have not been instructed on this subject by their constituents, according to the proviso at the end of the restrictive regulations, they beg leave to submit, for the adoption of the Conference, the following resolutions :—

"'*Resolved*, That if three-fourths of all the members of the several annual conferences who shall be present and vote on the subject shall concur herein, and as soon as the fact of such concurrence shall be certified by the secretaries of the several annual conferences, then the book agents and book committee in New-York shall be, and they are hereby, authorized and directed to settle with the agents of the Canada Conference, on the following principles and preliminaries, namely :—

"'1st. The dividend shall be made according to the proportion that the number of the travelling preachers in the Canada Conference bears to the number of the travelling preachers in the Methodist Episcopal Church in the United States, including in both estimates the superannuated preachers and those on trial.

"'2d. The amount of property to be divided shall be reckoned according to the first and largest estimate of stock in the late exhibit of the book agents, namely, $448,745 70½, deducting therefrom debts due from the Concern, annuities, &c., estimated at $15,728 18, and the whole of the publishing fund, amounting to $16,928 28, making a total deduction (including credits to be allowed M. Ruter and C. Holliday) of $35,178 77, and leaving an amount to be divided of about $413,566 93½.

"'3d. That the Canada Conference shall receive a full proportion of the unsaleable and saleable stock, and of the bad as well as the good debts, considering the stock and debts in Canada that belong to the Book Concern as so much of the dividend already paid, but to be estimated as forming a part of the general Book Concern, according to the manner of estimating the whole amount.

"'4. When the adjustment shall have been made, according to the foregoing preliminaries, it shall be deemed a final settlement of all claims which the Canada Conference may be supposed to have on the Book Concern, or any other funds or property of the Methodist Episcopal Church in the United States, in virtue of their former relation to us.

"'*Resolved*, That our superintendents be, and they are hereby, respectfully requested to present the foregoing preamble and resolution to the annual conferences for their concurrence, as contemplated in the premises.

"'The committee beg leave also to submit the following resolution:—

"'*Resolved, &c.*, That until the will of the annual conferences shall be ascertained, and a final settlement be made, the Canada Conference shall receive the same equal annual dividend of the profits of the Book Concern as heretofore.'

"5th. A motion for the adoption of this resolution was made, voted, and carried.

"On motion, The secretary is hereby directed to furnish the delegates from Canada with a copy of the decision of this Conference on that business."

On page 46 your Honours will find the minutes of the committee on the Canada claims. They are as follows:—

"*Minutes of Committee.*

"CINCINNATI, OHIO, *May* 6, 1836.

"Committee on Canada claims met on Friday evening, May 6th, at the Preachers' Office, Cincinnati. Committee consists of R. Payne, T. A. Morris, A. Griffith, M. Richardson, and C. Sherman. The whole committee present. C. Sherman chosen secretary. Rev. Mr. Lord presented to the committee a copy of the resolutions of the General Conference of 1828 and of 1832, on the subject of an appropriation from the Book Concern of the Methodist Episcopal Church to the Canada Conference, which was read. (See Doc. Nos. 1 and 2.) Copies of the resolutions of the annual conferences, concurring or non-concurring with the General Conference resolution, were then handed to the committee by Rev. B. Waugh, and read. (See Doc. No. 3.) The conferences concurring were as follow:—

New-England Conference, held June, 1832	Ayes	73	Noes	1
Maine Conference, held July 24, 1832	"	71	"	0
New-Hampshire Conference, held August 8, 1832	"	71	"	0
Oneida Conference, held 1833	"	77	"	2
Genesee Conference, held July, 1832	"	69	"	1
New-York Conference, held June 9, 1833	"	142	"	13
Six conferences.	For concurrence,	503	Against,	17

"The conferences non-concurring were as follow:—

Kentucky Conference, held Oct. 22, 1832	Non-concurring,	66	Concurring,	0
Indiana Conference, held October 17, 1832	"	36	"	0
Pittsburgh Conference, held Aug. 23, 1832	"	61	"	6
South Carolina Conference, held April 22, 1833	"	26	"	24
Mississippi Conference, held May 15, 1833	"	15	"	7
Ohio Conference	"	62	"	28
Holstein Conference, held March 29, 1833	"	34	"	8
Virginia Conference, held March 6, 1833	"	84	"	0
Baltimore Conference, held April 5, 1833	"	90	"	0
Philadelphia Conference, held April 24, 1833	"	89	"	1
Missouri Conference	"	24	"	2
Georgia Conference	"	41	"	13
Alabama Conference	"	22	"	3
Illinois Conference	"	19	"	2
Tennessee Conference	"	72	"	2
Fifteen conferences non-concurring.	Number for,	741	Against,	96
		17		503
Whole number in the several conferences against,		758	For,	599
" " " " for,		599		
Majority against granting Canada claims,		159		

"Brother Case then addressed the committee, making several remarks and statements in favour of the claims being answered. Committee was then addressed by brother Lord. After some information, obtained by brother Waugh, committee adjourned, to meet again next Tuesday evening.

(Signed,) C. SHERMAN, *Sec'y.*

"The report of the committee appointed upon the subject of the Canada claim was presented and adopted May 19, as follows:—

"The committee to whom was referred the communication from the conference of the Wesleyan Methodist Church in British North America, beg leave to report:—

"Your committee have given a serious, and they trust a candid, attention to the document referred to them. They have invited before them the president of the Canada Conference, the Rev. William Lord, and the delegate from Canada, the Rev. William Case, and have listened with pleasure to their remarks, and perused with close attention a communication purporting to set forth the grounds of these claims. But inasmuch as the last General Conference did distinctly avow that constitutional restrictions prohibited their action, and proceeded to lay the question before the several annual conferences, in order to obtain the decision of these primary bodies upon the subject, your committee were admonished that the task devolving upon them is limited to this single consideration, namely, Have the annual conferences determined against the claims of the Canada Conference?

"This point is determined by the votes of all the annual conferences, which, being properly authenticated, and having been carefully examined, stand as follows:—

In favour of concurring with the General Conference of 1832	599
Against concurring	758
Whole number of votes taken	1357

"This statement shows that, instead of three-fourths of the votes being in favour of obviating the constitutional restrictions, as the Discipline in such cases requires, a large majority have decided against it. And this decision your committee regard as final and conclusive against these claims.

"But inasmuch as the General Conference have ever claimed and exercised the right to regulate the discount at which our books may be sold to wholesale purchasers, and with a view to an amicable and final arrangement of all the difficulties which have existed on this subject, and especially with a sincere desire to go as far as justice to the Methodist Episcopal Church will authorize, to encourage and perpetuate the friendly and fraternal feelings which should ever exist between the different members of the great Methodist family, the committee submit to the consideration, and for the adoption, of the General Conference the following arrangement, mutually agreed to by the delegates from Canada and the book agents, and which we are assured will be satisfactory to our Canadian brethren, if sanctioned by this Conference.

"Whereas the Canada Conference, now in connexion with the Wesleyan Methodists of Great Britain, was formerly united to, and formed part of, the Methodist Episcopal Church; and whereas the union, which by mutual consent then subsisted, was dissolved at the earnest and repeated solicitations of the ministers and members of the Church in Canada, which was definitively determined upon by an act of the Canada Conference, who thereupon and subsequently did form a union with, and become a part of, the Wesleyan Methodist Connexion; and whereas there has been a difference of opinion between the Methodist Episcopal Church and the Canada Conference in regard to the claim which has been urged by the Canada Conference, of an interest in, and a portion of, the Methodist Book Concern; and whereas the decision of the several annual conferences, to whom the subject was referred by the General Conference of 1832, has been adverse to the claim of the Canada Conference, and has thereby precluded any further action of the General Conference on the ground of claim, as made by the Canada Conference; but whereas this General Conference cherishes an affectionate remembrance of the Canada brethren, and is desirous to manifest its fraternal regard in every suitable way; and whereas the Canada Conference did, at its last session, appoint its president, the Rev. William Lord, and the Rev. Egerton Ryerson, delegates to this General Conference to negotiate its claims on the Book Concern, and the Rev. William Case, having been duly appointed to take the place of Rev. E. Ryerson in the negotiation; and whereas the said Rev. William Lord, president of the Canada Conference, and the Rev. William Case, have full powers to bring to an amicable termination the question pending between the two connexions, therefore it is hereby declared to be mutually understood and agreed, that the following plan shall be considered as an arrangement for the full and final adjustment and settlement of the matter at issue between the Canada Conference and the Methodist Episcopal Church; to wit, The agents of the Methodist Book Concern shall furnish to the book-steward of the Canada Conference any of the books which may be issued from its press at the following rates, subject to the conditions and provisions hereinafter named:—

"1. The general alphabetical catalogue books, whether in sheets or bound, shall be sold at forty per cent. discount from the retail prices, as long as the present discount of one-third shall be made to wholesale purchasers; but should the discount be hereafter changed to one-fourth, then, in that case, the books sold to the book-steward of the Canada Conference shall be charged at a discount of one-third from the retail prices which shall from time to time be affixed to them respectively. Provided that this discount shall not apply to such books as may be reduced below the usual prices on account of rival publishers; and provided, also, that the Canada Conference shall give satisfactory security in regard to the payment of any debt which may be contracted with the Methodist Book Concern, within one year from the time such debt may be created. And it is also expressly understood and agreed, that no interest shall be demanded or paid on any such debts, unless payment shall be delayed beyond the period of credit before named, in which event interest shall be charged and paid, from and after the expiration of said credit term. It is also further provided, that all books which may be ordered by the book-steward of the Canada Conference shall be at the risk and expense of the said Conference, from the time they shall be forwarded from the Methodist Book Concern.

"2. Sunday-school books and tracts shall be furnished to the book-steward of the Canada Conference at a premium of eighteen per cent., to be paid in general catalogue books at *retail prices*; and it is hereby declared to be understood and agreed, that the same provisions and conditions are to be adjudged applicable to Sunday-school books and tracts as have been specified above in regard to books generally.

"3. It is understood and agreed, that the privileges herein secured to the Canada Conference shall be binding on the Methodist Book Concern until the first day of May, 1852, next ensuing the present date; *Provided*, also, that the said Canada Conference shall regularly and truly make annual settlements to the satisfaction of the agents of the Methodist Book-Concern, and not otherwise.

"4. Finally, it is hereby mutually understood and agreed, that the foregoing arrangement is considered as a full, and definite, and satisfactory adjustment of the question which has arisen between the Canada Conference and the Methodist Episcopal Church on the subject of the Methodist Book Concern.

"In testimony whereof, the agents of the Methodist Book-Concern, and the delegates of the Canada Conference, have mutually affixed their respective signatures, this eighteenth day of May, 1836, in the city of Cincinnati, Ohio.

(Signed) B. Waugh & T. Mason, *Agents.*
William Lord, } *Delegates from*
William Case, } *Canada.*

"May 23, 1832.—On motion of P. Akers, which was seconded, *Resolved*, that a copy of the resolution of the last General Conference by which the Canada Conference was allowed to dissolve connexion with the Methodist Episcopal Church in the United States; and also a copy of the acts of this General Conference on Canada affairs, accompany the resolutions about to be presented to the annual conferences."

I propose now, if your Honours please, to return to page 43, and to read from that and subsequent pages an address from the Canada Conference, held in 1833, to show that, notwithstanding their separation, the parties treated each other as members of the same body—the Methodist Episcopal Church—for all practical purposes.

"*To the Bishops and Members of the General Conference of the Methodist Episcopal Church in the United States.*

"Reverend Fathers and Brethren:—We rejoice to avail ourselves of this occasion to declare, in the words of the venerable Wesley in his last letter to America, 'that the Methodists are one people in all the world, and that it is their full determination so to continue,—

"Though mountains rise, and oceans roll,
To sever us in vain."'

"In connexion with you, we were born and nourished; in connexion with you, we have laboured and prospered; and from your example and liberality, and the counsels of two of your venerable bishops, and several of your highly esteemed preachers, we have derived assistance and advantages which have enabled us greatly to extend the work of God in this new country, and the grateful recollection of which will never be effaced from our minds.

"When the full period arrived in 1828, in which the welfare, harmony, and safety of our Church rendered it expedient for us to be organized into a separate and independent body, you candidly took into consideration our local circumstances, and generously complied with our wishes—and, at the same time continued to us the expression of your kindness and liberality. That separation, however, was not on our part, any more than on yours, a separation of doctrine, of discipline, of motive, or of affection, but only of political, geographical, and ecclesiastical boundary. Still with you we were one in heart, in aim, in doctrine, and discipline. Under the influence of this conviction and feeling, we sought to obtain a general superintendent from your connexion, and made successive applications to no less than four members of your conference to fill that highly important office over us. But all our applications were unsuccessful, and our efforts to establish and settle our economy were fruitless. In this unsettled state of anxious suspense, we have been involved for the last five years, during which time we have been with difficulty, but mercifully, preserved from agitation, division, and encroachment. Providence has at length opened the way for the settlement of our economy upon a permanent foundation. By the large influx of British emigration to this province, and especially of persons who had been connected with Methodist societies and congregations in Great Britain and Ireland, the attention of the Wesleyan Missionary Committee in London was particularly attracted, and pressing appeals were made to the Christian feelings and benevolence of the British Conference from many of their former flocks for a supply of those ordinances which they had enjoyed in the land of their fathers. These circumstances, together with the admitted and notorious fact of our inadequacy as a body, both in regard to men and means, to supply all the religious wants of the white settlements and Indian tribes, induced the Wesleyan Missionary Committee about a year since to determine on sending a number of missionaries into Upper Canada. For this purpose the committee sent the Rev. Robert Alder as their representative to this province, to inquire into its religious condition. Between Mr. Alder and this conference a negotiation was commenced, which has now resulted in a union between the Canadian and British connexion. This measure has been accomplished upon a principle of perfect equality, without any sacrifice of principle or independence on either side, and with merely those changes in one or two features of the prudential part of our economy, 'which our local circumstances require,'—as stated and provided for in the articles of separation from your connexion in 1828. So that, without departing from either the letter or spirit of the resolutions of your body, in generously granting our request for a separation, we have, through the Divine blessing, been enabled to adopt a plan—the only and most efficient plan—by which divisions may be prevented among our own societies, and misunderstandings with others; a plan which will secure the unity of Methodism throughout the province, and bring to our assistance a large addition of means and men to carry on the work of the Lord among the white population and the Indian tribes of North America; a plan which has been adopted unanimously and cordially both by this and the British Conference.

In this providential and gracious opening we recognise the peculiar hand of God, and we are persuaded you will rejoice with us in thus witnessing Methodism throughout the British empire, as throughout the United States, connected in a common bond of union, and sustained and extended under a common management. Nor are we in this necessary and beneficial arrangement the less united and grateful to you as our fathers, brethren, and benefactors; and we devoutly hope that no circumstance will occur which may tend to weaken our mutual confidence and affection in the final adjustment of those claims, the justice of which has been recognised and sanctioned by the majority of your body at two successive sessions.

"We shall rejoice to co-operate with you, and to assist you with native labourers, as far as in our power, until, by the blessing of God, the Western wilderness shall be illuminated by the light of the Gospel, and the banners of the Lamb shall be unfurled to the Pacific Ocean.

"We enjoy perfect harmony and peace throughout all our borders, and great prosperity in many places. Our Church members amount to 16,039, and the blessings of the Lord our God are abundantly upon us. We rejoice to hear of your great success, and most devoutly pray that you may go on prospering more and more.

"By order and on behalf of the Conference of the Wesleyan Methodist Church in British North America.

(Signed) "George Marsden, *President*.
Egerton Ryerson, *Secretary*.

"York, Upper Canada, *October* 9, 1833."

I will read next, if your Honours please, a few extracts in relation to alterations which have taken place from time to time in the restrictive rules:—

"May 22, 1828.—W. Fisk, for the committee to which had been referred the subject of recommending to the annual conferences some alterations in the restrictive rules, reported. The time of adjournment being near, it was moved and seconded to extend the session until six o'clock, and the motion was lost. It was then resolved, on motion, to extend the session for fifteen minutes. During the discussion, the time of adjournment having nearly arrived, it was resolved, on motion, to extend it ten minutes. A division of the above report was called for; and the question being taken on the first part, it was carried. The vote was then taken on the second and last part, and that was also carried.

"And then the Conference adjourned.

"The following is the report referred to above:—

"'The committee to whom was referred the subject embraced in a resolution suggesting the propriety of providing for the alteration of one of the rules commonly called the restrictive rules, beg leave to report the following resolution:—

"'*Resolved*, That this General Conference respectfully suggest to the several annual conferences the propriety of recommending to the next General Conference so to alter and amend the rules of our Discipline, by which the General Conference is restricted in its powers to make rules and regulations for the Church, commonly called the restrictive rules, as to make the proviso at the close of the restrictive rules, No. 6, read thus,—

"'*Provided nevertheless*, That upon the concurrent recommendation of three-fourths of all the members of the several annual conferences who shall be present and vote on such recommendation, then a majority of two-thirds of the General Conference succeeding shall suffice to alter any such regulations excepting the first article.

"'*And also*, whenever such alteration or alterations shall have first been recommended by two-thirds of the General Conference, so soon as three-fourths of the members of the annual conferences shall have concurred as aforesaid with such recommendation, such alteration or alterations shall take effect.

"'All which is respectfully submitted. W. Fisk, *Chairman*.'

"May 22, 1832.—The Committee on the Itinerancy beg leave to report the following, as the result of their deliberations on the subject recommended to them, viz.:

"'I. *Resolved*, That this General Conference recommend to the several annual conferences for their concurrence and adoption, as provided in the sixth article of the restrictive rules, the following resolution to amend the second article of the said restrictive rules:—

"'II. *Resolved*, That the second article of the restrictive rules be so altered as to read,—

" ' "They shall not allow of more than one representative for every fourteen members of the annual conference, nor allow for less number than one for every thirty: provided, nevertheless, that when there shall be in any annual conference a fraction of two-thirds the number which shall be fixed for the ratio of representation, such annual conference shall be entitled to an additional delegate for such fraction. And provided, also, that no conference shall be deprived the privilege of two delegates."

" 'III. *Resolved*, That the secretary furnish each of the bishops with a copy of these resolutions, and they are hereby respectfully requested to present the same to the several annual conferences, or cause the same to be presented at their next session, for their concurrence; and where the bishops or any two of the bishops shall have ascertained that three-fourths of all the members of the several annual conferences voting in the case have concurred with this General Conference, they shall certify the same, and cause such certificate to be printed in the minutes, and published three successive weeks in the Christian Advocate and Journal.

" 'IV. *Resolved*, That the ratio of representation for the next General Conference be one for every fourteen, provided the annual conferences concur in the alteration as above recommended by this conference.

" 'And that the Discipline in Section 3, Answer 1 to Question 2, on page 19, shall thereupon be so altered as to read,—

" ' "The General Conference shall be composed of one member for every fourteen members of each annual conference," ' &c.

"1836.—The ratio of representation was altered to one for every twenty-one; and to allow this, the second of the restrictive rules was changed to the following:—

" 'They shall not allow of more than one representative for every fourteen members of the annual conference, nor allow of a less number than one for every thirty: provided, nevertheless, that when there shall be in any annual conference a fraction of two-thirds the number which shall be fixed for the ratio of representation, such annual conference shall be entitled to an additional delegate for such fraction; and provided, also, that no conference shall be denied the privilege of two delegates,' "

Now, if your Honours please, I will read what relates to the subject of slavery. I will first read what appears in the Discipline as it stands on that subject. And first what is contained in the Discipline of 1840, under which, in fact, all these difficulties arose.

" *Of Slavery.*

" *Quest.* What shall be done for the extirpation of the evil of slavery?

"*Ans.* 1. We declare that we are as much as ever convinced of the great evil of slavery: therefore no slaveholder shall be eligible to any official station in our Church hereafter, where the laws of the State in which he lives will admit of emancipation, and permit the liberated slave to enjoy freedom.

"2. When any travelling preacher becomes an owner of a slave or slaves, by any means, he shall forfeit his ministerial character in our Church, unless he execute, if it be practicable, a legal emancipation of such slaves, conformably to the laws of the State in which he lives.

"3. All our preachers shall prudently enforce upon our members the necessity of teaching their slaves to read the word of God; and to allow them time to attend upon the public worship of God on our regular days of divine service.

"4. Our coloured preachers and official members shall have all the privileges which are usual to others in the district and quarterly conferences, where the usages of the country do not forbid it. And the presiding elder may hold for them a separate district conference, where the number of coloured local preachers will justify it.

"5. The annual conferences may employ coloured preachers to travel and preach where their services are judged necessary; provided that no one shall be so employed without having been recommended according to the form of Discipline.—Pp. 209, 210."

Now I turn, your Honours, to the extracts from "Minutes of several Conversations between the Rev. Thomas Coke, LL.D., the Rev. Francis Asbury, and others, at a Conference begun in Baltimore, in the State of Maryland, on Monday, the 27th

December, in the year 1784." This is the first Discipline of the Methodist Episcopal Church, adopted at what is called the "Christmas Conference."

"'*Quest.* 41. *Are there any directions to be given concerning the negroes?*

"'*Ans. Let every preacher, as often as possible, meet them in class. And let the assistant always appoint a proper white person as their leader. Let the assistants also make a regular return to theconference of the number of negroes in society in their respective circuits.*

"'*Quest.* 42. *What methods can we take to extirpate slavery?*

"'*Ans. We are deeply conscious of the impropriety of making new terms of communion for a religious society already established, excepting on the most pressing occasion: and such we esteem the practice of holding our fellow-creatures in slavery. We view it as contrary to the golden law of God on which hang all the law and the prophets, and the unalienable rights of mankind, as well as every principle of the revolution, to hold in the deepest debasement, in a more abject slavery than is perhaps to be found in any part of the world except America, so many souls that are all capable of the image of God.*

"'*We therefore think it our most bounden duty to take immediately some effectual method to extirpate this abomination from among us: and for that purpose we add the following to the rules of our society, viz:—*

"'1. *Every member of our society who has slaves in his possession, shall, within twelve months after notice given to him by the assistant, (which notice the assistants are required immediately, and without any delay, to give in their respective circuits,) legally execute and record an instrument, whereby he emancipates and sets free every slave in his possession who is between the ages of forty and forty-five immediately, or at farthest when they arrive at the age of forty-five.*

"'*And every slave who is between the ages of twenty-five and forty immediately, or at farthest at the expiration of five years from the date of the said instrument.*

"'*And every slave who is between the ages of twenty and twenty-five immediately, or at farthest when they arrive at the age of thirty.*

"'*And every slave under the age of twenty, as soon as they arrive at the age of twenty-five at farthest.*

"'*And every infant born in slavery after the above-mentioned rules are complied with, immediately on its birth.*

"'2. *Every assistant shall keep a journal, in which he shall regularly minute down the names and ages of all the slaves belonging to all the masters in his respective circuit, and also the date of every instrument executed and recorded for the manumission of the slaves, with the name of the court, book, and folio, in which the said instruments respectively shall have been recorded: which journal shall be handed down in each circuit to the succeeding assistants.*

"'3. *In consideration that these rules form a new term of communion, every person concerned, who will not comply with them, shall have liberty quietly to withdraw himself from our society within the twelve months succeeding the notice given as aforesaid: otherwise the assistant shall exclude him in the society.*

"'4. *No person so voluntarily withdrawn, or so excluded, shall ever partake of the supper of the Lord with the Methodists, till he complies with the above requisitions.*

"'5. *No person holding slaves shall, in future, be admitted into society or to the Lord's supper, till he previously complies with these rules concerning slavery.*

"'*N. B. These rules are to affect the members of our society no farther than as they are consistent with the laws of the States in which they reside.*

"'*And respecting our brethren in Virginia that are concerned, and after due consideration of their peculiar circumstances, we allow them two years from the notice given, to consider the expedience of compliance or non-compliance with these rules.*

"'*Quest.* 43. *What shall be done with those who buy or sell slaves, or give them away?*

"'*Ans. They are immediately to be expelled: unless they buy them on purpose to free them.*'—Pp. 42–44."

That your Honours will see was done by the conference which commenced its meeting in December of 1784. It was the annual conference. There was no General Conference at the time it was first organized. It was the act of the body of the Church represented by all its preachers.

The next annual conference met in 1785.

"1785.—At the annual conferences for 1785, it was concluded that the rule on slavery, adopted at the Christmas Conference, would do harm. It was, therefore, resolved to suspend its execution for the present, and a note to that effect was added to the annual minutes for that year. The conferences, however, still expressed 'the deepest abhorrence' of 'the practice,' and a determination 'to seek its destruction by all wise and prudent means.'—P. 80."

This provision never re-appeared, as I am instructed, in any future discipline.

I turn now to page 20 of the first of the Proofs, which contains extracts on this subject from Emory's History of the Discipline,

"For the provisions on this subject prior to 1784, see pp. 14, 15, 19, 21, 22. For the rules adopted at the Christmas Conference, see pp. 43, 44. Not more than six months had elapsed after the adoption of these last rules before it was thought necessary to suspend them. Accordingly, in the annual minutes for 1785 the following notice was inserted:—

"'It is recommended to all our brethren to suspend the execution of the minute on slavery till the deliberations of a future conference; and that an equal space of time be allowed all our members for consideration, when the minute shall be put in force.

"'N. B. We do hold in the deepest abhorrence the practice of slavery; and shall not cease to seek its destruction by all wise and prudent means.'

"This note does not seem to refer to Question 43, (1784,) as it, with the same answer, was retained in the Discipline of 1786. From this till 1796 no mention, it would seem, was made of the subject except in the General Rules. (See p. 181.)"

From the General Rules of the Society I will read an extract:—Discipline of 1840, p. 80:—

"There is only one condition previously required of those who desire admission into these societies, 'a desire to flee from the wrath to come, and to be saved from their sins.' But, wherever this is really fixed in the soul, it will be shown by its fruits. It is therefore expected of all who continue therein, that they should continue to evidence their desire of salvation,

"First, by doing no harm, by avoiding evil of every kind, especially that which is most generally practised; such as,

"The taking the name of God in vain.

"The profaning the day of the Lord, either by doing ordinary work therein, or by buying or selling.

"Drunkenness: or drinking spirituous liquors, unless in case of necessity.

"The buying and selling of men, women, and children, with an intention to enslave them.

"Fighting, quarrelling, brawling, brother going to law with brother; returning evil for evil; or railing for railing; the using many words in buying or selling.

"The buying or selling goods that have not paid the duty.

"The giving or taking things on usury, i. e., unlawful interest.

"Uncharitable or unprofitable conversation: particularly speaking evil of magistrates or of ministers.

"Doing to others as we would not they should do unto us."

I have read sufficient to show how it was then considered. On page 21 of the First of the Proofs we have the following:—

"1796.—The following section was introduced on the subject:—

"*Quest.* What regulations shall be made for the extirpation of the crying evil of African slavery?

"*Ans.* 1. We declare that we are more than ever convinced of the great evil of the African slavery which still exists in these United States, and do most earnestly recommend to the yearly conferences, quarterly meetings, and to those who have the oversight of districts and circuits to be exceedingly cautious what persons they admit to official stations, to require such security of those who hold slaves, for the emancipation of them, immediately or gradually, as the laws of the States respectively, and the circumstances of the case, will admit; and we do fully authorize all the yearly conferences to make whatever regulations they judge proper, in the present case, respecting the admission of persons to official stations in our Church."

We call your Honours' attention to this because it is one of the strongest expressions made use of to meet the difficulty. In case of future admissions to official station, security was to be required of those who held slaves for the emancipation of them, immediately or gradually, as the laws of the States respectively, and the circumstances of the case, will admit.

"'2. No slaveholder shall be received into society till the preacher who has the oversight of the circuit has spoken to him freely and faithfully on the subject of slavery.

"'Every member of the society who sells a slave shall immediately, after full proof, be excluded the society. And if any member of our society purchase a slave, the ensuing quarterly meeting shall determine on the number of years in which the slave so purchased would work out the price of his purchase. And the person so purchasing shall, immediately after such determination, execute a legal instrument for the manumission of such slave, at the expiration of the term determined by the quarterly meeting. And in default of his executing such instrument of manumission, or on his refusal to submit his case to the judgment of the quarterly meeting, such member shall be excluded the society. *Provided also*, that in the case of a female slave, it shall be inserted in the aforesaid instrument of manumission, that all her children who shall be born during the years of her servitude, shall be free at the following times, namely; every female child at the age of twenty-one, and every male child at the age of twenty-five. *Nevertheless*, if the member of our society executing the said instrument of manumission, judge it proper, he may fix the times of manumission of the children of the female slaves before mentioned at an earlier age than that which is prescribed above.

"'4. The preachers and other members of our society are requested to consider the subject of negro slavery with deep attention till the ensuing General Conference: and that they impart to the General Conference, through the medium of the yearly conferences, or otherwise, any important thoughts upon the subject, that the conference may have full light, in order to take further steps towards the eradicating this enormous evil from that part of the Church of God to which they are united.'

"1800.—The following new paragraphs were inserted:—

"'2. When any travelling preacher becomes an owner of a slave or slaves, by any means, he shall forfeit his ministerial character in our Church, unless he execute, if it be practicable, a legal emancipation of such slaves, conformably to the laws of the State in which he lives.

"'The annual conferences are directed to draw up addresses for the gradual emancipation of the slaves, to the legislatures of those States in which no general laws have been passed for that purpose. These addresses shall urge, in the most respectful, but pointed manner, the necessity of a law for the gradual emancipation of the slaves; proper committees shall be appointed, by the annual conferences, out of the most respectable of our friends, for the conducting of the business; and the presiding elders, elders, deacons, and travelling preachers, shall procure as many proper signatures as possible to the addresses, and give all the assistance in their power in every respect to aid the committees, and to further this blessed undertaking. Let this be continued from year to year, till the desired end be accomplished.'

"1804.—The following alterations were made:—

"The question reads,—'What shall be done for the extirpation of the evil of slavery?'

"In paragraph 1 (1796) instead of 'more than ever convinced,' we have 'as much as ever convinced;' and instead of 'the African slavery which still exists in these United States,' we have 'slavery.'

"In paragraph 4, (3 of 1796,) respecting the selling of a slave, before the words 'shall immediately,' the following clause is inserted:—'except at the request of the slave, in cases of mercy and humanity, agreeably to the judgment of a committee of the male members of the society, appointed by the preacher who has charge of the circuit.'

"The following new proviso was inserted in this paragraph:—'*Provided also*, that if a member of our society shall buy a slave with a certificate of future emancipation, the terms of emancipation shall, notwithstanding, be subject to the decision of the quarterly meeting conference.' All after '*nevertheless*' was struck out, and the following substituted:—'The members of our societies in the States of North Carolina, South Carolina, Georgia, and Tennessee, shall be exempted from the operation of the above rules.' The paragraphs about considering the subject of slavery and petitions to legislatures, (namely, No. 4 of 1796, and No. 6 of 1800,) were struck out, and the following added:—

"'5. Let our preachers, from time to time, as occasion serves, admonish and exhort all slaves to render due respect and obedience to the commands and interests of their respective masters.'

"1808.—All that related to slaveholding among private members (see 2 and 3 of 1796) struck out, and the following substituted:—

"'3. The General Conference authorizes each annual conference to form their own regulations relative to buying and selling slaves.'

"Paragraph 5 of 1804 was also struck out.

"1812.—Paragraph 3 of 1808 was altered so as to read,—

"'Whereas the laws of some of the States do not admit of emancipating of slaves, without a special act of the legislature; the General Conference authorizes each annual conference to form their own regulations relative to buying and selling slaves.'

"1816.—Paragraph 1 (see 1796) was altered so as to read,—

"'1. We declare that we are as much as ever convinced of the great evil of slavery; therefore no slaveholder shall be eligible to any official station in our Church hereafter, where the laws of the State in which he lives will admit of emancipation, and permit the liberated slave to enjoy freedom.'

"1820.—Paragraph 3, (see 1812,) leaving it to the annual conferences 'to form their own regulations about buying and selling slaves,' was struck out.

"1824.—The following paragraphs added:—

"'3. All our preachers shall prudently enforce upon our members the necessity of teaching their slaves to read the word of God; and to allow them time to attend upon the public worship of God on our regular days of divine service.

"'4. Our coloured preachers and official members shall have all the privileges which are usual to others in the district and quarterly conferences, where the usages of the country do not forbid it. And the presiding elder may hold for them a separate district conference, where the number of coloured local preachers will justify it.

"'5. The annual conferences may employ coloured preachers to travel and preach where their services are judged necessary; provided that no one shall be so employed without having been recommended according to the Form of Discipline.'—Pp. 274–279."

We now come down, if your Honours please, to the journal of the General Conference of 1840, page 56 of the first of the Proofs, and we approach to the very acts of dissension. We read these parts of the evidence with a view to show the actual state of the difficulty in which the society found itself in 1844, and whether there was a permanent or serious difficulty, or not.

"MAY 2.—O. Scott of the New-England Conference, presented a petition from persons residing in New-York on the subject of slavery. On the presenting of this petition, J. Early moved the appointment of a standing Committee on Slavery, to whom all papers, petitions, and memorials, upon that subject, shall be referred. Adopted. Ordered that the committee consist of twenty-eight members, one from each annual conference, and appointed by the respective delegations.

"FRIDAY, MAY 8.—E. Dorsey presented the memorial of the stewards and others of Westmoreland circuit, Baltimore Conference, complaining of the action of the Baltimore Annual Conference, in refusing to elect to ordination local preachers, on the single ground of their being slaveholders.

"The memorial was read, and ineffectual efforts made to procure other reference. After discussion it was, on motion, referred to a select committee of nine to consider and report thereon."

Your Honours will permit me to explain that the Westmoreland Circuit was in Virginia, but connected with the Baltimore Conference.

"WEDNESDAY, MAY 13.—On motion of J. A. Collins, the report of the Committee on the Judiciary, of 1836, in relation to a memorial from Westmoreland and Lancaster circuits, Baltimore Conference, was referred to the committee raised on the memorial from Westmoreland circuit to this Conference.

"THURSDAY, MAY 21.—N. Bangs, chairman of the Committee on Slavery, presented a report, which was read.

"O. Scott stated that the minority of the committee had a report which they wished to present. Moved that the report of the majority be laid on the table for the present. Carried.

"It was then moved that the report of the minority be read. After discussion, it was moved to lay this on the table. Carried.

"On motion, the report of the Committee on Slavery was again taken up. The first resolution accompanying the report was read.

"Moved to adjourn. Lost.

"O. Scott, rising to speak, and intimating that he would probably extend his remarks beyond fifteen minutes, it was, on motion, resolved to suspend the rule restricting a speaker to fifteen minutes, so as to permit brother Scott to proceed at his own discretion.

"Moved to adjourn. Lost.

"After brother Scott had proceeded some time with his remarks, he gave way for a motion to adjourn, which prevailed; and Conference adjourned, to meet to-morrow morning, at half-past eight o'clock."

THE COURT,—Where was that Conference held?

MR. LORD,—In the city of Baltimore. It commenced on the 1st of May, 1840.

MR. REVERDY JOHNSON,—The Conference of 1844 was held in this city.

MR. LORD continued to read as follows:—

"FRIDAY MORNING, MAY 22.—Conference proceeded to the consideration of the unfinished business of yesterday, it being the first resolution accompanying the report of the Committee on Slavery. The discussion was renewed.

"On motion, Conference resolved, that when it adjourned, it adjourn to meet this afternoon, at three o'clock.

"During the debate, brother Crowther being on the floor, and having spoken fifteen minutes, a motion was made that he have liberty to proceed with, and conclude his remarks. For this, a substitute was moved in these words, That the rule restricting speaking to fifteen minutes be suspended during the discussion of the subject before the Conference. Lost.

"The question recurring upon the original motion, it was withdrawn by the mover, but was immediately renewed and adopted."

I pass on to page 67 of the first of the Proofs for the continuation of the proceedings of this Conference:—

"MAY 28.—W. Capers, chairman of the Committee on the Address from the Wesleyan Methodist Connexion, made a report, accompanied with letters to the British and Canada Conferences, which were read. Moved to adopt the report and letters." (See appendix, Documents B. and C.)

"O. Scott called for a division on adopting the letter to the British Conference. H. Slicer moved to recommit the report. Lost. J. T. Mitchell offered the following resolution, which was adopted:—'Resolved, That the committee revise the letter to the British Conference, so as to refer to our literary institutions, and to the interchange of representatives.'

"The question was then taken on adopting the report of the committee.

"1. On the letter to the British Wesleyan Conference, a division was called for; and on motion, that part which does not refer to slavery was adopted. "That part relating to slavery was also adopted; one hundred and fourteen voting in the affirmative, and eighteen in the negative."

I now propose to read extracts from some documents which in these proceedings have been referred to; first, that which begins on page 58 of the first of the Proofs, and next, that which begins on page 64, which express the sentiments of the Conference at that period.

Mr. Johnson, Jun., read the following extract:—

"*Extract from Address of the Bishops to the General Conference of the Methodist Episcopal Church.*

"In a body so numerous as the Methodist connexion, embracing twenty-eight annual conferences, extended over these United States and Territories, and connected with different civil and domestic institutions, it is hardly expected that all should see 'eye to eye' relative to the meaning and administration of the Discipline of the Church, or the fitness and expediency of measures which may be adopted in conformity to such a state of things.

"It has been the constant aim and united endeavour of your general superintendents to preserve uniformity and harmony in these respects; and, as far as practicable, prevent conflicting action in all the official bodies in the Church. But although we record, with unfeigned gratitude to the God of all grace and consolation, the general peace, and harmony, and prosperity of the body since your last session, it becomes our painful duty to lay before you some exceptions to this happy and prosperous condition.

"At the last session of the General Conference the subject of slavery and its abolition was extensively discussed, and vigorous exertions made to effect new legislation upon it. But after a careful examination of the whole ground, *aided by the light of past experience*, it was the *solemn conviction* of the Conference that the interests of religion would not be advanced by any additional enactments in regard to it.

"In your Pastoral Address to the ministers and people at your last session, with great unanimity, and, as we believe, in the true spirit of the ministers of the peaceful Gospel of Christ, you solemnly advised the whole body to abstain from all abolition movements, and from agitating the exciting subject in the Church. This advice was in perfect agreement with the individual as well as associated views of your superintendents. But, had we differed from you in opinion, in consideration of the age, wisdom, experience, and official authority of the General Conference, we should have felt ourselves under a solemn obligation to be governed by your counsel. We have endeavoured, both in our official administration, and in our private intercourse with the preachers and members, to inculcate the sound policy and Christian spirit of your Pastoral Address. And it affords us great pleasure to be able to assure you, that our efforts in this respect have been very generally approved, and your advice cordially received and practically observed in a very large majority of the annual conferences, as will more fully appear to you on the careful examination of the journals of those bodies for the last four years. But we regret that we are compelled to say, that in some of the Northern and Eastern conferences, in contravention of your Christian and pastoral counsel, and of your best efforts to carry it into effect, the subject has been agitated in such forms, and in such a spirit, as to disturb the peace of the Church. This unhappy agitation has not been confined to the annual conferences, but has been introduced into quarterly conferences, and made the absorbing business of self-created bodies in the bosom of our beloved Zion. The professed object of all these operations is to free the Methodist Episcopal Church from the 'great moral evil of slavery,' and to secure to the enslaved the rights and privileges of free citizens of these United States. How far the measures adopted, and the manner of applying those measures, are calculated to accomplish such an issue, even if it could be effected by any action of ecclesiastical bodies, your united wisdom will enable you to judge.

"We cannot, however, but regard it as of unhappy tendency that either individual members or official bodies in the Church, should employ terms and pass resolutions of censure and condemnation on their brethren, and on public officers and official bodies, over whose actions they have no legitimate jurisdiction. It requires no very extensive knowledge of human nature to be convinced that if we would convert our fellow-men from the error of their ways, we must address them, not in terms of crimination and reproach, but in the milder language of respect, persuasion and kindness.

"It is justly due to a number of the annual conferences in which a majority, or a very respectable minority, of the members are professedly abolitionists, to say that they occupy a very different ground, and pursue a very different course from those of their brethren who have adopted ultra principles and measures in this unfortunate, and, we think, unprofitable controversy. The result of action had in such conferences on the resolution of the New-England Conference, recommending a very important change in our general rule on slavery, is satisfactory proof of this fact, and affords us strong and increasing confidence that the unity and peace of the Church are not to be materially affected by this exciting subject. Many of the preachers who were favourably disposed to the cause of abolition, when they saw the extent to which it was designed to carry these measures, and the inevitable consequence of their prosecution, came to a pause, reflected, and declined their co-operation. They clearly perceived that the success of the measures would result in the division of the Church; and for such an event they were not prepared. They have no disposition to criminate their brethren in the South, who are unavoidably connected with the institution of slavery, or to separate from them on that account. It is believed that men of ardent temperament, whose zeal may have been somewhat in advance of their knowledge and discretion, have made such advances in the abolition enterprise as to produce a reaction. A few preachers and members, disappointed in their expectations, and despairing of the success of their cause in the Methodist Church, have withdrawn from our fellowship, and connected themselves with associations more congenial with their views and feelings; and others, in similar circumstances, may probably follow their example. But we rejoice in believing that these secessions will be very limited, and that the great body of Methodists in these States will continue as they have been—one and inseparable. The uniformity and stability of our course should be such as to let all candid and thinking men see, that the *cause* of secessions from us is not a change of our doctrine or moral discipline—no imposition of new terms of communion—no violation of covenant engagements on the part of the Church. It is a matter worthy of particular notice, that those who have departed from us do not pretend that any material change in our system, with respect either to doctrine, discipline, or government, has taken place since they voluntarily united themselves with us. And it is ardently to be desired that no such innovation may be effected, as to furnish any just ground for such a pretension.

"The experience of more than half a century, since the organization of our ecclesiastical body, will afford us many important lights and landmarks, pointing out what is the safest and most prudent policy to be pursued in our onward course as regards African slavery in these States, and especially in our own religious community. This very interesting period of our history is distinguished by several characteristic features having a special claim to our consideration at the present time, particularly in view of the unusual excitement which now prevails on the subject, not only in the different Christian Churches, but also in the civil body. And, first: our general rule on slavery, which forms a part of the Constitution of the Church, has stood from the beginning unchanged, as testamentary of our sentiments on the principle of slavery and the slave trade. And in this we differ in no respect from the sentiments of our venerable founder, or from those of the wisest and most distinguished statesmen and civilians of our own and other enlightened and Christian countries. Secondly: in all the enactments of the Church relating to slavery, a due and respectful regard has been had to the laws of the States, never requiring emancipation in contravention of the civil authority, or where the laws of the States would not allow the liberated slave to enjoy his freedom. Thirdly: the simply holding or owning slaves, without regard to circumstances, has at no period of the existence of the Church subjected the master to excommunication. Fourthly: rules have been made from time to time, regulating the sale, and purchase, and holding of slaves, with reference to the different laws of the States where slavery is tolerated; which, upon the experience of the great difficulties of administering them, and the unhappy consequences both to masters and servants, have been as often changed or repealed. These important facts, which form prominent features of our past history as a Church, may very properly lead us to inquire for that course of action in future, which may be best calculated to preserve the peace and unity of the whole body, promote the greatest happiness of the slave population, and advance generally, in the slave-holding community of our country, the humane and hallowing influence of our holy religion. We cannot withhold from you, at this eventful period, the solemn conviction of our minds, that no new ecclesiastical legislation on the subject of slavery, at this time, will have a tendency to accomplish these most desirable objects. And we are fully persuaded that, as a body of Christian ministers, we shall accomplish the greatest good by directing our individual and united efforts, in the spirit of the first teachers of Christianity, to bring both master and servant under the sanctifying influence of the principles of that Gospel which teaches the duties of every relation, and enforces the faithful discharge of them by the strongest conceivable motives. Do we aim at the amelioration of the condition of the slave? How can we so effectually accomplish this, in our calling as ministers of the Gospel of Christ, as by employing our whole influence to bring both him and his master to a saving knowledge of the grace of God, and to a practical observance of those relative duties so clearly prescribed in the writings of the inspired apostles? Permit us to add, that, although we enter not into the political contentions of the day, neither interfere with civil legislation, nor with the administration of the laws, we cannot but feel a deep interest in whatever affects the peace, prosperity, and happiness of our beloved country. The union of these States, the perpetuity of the bonds of our national confederation, the reciprocal confidence of the different members of the great civil compact,—in a word, the *well-being* of the community of which we are members, should never cease to lie near our hearts, and for which we should offer up our sincere and most ardent prayers to the Almighty Ruler of the universe. But can we, as ministers of the Gospel, and servants of a Master 'whose kingdom is not of this world,' promote these important objects in any way so truly and permanently as by pursuing the course just pointed out? Can we, at this eventful crisis, render a better service to our country, than by laying aside all interference with relations authorized and established by the civil laws, and applying ourselves wholly and faithfully to what specially appertains to our 'high and holy calling;' to teach and enforce the moral obligations of the Gospel, in application to all the duties growing out of the different relations in society? By a diligent devotion to this evangelical employment, with an humble and steadfast reliance upon the aid of Divine influence, the number of 'believing masters' and servants may be constantly increased, the kindest sentiments and affections cultivated, domestic burdens lightened, mutual confidence cherished, and the peace and happiness of society be promoted. While, on the other hand, if past history affords us any correct rules of judgment, there is much cause to fear that the influence of our sacred office, if employed in interference with the relation itself, and consequently with the civil institutions of the country, will rather tend to prevent than to accomplish these desirable ends."

Mr. Lord,—If your Honours please, the extract from the address of the bishops, which has been read, is neither dated nor signed; but for the date and signatures, I refer you to the printed Minutes, or Journal of the General Conference, of 1840, page 151, and you will find that it was signed by R. R. Roberts, Joshua Soule, E. Hedding, James O. Andrew, B. Waugh, and Thomas A. Morris, being all the bishops of the Church at that time. It bears date, Baltimore, May 4, 1840.

The hour of three o'clock, the usual hour of adjournment, having arrived, the Court was adjourned until to-morrow, at ten o'clock, A. M.

SECOND DAY.—Tuesday, May 20, 1851.

Mr. Lord,—Before the adjournment yesterday, if your Honours please, we read an extract from the Address of the Bishops to the General Conference of the Methodist Episcopal Church, held in Baltimore in 1840. I now propose to read an extract from the Address of the British Conference to the bishops and members of the General Conference of the Methodist Episcopal Church in the United States of America, and an extract from an Address of the General Conference to the British

Conference. I refer your Honours to page 67 of the first of the Proofs, for the action of the General Conference of 1840, upon these documents.

"*From Address of the British Conference.*

"'But while we freely indulge in sentiments such as these, we cannot forget that on one subject especially—the subject of American slavery—you, our beloved brethren, are placed in circumstances of painful trial and perplexity. We enter, with brotherly sympathy, into the peculiar situation which you are now called to occupy. But on this question, we beg to refer you to what occurs in our Address to you from the conference of 1836, a proper copy of which will be handed to you by our representative; as also to the contents of our preceding letter of 1835. To the principles which we have affectionately but honestly declared in these two documents we still adhere, with a full conviction of their Christian truth and justice.

"'The time which has elapsed, and the events which have taken place, since the preparation of the above-mentioned papers, serve only to confirm us yet more in our views of the moral evil of slavery. Far be it from us to advocate violent and ill-considered measures. We are, however, strongly and unequivocally of opinion that it is, at this time, the paramount Christian duty of the ministers of our most merciful Lord in your country to maintain the *principle* of opposition to slavery with earnest zeal and unflinching firmness. May we not also be allowed, with the heart-felt solicitude of fraternal love, to entreat that you will not omit or qualify the noble testimony which we have extracted, in a note to our Address, from your Book of Discipline, but that you will continue to insert it there in its primitive and unimpaired integrity?'

"*From Address of the General Conference.*

"'We have considered, with affectionate respect and confidence, your brotherly suggestions concerning slavery, and most cheerfully return an unreserved answer to them. And we do so the rather, brethren, because of the numerous prejudicial statements which have been put forth in certain quarters to the wounding of the Church. We assure you then, brethren, that we have adopted no new principle or rule of discipline respecting slavery since the time of our apostolic Asbury; neither do we mean to adopt any. In our general rules, (called the 'General Rules of the United Societies,' and which are of constitutional authority in our Church,) '*the buying and selling of men, women, and children, with an intention to enslave them*,' is expressly prohibited; and in the same words, substantially, which have been used for the rule since 1792. And the extract of part ii, section 10, of our Book of Discipline, which you quote with approbation, and denominate 'a noble testimony,' is still of force to the same extent that it has been for many years; nor do we entertain any purpose to omit or qualify this section, or any part thereof. For while we should regard it a sore evil to divert Methodism from her proper work of '*spreading Scripture holiness over these lands*,' to questions of temporal import, involving the rights of Cæsar, yet are we not the less minded on that account to promote and set forward all humane and generous actions, or to prevent, to the utmost of our power, such as are evil and unchristian. It is our first desire, after *piety toward God*, to be '*merciful after our power; as we have opportunity, doing good of every possible sort, and as far as possible, to all men*'—'*to their bodies*,' but especially, and above all, '*to their souls*.'

"'Of these United States, (to the government and laws of which, 'according to the division of power made to them by the constitution of the Union, and the constitutions of the several States,' we owe, and delight to render, a sincere and patriotic loyalty,) there are several which do not allow of slavery. There are others in which it is allowed, and there are slaves; but the tendency of the laws, and the minds of the majority of the people, are in favour of emancipation. But there are others in which slavery exists so universally, and is so closely interwoven with their civil institutions, that both do the laws disallow of emancipation, and the great body of the people (the source of laws with us) hold it to be treasonable to set forth anything, by word or deed, tending that way. Each one of all these States is independent of the rest, and sovereign, with respect to its internal government, (as much so as if there existed no confederation among them for ends of common interest,) and therefore it is impossible to frame a rule on slavery proper for our people in all the States alike. But our Church is extended through all the States, and as it would be wrong and unscriptural to enact a rule of discipline in opposition to the constitution and laws of the State on this subject, so also would it not be equitable or Scriptural to confound the positions of our ministers and people (so different as they are in different States) with respect to the moral question which slavery involves.

"'Under the administration of the venerated Dr. Coke, this plain distinction was once overlooked, and it was attempted to urge emancipation in *all* the States; but the attempt proved almost ruinous, and was soon abandoned by the doctor himself. While, therefore, the Church has encouraged emancipation in those States where the laws permit it and allowed the freed-man to enjoy freedom, we have refrained, for conscience' sake, from all intermeddling with the subject in those other States where the laws make it criminal. And such a course we think agreeable to the Scriptures, and indicated by St. Paul's inspired instruction to servants in his First Epistle to the Corinthians, chap. vii, ver. 20, 21. For if servants were not to care for their servitude when they *might not* be free, though if they might be free they should use it *rather;* so, neither should masters be condemned for not setting them free when they *might not* do so, though *if* they *might* they should do so *rather*. The question of the evil of slavery, abstractedly considered, you will readily perceive, brethren, is a very different matter from a principle or rule of Church discipline to be executed contrary to, and in defiance of, the law of the land. Methodism has always been (except perhaps in the single instance above) eminently loyal and promotive of good order; and so we desire it may ever continue to be, both in Europe and America. With this sentiment we conclude the subject, adding only the corroborating language of your noble Missionary Society, by the revered and lamented Watson, in their instructions to missionaries, published in the Report of 1833, as follows:—

"'"As in the colonies in which you are called to labour a great proportion of the inhabitants are in a state of slavery, the committee most strongly call to your remembrance what was so fully stated to you when you were accepted as a missionary to the West Indies, that your only business is to promote the moral and religious improvement of the slaves to whom you may have access, without, in the least degree, in public or private, interfering with their civil condition."'"

I will now continue to read from the proceedings of the General Conference of 1840—page 68, of the first of the Proofs—the report of the Committee on the Westmoreland Petition, which was a case in which they had rejected a local preacher from ordination on the ground that he was a slave-holder.

"WEDNESDAY, JUNE 3.—H B. Bascom, chairman of the Committee on the Petition from Westmoreland, Va., presented a report, which was read and adopted.

"*Report on the Westmoreland Petition.*

"'The committee, to whom was referred the memorial and appeal of some fifteen official members of the Methodist Episcopal Church in Westmoreland circuit, Baltimore Conference, on the subject of alleged withholdment of right from a portion of the local ministry within the limits of that conference, and to whom was likewise referred the report of the judiciary committee upon a similar remonstrance from the same division of the Baltimore Conference, signed by about thirty official members of the Church, and addressed to the General Conference in 1836, after giving to the subject the attention its obvious importance demands, beg leave to report the following as the result of their deliberations:—

"'The particular portion, or rather general section of country in which these remonstrances have their origin, although belonging to the Baltimore Conference, is found within the limits of the state of Virginia; and the memorialists represent in strong but respectful terms, that local preachers within the jurisdiction of the Baltimore Conference, but residing in the commonwealth of Virginia, have, in considerable numbers, and for a succession of years, been rejected as applicants for deacons' and elders' orders in the ministry, solely on the ground of their being slaveholders or the owners of slaves. In the memorials referred to, it is distinctly stated, that election and ordination have been withheld from the applicants in question, on no other ground or pretence, than that of their being the owners of slave property; and it is further argued, that the Baltimore Conference avows this to be the only reason of the course they pursue, and which is complained of by the petitioners. The appellants allege further, that the laws of Virginia relating to slavery, forbid emancipation, except under restrictions, and subject to contingencies, amounting, to all intents and purposes, to a prohibition; and that the Discipline of the Church having provided for the ordination of ministers thus circumstanced, the course pursued by the Baltimore Conference operates as an abridgment of right, and, therefore, furnishes just ground of complaint. The memorialists regard themselves as clearly entitled to the protection of the well-known provisional exception to the general rule on this subject, found in the Discipline; and assume with confidence, and argue with firmness and ability, that no other objection being found to the character of candidates for ordination, it is a departure from the plain intentment of the law in the case, and a violation of not less express compact than of social justice, to withhold ordination for reasons which the provisions of the law plainly declare are not to be considered as a forfeiture of right. It is set forth in the argument of the appellants, that attaching themselves to the Church as citizens of Virginia, where, in the obvious sense of the Discipline, emancipation is impracticable, the holding of slaves, or failure to emancipate them, cannot plead in bar to the right of ordination, as is the case in States where emancipation, as defined and qualified by the rule in the case, is found to be practicable. In the latter case, the question is within the jurisdiction of the Church, inasmuch as the holding or not holding of property of this kind depends, not upon the constitution and regulation of civil property, but upon the will and purpose of individuals. Under such circumstances the conduct in question is voluntary, and in every final sense the result of choice. In the former, however, where emancipation is resisted by the prohibition of law, it may be otherwise; and in many instances is known to be, resulting entirely from the involuntary relations and circumstances of individuals connected with the very structures of civil polity, and the force and array of public opinion and popular interest. The memorialists advert to the fact, that we have in the Discipline two distinct classes of legislative provisions in relation to slavery—the one applying to owners of slaves where emancipation is practicable, consistently with the interests of master and slaves; and the other where it is impracticable without endangering such safety, and these interests on the part of both. With the former, known as the general rule on this subject, the petitioners do not interfere in any way, and are content simply to place themselves under the protection of the latter, as contracting parties with the Church; and the ground of complaint is, that the Church has failed to redeem the pledge of its own laws, by refusing or failing to promote to office ministers, in whose case no disability attaches on the ground of slavery, because the disability attaching in other cases is here removed by special provision of law, and so far leaves the right to ordination clear and undoubted, and hence the complaint against the Baltimore Conference. In further prosecution of the duty assigned them, your committee have carefully examined the law, and inquired into the system of slavery as it exists in Virginia, and find the representation of the memorialists essentially correct. The conditions with which emancipation is burdened in that commonwealth, preclude the practicability of giving freedom to slaves as contemplated in the Discipline, except in extremely rare instances—say one in a thousand, and possibly not more than one in five thousand. The exception in the Discipline is, therefore, strictly applicable to all the ministers and members of the Methodist Episcopal Church, holding slaves in Virginia, and they appear clearly entitled to the benefit of the rule made and provided in such cases.

"'As emancipation under such circumstances is not a requirement of Discipline, it cannot be made a condition of eligibility to office. An appeal to the policy and practice of the Church for fifty years past, will show incontestably, that, whatever may have been the convictions of the Church with regard to this great evil—the nature and tendency of the system of slavery—it has never insisted upon emancipation in contravention of civil authority; and it, therefore, appears to be a well-settled and long-established principle in the policy of the Church, that no ecclesiastical disabilities are intended to ensue, either to the ministers or members of the Church in those States where the civil authority forbids emancipation. The general rule, therefore, distinctly and invariably requiring emancipation as the ground of right and the condition of claim to ordination where the laws of the several States admit of emancipation and permit the liberated slave to enjoy freedom, and which, in the judgment of your committee, should always be carried into effect with unyielding firmness, does not apply to your memorialists, and cannot, by any fair construction of law, affect their rights.

"'On the other hand, your committee have given the most careful consideration to the position of the Baltimore Conference complained of by the appellants. The journals of the several sessions of the Baltimore Conference, for a series of years, have been carefully examined, and found to be silent on the subject of the rejections in question, except the single statement, that A, B, and C, from time to time, applied for admission or orders, and were rejected. We find no rule or reason of action, no evidence of preconcertion, no grounds or reasons of rejection, stated in any form, directly or indirectly. Nothing of this kind is avowed in, or found upon the face of the journals of that body. The charge of particular motives, it occurs to your committee, cannot be sustained in the instance of a deliberative body, say the Baltimore Conference, unless it appears in evidence that the motives have been avowed by a majority of the conference; and it is not in proof that the conference has ever had an action to this effect, whatever may have been the declaration of individuals sustaining the charge of the appellants. The fact charged, without reference to motives, that there had been a long list of rejections, both as regards admission into the travelling connexion and ordination, until the exception seems to be made a general rule, is undoubtedly true, and it is not denied by the defendants. The evidence, however, in relation to specific reasons and motives, is defective, and does not appear to sustain the charge of a contravention of right by any direct accredited action of the Baltimore Conference had in the premises.

"'That this view of the subject presents a serious difficulty, is felt by your committee, and must be so by all. The rule applicable in this case allows an annual conference to elect under the circumstances; but does not, and, from the very nature and ubiquity of the case, cannot require it. Among the unquestioned constitutional rights of our annual conferences, is that of acting freely, without any compulsory direction, in the exercise of individual franchise. Election here is plainly an assertion of personal right on the part of the different members composing the body, with regard to which, the claim to question or challenge motives does not belong even to the General Conference, unless the result has turned upon avowed considerations unknown to the law and rule in the case. The journal of the conference is the only part of its history of which this body has cognizance; and to extend such cognizance to the reasons and motives of individual members of conferences not declared to be the ground of action by a majority, would be to establish a rule at once subversive of the rights and independence of annual conferences. In the very nature of the case an annual conference must possess the right of free and uncontrolled determination, not only in the choice of its members, but in all its elections, and, keeping within the limits and restrictions of its charter as found in the Discipline, can only be controlled in the exercise of such rights by moral and relative considerations connected with the intelligence and interests of the body.

"'The memorialists prayed the last General Conference, and they again ask this, to interfere authoritatively, by change or construction of rule, so as to afford relief; and in failure to do so, in the memorial of 1836, they ask to be set off to the Virginia Conference as the only remaining remedy. In their present petition they are silent on the subject of a transfer to Virginia. Under all the circumstances of the case, and taking into the account the probabilities of future action in the premises, your committee cannot but regard this as the only conclusive remedy. But how far this may be considered as relatively practicable, or whether advisable, in view of all the interests involved, the committee have no means of determining, and therefore leave it to the judgment of those who have. That the petitioners, in accordance with the provisions of the Discipline, whether said provisions be right or wrong, are entitled to remedy, your committee cannot for a moment doubt, inasmuch as they are labouring, and have been for years, under practical disabilities actually provided against by the Discipline of the Church. The alleged grievance is by the petitioners themselves regarded as one of administration, not of law. No change of legislation is asked for, unless this body prefer it; and it does not appear to your committee to be called for by any view of the subject they have been able to take.

"'Your committee are unwilling to close this brief view of the subject, without anxiously suggesting that, as it is one of the utmost importance and intense delicacy in its application and bearings throughout our entire country, involving in greater or less degree the hopes and fears, the anxieties and interests of millions, it must be expected that great variety of opinions and diversity of conviction and feeling will be found to exist in relation to it, and most urgently call for the exercise of mutual forbearance and reciprocal good-will on the part of all concerned. May not the principles and causes giving birth and perpetuity to great moral and political systems or institutions be regarded as evil, even essentially evil, in every primary aspect of the subject, without the implication of moral obliquity on the part of those involuntarily connected with such systems and institutions, and providentially involved in their operation and consequences? May not a system of this kind be jealously regarded as in itself more or less inconsistent with natural right and moral rectitude, without the imputation of guilt and derelict motive, in the instance of those who, without any choice or purpose of their own, are necessarily subjected to its influence and sway?

"'Can it be considered as just or reasonable to hold individuals responsible for the destiny of circumstances over which they have no control? Thus conditioned in the organic arrangements and distributions of society, is there any necessary connexion between the moral character of the individual and that of the system? In this way the modifying influence of unavoidable agencies or circumstances in the formation of character is a well-known principle, and one of universal recognition in law, morals, and religion, and upon which all administration of law, not unjust and oppressive, must proceed. And your committee know no reason why the rule is inapplicable, or should not obtain, in relation to the subject of this report. In conclusion, your committee would express the deliberate opinion that, while the general rule on the subject of slavery, relating to those States only whose laws admit of emancipation and permit the liberated slave to enjoy freedom, *should be firmly and constantly enforced*, the exception to the general rule, applying to those States where emancipation, as defined above, is not practicable, should be recognised and protected with equal *firmness* and *impartiality*. The committee respectfully suggest to the Conference the propriety of adopting the following resolution:—

"'Resolved, by the delegates of the several annual conferences in General Conference assembled, That under the provisional exception of the general rule of the Church on the subject of slavery, the simple holding of slaves, or mere ownership of slave property, in States or Territories where the laws do not admit of emancipation and permit the liberated slave to enjoy freedom, constitutes no legal barrier to the election or ordination of ministers to the various grades of office known in the ministry of the Methodist Episcopal Church, and cannot therefore be considered as operating any forfeiture of right in view of such election and ordination.'"

I beg your Honours' attention to the phrase, "constitutes no legal barrier to the election or ordination of ministers to the various grades of office known in the ministry of the Methodist Episcopal Church."

I now proceed to quote from the acts of the General Conference of 1844, upon the case of Mr. Harding, which arose in the Baltimore Conference, which, I believe, has been called the "Breakwater Conference." This General Conference commenced its sittings in the city of New-York, on Wednesday, May 1, 1844, on which day Bishops Soule, Hedding, Andrew, Waugh, and Morris, were present. From the Minutes it appears that this Conference was flooded with petitions upon the subject of slavery; and on the 4th of May this precise and particular case came up.—(*P. 75, first of the Proofs.*)

"SATURDAY, MAY 4, 1844.—J. A. Gere presented the appeal of Francis A. Harding, of the Baltimore Conference; which, on motion, the Conference made the special order for Tuesday next.

"TUESDAY, MAY 7.—On motion, the rule of business was suspended to take up the special order of the day, namely: The appeal of Francis A. Harding, of the Baltimore Conference.

"J. Early announced that the appellant was present, and had spoken to W. A. Smith of the Virginia Conference, to act as his representative, in presenting and prosecuting the appeal.

"The journal of the Baltimore Conference, unfolding its action in regard to the appellant, and from which he appeals, was read by the Secretary. From this it appears that F. A. Harding had been suspended from his ministerial standing for refusing to manumit certain slaves which came into his possession by his marriage. On motion of S. Luckey and J. B. Finley, the appeal was admitted and entertained.

"W. A. Smith, in behalf of the appellant, made a statement, and argued the case until near the hour of adjournment. When he had concluded, J. A. Collins moved that the case be postponed, and made the special order for to-morrow, to be taken up immediately after the reading of the journal. Adopted.

"Wednesday, May 8.—On motion, the journal of yesterday was so amended as to read, 'the order of business according to the rule was suspended, to take up the order of the day, namely: the appeal of F. A. Harding.' The journal as amended was approved and confirmed.

"The consideration of the appeal case before the Conference yesterday was resumed.

"J. A. Collins, in behalf of the Baltimore Conference in this case, addressed the Conference in reply to W. A. Smith, and in defence of the action of the Baltimore Conference, until eleven o'clock. H. Slicer, A. Griffith, and T. B. Sargent, were also heard for the Baltimore Conference.

"When the delegates of the Baltimore Conference had spoken, the place was given to the representative of the appellant to rejoin. At this point, J. Early moved that the further consideration of this case be postponed until to-morrow morning at ten o'clock, and that it be made the special order for that time. J. A. Collins moved to amend, by inserting, instead of ten o'clock, 'immediately after the reading of the journal.' This was lost. N. Rounds moved to amend by inserting 'three o'clock to-morrow afternoon.' J. A. Collins moved further to amend by inserting '*this* afternoon.' As a substitute, W. Capers moved, that the Conference attend to this business to-morrow morning, immediately after reading the journal. W. M'Mahan moved, that when the Conference adjourn, it adjourn to meet the American Bible Society, to-morrow morning at ten o'clock. This motion was laid on the table. Finally, at fifteen minutes before one o'clock, E. R. Ames moved that Conference do now adjourn; which motion was adopted, and Conference separated after prayer by brother Spaulding.

"Friday, May 10.—The appeal of F. A. Harding was resumed. By consent of W. A. Smith, the representative of the appellant, J. A. Collins, who acted in behalf of the Baltimore Conference, was allowed to make a further response for the Baltimore Conference to the statement and defence of W. A. Smith. He spoke until within five minutes of eleven o'clock.

"When W. A. Smith was about to reply, Conference, on motion of T. Crowder, resolved to prolong the session until he should have concluded his rejoinder.

"W. A. Smith, on behalf of the appellant, was then heard in reply to the representative of the Baltimore Conference. He spoke until after one o'clock; and the pleadings on both sides were closed.

"Saturday, May 11.—On motion of E. R. Ames, the rules of Conference were suspended for the purpose of taking up the appeal of F. A. Harding. W. A. Smith came forward when the appeal was resumed, and asked leave to make further statements in regard to the appellant. A motion to grant leave was offered and carried. When the Conference had heard Mr. Smith, J. Early offered the following resolution, namely:—

"'Resolved, That the act of the Baltimore Annual Conference, by which F. A. Harding was suspended from his ministerial functions, be, and the same is, hereby reversed.'

"The yeas and nays were called for, and ordered by a vote of Conference; and the secretary proceeded to call the list by conferences, in the order in which they stand in the Discipline, in the chapter on boundaries. The secretaries reported the vote as follows:—*Nays* 117, against reversing the decision of the Baltimore Conference; and 56 *yeas*, in favour of reversing that decision."

I omit the lists of the names of those who voted, and proceed to read the subsequent proceedings (p. 79):—

"When S. Olin's name was called, he asked to be excused from voting on this question, because indisposition had prevented him from hearing the whole case. He was, on motion, excused.

"J. A. Gere also asked to be excused from voting, because he had once sat in judgment on the case, and had been called upon as a witness. He was not excused.

"It appeared, on calling the list, that J. G. Dow, R. Paine, and L. Scott were absent.

"N. Bangs and S. Dunwody were reported sick.

"So the motion to reverse the act of the Baltimore Annual Conference was lost by the above vote of 117 to.56.

"The chair decided that this vote virtually affirmed the action of the Baltimore Annual Conference, in suspending Francis A. Harding from his ministerial standing. W. Capers took an appeal from the decision of the chair. The appeal was put, and the decision of the chair sustained, by a vote of 111 for sustaining the decision, and 53 against sustaining it. So the vote virtually affirmed the action of the Baltimore Conference on suspending F. A. Harding."

In connexion with this, I call your Honours' attention to the question of Maryland Law which is involved in it. The debates of the General Conference of 1844 (pp. 21, 22) show that legal opinions were produced from the Honourable William D. Merrick, U. S. Senator, and Mr. Edmund Key, showing that Mr. Harding could not manumit his slaves. These opinions were produced before a committee of the Baltimore Conference, which was appointed to investigate the case of Mr. Harding. Mr. Merrick's opinion is in these words :—

"At the request of Mr Harding, I have to state that, under the laws of Maryland, no slave can be emancipated to remain in that State, nor unless provision be made by the person emancipating him for his removal from the State, which removal must take place, unless for good and sufficient reason the competent authorities grant permission to the manumitted slave to remain.

"There has lately (winter of 1843) been a statute enacted by the State legislature, securing to married females the property (slaves of course included) which was theirs at the time of their marriage, and protecting it from the power and liabilities of their husbands.

(Signed) "William D. Merrick."

The opinion of Judge Key is as follows :—

"The Rev. Mr. Harding having married Miss Swan, who, at the time of her marriage, was entitled to some slaves, I am requested to say, whether he can legally manumit them or not? By an act of Assembly, no person can manumit a slave in Maryland; and by another act of our Assembly, a husband has no other or further right to his wife's slaves than their labour, while he lives. He can neither sell nor liberate them. Neither can he and his wife, either jointly or separately, manumit her slaves, by deed, or otherwise. A reference to the Acts of Assembly of Maryland will show this.

"Edmund Key.

"*Prince George County, April 25th,* 1844."

The law of Maryland, on the subject of slavery, is also set forth in the debates of the General Conference of 1844: indeed, there are several of them, which appear to have been copied from books in the library of the Historical Society in this city. The first which I shall read is chap. 293 :—

"Sec. 1. *Be it enacted by the General Assembly of Maryland,* That from and after the passage of this act, any married woman may become seized or possessed of any property, real or of slaves, by direct bequest, demise, gift, purchase, or distribution, in her own name, and as of her own property; *provided,* the same does not come from her husband after coverture.

"Sec. 2. *And be it enacted,* That hereafter, when any woman possessed of a property in slaves, shall marry, her property in such slaves, and their natural increase, shall continue to her, notwithstanding her coverture; and she shall have, hold, and possess the same as her separate property, exempt from any liability for the debts or contracts of the husband.

"Sec. 3. *And be it enacted,* That when any woman during coverture shall become entitled to, or possessed of, slaves by conveyance, gift, inheritance, distribution, or otherwise, such slaves, together with their natural increase, shall enure and belong to the wife in like manner as is above provided as to slaves which she may possess at the time of marriage.

"Sec. 4. *And be it enacted,* That the control and management of all such slaves, the direction of their labour, and the receipts of the productions thereof, shall remain to the husband agreeably to the laws heretofore in force. All suits to recover the property or possession of such slaves, shall be prosecuted or defended, as the case may be, in the joint names of the husband and wife; in case of the death of the wife, such slaves shall descend and go to her children, and their descendants, subject to the use of the husband during life, without liability to his creditors; and if she die without leaving children living, or descendants of such children living, they shall descend and go to the husband.

"Sec. 5. *Be it enacted,* That the slaves owned by a femme-covert under the provisions of this act, may be sold by the joint deed of the husband and wife, executed, proved, and recorded agreeably to the laws now in force in regard to the conveyance of real estate of femme-coverts, and not otherwise.

"Sec. 6. *And be it enacted,* That a wife shall have a right to make a will, and give all her property, or any part thereof, to her husband, and to other persons, with the consent of the husband subscribed to said will; *provided always,* that the wife shall have been privately examined by the witnesses to her will, apart and out of the presence and hearing of her husband, whether she doth make the same will freely and voluntarily, and without being induced thereto by fear or threats of, or ill usage by, said husband, and says she does it willingly and freely; *provided,* that no will under this act shall be valid, unless made at least sixty days before the death of the testatrix."

And then, on the subject of manumission, we have an extract from the laws of Maryland, from Dorsey's "Laws of Maryland," in 1831. I read from the debates of the Conference of 1844, p. 24:—

" '*And be it enacted,* That it shall hereafter be the duty of every clerk of a county in this State, whenever a deed of manumission shall be left in his office for record, and of every register of wills in every county of this State, whenever a will manumitting a slave or slaves shall be admitted to probate, to send, within five days thereafter (under a penalty of ten dollars for each and every omission so to do, to be recovered before any justice of the peace, one half whereof shall go to the informer, and the other half to the State) an extract from such deed or will, stating the names, number, and ages of the slave or slaves so manumitted, a list whereof, in the case of the will so proved, shall be filed therewith by the executor or administrator to the board of managers for Maryland for removing the people of colour of said State; and it shall be the duty of said board, on receiving the same, to notify the American Colonization Society, or the Maryland State Colonization Society thereof, and to propose to such society, that they shall engage, at the expense of said society, to remove said slave or slaves so manumitted to Liberia; and if the said society shall so engage, then it shall be the duty of the said board of managers to have the said slave or slaves delivered to the agent of such society, at such place as the said society shall appoint for receiving such slave or slaves, for the purpose of such removal, at such time as the said society shall appoint; and in case the said society shall refuse so to receive and remove the person or persons so manumitted and offered; or in case the said person or persons shall refuse so to be removed, then it shall be the duty of the said board of managers to remove the said person or persons to such other place or places beyond the limits of this State, as the said board shall approve of, and the said person or persons shall be willing to go to, and provide for their reception and support such place or places as the board may think necessary, until they shall be able to provide for themselves, out of any money that may be earned by their hire, or may be otherwise provided for that purpose; and in case the said person or persons shall refuse to be removed to any place beyond the limits of this State, and shall persist in remaining therein, then it shall be the duty of said board to inform the sheriff of the county wherein such person or persons may be, of such refusal, and it shall thereupon be the duty of said sheriff forthwith to arrest, or cause to be arrested, the said person or persons so refusing to emigrate from this State, and transport the said person or persons beyond the limits of this State; and all slaves shall be capable of receiving manumission for the purpose of removal as aforesaid, with their consent, of whatever age, any law to the contrary notwithstanding.' Chap. 281, sec. 3.' "

We find a supplement to this law in 1832:—

"'CHAP. 145, SEC. 1. *Be it enacted by the General Assembly of Maryland*, That whenever the board of managers, appointed under the act to which this is a supplement, shall inform the sheriff of any county of the refusal to remove any person or persons therein mentioned, and shall provide a sum sufficient to defray the removal of said person or persons beyond the limits of the State, every sheriff then failing to comply, within the term of one month, with the duties prescribed in the third section of the act aforesaid, shall forfeit fifty dollars for every person he shall neglect so to remove, to be recoverable in the county court, by action of debt on indictment.

"'SEC. 2. *And be it enacted*, That nothing herein contained shall be construed to repeal any part of the act to which this is a supplement.'

"The foregoing is a copy, corrected by myself, from the acts referred to, as published in Dorsey's Laws of Maryland.

"GEORGE H. MOORE,
Assistant Librarian New-York Historical Society."

We have now, may it please your Honours, finished the case of Mr. Harding, and we come to the case of Bishop Andrew. I read from page 80 of the first of the Proofs:—

"MONDAY, MAY 20.—J. A. Collins offered the following resolution, which was adopted, viz.:—

"'Whereas it is currently reported, and generally understood, that one of the bishops of the Methodist Episcopal Church has become connected with slavery; and whereas it is due to this General Conference to have a proper understanding of the matter; therefore,

"'Resolved, That the Committee on the Episcopacy be instructed to ascertain the facts in the case, and report the results of their investigation to this body to-morrow morning.

JOHN A. COLLINS,
J. B. HOUGHTALING.'

"TUESDAY, MAY 21.—The Committee on Episcopacy presented a further report, No. 3, which was read, and on motion of J. A. Collins, laid on the table to be the order of the day for to-morrow.

"WEDNESDAY, MAY 22.—As no reports from select committees were offered, on motion of A. Griffith, Conference proceeded to consider the order of the day, viz., the report No. 3 of the Committee on Episcopacy. It reads as follows:—

"'The Committee on Episcopacy, to whom was referred a resolution, submitted yesterday, instructing them to inquire whether any one of the superintendents is connected with slavery, beg leave to present the following as their report on the subject:—

"'The committee had ascertained, previous to the reference of the resolution, that Bishop Andrew is connected with slavery, and had obtained an interview with him on the subject; and having requested him to state the whole facts in the premises, hereby present a written communication from him in relation to this matter, and beg leave to offer it as his statement and explanation of the case.

'*To the Committee on Episcopacy*:—

'Dear Brethren,—In reply to your inquiry, I submit the following statement of all the facts bearing on my connexion with slavery. Several years since an old lady, of Augusta, Georgia, bequeathed to me a mulatto girl, in trust that I should take care of her until she should be nineteen years of age; that *with her consent* I should then send her to Liberia; and that in case of her refusal, I should keep her, and make her as free as the laws of the State of Georgia would permit. When the time arrived, she refused to go to Liberia, and of her own choice remains *legally* my slave, although I derive no pecuniary profit from her. She continues to live in her own house on my lot; and has been, and is at present, at perfect liberty to go to a free State at her pleasure; but the laws of the State will not permit her emancipation, nor admit such deed of emancipation to record, and she refuses to leave the State. In her case, therefore, I have been made a slaveholder legally, but not with my own consent.

'2dly. About five years since, the mother of my former wife left to her daughter, *not to me*, a negro boy; and as my wife died without a will more than two years since, by the laws of the State he becomes legally my property. In this case, as in the former, emancipation is impracticable in the State; but he shall be at liberty to leave the State whenever I shall be satisfied that he is prepared to provide for himself, or I can have sufficient security that he will be protected and provided for in the place to which he may go.

'3dly. In the month of January last I married my present wife, she being at the time possessed of slaves, inherited from her former husband's estate, and belonging to *her*. Shortly after my marriage, being unwilling to become their owner, regarding them as strictly hers, and the law not permitting their emancipation, I secured them to her by a deed of trust.

'It will be obvious to you, from the above statement of facts, that I have neither bought nor sold a slave; that in the only two instances in which I am legally a slaveholder, emancipation is impracticable. As to the servants owned by my wife, I have no legal responsibility in the premises, nor could my wife emancipate them if she desired to do so. I have thus plainly stated all the facts in the case, and submit the statement for the consideration of the General Conference. Yours respectfully,

'JAMES O. ANDREW.'

"'All which is respectfully submitted.

"'ROBERT PAINE, *Chairman*.'

"A. Griffith and J. Davis offered the following preamble and resolution, which were read and debated:—

"'Whereas the Rev. James O. Andrew, one of the bishops of the Methodist Episcopal Church, has become connected with slavery, as communicated in his statement in his reply to the inquiry of the Committee on the Episcopacy, which reply is embodied in their report, No. 3, offered yesterday; and whereas it has been, from the origin of said Church, a settled policy and the invariable usage to elect no person to the office of bishop who was embarrassed with this "great evil," as under such circumstances it would be impossible for a bishop to exercise the functions and perform the duties assigned to a general superintendent with acceptance, in that large portion of his charge in which slavery does not exist; and whereas Bishop Andrew was himself nominated by our brethren of the slaveholding States, and elected by the General Conference of 1832, as a candidate, who, though living in the midst of a slaveholding population, was nevertheless free from all personal connexion with slavery; and whereas this is, of all periods in our history as a Church, the one least favourable to such an innovation upon the practice and usage of Methodism as to confide a part of the itinerant general superintendency to a slaveholder; therefore,

"'Resolved, That the Rev. James O. Andrew be, and he is hereby affectionately requested to resign his office as one of the bishops of the Methodist Episcopal Church.'

"When brother Griffith, in favour of his resolution, had spoken as long as the rule allowed, a motion was made to permit him to proceed. G. Filmore offered as a substitute for this, that the rule which restricts a speaker to fifteen minutes, be suspended during the discussion of this subject. The substitute prevailed, by a vote of one hundred and three.

"On motion of N. Bangs, it was resolved, that when we adjourn, it be to meet again this afternoon at half-past three o'clock, one hundred and four voting for it.

"W. Capers then moved, that we do now adjourn. Lost.

"J. P. Durbin moved to reconsider the vote by which we resolved to meet this afternoon. This was lost.

"The motion for adjournment was renewed and carried; and Conference adjourned with prayer by brother Tippett.

"WEDNESDAY AFTERNOON, MAY 22.—Conference met, pursuant to adjournment, at half-past three o'clock, Bishop Soule in the chair, and was opened with religious services by brother Fowler.

"The chair called for reports from standing and select committees. None being offered, W. Cooper moved that the resolution under discussion this morning be postponed, and made the order of the day for to-morrow morning. Lost. The consideration was resumed, and several speakers were heard.

"On motion of J. A. Collins, Conference adjourned with prayer by brother Bond.

"THURSDAY MORNING, MAY 23.—Conference met at the regular hour, Bishop Hedding in the chair, and was opened with religious exercises by brother Robinson.

"The journal of yesterday afternoon was read and approved.

"The chair called for reports from standing and select committees. None were presented.

"Conference resumed the consideration of the resolution under discussion yesterday, viz., the resolution offered by brothers Griffith and Davis on Wednesday.

"J. B. Finley offered a substitute for the resolution, in the following words, viz.:—

"'Whereas the Discipline of our Church forbids the doing anything calculated to destroy our itinerant general superintendency, and whereas Bishop Andrew has become connected with slavery by marriage and otherwise, and this act having drawn after it circumstances which, in the estimation of the General Conference, will greatly embarrass the exercise of his office as an itinerant general superintendent, if not in some places entirely prevent it; therefore,

"'Resolved, That it is the sense of this General Conference that he desist from the exercise of this office so long as this impediment remains.

"'J. B. Finley,
J. M. Trimble.'

"A discussion on the above substitute ensued, occupying the morning session. A few minutes before one o'clock, when W. D. Cass was speaking, it was resolved to continue the session five minutes after the regular time, for the purpose of hearing a statement which J. Early wished to make. When this was made, Conference adjourned with prayer by brother Steele.

"Friday, May 24.—The order of the day, namely, the above-named substitute, (Finley's,) was resumed, and its discussion continued until one o'clock, when Conference adjourned with prayer by brother Ferguson.

"Saturday, May 25.—The order of the day, namely, the substitute of brothers Finley and Trimble, for the resolution offered by brothers Griffith and Davis, was resumed.

"During the discussion, J. P. Durbin asked leave of absence, on account of family affliction. The leave was granted.

"After the consideration of the substitute had been resumed, G. Baker moved that the vote by which the rule limiting a speaker to fifteen minutes had been suspended, be reconsidered. On motion of J. E. Evans, the proposal to reconsider was laid on the table. The discussion was continued until fifteen minutes before the hour of adjournment, when, on motion of L. M. Lee, Conference adjourned with prayer by brother Bush.

"Monday, May 27.—The whole session was occupied in discussing the substitute under consideration for some days past.

"Tuesday Morning, May 28.—Conference resumed the consideration of Finley's substitute. J. A. Collins, who was speaking at the adjournment yesterday, concluded his remarks, and was followed by E. W. Sehon, W. Winans, and J. B. Finley. Bishop Andrew also addressed the Conference.

"At the request of T. Crowder, brother Finley gave way to permit him to offer the following resolution:—

"'Resolved, That when this Conference adjourn, it adjourn to meet again at half-past three o'clock.'

"The resolution prevailed. P. Cartwright obtained the floor, but the hour of adjournment having come, Conference adjourned with prayer by brother A. D. Peck.

"Tuesday Afternoon, May 28.—The subject under consideration at the adjournment was resumed, and discussed by P. Cartwright and J. Stamper.

"When P. Cartwright had concluded his remarks, P. Crandall offered a resolution, that the discussion on this question close at half-past five o'clock this afternoon. J. A. Collins rose to a point of order, whether the resolution could be entertained, the Conference having no rule for the previous question. The chair decided that the resolution was not in order. From this decision J. B. Houghtaling appealed; and the decision of the chair was sustained by a vote of one hundred and three.

"S. Dunwody obtained the floor, but gave way for a motion to adjourn, which was withdrawn to permit Bishop Soule to make a few remarks, asking leave of the Conference, before the final action, to make some remarks on the subject now under consideration. J. Early moved that Bishop Soule and all the other bishops be at liberty to address the Conference on the subject now under consideration, at any time after brother Dunwody has concluded his remarks.

"Without taking the vote, on motion, Conference adjourned with the benediction by Bishop Waugh,

"WEDNESDAY MORNING, MAY 29.—Conference took up the resolution of J. Early, which was under discussion when Conference adjourned. A motion was made to lay the resolution on the table, which prevailed. J. S. Porter moved to reconsider the last vote. Carried. J. P. Durbin moved the previous question, which being sustained, the vote on the resolution before the Conference was taken, and the resolution was adopted.

"The Conference renewed the consideration of the substitute offered by J. B. Finley. S. Dunwody addressed the Conference, and was followed by Bishop Soule.

"N. Bangs moved, that when Conference adjourn, it adjourn to meet again at half-past three o'clock this afternoon. Carried.

"Bishop Soule having concluded his remarks, the Conference adjourned with the benediction by brother Dunwody."

I will hereafter read the remarks of Bishop Soule from the debates of the General Conference of 1844; but, before doing so, I beg your Honours to notice the dates of the proceedings which have been read, that you may see how long the discussion continued.

"WEDNESDAY AFTERNOON, MAY 29.—Conference resumed the consideration of the substitute of J. B. Finley. J. P. Durbin addressed the Conference, after some explanation by W. A. Smith, A. B. Longstreet, and others. W. Capers then obtained the floor, but gave way for a motion to adjourn, which being put was carried.

"THURSDAY, MAY 30.—The consideration of Finley's substitute was resumed, W. Capers having the floor, who addressed the Conference. When he had concluded, G. Peck obtained the floor, but yielded it to J. Hobart, who moved the previous question. J. P. Durbin moved, that on the vote whether the main question shall now be put, the ayes and noes be taken. The ayes and noes were ordered by a vote of one hundred and seventeen.

"The list was called, and ninety-eight answered in favour of putting the main question, and eighty against it.

"So the motion to take the main question was lost, not having a majority of two-thirds.

"At this moment Bishop Hedding suggested that the Conference have no afternoon session, and thus allow the bishops time to consult together, with a hope that they might be able to present a plan of adjusting our present difficulties. The suggestion was received with general and great cordiality; and, on motion, the discussion of the substitute under consideration was postponed until to-morrow morning.

"FRIDAY, MAY 31.—Bishop Waugh, in behalf of the bishops, presented the following communication, which was read by himself, and also by the Secretary:—

"'*To the General Conference of the Methodist Episcopal Church.*

"'REV. AND DEAR BRETHREN,—The undersigned respectfully and affectionately offer to your calm consideration the result of their consultation this afternoon in regard to the unpleasant and very delicate question which has been so long and so earnestly debated before your body. They have, with the liveliest interest, watched the progress of the discussion, and have awaited its termination with the deepest solicitude. As they have pored over this subject with anxious thought, by day and by night, they have been more and more impressed with the difficulties connected therewith, and the disastrous results which, in their apprehension, are the almost inevitable consequences of present action on the question now pending before you. To the undersigned it is fully apparent that a decision thereon, whether affirmatively or negatively, will most extensively disturb the peace and harmony of that widely-extended brotherhood which has so effectively operated for good in the United States of America and elsewhere during the last sixty years, in the development of a system of active energy, of which union has always been a main element. They have, with deep emotion, inquired, Can anything be done to avoid an evil so much deprecated by every friend of our common Methodism? Long and anxiously have they waited for a satisfactory answer to this inquiry, but they have paused in vain. At this painful crisis they have unanimously concurred in the propriety of recommending the postponement of further action in the case of Bishop Andrew until the ensuing General Conference. It does not enter into the design of the undersigned to argue the propriety of their recommendation; otherwise, strong and valid reasons might be adduced in its support. They cannot but think that if the embarrassment of Bishop Andrew should not cease before that time, the next General Conference, representing the pastors, ministers, and people of the several annual conferences, after all the facts in the case shall have passed in review before them, will be better qualified than the present General Conference can be to adjudicate the case wisely and discreetly. Until the cessation of the embarrassment, or the expiration of the interval between the present and the ensuing General Conference, the undersigned believe that such a division of the work of the general superintendency might be made, without any infraction of a constitutional principle, as would fully employ Bishop Andrew in those sections of the Church in which his presence and services would be welcome and cordial. If the course pursued on this occasion by the undersigned be deemed a novel one, they persuade themselves that their justification, in the view of all candid and peace-loving persons, will be found in their strong desire to prevent disunion, and to promote harmony in the Church.

"'Very respectfully and affectionately submitted,

"'Joshua Soule,
Elijah Hedding,
B. Waugh,
T. A. Morris.

"'*Thursday Afternoon, May* 30, 1844.'

"J. A. Collins moved that the consideration of the communication just read be postponed until to-morrow morning, and that the communication itself be printed forthwith. A third reading was called for, and ordered by the Conference. I. Winner moved to amend the above resolution by striking out 'to-morrow morning,' and inserting 'four o'clock this afternoon.' This amendment, on motion of J. Stamper, was laid on the table. T. Stringfield called for a division of the resolution; and that part which relates to the printing was adopted. The other member of the resolution was also adopted.

"Saturday, June 1.—At this juncture all the bishops on the platform addressed the Conference, in the following order:—

"Bishop Hedding said he wished to withdraw his name from the Address of the Bishops, presented yesterday. He had not been argued or persuaded into signing it, but had attached his name of his own free will and accord, because he thought it would be a peace measure; but facts had come to his knowledge since, which led him to believe that such would not be the case. Again: he thought it would be adopted without debate, but he was convinced now that it would give rise to much discussion, and therefore he wished to withdraw his name from the paper on the table.

"Bishop Waugh followed, and said he came into the measure, as his venerated and honoured colleague did, without persuasion or restraint. He considered it as the last resort to promote the future peace of the Church. He admitted he had not been very sanguine on the subject, and if it failed, he would not be disappointed. Still he did not desire to withdraw his name; he would regret if the communication should be the cause of lengthened debate, and in that case *might* feel called upon to withdraw his name from the document. At present he was content to let it remain.

"Bishop Morris succeeded, and said he wished his name to stand on that paper, as a testimony that he had done what he could to preserve the unity and peace of the Church.

"Bishop Soule added, that his colleagues would certainly say, that they adopted the paper as freely as he did. He put his name to that document under the same circumstances as they did. He had not changed his views or convictions in any way, He wished his signature to *stand* to that document, which had now gone forth to the American people through a thousand mediums.

"N. Bangs moved to lay the Address on the table. J. Early moved that the question of laying it on the table be taken by ayes and noes. This prevailed. The vote was then taken, and ninety-five affirmative and eighty-four negative votes were given. So the Address of the Bishops was laid on the table.

"J. A. Collins moved to take up the substitute of J. B. Finley, which had been laid on the table by a vote some days ago. J. C. Evans moved the previous question on taking up the substitute. The call for the previous question was sustained by two-thirds voting affirmatively; and the substitute was taken up by another vote. J. T. Peck moved the previous question on the substitute, and the words, 'Shall the main question now be put?' applied to the substitute, according to the resolution establishing the previous question. A motion that the vote whether the main question now be taken shall be by yeas and nays, was lost by a vote of 128 to 47. The call for the previous question was sustained by the requisite majority, and the vote on the substitute being ordered, it was moved to take this vote by yeas and nays. The yeas and nays were ordered. The list by conferences was called, and the vote on the substitute was decided by 110 yeas, and 68 nays. So conference adopted the substitute of James B. Finley, which is in these words:—

"'Whereas the Discipline of our Church forbids the doing anything calculated to destroy our itinerant general superintendency, and whereas Bishop Andrew has become connected with slavery by marriage and otherwise, and this act having drawn after it circumstances which, in the estimation of the General Conference, will greatly embarrass the exercise of his office as an itinerant general superintendent, if not in some places entirely prevent it; therefore,

"'*Resolved*, That it is the sense of this General Conference that he desist from the exercise of his office so long as this impediment remains.'

"During the call for yeas and nays, J. C. Clark asked to be excused from voting, as he was compelled, by the want of health in some members of his family, to remove from Texas. Conference by a vote declined excusing him."

If your Honours please, I beg leave here to read two resolutions which were offered in that Conference. I read from book of Proofs, No. 2, pp. 6, 7.

"*Mr. Drake's resolution proposed, but not acted on, in General Conference of* 1844.

"'Whereas there have been found difficulties of a serious nature in the bishops of the Methodist Episcopal Church exercising a general superintendency; therefore,

"'*Resolved*, That the General Conference recommend the episcopacy to assign to each superintendent his sphere of labour for the next four years.'

"This proposition, not being in order, was offered as a suggestion, and no action was had on it.

"*Mr. Durbin's resolve not passed in that Conference.*

"'*Resolved*, That the case of Bishop Andrew be referred to the Church, and that the judgment of the next General Conference be deemed and taken to be the voice of the Church, whether Bishop Andrew shall continue to exercise his functions as a general superintendent in the Methodist Episcopal Church while he sustains the relation to slavery as stated in his communication to the Conference, as reported to the Conference by the Committee on Episcopacy.'"

I now return to the first of the Proofs, page 94.

"L. Pierce gave notice that a Protest would be presented by the minority on this vote, at as early a day as practicable; to be entered on the journals of the Conference.

"W. Winans moved that the Conference do now adjourn. This motion was carried. After prayer by brother Sovereign, conference adjourned until Monday morning, at half-past eight o'clock.

"Monday, June 3.—The following resolutions were offered by H. Slicer and T. B. Sargent:—

"'1. *Resolved*, That it is the sense of this General Conference that the vote of Saturday last, in the case of Bishop Andrew, be understood as advisory only, and not in the light of a judicial mandate.

"'2. *Resolved*, That the final disposition of Bishop Andrew's case be postponed until the General Conference of 1848, in conformity with the suggestion of the bishops in their Address to the Conference on Friday, 31st May.

"'H. Slicer,
T. B. Sargent.

"'*June* 3, 1844.'

"It was moved to lay these resolutions on the table for the present. On the question of laying them on the table, the yeas and nays were called for, and ordered.—Ayes 75, Noes 68.

"So the resolutions, for the present, are laid on the table."

I believe that they were never afterwards called up again, so that the Conference resolved not to put that construction upon its acts.

"Dr. Capers offered a series of resolutions, which were read, and lie on the table, under the rule. They are as follows:—

"'Be it resolved by the delegates of all the annual conferences in General Conference assembled:

"'That we recommend to the annual conferences to suspend the constitutional restrictions which limit the powers of the General Conference so far, and so far only, as to allow of the following alterations in the government of the Church, namely:—

"'That the Methodist Episcopal Church in these United States and territories, and the republic of Texas, shall constitute two General Conferences, to meet quadrennially, the one at some place *south*, and the other *north* of the line which now divides between the States commonly designated as free States and those in which slavery exists.

"'2. That each one of the two General Conferences thus constituted shall have full powers, under the limitations and restrictions which are now of force and binding on the General Conference, to make rules and regulations for the Church, within their territorial limits respectively, and to elect bishops for the same.

"'3. That the two General Conferences aforesaid, shall have jurisdiction as follows:—The Southern General Conference shall comprehend the States of Virginia, Kentucky, and Missouri, and the States and Territories lying southerly thereto, and also the republic of Texas, to be known and designated by the title of the Southern General Conference of the Methodist Episcopal Church of the United States. And the Northern General Conference to comprehend all those States and Territories lying north of the States of Virginia, Kentucky, and Missouri, as above, to be known and designated by the title of the Northern General Conference of the Methodist Episcopal Church in the United States.

"'4. And be it further resolved, That as soon as three-fourths of all the members of all the annual conferences voting on these resolutions, shall approve the same, the said Southern and Northern General Conferences shall be deemed as having been constituted by such approval; and it shall be competent for the Southern annual conferences to elect delegates to said Southern General Conference, to meet in the city of Nashville, Tenn., on the first of May, 1848; or sooner, if a majority of two-thirds of the members of the annual conferences composing that General Conference shall desire the same.

"'5. And be it further resolved, as aforesaid, That the Book Concerns at New-York and Cincinnati shall be held and conducted as the property and for the benefit of all the annual conferences as heretofore—the editors and agents to be elected once in four years at the time of the session of the Northern General Conference, and the votes of the Southern General Conference to be cast by the delegates of that Conference attending the Northern for that purpose.

"'6. And be it further resolved, That our Church organization for foreign missions shall be maintained and conducted jointly between the two General Conferences as one Church, in such manner as shall be agreed upon from time to time between the two great branches of the Church as represented in the said two Conferences.'

"On motion of N. Bangs, the resolutions offered by W. Capers this morning were referred to a select committee of nine, who were instructed to report on them as soon as practicable."

It was in reference to these resolutions that the report was made by a committee of nine, which we call a "Plan of Separation."

MR. FANCHER,—The committee of nine to which those resolutions were referred, as is shown by the proceedings which have been read, did not make a report. That committee could not agree. The Plan of Separation was reported by another committee of nine.

Mr. Lord,—That is shown by the journal.

"Wednesday, June 5.—W. Capers returned certain resolutions to the Conference, on which a special committee was appointed, stating that the committee could not agree on a report which they judged would be acceptable to the Conference.—See *Journal of June* 3, p. 86.

"A. B. Longstreet, in behalf of the delegations from the Southern and South-Western conferences, presented the following declaration, which was read":—

I beg your Honours to mark this. It is called a "Declaration."

"The delegates of the conferences in the slave-holding States take leave to *declare* to the General Conference of the Methodist Episcopal Church, that the continued agitation of the subject of slavery and abolition in a portion of the Church; the frequent action on that subject in the General Conference; and especially the extra-judicial proceedings against Bishop Andrew, which resulted, on Saturday last, in the virtual suspension of him from his office as superintendent, must produce a state of things in the South, which renders a continuance of the jurisdiction of this General Conference over these conferences inconsistent with the success of the ministry in the slave-holding States."

This was signed by fifty-two gentlemen from the Southern conferences, whose names may be found on pp. 97, 98.

"A motion was made by C. Elliott to refer this declaration to a committee of nine. This gave rise to some discussion; and the previous question was moved, and the call sustained. The select committee of nine was ordered, and the paper referred to them.

"J. B. M'Ferrin offered the following resolution:—

"'Resolved, That the committee appointed to take into consideration the communication of the delegates from the Southern conferences be instructed, provided they cannot in their judgment devise a plan for an amicable adjustment of the difficulties now existing in the Church, on the subject of slavery, to devise, if possible, a constitutional plan for a mutual and friendly division of the Church.

"'J. B. M'Ferrin,
Tobias Spicer.'

"T. Crowder's motion to strike out the word 'constitutional' did not prevail, and the resolution was adopted.

"The chair announced the following brethren as the select Committee of nine,—Robert Paine, Glezen Filmore, Peter Akers, Nathan Bangs, Thomas Crowder, Thomas B. Sargent, William Winans, Leonidas L. Hamline, and James Porter."

Of this committee, I may mention, five voted against Bishop Andrew and four for him. It was therefore a committee of a compromise character.

"Thursday, June 6.—J. Early asked that H. B. Bascom have leave to read to the Conference the Protest that L. Pierce, on Saturday, gave notice would be presented by the Southern delegates. When the reading by Dr. Bascom was finished, the Chair decided that the Protest be entered upon the journal.

"Mr. Simpson offered the following resolution, which was adopted:—

"'Resolved, That the Conference appoint brothers Olin, Durbin, and Hamline, a committee to prepare a statement of the facts connected with the proceedings in the case of Bishop Andrew; and that they have liberty to examine the Protest just presented by the Southern brethren."'

With the permission of your Honours, my venerable friend, Dr. Smith, will read the Protest to which these proceedings refer.

The Rev. Dr. Smith read it as follows:—

"THE PROTEST.

"*Protest of the Minority of the General Conference against the Action of that Body in the case of Bishop Andrew.*

"In behalf of thirteen annual conferences of the Methodist Episcopal Church, and portions of the ministry and membership of several other conferences, embracing nearly five thousand ministers, travelling and local, and a membership of nearly five hundred thousand, constitutionally represented in this General Conference, we, the undersigned, a minority of the delegates of the several annual conferences in General Conference assembled, after mature reflection, impelled by convictions we cannot resist, and in conformity with the rights and usages of minorities, in the instance of deliberative assemblies and judicial tribunals, in similar circumstances of division and disagreement, *do most solemnly, and in due form, protest* against the recent act of a majority of this General Conference, in an attempt, as understood by the minority, to degrade and punish the Rev. James O. Andrew, one of the bishops of the Methodist Episcopal Church, by declaring it to be the sense or judgment of the General Conference that he desist from the exercise of his episcopal functions, without the exhibition of any alleged offence against the laws or discipline of the Church, without form of trial, or legal conviction of any kind, and in the absence of any charge of want of qualification or faithfulness in the performance of the duties pertaining to his office.

"We *protest* against the act of the majority in the case of Bishop Andrew, as extra-judicial to all intents and purposes, being both without law and contrary to law. We *protest* against the act, because we recognise in this General Conference no right, power, or authority, ministerial, judicial, or administrative, to suspend or depose a bishop of the Methodist Episcopal Church, or otherwise subject him to any official disability whatever, without the formal presentation of a charge or charges, alleging that the bishop to be dealt with has been guilty of the violation of some law, or at least some disciplinary obligation of the Church, and also upon conviction of such charge, after due form of trial. We *protest* against the act in question as a violation of the fundamental law, usually known as the compromise law of the Church, on the subject of slavery—the only law which can be brought to bear upon the case of Bishop Andrew, and the assertion and maintenance of which, until it is constitutionally revoked, is guaranteed by the honour and good faith of this body, as the representative assembly of the thirty-three annual conferences known as contracting parties in the premises.

"*And we protest against the act further*, as an attempt to establish a dangerous precedent, subversive of the union and stability of the Methodist Episcopal Church, and especially as placing in jeopardy the general superintendency of the Church, by subjecting any bishop of the Church at any time to the will and caprice of a majority of the General Conference, not only without law, but in defiance of the restraints and provisions of law. The undersigned, a minority of the General Conference, in *protesting*, as they do, against the late act of the majority, in the virtual suspension of Bishop Andrew, regard it as due to themselves and those they represent, as well as the character and interests of the Church at large, to declare, by solemn and formal avowal, that after a careful examination of the entire subject, in all its relations and bearings, they protest as above, for the reasons and upon the grounds following, viz:—1st. The proceeding against Bishop Andrew in this General Conference has been upon the assumption that he is connected with slavery—that he is the legal holder and owner of slave property. On the subject of slavery in the Methodist Episcopal Church, both as it regards the ministry and membership, we have special law, upon which the adjudication of all questions of slavery must, by intention of law, proceed. The case of Bishop Andrew, therefore, presents a simple question of law and fact, and the undersigned cannot consent that the force of circumstances, and other merely extrinsic considerations, shall be allowed to lead to any issue, except that indicated by the law and the facts in the case. In the late act of the majority, law, express law, is appealed from, and expediency in view of circumstances—relative propriety—assumed necessity, is substituted in its place as a rule of judgment. It is assumed, and the assumption acted upon, that expediency may have jurisdiction even in the presence of law—the law, too, being special, and covering the case in terms. In the absence of law, it might be competent for the General

Conference to act upon other grounds; this is not disputed, nor yet that it would have been competent for the Conference to proceed upon the forms of law—but that the terms and conditions of a special enactment, having all the force of a common public charter, can be rightfully waved in practice, at the promptings of a fugitive, unsettled expediency, is a position the undersigned regard, not merely as erroneous, but as fraught with danger to the best interests of the Church.

"The law of the Church on slavery has always existed, since 1785, but especially since 1804, and in view of the adjustment of the whole subject in 1816, as a *virtual, though informal, contract of mutual concession and forbearance* between the North and the South, then, as now, known and existing as distinct parties, in relation to the vexed questions of slavery and abolition;—those conferences found in States where slavery prevailed constituting the Southern party, and those in the non-slaveholding States, the Northern, exceptions to the rule being found in both. The rights of the legal owners of slaves, in all the slaveholding States, are guaranteed by the Constitution of the United States, and by the local constitutions of the States respectively, as the supreme law of the land, to which every minister and member of the Methodist Episcopal Church within the limits of the United States' government professes subjection, and pledges himself to submit, as an article of Christian faith, in the common creed of the Church. Domestic slavery, therefore, wherever it exists in this country, is a civil regulation, existing under the highest santcions of constitutional and municipal law known to the tribunals of the country; and it has always been assumed at the South, and relied upon as correct, that the North, or non-slaveholding States, had no right, civil or moral, to interfere with relations and interests thus secured to the people of the South by all the graver forms of law and social order, and that it cannot be done without an abuse of the constitutional rights of citizenship. The people of the North, however, have claimed to think differently, and have uniformly acted toward the South in accordance with such opposition of opinion. Precisely in accordance, too, with this state of things, as it regards the general population of the North and South, respectively, the Methodist Episcopal Church has been divided in opinion and feeling on the subject of slavery and abolition, since its organization in 1784: two separate and distinct parties have always existed. The Southern conferences, in agreeing to the main principles of the compromise law in 1804 and 1816, conceded, by express stipulation, their right to resist Northern interference in any form, upon the condition, pledged by the North, that while the *whole Church*, by common consent, united in proper effort for the mitigation and final removal of the evil of slavery, the North was not to interfere, by excluding from membership or ministerial office in the Church persons owning and holding slaves in States where emancipation is not practicable, and where the liberated slave is not permitted to enjoy freedom. Such was the compact of 1804 and 1816, finally agreed to by the parties after a long and fearful struggle, and such is the compact now—the proof being derived from history and the testimony of living witnesses. And is it possible to suppose that the original purpose and intended application of the law was not designed to embrace every member, minister, order, and officer of the Methodist Episcopal Church? Is the idea of excepted cases allowable by fair construction of the law? Do not the reasons and intendment of the law place it beyond doubt, that every conceivable case of alleged misconduct that can arise, connected with slavery or abolition, is to be subjected, by consent and contract of parties, to the jurisdiction of this great conservative arrangement?

"Is there anything in the law or its reasons creating an exception in the instance of bishops? Would the South have entered into the arrangement, or in any form consented to the law, had it been intimated by the North, that bishops must be an exception to the rule? Are the virtuous dead of the North to be slandered by the supposition, that they intended to except bishops, and thus accomplished their purposes, in negotiation with the South, by a resort to deceptive and dishonourable means? If bishops are not named, no more are presiding elders, agents, editors —or, indeed, any other officers of the Church, who are nevertheless included, although the same rule of construction would except them also. The enactment was for an entire people, east, west, north, and south. It was for the Church, and every member of it—for the common weal of the body—and is therefore universal and unrestricted in its application; and no possible case can be settled upon any other principles, without a direct violation of this law both in fact and form.

The law being what we have assumed, any violation of it, whatever may be its form or mode, is as certainly a breach of good faith as an infringement of law. It must be seen, from the manner in which the compromise was effected, in the shape of a law, agreed to by equal contracting parties,—'the several annual conferences,'—after a long and formal negotiation, that it was not a mere legislative enactment, a simple decree of a General Conference, but partakes of the nature of a grave compact, and is invested with all the sacredness and sanctions of a solemn treaty, binding respectively the well-known parties to its terms and stipulations. If this be so—and with the evidence accessible who can doubt it?—if this be so, will it prove a light matter for this General Conference to violate or disregard the obligation of this *legal compromise*, in the shape of public recognised law? Allow that the present parties in this controversy cannot be brought to view the subject of the law in question in the same light, can such a matter end in a mere difference of opinion as it respects the immediate parties? The law exists in the Discipline of the Church—the law is known, and its reasons are known, as equally binding upon both parties; and what is the likelihood of the imputation of bad faith under the circumstances? What the hazard, that such imputation, as the decision of public opinion, it may be from a thousand tribunals, will be brought to bear, with all the light and force of conviction, upon any act of this body, in violation of the plain provisions of long-established law, originating in treaty, and based upon the principles of *conventional compromise?*

"In proportion to our love of truth, of law, and order, are we not called upon to pause and weigh well the hazard, before, as a General Conference, we incur it beyond change or remedy? The undersigned have long looked to the great *conservative law* of the Discipline on the subject of slavery and abolition, as the only charter of *connexional union* between the North and the South; and whenever this bond of connexion is rendered null and void, no matter in what form, or by what means, they are compelled to regard the Church, to every practical purpose, as already divided without the intervention of any other agency. By how far, therefore, they look upon the union of the Methodist Episcopal Church as essential to its prosperity, and the glory and success of American Methodism, by so far they are bound to *protest* against the late act of the General Conference in the irregular suspension of Bishop Andrew, as not only without law, but in direct contravention of legal stipulations known to be essential to the unity of the Church. And they are thus explicit in a statement of facts, that the responsibility of division may attach where in justice it belongs. The minority making this Protest, are perfectly satisfied with the law of the Church affecting slavery and abolition. They ask no change. They need—they seek no indulgence in behalf of the South. Had Bishop Andrew been suspended according to law, after due form of trial, they would have submitted without remonstrance, as the friends of law and order.

"*They except and protest, further*, against the lawless procedure, as they think, in the case of Bishop Andrew, because, apart from the injustice done him and the South, by the act, other and graver difficulties, necessarily incidental to this movement, come in for a share of attention. The whole subject is, in the very nature of things, resolved into a single original question: Will the General Conference adhere to, and in good faith assert and maintain, the compromise law of the Church on the vexed question dividing us—or will it be found expedient generally, as in the case of Bishop Andrew, to lay it aside, and tread it under foot? No question on the subject of slavery and abolition can be settled until the General Conference shall settle *this* beyond the possibility of evasion. In the present crisis, it is the opinion of the undersigned, that every bishop of the Methodist Episcopal Church, and every member of this General Conference, is especially called upon by all the responsibilities of truth and honour to declare himself upon the subject; and they deem it proper, respectfully and urgently, to make such call a part of this Protest. When so much depends upon it, can the General Conference, as the organ of the supreme authority of the Church, remain silent without incurring the charge of trifling both with its interests and reputation? Law always pledges the public faith of the body ostensibly governed by it to the faithful assertion and performance of its stipulations; and the compromise law of the Discipline, partaking, as it does, of the nature of the law of treaty, and embracing, as has been seen, all possible cases, pledges the good faith of every minister and member of the Methodist Episcopal Church, against saying or doing anything tending to annul the force or thwart the purposes of its enactment. The only allowable remedy of those who object to the law, is to seek a constitutional change of the law; and in failure, to submit, or else retire from the Church. All attempts to resist, evade, or defeat the objects and intended application of the law, until duly revoked, must be regarded as unjust and revolutionary, because an invasion of well-defined conventional right. And the undersigned except to the course of the majority in the informal prosecution of Bishop Andrew, and the anomalous quasi suspension it inflicts, as not only giving to the compromise a construction rendering it entirely ineffective, but as being directly subversive of the great bond of union which has held the North and South together for the last forty years. Turning to the confederating annual conferences of 1804, and the vexed and protracted negotiations which preceded the General Conference of that year, and finally resulted in the existing law of the Discipline, regulating the whole subject, and glancing at nearly half a million of Methodists, now in the South, who have come into the Church with all their hopes and fears, interests and associations, their property, character, and influence, reposing in safety upon the publicly-pledged faith of the Methodist Episcopal Church, only to be told that this is all a dream, that a part of what was pledged was never intended to be allowed; and that the whole is at all times subject to the discretion of a dominant majority, claiming, in matter of right, to be without and above law, competent not merely to make all rules and regulations for the proper government of the Church, but to govern the Church without rule or regulation, and punish and degrade without even the alleged infringement of law, or the form of trial, if it be thought expedient, presents a state of things filling the undersigned with alarm and dismay. Such views and facts, without adducing others, will, perhaps, be sufficient to show the first and principal ground occupied by the minority in the Protest. They cannot resist the conviction that the majority have failed to redeem the pledge of public law given to the Church and the world by the Methodist Episcopal Church.

"2. The undersigned are aware that it is affirmed by some of the majority, but meanwhile denied by others, and thus a mooted, unsettled question among themselves, that the resolution censuring and virtually suspending Bishop Andrew, as understood by the minority, is mere matter of advice or recommendation; but so far from advising or recommending anything, the language of the resolution, by fair and necessary construction, is imperative and mandatory in form, and, unqualified by anything in the resolution itself, or in the preamble explaining it, conveys the idea plainly and most explicitly, that it is the judgment and will of the Conference that Bishop Andrew shall cease to exercise the office of bishop until he shall cease to be the owner of slaves. '*Resolved*, That it is the sense of this conference that he desist.' That is, having rendered himself unacceptable to the majority, it is their judgment that he retire from the bench of bishops and their field of action.

"No idea of request, advice, or recommendation, is conveyed by the language of the preamble or resolution, and the recent avowal of an intention to advise is, in the judgment of the undersigned, disowned by the very terms in which, it is said, the *advice* was given. The whole argument of the majority, during a debate of twelve days, turned upon the right of the Conference to displace Bishop Andrew without resort to formal trial. No one questioned the legal right of the Conference to advise; and if this only was intended, why the protracted debate upon the subject? But further: a resolution respectfully and affectionately requesting the bishop to resign had been laid aside, to entertain the substitute under notice; a motion, too, to declare the resolution advisory was promptly rejected by the majority; and in view of all these facts, and the *entire* proceedings of the majority in the case, the undersigned have been compelled to consider the resolution as a mandatory judgment, to the effect that Bishop Andrew desist from the exercise of his episcopal functions. If the majority have been misunderstood, the language of their own resolution, and the position they occupied in debate, have led to the misconception; and truth and honour, not less than a most unfortunate use of language, require that they explain themselves.

"3. We except to the act of the majority, because it is assumed that conscience and principle are involved, and require the act complained of, as expedient and necessary under the circumstances. Bishop Andrew being protected by the law of the Church, having cognizance of all offences connected with slavery, such connexion in his case, in the judgment of all jurisprudence, can only be wrong in the proportion that the law is bad and defective. It is not conceived by the minority how conscience and principle can be brought to bear upon Bishop Andrew, and not upon the *law* and the *Church* having such law. They are obliged to believe that the law and the source from which it emanates must become the object of exception and censure before Bishop Andrew, who has not offended against either, unless the Church is against the law, can be subjected to trial, at the bar of the conscience and principles of men who profess subjection and approval, in the instance both of the law and the Church.

"The undersigned can never consent, while we have a plain law, obviously covering an assumed offence, that the offence shall be taken, under plea of principle, out of the hands of the law, and be resubjected to the conflicting opinions and passions which originally led to a resort to law, as the only safe standard of judgment. They do not understand how conscience and principle can attach grave blame to action not disapproved by the law—express law too, made and provided in the case—without extending condemnation to the law itself, and the body from which it proceeds. The Church can hardly be supposed to have settled policy and invariable custom, in contravention of law; the avowal of such custom and policy, therefore, excluding from the episcopacy any and every man, in any way connected with slavery, is mere *assumption*. No contract, agreement, decree, or purpose of this kind, is of record, or ever existed. No such exaction, in terms or by implication, was ever made by the North, or conceded by the South. No conventional understanding ever existed to this effect, so far as the South is concerned, or has been informed. That it has long, perhaps always, been the purpose of the North, not to elect a slaveholder to the office of bishop, is admitted. But as no law gave countenance to anything of the kind, the South regarded it as a mere matter of social injustice, and was not disposed to complain. The North has always found its security in numbers, and the untrammelled right of suffrage, and to this the South has not objected. The assumption, however, is entirely different, and is not admitted by the South, but is plainly negatived by the law and language of the Discipline, as explained by authority of the General Conference.

"No such concession, beyond peaceable submission to the right of suffrage, exercised by the majority, will ever be submitted to by the South, as it would amount to denial of equal abstract right, and a disfranchisement of the Southern ministry, and could not be submitted to without injury and degradation. If, then, the North is not satisfied with the negative right conceded to the South by law in this matter, the minority would be glad to know what *principle* or *policy* is likely to introduce beyond the existing provisions of law. As the contingency which has occasioned the difficulty in the case of Bishop Andrew, and to which every Southern minister is liable at any time, does not, and cannot fall under the *condemnation* of existing law, and he cannot be punished, nor yet subjected to any official disability, without an abuse of both right and power, on the part of this General Conference, the minority are compelled to think that the majority ought to be satisfied with the consciousness and declaration, that they are in no way responsible for the contingency, and thus, at least, allow Bishop Andrew the benefit of their own legislation, until they see proper to change it. This attempt by the majority to protect a lawless prosecution from merited rebuke, by an appeal to conscience and principle, condemning Bishop Andrew, while the law and the Church, shielding him from the assault, are not objected to, is looked upon by the minority as a species of moral, we will not say legal, casuistry, utterly subversive of all the principles of order and good government.

"4. The act of the majority was ostensibly resorted to, because, as alleged, the Church in the Middle and Northern conferences will not submit to any, the slightest connexion with slavery. But if connexion with slavery is ruinous to the Church in the North, that ruin is already wrought. Who does not know that the very Discipline, laws, and legislation of the Church necessarily connect us all with slavery? All our provisional legislation on the subject has proceeded on the assumption that slavery is an element of society—a principle of action—a household reality in the Methodist Episcopal Church in the United States. It is part and parcel of the economy of American Methodism, in every subjective sense. It has given birth to law and right, conventional arrangements, numerous missions, and official trusts. Every bishop, every minister, every member of the Church is of necessity connected with slavery. Each is brother and co-member, both with slave and master, by the very laws and organization of the Church.

"If, then, connexion with slavery is so disastrous, the only remedy is to purify the Church by reorganization, or get out of it as soon as possible. And would not this aversion to slavery—would not conscience and principle, so much plead in this controversy—appear much more consistent in every view of the subject, in striking at the root of the evil, in the organic structure of the Church, than in seeking its personification in Bishop Andrew, protected although he be by the law, and proceeding to punish him, by way of calling off attention from the known toleration of the same thing, in other aspects and relations?

"Impelled by conscience and principle to the illegal arrest of a bishop, because he has incidentally, by bequest, inheritance, and marriage, come into possession of slave property, in no instance intending to possess himself of such property, how long will conscience and principle leave other ministers, or even lay members, undisturbed, who may happen to be in the same category with Bishop Andrew? Will assurances be given that the lawlessness of expediency, controlled, as in such case it must be, by prejudice and passion, will extend no further—that there shall be no further curtailment of right as it regards the Southern ministry? Yet what is the security of the South in the case? Is the public faith of this body, as instanced in the recent violations of the compromise law, to be relied upon as the guarantee for the redemption of the pledge? What would such pledge or assurance be but to remind the South that any departure at all from the great conservative pledge of law, to which we appeal, was much more effectually guarded against originally, than it is possible to guard against any subsequent infringement, and to make the South feel further that disappointment in the first instance must compel distrust with regard to the future? The Church having specific law on the subject, all questions involving slavery must inevitably, by intention of law, come within the purview of such special provision, and cannot be judged of by any other law or standard, without a most daring departure from all the rules and sobrieties of judicial procedure, and the undersigned accordingly except to the action of the majority in relation to Bishop Andrew, as not only without sanction of law, but in conflict with rights created by law.

"5. As the Methodist Episcopal Church is now organized, and according to its organization since 1784, the episcopacy is a co-ordinate branch, the executive department proper of the government. A bishop of the Methodist Episcopal Church is not a mere creature—is in no prominent sense an officer of the General Conference. The General Conference, as such, cannot constitute a bishop. It is true the annual conferences select the bishops of the Church, by the suffrage of their delegates, in General Conference assembled; but the General Conference, in its capacity of a representative body or any other in which it exists, does not possess the power of ordination, without which a bishop cannot be constituted.

"The bishops are beyond a doubt an integral constituent part of the General Conference, made such by law and the constitution; and because elected by the General Conference, it does not follow that they are subject to the will of that body, except in conformity with legal right and the provisions of law, in the premises. In this sense, and so viewed, they are subject to the General Conference, and this is sufficient limitation of their power, unless the government itself is to be considered irregular and unbalanced in the co-ordinate relations of its parts. In a sense by no means unimportant the General Conference is as much the creature of the episcopacy, as the bishops are the creatures of the General Conference. Constitutionally the bishops alone have the right to fix the time of holding the annual conferences, and should they refuse or neglect to do so, no annual conference could meet, according to law, and, by consequence, no delegates could be chosen, and no General Conference could be chosen, or even exist. And because this is so, what would be thought of the impertinent pretension, should the episcopacy claim that the General Conference is the mere creature of their will? As *executive officers* as well as *pastoral overseers,* the bishops belong to the Church as such, and not to the General Conference as one of its councils or organs of action merely.

"The General Conference is in no sense the Church, not even representatively. It is merely the representative organ of the Church, with limited powers to do its business, in the discharge of a delegated trust.

"Because bishops are in part constituted by the General Conference, the power of removal does not follow. Episcopacy even in the Methodist Church is not a mere appointment to labour. It is an official consecrated station, under the protection of law, and can only be dangerous as the law is bad, or the Church corrupt. The power to appoint does not necessarily involve the power to remove; and when the appointing power is derivative, as in the case of the General Conference, the power of removal does not accrue at all, unless by consent of the co-ordinate branches of the government, expressed by law, made and provided in the case. When the legislature of a State, to appeal to analogy for illustration, appoints a judge or senator in congress, does the judge or senator thereby become the officer or creature of the legislature, or is he the officer or senatorial representative of the State, of which the legislature is the mere organ? And does the power of removal follow that of appointment? The answer is negative, in both cases, and applies equally to the bishops of the Methodist Episcopal Church, who, instead of being the officers and creatures of the General Conference, are *de facto* the officers and servants of the Church, chosen by the General Conference, as its organ of action, and no right of removal accrues, except as they fail to accomplish the *aims* of the Church in their appointment, and then only in accordance with the provisions of law. But when a bishop is suspended, or informed that it is the wish or will of the General Conference that he cease to perform the functions of bishop, for doing what the law of the same body allows him to do, and of course without incurring the hazard of punishment, or even blame, then the whole procedure becomes an outrage upon justice, as well as law.

"The assumption of power by the General Conference beyond the warrant of law, to which we object, and against which we protest, will lead, if carried into practice, to a direct violation of one of the restrictive rules of the constitution. Suppose it had been the 'sense' of this General Conference, when the late communication from the bishops was respectfully submitted to the Conference, that such communication was an interference with their rights and duties—an attempt to tamper with the purity and independence, and therefore an outrage upon the claims and dignity of the Conference not to be borne with. And proceeding a step further, suppose it had been the 'sense' of the Conference that they *all* desist from performing the functions of bishops until the 'impediment' of such offence had been removed—assume this, (and, so far as mere law is concerned, no law being violated in either case, it was just as likely as the movement against Bishop Andrew,) and had it taken place, what had become of the general superintendency? If a bishop of the Methodist Episcopal Church may, without law, and at the instance of mere party expediency, be suspended from the exercise of the appropriate functions of his office, for one act, he may for another. Admit this doctrine, and by what tenure do the bishops hold office? One thing is certain, whatever other tenure there may be, they do not hold office *according to law.*

"The provisions of law and the faithful performance of duty, upon this theory of official tenure, afford no security. Admit this claim of absolutism, as regards right and powers on the part of the General Conference, and the bishops of the Methodist Episcopal Church are slaves, and the men constituting this body their masters and holders. They are in office only at the discretion of a majority of the General Conference, without the restraints or protection of law. Both the law and themselves are liable and likely at any time to be overborne and trampled upon together, as exemplified in the case of Bishop Andrew. If the doctrine against which we protest be admitted, the episcopal office is, at best, but a quadrennial term of service, and the undersigned are compelled to think that a man who would *remain* a bishop, or allow himself to be *made one*, under such circumstances, 'desires a good work,' and is prepared for *self-sacrifice*, quite beyond the comprehension of ordinary piety.

"As it regards Bishop Andrew, if it shall be made to appear that the action in his case was intended only to *advise* and *request* him to desist from his office, it does not in any way affect the real or relative character of the movement. When a body claiming the right to compel, asks the resignation of an officer, the request is to all official and moral purposes *compulsory*, as it loads the officer with disability, and gives notice of assumed unworthiness, if not criminality. The request has all the force of a mandate, inasmuch as the officer is by such request compelled either to resign or remain in office contrary to the known will of the majority. A simple request, therefore, under the circumstances supposed, carries with it all the force of a decree, and is so understood, it is believed, by all the world.

"To request Bishop Andrew to resign, therefore, in view of all the facts and relations of the case, was, in the judgment of the minority, to punish and degrade him; and they maintain that the whole movement was without authority of law, is hence of necessity null and void, and therefore not binding upon Bishop Andrew, or the minority protesting against it.

"6. We protest against the act of the majority, instructing Bishop Andrew to desist from the exercise of his office, not merely on account of the injustice and evil connecting with the act itself, but because the act must be understood as the exponent of principles and purposes, as it regards the union of the North and South in the Methodist Episcopal Church, well-nigh destroying all hope of its perpetuity. The true position of the parties in relation to a long-existing conventional arrangement, on the subject of slavery and abolition, has been fully under notice; and when men of years and wisdom, experience and learning—men of no common weight of character, and with a well-earned aristocracy of Church influence thrown about them, assume and declare, in action as well as debate, that what a plain law of the Church—the only law applicable in the case—sustained and enforced, too, by an explanatory decree of this body, at a previous session—*decides* shall *not* be a disqualification for office, in any grade in the ministry,—when such men, the law and decision of the General Conference notwithstanding, are heard declaring that what law provides for and protects nevertheless *always has been* and *always shall be* a disqualification, what further evidence is wanting to show that the *compromise basis of union*, from which the South has never swerved, has been abandoned both by the Northern and Middle Conferences, with a few exceptions in the latter, and that principles and purposes are entertained by the majority, driving the South to extreme action, in defence both of their rights and reputation? And how far the long train of eventful sequences, attendant upon the threatened result of division, may be traceable to the Northern and Middle Conferences, by the issue thus provoked, is a question to be settled not by us, but by our contemporaries and posterity.

"It is matter of history, with regard to the past, and will not be questioned, that now, as formerly, the South is upon the basis of the Discipline, on the subject of slavery. The minority believe it equally certain that this is not true with regard to the North proper especially. In view, then, of the unity of the Methodist Episcopal Church, which party has been, in equity, entitled to the sympathy and protection of the Middle and *umpire* conferences?—those who through good and evil report have kept good faith and adhered to law, or those whose opinions and purposes have led them to seek a state of things in advance of law, and thus dishonour its forms and sanctions?

"7. In proportion as the minority appreciate and cling to the unity of the Methodist Episcopal Church, they are bound, further, to except to the position of the majority, in this controversy. Allow that Bishop Andrew, without however any infringement of law, is, on account of his connexion with slavery, unacceptable in the Northern conferences. It is equally known to the majority that any bishop of the Church, either violating, or submitting to a violation of the compromise charter of union between the North and the South, without proper and public remonstrance, cannot be acceptable in the South, and need not appear there. By pressing the issue in question, therefore, the majority virtually dissolve the government of the Methodist Episcopal Church, because in every constitutional aspect it is sundered by so crippling a co-ordinate branch of it as to destroy the itinerant general superintendency altogether. Whenever it is clearly ascertained that the compromise law of the Church, regulating slavery and abolition, is abandoned, every bishop, each of the venerable and excellent men who now adorn the Church and its councils, *ceases* to be a general superintendent: the law of union, the principle of gravitation, binding us together, is dissolved, and the general superintendency cf the Methodist Episcopal Church is no more!

"8. The South have not been led thus to protest merely because of the treatment received by Bishop Andrew, or the kindred action of this body in other matters. The abandonment of the compromise—the official refusal by the majority, as we have understood them, to abide the arbitrament of law—is their principal ground of complaint and remonstrance. If the minority have not entirely misunderstood the majority, the abolition and anti-slavery principles of the North will no longer allow them to submit to the law of the Discipline on the general subject of slavery and abolition; and if this be so, if the compromise law be either repealed or allowed to remain a dead letter, *the South cannot submit, and the absolute necessity of division is already dated.* And should the exigent circumstances in which the minority find themselves placed, by the facts and developments alluded to in this remonstrance, render it finally necessary that the Southern conferences should have a *separate, independent* existence, it is hoped that the character and services of the minority, together with the numbers and claims of the ministry and membership of the portion of the Church represented by them, not less than similar reasons and considerations on the part of the Northern and Middle conferences, will suggest the high moral fitness of meeting this great emergency with strong and steady purpose to do justice to all concerned. And it is believed that, approaching the subject in this way, it will be found practicable to devise and adopt such measures and arrangements, present and prospective, as will secure an amicable division of the Church upon the broad principles of right and equity, and destined to result in the common good of the great body of ministers and members found on either side *the line of separation.*"

Mr. Wood,—There was a reply to that Protest, which I suppose is properly our evidence, but I think there is great propriety in having them read together; and the court will then have the whole ecclesiastical argument before it.

Mr. Lord,—I will agree to that; but there is a short letter which was presented to the Conference from Dr. Bascom, which I will read first in this connexion.

Judge Nelson,—I think the counsel on the part of the plaintiffs had better go on, without mixing up the case on the other side with that on which he means to rely.

Mr. Lord,—This would not be so mixing it up, may it please your Honours. This paper will tend to show how things then stood at that Conference, and perhaps it is just that it should now be read—it certainly will be convenient—that your Honours may see the feeling which prevailed on both sides before the separation was effected.

Judge Nelson,—We do not object.

Mr. Lord,—If your Honours please, I will first read Dr. Bascom's letter :—

"'*Rev. Bishops Soule, Hedding, Waugh, and Morris:*

"'My Dear Brethren,—That part of the *Protest*, presented to the General Conference yesterday, which relates to the bishops of the Methodist Episcopal Church maintaining the *compromise law* of the Discipline, on the subject of *slavery and abolition*, was intended as the *declaration of a principle*, to which it is the purpose of the South to adhere; but was not intended to convey the idea, that any member of the *existing bench of bishops* was in any way delinquent with regard to the law of the Church in question. If any such impression has been made, in any quarter, it is deeply regretted. It is the opinion of the writers and signers of the *Protest* alluded to, that the bishops addressed in this communication have, at different times, and in different forms, sufficiently *declared* themselves on the subject under notice; and so far from intending to impugn the bishops in any way, the minority signing the Protest are ready at all times to endorse the purity and impartiality with which they have maintained and enforced the law and doctrine of the Church, on the subject of slavery and abolition.

"'In behalf of the Southern delegations signing the Protest, very truly and respectfully, H. B. Bascom.

"'*New-York, June 7, 1844.*'"

The Rev. Dr. Peck then read the following, at the request of Mr. Fancher :—

"REPLY TO THE PROTEST.

"*Report of the Committee appointed to prepare a Statement of the Facts connected with the Proceedings in the Case of Bishop Andrew.*

"The committee appointed to prepare a statement of the facts in the case of Bishop Andrew, and to examine the Protest of the minority, regret that the circumstances under which they have been compelled to act have prevented their preparing so complete a report as the importance of the subject demands. The Protest was not placed under their command until Friday afternoon, and immediately afterward two of the original committee had to withdraw, one of them being ill, and the other having been elected bishop; nor were their places supplied until Saturday evening. It is under these disadvantages, and amid the pressure of important Conference business, that they have been required to prepare a document in relation to some of the most important questions that have ever engaged the attention of the Church. It is believed, however, that the following statement of *law* and *facts* will be a sufficient notice of the Protest which has been referred to them.

"As the proceedings of the General Conference in the case of Bishop Andrew were not judicial, its decision has gone forth to the public unaccompanied by the reasons and facts upon which this action was founded. This deficiency is but partially supplied by the published reports of the debate on the subject. The speakers who advocated the resolution were restrained by a praiseworthy delicacy from all avoidable allusions which might give pain to the respected individual concerned, or awaken unpleasant emotions in any quarter. It is but natural that, under these circumstances, some misunderstanding should prevail as to the merits of the case. The following statement, it is believed, contains nothing, at least so far as facts are concerned, which will not be cheerfully confirmed by all parties, and will throw light upon the true position of the authors of the Protest.

"From the first institution of the episcopacy of the Methodist Episcopal Church, no slaveholder has been elected to that dignity, though, in several instances, candidates, otherwise eminently fitted for the station, have failed of success solely on account of this impediment. Since the period referred to, nine bishops have been elected, who were natives of the United States. Of these only three have been Northern men, while six were natives of slaveholding States. Not one, however, was a slaveholder; a remarkable fact, which shows very clearly, that while much more than their just claim has been conceded to the slaveholding portions of the Church, a decided and uniform repugnance has, from the first, been felt and manifested to the occupancy of that high office by a slaveholder.

"It is known and acknowledged by all Southern brethren, that Bishop Andrew was nominated by the delegates from the South Carolina and Georgia Conferences, as a Southern candidate for whom Northern men might vote, without doing violence to their principles, as he was no slaveholder. Bishop Andrew himself perfectly understood the ground of his election, and often said that he was indebted to his poverty for his promotion. Since the year 1832, the anti-slavery sentiment in the Church, as well as in the whole civilized world, has constantly and rapidly gained ground; and within the last year or two it has been roused to a special and most earnest opposition to the introduction of a slaveholder into the episcopal office—an event which many were led to fear, by certain intimations published in the Southern Christian Advocate, the Richmond Christian Advocate, and perhaps some other Methodist periodicals. This opposition produced the profoundest anxiety through most of the non-slaveholding conferences. The subject was discussed everywhere, and the dreaded event universally deprecated as the most fearful calamity that ever threatened the Church. Many conferences instructed their delegates to use all possible means to avert such an evil. Other conferences, and many thousand laymen, sent up petitions and memorials to the same effect to the present General Conference. Such was the state of sentiment and of apprehension in the Northern portion of the Church, when the delegates to the General Conference learned, on reaching this city, that Bishop Andrew had become a slaveholder. The profound grief, the utter dismay, which was produced by this astounding intelligence, can be fully appreciated only by those who have participated in the distressing scenes which have since been enacted in the General Conference.

"When the first emotions of surprise and sorrow had so far subsided as to allow of sober thought and inquiry, it was ascertained that Bishop Andrew had been a slaveholder for several years. Soon after his election to the episcopacy, a lady of Augusta bequeathed him a female slave, on condition that she should be sent to Liberia at nineteen years of age, if her consent to emigrate could be obtained—otherwise she was to be made as free as the laws of Georgia would permit. She refused to emigrate, has since married, and is now enjoying all the privileges provided for in the will of her former mistress:—she is, and must be, a slave—she and her children—and liable to all that may befall slaves. Another slave Bishop Andrew has inherited from the mother of his former wife, and by his recent marriage he has become the owner of (it was said on the floor of the General Conference) fourteen or fifteen more. These belonged to Mrs. Andrew in her own right before her marriage. That act, according to the laws of Georgia, made them the property of Bishop Andrew, to keep or dispose of as he pleased. He conveyed them to a trustee, for the joint use of himself and wife, of whom the survivor is to be the sole owner. This conveyance was made for the security of Mrs. Andrew, and with no view either to satisfy or to mislead the opinions of the Northern Church. So much, at least, Bishop Andrew was understood to say to the Conference. His known integrity forbids the suspicion that he would attempt to disguise the real character of the transaction; and the fact that the earnings of the slaves, as well as the reversionary title to them, are his, demonstrates that this arrangement was not made with any view to satisfy the well-known sentiments of the Church against a slaveholding bishop. It is manifest from this statement, which is believed to be strictly correct, that Bishop Andrew's connexion with slavery is not, as the Protest intimates, merely an "assumption," but that he is the owner of slaves, in the full and proper sense of that term. His title was acquired by bequest, by inheritance, and by marriage, which are by far the most common grounds of ownership in slaves. All the usual and necessary conditions of slavery have their fulfilment in the relation of these persons to Bishop Andrew. Their labour and their earnings are subject to his control, and inure to his benefit and that of his family. They are now liable, or they may be hereafter, to be sold; they and their offspring are doomed, as the case now stands, to a bondage that is perpetual, and they are liable and likely to descend to his heirs. Beyond all reasonable doubt, the condition of Bishop Andrew's slaves will be attended, while he lives, with all the alleviations—and these are many and great—which a very benevolent and Christian master can provide. Still it must be slavery. In the view of the law of the land, and of the law of the Discipline, in all its more weighty and permanent consequences to the bondman, it is and must be slavery. It was said repeatedly on the floor of the Conference, that the deed of trust had put it quite beyond Bishop Andrew's power to free his slaves, even if there were no other obstacle. So then, should the stringent laws of Georgia against emancipation be relaxed or repealed by her next legislature, the rule of the Discipline, which would then become imperative on Bishop Andrew, could not, and would not, be satisfied, and the Church must still have a slaveholding bishop, in spite, not only of its known will, but of its standing laws.

"It was the almost unanimous opinion of the delegates from the non-slaveholding conferences that Bishop Andrew could not continue to exercise his episcopal functions under existing circumstances, without producing results extensively disastrous to the Church in the North; and from this opinion the brethren of the South did not dissent. For a while the hope was entertained that the difficulty would be quietly removed by his resigning his office, which it was known he had previously desired to do. But this hope was dissipated by the intelligence that the delegates from the conferences in the slaveholding States had been convened, and that they had unanimously advised him not to resign. Various efforts were then made in private to devise some method to relieve the case, but they all proved abortive, and nothing remained but that it must come before the General Conference. The bishops themselves, in their united Address to the Conference, had urged it to ascertain whether there has been any departure from the essential principles 'of the general itinerant superintendency,' and had declared of that superintendency that 'the plan of its operation is *general, embracing the whole work in connexional order, and not diocesan or sectional.* Consequently any division of the work into districts, or otherwise, so as to create a particular charge, with any other view, or in any order, than as a prudential measure to secure to all the conferences the annual visits of the superintendents, would be an innovation on the system'—that '*our superintendency must be itinerant, and not local*:'—that 'it was wisely provided in the system of Methodism, from its very foundation, that it should be the duty of superintendents '*to travel through the Connexion at large.* The question then presented itself, how the case of Bishop Andrew could be so disposed of as to preserve this itinerant general superintendency? If the General Conference had even been disposed to evade it, the consideration of it was forced upon them by the episcopal Address itself.

"A diversity of sentiment existed as to the proper method of treating the case.

"Some, at least, believed—perhaps few doubted—that sufficient ground existed for impeachment on a charge of 'improper conduct' under the express provisions of the Discipline. The opinion was certainly entertained in several quarters that it was 'improper' for the shepherd and bishop of eleven hundred thousand souls, either deliberately or heedlessly, to place himself in direct and irreconcilable conflict with the known and cherished moral sentiments of a large majority of his vast flock. Such, however, was the prevalence of moderate counsels, that no proposal was made either to impeach or punish, and such the controlling influence of forbearance and kindness, that it is believed not one word was uttered during the entire debate of nearly a fortnight derogatory to the character, or justly offensive to the feelings of Bishop Andrew. The transaction which had brought such distress upon the Church, and threatened such extensive ruin, was dealt with merely as a fact—as a practical difficulty—for the removal or palliation of which it was the duty of the General Conference to provide. It was in this spirit, and for such ends, that the following preamble and resolution were passed :—

"'Whereas, the Discipline of our Church forbids the doing anything calculated to destroy our itinerant general superintendency, and whereas Bishop Andrew has become connected with slavery by marriage and otherwise, and this act having drawn after it circumstances which in the estimation of the General Conference will greatly embarrass the exercise of his office as an itinerant general superintendent, if not in some places entirely prevent it ; therefore,

"'Resolved, That it is the sense of this General Conference that he desist from the exercise of this office so long as this impediment remains.

"'J. B. Finley,
J. M. Trimble.'

"The action of the General Conference was neither judicial nor punitive. It neither achieves nor intends a deposition, nor so much as a legal suspension. Bishop Andrew is still a bishop ; and should he, against the expressed sense of the General Conference, proceed in the discharge of his functions, his official acts would be valid.

"Such are the facts in the case of Bishop Andrew. We now proceed to notice the law. Nearly all the objections raised in the Protest against the action of the General Conference may be reduced to two, viz. :—that that body has violated the *constitutional* and the *statutory* law of the Church. That it has violated the constitutional law the Protest attempts to prove by representing its late action as a breach of what it calls 'the compromise law of the Church on the subject of slavery ;' meaning, as is supposed, the section on slavery, particularly that paragraph which relates to travelling preachers. The entire language on this subject is evidently formed so as to make the impression on any reader not intimately acquainted with the history and Discipline of the Methodist Episcopal Church, that there has been some period (whether 1804 or 1816 does not clearly appear from the Protest) when the question of slavery was settled in the Methodist Episcopal Church as it was in the General Government at the adoption of the federal constitution,—that 'the confederating annual conferences,' 'after a vexed and protracted negotiation,' met in convention, and the section on slavery 'was finally agreed to by the parties, after a long and fearful struggle,' as 'a compact,' 'a treaty,' which cannot be altered by the General Conference until certain constitutional restrictions are removed. So that now any interference on the part of that body with the question of slavery in the Southern Conferences is as unconstitutional as it is admitted would be the interference of the General Government with the question in the Southern States.

"After the boldness with which this doctrine is advanced, and the confidence with which it is relied upon as 'the first and principal ground occupied by the minority in this Protest,' it will be difficult for the uninitiated to believe, that it is as unfounded in fact as it is ingenious in its 'legal casuistry.' It is indeed true, that the question of slavery had been long and anxiously agitated in the Church, and the various General Conferences had endeavoured to adjust the matter so as to promote the greatest good of all parties ; but this very fact goes to disprove the position assumed in the Protest : for as the attention of the Church had been thus strongly called to the subject, if it had been the intention to guard the question of slavery by constitutional provisions, it would have been done when the Church actually did meet to frame a constitution. But nothing of the kind appears. For when, in 1808, it was resolved that the General Conference, instead of consisting, as before, of all the travelling elders, should be a delegated body, and when it was determined that that body (unlike the General Government, which had no powers but such as are expressly conferred) should have all powers but such as are expressly taken away,—

when this vast authority was about to be given to the General Conference, among 'the limitations and restrictions' imposed, *there is not one word on the subject of slavery; nor was any attempt made to introduce any such restriction.* The only provision anywhere established by that General Conference of constitutional force, was the general rule forbidding the buying and selling of human beings with an intention to enslave them. So that, in direct opposition to the assertion of the Protest, we maintain that the section on slavery is 'a mere legislative enactment, a simple decree of a General Conference,'' as much under its control as any other portion of the Discipline not covered by the restrictive rules. If additional proof of the truth of this position were needed it might be adduced in the fact that that section which the Protest represents to have been settled in 1804, was not only altered at the General Conference or convention of 1808, but also at the delegated General Conferences of 1812, 1816, 1820, and 1824. And although the Protest speaks of it as '*usually known*' by the name of 'the compromise act,' the greater part of this General Conference have never heard either that appellation or that character ascribed to it until the present occasion.

"But although this General Conference cannot admit that any portion of the section on slavery is constitutional in its character, and therefore could not under any circumstances allow the imputation of the Protest that they have violated the constitution of the Church, yet they do admit that it is *law*—law too which the General Conference (though possessing full powers in the premises) has never altered except at the above periods, and then, in each instance, for the further indulgence of the South. The question then comes up, whether this General Conference, as the Protest maintains, has in effect suddenly reversed the legislation of the Church, not indeed by altering the law, but by practically disregarding it. The portion of the law particularly in question is the following paragraph:—

"'When any travelling preacher becomes an owner of a slave or slaves, by any means, he shall forfeit his ministerial character in our Church, unless he execute, if it be practicable, a legal emancipation of such slaves, conformably to the laws of the State in which he lives.'

"This it is alleged fully covers the case of Bishop Andrew, and therefore he ought to have been left in the quiet and unquestionable enjoyment of his rights. Were it even true, that proceedings, either judicial or 'extra-judicial,' have been had in his case, we should not hesitate to join issue here, and maintain that this law does not protect him. The Protest asks, 'Is there anything in the law or its reasons creating an exception in the instance of bishops?' We answer, There is in both. So far as judicial proceedings are concerned, the Discipline divides the Church into four classes—private members, local preachers, travelling preachers, and bishops; and establishes distinct tribunals, and different degrees of responsibility for each. The section on slavery applies only to officers of the Church, and therefore private members are not named at all, but special provision is made in the case of local and travelling preachers. How happens it that bishops are not named at all? Are they necessarily included in the title 'travelling preachers?' In common parlance they may sometimes be thus designated, but in the Discipline it is not so understood, even in regard to matters much less important than this, in evidence of which we need only advert to the fact, that the General Conference of 1836 did not consider that the allowance of bishops was provided for under the general title of 'travelling preachers,' and they therefore inserted them accordingly. To explain why no mention is made of 'bishops,' it is not necessary, as the Protest supposes, 'to slander the virtuous dead of the North,' as if they excluded them intentionally 'by a resort to deceptive and dishonourable means.' It is a much more natural and reasonable explanation, that at that day, when the Church could hardly tolerate slavery in any class of the ministry, 'the virtuous dead' both of the North and of the South did not dream that it would ever find its way into the episcopacy.

"But though the *language* of the law does not include bishops, yet if the 'reason' and spirit of it did, we might be disposed to allow them the benefit of it. But this is not the case. The whole tenor of the Discipline of the Methodist Episcopal Church is adverse to slavery. Even the Protest has admitted (irreconcilable as the admission is with another portion of the same instrument) that, at the time of the alleged 'compact,' 'the whole Church by common consent united in proper effort for the *mitigation and final removal* of the evil of slavery.' But let the Discipline speak for itself. The mildest form in which the question at the head of the section on slavery has ever been expressed, is the present, namely, 'What shall be done for the *extirpation* of the evil of slavery ?' And the very Conference of 1804, which enacted the so-called 'compromise law,' as well as that of 1800, when the paragraph relating to travelling preachers was really adopted, were each convened under a request from the preceding General Conference, that the whole Church would aid that body in obtaining 'full light in order to take further steps toward the *eradicating this enormous evil* from that part of the Church of God to which they are united.' It is obvious, therefore, that connexion with slavery is tolerated no further than seems necessary. In the case of ordinary travelling preachers, there appeared to be a necessity for some indulgence. They might become owners of slaves in the providence of God ; the laws of the States might not allow emancipation ; and they had no power to choose their own place of residence. But no such 'reason' could apply to a bishop, for he has always been allowed to live where he pleases. Again: travelling preachers encumbered with slaves labour among people similarly situated, and who would, not, therefore, be likely to object to them on that account. But a bishop, by the *constitution* of the Church, is required to labour in every part of the Connexion ; and in by far the larger portion of it the services of a slaveholding bishop would not be acceptable. So here again the 'reason' of the case does not apply to a bishop. There is not, therefore, as the Protest so roundly asserts, any 'express' or 'specific law' in the case ; and therefore, as the Protest itself admits, 'in the absence of law it might be competent for the General Conference to act on other grounds.' With the failure to prove any 'specific law' authorizing a bishop to hold slave property, the third and fourth arguments of the Protest, which are founded on this assumption, fail also.

"But, perhaps, it is not so much the law of the Discipline which the Protest claims to cover Bishop Andrew, as the law of the land. For it declares, 'The rights of the legal owners of slaves in all the slaveholding States are guaranteed by the Constitution of the United States, and by the local constitutions of the States respectively, as the supreme law of the land, to which every minister and member of the Methodist Episcopal Church, within the limits of the United States government, professes subjection, and pledges himself to submit as an article of the Christian faith, in the common creed of the Church.' If by this is meant that the law of the land *allows* citizens to hold slaves, it is admitted. But so also it allows them to keep theatres and grog-shops, so that this is no ground of argument. But if it mean that the law of the land *requires* citizens to keep slaves, (the only interpretation which can make the argument available,) it is denied. And until it can be shown that the Methodist Episcopal Church by its action, legislative, judicial, or executive, requires any citizen to do what the law of the land requires him not to do, it is unjust to attempt to get up popular clamor against it, as if it came in conflict with the civil authority.

"This course of reasoning has been pursued thus far, not so much because it was deemed necessary for the vindication of the Conference, as to avoid sanctioning, by silence, the erroneous exposition which the Protest presents of the constitution and the law of the Church. For it has been already seen that Bishop Andrew has been subjected to no trial, and no penalty has been inflicted. At present, it is plain that the Conference has done nothing to depose, or even suspend Bishop Andrew. His name will appear in official publications with those of the other bishops, and with them he will derive his support from the funds of the Church. In order to make out that the General Conference had no right to take such action as they have in Bishop Andrew's case, the authors of the Protest have been driven to the necessity of claiming for the Methodist episcopacy powers and prerogatives never advanced before, except by those who wished to make it odious, and which have always been repudiated by its chosen champions. The Protest maintains that 'the episcopacy is a co-ordinate branch of the government ;' for which no argument is adduced save this—that it is, in general, the province of bishops to ordain bishops. A sufficient answer to which may be found in the principle of Methodist polity, stated in the Address of the Bishops to the present General Conference, that orders (the principle applies to bishops, though not expressly named, as well as to elders and deacons) are 'conferred' by the election, and only 'confirmed' by the ordination ; and that when the election has been made, the bishop 'has no discretional authority ; but is under *obligation* to ordain the person elected, whatever may be his own judgment of his qualifications.' And if all the bishops should refuse to ordain the person elected by the General Conference, that body would unquestionably have the right to appoint any three elders to ordain him, as is provided 'in case there be no bishop remaining in our Church.' The Protest declares, that 'the bishops are, beyond doubt, an integral, constituent part of the General Conference, made such by law and the constitution.' If the words 'General Conference' be not a mere clerical error, the assertion is sufficiently refuted by the answer in the Discipline to the question, 'Who shall compose the General Conference?' and by the practice of the bishops themselves, who disclaim a right to give even a casting vote, or even to speak in General Conference, except by permission. The Protest maintains that, 'in a sense by no means unimportant, the General Conference is as much the *creature* of the episcopacy, as the bishops are the creatures of the General Conference.' The proof adduced for which is, that 'constitutionally the bishops alone have the right to fix the time of holding the annual conferences; and should they refuse, or neglect to do so, no annual conference could meet according to law; and, by consequence, no delegates could be chosen, and no General Conference could be chosen, or even exist.' That is to say, because, for the convenience of the bishops in performing their tour, they are allowed to say *at what time in the year* an annual conference shall meet, therefore they have the power to prevent such body from meeting at all, though, from its very name, it must meet once a year!—that, by preventing the meeting of annual conferences, they might prevent the organization of any General Conference; and thus, escaping all accountability for their delinquencies, might continue to lord it over God's heritage, until themselves and the Church should die a natural death. We can easily perceive, were this reasoning legitimate, that the bishops might *destroy*, not only the General Conference, but the Church; but are at a loss to discover how it proves that they can *create* either. We must protest against having any argument of ours adduced as analogous to this.

"The Protest maintains that 'the General Conference has no right, power, or authority, ministerial, judicial, or administrative,' in any way to subject a bishop 'to any official disability whatever, without the formal presentation of a charge or charges, alleging that the bishop to be dealt with has been guilty of the violation of some law, or at least some disciplinary obligation of the Church, and also upon conviction of such charge, after due form of trial.' To those who are not familiar with the Methodist economy, this might seem plausible. But it is, in reality, an attempt to except, from the action of a general system, those who, least of all, ought to be excepted. The cardinal feature of our polity is the itinerancy.

"To sustain this system, it is essential that the classes should receive the leaders that are appointed by the preacher, that the societies should receive the preachers that are stationed over them by the bishops, that the annual conferences should receive the bishops that are sent to them by the General Conference. Unless, therefore, the utmost care be taken by those who have authority in the premises, that these parties shall severally be acceptable to those among whom they labour, there is great danger that those who are injured by such neglect may seek redress by revolutionary measures. For this reason the officers of the Methodist Church are subjected regularly to an examination unknown, it is believed, among other denominations. Not only is provision made for formal trials, in cases of crimes and misdemeanors, but there is a special arrangement for the correction of other obstructions to official usefulness. At every annual conference the character of every travelling preacher is examined; at every General Conference that of every bishop. And the object is to ascertain not merely whether there is ground for the formal presentation of charges, with a view to a regular trial; but whether there is 'any objection'—anything that might interfere with the acceptance of the officer in question among his charge. And it is doctrine novel and dangerous in the Methodist Church, that such difficulties cannot be corrected, unless the person objected to be formally arraigned under some specific law, to be found in the concise code of the Discipline—doctrine not the less dangerous, because it is applied where 'objections,' unimportant in others, might be productive of the most disastrous consequences. Will the Methodist Church sanction the doctrine, that while all its other officers, of whatever name or degree, are subjected to a sleepless supervision,—are counselled, admonished, or changed, 'as necessity may require, and as the Discipline directs,'—a bishop, who decides all questions of law in annual conferences; who, of his mere motion and will, controls the work and the destiny of four thousand ministers; who appoints and changes at pleasure the spiritual guides of four millions of souls—that the depositary of these vast powers, whose slightest indiscretions or omissions are likely to disturb the harmony and even impair the efficiency of our mighty system of operations, enjoys a virtual impunity for all delinquencies or misdoings not strictly criminal?

"It is believed that an attempt to establish such an episcopal supremacy would fill not only a part, but the whole of the Church 'with alarm and dismay.' But this doctrine is not more at variance with the genius of Methodism than it is with the express language of the Discipline, and the exposition of it by all our standard writers. The constitution of the Church provides that 'the General Conference shall have full powers to make rules and regulations for our Church,' under six 'limitations and restrictions,' among which the only one relating to the episcopacy is this: 'They shall not change or alter any part, or rule of our government, so as to do away episcopacy, or destroy the plan of our itinerant general superintendency.' As there is nothing in the restrictive rules to limit the full powers of the General Conference in the premises, so is there nothing in the special provision respecting the responsibility of a bishop. In reply to the question, 'To whom is a bishop amenable for his conduct?' the Discipline declares, 'To the General Conference, who have power to expel him for improper conduct, if they see it necessary.' And this, be it remembered, is all that is said respecting the jurisdiction over a bishop, with the exception of a rule for his trial, in the interval of a General Conference, if he be guilty of immorality. In full accordance with the plain meaning of these provisions is the language of all the standard writers on Methodist polity.

"Bishop Emory—a man of whom it is no injustice to the living or the dead to say, that he was a chief ornament and light of our episcopacy; that he brought to the investigation of all ecclesiastical subjects a cool, sagacious, powerful, practical intellect—fully sustains the positions we have assumed in behalf of the powers of the General Conference over the bishops of our Church. He gives an unqualified assent to the following passages from the notes to the Discipline, prepared by Bishops Asbury and Coke, at the request of the General Conference: 'They (our bishops) are entirely dependent on the General Conference:' 'their power, their usefulness, themselves, are entirely at the mercy of the General Conference.'

"Dr. Emory also quotes some passages from a pamphlet, by the Rev. John Dickens, which, he says, was published by the unanimous request of the Philadelphia Conference, and may be considered as expressing the views both of that conference and of Bishop Asbury, his intimate friend. Mr. Dickens affirms, that the bishops derive their power from the election of the General Conference, and not from their ordination; and that the Conference has, on that ground, power to remove Bishop Asbury, and appoint another, 'if they see it necessary.' He affirms that Bishop Asbury 'derived his official power from the Conference, and therefore his office is at their disposal;'—Mr. Asbury was 'responsible to the General Conference, who had power to remove him, if they saw it necessary;' 'he is liable every year to be removed.'

"The above quotations show very clearly the sentiments of Asbury, and Coke, and Dickens on this question—men chiefly instrumental in laying the foundations of our polity.

"Equally clear and satisfactory is the testimony of another venerable bishop, who still lives, in the full exercise of his mental powers and benignant influence, to guide and bless the Church,—'The superintendents now have no power in the Church above that of elders, except what is connected with presiding in the Conference, fixing the appointments of the preachers, and ordaining:'—'They are the servants of the elders, and go out and execute their commands:'—'The General Conference may expel a bishop not only for immoral, but for "*improper* conduct," which means a small offence below a crime; for which not even a child or a slave can be expelled but after repeated admonitions:'—'The travelling preachers gave the bishop his power, they continue it in his hands, and they can reduce, limit, or transfer it to other hands, whenever they see cause.' Such is the language of Bishop Hedding, who only concurs in the moderate, truly Methodistic views of Bishops Asbury, Coke, and Emory.

"It is believed that this statement of the facts and the law in the case, will afford a satisfactory answer to all the positions and reasonings of the Protest; and, after having thus presented it, the majority are perfectly willing to abide 'the decision of our contemporaries, and of posterity.' They cannot, however, close these remarks, without expressing their regret that the minority, not content with protesting against the action of the General Conference, as 'lawless,' as 'without law, and contrary to law,' as such 'a violation of the compromise law' that 'the public faith of this body can no longer be relied upon as the guarantee for the redemption of the pledge, 'that there shall be no further curtailment of right as regards *the Southern ministry*,' —that, not content with thus harshly assailing the proceedings of the General Conference, they have even refused to the bishops, whom they have invested with such exalted prerogatives, the quiet possession of their thoughts and feelings, but have thrown out the significant intimation, 'that any bishop of the Church, either violating, or submitting to the violation of the compromise charter of union between the North and South, without proper and public remonstrance, cannot be acceptable in the South, and *need not appear there*.' We shall be slow to believe, that even their constituents will justify them in thus virtually deposing, not one bishop only, but several, by a process which is even worse than 'extra-judicial.'

"When all the law, and the facts in the case, shall have been spread before an impartial community, the majority have no doubt that they *will* fix '*the responsibility of division*,' should such an unhappy event take place, 'where in justice *it belongs*.' They will ask, Who first introduced slavery into the episcopacy? And the answer will be, *Not the General Conference*. Who opposed the attempt to withdraw it from the episcopacy? *Not the General Conference*. Who resisted the measure of peace that was proposed—the mildest that the case allowed? *Not the majority*. Who first sounded the knell of division, and declared that it would be impossible longer to remain under the jurisdiction of the Methodist Episcopal Church? *Not the majority*.

"The proposition for a peaceful separation, (if any must take place,) with which the Protest closes, though strangely at variance with much that precedes, has already been met by the General Conference. And the readiness with which that body (by a vote which would doubtless have been unanimous but for the belief which some entertained of the unconstitutionality of the measure) granted all that the Southern brethren themselves could ask, in such an event, must forever stand as a practical refutation of any assertion that the minority have been subjected to the tyranny of a majority.

"Finally, we cannot but hope that the minority, after reviewing the entire action of the Conference, will find that, both in their Declaration and their Protest, they have taken too strong a view of the case; and that, by presenting it in its true light before their people, they may be able to check any feelings of discord that may have arisen, so that the Methodist Episcopal Church may still continue as one body, engaged in its proper work of 'spreading Scriptural holiness over these lands.'

"J. P. Durbin, *Chairman*.
Geo. Peck,
Chas. Elliott."

Mr. Lord,—I will now give your Honours the dates of these papers, as they may be worthy of noting:—

The "Declaration," your Honours will find to have been put in on the 5th of June, 1844. The date of the passage of Mr. Finley's resolution was the 1st of June. The committee of nine to consider a plan of separation, was appointed on the 5th of June. The Protest was brought in on the 6th of June, and the Reply on the 10th of the same month. I propose also to give the date of some other papers that I shall presently read. The election of two bishops—Bishops Hamline and Janes—took place on the 7th of June.—Page 128 of Journal of the General Conference of 1844.

I will now proceed to read from page 123 of the first of the Proofs:—

"Thursday, June 6.—Bishop Soule presented the following communication:—

"'*To the General Conference*.

"'Rev. and Dear Brethren,—As the case of Bishop Andrew unavoidably involves the future *action* of the superintendents, which, in their judgment, in the present position of the bishop, they have no discretion to decide upon; they respectfully request of this General Conference *official* instruction, in answer to the following questions:—

"'1. Shall Bishop Andrew's name remain as it now stands in the Minutes, Hymn Book, and Discipline, or shall it be struck off of these official records?

" '2. How shall the bishop obtain his support? As provided for in the form of Discipline, or in some other way?

" '3. What work, if any, may the bishop perform; and how shall he be appointed to the work?

" 'JOSHUA SOULE,
ELIJAH HEDDING,
BEVERLY WAUGH,
THOMAS A. MORRIS.'

"J. T. Mitchell offered the following resolutions, in reply to the several inquiries of the superintendents :—

" '1. *Resolved*, as the sense of this Conference, that Bishop Andrew's name stand in the Minutes, Hymn Book, and Discipline, as formerly.

" '2. *Resolved*, That the rule in relation to the support of a bishop and his family, applies to Bishop Andrew.

" '3. *Resolved*, That whether in any, and if any, in what work, Bishop Andrew be employed, is to be determined by his own decision and action in relation to the previous action of this Conference in his case.'

"D. B. Randall offered an amendment, which was laid on the table.

"The yeas and nays were ordered. During the call, J. G. Dow, F. G. Hibbard, and G. Smith, asked to be excused from voting. Conference refused to excuse them.

"The *first* resolution was adopted—ayes 155, noes 17.

"A motion to adjourn was made and lost.

"The *second* resolution was read, and the yeas and nays were ordered. During the call E. Robinson objected to being compelled to vote. A motion was made to excuse him, but was lost. F. G. Hibbard and J. Spaulding asked to be excused from voting. Conference refused to excuse them.

"The resolution was adopted—yeas 152, nays 14.

"A motion to adjourn was made and lost.

"The *third* resolution was read. J. T. Peck offered a substitute, which, on motion of J. S. Porter, was laid on the table. H. Slicer offered a substitute, which, on motion of T. Crowder, was laid on the table. J. A. Collins offered a substitute, which, on motion of J. T. Peck, was laid on the table. T. Crowder moved the previous question, which prevailed. The yeas and nays were ordered, and the vote taken.

"D. B. Randall, who voted in the negative, asked and obtained leave to change his vote, not having understood the question; being sick and obliged to be absent during a part of the discussion. He then voted in the affirmative.

"The resolution was adopted—ayes 103, noes 67."

On Monday, June the 10th, the two newly-elected bishops were ordained. I will read a few passages from the journal of the Conference, under that date :—pp. 138–9.

"On motion of J. Early, the order of business was suspended, the hour for ordaining the bishops elect having arrived.

"Brothers Hamline and Janes, the bishops elect, were invited to chairs in front of the altar, the former sitting between brothers Pickering and Filmore, and the latter between brothers L. Pierce and Capers.

"The Collect and Epistle were read by Bishop Waugh, the Gospel by Bishop Morris, and the questions and prayers by Bishops Soule and Hedding.

"Brother Hamline was presented by brothers Pickering and Filmore, and brother Janes by brothers Pierce and Capers.

"The imposition of hands was by the four bishops, Soule, Hedding, Waugh, and Morris.

"Thus Leonidas Lent Hamline and Edmund Storer Janes were solemnly ordained superintendents or bishops of the Methodist Episcopal Church."

I again return to the first of the Proofs, (p. 125,) and ask your Honours' attention to the phraseology. The report, it will be seen, was made on the "Declaration :"—

"SATURDAY, JUNE 8.—On motion of R. Paine, the special order of the day was dispensed with, and the report of the select committee of nine, on the declaration of fifty-one brethren, from the Southern conferences, was taken up. The report was read again.

"C. Elliott moved the adoption of the report of the committee of nine. The *first* resolution was read. The rule was suspended to allow P. Cartwright to extend his remarks. On the first resolution the previous question was moved, and the call was sustained. The yeas and nays were ordered and taken. Ayes, 147; noes, 22.

"On motion of R. Paine, the vote by yeas and nays was reconsidered. On further motion, the resolution was amended, by striking out the words, 'delegates from the,' and inserting 'annual.' The discussion was resumed on the amended resolution."

If your Honours will turn to p. 128, you will see how it was amended. The resolutions are there printed as they were amended. After the figure it originally read: "Should the delegates from the conferences," &c. They struck out "the delegates from" and inserted "annual." "The delegates" could only mean those who were then present. That becomes a very material fact in respect to one of the claims set up in this matter. It was originally proposed that if the delegates then present should find it necessary to unite in a distinct ecclesiastical connexion, the rule there set forth should be observed; but, on the motion of Mr. Paine, one of the Southern delegates, it was determined that, instead of it being left to them, it should be left to the annual conferences.

Mr. Fancher,—It was not on the motion of Mr. Paine.

Mr. Lord,—On the motion of Mr. Paine the vote was reconsidered; and in the same connexion it is stated, "on further motion, the resolution was amended," &c., and therefore I supposed it to be Mr. Paine's motion.

Mr. Fancher,—The record does not show whose motion it was.

Mr. Lord continued:—

"On motion, it was resolved to meet again at half-past three o'clock this afternoon.

"The previous question was moved on the amended resolution, and the call was sustained, and the resolution adopted by one hundred and thirty-five affirmative to eighteen negative votes.

"On the second resolution, J. T. Mitchell moved to amend, by inserting, 'and private members.' The amendment was laid on the table."

By turning to p. 129, your Honours will see how that reads. If the amendment had been adopted, it would have stood thus:—

"'2. That ministers, local and travelling, of every grade and office in the Methodist Episcopal Church, "*and private members*," may, as they prefer, remain in that Church, or, without blame, attach themselves to the Church, South.'

"On motion of J. A. Collins, the session was prolonged fifteen minutes.

"The second resolution was adopted by one hundred and thirty-nine affirmative to seventeen negative votes.

"A motion to adjourn was lost.

"The yeas and nays were ordered on the third resolution.

"The previous question was moved, and the call sustained.

"The session was further prolonged until the call of the roll was completed, and the vote finished.

"The third resolution was adopted by one hundred and forty-seven yeas to twelve nays.

"Adjourned with the benediction by brother Pickering.

"SATURDAY AFTERNOON, JUNE 8.—Conference met at half-past three o'clock, pursuant to adjournment, Bishop Morris in the chair, and was opened with religious exercises by brother Simpson.

"The journal of the morning was read and approved.

"On motion of M. Simpson, G. Peck and C. Elliott were put in place of S. Olin and L. L. Hamline, on the select committee of three to prepare a statement of the action of this Conference in the case of Bishop Andrew.

"On motion, the special order of business, on which Conference adjourned this morning, was resumed.

"The *fourth* resolution of the report of the select committee of nine was adopted.

"On the *fifth* resolution the yeas and nays were ordered. It was adopted by one hundred and fifty-three yeas to thirteen nays.

"The *sixth, seventh, eighth,* and *ninth* resolutions were adopted.

"To the *tenth* resolution D. B. Randall moved an amendment which was adopted, and is incorporated with the resolution.

"The *eleventh* and *twelfth* resolutions were adopted. On motion, the order of the eleventh and twelfth resolutions was inverted, so as to make the latter stand first.

"The preamble of the report was adopted.

"The blank in the *seventh* resolution was filled up with "three;" and N. Bangs, G. Peck, and G. Filmore, were appointed commissioners under the seventh resolution. G. Filmore tendered his resignation, which was accepted, and J. B. Finley appointed in his place.

"On motion of W. Winans, the Secretary was requested to prepare and furnish to J. Early a copy of the "Declaration" so often referred to, and of the report just adopted.

"B. M. Drake offered a resolution, which, on motion, was laid on the table."

That was one of the resolutions which I read from one book.

"J. Porter moved a reconsideration of the first resolution, with a view of offering a substitute. The motion to reconsider was laid on the table.

"The report as a whole was adopted. It is as follows:—

"'The select committee of nine, to consider and report on the Declaration of the delegates from the conferences of the slaveholding States, beg leave to submit the following report:—

"'Whereas a Declaration has been presented to this General Conference, with the signatures of *fifty-one* delegates of the body, from thirteen annual conferences in the slaveholding States, representing that, for various reasons enumerated, the objects and purposes of the Christian ministry and Church organization cannot be successfully accomplished by them under the jurisdiction of this General Conference as now constituted; and

"'Whereas, in the event of a separation, a contingency to which the Declaration asks attention as not improbable, we esteem it the duty of this General Conference to meet the emergency with Christian kindness and the strictest equity; therefore,

"'*Resolved*, by the delegates of the several annual conferences in General Conference assembled,

"'1. That, should the annual conferences in the slaveholding States find it necessary to unite in a distinct ecclesiastical connexion, the following rule shall be observed with regard to the northern boundary of such connexion:—All the societies, stations, and conferences adhering to the Church in the South, by a vote of a majority of the members of said societies, stations, and conferences, shall remain under the unmolested pastoral care of the Southern Church; and the ministers of the Methodist Episcopal Church shall in no wise attempt to organize Churches or societies within the limits of the Church South, nor shall they attempt to exercise any pastoral oversight therein; it being understood that the ministry of the South reciprocally observe the same rule in relation to stations, societies, and conferences adhering, by a vote of a majority, to the Methodist Episcopal Church; provided, also, that this rule shall apply only to societies, stations, and conferences bordering on the line of division, and not to interior charges, which shall in all cases be left to the care of that Church within whose territory they are situated.

"'2. That ministers local and travelling, of every grade and office in the Methodist Episcopal Church, may, as they prefer, remain in that Church, or, without blame, attach themselves to the Church, South.

" '3. *Resolved*, by the delegates of all the annual conferences in General Conference assembled, That we recommend to all the annual conferences, at their first approaching sessions, to authorize a change of the sixth restrictive article, so that the first clause shall read thus :—" They shall not appropriate the produce of the Book Concern, nor of the Chartered Fund, to any other purpose other than for the benefit of the travelling, supernumerary, superannuated, and worn-out preachers, their wives, widows, and children, and to such other purposes as may be determined upon by the votes of two-thirds of the members of the General Conference."

" '4. That whenever the annual conferences, by a vote of three-fourths of all their members voting on the third resolution, shall have concurred in the recommendation to alter the sixth restrictive article, the agents at New-York and Cincinnati shall, and they are hereby authorized and directed to deliver over to any authorized agent or appointee of the Church, South, should one be organized, all notes and book accounts against the ministers, Church members, or citizens within its boundaries, with authority to collect the same for the sole use of the Southern Church ; and that said agents also convey to the aforesaid agent or appointee of the South, all the real estate, and assign to him all the property, including presses, stock, and all right and interest connected with the printing establishments at Charleston, Richmond, and Nashville, which now belong to the Methodist Episcopal Church.

" '5. That when the annual conferences shall have approved the aforesaid change in the sixth restrictive article, there shall be transferred to the above agent of the Southern Church so much of the capital and produce of the Methodist Book Concern as will, with the notes, book accounts, presses, &c., mentioned in the last resolution, bear the same proportion to the whole property of said Concern that the travelling preachers in the Southern Church shall bear to all the travelling ministers of the Methodist Episcopal Church ; the division to be made on the basis of the number of travelling preachers in the forthcoming minutes.

" '6. That the above transfer shall be in the form of annual payments of $25,000 per annum, and specifically in stock of the Book Concern, and in Southern notes and accounts due the establishment, and accruing after the first transfer mentioned above ; and until the payments are made, the Southern Church shall share in all the net profits of the Book Concern, in the proportion that the amount due them, or in arrears, bears to all the property of the Concern.

" '7. That Nathan Bangs, George Peck, and James B. Finley be, and they are hereby appointed commissioners to act in concert with the same number of commissioners appointed by the Southern organization, (should one be formed,) to estimate the amount which will fall due to the South by the preceding rule, and to have full powers to carry into effect the whole arrangements proposed with regard to the division of property, should the separation take place. And if by any means a vacancy occurs in this board of commissioners, the Book Committee at New-York shall fill said vacancy.

" '8. That whenever any agents of the Southern Church are clothed with legal authority or corporate power to act in the premises, the agents at New-York are hereby authorized and directed to act in concert with said Southern agents, so as to give the provisions of these resolutions a legally binding force.

" '9. That all the property of the Methodist Episcopal Church in meeting-houses, parsonages, colleges, schools, conference funds, cemeteries, and of every kind within the limits of the Southern organization, shall be forever free from any claim set up on the part of the Methodist Episcopal Church, so far as this resolution can be of force in the premises.

" '10. That the Church so formed in the South shall have a common right to use all the copy-rights in possession of the Book Concerns at New-York and Cincinnati, at the time of the settlement by the commissioners.

" '11. That the book agents at New-York be directed to make such compensation to the conferences South, for their dividend from the Chartered Fund, as the commissioners above provided for shall agree upon.

" 'That the bishops be respectfully requested to lay that part of this report requiring the action of the annual conferences, before them as soon as possible, beginning with the New-York Conference.' "

That is all we shall read from the Book of Proofs No. 1. What remains, belongs to our friends on the other side, if they think it necessary to introduce it. I will now proceed to read that part of the evidence which relates to the organization of the Church under this Plan of Separation. I read from the Book of Proofs No. 2, page 1 :—

"1. *History of proceedings of the Delegates from slaveholding States, at their meeting in the City of New-York, on the day after the adjournment of the General Conference of* 1844.

"At that meeting, they adopted the following plan of action as proper to be recommended to the conferences represented by them :—

"'With a view to promote uniformity of action in the premises, we beg leave to submit to your consideration the expediency of concurring in the following plan of procuring the judgment of the Church within the slaveholding States, as to the propriety of organizing a Southern division of the Methodist Episcopal Church in the United States, and of effecting such an organization should it be deemed necessary :—

"'1. There shall be a convention held in Louisville, Kentucky, to commence the 1st of May, 1845,—composed of delegates from the several annual conferences within the slaveholding States, appointed in the ratio of one for every eleven members.

"'2. These delegates shall be appointed at the ensuing session of the several annual conferences enumerated, each conference providing for the expenses of its own delegates.

"'3. These several annual conferences shall instruct their delegates to the proposed convention on the points on which action is contemplated—conforming their instructions, as far as possible, to the opinions and wishes of the membership within their several conference bounds.'

"They also sent abroad the following address :—

"'ADDRESS

"'*To the Ministers and Members of the Methodist Episcopal Church, in the Slaveholding States and Territories.*

"'The undersigned, delegates in the late General Conference of the Methodist Episcopal Church, from *thirteen* annual conferences in slaveholding States and Territories, would most respectfully represent—that the various action of the *majority* of the General Conference, at its recent session, on the subject of *slavery and abolition,* has been such as to render it necessary, in the judgment of those addressing you, to call attention to the *proscription and disability* under which the Southern portion of the Church must of necessity labour in view of the action alluded to, unless some measures are adopted to free the minority of the South from the oppressive jurisdiction of the majority in the North, in this respect.

"'The proceedings of the majority, in several cases involving the question of slavery, have been such as indicate most conclusively that the legislative, judicial, and administrative action of the General Conference, as now organized, will always be extremely hurtful, if not finally ruinous, to the interests of the Southern portion of the Church; and must necessarily produce a state of conviction and feeling in the slaveholding States, entirely inconsistent with either the peace or prosperity of the Church.

"'The opinions and purposes of the Church in the North on the subject of slavery, are in direct conflict with those of the South, and unless the South will submit to the dictation and interference of the North, greatly beyond what the existing law of the Church on slavery and abolition authorizes, there is no hope of anything like union or harmony. The debate and action of the General Conference in the case of the Rev. Mr. Harding, of the Baltimore Conference; the debate and action in the case of Bishop Andrew; and the opinions and purposes avowed and indicated in a *manifesto* of the majority, in reply to a *Protest* from the minority against the proceedings complained of,—together with hundreds of petitions from the East, North, and West, demanding that slavery, in all its possible forms, be separated from the Church;—these, and similar demonstrations, have convinced the undersigned, that they cannot remain silent or inactive without hazard and injustice to the different portions of the Church they represent.

"'They have, therefore, thought proper to invoke the attention of the Church in the South to a state of things they are compelled to regard as worthy the immediate notice and action of the Church throughout all the slaveholding states and territories. The subject of slavery and abolition, notwithstanding the plain law of the Discipline on the subject, was agitated and debated in the late General Conference, for *five successive weeks;* and even at the very close of the session, the aspect of things was less satisfactory and more threatening to the South than at any former period; and under such circumstances of mutual distrust and disagreement, the General Conference adjourned.

"'Some time before the adjournment, however, upon a *Declaration* made by the Southern delegations,' setting forth the impossibility of enduring such a state of things much longer, the General Conference, by a very large and decided majority, agreed to a *plan of formal and pacific separation,* by which the Southern conferences are to have a distinct and independent organization of their own, in no way subject to Northern jurisdiction. It affords us pleasure to state that there were those found among the majority who met this proposition with every manifestation of justice and liberality. And should a similar spirit be exhibited by the annual conferences in the North, when submitted to them, as provided for in the Plan itself, there will remain no legal impediment to its peaceful consummation.

"'This Plan is approved by the undersigned as the best, and, indeed, all that can be done at present, in remedy of the great evil under which we labour. Provision is made for a peaceable and constitutional division of Church property of every kind. The Plan does not decide that division shall take place; but simply, and it is thought securely, provides that it may, if it be found necessary. Of this necessity, you are to be the judges, after a careful survey and comparison of all the reasons for and against it.

"'As the undersigned have had opportunity and advantages which those at a distance could not possess, to form a correct judgment in the premises, and it may be expected of them that they express their views fully on the subject, they do not hesitate to say, that they regard a separation at no distant day as inevitable; and further, that the Plan of Separation agreed upon is as eligible as the Southern conferences have any right to expect at any time. We most respectfully, therefore, and with no common solicitude, beseech our brethren of the ministry and membership in the slaveholding States, to examine this matter carefully, and weighing it well in all its bearings, try to reach the conclusion most proper under the circumstances. Shall that which, in all moral likelihood, must take place soon, be attempted now, or are there reasons why it should be postponed?

"'We deprecate all excitement; we ask you to be calm and collected, and to approach and dispose of the subject with all the candour and forbearance the occasion demands. The separation proposed is *not* schism, it is *not* secession. It is a state or family, separating into two different states or families, by mutual consent. As the "Methodist Episcopal Church" will be found north of the dividing line, so the "Methodist Episcopal Church" will be found south of the same line.

"'The undersigned have clung to the cherished unity of the Church with a firmness of purpose and force of feeling which nothing but invincible necessity could subdue. If, however, nominal unity must co-exist with unceasing strife and alienated feeling, what is likely to be gained by its perpetuation? Every minister and member of the Church in slave-holding States must perceive at once, that the constant, not to say interminable, agitation of the slavery and abolition question in the councils of the Church, and elsewhere, must terminate in incalculable injury to all the Southern conferences. Our access to slave and master is to a great extent cut off. The legislation of the Church in conflict with that of the State—Church policy attempting to control public opinion and social order—must generate an amount of hostility to the Church, impossible to be overcome, and slowly but certainly diminish both the means and the hope of usefulness and extension on the part of the Church.

"'Disposed, however, to defer to the judgment of the Church, we leave this subject with you. Our first and most direct object has been to bring it fully before you, and, giving you an opportunity to judge and determine for yourselves, await your decision. The minority from the South in the late General Conference, were most anxious to adjourn the decision in the case of Bishop Andrew, with all its attendant results, to the annual conferences and to the Church at large, to consider and decide upon during the next four years—as no charge was presented against the bishop, and especially as this measure was urgently recommended by the whole bench of bishops, although Bishop Hedding subsequently withdrew his name. The proposition, how ever, to refer the whole subject to the Church, was promptly rejected by the majority, and immediate action demanded and had. But as all the facts connected with the equivocal suspension of Bishop Andrew, will come before you in other forms, it is unnecessary to detail them in this brief address, the main object of which is to place before you, in a summary way, the principal facts and reasons connected with the proposed separation of the Southern conferences into a distinct organization.'

"Adopted at a meeting of the Southern delegations, held in New-York, at the close of the General Conference, June 11, 1844, and ordered to be published.

"Signed on behalf of the Kentucky, Missouri, Holston, Tennessee, North Carolina, Memphis, Arkansas, Virginia, Mississippi, Texas, Alabama, Georgia, and South Carolina Annual Conferences.

"*Kentucky*, H. B. Bascom, William Gunn, H. H. Kavanaugh, E. Stevenson, B. T. Crouch, G. W. Brush. *Missouri*, W. W. Redman, W. Patton, J. C. Berryman, J. M. Jameson. *Holston*, E. F. Sevier, S. Patton, T. Stringfield. *Tennessee*, R. Paine, J. B. M'Ferrin, A. L. P. Green, T. Maddin. *North Carolina*, B. T. Blake, J. Jamieson, P. Doub. *Memphis*, G. W. D. Harris, S. S. Moody, W. M'Mahon, Thomas Joyner. *Arkansas*, J. C. Parker, W. P. Ratcliffe, A. Hunter. *Virginia*, J. Early, T. Crowder, W. A. Smith, L. M. Lee. *Mississippi*, W. Winans, B. M. Drake, J. Lane, G. M. Rogers. *Texas*, Littleton Fowler. *Alabama*, J. Boring, J. Hamilton, W. Murrah, G. Garrett. *Georgia*, G. F. Pierce, W. J. Parks, L. Pierce, J. W. Glenn, J. E. Evans, A. B. Longstreet. *South Carolina*, W. Capers, W. M. Wightman, C. Betts, S. Dunwody, H. A. C. Walker."

If your Honours please, I propose now to show the action of the several Southern conferences upon the subject. I begin to read on page 7.

"The Kentucky Conference was the first in the Southern division of the Church to meet after the adjournment of the General Conference. It convened on the 11th of September, 1844, and adopted the following resolutions, with but one dissenting vote:—

"'*Report of the Committee on Division.*

"'The committee to whom was referred the subject of the division of the Church into two separate General Conference jurisdictions, and kindred subjects, have had the same under serious consideration, and beg leave to report:—

"'That, enlightened as the conference is presumed to be, on the merits of the very important subject upon which your committee have been called to act, it was not deemed expedient to delay this report by an elaborate and argumentative investigation of the matters committed to them, in their various relations, principles, and bearings; they, therefore, present the result of their deliberations to the conference by offering for adoption the following resolutions:—

"'1. *Resolved*, That it is the deliberate judgment of this conference, that the action of the late General Conference, virtually deposing Bishop Andrew, and also their action in confirming the decision of the Baltimore Conference, in the case of the Rev. F. A. Harding, are not sustained by the Discipline of our Church, and that we consider those proceedings as constituting a highly dangerous precedent.

"'2. *Resolved*, That we deeply regret the prospect of division growing out of these proceedings, and that we do most sincerely hope and pray that some effectual means, not inconsistent with the interests and honour of all concerned, may be suggested and devised, by which so great a calamity may be averted, and to this end we recommend that our societies be freely consulted on the subject.

"'3. *Resolved*, That we approve the holding of a convention of delegates from the conferences in the slaveholding States, in the city of Louisville, on the first day of May next, agreeably to the recommendation of the Southern and South-western delegates in the late General Conference; and that the ratio of representation proposed by said delegates—to wit, one delegate for every eleven members of conference—be and the same is hereby adopted; and that this conference will elect delegates to the proposed convention upon said basis.

"'4. *Resolved*, That should a division be found to be indispensable, the delegates of this conference are hereby required to act under the following instructions, to wit: that the Southern and South-western conferences shall not be regarded as a secession from the Methodist Episcopal Church, but that they shall be recognised in law, and to all intents and purposes, as a co-ordinate branch of the Methodist Episcopal

Church in the United States of America, simply acting under a separate jurisdiction. And further, that being well satisfied with the Discipline of the Church as it is, this conference instruct its delegates not to support or favour any change in said Discipline by said convention.

"'5. *Resolved,* That unless we can be assured that the rights of our ministry and membership can be effectually secured according to Discipline, against future aggressions, and reparation be made for past injury, we shall deem the contemplated division unavoidable.

"'6. *Resolved,* That we approve the course of our delegates in the late General Conference in the premises, and that we tender them our thanks for their faithful and independent discharge of duty in a trying crisis.

"'7. *Resolved,* That the secretary of this conference be directed to have these resolutions published in such of our Church papers as may be willing to insert them.

"'All of which is respectfully submitted. M. M. HENKLE, *Chairman.*'

"*Further Action in Reference to the Contemplated Convention.*

"'*Resolved, by the Kentucky Annual Conference,* That should the proposed convention, representing the annual conferences of the Methodist Episcopal Church, in the slaveholding States, appointed to assemble in the city of Louisville, the first of May, 1845, proceed to a separate organization, as contingently provided for in the resolutions of this body on yesterday, then and in that event, the convention shall be regarded as the regular General Conference, authorized and appointed by the several annual conferences of the Southern division of the Church, and as possessing all the rights, powers, and privileges of the General Conference of the Methodist Episcopal Church in the United States, and subject to the same restrictions, limitations, and restraints.

"'*Resolved,* That in order to secure the constitutional character and action of the convention as a General Conference proper, should a separate organization take place, the ratio of representation as now found in the 2d restrictive rule, one for every twenty-one, shall prevail and determine the number of constitutional delegates, taking and accrediting as such the proper number from each annual conference first elected in order, and that the supernumerary delegates be regarded as members of the convention to deliberate, etc., but not members of the General Conference proper, should the convention proceed to a separate organization in the South—*Provided,* nevertheless, that should any delegate or delegates, who would not be excluded from the General Conference proper, by the operation of the above regulation, be absent, then any delegate or delegates present, not admitted by said regulation as member or members of the constitutional General Conference, may lawfully take the seat or seats of such absent delegates, upon the principle of the selection named above.

"'*Resolved, by the Kentucky Annual Conference,* That we respectfully invite the bishops of the Methodist Episcopal Church, who may feel themselves disposed to do so, to be in attendance at the contemplated convention, to be held in the city of Louisville, Ky., in May, 1845.

"'*Resolved, by the Kentucky Annual Conference,* That we appoint the Friday immediately preceding the day fixed for the meeting of the proposed General Convention of the delegates of the conferences, as a day of fasting and prayer for the blessing of Almighty God on the said convention.'

"The Missouri Conference adopted the following report and resolutions, from the Committee on Division:—

"*Report of the Committee on Division.*

"'The committee to whom was referred the subject of a division of the Church into two separate General Conference jurisdictions, together with the causes and circumstances connected with the same, have bestowed upon it, in the most prayerful and religious manner, all the time and attention they could command for the purpose, and beg leave to present the following as their report:—

"'That inasmuch as the conference is presumed to be well informed on the merits of the very important subject upon which the committee has been called to act, it was not deemed necessary to delay this report by an extended and argumentative investigation of the matters committed to them, in their various relations, principles, and bearings; they would, therefore, present the result of their deliberations to the conference by offering for adoption the following resolutions:—

"'*Resolved,* That we have looked for many years, with painful apprehension and disapproval, upon the agitation of the slavery and abolition subject in our General Conference, and now behold with sorrow and regret, the disastrous results which it has brought about.

"'*Resolved*, That while we accord to the great majority of our Northern brethren the utmost purity of intention, and while we would carefully refrain from all harsh denunciations, we are compelled to pronounce the proceedings of the late General Conference against Bishop Andrew, extra-judicial and oppressive.

"'*Resolved*, That we deeply regret the prospect of separation growing out of these proceedings, and that we do most sincerely hope and pray that some effectual means not inconsistent with the interests and honour of all concerned, may be suggested and devised, by which so great a calamity may be averted; and to this end we recommend that our societies be freely consulted on this subject.

"'*Resolved*, That we approve the holding of a convention of delegates from the conferences in the slaveholding States, in the city of Louisville, Kentucky, on the 1st day of May next, agreeably to the recommendation of the delegates from the Southern and South-western conferences, in the late General Conference; and that the ratio of representation proposed by said delegates—to wit, one delegate for every eleven members of the conference—be, and the same is hereby adopted; and that this conference will elect delegates to the proposed convention upon said basis.

"'*Resolved*, That our delegates act under the following instructions, to wit: to oppose the division of the Church, unless such division, under all the circumstances of the case, be found to be indispensable, (and consequently unavoidable;) and should such necessity be found to exist, and the division be determined on, then, and in that event, that the Southern and South-western conferences shall not be regarded as a secession from the Methodist Episcopal Church, but that they shall be recognised in law, and to all intents and purposes, as a co-ordinate branch of the Methodist Episcopal Church in the United States of America, simply acting under a separate jurisdiction. And further, that being well satisfied with the Discipline of the Church as it is, this conference instruct its delegates not to support or favour any change in said Discipline by said convention.

"'*Resolved*, That unless we can be assured that the rights of our ministry and membership can be effectually secured according to the Discipline, against future aggressions, we shall deem the contemplated division as unavoidable.

"'*Resolved*, That should the proposed convention, representing the annual conferences of the Methodist Episcopal Church in the slaveholding States, appointed to assemble at the city of Louisville, Kentucky, the 1st of May, 1845, proceed to a separate organization, as contingently provided for in the foregoing resolutions, then, in that event, the convention shall be regarded as the regular General Conference, authorized and appointed by the several annual conferences of the Southern division of the Church, and as possessing all the rights, powers, and privileges of the General Conference of the Methodist Episcopal Church in the United States of America, and subject to the same restrictions, limitations, and restraints.

"'*Resolved*, That in order to secure the constitutional character and action of the convention as a General Conference proper, should a separate organization take place, the ratio of representation as now found in the second restrictive rule, one for every twenty-one, shall prevail and determine the constitutional delegates, taking and accrediting as such the proper number from each annual conference, first elected in order, and that the supernumerary delegates be regarded as members of the convention to deliberate, but not members of the General Conference proper, should the convention proceed to a separate organization in the South. *Provided*, nevertheless, that should any delegate or delegates who would not be excluded from the General Conference proper, by the operation of the above regulation, be absent, then any delegate or delegates present, not admitted by said regulations as a member or members of the constitutional General Conference, may lawfully take the seat or seats of such absent delegates, upon the principle of selection named above.

"'*Resolved*, That we have read with deep regret the violent proceedings of some of our Southern brethren, in their primary meetings, against some of our bishops and others; and that we do most cordially invite to our pulpits and firesides all our bishops and Northern brethren, who, in the event of a division, shall belong to the Northern Methodist Episcopal Church.

"'*Resolved*, That the preachers shall take up public collections in all their circuits and stations, sometime before the first day of March next, for the purpose of defraying the expenses of the delegates to the above-named convention, and pay over the same to the delegates, or the respective presiding elders, so that the delegates may receive the same before starting to the convention.

"'Wm. Patten, Andrew Monroe, J. Boyle, W. W. Redman, John Glannville, E. Perkins, T. W. Chandler, Jas. G. T. Dunleavy, John Thatcher.—*Committee.*'

"The following resolutions were offered and immediately adopted by the conference:—

"'*Resolved,* That we approve the course of our delegates in their action at the late General Conference, in the case of Bishop Andrew, and the part they took in the subsequent acts of the Southern delegates, growing out of the proceedings of the majority, and they are hereby entitled to our hearty thanks for their manly course in a trying crisis.

"'*Resolved,* That we invite the bishops of our Church, who may feel free to do so, and they are hereby invited, to attend the contemplated convention at Louisville, Kentucky.

J. H. Linn,
R. Boyd.'

"The Holston Conference adopted the following report and resolutions from the Committee on Separation:—

"*Report of the Committee on Separation.*

"'The committee to whom was referred the subject of Church separation and other matters connected therewith, would respectfully submit the following report:—

"'In common with our brethren all over our widely-extended Zion, our hearts are exceedingly pained at the prospect of disunion, growing out of the action of the late General Conference in the case of Bishop Andrew. Your committee believe this action to be extra-judicial, and forming a highly-dangerous precedent. The aspect of affairs at the close of the General Conference, was indeed gloomy; and while we have sought for light from every possible source, we cannot believe that our Church papers are the true exponents of the views and feelings of the whole South, or of the whole North. We would respect the opinions of our brethren everywhere, but we feel that we shall not be doing justice to ourselves, the Church, or the world, if we do not express independently, and in the fear of God, our own sentiments on this important subject. We are not prepared to see the Church of our love and choice, which has been so signally blessed of God, and cherished by the tears, prayers, and untiring efforts of our fathers, lacerated and torn asunder, without one more effort to bind up and heal her bleeding wounds. Therefore,

"'*Resolved,* That we approve of the proposed convention to be holden at Louisville, Kentucky, May 1st, 1845; and will elect delegates to said convention, according to the ratio agreed upon at the last General Conference by the Southern delegates.

"'*Resolved,* That the conferences in the non-slaveholding States and territories, be, and they are hereby respectfully requested to elect one delegate from each annual conference, (either in conference capacity or by the presiding elders,) to meet with one delegate from each of the slaveholding conferences, in the city of Louisville, Kentucky, on the first day of May, 1845, to devise some plan of compromise. And, in the event that the non-slaveholding conferences, or any number of them, which, with the slaveholding conferences, shall make a respectable majority of all the annual conferences, shall so elect delegates,—then, and in that case, the delegates which we will elect from this conference to the Louisville convention, shall appoint one of their number on said committee of compromise. And the Southern and South-western conferences are respectfully requested to agree to act upon this plan.

"'*Resolved,* That if nothing can be effected on the foregoing plan, then the delegates from this conference are instructed to propose to the Louisville convention the following or some similar plan, as the basis of connexion between the two General Conferences—proposed in case of separate organization:—The said General Conferences shall appoint an equal number of delegates, (say ten,) who shall meet together in the interim of the General Conferences, to whom shall be referred for adjustment all matters of difference between the two General Conferences, or those Churches over which they exercise jurisdiction, their decisions or propositions for adjustment to be referred for ultimate action to the General Conferences before mentioned; and when both General Conferences have confirmed their decision, it shall be final and binding on both parties.

"'*Resolved*, That if both the foregoing propositions should fail, then the delegates from this conference are instructed to support the plan of separation proposed by the late General Conference. And in so doing, we positively disavow secession, but declare ourselves, by the act of the General Conference, a co-ordinate branch of the Methodist Episcopal Church. And in the event of either the second or third proposition obtaining, the delegates from this conference are instructed not to favour any—even the least—alteration of our excellent Book of Discipline, except in so far as may be necessary to form a separate organization.

"'*Resolved*, That our delegates to the late General Conference merit the warmest expression of our thanks, for their prudent, yet firm course in sustaining the interests of our beloved Methodism in the South.

"'*Resolved*, That we warmly commend the truly Christian and impartial course of our bishops at the late General Conference, and we affectionately invite all our superintendents to attend the convention to be holden at Louisville, Kentucky.

"'All which is respectfully submitted.

"'T. K. Catlett, T. Sullins, A. H. Mathes, Ephm. E. Wiley, David Fleming, C. Fulton, R. M. Stevens, Jas. Cumming, O. F. Cunningham.'"

If your Honours please, I will now endeavour to abridge the reading. I refer your Honours to page 113. There was action by the Conferences of Kentucky and Missouri, Holston and Tennessee, in 1845, subsequent to the Louisville convention.

"Next, the Holston Conference met."

JUDGE NELSON,—Where is the Holston Conference?

The Hon. THOMAS EWING, (who being counsel for the defendants in a correlative case in Ohio, attended the trial of this suit to watch its progress,)—It embraces East Tennessee, part of Georgia, and other contiguous territory.

MR. LORD continued:—

"Next, the Holston Conference met: Bishop Andrew presided, and the conference adopted the following preamble and resolutions, with but one negative vote; and the brother who gave the negative vote, afterwards gave in his adhesion to the Methodist Episcopal Church, South, and took work of the conference as usual:—

"The following preamble and resolutions were offered by Samuel Patten, and adopted by a vote of 51 in the affirmative, and 1 in the negative. Several members were not in attendance at the conference.

"'Whereas, the long-continued agitation on the subject of slavery and abolition in the Methodist Episcopal Church did, at the General Conference of said Church, held in the city of New-York, in May, 1844, result in the adoption of certain measures by that body, which seriously threatened a disruption of the Church; and to avert this calamity, said General Conference did advise and adopt a plan contemplating the peaceful separation of the South from the North; and constituting the conferences in the slave-holding States the sole judges of the necessity of such separation: and, whereas, the conferences in the slave-holding States, in the exercise of the right accorded to them by the General Conference, did, by their representatives in convention at Louisville, Kentucky, in May last, decide that separation was necessary, and proceeded to organize themselves into a separate and distinct ecclesiastical connexion, under the style and title of the Methodist Episcopal Church, South, basing their claim to a legitimate relation to the Methodist Episcopal Church in the United States, upon their unwavering adherence to the Plan of Separation, adopted by the General Conference of said Church, in 1844, and their devotion to the doctrines, discipline, and usages of the Church as they received them from their fathers.

"'And as the Plan of Separation provides that the conferences bordering on the geographical line of separation, shall decide their relation by the votes of the majority—as, also, that ministers of every grade shall make their election North or South without censure—therefore,

"'1. *Resolved*, That we now proceed to determine the question of our ecclesiastical relation, by the vote of the conference.

" '2. That we, the members of the Holston Annual Conference, claiming all the rights, powers, and privileges of an annual conference of the Methodist Episcopal Church in the United States, do hereby make our election with, and adhere to the Methodist Episcopal Church, South.

" '3. That while we thus declare our adherence to the Methodist Episcopal Church, South, we repudiate the idea of secession in any schismatic or offensive sense of the phrase, as we neither give up nor surrender any thing which we have received as constituting any part of Methodism, and adhere to the Southern ecclesiastical organization, in strict accordance with the provisions of the Plan of Separation, adopted by the General Conference of the Methodist Episcopal Church, at its session in New-York, in May, 1844.

" '4. That we are satisfied with our Book of Discipline as it is, on the subject of slavery and every other vital feature of Methodism, as recorded in that book; and that we will not tolerate any changes whatever, except such verbal or unimportant alterations as may, in the judgment of the General Conference, facilitate the work in which we are engaged, and promote uniformity and harmony in our administration.

" '5. That the journals of our present session, as well as all our official business, be henceforth conformed in style and title to our ecclesiastical relations.

" '6. That it is our desire to cultivate and maintain fraternal relations with our brethren of the North. And we do most sincerely deprecate the continuance of paper warfare, either by editors or correspondents, in our official Church papers, and devoutly pray for the speedy return of peace and harmony in the Church, both North and South.

" '7. That the Holston Annual Conference most heartily commend the course of our beloved bishops, Soule and Andrew, during the recent agitations which have resulted in the territorial and jurisdictional separation of the Methodist Episcopal Church, and that we tender them our thanks for their steady adherence to principle and the best interests of the slave population.

" 'DAVID ADAMS.' "

I will not read all the resolutions of the various conferences, but refer your Honours to them. The adhering resolutions of the Tennessee Conference will be found on pp. 16, 17, 18, and 19. They state "that the actions of the late General Conference, together with the entire merits of the proceedings of that body, leading to the contemplated separation of the Church, have been fully and fairly presented to our people, and that both the ministry and membership within our bounds have, with great solicitude and prayerful anxiety, investigated the subject in its various relations, principles, and bearings;" and that they consider a separate organization proper. I refer particularly to the second resolution, which is on page 17; to the third resolution on the same page; and to the fourth resolution on page 18, as indicating the character of the separation. The sixth resolution provides for a General Conference, in a contingency there contemplated; and the seventh resolution shows that they adopted the same mode of representation in the General Conference. They dissented from the medium scheme of the Holston Conference, as, indeed, they all did.

The next is the Memphis Conference, page 20. They appointed a committee to examine and report upon the subject, and a series of resolutions was reported and adopted, in which, amongst other things, they approved the holding of a convention of delegates from the conferences in the slave-holding States, in the city of Louisville, Kentucky, agreeably to the recommendation of the Southern and South-Western delegates in the late General Conference. Those resolutions will be found on pp. 21, 22, and 23.

The resolutions of the Mississippi Conference are the next in order, page 24. These documents are all prefaced with a short statement, that an investigation and examination of the subject had been made. The resolutions commence on page 25. The first and second resolutions declare "that the decision of the late General Conference, in the cases of the Rev. F. A. Harding and Bishop Andrew, was unauthorized by the

Discipline of the Methodist Episcopal Church; and that a tame submission to them, upon the part of the Church in the slave-holding States, would prevent our access to the slaves, and expose us to suspicions destructive to our general usefulness;" and "that as no authorized plan of compromise has been suggested by the North, and as all the propositions made by the Southern delegates were rejected, we regard a separation as inevitable, and approve the holding of a convention to meet in Louisville." The third resolution contains instructions to their delegates to such convention.

The next is the Arkansas Conference, whose resolutions will be found upon pp. 27, 28, and 29.

The Virginia resolutions are on pp. 30, 31, and 32.

The North Carolina Conference adopted the report of their committee, in which they "deeply regret the division of the Methodist Episcopal Church, which the course of the majority in the late General Conference renders not only necessary but inevitable." I would particularly call attention to what they say on page 34:—

"Nothing was left for the South to do, but to pass from under the jurisdiction of so wayward a power, to the regulations and government of our old, wholesome, and Scriptural Discipline. This, we sorrow when we say it, has opened a great gulf—we fear an impassable gulf—between the North and the South. This consolation, however, if no other, they have—the good Book of Discipline, containing the distinctive features of the Methodist Episcopal Church, shall still lie on the South side. Compelled by circumstances which could neither be alleviated nor controlled —which neither the entreaties of kindness nor the force of truth could successfully resist—we hesitate not to decide on being forever separate from those whom we not only esteem, but love. Better far that we should suffer the loss of union, than that thousands, yea millions of souls should perish."

Their resolutions follow.

The proceedings and resolutions of the South Carolina Conference, which will be found on the 35th and subsequent pages, show how they came to their conclusion. It appears that in all the circuits and stations of that conference, and in other meetings and at preaching places where there was a society, the subject had been talked over, and on all occasions there had been but one voice uttered, one opinion expressed. On pages 36 and 37, your Honours will find a statement of the manner in which they came to their conclusion; and considering where it comes from, it is a very moderate document indeed. Their resolutions are on pages 38 and 39, and they show that they cordially agreed in the necessity of a separation. I would very gladly read all these resolutions if it were consistent with a proper economy of time. Their resolutions, however, show that the subject had been deliberately considered.

The next is the Indian Mission Conference, which lies, I believe, west of the Mississippi. They elected delegates to represent the Indian Mission Conference in the contemplated convention to be held in Louisville, Kentucky.—Pp. 40, 41.

The Georgia Conference discuss the subject fully in their report, pp. 42, 43, 44; and on pp. 45, 46, 47 are their resolutions, by which they authorize the Southern organization of the Church.

The resolutions of the Florida Conference will be found on pp. 47, 48; those of the Texas Conference on pp. 49, 50; and those of the Alabama Conference, on pp. 50, 51, 52, and 53. There were fifteen or sixteen Southern conferences that appointed delegates, who were instructed and recommended to form a Southern organization of the Church. They met, and extracts from the journal of their proceedings will be found on page 54 of the book from which I have been reading—Proofs, No. 2. Perhaps it is proper that I should read the address of Bishop Soule, which he delivered to that Convention on the second day of its session, the second of May, 1845.

"I rise on the present occasion to offer a few remarks to this convention of ministers, under the influence of feelings more solemn and impressive than I recollect ever to have experienced before. The occasion is certainly one of no ordinary interest and solemnity. I am deeply impressed with a conviction of the important results of your deliberations and decisions in relation to that numerous body of Christians and Christian ministers you here represent, and to the country at large. And knowing, as I do, the relative condition of the vast community where your acts must be extensively felt, I cannot but feel a deep interest in the business of the convention, both as it respects yourselves, and the millions who must be affected by your decisions. With such views and feelings, you will indulge me in an expressisn of confident hope that all your business will be conducted with the greatest deliberation, and with that purity of heart, and moderation of temper, suitable to yourselves, as a body of Christian ministers, and to the important concerns which have called you together in this city.

"The opinion which I formed at the close of the late General Conference, that the proceedings of that body would result in a division of the Church, was not induced by the impulse of excitement; but was predicated of principles and facts, after the most deliberate and mature consideration. That opinion I have freely expressed. And however deeply I have regretted such a result, believing it to be inevitable, my efforts have been made, not to prevent it, but rather that it be attended with the least injury, and the greatest amount of good which the case would admit. I was not alone in this opinion. A number of aged and influential ministers entertained the same views. And, indeed, it is not easy to conceive how any one, intimately acquainted with the facts in the case, and the relative position of the North and South, could arrive at any other conclusion. Nothing has transpired since the close of the General Conference to change the opinion I then formed; but subsequent events have rather confirmed it. In view of the certainty of the issue, and at the same time ardently desirous that the two great divisions of the Church might be in peace and harmony within their own respective bounds, and cultivate the spirit of Christian fellowship, brotherly kindness, and charity for each other, I cannot but consider it an auspicious event that the sixteen annual conferences, represented in this convention, have acted with such extraordinary unanimity in the measures they have taken in the premises. In the Southern conferences which I have attended, I do not recollect that there has been a dissenting voice with respect to the *necessity* of a separate organization; and although their official acts in deciding the important question, have been marked with that clearness and decision which should afford satisfactory evidence that they have acted under a solemn conviction of duty to Christ, and to the people of their charge, they have been equally distinguished by moderation and candour. And as far as I have been informed, all the other conferences have pursued a similar course.

"It is ardently to be desired that the same unanimity may prevail in the counsels of this convention as distinguished, in such a remarkable manner, the views, and deliberations, and decisions of your constituents. When it is recollected that it is not only for yourselves, and the present ministry and membership of the conferences you represent, that you are assembled on this occasion, but that millions of the present race, and generations yet unborn, may be affected, in their most essential interests, by the results of your deliberations, it will occur to you how important it is that you should 'do all things as in the immediate presence of God.' Let all your acts, dear brethren, be accompanied with much prayer for that *wisdom which is from above*.

"While you are thus impressed with the importance and solemnity of the subject which has occasioned the convention, and of the high responsibility under which you act, I am confident you will cultivate the spirit of Christian moderation and forbearance; and that in all your acts you will keep strictly within the limits and provisions of the 'Plan of Separation' adopted by the General Conference with great unanimity and apparent Christian kindness. I can have no doubt of the firm adherence of the ministers and members of the Church in the conferences you represent, to the doctrine, rules, order of government, and forms of worship contained in our excellent Book of Discipline. For myself, I stand upon the basis of Methodism as contained in this book, and from it I intend never to be removed I cannot be insensible to the expression of your confidence in the resolution you have unanimously adopted, requesting me to preside over the convention in conjunction with my colleagues. And after having weighed the subject with careful deliberation, I have resolved to accept your invitation, and discharge the duties of the important trust to the best of my ability. My excellent colleague, Bishop Andrew, is of the same mind, and will cordially participate in the duties of the chair.

"I am requested to state to the convention, that our worthy and excellent colleague, Bishop Morris, believes it to be his duty to decline a participation in the presidential duties. He assigns such reasons for so doing as are, in the judgment of his colleagues, perfectly satisfactory; and it is presumed they would be considered in the same light by the convention. In conclusion, I trust that all things will be done in that spirit which will be approved of God; and devoutly pray that your acts may result in the advancement of the Redeemer's kingdom, and the salvation of the souls of men."

Bishop Soule then took the chair, and from the record of their proceedings I read the following:—

"On motion of J. Early and W. A. Smith, it was

"'*Resolved*, That a committee of *two* members, from each annual conference represented in this convention, be appointed, whose duty it shall be to take into consideration the propriety and necessity of a Southern organization, according to the Plan of Separation adopted by the late General Conference, together with the acts of the several annual conferences on this subject, and report the best method of securing the objects contemplated in the appointment of this convention.'

"MONDAY MORNING, MAY 5.—On motion of Dr. William Winans, it was

"'*Resolved*, That the Committee on Organization be instructed to inquire whether or not anything has transpired, during the past year, to render it possible to maintain the unity of the Methodist Episcopal Church, under the same General Conference jurisdiction, without the ruin of Southern Methodism.'

"On motion of Benjamin M. Drake, it was

"'*Resolved*, That the Committee on Organization be, and are hereby instructed to inquire into the propriety of reporting resolutions in case a division should take place, leaving the way open for re-union on terms which shall not compromise the interests of the *Southern*, and which shall meet, as far as may be, the views of the *Northern* portion of the Church.'

"Dr. William A. Smith and Dr. Lovick Pierce presented the following resolution, which, at their request, was laid on the table, to be taken up on to-morrow morning.

"'*Resolved*, by the delegates of the several annual conferences in the Southern and South-western states, in General Convention assembled, That we cannot sanction the action of the late General Conference of the Methodist Episcopal Church, on the subject of slavery, by remaining under the ecclesiastical jurisdiction of that body, without deep and lasting injury to the interests of the Church and the country; we, therefore, hereby instruct the Committee on Organization, that if, upon careful examination of the whole subject, they find that there is no reasonable ground to hope that the Northern majority will recede from their position and give some safe guarantee for the future security of our civil and ecclesiastical rights, they report in favour of a separation from the ecclesiastical jurisdiction of the said General Conference.'

"WEDNESDAY MORNING, MAY 14.—The resolution of Dr. Smith was then taken up, and after a few remarks in its support by Joseph Boyle and Jesse Green, of the Missouri Conference, and Littleton Fowler, of the Texas Conference, was adopted, with one dissenting voice.

"SATURDAY MORNING, MAY 17.—On motion of John Early, of the Virginia Conference, the report of the Committee on Organization was taken up, and the convention resolved to act on it by *yeas* and *nays*—sick and absent members being permitted to enter their votes at some subsequent period during the season.

"The first resolution was read, and on motion of John Early, was adopted as follows:—

"'*Be it resolved, by the delegates of the several annual conferences of the Methodist Episcopal Church in the slaveholding States, in General Convention assembled,* That it is right, expedient, and necessary, to erect the annual conferences represented in this convention, into a distinct ecclesiastical connexion, separate from the jurisdiction of the General Conference of the Methodist Episcopal Church, as at present constituted; and accordingly, we, the delegates of said annual conferences, acting under the provisional Plan of Separation adopted by the General Conference of 1844, do solemnly *declare* the jurisdiction hitherto exercised over said annual conferences, by the General Conference of the Methodist Episcopal Church, *entirely dissolved;* and that said annual conferences shall be, and they hereby *are constituted*, a separate ecclesiastical connexion, under the provisional Plan of Separation aforesaid, and based upon the Discipline of the Methodist Episcopal Church, comprehending the doctrines and entire moral, ecclesiastical, and economical rules and regulations of said Discipline, except only, in so far as verbal alterations may be necessary to a distinct organization, and to be known by the style and title of the METHODIST EPISCOPAL CHURCH, SOUTH.'—Yeas 94; nays 3.

"The second resolution was then read, and, on motion of Thomas Crowder, of the Virginia Conference, adopted as follows:—

"'*Resolved*, That we cannot abandon or compromise the principles of action, upon which we proceed to a separate organization in the South; nevertheless, cherishing a sincere desire to maintain Christian union and fraternal intercourse with the Church, North, we shall always be ready, kindly and respectfully, to entertain, and duly and carefully consider, any proposition or plan, having for its object the union of the two great bodies, in the North and South, whether such proposed union be *jurisdictional* or *connexional*.'—Yeas, 97; nays, none.

"The Committee on Organization then presented an additional report, which was amended and adopted, in the following form:—

"'1. *Resolved*, That this convention request the bishops, presiding at the ensuing session of the border conferences of the Methodist Episcopal Church, *South*, to incorporate into the aforesaid conferences any societies or stations adjoining the line of division, provided such societies or stations, by a majority of the members, according to the provisions of the Plan of Separation adopted by the late General Conference, request such an arrangement.

"'2. *Resolved*, That answer 2d of 3d section, chapter 1st of the Book of Discipline, be so altered and amended as to read as follows:—

"'The General Conference shall meet on the first day of May, in the year of our Lord, 1846, in the town of Petersburg, Virginia, and thenceforward in the month of April or May, once in four years successively; and in such place and on such day as shall be fixed on by the preceding General Conference, &c.

"'3. *Resolved further*, That the first answer in the same chapter be altered by striking out the word '*twenty-one*,' and inserting in its place *fourteen*.'—Yeas, 97; nays, none.

"MONDAY MORNING, MAY 19.—The Committee on Organization then made an additional report, as follows:—

"'The Committee on Organization beg respectfully to report the following resolutions for adoption by the convention:—

"'1. *Resolved*, That Bishops Soule and Andrew be, and they are hereby respectfully and cordially requested by this convention, to unite with and become regular and constitutional bishops of the Methodist Episcopal Church, South, upon the basis of the Plan of Separation adopted by the late General Conference.

"'2. *Resolved*, That should any portion of an annual conference on the line of separation, not represented in this convention, adhere to the Methodist Episcopal Church, South, according to the Plan of Separation adopted at the late General Conference, and elect delegates to the General Conference of the Church in 1846, upon the basis of representation adopted by this convention, they shall be accredited as members of the General Conference.

"'3. *Resolved*, That a committee of three be appointed, whose duty it shall be to prepare and report to the General Conference of 1846, a revised copy of the present Discipline, with such changes as are necessary to conform it to the organization of the Methodist Episcopal Church, South. Respectfully submitted.

"'JOHN EARLY, *Chairman*.'

"The first resolution was then adopted:—Yeas, 95; nays, none; absent, 5."

Then follows the adhesion of Bishop Soule, or rather his letter, which it is not necessary to read; and a similar letter from Bishop Andrew, both of which may be considered as read and in evidence. Neither do I intend to read the Pastoral Address which was prepared by that convention, beginning on page 62; but I wish it to be considered as read, as a declaration of the character of the new organization.

There is another document, beginning on page 67, which, if time would permit, I should with pleasure read. It is their manifesto; and able as are the other papers, I consider this one of the most able. By this document, which is understood to be the production of the pen of the late Bishop Bascom, nearly all the argument on our side may be considered as anticipated. It is a very long document, extending from page 67 to page 101, and contains a full discussion of the case. I crave your Honours' attention to this report, as being, if nothing else, an argument which sets the case in a clear and strong light.

The Southern Church having been organized, the bishops—not of the Southern but of the Northern Church—met in council on the 2d of July, 1845, in New-York. Your Honours will recollect that the organization of the Church, South, was completed in May; and in July the bishops met in council, of whose proceedings I will read an extract from pp. 101, 102, book of Proofs, No. 2:—

"This council met in the city of New-York, July 2d, 1845, and was attended by Bishops Hedding, Waugh, Morris, and Janes. Bishop Hamline sent his opinion in writing on the points to be acted on by the council, Bishop Soule did not attend, and Bishop Andrew, being suspended, was not invited. Besides agreeing on a new plan of visitation, the bishops adopted the following resolutions, intended for the government of their own administration:—

"'1. *Resolved*, That the plan reported by the select committee of nine at the last General Conference, and adopted by that body, in regard to a distinct ecclesiastical connexion, should such a course be found necessary by the annual conferences in the slaveholding States, is regarded by us as of binding obligation in the premises, so far as our administration is concerned.

"'2. *Resolved*, That in order to ascertain fairly the desire and purpose of those societies bordering on the line of division, in regard to their adherence to the Church, North or South, due notice should be given of the time, place, and object of the meeting for the above purpose, at which a chairman and secretary should be appointed, and the sense of all the members present be ascertained, and the same be forwarded to the bishop who may preside at the ensuing annual conferences; or forward to such presiding bishop a written request to be recognised and have a preacher sent them, with the names of the majority appended thereto.

"'A true copy. EDMUND S. JANES, *Sec'y.*'"

Then appears Bishop Soule's letter of invitation to Bishop Andrew to perform episcopal functions, and Bishop Andrew's reply, accepting the office of bishop in that Church. They are merely necessary to show the organization of the Church as an episcopal Church. Your Honours will consider them as read for that purpose.

There is then the action of the conferences of Kentucky, Missouri, Holston, and Tennessee, in 1845, subsequent to the Louisville convention.—P. 108. I will not read them, but your Honours will take them as read, showing the completeness of its organization. All these documents are of the same character, showing the completeness of the organization of the new Church.

I next refer your Honours to page 117, where you will find this title:—

"9. The Journal of the General Conference of the Methodist Episcopal Church, South, at Petersburgh, Va., in May, 1846, printed. (To be referred to.)"

There is here a reference to the conference journal, South. It was set up in the answer of the defendants, that this suit is not brought by the authority of the Church, South. I therefore refer to the journal of that Conference, to show that this suit was authorized. It is a mere formal matter of proof.

On page 96 of the Journal of the General Conference of the Methodist Episcopal Church, South, held in 1846, at Petersburg, in the State of Virginia, will be found the following :—

"The Report of the Committee on Finance, in reference to the appointment of commissioners, being taken up, the blank in the fourth resolution, on motion of Dr. Smith, was filled with the name of John Early. The report was then adopted, as follows, viz. :—

"'The Finance Committee submit their Fourth Report, as follows :—

"'1. *Resolved,* by the delegates of the several annual conferences of the Methodist Episcopal Church, South, in General Conference assembled, That three commissioners be appointed in accordance with the Plan of Separation adopted by the General Conference of the Methodist Episcopal Church, in 1844, to act in concert with the commissioners appointed by the said Methodist Episcopal Church, to estimate the amount due to the South, according to the aforesaid Plan of Separation; and to adjust and settle all matters pertaining to the division of the Church property and funds, as provided for in the Plan of Separation, with full powers to carry into effect the whole arrangement with regard to said division.

"'2. *Resolved,* That the commissioners of the South shall forthwith notify the commissioners and book agents of the Methodist Episcopal Church of their appointment, and of their readiness to adjust and settle the matters aforesaid; and should no such settlement be effected before the session of the General Conference of the Methodist Episcopal Church, in 1848, said commissioners shall have power and authority, for and in behalf of this Conference, to attend the General Conference of the Methodist Episcopal Church, to settle and adjust all questions involving property or funds, which may be pending between the Methodist Episcopal Church and the Methodist Episcopal Church, South.

"'3. *Resolved,* That should the commissioners appointed by this General Conference, after proper effort, fail to effect a settlement as above, then, and in that case, they shall be, and are hereby authorized, to take such measures as may best secure the just and equitable claims of the Methodist Episcopal Church, South, to the property and funds aforesaid.

"'4. *Resolved,* That John Early be, and he is hereby authorized, to act as the agent or appointee of the Methodist Episcopal Church, South, in conformity to the Plan of Separation, adopted by the General Conference of 1844, to receive, and hold in trust, for the use and benefit of the Methodist Episcopal Church, South, all property and funds of every description which may be paid over to him by the agents of the Methodist Episcopal Church.

"'5. *Resolved,* That the commissioners, appointee, and book-agent, report to the next General Conference of the Methodist Episcopal Church, South.

"'6. *Resolved,* That should a vacancy occur in the board of commissioners, or in the office of appointee, hereinbefore provided for, by death or otherwise, in the interim of the General Conference, then, and in that case, the remaining members of the board shall have power to fill such vacancy, with the approbation of one or more of the bishops. W. A. SMITH, *Chairman.*'"

The other documents in this case are also merely formal, being an application of our commissioners to their commissioners—page 117 of second of Proofs—dated Cincinnati, Ohio, August 25th, 1846; and their reply, dated New-York, October 14, 1846. Your Honours will see that the Northern commissioners took what appears to us to be very strange ground on the subject. They declined having anything to do with it. Then the Southern commissioners appeared at Pittsburgh, and addressed a communication to the General Conference of 1848, asking for a settlement—page 124. To this no reply was received. They then addressed another letter, of the 18th May, 1848—page 125—which letter, and the reply which they received, I will read.

"12. *The letter of H. B. Bascom, and others, commissioners, to N. Bangs, and others, dated Pittsburgh, May 18th, 1848, and the reply thereto, dated Pittsburgh, May 20th,* 1848.

"'PITTSBURGH, 18*th May*, 1848.

"'The undersigned, commissioners of the Methodist Episcopal Church, South, appointed by the General Conference of said Church, in accordance with the Plan of Separation adopted by the General Conference of the Methodist Episcopal Church, in 1844, would respectfully represent to the Rev. Nathan Bangs, George Peck, and James B. Finley, commissioners on the part of the Methodist Episcopal Church, that it is important their stay in the city should not be prolonged beyond the period necessary to accomplish, as far as may be found practicable, the objects of their commission; and with a view to a correct decision in the case, the undersigned beg leave to inquire—1st. Whether as commissioners appointed by the General Conference of 1844, to act in concert with a similar board of commissioners in behalf of the Church, South, provided for in the Plan of Separation, you regard yourselves as authorized to act in the premises, under the authority above, and if so, in what form? 2d. Should your answer to this inquiry be in the negative, we would respectfully ask, have you anything to propose to us, as commissioners of the Methodist Episcopal Church, South, designed to carry into effect the provisions of the Plan of Separation, having reference to the division of the Church property? Very truly and respectfully,

"'H. B. BASCOM,
A. L. P. GREEN,
C. B. PARSONS.

"'REV. N. BANGS, GEORGE PECK, and JAS. B. FINLEY.'

"'PITTSBURGH, *May 20th*, 1848.

"'*Rev. Messrs. H. B. Bascom, D.D., A. L. P. Green, and C. B. Parsons:—*

"'GENTLEMEN,—The undersigned have the honour to acknowledge the receipt of your communication of the 18th inst., and would respectfully reply:—

"'1. That the conditions upon which their powers, as 'commissioners,' appointed by the General Conference at its session of 1844, were made to depend, having failed, they have not, and never had, power to act in the matter in question.

"'2. In accordance with the above view, they would respectfully say that they have nothing to "propose" to you touching these matters. With sentiments of esteem, yours,

"'GEORGE PECK,
JAMES B. FINLEY.'"

We also produce the Discipline of the Methodist Episcopal Church, South, with a view of showing that there is no difference in doctrine, organization, or discipline of the Church. There is only one note, I believe, added on the subject of slavery. I believe it is not worthy of notice, and yet, perhaps, in fairness I ought to state it. I will show it to your Honours afterwards. I need not now detain the Court to state it.

This, your Honours, is the evidence on our part.

JUDGE NELSON,—Is there any evidence to be offered on the part of the defendants?

MR. EWING,—Yes, sir.

JUDGE NELSON,—How long will it occupy?

MR. EWING,—Perhaps we can read it in half an hour, or a little more.

The Court then adjourned.

[NOTE BY THE REPORTER.—As Mr. Lord referred to various documents, pointing the Court to the pages where they may be found, and desired that they might be considered as read, without consuming the time necessary to read them, there is great propriety, in the judgment of the Reporter, in the incorporation of them in this report. They are, therefore, appended. The first document to which he referred, comprises the report and resolutions from the Committee on Separation, which were adopted by the Tennessee Conference.] Second of Proofs, pp. 16, 17, 18, 19, and 20.

"The committee to whom was referred the proposed division of the Methodist Episcopal Church into two separate and distinct General Conference jurisdictions, and kindred subjects, having had the same under mature consideration, beg leave to submit the following:—

"Apprised as we are, that the actions of the late General Conference, together with the entire merits of the proceedings of that body, leading to the contemplated separation of the Church, have been fully and fairly presented to our people, and that both the ministry and membership within our bounds have, with great solicitude and prayerful anxiety, investigated the subject in its various relations, principles, and bearings, we deem it entirely inexpedient at present to enter into detail or to prepare an elaborate investigation of the very important matters committed to us; therefore your committee present the result of their deliberations to the conference, by the offering for your consideration and adoption, the following resolutions:—

"1. *Resolved*, That it is the candid and deliberate judgment of this conference, that the action of the late General Conference, by which Bishop Andrew was virtually deposed, as well as their action in confirming the decision of the Baltimore Conference in the case of the Rev. F. A. Harding, is not sustained by the Discipline of our Church, and that we consider such extra-judicial proceedings as constituting a highly-dangerous precedent.

"2. That under the great affliction caused by these unfortunate proceedings, we did most ardently hope and pray that the calamitous consequences might have been averted. But since the only plausible plan of reconciliation, the proposition unanimously recommended by our beloved superintendents, was put down by the majority in the late General Conference, we honestly confess we see at present no prospect to avoid a separation.

"3. That we approve the holding a convention of delegates from all the conferences in the slaveholding States, in the city of Louisville, on the first day of May next, agreeably to the recommendation of the Southern and South-Western delegates in the late General Conference; and that the ratio of representation proposed by said delegates—to wit, one delegate for every eleven members of conference—be, and the same is hereby adopted; and this conference will elect delegates to the proposed convention upon said basis.

"4. That should a division be found to be indispensable, the delegates of this conference are required to act under the following instruction,—to wit, that the Southern and South-western conferences shall not be regarded as a secession from the Methodist Episcopal Church, but that they shall be recognised in law, and to all intents and purposes, as a co-ordinate branch of the Methodist Episcopal Church in the United States of America, simply acting under a separate jurisdiction. And, furthermore, as we are well satisfied with the Discipline of our Church as it is, this conference instruct its delegates not to support or favour any change in said Discipline by said convention; except in so far as may be necessary to conform it in its economical arrangements to the new organization.

"5. That unless we can be well assured that the rights of our ministry and membership can be effectually secured according to Discipline against future aggression, and full reparation be made for past injury, we shall deem the contemplated division unavoidable.

"6. That should the proposed convention, representing the annual conferences of the Methodist Episcopal Church in the slaveholding States, appointed to assemble in the city of Louisville, the first day of May next, proceed to a separate organization, as contingently provided for in the foregoing resolutions, then, and in that event, the convention shall be regarded as the regular General Conference, authorized and appointed by the several annual conferences of the Southern division of the Church in the United States, as possessing all the rights and privileges of the General Conference of the Methodist Episcopal Church, in the United States of America, and subject to the same constitutional limitations and restrictions.

"7. That in order to secure the constitutional character and action of the convention, as a General Conference proper, should a separate organization take place, the ratio of representation, as now found in the second restrictive rule, one for every twenty-one, shall prevail and determine the number of constitutional delegates, taking and accrediting as such the proper number from the annual conference first elected in order; and that the supernumerary delegates be regarded as members of the convention to deliberate, but not members of the General Conference proper, should the convention proceed to a separate organization in the South. *Provided*, nevertheless, that should any delegate or delegates who would not be excluded from the General Conference proper, by the operation of the above regulation, be absent, then any delegate or delegates present, not admitted by said regulation as member or members of the constitutional General Conference, may lawfully take the seat or seats of such absent delegates, upon the principle of selection named above.

"8. That we do most cordially approve of the course of our delegates in the late General Conference, in the premises, and that we tender them our sincere thanks for their faithful and independent discharge of duty in a trying crisis.

"9. That the secretary of this conference be directed to have the foregoing preamble and resolutions published in the South-Western Christian Advocate.

"All which is respectfully submitted.

"F. E. Pitts, Joshua Boucher, F. G. Ferguson, G. W. Dye, P. P. Neely, W. D. F. Sawrie, Jno. W. Hanner, A. F. Driskill, R. L. Andrews."

The following resolutions were adopted by the conference:—

"'*Resolved*, That this conference invite the bishops of the Methodist Episcopal Church, to attend the convention at Louisville, Kentucky.

"'*Resolved*, That the preacher in charge of each circuit and station, shall lift a collection before the first day of April next, to defray the expenses of our delegates to the convention at Louisville, Kentucky. The funds so collected shall be handed over to the nearest delegate, or forwarded to the editor of the South-Western Christian Advocate, and shall be equally distributed among the delegates in proportion to their expenses; and should any surplus accrue, it shall be returned to the conference at its next session, and shall be applied as the other conference funds, in making up the deficiency of our preachers, &c.'"

On the resolution of the Holston Conference, suggesting a plan of a compromise, it was unanimously

"'*Resolved*, That sympathizing as we do with our brethren of the Holston Conference in the feeling of deep regret for the necessity of a separation of the Southern portion of our Church from the Northern, and willing as we would be to preserve the union of our beloved Church, upon principles safe and just to ourselves and conservative of the Discipline; yet, inasmuch as any proposition for a compromise of existing difficulties, which might be proposed with any probability of success, should come in an authoritative manner from the Northern section of the Church, and believing the plan proposed by the Holston Conference, would, if generally adopted by the South, utterly fail to meet the object contemplated, therefore we cannot agree to the proposition.'"

The proceedings of the Memphis Conference, to which the learned gentleman referred, are as follows:—

"The committee to whom was referred the subject of the division of the Church into two separate General Conference jurisdictions, and all matters connected therewith, after solemnly and prayerfully deliberating upon the same, present the following report:—Inasmuch as the conference is presumed to be well informed on the merits of the subject, we deem it unnecessary to consume time, by entering into an extended and argumentative investigation of the various relations, principles, and bearings of the same, but proceed at once to offer the following resolutions for the action of the conference:—

"*Resolved*, 1. That it is the deliberate judgment of this conference, that the action of the late General Conference of the Methodist Episcopal Church, virtually deposing Bishop Andrew, and also their action in affirming the decision of the Baltimore Annual Conference in the case of the Rev. F. A. Harding, are not sustained by the Discipline of our Church, and that we consider these proceedings as constituting a highly-dangerous precedent.

"2. That we deeply regret the prospect of division growing out of these proceedings, and do most sincerely and devoutly pray to the great Head of the Church, that some effectual means, not inconsistent with the interests of the cause of Christ, or the honour of all concerned, may be suggested and devised, by which so great a calamity may be averted, and our long-cherished union preserved and perpetuated.

"3. That we approve the holding a convention of delegates from the conferences in the slaveholding States, in the city of Louisville, Kentucky, on the first day of May next, agreeably to the recommendation of the Southern and South-Western delegates in the late General Conference; and that the ratio of representation proposed by said delegates—to wit, one delegate for every eleven members of conference—be, and the same is hereby adopted; and that this conference will elect delegates to the proposed convention on said basis.

"4. That should a division be found to be indispensable, the delegates of this conference are hereby required to act under the following instructions, to wit: that the Southern and South-Western conferences shall not be regarded as having by such division *seceded* from the Methodist Episcopal Church; but they shall be recognised in law, and to all intents and purposes, as a co-ordinate branch of the Methodist Episcopal Church in the United States of America, simply acting under a separate jurisdiction. And further, that being well satisfied with the Discipline of the Church as it now is, this conference instructs its delegates not to support or favour any change in said Discipline by said convention, only so far as is necessary to perfect a Southern organization.

"5. That unless we can be assured that the rights of our ministry and membership will be effectually secured, according to Discipline, against future aggressions, and full reparation be made for past injury, we shall deem the contemplated division unavoidable.

"6. That should the proposed convention, representing the annual conferences of the Methodist Episcopal Church in the slaveholding States, appointed to assemble at the city of Louisville, on the first day of May, 1845, proceed to a separate organization, as contingently provided for in the foregoing resolutions; then, and in that event, the convention shall be regarded as the regular General Conference, authorized and appointed by the several annual conferences of the Southern division of the Church, and as possesssing all the rights, powers, and privileges of the General Conference of the Methodist Episcopal Church in the United States of America, and subject to the same restrictions, limitations, and restraints.

"7. That in order to secure the constitutional character and action of the convention, as a General Conference proper, should a separate organization take place, the ratio of representation as it now stands in the second restrictive rule, one for every twenty-one, shall prevail, and determine the constitutional delegates, taking as such the proper number from each annual conference, first elected in order, and that the remaining delegates be regarded as members of the convention to deliberate, but not members of the General Conference proper, should the convention proceed to a separate organization in the South. *Provided*, nevertheless, that should any delegate or delegates who would not be excluded from the General Conference proper, by the operation of the foregoing regulation, be absent, then any delegate or delegates present, not admitted by said regulation as a member or members of the constitutional General Conference, may lawfully take the seat or seats of such absent delegates upon the principles of selection before named.

"8. That we have witnessed with sorrow and disapprobation, alike the violence manifested by some at the South, and the ultraism displayed by others at the North; and that we regret exceedingly that any annual conference should have deemed it necessary to refuse to concur in the recommendation of the late General Conference to alter the sixth restrictive article: nevertheless, we shall entertain for our brethren of the North the feeling of Christian kindness and brotherly love.

"9. That we heartily approve the entire course pursued by our delegates at the late General Conference.

"10. That we cordially invite such of our bishops as may deem it proper, to be present at the contemplated convention in Louisville.

"11. That it be made the duty of each preacher to take up a public collection in every congregation under his charge, for the purpose of defraying the expenses of the delegates to the convention; and that such collections be taken up previous to the first Sabbath in April next, and immediately transmitted to some one of the delegates; and that the delegates be required to report to the next annual conference the sums received by them for this purpose, together with the amount expended by them in attending said convention.

"12. That the secretary of this conference be instructed to forward the foregoing to the South-Western Christian Advocate for publication, with a request that all other Church papers copy.

"Moses Brock, Joseph Travis, Thomas Smith, M. J. Blackwell, J. T. Baskerville, D. J. Allen, B. H. Hubbard, William Pearson, A. T. Scruggs."

The Mississippi Conference adopted the following preamble and resolutions:—

"The committee to whom was referred the subject of the contemplated division of the Methodist Episcopal Church, have endeavoured to examine the subject carefully, and in a spirit of reliance upon the teachings of the word of God for direction.

"Your committee can but deplore the existence of such causes as compel the Church of our choice to meditate a severance of that union which has so long existed, and which, under God, has contributed so efficiently to the spread of Scriptural holiness through these lands. But we are fully convinced that justice to ourselves, as well as compassion for the slaves, demand an unqualified disapproval of the action of the late General Conference—first, in confirming the decision of the Baltimore Conference, in the case of Rev. F. A. Harding; and secondly, in virtually suspending Bishop Andrew from the episcopacy, not only without law or usage, but in direct contravention of all law, and in defiance of a resolution adopted by the General Conference of 1840, which provides, 'that under the provisional exception of the general rule of the Church on the subject of slavery, the simple holding of slaves, or mere ownership of slave property, in the States or Territories where the laws do not admit of emancipation and permit the liberated slave to enjoy freedom, constitutes no legal barrier to the election or ordination of ministers to the various grades of office known in the ministry of the Methodist Episcopal Church, and cannot therefore be considered as operating any forfeiture of right in view of such election and ordination.'

"With the abstract question of slavery we are not now concerned, nor do we regard it as a subject on which the Church has a right to legislate; neither are we disposed in this report to state the full extent of our grievances, or to investigate the reasons which impose upon us the necessity of planning an amicable separation. Your committee deeply regret the injury which may be inflicted upon our beloved Zion by the intemperate and unjust denunciation of the *whole North* by those who have occasion to complain of the illegal and oppressive course pursued by the majority of the late General Conference, and most earnestly recommend the exercise of that charity which 'suffereth long and is kind.' As the result of our prayerful examination of the subject in all its bearings, we offer the following resolutions for your consideration and adoption:—

"*Resolved*, 1. That the decisions of the late General Conference in the cases of Rev. F. A. Harding and Bishop Andrew, were unauthorized by the Discipline of the Methodist Episcopal Church, and that a tame submission to them upon the part of the Church in the slaveholding States, would prevent our access to the slaves, and expose us to suspicions destructive to our general usefulness.

"*Resolved*, 2. That as no authorized plan of compromise has been suggested by the North, and as all the propositions made by the Southern delegates were rejected, we regard a separation as inevitable, and approve the holding of a convention, to meet in Louisville, Kentucky, on the first day of May next, agreeably to the recommendation of the Southern and South-Western delegates to the late General Conference; and that the ratio of representation proposed by said delegates—to wit, one delegate for every eleven members of the annual conferences—be, and the same is hereby adopted, and that this conference will elect delegates to the proposed convention upon said basis. *Provided*, however, that if, in the providence of God, any plan of compromise, which in the judgment of our delegates will redress our grievances, and effectually secure to us the full exercise and peaceable enjoyment of all our disciplinary rights, should be proposed in time to prevent disunion, we will joyfully embrace it.

"*Resolved*, 3. That our delegates to said convention shall be empowered to co-operate with the delegates to said convention from the other conferences, in adopting such measures as they shall deem necessary for the complete organization of a Southern Church, provided that it conform in all its essential features to the Discipline of the Methodist Episcopal Church.

"*Resolved*, 4. That the course pursued by our immediate representatives in the late General Conference, was and is approved by us.

"*Resolved*, 5. That the conciliatory spirit evinced by our general superintendents entitles them to the unqualified approbation of the whole Church, and that we do most cordially invite them to attend the proposed convention.

"All of which is respectfully submitted.

"D. O. Shattuck, William H. Watkins, John G. Jones, B. Pipkin, L. Campbell, John N. Hamill, A. T. M. Fly, David M. Wiggins, W. G. Gould."

"Eighty-one voting concurring in the change of the sixth restrictive rule—none non-concurring."

"*Resolved*, That the first Friday in May next be set apart as a day of special fasting and prayer for the superintendence and direction of Divine Providence, with regard to our Church difficulties, that the delegates may act so as to bring the greatest glory to God and the most good to his Church."

"The committee to whom was referred the resolutions of the Holston Conference, have had the same under consideration, and although we hold ourselves in readiness to accept any plan of pacification which obliterates the distinction between Northern and Southern Methodists, we do not regard the resolution of the Holston Conference as sanctioned by the North, or practicable in itself. Therefore,

"*Resolved*, That this conference do not concur.

"D. O. Shattuck, Willlam Hamilton Watkins, John G. Jones, B. Pipkin, L. Campbell, J. N. Hamill, A. T. M. Fly, D. M. Wiggins, Wm. G. Gould."

"Seventy-three non-concurring—none concurring."

The following report and resolutions were adopted by the Arkansas Conference :—

"The committee to whom were referred the several subjects connected with the prospective division of the Methodist Episcopal Church, have had the same under calm and prayerful consideration, and beg leave to present the following as the result of their honest deliberations.

"Being well convinced that the members of this body have not been inattentive to the proceedings of the General Conference, and that they have not failed to derive some information from the numerous addresses and communications that have appeared in our periodicals, your committee have not been disposed to waste their time, nor insult your judgments, by detailing the many circumstances, which, were you differently situated, would require amplification,—they, therefore, present to your minds for consideration and action, the subjoined resolutions :—

"1. *Resolved*, That it is the decided opinion of this conference, that the Discipline of the Methodist Episcopal Church does not sustain the action of the late General Conference in the cases of Rev. F. A. Harding and Bishop Andrew.

"2. *Resolved*, That we approve the suggestions of the bishops, as well as the request of several Southern delegates, which contemplated the postponing of the action of the General Conference, until the wishes of the whole Church could be consulted.

"3. *Resolved*, That, as we see no probability that reparation will be made for past injuries, and no security given that the rights and privileges of the ministry and membership in the slaveholding conferences will be equally respected, we believe it is the imperative duty, if not the only alternative, of the South, to form a separate organization. Nevertheless, should honourable and satisfactory propositions for pacification be made by the North, we shall expect our delegates to favour the perpetuation of the union.

"4. *Resolved*, That we approve the holding of a convention of delegates from the conferences in the slaveholding States, in the city of Louisville, Kentucky, on the first day of May, 1845, agreeably to the recommendation of the delegates from the Southern and South-Western conferences, in the late General Conference.

"5. *Resolved*, That should the proposed convention, representing the Methodist Episcopal Church in the slaveholding States, appointed to assemble at Louisville, Kentucky, the first day of May, 1845, proceed to a separate organization, as contingently provided for in the foregoing resolutions, then, in that event, the convention shall be regarded as the regular General Conference authorized and appointed by the several annual conferences in the Southern division of the Church, and as possessing all the rights, powers, and privileges of the General Conference of the Methodist Episcopal Church in the United States of America, and subject to the same restrictions, limitations, and restraints.

"6. *Resolved*, That in order to secure the constitutional character and action of the convention as a General Conference proper, should a separate organization take place, the ratio of representation, as now found in the second restrictive rule, one for every twenty-one, shall prevail and determine the constitutional delegates, taking and accrediting as such the proper number from each annual conference, first elected in order; and that the supernumerary delegates be regarded as members of the convention to deliberate, but not members of the General Conference proper, should the convention proceed to a separate organization in the South. *Provided*, nevertheless, that should any delegate or delegates who would not be excluded from the General Conference proper, by the operation of the above regulation, be absent, then any delegate or delegates present, not admitted by said regulation as a member or members of the constitutional General Conference, may lawfully take the seats of such absent delegates, upon the principle of selection named above.

"7. *Resolved*, That, as we are well satisfied with the Discipline of the Methodist Episcopal Church as it is, we hereby instruct our delegates to said convention not to favour any change therein.

"8. *Resolved*, That, though we feel ourselves aggrieved, and have been wounded, *without cause*, in the house of our friends, we have no disposition to impute wrong motives to the majority in the late General Conference, and no inclination to endorse those vindictive proceedings had in some portions of the South, believing it to be the duty of Christians, under all circumstances, to exercise that *charity* which *beareth all things*.

"9. *Resolved*, That the preachers take up collections on their several circuits and stations, at an early period, and hand the money collected to their presiding elders, that the delegates may receive the whole amount collected before they shall be required to start for Louisville.

"10. *Resolved*, That we tender our warmest thanks to our representatives in the late General Conference, for the stand which they took, with others, in defence of our Disciplinary rights.

"11. *Resolved*, That the bishops generally be, and they hereby are, requested, if it be congenial with their feelings, to attend the convention at Louisville.

"12. *Resolved*, That we recommend to our people the observance of the first of May next as a day of humiliation and prayer, that the Divine presence may attend the deliberations of the convention.

"John Harrell, Fountain Brown, J. B. Annis, Jacob Custer, Alexander Avery, J. F. Truslow."

The Virginia Conference adopted the following preamble and resolutions:—

"The committee to whom was referred the resolutions of the late General Conference, recommending to all the annual conferences at their first approaching sessions, to authorize a change of the sixth restrictive article, so that the first clause shall read, 'They shall not appropriate the produce of the Book Concern nor of the Chartered Fund to any purpose, other than the travelling, supernumerary, superannuated, and worn-out preachers, their wives, widows, and children, and to such other purposes as may be determined on by the votes of two-thirds of the members of the General Conference,'—and to whom was also referred the Address of the Southern delegates in the late General Conference, recommending a Southern Convention, to be held in Louisville, Kentucky, on the first day of May, 1845; together with the proceedings of various primary and quarterly conference meetings within the bounds of the Virginia Conference on the subject of a separation from the ecclesiastical jurisdiction of the General Conference of the Methodist Episcopal Church, beg leave to report:—

"That, having maturely considered these subjects, they do not deem it necessary to present an argument upon the various topics submitted to them; but that the duty assigned them will probably be more satisfactorily accomplished in the following series of resolutions, namely:—

"*Resolved*, 1. That we concur in the recommendation of the late General Conference to change the sixth restrictive article of the Discipline of our Church.

"*Resolved*, 2. That, from the ample sources of information before your committee, in numerous primary meetings, which have been held in various charges within our pastoral limits, and the proceedings of quarterly meeting conferences, which we have the most sufficient reason to regard as a fair and full exponent of the mind and will of the membership upon the subject of the action of the recent General Conference, and the propriety of division,—we are of opinion, that it is the mind of the laity of the Church, with no exception sufficient to be regarded as the basis of action, that, whilst they seriously deprecate division, considered relatively, and most earnestly wish that some ground of permanent union could have been found, they see no alternative, and therefore approve of a peaceable separation in the present circumstances of our condition; and in *this opinion* and *this determination* your committee unanimously concur.

"*Resolved*, 3. That we concur in the recommendation of the Southern delegates in the late General Conference, that there be a Southern Convention, to be held in Louisville, Kentucky, on the first day of May, 1845; and *in the objects of this convention, as are contemplated in the address of the Southern delegates.*

"*Resolved*, 4. That while we do not propose to dissolve our connexion with the Methodist Episcopal Church, but only *with the General Conference* of the Methodist Episcopal Church, we are, therefore, entitled to our full proportion of all the rights and privileges appertaining to the property of the Church. Nevertheless, our delegates to the convention to be held in Louisville, Kentucky, in May, 1845, are hereby instructed not to allow the question of property to enter into the calculation whether or not we shall exist as a separate organization.

"*Resolved*, 5. That the action of the late General Conference in the case of Bishop Andrew, was in violation of the provisional rule of the Discipline on the subject of slavery, and in derogation of the dignity and authority of the episcopal office: it was, therefore, equally opposed to the rights of the Southern portion of the Church, and to those of the incumbents of the episcopal office. But more than this: it was an effort to accomplish, by legislative action, what it was only competent for them to do, *if at all*, by regular judicial process: the very attempt was an acknowledgment that there was no rule of Discipline, under which he could either be deposed or censured, and that the General Conference, being unrestrained by the authority of law, was supreme. Thus, both the episcopal office and its incumbents were taken from under the protection of the constitutional restriction, and the provisional rule of Discipline, by which it was made a co-ordinate branch of the government, and placed at the caprice of a majority, which claims that its mere will is the law of the Church.

"Bishop Andrew, therefore, in refusing to resign his office, or otherwise yield to this unwarranted assumption of authority on the part of the General Conference, has taken a noble stand upon the platform of constitutional law, in defence of the episcopal office and the rights of the South, which entitles him to the cordial approbation and support of every friend of the Church; and we hereby tender him a unanimous expression of our admiration of his firmness in resisting the misrule of a popular majority.

"*Resolved*, 6. That we cordially approve the course of the Southern and South-Western delegates of the late General Conference, in resisting with so much constancy and firmness the encroachments of the majority upon the rights of the South, and for so faithfully warning them against the tendency of those measures, which we fear do inevitably draw after them the dissolution of our ecclesiastical union.

"John Early, Thomas Crowder, jr., Wm. A. Smith, Abram Penn, George W. Nolley, Anthony Dibrell, H. B. Cowles, D. S. Doggett, Jos. H. Davis."

"The recommendation to change the sixth restrictive article was concurred in—eighty-one in favour, and none against it, and the whole report of the committee was unanimously adopted by the conference."

The North Carolina Conference adopted the following report and resolutions:—

"The committee to whom the resolution of the late General Conference, respecting the alteration of the sixth restrictive rule, the report of the select Committee of Nine, on the declaration of the Southern delegates, and the reports of numerous voluntary meetings, both of ministers and people, within the bounds of North Carolina Conference, were referred, beg leave to report:—

"Your committee deeply regret the division of the Methodist Episcopal Church, which the course of the majority in the late General Conference renders not only necessary but inevitable. The unity of the Church, so long the boast and praise of Methodism, was a feature greatly admired, and more than esteemed by Southern Methodists. For its promotion and preservation they were willing to surrender anything but principle—vital principle. *This* they could not do!—*this* they durst not do! The course of the late General Conference demanded a submission on the part of the ministers in the slaveholding conferences, which the Discipline did not require, and the institutions of the South absolutely forbade. To have yielded, therefore, would have opened a breach in Methodism wholly subversive of the Church, and greatly mischievous to the civil community—to have yielded would have been ruin! This, therefore, they *refused to do;* absolutely refused! With the Discipline in their hands, sustained and upheld by it, they protested against the proceedings of the majority, with an unfaltering and manly voice, declaring them to be not only unauthorized, but unconstitutional. The protestation, however, just and legal as it was, authorized and borne out by the Discipline, was altogether unavailing. Nothing was left for the South to do, but to pass from under the jurisdiction of so wayward a power, to the regulations and government of our old, wholesome, and Scriptural Discipline. This, we sorrow when we say it, has opened a great gulf—we fear an impassable gulf—between the North and the South. This consolation, however, if no other, they have—the good Book of Discipline, containing the distinctive features of the Methodist Episcopal Church, shall still lie on the South side. Compelled by circumstances which could neither be alleviated nor controlled—which neither the entreaties of kindness nor the force of truth could successfully resist—we hesitate not to decide on being forever separate from those whom we not only esteem, but love. Better far that we should suffer the loss of union, than that thousands, yea millions of souls should perish.

"From the reports of quarterly meeting conferences and numerous voluntary meetings within the bounds of the North Carolina Conference, both of ministers and people, we feel assured that it is the mind of our people and preachers fully to sustain the action of the Southern and South-Western delegates, as set forth in the Declaration and Protest; and therefore,

"1. *Resolved,* That the time has come for the ministers of the Methodist Episcopal Church in the slaveholding States, to refuse to act in union with the North.

"2. *Resolved,* That we concur in the proposed alteration of the sixth restrictive rule of the Discipline.

"3. *Resolved,* That we concur in the recommendation to hold a convention in Louisville, Kentucky, in May, 1845.

"4. *Resolved,* That this conference elect delegates to said convention according to the basis of representation recommended.

"5. *Resolved,* That the action of the late General Conference, in the case of Bishop Andrew, was a violation of the rule of Discipline on the subject of slavery, and derogatory to the dignity of the episcopal office, by throwing it from under the protection of law, and exposing it to the reproach and obloquy of misrule and lawless power. The bishop, therefore, acted justly and honourably in resisting such action, and declining obedience to the resolution of said conference; and for thus guarding and respecting the rights of the South, both of ministers and people, he is entitled to our highest regards.

"All which is respectfully submitted.

"H. G. Leigh, S. S. Bryant, James Jameson, P. Doub, Bennet T. Blake, James Reid, D. B. Nicholson, R. J. Carson, William Carter."

"The above report was *unanimously* adopted by the conference. On the question of concurrence in altering the sixth restrictive rule, the vote was: ayes 58—nays none.

S. S. Bryant,
Secretary of North Carolina Annual Conference."

The following preamble and resolutions were adopted by the South Carolina Conference :—

"The committee to whom was referred the general subject of the difficulties growing out of the action of the late General Conference on the case of Bishop Andrew and brother Harding ; and, in particular, the report of the select committee on the Declaration of the Southern and South-Western delegates of the General Conference, as adopted by the conference, and the proceedings of numerous quarterly conferences, and other meetings, in all parts of our annual conference district ; respectfully offer the following report :—

"It appears to your committee, on the evidence of numerous documents, and the testimony of the preachers, in open conference, that in all the circuits and stations of this conference district, the people have expressed their minds with respect to the action of the General Conference, and the measures proper to be adopted in consequence of that action. Resolutions to that effect have been adopted by the quarterly conferences of all the circuits and stations, without any exception ; and in many, perhaps in most of them, by other meetings also, which have been called expressly for the purpose ; and in some of them, by meetings held at every preaching-place where there was a society. And on all these occasions, there has been but one voice uttered—one opinion expressed—from the sea-board to the mountains, as to the unconstitutionality and injurious character of the action in the case above-named. the necessity which that action imposes for a separation of the Southern from the Northern conferences, and the expediency and propriety of holding a convention at Louisville, Kentucky, and of your sending delegates to it, agreeably to the proposition of the Southern and South-Western delegates of the late General Conference.

"Your committee, also, have made diligent inquiry, both out of conference and by calling openly in conference, for information from the preachers, as to the number, if any, of local preachers, or other official members, or members of some standing among us, who should have expressed, in the meetings or in private, a different opinion from that which the meetings have proclaimed. And the result of this inquiry has been, that, in the whole field of our conference district, one individual only has been heard to express himself doubtfully, as to the expediency of a separate jurisdiction for the Southern and South-Western conferences ; not even one as to the character of the General Conference action. Nor does it appear that this unanimity of the people has been brought about by popular harangues, or any schismatic efforts of any of the preachers, or other influential persons ; but that it has been as spontaneous as universal, and from the time that the final action of the General Conference became known, at every place. Your committee state this fact thus formally, that it may correct certain libellous imputations which have been cast on some of our senior ministers, in the Christian Advocate and Journal ; as well as for the evidence which it furnishes of the necessity of the measures which are in progress for the relief of the Church in the South and South-West.

"Your committee also consider it due to state, that it does not appear that the action of the General Conference in the cases of the bishop and of brother Harding, proceeded of ill will, as of purpose to oppress us ; nor of any intended disregard of the authority of the Scriptures or of the Discipline, as if to effect the designs of a politico-religious faction, without warrant of the Scriptures, and against the Discipline and peace of the Church : but they consider that action as having been produced out of causes which had their origin in the fanatical abolitionism of Garrison aud others ; and which, being suffered to enter and agitate the Church, first in New-England, and afterwards generally at the North, worked up such a revival of the anti-slavery spirit as had grown too strong for the restraints of either Scripture or Discipline, and too general through the Eastern, Northern, and North-Western conferences to be resisted any longer by the easy, good-natured prudence of the brethren representing those conferences in the late General Conference. Pressed beyond their strength, whether little or much, they had to give way ; and reduced (by the force of principles which, whether by their own fault or not, had obtained a controlling power) to the alternative of breaking up the Churches of their own conference districts, or adopting measures which they might hardly persuade themselves could be endured by the South and South-West, they determined on the latter. The best of men may have their judgments perverted ; and it is not wonderful that, under such stress of circumstances, the majority should have adoped a new construction of both Scripture and Discipline, and persuaded themselves, that in pacifying the abolitionists, they were not unjust to their Southern brethren. Such, however, is unquestionably the character of the measures they adopted; and which the Southern Churches cannot possibly submit to, unless the majority who enacted them could also have brought us to a conviction that we ought to be bound by their judgment, against our consciences and calling of God, and the warrant of Scripture, and the provisions of the Discipline. But while we believe that our paramount duty in our calling of God, positively forbids our yielding the Gospel in the Southern States, to the pacification of abolitionism in the Northern; and the conviction is strong and clear in our own minds, that we have both the warrant of Scripture and the plain provisions of the Discipline to sustain us; we see no room to entertain any proposition for compromise, under the late action in the cases of Bishop Andrew and brother Harding, and the principles avowed for the maintenance of that action, short of what has been shadowed forth in the report of the select committee which we have had under consideration, and the measures recommended by the Southern and South-Western delegates at their meeting after the General Conference had closed its session.

"Your committee do, therefore, recommend the adoption of the following resolutions:—

"1. *Resolved*, That it is necessary for the annual conferences in the slaveholding States and Territories, and in Texas, to unite in a distinct ecclesiastical connexion, agreeably to the provisions of the report of the select committee of nine of the late General Conference, adopted on the 8th day of June last.

"2. *Resolved*, That we consider and esteem the adoption of the report of the aforesaid committee of nine, by the General Conference, (and the more for the unanimity with which it was adopted,) as involving the most solemn pledge which could have been given by the majority to the minority and the Churches represented by them, for the full and faithful execution of all the particulars specified and intended in that report.

"3. *Resolved*, That we approve of the recommendation of the Southern delegates, to hold a convention in Louisville, on the 1st day of May next, and will elect delegates to the same on the ratio recommended in the address of the delegates to their constituents.

"4. *Resolved*, That we earnestly request the bishops, one and all, to attend the said convention.

"5. *Resolved*, That while we do not consider the proposed convention competent to make any change or changes in the Rules of Discipline, they may nevertheless indicate what changes, if any, are deemed necessary under a separate jurisdiction of the Southern and South-Western conferences. And that *it is necessary* for the convention to resolve on, and provide for, a separate organization of these conferences under a General Conference to be constituted and empowered in all respects *for the government of these conferences*, as the General Conference hitherto has been with respect to *all* the annual conferences—according to the provisions and intentions of the late General Conference.

"6. *Resolved*, That as, in common with all our brethren of this conference district, we have deeply sympathized with Bishop Andrew in his afflictions, and believe him to have been blameless in the matter for which he has suffered, so, with them, we affectionately assure him of our approbation of his course, and receive him as not the less worthy, or less to be honoured in his episcopal character, for the action which has been had in his case.

"7. *Resolved*, That we recognise in the wisdom and prudence, the firmness and discretion, exhibited in the course of Bishop Soule, during the General Conference—as well as in former instances, wherein he has proved his devotion to the great principles of constitutional right in our Church—nothing more than was to be expected from the bosom friend of Asbury and M'Kendree.

"8. *Resolved*, That, in common with the whole body of our people, we approve of the conduct of our delegates, both during the General Conference, and subsequently.

"9. *Resolved*, That we concur in the recommendation of the late General Conference for the change of the sixth article of the restrictive rules in the book of Discipline, so as to allow an equitable pro rata division of the Book Concern.

"W. Capers, W. Smith, H. Bass, N. Talley, H. A. C. Walker, C. Betts, S. W. Capers, S. Dunwody, R. J. Boyd, *Committee*."

The Indian Mission Conference adopted the following resolutions:—

"The committee to whom was referred the action of the late General Conference relating to an amicable division of the Methodist Episcopal Church in the United States, beg leave to report the following resolutions for adoption by the conference:—

"1. *Resolved*, That we concur in the proposed alteration in the sixth restrictive article of the Discipline.

"2. *Resolved*, That we approve of the course pursued by the minority of the late General Conference.

"3. *Resolved*, That we elect delegates to represent the Indian Mission Conference in the contemplated convention to be held in Louisville, Kentucky, in May next.

"4. *Resolved*, That this conference do deeply deplore the necessity for division of any kind in the Methodist Episcopal Church; and that we will not cease to send up our prayers to Almighty God for his gracious interposition, and that he may guide the affairs of the Church to a happy issue.

"J. C. BERRYMAN, *Chairman*."

"The above report having been read, was taken up section by section, and disposed of as follows:—The first resolution was adopted, ayes 14; nays 1. The second resolution was adopted, ayes 11; nays 3; declined voting, 4. The third resolution was adopted, ayes 16. The fourth resolution was adopted, ayes 17. The preamble and resolutions were then adopted by the conference as a whole.

"The conference then proceeded, in accordance with the third resolution, to elect delegates to attend the proposed convention in Louisville, in May next. On counting the votes, it appeared that the whole number of votes given was twenty-one, of which number William H. Goode had received twenty, Edward T. Peery eighteen, scattering four. Whereupon, W. H. Goode and E. T. Peery, having received a majority of all the votes given, were declared duly elected. D. B. Cumming was then elected reserved delegate.

"The following resolutions were on the next day unanimously adopted, at the request of the delegates elect:—

"'*Resolved*, That in view of the condition of the Church, at the present trying crisis, the members of this conference will, when practicable, as near as may be, at the hour of twilight, in the evening of each day, until the close of the approaching convention at Louisville, meet each other at a throne of grace, and devoutly implore the blessing of God upon our assembled delegates in the discharge of their important duties.

"'*Resolved*, That the Friday preceding the opening of said convention, be set apart as a day of fasting and supplication to Almighty God for the continued unity, peace, and prosperity of the Methodist Episcopal Church; and that our members throughout this conference be requested to join us in the devotions of that day.

"'WM. H. GOODE,
E. T. PEERY.'"

The following preamble and resolutions were unanimously adopted by the Georgia Conference:—

"The committee appointed to take into consideration the difficulties of the Church, as growing out of the action of the General Conference in the case of Bishop Andrew, and to submit some recommendations to the annual conference for their adoption, beg leave to report:—

"The action of the majority in the last General Conference of the Methodist Episcopal Church, in the cases of Bishop Andrew and the Rev. Mr. Harding, has rendered it *indispensable* that the conferences, within whose limits slavery exists, should cease to be under the jurisdiction of that body. They must either abandon the people collected under their ministry, and committed to their pastoral care, and the vast and widening field of missionary labour among the slaves—a field to which their attention is imperatively called by their sympathies as Christians, their sense of ministerial obligation as preachers of the Gospel, and their interests and duties as citizens—or they must live under the control of an ecclesiastical body, separate and distinct from, and independent of, the conferences lying within the States and Territories where slavery is not allowed by law. In view of the relations before stated, that distinct organization is required by a *necessity* strict and *absolute*, and upon that issue we place it, before the Church and the world. The exigence which brings it upon us, arose, not out of our acts or designs; no collateral considerations of expedience abated our zeal in withstanding it; no collateral issues upon points involved, affected our determination to maintain the unity of the Church under one organization as heretofore existing; no pride of opinion, speculative differences, nor personal motives, have conducted us to this conclusion. We did not seek to effect any changes in the doctrine or Discipline of our Church; we did not ask any boon at the hands of the General Conference, nor any exemption from the operation of the laws which were common to the whole Connexion; and whatever consequences, affecting the Church or the civil community, may result from our movement, we confidently look for acquittal to the judgment of posterity, and the decision of the sober and unprejudiced among our contemporaries.

"The General Conference violated the law of the Church: first, by confirming the decision of the Baltimore Conference, suspending the Rev. Mr. Harding from his connexion with that conference as a travelling preacher therein, because he would not give freedom to slaves, which by the laws of the land he could not manumit; and secondly, by passing a resolution intended to inhibit Bishop Andrew from the exercise of his episcopal functions for the same reasons; in both cases contrary to the express provisions of the Discipline, which allows preachers to hold slaves wherever they are not permitted by the laws of the land to enjoy freedom when manumitted; and in both cases striking an effective blow at the fundamental principle of the economy of Methodism, as it destroys that general itinerancy of the preachers, which is its most distinguished peculiarity; for under their decision, preachers holding slaves in conferences where by the law of the Discipline they are allowed so to do, may not be transferred to conferences within whose limits slavery does not exist.

"By the same decision, both preachers and lay-members holding slaves are thrown into an odious and dishonoured caste, the first deprived of office therefor, and the religious character of both impeached, and thrown under suspicion thereby; to which must be added, as an evil not lightly to be regarded, nor slightly overlooked, that in connexion with the fanatical movements of abolitionists in the North, East, and West, it is well fitted to excite slaves to disaffection and rebellion, making it imperative upon governments and citizens to prohibit all communication between slaves and preachers, who either teach such doctrine, or impliedly admit it to be true by submitting to such dishonour and deprivation. Secondly. That in the case of Bishop Andrew, the General Conference have violated the Discipline of the Church and invaded personal rights, which are secured by the laws of every enlightened nation, if not by the usages of every savage people on earth. They tried and sentenced Bishop Andrew without charges preferred, or a cognizable offence stated. If it is even admitted that they intended to charge him with 'improper conduct,' as a phrase used in the Discipline to embrace every class of offences for which a bishop is amenable to the General Conference, and on conviction liable to be expelled, they did not *formally* prefer that charge; if they intended to specify his 'connexion with slavery,' as the substantive offence under that charge, a 'connexion with slavery' is not a cognizable offence under any law of our Church, written or unwritten, statutory or prescriptive, and the only 'connexion with slavery' attempted to be established in his case, is expressly permitted by the Discipline in section 10th, part 2d, on slavery. If they claimed the right to declare in their legislative capacity, that 'such a connexion with slavery' was an offence in a bishop, they could only extend it to him *retrospectively by ex post facto enactment*, and even then it was not *promulgated* until the very moment in which they pronounced his sentence by a majority vote. But we cannot admit that the framers of our Discipline ever intended to subject a bishop to the monstrous injustice of being liable to be *expelled* by the General Conference, exercising original jurisdiction, for an *impropriety* short of immorality or official delinquency, whilst they so cautiously secured his official and personal rights in all cases where that body has appellate cognizance of charges for positive immoralities; and we are confident that a fair and rational construction of the 4th and 5th questions, and their answers in the 4th section of the 1st chapter of the Discipline, will make 'improper conduct,' in the answer to the 4th question, and 'immorality,' in the 5th, descriptive of the same class of offences in the mind of the lawmaker, who could never have intended to subject that venerable officer to expulsion for offences so light, that they could not be considered immoralities or official delinquencies, and so entirely dependent for their very existence upon the caprice or varying notions of every General Conference, that they could not either be classified or designated.

"The foregoing views we consider the embodiment of public opinion throughout our conference. The sentiments of our people in primary meetings, in quarterly conferences, as expressed in the most solemn forms, sustain the course of our delegation in the General Conference, and approve and even demand an organization which shall transfer the slaveholding conferences from the jurisdiction of the North. The unanimity of the people we verily believe to be without a parallel in the history of Church action, and therefore feel ourselves perfectly justified in recommending to your body the adoption of the following resolutions, viz :—

"1. *Resolved*, That we will elect delegates to the convention to be held in Louisville, in Kentucky, on the 1st of May next, upon the basis of representation proposed and acted on by the other conferences ; viz., one delegate for every eleven members of our conference.

"2. *Resolved*, That our delegates be instructed to co-operate with the delegates from the other Southern and South-Western conferences, who shall be represented in the convention, in effecting the organization of a General Conference, which shall embrace those annual conferences, and in making all necessary arrangements for its going into operation, as soon as the acts of the said convention shall have been reported by the several delegations to their constituents, and accepted by them, according to such arrangements as may be made by the convention for carrying the same into effect.

"3. *Resolved*, That our delegates be instructed to use all prudent precautions to secure that portion of the Book Concern and Chartered Fund of the Methodist Episcopal Church, to which the annual conferences represented in the convention, shall be unitedly entitled, and all the property to which the several annual conferences are entitled to them severally ; and that to this end, they be requested to obtain the written opinions of one or more eminent lawyers ; but that in the event they must either abandon the property, or remain under the jurisdiction of the General Conference of the Methodist Episcopal Church, constituted as it now is, they be left to the exercise of a sound discretion in the premises.

"4. *Resolved*, That our delegates make a report to this body at its next session, of all their acts and doings in the aforesaid convention, and this body shall not be bound by any arrangements therein made, until after it shall have accepted and approved them in conference assembled.

"5. *Resolved*, That our delegates be, and they are hereby instructed not to agree to any alterations in the Discipline of the Methodist Episcopal Church, but that the Discipline adopted under the new organization, shall be that known and recognised as the Discipline of the Methodist Episcopal Church in the United States, with such modifications only as are necessary formally to adapt it to the new organization.

"6. *Resolved*, That we consider ourselves as an integral part of the Methodist Episcopal Church in the United States, and that we have done no act, nor do we authorize any act to be done in our name, by which our title to be so considered shall be forfeited, unless in the event contemplated in the last clause of the third resolution it becomes necessary so to do.

"7. *Resolved*, That we highly appreciate the devotion of our venerable senior bishop to the constitution and Discipline of the Church, and his uncompromising firmness in maintaining both the one and the other, and hereby assure him of our increased confidence and affection.

"8. *Resolved*, That our beloved Bishop Andrew has endeared himself to the preachers and people of the Southern Church, by resisting the constitutional dictation of the majority of the late General Conference, and that we cordially approve his whole action in the case, and welcome him to the unrestricted exercise of his episcopal functions among us.

"9. *Resolved*, That the course of our delegates in the trying circumstances by which they were surrounded during the last session of the General Conference, meets our entire approbation.

"10. *Resolved*, That we concur in the alteration of the sixth restrictive rule, as recommended by the resolution of the General Conference.

"11. *Resolved*, That we do not concur with the Holston Conference in the resolution proposed by them, regarding it as tending only to embarrass the action of the convention, without the slighest promise of good to either division of the Church.

"L. Pierce, Thomas Samford, Ignatius A. Few, Samuel Anthony, Isaac Boring, George F. Pierce, Joan W. Talley, W. D. Matthews, J. B. Payne, Josiah Lewis."

"It was further resolved, that the bishops of the Methodist Episcopal Church be requested to attend the convention of Southern delegates to be held at Louisville in May next."

The following report was unanimously adopted by the Florida Conference :—

"The committee to whom was referred the subject of the action of the late General Conference in the cases of Bishop Andrew and F. A. Harding; also the report of the committee of nine in the late General Conference on the subject of a peaceable separation of the Church; also the resolution of the Holston Conference on the same subject, submit the following resolutions, to wit :—

"1. *Resolved,* That we disapprove of the course of the late General Conference in the cases of Bishop Andrew and F. A. Harding.

"2. That we heartily approve the proposed Plan of Separation as adopted by the General Conference, under which the Southern and South-Western conferences are authorized to unite in a distinct ecclesiastical connexion.

"3. That we are satisfied that the peace and success of the Church in the South demand a separate and distinct organization.

"4. That we commend and admire the firm and manly course pursued by Bishop Andrew under the trials he has had to encounter, and that we still regard him as possessing all his episcopal functions.

"5. That the course pursued by our venerable senior superintendent, Bishop Soule, in defending the Discipline of our Church, has served but to endear him to us more and more, and we heartily approve his course in inviting Bishop Andrew to assist him in his episcopal visitations.

"6. That we tender our warmest thanks to all those brethren who voted in the minority in Bishop Andrew's case.

"7. That we approve of the proposed convention to be held in Louisville the first of May next, and will proceed to elect delegates to said convention.

"8. That *we do not* concur in the resolution of the Holston Conference, proposing the election of delegates for forming a plan of compromise.

"9. That *we do* concur in the recommendation of the late General Conference for the change of the sixth article in the restrictive rules in the Book of Discipline, allowing an equitable *pro rata* division of the Book Concern.

"P. P. Smith, T. C. Benning, R. H. Lucky, J. W. Yarbrough, R. H. Howren, W. W. Griffin, A. Peeler, A. Martin, S. P. Richardson."

The Texas Conference adopted the following report and resolutions :—

"The committee to whom were referred certain acts of the late General Conference, causing and providing for a division of the Methodist Episcopal Church, or the General Conference thereof, and sundry communications pertaining thereto, have had the same under solemn and prayerful consideration, and beg leave to present the following report :—

"In view of the numerous expositions and arguments, *pro* and *con*, with which the Christian Advocates have teemed for some months, on the merits of the highly-important subject upon which your committee have been called to act, they presume that the conference is too well enlightened to need an elaborate and argumentative investigation of them, in their multifarious relations and bearings; they, therefore, respectfully present the following resolutions, as the result of their deliberations :—

"*Resolved,* 1. That we approve of the course of the Southern and South-Western delegates in the late General Conference; and that their independent and faithful discharge of duty, in a trying crisis, commands our admiration and merits our thanks.

"2. That we deeply deplore the increasingly-fearful controversy between the Northern and Southern divisions of the Methodist Episcopal Church, on the institution of domestic slavery, and that we will not cease to pray most fervently to the great Head of the Church for his gracious interposition in guiding this controversy to a happy issue.

"3. That we approve the appointment of a convention of delegates from the conferences in the slaveholding States, in the city of Louisville, on the first of May next, by the Southern and South-Western delegates in the late General Conference; and also, the ratio of representation proposed by said delegates—to wit, one delegate for every eleven members of the Conference; and that we will elect delegates to the proposed convention upon said basis, to act under the following instructions, to wit: To endeavour to secure a compromise between the North and South; to oppose a formal division of the Church before the General Conference of 1848, or a general convention can be convened to decide the present controversy. But should a division be deemed unavoidable, and be determined on by the convention, then, being well satisfied with the Discipline of the Church, as it is, we instruct our delegates not to support or favour any change in said Discipline, by said convention, other than to adapt its fiscal economy to the Southern organization.

"4. That we approve of the dignified and prudent course of the bench of bishops, who presided in the late General Conference.

"5. That it is the sense of this conference, that the Rev. John Clarke, one of our delegates to the late General Conference, entirely misrepresented our views and sentiments, in his votes in the cases of Rev. F. A. Harding and Bishop Andrew.

"6. That we appoint the Friday immediately preceding the meeting of the proposed general convention of the delegates of the Southern and South-Western conferences, as a day of fasting and prayer for the blessing of Almighty God on said convention, that it may be favoured with the healthful influence of his grace, and the guidance of his wisdom.

"Chauncey Richardson, Robert Alexander, Samuel A. Williams:"

The Alabama Conference adopted the following preamble and resolutions.—

"The committee appointed by the conference to take into consideration the subject of a separate jurisdiction for the Southern conferences of the Methodist Episcopal Church, beg leave to report: That they have meditated with prayerful solicitude on this important matter, and have solemnly concluded on the necessity of the measure. They suppose it to be superfluous to review formally all the proceedings which constitute the unhappy controversy between the Northern and Southern portions of our Church, inasmuch as their sentiments can be expressed in one sentence,—They endorse the unanswerable Protest of the minority in the late General Conference. They believe that the doctrines of that imperishable document cannot be successfully assailed. They are firm in the conviction that the action of the majority in the case of Bishop Andrew was unconstitutional. Being but a delegated body, the General Conference has no legitimate right to tamper with the office of a general superintendent—his amenableness to that body and liability to expulsion by it, having exclusive reference to mal-administration, ceasing to travel, and immoral conduct. They are of opinion that Bishop Andrew's connexion with slavery can come under none of these heads. If the entire eldership of the Church, in a conventional capacity, were to constitute non-slaveholding or even abolitionism a tenure by which the episcopal office should be held, or if they were to abolish the office, they doubtless could plead the abstract right thus to modify or revolutionize the Church in its supreme executive administration; but before the General Conference can justly plead this right, it must show when and where such plenary power was delegated to it by the *only fountain of authority—the entire pastorate of the Church.* Your committee are, therefore, of opinion, that the General Conference has no more power over a bishop, except in the specified cases of mal-administration, ceasing to travel, and immorality, than over the episcopacy, as an integral part of our ecclesiastical polity. It can no more depose a bishop for slaveholding than it can create a new Church.

"Your committee deeply regret that these 'conservative' sentiments did not occur to the majority in the late General Conference, and that the apologists of that body, since its session, have given them no place in their ecclesiastical creed, but on the contrary have given fearful evidence that the proceedings in the case of Bishop Andrew are but the incipiency of a course, which, when finished, will leave not a solitary slaveholder in the communion which shall be unfortunately under their control. The foregoing sentiments and opinions embody the general views expressed most unequivocally throughout the conference district since the late General Conference, by the large body of the membership, both in *primary meetings* and quarterly conferences.

"The committee, therefore, offer to the calm consideration and mature action of the Alabama Annual Conference, the following series of resolutions:—

"1. *Resolved*, That this conference deeply deplores the action of the late General Conference of the Methodist Episcopal Church in the case of our venerable superintendent, Bishop Andrew, believing it to be unconstitutional, being as totally destitute of warrant from the Discipline as from the word of God.

"2. That the almost-unanimous agreement of Northern Methodists with the majority, and Southern Methodists with the minority of the late General Conference, shows the wisdom of that body in suggesting a duality of jurisdiction to meet the present emergency.

"3. That this conference agrees to the proposition for the alteration of the sixth restrictive rule of the Discipline.

"4. That this conference approves of the projected convention at Louisville, in May next.

"5. That this conference most respectfully invites all the bishops to attend the proposed convention at Louisville.

"6. That this conference is decided in its attachment to Methodism, as it exists in the Book of Discipline, and hopes that the Louisville convention will not make the slightest alteration, except so far as may be absolutely necessary for the formation of a separate jurisdiction.

"7. That every preacher of this conference shall take up a collection in his station or circuit, as soon as practicable, to defray the expenses of the delegates to the convention; and the proceeds of such collection shall be immediately paid over to the nearest delegate or presiding elder, and the excess or deficit of the collection for the said expenses shall be reported to the next conference, which shall take action on the same.

"8. That the Friday immediately preceding the session of the convention, shall be observed in all our circuits and stations, as a day of fasting and prayer for the blessings of God upon its deliberations.

"9. That whilst this conference fully appreciates the commendable motives which induced the Holston Conference to suggest another expedient to compromise the differences existing between the Northern and Southern divisions of the Church, it nevertheless cannot concur in the proposition of that conference concerning that matter.

"10. That this conference fully recognises the right of our excellent superintendent, Bishop Soule, to invite Bishop Andrew to share with him the responsibilities of the episcopal office; and while the conference regrets the absence of the *former*, it rejoices in being favoured with the efficient services of the *latter*—it respectfully tenders these 'true yoke-fellows' in the superintendency the fullest approbation, the most fervent prayers, and the most cordial sympathies.

"Thos. O. Summers, A. H. Mitchell, E. V. Levert, J. Hamilton, E. Hearn, W. Murrah, J. Boring, Geo. Shaeffer, C. McLeod."

Bishop Soule's letter of adhesion, and Bishop Andrew's letter, both of which were addressed to the convention at Louisville, are as follows:—

"Dear Brethren,—I feel myself bound in good faith, to carry out the official plan of episcopal visitations as settled by the bishops in New-York, and published in the official papers of the Church, until the session of the first General Conference of the Methodist Episcopal Church, South; from which time it would be necessary that the plan should be so changed as to be accommodated to the jurisdiction of the two distinct General Conferences. That when such Southern General Conference shall be held, I shall feel myself fully authorized by the Plan of Separation, adopted by the General Conference of 1844, to unite myself with the Methodist Episcopal Church, South, and if received by the General Conference of said Church, to exercise the functions of the episcopal office within the jurisdiction of said General Conference.

"*Louisville, Ky., May* 19, 1845. Joshua Soule."

"Dear Brethren,—I decidedly approve the course which the convention has taken in establishing the Methodist Episcopal Church, South, believing, as I do most sincerely, that it will tend, under God's blessing, to the wider spread and more efficient propagation of the Gospel of the grace of God. I accept the invitation of the convention to act as one of the superintendents of the Methodist Episcopal Church, South, and pledge myself, in humble dependence upon Divine grace, to use my best efforts to promote the cause of God in the interesting and extensive field of labour assigned me.

"May the blessing of God be upon us mutually, in our laborious field of action, and, finally, may we all, with our several charges, be gathered to the home of God and the good in heaven! Affectionately your brother and fellow-labourer,

"*Louisville, May*, 1845. JAMES O. ANDREW."

The Pastoral Address referred to by Mr. Lord was in these words:—

"To the ministers of the several annual conferences of the Methodist Episcopal Church, South, and to all the brethren of their pastoral oversight, the convention of said annual conferences address this letter, with Christian salutation.

"We gratefully regard it matter of congratulation, beloved brethren, for which our thanks should be offered at the throne of grace, that we have been enabled to conduct the business confided to us by you, with great harmony, and except, perhaps, some inconsiderable shades of difference on points of minor import, with unexampled unanimity. Our agreement on all questions of importance, has probably been as perfect as the weakness of human knowledge might allow, or reason should require.

"For full information of all that we have done, we refer you to the journal of our proceedings, and the documents which accompany it; particularly the reports of the committee on organization and on missions. This latter interest we have made the subject of a special letter, wishing to bring it immediately to the notice of all our Churches and congregations, (to whom we have requested the letter might be read,) to engage their instant liberality.

"We made it a point of early inquiry, in the course of our proceedings, to ascertain with what unanimity the annual conferences represented by us, and the entire body of the ministry and membership within their general bounds, were known to have concurred in sustaining the Declaration of the Southern delegates in the late General Conference, and in approving of the Plan provided by that Conference for our being constituted a distinct ecclesiastical connexion, separate from the North. The committee on organization, being composed of two members from each of the annual conferences, was furnished with ample means of obtaining satisfactory information. The members of the committee held meetings with their several delegations apart, and on a comparison of their several reports carefully made, it was found, that both as to the members of the annual conferences, and the local ministry and membership of our entire territory, the declaration had been sustained, and a separate organization called for, by as great majority as *ninety-five to five*. Nor did it appear that *even five in a hundred* were disposed to array themselves against their brethren, whose interests were identical with their own; but that part were Northern brethren sojourning in our borders, and part were dwelling in sections of the country where the questions involved did not materially concern their Christian privileges, or those of the slaves among them. So great appears to have been the unanimity of opinion prevailing, both among the pastors and the people, as to the urgent necessity of the great measure which we were deputed to effect, by organizing on the basis of the Discipline, and the Plan provided by the late General Conference, THE METHODIST EPISCOPAL CHURCH, SOUTH.

"That on so grave a question, concerning interests so sacred, and affecting so numerous a people, spread over the vast extent of the country from Missouri to the Atlantic Ocean, and from Virginia to Texas, there should be found some who dissent, is what we could not but expect. But that the number dissenting should have been so small, compared to the number of those who have required us to act, is, at least to our minds, conclusive proof of the absolute necessity of this action, as affording the only means left in our power to preserve the Church in the more Southern States from hopeless ruin. Indeed the action of the late General Conference, without the intervention of the Declaration of the Southern delegates, and the provisional Plan for a separate Southern connexion, must have immediately broken up all our missions to the people of colour, and subjected their classes in most of the Southern circuits to ruinous deprivations. Of this, the evidence has been unquestionable. And it must appear to you, brethren, that for whatever reason so great an evil was threatened for a cause which the Southern delegates did nothing to produce, but resisted in the General Conference, *that* evil could not fail of being inflicted with redoubled violence, and to a still greater extent, if we, having a platform legally furnished for a separate organization, should hesitate a moment to avail ourselves of it. It would be, in effect, to put ourselves, in relation to the laws and policy of the Southern people, in the same position which was so injuriously offensive in our Northern brethren, while it could not be plead in extenuation of the fault, that we were Northern men, and ignorant of the state of affairs at the South. Into such a position we could not possibly put ourselves; nor can we think that reasonable men would require us to do so.

"We avow, brethren, and we do it with the greatest solemnity, that while we have thus been laid under the imperative force of an absolute necessity to organize the Southern and South-Western conferences into an independent ecclesiastical connexion, whose jurisdiction shall be exclusive of all interference on the part of the North, we do not withdraw from the true Christian and catholic pale of the Methodist Episcopal Church. And that whilst we have complained, with grievous cause, of the power of the majority of the General Conference, as that power has been construed and exercised, we have not complained, and have no complaint, against the Church in itself. The General Conference, or a majority thereof, is not the Church. Nor is it possible that that should be the Methodist Episcopal Church, which withdraws the ministry of the Gospel from the poor, and turns her aside from her calling of God, 'to spread Scripture holiness over these lands,' in order to fulfil some other errand, no matter what. We could not be Methodists at all, as we have been taught what Methodism is, if, with our knowledge of its nature, its aim, its constitution, its discipline, and of the ruin inevitable to the work of the ministry in most of the Southern States, if not in all of them, we should still cleave to a Northern jurisdiction; we nevertheless could not be persuaded to yield the Gospel for a jurisdictional affinity with brethren, who, we believe in our hearts, cannot govern us without great injury to the cause of Christ in most parts of our work. If we err, it is the spirit of Methodism which prompts us to the error. We 'call God for a record,' that, as far as we know our hearts, we intend nothing, we desire nothing, we do nothing, having any other object or aim, but that the Gospel may be preached, without let or hindrance, in all parts of our country, and especially to the poor. There is nothing belonging of right to the Church—her doctrines, her discipline,her economy, her usages, her efficiency—which we do not cherish in our inmost hearts. It is not the Church, not anything proper to the Church, in her character as Christ's body, and consecrated to the promotion of his cause in the earth, which we would disown, or depart from, or oppose; but only such a position *in* the Church as some of her sons would force us into, antagonistic to her principles, her policy, and her calling of God. Nor yet can we be charged with any factious or schismatic opposition to the General Conference, for we have done nothing, and mean to do nothing, not authorized by express enactment of that body, in view of the very emergency which compels our action.

"It had been too much to expect, considering the weakness of men, that, suddenly roused to resistance, as the Southern Churches were, by the unlooked-for action in the cases of Bishop Andrew and brother Harding, there should not, in some instances, have escaped expressions of resentment and unkindness. Or that, put to the defence of the majority of the General Conference, where the evil complained of was so serious, the advocates of that majority should not sometimes have expressed themselves in terms which seemed harsh and unjust. We deeply deplore it, and pray that, for the time to come, such exhibitions of a mortifying frailty may give place to Christian moderation. We invoke the spirit of peace and holiness. That brother shall be esteemed as deserving best, who shall do most for the promotion of peace. Surely this is a time of all others, in our day, when we should seek and pursue peace. A continuance of strife between North and South must prove prejudicial on both sides. The separation is made—formally, legally made—and let peace ensue. In Christ's name let there be peace. Whatever is needful to be done, or worth the doing, may be done in peace. We especially exhort brethren of the border conferences and societies, to forbear each other in love, and labour after peace. Let every one abide by the law of the General Conference, with respect to our bounds, and choose for himself with Christian temper, and permit others to choose without molestation, between North and South. Our chief care should be to maintain 'the unity of the Spirit in the bond of peace.' Methodism, preserved in what makes it one the world over—the purity of its doctrines, the efficiency of its discipline, its unworldliness, its zeal for God, its self-devotion—is of infinitely greater value than a question of boundary or General Conference jurisdiction merely.

"And now, brethren, beseeching you to receive the word of exhortation which we have herein briefly addressed to you, and humbly invoking the blessings of God upon you, according to the riches of his grace in Christ our Lord, praying for you, as we always do, that you may abound in every good work, and confiding in your prayers for us, that we may be found one with you in faith and charity at the appearing of Jesus Christ, we take leave of you, and return from the work which we have now fulfilled, to renew our labours with you and among you in the Lord.

"James O. Andrew, *President*.

"Thomas O. Summers, *Secretary*.

"Louisville, *Kentucky*, May 16, 1845."

The report of the Committee on Organization, on page 67, which Mr. Lord commended to the attention of the Court as an able document, containing nearly all the argument on that side, is in these words:—

"The committee appointed to inquire into the propriety and necessity of a separate organization of the annual conferences of the Methodist Episcopal Church in the slaveholding States, for the purpose of a separate General Conference connexion and jurisdiction, within the limits of said States and conferences, having had the entire subject under careful and patient consideration, together with the numerous petitions, instructions, resolutions, and propositions for adjustment and compromise, referred to them by the convention, offer the following as their

"REPORT.

"In view of the extent to which the great questions in controversy, between the North and the South of the Methodist Episcopal Church, have been discussed, and by consequence must be understood by the parties more immediately interested, it has not been deemed necessary by the committee to enter into any formal or elaborate examination of the general subject, beyond a plain and comprehensive statement of the facts and principles involved, which may place it in the power of all concerned, to do justice to the convictions and motives of the Southern portion of the Church, in resisting the action of the late General Conference on the subject of slavery, and its unconstitutional assumption of right and power in other respects; and also presenting, in a form as brief and lucid as possible, some of the principal grounds of action, had in view by the South, in favouring the provisional Plan of Separation, adopted by the General Conference at its last session.

"On the subject of the legitimate right, and the full and proper authority of the convention to institute, determine, and finally act upon the inquiry, referred to the committee to deliberate and report upon, the committee entertain no doubt whatever. Apart from every other consideration which might be brought to bear upon the question, the General Conference of 1844, in the Plan of jurisdictional Separation adopted by that body, gave full and express authority to 'the annual conferences in the slaveholding States,' to judge of the propriety, and decide upon the necessity, of organizing a 'separate ecclesiastical connexion' in the South. And not only did the General Conference invest this right in 'the annual conferences in the slaveholding States,' without limitation or reserve, as to the *extent* of the investment, and *exclusively* with regard to every other division of the Church, and all other branches or powers of the government, but left the method of official determination and the mode of action, in the exercise or assertion of the right, to the free and untrammelled discretion of the conferences interested. These conferences, thus accredited by the General Conference to judge and act for themselves, confided the right and trust of decision and action, in the premises, to delegates regularly chosen by these bodies respectively, upon a uniform principle and fixed ratio of representation, previously agreed upon by each, in constitutional session, and directed them to meet in general convention, in the city of Louisville, May, 1845, for this and other purposes, authorized by the General Conference, at the same time and in the same way. All the right and power, therefore, of the General Conference, in any way connected with the important decision in question, were duly and formally transferred to 'the annual conferences in the slaveholding States,' and exclusively invested in them. And as this investment was obviously for the purpose, that such right and power might be exercised by them, in any mode they might prefer, not inconsistent with the terms and conditions of the investment, the delegates thus chosen, one hundred in number, and representing sixteen annual conferences, under commission of the General Conference, here and now assembled in convention, have not only all the right and power of the General Conference, as transferred to 'the annual conferences in the slaveholding States,' but in addition, all the right and power of necessity inherent in these bodies, as constituent parties, giving birth and power to the General Conference itself, as the common federal council of the Church. It follows hence, that for all the purposes specified and understood in this preliminary view of the subject, the convention possesses all the right and power, both of the General Conference and the sixteen 'annual conferences in the slaveholding States,' jointly and severally considered. The ecclesiastical and conventional right, therefore, of this body, to act in the premises, and act conclusively, irrespective of the whole Church, and all its powers of government beside, is clear and undoubted. As the *moral* right, however, to act as proposed in the General Conference Plan of jurisdictional Separation, rests upon entirely different grounds, and will perhaps be considered as furnishing the only allowable warrant of action, notwithstanding constitutional right, it may be necessary at least to glance at the grave moral reasons, creating the necessity, the high moral compulsions, by which the Southern conferences and Church have been impelled to the course of action, which it is the intention of this report to explain and vindicate, as not only right and reasonable, but indispensable to the character and welfare of Southern Methodism.

"The preceding statements and reasoning, present no new principle or form of action in the history of the Church. Numerous instances might be cited, in the constitutional history of Church polity, in which high moral necessity, in the absence of any recognised conventional right, has furnished the only and yet sufficient warrant for ecclesiastical movements and arrangements, precisely similar in character with that contemplated in the plan of a separate Southern Connexion of the Methodist Episcopal Church, adopted by the late General Conference. Wesleyan Methodism, in all its phases and aspects, is a most pertinent illustration of the truth we assume, and the fitness and force of the example must go far to preclude the necessity of any other proof. It was on the specific basis of such necessity, without conventional right, that the great Wesleyan Conference arose in England. It was upon the same basis, as avowed by Wesley, that the American Connexion became separate and independent, and this Connexion again avows the same principle of action, in the separation and establishment of a Methodist Episcopal Church in Canada, whose organization took place by permission and direction of the same authority, under which this convention is now acting for a similar purpose.

"Should it appear in the premises of the action proposed, that a high moral and religious duty is devolved upon the ministry and membership of the Methodist Episcopal Church, in the South,—devolved upon us by the Great Head of the Church, and the providential appointments of our social condition, which we cannot neglect without infidelity to a high moral trust, but which we cannot fulfil in connexional union with the Northern portion of the Church, under the same General Conference jurisdiction, owing to causes connected with the civil institutions of the country, and beyond the control of the Church,—*then* a strong moral necessity is laid upon us, which assumes the commanding character of a positive duty, under sanction of Divine right, to dissolve the ties and bonds of a single General Conference jurisdiction, and in its place substitute one in the South, which will not obstruct us in the performance of duty, or prevent us from accomplishing the great objects of the Christian ministry and Church organization. From a careful survey of the entire field of facts and their relations—the whole range of cause and effect, as connected with the subject-matter of this report—it is confidently believed that the great warrant of *moral necessity*, not less than unquestionable ecclesiastical right, fully justified this convention in the position they are about to take, as a separate organic division of the Methodist Episcopal Church, by authority of its chief synod,—'the delegates of all the several annual conferences in General Conference assembled.' One of the two main issues, which have decided the action of the Southern conferences, relates, as all know, to the assumed right of the Church to control the question of slavery, by means of the ordinary and fluctuating provisions of Church legislation, without reference to the superior control of State policy and civil law. From all the evidence accessible in the case, the great masses of the ministry and membership of the Methodist Episcopal Church, North and South, present an irreconcilable opposition of conviction and feeling on the subject of slavery, so far as relates to the rights of the Church to interfere with the question—the one claiming unlimited right of interference to the full extent the Church may, at any time or from any cause, be concerned; and the other resisting alike the assumption or exercise of any such right, because, in nearly all the slaveholding States, such a course of action must bring the Church in direct conflict with the civil authority, to which the Church has pledged subjection and support in the most solemn and explicit forms, and from the obligations of which she cannot retreat without dishonouring her own laws, and the neglect and violation of some of the plain and most imperative requirements of Christianity. Under such circumstances of disagreement—in such a state of adverse conviction and feeling on the part of the North and South of the Church—it is believed that the two great sections of the Church, thus situated, in relation to each other, by causes beyond the control of either party, cannot remain together and successfully prosecute the high and common aims of the Christian ministry and Church organization, under the same General Conference jurisdiction. The manifest want of uniformity of opinion and harmony of co-operation, must always lead, as heretofore, to struggles and results directly inconsistent with the original intention of the Church, in establishing a common jurisdiction, to control all its general interests. And should it appear that, by a division and future duality of such jurisdiction, as authorized by the late General Conference, the original purposes of the Church can better be accomplished, or rather, that they can be accomplished in no other way, how can the true and proper unity of the Church be maintained except by yielding to the necessity, and having a separate General Conference jurisdiction for each division? By the Southern portion of the Church generally, slavery is regarded as strictly a civil institution, exclusively in custody of the civil power, and as a regulation of State beyond the reach of Church interference or control, except as civil law and right may be infringed by ecclesiastical assumption. By the Northern portion of the Church, individuals are held responsible for the alleged *injustice* and *evil* of relations and rights, created and protected by the organic and municipal laws of the government and country, and which relations and rights, in more than two-thirds of the slaveholding States, are not under individual control in any sense or to any extent.

"Both portions of the Church are presumed to act from principle and conviction, and cannot, therefore, recede; and *how*, under *such* circumstances, is it possible to prevent the most fearful disunion, with all the attendant evils of contention and strife, except by allowing each section a separate and independent jurisdiction, the same in character and purpose with the one to which both have hitherto been subject? What fact, truth, or principle, not merely of human origin, and therefore of doubtful authority, can be urged, as interposing any reasonable obstacle to a change of jurisdiction, merely *modal* in character, and simply designed to adapt a single principle of Church government, not pretended to be of Divine obligation or Scripture origin, to the character and features of the civil government of the country? Nothing essential to Church organization; nothing essentially distinctive of Methodism,—even American Methodism,—is proposed to be disturbed, or even touched, by the arrangement. It is a simple division of general jurisdiction, for strong moral reasons, arising out of the civil relations and position of the parties, intending to accomplish for both, what it is demonstrated by experiment cannot be accomplished by one common jurisdiction, as now constituted, and should, therefore, under the stress of such moral necessity, be attempted in some other way.

"The question of slavery, more or less intimately interwoven with the interests and destiny of nine millions of human beings, in the United States, is certainly of sufficient importance, coming up as it has in the recent history of the Methodist Episcopal Church, and as it does in the deliberations of this convention, to authorize any merely *modal* or even organic changes in the government of the Church, should it appear obvious that the original and avowed purposes of the Church will be more effectively secured and promoted by the change proposed, than by continuing the present or former system. The evidence before the committee, establishes the fact in the clearest manner possible, that, throughout the Southern conferences, the ministry and membership of the Church, amounting to nearly 500,000, in the proportion of about ninety-five in the hundred, deem a division of jurisdiction indispensable to the welfare of the Church, in the Southern and South-Western conferences of the slaveholding States; and this fact alone, must go far to establish the *right*, while it demonstrates the *necessity*, of the separate jurisdiction, contemplated in the Plan of General Conference, and adopted by that body in view of such necessity, as likely to exist The interests of State, civil law, and public opinion, in the South, imperiously require, that the Southern portion of the Church shall have no part in the *discussion* and agitation of this subject in the chief councils of the Church. In this opinion, nearly universal in the South, we *concur*.

"Christ and his apostles—Christianity and its inspired and early teachers—found slavery in its most offensive and aggravated forms, as a civil institution, diffused and existing throughout nearly the entire field of their administrations and influence; and yet, in the New Testament and earlier records of the Church, we have no legislation—no interference—no denunciation with regard to it, not even remonstrance against it. They found it wrought up and vitally intermingled with the whole machinery of civil government and order of society—so implicated with 'the powers that be,' that Infinite Wisdom, and the early pastoral guides of the Church, saw just reason why the Church should not interfere beyond a plain and urgent enforcement of the various duties growing out of the peculiar relation of master and slave, leaving *the relation* itself, as a civil arrangement, untouched and unaffected, except so far as it seems obviously to have been the Divine purpose to remove every form and degree of wrong and evil connected with the institutions of human government, by a faithful inculcation of the doctrines and duties of Christianity, without meddling in any way with the civil polity of the countries into which it was introduced. A course precisely similar to this, the example of which should have been more attractive, was pursued by the great founder of Methodism, in all slaveholding countries in which he established societies. Mr. Wesley never deemed it proper to have any rule, law, or regulation on the subject of slavery, either in the United States, the West Indies, or elsewhere. The effects of the early and unfortunate attempts of the Methodist Church to meddle and interfere, in the *legislation* and *practice* of government and discipline, with the institution of slavery in the United States, are too well known to require comment. Among the more immediate results of this short-sighted, disastrous imprudence, especially from 1780 to 1804, may be mentioned the watchful jealousy of civil government, and the loss of public confidence throughout a very large and influential portion of the whole Southern community. These, and similar developments, led the Church, by the most careful and considerate steps, to the adoption, gradually, of a medium compromise course of legislation on the subject; until the law of slavery, as it now exists in the *letter* of Discipline, became, by the last material act of legislation in 1816, the great compromise bond of union between the North and the South on the subject of slavery. The whole law of the Church—all there is in the statute-book, to govern North and South on this subject—is the following:—*First:* The general rule, which simply prohibits 'the buying or selling of men, women, or children, with an *intention to enslave them.*' *Second:* 'No slaveholder shall be eligible to any official station in our Church hereafter, where the laws of the State in which he lives admit of emancipation, and permit the liberated slave to enjoy freedom. When any travelling preacher becomes an owner of a slave or slaves, by any means, he shall forfeit his ministerial character in our Church, unless he execute, if it be practicable, a legal emancipation of such slaves, conformably to the laws of the State in which he lives.'

"Here is the law, the *whole*, the *only* law of the Church, containing, first, a *prohibition*, and, second, a *grant*. The prohibition is, that no member or minister of the Church, is allowed to purchase or sell a human being, who is to be *enslaved*, or *reduced to a state of slavery*, by such purchase or sale. And further, that no minister, in *any of the grades* of ministerial office, or other person, having official standing in the Church, can, if he be the owner of a slave, be allowed to sustain such official relation to the Church, unless he shall legally provide for the emancipation of such slave or slaves, if the laws of the State in which he lives will admit of legal emancipation, and permit the liberated slave to enjoy freedom. Such is the plain *prohibition* of law, binding upon all. The *grant* of the law, however, is equally plain and unquestionable. It is, that persons *may* purchase or sell men, women, or children, provided such purchase or sale does not involve the fact or intention of enslaving them, or of *reducing the subjects* of such purchase or sale *to a state of slavery*. The intention of the law no doubt is, that this may be done from motives of humanity, and not by any means for the purpose of gain. But further, the law distinctly provides, that every minister, *in whatever grade of office*, and every person having *official standing of any kind* in the Methodist Episcopal Church, being the owner or owners of slave property, shall be protected against any forfeiture of right, on this account, where the laws of the State do not admit of legal emancipation, and allow the liberated slave to enjoy freedom in the State in which he is emancipated. Here is the plain *grant of law* to which we allude. From the first agitation of the subject of slavery in the Church, the Northern portion of it has been disposed to insist upon further *prohibitory* enactments. The South, meanwhile, has always shown itself ready to go as far, by way of prohibition, as the law in question implies, but has uniformly resisted any attempt to impair Southern rights under protection of the grant of law to which we have asked attention. Under such circumstances of disagreement and difficulty, the conventional and legislative adjustment of the question, as found in the General Rule, but especially the tenth section of the Discipline, was brought about, and has always been regarded in the South as a great compromise arrangement, without strict adherence to which, the North and the South could not remain together under the same general jurisdiction. That we have not mistaken the character of the law, or misconstrued the intention and purposes of its enactment, at different times, we think entirely demonstrable from the whole history both of the legistation of the Church and the judicial and executive administration of the government. The full force and bearing of the law, however, were more distinctly brought in view, and authoritatively asserted, by the General Conference of 1840, after the most careful examination of the whole subject, and the judicial determination of that body, connected with the language of the Discipline, just quoted, gives in still clearer light *the true and only law of the Church* on the subject of slavery. After deciding various other principles and positions incidental to the main question, the decision is summed up in the following words:—'While the general rule (or law) on the subject of slavery, relating to those States whose laws admit of emancipation, and permit the liberated slave to enjoy freedom, should be firmly and constantly enforced, the exception to the general rule (or law) applying to those States where emancipation, as defined above, is *not practicable*, should be recognised and protected with equal firmness and impartiality; therefore—

"'*Resolved by the several annual conferences in General Conference assembled*, That under the provisional exception of the general rule (or law) of the Church, on the subject of slavery, the simple holding of slaves, or mere ownership of slave property, in States or Territories where the laws do not admit of emancipation and permit the liberated slave to enjoy freedom, constitutes *no legal barrier* to the election or ordination of ministers to the various grades of office known in the ministry of the Methodist Episcopal Church, and cannot, therefore, be considered as operating *any forfeiture* of right, in view of such election and ordination.' This decision of the General Conference was not objected to or dissented from by a single member of that body. It was the unanimous voice of the great representative and judicial council of the Church, then acting in the character of a high court of appeals for the decision of an important legal question. It will be perceived how strikingly the language of this decision accords with *both* the features of the law of slavery which we have thought important to notice—the *prohibition* and the *grant* of law in the case; what may *not* be done as the general rule, and at the same time what *may be done*, under the provisional exception to the general law, without forfeiture of right of any kind. It is also worthy of particular notice, that besides the plain assurance of the original law, that where emancipation is not legally practicable, and the emancipated slave allowed to enjoy freedom, or where it is practicable to emancipate, but the emancipated slave cannot enjoy freedom, emancipation is not required of any owner of slaves in the Methodist Episcopal Church, from the lowest officer up to the bishop, but the rights of all thus circumstanced are protected and secured, notwithstanding their connexion with slavery. Besides this, the full and elaborate decision of the General Conference, as a grave and formal adjudication had upon all the issues involved in the question, published to all who where in, or might be disposed to enter the Church, that the law of slavery applied to States where emancipation is impracticable, and the freed slave not allowed to enjoy freedom, this clear and unambiguous decision, by the highest authority of the Church, *leaves* the owner of slaves upon the ground—upon a basis—of the most perfect equality with *other* ministers of the Church having no connexion with slavery. Such, then, is the law; such its construction; such the official and solemn pledge of the Church. And these had, to a great extent, restored the lost confidence and allayed the jealous apprehensions of the South, in relation to the purposes of the Church respecting slavery. There was in the South no disposition to disturb, discuss, or in any way agitate the subject. The law was not objected to or complained of, but was regarded as a settled compromise between the parties, a medium arrangement on the ground of mutual concession, well calculated to secure and promote the best interests of the Church, North and South.

"That this law—this great compromise conservative arrangement, which had been looked to as the only reliable bond of jurisdictional union between the North and South for nearly half a century—was practically disregarded and abandoned by the last General Conference, in the memorable cases of Harding and Andrew, both by judicial construction and virtual legislation, manifestly inconsistent with its provisions and purposes, and subversive of the great objects of its enactment, has been too fearfully demonstrated by various forms of proof, to require more than a brief notice in this report. The actual position of the Church was suddenly reversed, and its long-established policy entirely changed. The whole law of the Church and the most important adjudications had upon it, were treated as null and obsolete, and that body proceeded to a claim of right, and course of action, amounting to a virtual repeal of all law, and new and capricious legislation on the most difficult and delicate question ever introduced into the councils of the Church, or named upon its statute-book.

"By no fair construction of the law of slavery as given above, could the Church be brought in conflict with civil legislation on the subject. It is true, as demanded by the convictions and opinions of the Church, testimony was borne against the evil of slavery, but it was done without conflicting with the polity and laws of any portion of the country. No law, for example, affected the lay-membership of the Church with regard to slaveholding; the Church gave its full permission that the private members of the Church might own and hold slaves at discretion; and the inference is indubitable, that the Church did not consider simple slaveholding *as a moral evil*, personally attaching to the mere fact of being the owner or holder of slaves. The evil charged upon slavery must of necessity have been understood of other aspects of the subject, and could not imply moral obliquity, without impeaching the integrity and virtue of the Church. Moreover, where the laws precluded emancipation, the ministry were subjected to no disabilities of any kind, and the requirements of the Church, in relation to slavery, were not at least in anything like direct conflict with civil law. In contravention, however, of the plain and long-established law of the Church, the action of the General Conference of 1844, in the well-known instances cited, brought the Church into a state of direct and violent antagonism with the civil authority and the rights of citizenship, throughout all the slaveholding States. This was not done by the repeal of existing law, or additional legislation by direct enactment, but in a much more dangerous form, by the simple process of resolution by an irresponsible majority, requiring Southern ministers as slaveholders, in order to Church eligibility and equality of right with non-slaveholding ministers of the Church, to do what cannot be done without a violation of the laws of the States in which they reside, and is not required or contemplated, but expressly excepted, and even provided against, by the law of the Church.

"It will thus appear that the entire action of the General Conference on the subject of slavery, was in direct conflict with the law, both of the Church and the land, and could not have been submitted to by the South, without the most serious detriment to the interests of the Church. The action in the instance of Bishop Andrew, was, in the strongest and most exceptionable sense, extra-judicial. It was not pretended that Bishop Andrew had violated any law of the Church; so far from this, the only law applicable to the case, gave, as we have seen, ample and explicit assurance of protection. So to construe law, or so proceed to act without reference to law, as to abstract from it its whole protective power, and deprive it of all its conservative tendencies in the system, is one of the most dangerous forms of legal injustice, and, as a principle of action, must be considered as subversive of all order and government. The late General Conference required of Bishop Andrew, the same being equally true in the case of Harding, as the condition of his being acceptable to the Church, the surrender of rights secured to him, both by civil and ecclesiastical law. The purposes of law were contravened and destroyed, and its prerogative and place usurped by mere opinion.

"The requisition in the case was not only extra-judicial, being made in the absence of anything like law authorizing the measure, but being made at the same time against law, it was usurpation; and so far as the proceeding complained of is intended to establish a principle of action with regard to the future, it gives to the General Conference all the attributes of a despotism, claiming the right to govern *without, above*, and *against law*. The doctrine avowed at the late General Conference, and practically endorsed by the majority, that that body may, by simple resolution, advisory, punitive, or declaratory, repeal an existing law in relation to a particular case, leaving it in full force with regard to other cases ; or may enact a new and different law, and apply it judicially to the individual case, which led to the enactment, and all in a moment, by a single elevation of the hand, is a position, a doctrine so utterly revolutionary and disorganizing, as to place in jeopardy at once, both the interests and reputation of the Church. The action in the case of Bishop Andrew, not only assumed the character, and usurped the place of law, but was clearly an instance of *ex post facto* legislation, by making that an offence after the act, which was not such before. The conduct charged as an offence, was at the time, and continues to be, under the full protection of a well-understood and standing law of the Church, and yet this conduct was made criminal and punishable by the retrospective action of the Conference to which we allude. The officially-expressed will of the General Conference, intended to govern and circumscribe the conduct of Bishop Andrew, without reference to existing law, and indeed contrary to it, was made the rule of action, and he found guilty of its violation, by acts done before he was made acquainted with it. The conduct charged was in perfect consistency with the law of the Church, and could only be wrought into an offence by an *ex post facto* bearing of the after action of the General Conference.

"Bishop Andrew became the owner of slave property involuntarily, several years before his marriage, and as the *fact*, and not the *extent* of his connexion with slavery, constituted his offence, it follows, that for a relation in which he was placed by the action of others, and the operation of civil law, and in which, as a citizen of Georgia, he was compelled to remain, or be brought in conflict with the laws of the State, he *was*, in violation of the pledge of public law, as we have shown, arrested and punished by the General Conference. That body, by direct requirement, such at least by implication, commanded him to free his slaves, or suffer official degradation. The law of Georgia required him to hold his slaves, or transfer them to be held as such by others, under heavy and painful penalties to master and slave. To avoid ecclesiastical punishment and disability, the Church required him either to leave the State of his residence, or violate its laws. In this way, taking the judicial decision in Harding's case, and the anomalous action in Bishop Andrew's, the Church is placed in most offensive conflict with the civil authority of the state. Can any country or government safely allow the Church to enforce disobedience to civil law, as a Christian duty? If such attempts are made to subordinate the civil interests of the state to the schemes and purposes of Church innovation, prompted and sustained by the bigotry and fanaticism of large masses of ignorant and misguided zealots engaged in the conflict in the name of God and conscience, and for the ostensible purposes of religious reform, what can be the stability of civil government, or the hopes of those seeking its protection? And what, we ask, must be the interests of the South, in connexion with such movements?

"In the instance of slavery in this country, it is but too well-known, that such antagonism as is indicated by the preceding facts and developments between the purposes of the Church and the policy of the State, must result in the most disastrous consequences to both. The slavery of the Southern States can never be reduced in amount, or mitigated in form, by such a state of things. The Southern States have the sole control of the question, under the authority and by contract of the federal constitution, and all hope of removing the evil of slavery, without destroying the national compact and the union of the States, must connect with the individual sovereignty of the Southern States, as parties to the federal compact, and the independent policy of each State in relation to slavery, as likely to be influenced by moral and political reasons and motives, brought to bear, by proper means and methods, upon the understanding and moral sense of the Southern people. All trespass upon right—whether as it regards the rights of property or of character—everything like aggression, mere denunciation or abuse, must of necessity tend to provoke further resistance on the part of the South, and lessen the influence the North might otherwise have upon the great mass of the Southern people, in relation to this great and exciting interest. The true character and actual relations of slavery in the United States, are *so predominantly civil and political*, that any attempt to treat the subject or control the question upon purely moral and ecclesiastical grounds, can never exert any salutary influence South, except in so far as the moral and ecclesiastical shall be found strictly subordinate to the civil and political. This mode of appeal, it is believed, will never satisfy the North. The whole Northern portion of the Church, speaking through their guides and leaders, is manifesting an increasing disposition to form issues upon the subject, so utterly inconsistent with the rights and peace of the slaveholding States, that by how far the Methodist Episcopal Church, in the South, may contribute to the bringing about of such a state of things, or may fail to resist it, the influence of Methodism must be depressed, and the interests of the Church suffer. In addition, then, to the fact, that we have already received an amount of injury, beyond what we can bear, except under a separate organization, we have the strongest grounds of apprehension, that unless we place ourselves in a state of defence, and prepare for independent action, under the distinct jurisdiction we are now authorized by the General Conference to resolve upon and organize, we shall soon find ourselves so completely subjected to the adverse views and policy of the Northern majority, as to be left without right or remedy, except as a mere secession from the Church. Now, the case is entirely different, as we propose to do nothing not authorized in the General Conference Plan of Separation, either expressly or by necessary implication. The general view thus far taken of the subject, is intended to show, that 'the annual conferences in the slaveholding States,' embracing the entire Church, South, have found themselves placed in circumstances, by the action of the General Conference in May last, which, according to the Declaration of the Southern delegates, at the time, render it impracticable to accomplish the objects of the Christian ministry and Church organization under the present system of General Conference control, and showing by the most clear and conclusive evidence, that there exists the most urgent necessity for the 'separate ecclesiastical connexion,' constitutionally provided for by the General Conference upon the basis of the Declaration, just adverted to. At the date of the Declaration, the Southern delegates were fully convinced that the frequent and exciting agitation and action in that body on the subject of slavery and abolition—as in Harding's case, and especially the proceedings in the case of Bishop Andrew—each being regarded as but a practical exposition of the principle of the majority—rendered a *separate organization* indispensable to the success of Methodism in the South. The truth of the Declaration, so far from being called in question, by the majority, was promptly conceded in the immediate action the Conference had upon it, assigning the Declaration as the sole ground or reason of the action, which terminated in the adoption of the Plan of Separation, under which we are now acting, as a convention, and from the spirit and intention of which, it is believed to be the purpose of the convention not to depart, in any of its deliberations or final acts. Although the action of this General Conference on the subject of slavery, and the relative adverse position of the parties North and South, together with the irritating and exasperating evils of constant agitation and frequent attempts at legislation, are made, in the Declaration, the grounds of the avowal, that a separate organization was necessary to the success of the ministry in the slaveholding States, it was by no means intended to convey the idea, or make the impression, that no other causes existed rendering a separate organization proper and necessary; but as the action of the Conference on the subject of slavery, was certain to involve the Church in the South in immediate and alarming difficulty, and it was believed that this could be so shown to the majority, as to induce them to consent to some course of action in remedy of the evil, the complaint of the declaration was confined to the simple topic of slavery. It will be perceived that the case of Bishop Andrew, although prominently introduced, is not relied upon as exclusively furnishing the data of this conclusion at which we have arrived. The entire action of the General Conference, so frequently brought to view, and which is made the ground of dissent and action, both in the Protest and Declaration of the Southern delegates, must be understood, as belonging to the premises and language employed, as including all the principles avowed as well as the action had by the late General Conference on the subject of slavery. The attempt to disclaim the judicial character of the action in Bishop Andrew's case, and show it to be merely advisory, cannot affect the preceding reasoning: for, first, the disclaimer is as equivocal in character as the original action; and, secondly, the reasoning in support of the disclaimer negatives the supposition of mere advice, because it involves issues coming legitimately within the province of judicial process and legal determination; and, thirdly, Bishop Andrew is, by the explanation of the disclaimer itself, held as responsible for his conduct, in view of the alleged advice, as he could have been held by the original action without the explanation. While, therefore, the explanation giving the original action an *advisory* character, notwithstanding the inconsistency involved, fully protects Bishops Soule and Andrew from even the shadow of blame in the course they have pursued, the entire action in the case, and especially when connected with the case of Harding, as alluded to in the Declaration, fully sustains the general view of the subject we have taken in this report. The Southern delegates at the General Conference, in presenting to that body their Declaration and Protest, acted, and they continue to act, as the representatives of the South, under the full conviction that the principles and policy avowed by the Northern majority, are such as to render their *public* and *practical renunciation* by the Southern Methodist ministry and people, necessary to the safety, not less than the success of the Church in the South.

"Other views of the subject, however, must claim a share of our attention. Among the many weighty reasons which influence the Southern conferences in seeking to be released from the jurisdiction of the General Conference of the Methodist Episcopal Church, as now constituted, are the novel, and, as we think, dangerous doctrines, practically avowed and endorsed by that body and the Northern portion of the Church generally, with regard to the *constitution* of the Church, and the constitutional rights and powers respectively of the episcopacy and the General Conference. In relation to the first, it is confidently, although most unaccountably, maintained that the six short *restrictive rules*, which were adopted in 1808, and first became obligatory, as an amendment to the constitution, in 1812, are in fact the *true* and *only* constitution of the Church. This single position, should it become an established principle of action to the extent it found favour with the last General Conference, must subvert the government of the Methodist Episcopal Church. It must be seen at once, that the position leaves many of the organic laws and most important institutions of the Church entirely unprotected, and at the mercy of a mere and ever-fluctuating majority of the General Conference. Episcopacy, for example, although protected in the abstract, in general terms, may be entirely superseded or destroyed by the simple omission to elect or consecrate bishops, neither of which is provided for in the restrictive articles. The whole itinerant system, except general superintendency, is without protection in the restrictive rules; and there is nothing in them preventing the episcopacy from restricting their superintendency to *local* and *settled* pastors, rather than a travelling ministry, and thus destroying the most distinctive feature of Wesleyan Methodism. So far as the restrictive rules are concerned, the annual conferences are without protection, and might also be destroyed by the General Conference at any time. If the new constitutional theory be correct, class-leaders and private members are as eligible, upon the basis of the constitution, to a seat in the General Conference, as any ministers of the Church. Societies, too, instead of annual conferences, may elect delegates, and may elect *laymen* instead of ministers, or local instead of travelling ministers. Very few indeed of the more fundamental and distinguishing elements of Methodism, deeply and imperishably imbedded in the affection and veneration of the Church, and vital to its very existence, are even alluded to in the restrictive articles. This theory assumes the self-refuted absurdity, that the General Conference is in fact the government of the Church, if not the Church itself. With no other constitution than these mere restrictions upon the powers and rights of the General Conference, the government and discipline of the Methodist Episcopal Church, as a system of organized laws and well-adjusted instrumentalities for the spread of the Gospel and the diffusion of piety, and whose living principles of energy and action have so long commanded the admiration of the world, would soon cease even to exist. The startling assumption, that a bishop of the Methodist Episcopal Church, instead of holding office under the constitution, and by tenure of law, and the faithful performance of duty, is nothing in his character of bishop, but a mere officer, at will, of the General Conference, and may accordingly be deposed at any time, with or without cause, accusation, proof, or form of trial, as a dominant majority may capriciously elect, or party interests suggest; and that the General Conference may do, by right, whatever is not prohibited by the restrictive rules; and, with this single exception, possess power, 'supreme and all-controlling,' and this, in all possible forms of its manifestation, legislative, judicial, and executive; the same men claiming to be at the same time both the fountain and functionaries of all the powers of government, which powers, thus mingled and concentrated into a common force, may at any time be employed at the prompting of their own interests, caprice, or ambition;—such wild and revolutionary assumptions, so unlike the faith and discipline of Methodism, as we have been taught them, we are compelled to regard as fraught with mischief and ruin to the best interests of the Church, and as furnishing a strong additional reason why we should avail ourselves of the warrant we now have, but may never again obtain, from the General Conference, to 'establish an ecclesiastical connexion,' embracing only the annual conferences in the slaveholding States.

"Without intending anything more than a general specification of the disabilities, under which the Southern part of the Church labours, in view of existing difficulties, and must continue to do so until they are removed, we must not omit to state, that should we submit to the action of the late General Conference, and decline a separate organization, it would be to place and finally confirm the whole Southern ministry in the relation of an *inferior caste*, the effect of which, in spite of all effort to the contrary, would be such a relation, if not (as we think) real degradation, of the ministry, as to destroy its influence to a great, a most fearful extent throughout the South. A practical proscription, under show of legal right, has long been exercised towards the South, with regard to the higher offices of the Church, especially the episcopacy. To this, however, the South submitted with patient endurance, and was willing further to submit, in order to maintain the peace and unity of the Church, while the *principle* involved was disavowed, and decided to be unjust, as by the decision of the General Conference in 1840. But when, in 1844, the General Conference declared by their action, without the forms of legislative or judicial process, that the mere providential ownership of slave property, in a State where emancipation is legally prohibited under all circumstances, and can only be effected by special legislative enactment, was hereafter to operate as a forfeiture of right in all similar cases, the law of the Church and the decision of the preceding General Conference to the contrary notwithstanding, the Southern ministry were compelled to realize, that they were deliberately fixed by the brand of common shame, in the degrading relation of standing inferiority to ministers, not actually, nor yet liable to be, connected with slavery, and that they were published to the Church and the world as belonging to a *caste* in the ministry, from which the higher officers of the Church could never be selected.

"To submit, under such circumstances, would have been a practical, a most humiliating recognition of the *inferiority of caste*, attempted to be fixed upon us by the Northern majority, and would have justly authorized the inference of a want of conscious integrity and self-respect, well calculated to destroy both the reputation and influence of the ministry in all the slaveholding States. It may be no virtue to avow it, but we confess we have no humility courting the grace of such a baptism. The higher objects, therefore, of the Christian ministry, not less than conscious right and self-respect, demanded resistance on the part of the Southern ministry and Church; and these unite with other reasons, in vindicating the plea of necessity, upon which the meeting and action of this convention are based, with the consent and approval of the General Conference of the Methodist Episcopal Church. The variety of interests involved, renders it necessary that the brief view of the subject we are allowed to take, be varied accordingly.

"Unless the Southern conferences organize as proposed, it is morally certain, in view of the evidence before the committee, that the Gospel, now regularly and successfully dispensed by the ministers of these conferences to about a million of slaves, in their various fields of missionary enterprise and pastoral charge, must, to a great extent, be withheld from them, and immense masses of this unfortunate class of our fellow-beings be left to perish, as the result of Church interference with the civil affairs and relations of the country.

"The committee are compelled to believe, that the mere division of jurisdiction, as authorized by the General Conference, cannot affect either the moral or legal unity of the great American family of Christians, known as the Methodist Episcopal Church, and this opinion is concurred in by the ablest jurists of the country. We do nothing but what we are *expressly authorized to do* by the supreme, or rather highest legislative power of the Church. Would the Church authorize us to do wrong? The division relates only to the power of general jurisdiction, which it is not proposed to destroy or even reduce, but simply to invest it in two great organs of Church action and control, instead of one as at present. Such a change in the present system of general control, cannot disturb the moral unity of the Church; for it is strictly an *agreed modification* of General Conference jurisdiction, and such agreement and consent of parties must preclude the idea of disunion. In view of *what* is the alleged disunion predicated? Is the purpose and act of becoming a separate organization proof of disunion or want of proper Church unity? This cannot be urged with any show of consistency, inasmuch as 'the several annual conferences in General Conference assembled,' that is to say, the Church through only its constitutional organ of action, on all subjects involving the power of legislation, not only agreed to the separate organization South, but made full constitutional provision for carrying it into effect. It is a separation by consent of parties, under the highest authority of the Church. Is it intended to maintain, that the unity of the Church depends upon the modal uniformity of the jurisdiction in question? If this be so, the Methodist Episcopal Church has lost its unity at several different times. The general jurisdiction of the Church has undergone modifications, at several different times, not less vital, if not greatly more so, than the one now proposed. The high conventional powers, of which we are so often reminded, exercised in the organization of the Methodist Episcopal Church, were in the hands of a conference of unordained lay preachers, under the sole superintendence of an appointee of Mr. Wesley. This was the first General Conference type and original form of the jurisdiction in question. The jurisdictional power now proposed by the General Conference, was for years exercised by small annual conferences, without any defined boundaries, and acting separately on all measures proposed for their determination. This general power of jurisdiction next passed into the hands of the bishops' council, consisting of some ten persons, where it remained for a term of years. Next, it passed into the hands of the whole itinerant ministry, in full connexion, and was exercised by them, in collective action, as a General Conference of the whole body, met together at the same time. The power was afterwards vested in the whole body of travelling elders, and from thence finally passed into the hands of delegates, elected by the annual conferences, to meet and act quadrennially as a General Conference, under constitutional restrictions and limitations. Here are several successive re-organizations of General Conference jurisdiction, each involving a much more material change than that contemplated in the General Conference plan, by authority of which this Convention is about to erect the sixteen annual conferences in the slaveholding States into a separate organization. We change no principle in the existing theory of General Conference jurisdiction. We distinctly recognise the jurisdiction of a delegated General Conference, receiving its appointment and authority from the whole constituency of annual conferences. The only change in fact or form, will be, that the delegates of the 'annual conferences in the slaveholding States,' as authorized in the Plan of Separation, will meet in one General Conference assembly of their own, and act in behalf only of their own constituency, and in the regulation of their own affairs, consistently with the good faith and fealty they owe the authority and laws of the several States in which they reside, without interfering with affairs beyond their jurisdiction, or suffering foreign interference with their own. And in proceeding to do this, we have all the authority it was in the power of the Methodist Episcopal Church to confer. We have, also, further, example and precedent in the history of Methodism, to show that there is nothing irregular or inconsistent with Church order or unity in the separation proposed. The great Wesleyan Methodist family, everywhere one in faith and practice, already exists under several distinct and unconnected jurisdictions—there is no jurisdictional or connexional union between them; and yet it has never been pretended that these several distinct organizations were in any sense inconsistent with Church unity. If the Southern conferences proceed, then, to the establishment of another distinct jurisdiction, without any change of doctrine or discipline, except in matters necessary to the mere economical adjustment of the system, will it furnish any reason for supposing that the real unity of the Church is affected by what all must perceive to be a simple division of jurisdiction? When the conferences in the slaveholding States are separately organized as a distinct ecclesiastical Connexion, they will only be what the General Conference authorized them to be. Can this be irregular or subversive of Church unity? Acting under the provisional Plan of Separation, they must, although a separate organization, remain in essential union with, and be a part and parcel of, the Methodist Episcopal Church, in every Scriptural and moral view of the subject; for what they do is with the full consent, and has the official sanction of the Church as represented in the General Conference.

The jurisdiction we are about to establish and assert as separate and independent, is expressly declined and ceded by the General Conference, as originally its own, to the Southern Conferences, for the specific purpose of being established and asserted in the manner proposed. All idea of secession, or an organization alien in right or relation to the Methodist Episcopal Church, is forever precluded by the terms and conditions of the authorized Plan of Separation. In whatever sense we are *separatists* or *seceders*, we are such by authority—the *highest* authority of the Methodist Episcopal Church. To whatever extent, or in whatever aspect we are not true and faithful ministers and members of that Church, such delinquency or misfortune is authenticated by her act and approval, and she declares us to be 'without blame.' 'Ministers of every grade and office in the Methodist Episcopal Church, may, as they prefer, without blame, attach themselves to the Church, South.' Bishops, elders, and deacons, come into the Southern organization at their own election, under permission from the General Conference, not only accredited as ministers of the Methodist Episcopal Church, but with credentials *limiting* the exercise of their functions *within the Methodist Episcopal Church.* Is it conceivable that the General Conference would so act and hold such language in relation to an ecclesiastical Connexion, which was to be regarded as a secession from the Church? Do not such act and language, and the whole Plan of Separation, rather show that, as the South had asked, so the General Conference intended to authorize, a simple division of its own jurisdiction, and nothing more?

"All idea of secession, or schism, or loss of right or title, as ministers of the Methodist Episcopal Church, being precluded by the specific grant or authority under which we act, as well as for other reasons assigned, many considerations might be urged, strongly suggesting the *fitness* and *propriety* of the separate jurisdiction contemplated, rendered *necessary*, as we have seen, upon *other* and *different* grounds; and among these the increased value of the representative principle, likely to be secured by the change, is by no means unworthy of notice. At the first representative General Conference, thirty-three years ago, each delegate represented five travelling ministers and about two thousand members, and the body was of convenient size for the transaction of business. At the late General Conference, each delegate was the representative of twenty-one ministers and more than five thousand members, and the body was inconveniently large for the purpose of deliberation and action. Should the number of delegates in the General Conference be increased with the probable growth of the Church, the body will soon become utterly unwieldy. Should the number be reduced, while the ministry and membership are multiplying, the representative principle would become to be little more than nominal, and, in the same proportion, without practical value. Besides that the proposed re-organization of jurisdiction will remedy this evil, at least to a great extent, it will result in the saving of much time and expense, and useful services to the Church, connected with the travel and protracted sessions of the General Conference, not only as it regards the delegates, but also the bench of bishops, whose general oversight might become much more minute and pastoral in its character, by means of such an arrangement. When, in 1808, the annual conferences resolved upon changing the form of General Conference jurisdiction, the precise reasons we have just noticed were deemed sufficient ground and motive for the change introduced; and as we are seeking only a similar change of jurisdiction, although for other purposes as well as this, the facts to which we ask attention are certainly worthy of being taken into the estimate of advantages likely to result from a separate and independent organization, especially as the ministry and membership, since 1808, have increased *full seven hundred per centum*, and should they continue to increase, in something like the same ratio, for thirty years to come, under the present system of General Conference jurisdiction, some such change as that authorized by the late General Conference must be resorted to, or the Church resign itself to the virtual extinction of the representative principle, as an important element of government action.

"In establishing a separate jurisdiction as before defined and explained, so far from affecting the moral oneness and integrity of the great Methodist body in America, the effect will be to secure a very different result. In resolving upon a separate Connexion, as we are about to do, the one great and controlling motive is to restore and perpetuate the peace and unity of the Church. At present we have neither; nor are we likely to have, should the Southern and Northern conferences remain in connexional relation, as heretofore. Inferring effects from causes known to be in existence and active operation, agitation on the subject of slavery is certain to continue, and frequent action in the General Conference is equally certain, and the result, as heretofore, will be excitement and discontent, aggression and resistance. Should the South retire and decline all further conflict, by the erection of the Southern conferences into a separate jurisdiction, as authorized by the General Conference plan, agitation in the Church cannot be brought in contact with the South, and the former irritation and evils of the controversy must, to a great extent, cease, or at any rate so lose their disturbing force as to become comparatively harmless. Should the Northern Church continue to discuss and agitate, it will be within their own borders and among themselves, and the evil effects upon the South must, to say the least, be greatly lessened. At present, the consolidation of all the annual conferences, under the jurisdictional control of one General Conference, always giving a decided Northern majority, places it in the power of that majority to manage and control the interests of the Church, in the slaveholding States, as they see proper, and we have no means of protection against the evils certain to be inflicted upon us, if we judge the future from the past. The whole power of legislation is in the General Conference, and as that body is now constituted, the annual conferences of the South are perfectly powerless in the resistance of wrong, and have no alternative left them but unconditional submission. And such submission to the views and action of the Northern majority on the subject of slavery, it is now demonstrated, must bring disaster and ruin upon Southern Methodism, by rendering the Church an object of distrust on the part of the state. In this way, the assumed *conservative power* of the Methodist Episcopal Church, with regard to the *civil union* of the States, is to a great extent destroyed, and we are compelled to believe that it is the *interest* and becomes the *duty* of the Church in the South to seek to exert *such conservative influence* in some *other* form; and after the most mature deliberation and careful examination of the whole subject, we know of nothing so likely to effect the object, as the jurisdictional separation of the great Church parties, unfortunately involved in a religious and ecclesiastical controversy about an affair of state—a question of civil policy—over which the Church has no control, and with which, it is believed, she has no right to interfere. Among the nearly five hundred thousand ministers and members of the conferences represented in this convention, we do not know *one* not *deeply* and *intensely* interested in the *safety* and *perpetuity* of the *National Union*, nor can we for a moment hesitate *to pledge them all* against *any* course of *action* or *policy*, not calculated, in their judgment, *to render that union as immortal as the hopes of patriotism would have it to be!*

"Before closing the summary view of the whole subject taken in this report, we cannot refrain from a brief notice of the relations and interests of Southern border conferences. These, it must be obvious, are materially different from those of the more Southern conferences. They do not, for the present, feel the pressure of the strong necessity impelling the South proper to immediate separation. They are, however, involved with regard to the subject-matter of the controversy, and committed to well-defined principles, in the same way, and to the same extent, with the most Southern conferences. They have with almost perfect unanimity, by public official acts, protested against the entire action of the late General Conference on the subject of slavery, and in reference to the relative rights and powers of episcopacy and the General Conference, as not only *unconstitutional*, but *revolutionary*, and, therefore, dangerous to the best interests of the Church. They have solemnly declared, by approving and endorsing the Declaration, the Protest, and Address of the Southern delegates, that the objects of their ministry cannot be accomplished, under the existing jurisdiction of the General Conference, without reparation for past injury and security against future aggression; and unless the border conferences have good and substantial reasons to believe such reparation and security not only *probable*, but so certain as to remove *reasonable* doubt, they have, so far as *principle* and pledge are concerned, the same motive for action with the conferences South of them. Against the principles thus avowed by every one of the conferences in question, the anti-slavery and abolition of the North have, through official Church organs, declared the most open and undisguised hostility, and these conferences are reduced to the necessity of deciding upon *adherence* to the principles they have officially avowed, or of a resort to expediency to adjust difficulties in some unknown form, which they have said could only be adjusted by substantial reparation for past injury, and good and sufficient warrant against future aggression. The question is certainly one of no common interest. Should any of the border conferences, or societies South, affiliate with the North, the effect, so far as we can see, will be to transfer the seat of war to the remoter South—to these border districts; and what, we ask, will be the security of these districts against the moral ravages of such a war? What protection or security will the *Discipline*, or the *conservatism* of the middle conferences afford? Of what avail were *these* at the last General Conference, and has *either* more influence now than then? The controversy of a large and rapidly-increasing portion of the North, is not so much with the *South* as with the *Discipline*, because it tolerates slavery *in any form* whatever; and should the Southern conferences remain under the present common jurisdiction, or any slaveholding portions of the South unite in the Northern Connexion in the event of division, it requires very little discernment to see that *this controversy* will never cease until every slaveholder or every abolitionist is out of the Connexion. Besides, the border conferences have a great and most delicate interest at stake, in view of their *territorial*, and *civil*, and *political* relations, which it certainly behooves them to weigh well and examine with care in coming to the final conclusion, which is to identify them with the North or the South. Border districts going with the North, after and notwithstanding the action of the border conferences, must, in the nature of things, as found in the Methodist Episcopal Church, affiliate, to a great extent, with the entire aggregate of Northern anti-slavery and abolition, as now embarked against the interests of the South; as also with all the recent official violations of right, of law, and Discipline, against which the South is now contending. In doing this, they must of necessity, if we have reasoned correctly, elect, and contribute their influence, to retain in the Connexion of their choice all the principles and elements of strife and discord which have so long and fearfully convulsed the Church. Will this be the election of Southern border sections and districts, or will they remain where, by location, civil and political ties and relations, and their own avowed principles, they properly belong—firmly planted upon the long and well-tried platform of the Discipline of our common choice, and from which the Methodism of the South has never manifested any disposition to swerve? To the Discipline the South has always been loyal. By it she has *abided* in every trial. Jealously has she cherished and guarded that "form of sound words"—the faith, the ritual, and the government of the Church. It was Southern defence against Northern invasion of the Discipline, which brought on the present struggle; and upon the Discipline, the whole Discipline, the South proposes to organize, under authority of the General Conference, a separate Connexion of the Methodist Episcopal Church. The result, from first to last, has been consented to on the part of the South with the greatest reluctance.

"After the struggle came on, at the late General Conference, the Southern delegates, as they had often done before, manifested the most earnest desire, and did all in their power, to maintain jurisdictional union with the North, without sacrificing the interests of the South: when this was found impracticable, a *connexional* union was proposed, and the rejection of this, by the North, led to the *projection* and *adoption* of the present General Conference Plan of Separation. Every overture of compromise, every plan of reconciliation and adjustment, regarded as at all eligible, or likely to succeed, was offered by the South and rejected by the North. All subsequent attempts at compromise, have failed in like manner, and the probability of any such adjustment, if not extinct, is lessening every day, and the annual conferences in the slaveholding States are thus left to take their position upon the ground assigned them by the General Conference of 1844, as a distinct ecclesiastical Connexion, ready and most willing to treat with the Northern division of the Church, at any time, in view of adjusting the difficulties of this controversy, upon terms and principles which may be safe and satisfactory to both.

"Such we regard as the *true position of the annual conferences* represented *in this convention. Therefore, in view of all the principles and interests involved*, appealing to the *Almighty Searcher of hearts, for the sincerity of our motives, and humbly invoking the Divine blessing upon our action*,

"*Be it resolved, by the delegates of the several annual conferences of the Methodist Episcopal Church, in the slaveholding States, in General Convention assembled*, That it is right, expedient, and necessary, to erect the annual conferences, represented in this convention, into a distinct ecclesiastical Connexion, separate from the jurisdiction of the General Conference of the Methodist Episcopal Church, as at present constituted; and, accordingly, we, the delegates of said annual conferences, acting under the provisional Plan of Separation adopted by the General Conference of 1844, do solemnly *declare* the jurisdiction hitherto exercised over said annual conferences, by the General Conference of the Methodist Episcopal Church, *entirely dissolved*; and that said annual conferences shall be, and they hereby *are constituted* a separate ecclesiastical Connexion, under the provisional Plan of Separation aforesaid, and based upon the Discipline of the Methodist Episcopal Church, comprehending the doctrines, and entire moral, ecclesiastical, and economical rules and regulations of said Discipline, except only in so far as verbal alterations may be necessary to a distinct organization, and to be known by the style and title of the *Methodist Episcopal Church, South.*

"*Resolved*, That Bishops Soule and Andrew be, and they are hereby respectfully and cordially requested by this convention to unite with, and become regular and constitutional bishops of the Methodist Episcopal Church, South, upon the basis of the Plan of Separation adopted by the late General Conference.

Resolved, That this convention request the bishops presiding at the ensuing sessions of the border conferences of the Methodist Episcopal Church, South, to incorporate into the aforesaid conferences any societies, or stations adjoining the line of division, provided such societies or stations, by the majority of the members, according to the provisions of the Plan of Separation aforesaid, request such an arrangement.

"*Resolved*, That answer the 2d of 3d Section, Chapter 1st, of the Book of Discipline be so altered and amended as to read as follows: 'The General Conference shall meet on the 1st of May, in the year of our Lord, 1846, in the town of Petersburg, Va., and thenceforward, in the month of April or May, once in four years successively, and in such place and on such day as shall be fixed on by the preceding General Conference,' &c.

"*Resolved*, That the first answer in the same chapter, be altered by striking out the word '*twenty-one*,' and inserting in its place the word '*fourteen*,' so as to entitle each annual conference to one delegate for every fourteen members.

"*Resolved*, That a committee of three be appointed, whose duty it shall be to prepare and report to the General Conference of 1846, a revised copy of the present Discipline, with such changes as are necessary to conform it to the organization of the Methodist Episcopal Church, South.

"*Resolved*, That while we cannot abandon or compromise the principles of action upon which we proceed to a separate organization in the South, nevertheless, cherishing a sincere desire to maintain Christian union and fraternal intercourse with the Church, North, we shall always be ready, kindly and respectfully to entertain, and duly and carefully consider, any proposition or plan, having for its object, the union of the two great bodies, in the North and South, whether such proposed union be *jurisdictional* or *connexional*."

The following are Bishop Soule's letter of invitation to Bishop Andrew to perform episcopal functions, and Bishop Andrew's reply:—

"LEBANON, OHIO, Sept. 26, 1844.

"*To the Rev. James O. Andrew, D.D., Bishop of the Methodist Episcopal Church.*

"MY DEAR BISHOP,—Since the close of the recent eventful session of the General Conference, I have been watching, with deep solicitude, the 'signs of the times,' and tracing causes, as far as I was able, to their ultimate issues. Some *general* results, growing out of the action of the Conference, it required no prophetic vision to foresee. To prevent the measures which, in my judgment, would lead to these results with demonstrative certainty, I laboured day and night with prayers and tears, till the deed was done,—the eventful resolution passed. From that perilous hour my hands hung down, discouragement filled my heart, and the last hope of the *unity* of our beloved Zion well-nigh fled from *earth* to *heaven*. My last effort to avert the threatening storm appears in the joint recommendation of all the bishops to suspend all action in the case until the ensuing General Conference. At the presentation of this document some brethren perceived that instead of *light*, the darkness around them was increased tenfold. *Others will judge*, have judged already. And those who come after us will examine the history of our acts. The document was *respectfully* laid upon the table, probably under the influence of deep regret that 'our bishops should enter the arena of controversy in the General Conference.' *But it cannot—does not sleep there.* I have heard many excellent ministers, and distinguished laymen in our own communion, not in the slave States, refer to it as a measure of sound Christian policy, and with deep regret that the Conference had not adopted it. Many of our Northern brethren seem now deeply to deplore the division of their Church. O that there had been *forethought*, as well as *afterthought!* I have seen various plans of compromise for the adjustment of our differences and preservation of the unity of the Church. The most prominent plan provides that a fundamental article in the treaty shall be, that no abolitionist or slaveholder shall be eligible to the office of a bishop in the Methodist Episcopal Church. Alas for us! Where are our men of wisdom, of experience? Where are our fathers and brethren who have analyzed the elements of civil or ecclesiastical compacts? Who are the 'high contracting parties?' and will they create a *caste* in the constitutional eldership in the Church of Christ? Will this tend to harmonize and consolidate the body? Brethren, North and South, *will know* that the *cause* must be removed that the *effect* may cease; that the *fountain* must be dried up before the *stream* will cease to flow. But I must pause on this subject. The time has not fully arrived for me to define my position in regard to the causes and remedies of the evils which now agitate and distract our once-united and peaceful body. Still I trust I have given such proofs at different times, and under different circumstances, as not to render my position *doubtful* in the judgment of sober, discriminating men, either North or South. The General Conference spake in the language of wisdom and sound Christian policy, when, in the pastoral address of 1836, it solemnly and affectionately *advised* the ministers and members of the Church to abstain from all agitation of the exciting subject of slavery and its abolition. Nor was the adoption of the report of the committee on the memorial of our brethren from a portion of Virginia, within the bounds of the Baltimore Conference, less distinguished by the same characteristics of our holy Christianity, and the sound policy of our Discipline in providing for the case.

"It has often been asked, through the public journals, and otherwise, 'Why Bishop Andrew was not assigned his regular portion of the episcopal work for the four ensuing years, on the plan of visitation formed by the bishops, and published in the official papers?' It devolves on the majority of my colleagues in the episcopacy, (if, indeed, we have an episcopacy,) rather than on me, to answer this question. Our difference of opinion in the premises, I have no doubt, was in Christian honesty and sincerity. Dismissing all further reference to the *painful* past till I see you in the South, let me now most cordially invite you to meet me at the Virginia Conference, at Lynchburg, November 13th, 1844, should it please a gracious Providence to enable me to be there. And I earnestly desire that you would, if practicable, make your arrangements to be with me at all the Southern conferences in my division of the work for the present year, where I am sure your services will not be 'unacceptable.' I am the more solicitous that you should be at Lynchburg from the fact that my present state of health creates a doubt whether I shall be able to reach it. I am now labouring, and have been for nearly three weeks, under the most severe attack of asthma which I have had for six or seven years,—some nights unable to lie down for a moment. Great prostration of the vital functions, and indeed of the whole physical system, is the consequence. But no effort of mine shall be wanting to meet my work; and the inducements to effort are greatly increased by the present position of the Church, and the hope of relief from my present affliction by the influence of a milder and more congenial climate. I cannot conclude without an expression of my sincere sympathy for you, and the second of your joys and sorrows, in the deep affliction through which you have been called to pass. May the grace of our Lord Jesus Christ sustain you both. Yours with sentiments of affection and esteem,

"JOSHUA SOULE."

"CHARLESTON, S. C., Nov. 4, 1844.

"MY DEAR BROTHER,—I perceive from the resolutions passed at the various Church meetings in the South, that there is a very general expression of opinion in favour of my taking my appropriate share of episcopal labour; and as I have received, both from public meetings and individual correspondents, from ministers and laymen, the most earnest and affectionate invitations to attend the sessions of most of the Southern and South-Western conferences, I deem it due to all concerned to state definitely the course I have pursued, and had resolved to pursue, till the meeting of the convention at Louisville, Kentucky. Immediately after the passing of the memorable resolution in my case in the late General Conference, I left the city of New-York, and spent the next day, which was the Sabbath, at Newark, New-Jersey, to fulfil an engagement previously made; after which I returned to the bosom of my family in Georgia. From Newark I addressed a letter to Bishop Soule, assigning the reasons for my departure, and stating in substance to the following effect, viz: That I did not know whether the bishops would feel authorized, in view of the recent action of the General Conference, to assign me a place among them for the next four years, unless that body should condescend to explain its action more definitely; but that if the bishops should see proper to assign me my share in the episcopal visitations, I should be glad that they would let my work commence as late in the season as convenient, inasmuch as I had been absent from my family most of the time for the last twelve months; but that if they did not feel authorized, in view of the action of the General Conference, to give me work, I should not feel hurt with them. It will be remembered that there was subsequently introduced into the Conference a resolution intended to explain the meaning of the former one as being simply *advisory;* this was promptly laid on the table, which left no doubt of the correctness of the opinion I had previously formed, that the General Conference designed the action as *mandatory.* I understand that the Southern delegates afterwards notified the bishops in due form, that if they should give me my portion of the episcopal work, I should attend to it. The plan of episcopal visitation, however, was drawn up and subsequently published without my name, as is well known. I have heard it rumoured, indeed, that this plan was so arranged that I could be taken into it at *any time* when I should signify a wish to be so introduced; and some anonymous correspondents of the Western and Southern Christian Advocates have expressed themselves in a manner which indicated some surprise, that I had not availed myself of this kind provision of the episcopal board. Now, in reply to all this I have only to say, that I presume those gentlemen are mistaken entirely as to the practicability of any such arrangement; for if the bishops had contemplated the possibility of any such change in their plan, it is but fair to infer that either they would have appended to their published arrangement some note to that effect, or else that they would have informed me of it by letter; and forasmuch as they have done neither, I presume that the aforementioned rumour is altogether without foundation. However, I may be mistaken in this judgment, and I know nothing of the plans of the bishops, other than what is published, not having received a line from one of them since the General Conference, save the accompanying letter from Bishop Soule. In view of all these facts, I came deliberately to the conclusion that the bishops thought it most prudent, under the circumstances, not to invite me to perform any official action; and as I wished to be the cause of no unpleasant feeling to the bishops or preachers, I determined not to visit any of the annual conferences at their respective sessions. At the urgent solicitation, however, of many of the preachers of the Kentucky Conference, I so far changed my determination as to make an effort to reach that conference about the last day or two of the session; but a very unexpected detention on the road prevented the accomplishment of my purpose. Further reflection brought me back to my original purpose; and I abstained from visiting Holston and Missouri. On the important questions which now agitate us, I wished the conferences to act in view of the great facts and principles involved, apart from any influence which my personal presence among them might produce. I had laid out my plan of work for the winter: I designed to visit different portions of the Church in the slaveholding States, and publish among them, as I was able, the unsearchable riches of Christ. The foregoing communication from Bishop Soule furnishes me a sufficient reason to change my arrangements, and to attend, in connexion with him, the conferences allotted to him during the winter, in the distribution of episcopal labour.

"And now permit me, in conclusion, to tender to my brethren, both of the South and South-West, my most cordial and grateful acknowledgments for their kind expressions of sympathy for me, in the storm through which I have been passing, and to invoke their most fervent and continued prayers for me and mine, and especially for the Church of God. I thank them for the many affectionate invitations to attend their conferences, and most joyfully would I have been with them but for the reasons indicated above. May God abundantly bless us, and guide us into the way of truth and peace.

James O. Andrew."

The action of the conferences of Kentucky, Missouri, Holston, and Tennessee, in 1845, subsequent to the Louisville Convention, from which an extract was read, is thus set forth.—Page 108.

"We now come to notice the movements of conferences in the slaveholding States, and which were represented in the Louisville Convention. The first in order of these is Kentucky. It met September 10, 1845, in Frankfort, Kentucky, and was attended by Bishops Soule and Andrew. On the first day of the session the following preamble and resolutions were offered to the conference, and adopted:—

"'Whereas, the long-continued agitation and excitement on the subject of slavery and abolition in the Methodist Episcopal Church, and especially such agitation and excitement in the last General Conference, in connexion with the civil and domestic relations of Bishop Andrew, as the owner of slave property, by inheritance and marriage, assumed such form, in the action had in the case of Bishop Andrew, as to compel the Southern and South-Western delegates in that body to believe, and formally and solemnly to declare, that a state of things must result therefrom which would render impracticable the successful prosecution of the objects and purposes of the Christian ministry and Church organization in the annual conferences within the limits of the slaveholding States,—upon the basis of which declaration the General Conference adopted a provisional Plan of Separation, in view of which said conferences might, if they found it necessary, form themselves into a separate General Conference jurisdiction; and whereas, said conferences, acting first in their separate conference capacity, as distinct ecclesiastical bodies, and then collectively, by their duly-appointed delegates and representatives, in general convention assembled, have found and declared such separation necessary, and have further declared a final dissolution, in fact and form, of the jurisdictional connexion hitherto existing between *them* and the General Conference of the Methodist Episcopal Church as heretofore constituted, and have organized the Methodist Episcopal Church, South, upon the unaltered basis of the doctrines and Discipline of the Methodist Episcopal Church in the United States before its separation, as authorized by the General Conference; and whereas, said Plan of Separation, as adopted by the General Conference, and carried out by the late convention of Southern delegates in the city of Louisville, Kentucky, and also recognised by the entire episcopacy as authoritative and of binding obligation in the whole range of their administration, provides that conferences bordering on the line of division between the two connexions—North and South—shall determine, by vote of a majority of their members respectively, to which jurisdiction they will adhere; therefore, in view of all the premises, as one of the border conferences, and subject to the above-named rule,—

"'*Resolved by the Kentucky Annual Conference of the Methodist Episcopal Church,* That in conforming to the General Conference Plan of Separation, it is necessary that this conference decide by a vote of a majority of its members to which Connexion of the Methodist Episcopal Church it will adhere, and that we now proceed to make such decision.

"'*Resolved,* That any member or members of this conference declining to adhere to that Connexion to which the majority shall by regular, official vote decide to adhere, shall be regarded as entitled, agreeably to the Plan of Separation, to hold their relation to the other ecclesiastical Connexion—North or South, as the case may be—without blame or prejudice of any kind, unless there be grave objections to the moral character of such member or members before the date of such formal adherence.

"'*Resolved,* That agreeably to the provisions of the General Conference Plan of Separation, and the decisions of the episcopacy with regard to it, any person or persons, from and after the act of non-concurrence with the majority, as above, cannot be entitled to hold membership, or claim any of the rights or privileges of membership, in this conference.

"'*Resolved,* That, as a conference, claiming all the rights, powers, and privileges of an annual conference of the Methodist Episcopal Church, we *adhere* to the Methodist Episcopal Church, South, and that all our proceedings, records, and official acts, hereafter, be in the name and style of the Kentucky Annual Conference of the Methodist Episcopal Church, South.

"'Frankfort, Kentucky, September 10, 1845.'

"The vote on the 4th—the *adhering* resolution—being taken by ayes and noes, stood, ayes 77, noes 6. Four of the six who voted in the negative afterwards adhered personally to the South; but *three* persons who did not vote on conference adherence—one being absent, and two being probationers—personally adhered to the North. Here the result was very different from the predictions of one party and the apprehensions of the other. The unanimity of sentiment in the conference, and the delightful harmony which prevailed, wielded a mighty influence in promoting harmony in the societies and throughout the conference. On a line of border of several hundreds of miles, there was found but one small society adhering to the North, while in nearly all the others not a murmur or complaint was heard. A paper in Kentucky, which had employed all its influence previously against the South, from this time acquiesced, and faithfully co-operated with the conference. True, the conference had lost two effective men—two young men who might in time have become useful, and a venerable *superannuate*, for whose support during life the conference gave a generous pledge; but they had gained *five* (and afterwards gained *three*) from the North, all men of experience, weight, and talents.

"The second border conference to act on the question of adherence was Missouri. Here it was claimed that the Northern party would have a conference at any rate; for if they could not secure a majority, they would organize with a *minority*, transact the regular business of the Missouri Conference, and draw the dividend from the Book Concern. The better to accomplish their purposes, Bishop Morris was written to and invited to attend the conference, with a desire that he would take charge of the Northern party. To this invitation he gave the following noble response:—

"*Bishop Morris's Letter.*

"'BURLINGTON, IOWA, September 8, 1845.

"'Rev. Wilson S. McMurry—Dear Brother,—Your letter of the first instant is now before me. The resolutions to which you refer did pass in the meeting of the bishops at New-York, in July, unanimously. We all believe they are in accordance with the Plan of Separation adopted by the General Conference. Whether that Plan was wise or foolish, constitutional or unconstitutional, did not become us to say, it being our duty, as bishops, to know what the General Conference ordered to be done in a certain contingency which has actually transpired, and to carry it out in good faith. It is, perhaps, unfortunate that the resolutions were not immediately published, but it was not thought necessary by a majority at the time they passed. Still, our administration will be conformed to them. Bishop Soule's notice was doubtless founded upon them.

"'As I am the responsible man at Indiana Conference, October 8, it will not be in my power to attend Missouri Conference; nor do I think it important to do so. Were I there, I could not, with my views of propriety and responsibility, encourage subdivision. If a majority of the Missouri Conference resolve to come under the Methodist Episcopal Church, South, that would destroy the identity of the Missouri Conference as an intregal part of the Methodist Episcopal Church. As to having two Missouri Conferences, each claiming to be the true one, and demanding the dividends of the Book Concern, and claiming the Church property, that is the very thing that the General Conference designed to prevent, by adopting the amicable Plan of Separation. It is true that the minority preachers have a right, according to the general rule in the Plan of Separation, to be recognised still in the Methodist Episcopal Church, but in order to that they must go to some adjoining conference in the Methodist Episcopal Church. The border charges may also, by a majority of votes, decide which organization they will adhere to, and if reported in regular order to the conference from which they wish to be supplied, or to the bishops presiding, they will be attended to, on either side of the line of separation. But if any brethren suppose the bishops will send preachers from the North to interior charges, South, or to minorities of border charges, to produce disruption; or that they will encourage minority preachers on either side of the line to organize opposition lines, by establishing one conference in the bounds of another, they are mis-led. That would be departing from the plain letter of the rule prescribed by the General Conference, in the premises. Editors may teach such nullification and answer for it, if they will; but the bishops all understand their duty better than to endorse such principles. I acknowledge that, under the practical operation of the Plan of Separation, some hard cases may arise; but the bishops do not make, and have not the power to relieve them. It is the fault of the rule, and not of the executive administration of it. In the meantime, there is much more bad feeling indulged in respecting the separation, than there is necessity for. If the Plan of Separation had been carried out in good faith and Christian feeling on both sides, it would scarcely have been felt any more than the division of an annual conference. It need not destroy confidence or embarrass the work, if the business be managed in the spirit of Christ. I trust the time is not very far distant when brethren, North and South, will cease their hostilities, and betake themselves to their prayers and other appropriate duties in earnest. Then, and not till then, may we expect the Lord to bless us as in former days.

" 'I am, dear brother, Yours respectfully and affectionately,

" 'THOMAS A. MORRIS.'

" Bishop Soule presided over the conference; and when the question of adherence was taken up, the letter of Bishop Morris was read, and, as may be supposed, not without effect.

" The same resolutions substantially adopted by Kentucky Conference, were introduced and adopted by this conference, only 14 voting in the negative, including absentees."

The passages in relation to the Holston Conference were read by Mr. Lord, and are given in their proper place. The conclusion of the extracts is as follows:—

" The Tennessee Conference, which met October 22, 1845, though not a border conference, adopted the following preamble and resolutions, by a unanimous vote:—

" 'WHEREAS, the agitation of the questions of slavery and abolition for the last several years, has created great excitement in the Methodist Episcopal Church, destructive of her peace and harmony; and whereas, the General Conference of 1844 did, by extra-judicial act, virtually suspend the Rev. James O. Andrew, one of the bishops of said Church, for an act in which he was fully sustained by the law and constitution of the Church, and did thereby render a continuance of the conferences in the slaveholding States under the jurisdiction of said General Conference, inconsistent with the interests of our holy religion, and the great purposes of the Christian ministry; and whereas, the said General Conference adopted a plan for a constitutional and peaceable division of the Methodist Episcopal Church into two separate and distinct ecclesiastical jurisdictions; and whereas, the conferences in the slaveholding States did adjudge such separation imperiously necessary, and did appoint delegates from their respective bodies to meet in General Convention at Louisville, Kentucky, on the first day of May, 1845; and whereas, said convention did proceed to declare the separation right, expedient, and necessary for the prosperity of the Southern Church, and did proceed, according to the Plan of Separation provided by the General Conference of 1844, to adopt measures for the organization of a separate and distinct ecclesiastical jurisdiction, known by the name and under the style of "The Methodist Episcopal Church, South," based on the doctrines and economy of the Methodist Episcopal Church, as set forth in the Discipline of said Church; therefore,

" '1. *Resolved*, That we approve the Plan of Separation as reported by the Committee of Nine, and adopted by the General Conference of 1844.

" '2. That we most cordially approve of the entire proceedings of the Southern delegates in the convention at Louisville, in May, 1845, and that we *solemnly declare* our adherence to the said Southern organization.

" '3. That our journals and all our official records be kept in the name and under the style of the Tennessee Annual Conference of the Methodist Episcopal Church, South.

" '4. That we will, at this session, elect delegates to the General Conference of the Methodist Episcopal Church, South, to be held at Petersburg, Va., on the first day of May, 1846, according to the ratio of representation (one for every fourteen members of the conference) fixed at the Louisville convention.

" '5. That we, as ever, heartily believe in the doctrines and approve the government of the Methodist Episcopal Church, as set forth in our articles of faith, and taught in the Discipline, and that we will resist any and every attempt to change any cardinal features of Methodism, as handed down to us by "our fathers."

"'6. That we highly approve of the course pursued by Bishops Soule and Andrew in their administration, since the occurrence of the difficulties in the General Conference of 1844, and that we sympathize with them in the unjust and ungenerous persecution which has been so bitterly carried on against them in certain portions of the North.

"'7. That we properly appreciate the conservative course pursued by the bench of bishops, pending the difficulties which for the last eighteen months have so agitated the Church, and specially do we commend their purpose of carrying out, so far as their administration is concerned, the Plan of Separation adopted by the General Conference of 1844.

ROBERT PAINE,
J. B. MCFERRIN.'"

The communication from H. B. Bascom, and others, commissioners, to N. Bangs, and others, commissioners, dated Cincinnati, Ohio, August 25, 1846, and the reply thereto, dated New-York, October 14th, 1846—page 117, second of Proofs—to which Mr. Lord referred, are as follows:—

"The General Conference of 1844, in the provisional Plan of a division of the Church property with the South, appointed three commissioners in behalf of the Northern branch of the Church to act co-operatively with like commissioners to be appointed on the part of the South. Our Southern General Conference of May last appointed commissioners accordingly, who met in Cincinnati in August last, and addressed the following communication to the commissioners of the North—personally and privately. Rev. J. B. Finley, one of the Northern commissioners, has responded through the Western Advocate, and we now deem it proper to let our readers see the communication of our commissioners, and Mr. Finley's reply in connexion. The argument of commissioner Finley is sufficiently original. In substance it is, 1. The conferences voted against the change. 2. The commissioners had no means of knowing how the conferences voted. 3. Nobody had any authority to give them the information. 4. The South had forfeited all claim to the benefits of such vote if it was given.

"'The undersigned, commissioners appointed by the late General Conference of the Methodist Episcopal Church, South, in accordance with the Plan of Separation adopted by the General Conference of the Methodist Episcopal Church in 1844, to act in concert with the commissioners of said Methodist Episcopal Church, specially appointed for the purpose, in estimating the amount of property and funds due to the Methodist Episcopal Church, South, according to the Plan of Separation aforesaid, and to adjust and settle all matters pertaining to the division of the Church property and funds as agreed upon and provided for in said Plan, with full powers at the same time to carry into effect the whole arrangement, with regard to said division of property, would respectfully give notice to the Rev. Dr. Bangs, Dr. Peck, and Rev. James B. Finley, commissioners, and the Rev. George Lane and C. B. Tippett, book agents of the Methodist Episcopal Church, that they are prepared to act in concert with them, as the Plan of Separation contemplates and requests, in an amicable attempt, to settle and adjust all the matters and interests to which the appointment of each Board of Commissioners relates—that is to say, all questions involving property and funds which may be pending between the Methodist Episcopal Church, and the Methodist Episcopal Church, South. And as necessary to such a result, in the judgment of the commissioners, South, they would respectfully suggest and urge the propriety and necessity of a joint meeting of the Board of Commissioners, North and South, at a period as early as practicable, that the intention of the Plan of Separation, in this respect, may not be defeated by unnecessary delay. It has been the aim of the General Conference of the Methodist Episcopal Church, South, to see that all the terms and stipulations of the Plan of Separation be strictly complied with on their part, and provision has been accordingly made that the Rev. John Early, book agent of the Methodist Episcopal Church, South, and its appointee to receive the property and funds falling due to the South, be duly and properly clothed with the legal and corporate powers required by the Plan of Separation. And the undersigned commissioners are not able to perceive any valid reason or reasons why the negotiation respecting the division of property should not proceed in the hands of the joint commissioners without delay, and hence request the joint meeting of the commissioners of the bodies they represent to judge and determine whether the annual conferences have authorized the change of the sixth restrictive rule, and as no such decision can be had until given by them, it seems important that such decision should be given by them as soon as practicable, and we know of no mode of conclusive action in the case, except by a joint meeting of the commissioners. The Plan of Separation provides for no intermediate action between that of the annual conferences, and that to be had by the commissioners, and unless the commissioners *North* are in possession of information, clear and satisfactory, that the action of the annual conferences, in the aggregate *vote* given by them, is adverse to the recommendation of the General Conference, it is obviously made their duty, by the Plan of Separation, to meet and decide the question. From all the information in our possession, we see no reason why we should not act upon the assumption, that the proposed change in the restrictive rule has been authorized. The language of the Discipline is, "Upon the concurrent recommendation of three-fourths of all the members of the several annual conferences, who shall be present *and vote* upon such recommendations." The language of the Plan of Separation is, "Whenever the annual conferences, by a vote of three-fourths of all their members *voting* on the third resolution." It follows hence, that both by the language of the Discipline and that of the Plan of Separation, the question was to be settled by the aggregate vote of those members of the several annual conferences, who were present in their annual sessions, when the question came up, and *actually voted* upon it. If any refused or failed to vote, with such we have nothing to do—they cannot be regarded as either for or against the measure. They declined the right of suffrage by refusing to act, and the determination of the question rests with those who were present *and voted* in accordance with the law. In the instance of several annual conferences, the vote was contingent, and future events, now to be judged of by the commissioners, were to give an *affirmative* or *negative* character to their votes. In the instance of two of these at least (and we believe it to be equally true of four) it is susceptible of the clearest proof, that, by their *own official showing*, their votes must, beyond all doubt, be counted in the affirmative, or not at all; and in either case, and indeed without reference to either, taking no account of the conferences which refused to vote, it is believed the constitutional majority of all the votes given was in favour of the change, and it will, it seems to us, devolve upon the commissioners of the Methodist Episcopal Church, to make the contrary appear before they can in good faith refuse to carry into effect the Plan of Separation. To settle this question fairly and honourably, and in accordance with the facts in the case, it is believed that a meeting of the commissioners is indispensable. To this we may add, that the most weighty considerations, both of justice and humanity, demand alike that the question be settled as early as possible, as the dividends to which we are declared entitled by the Plan of Separation, and which that Plan pledges shall be paid to us, until the division of property shall actually take place, have already been withheld, and our "travelling, supernumerary, superannuated, and worn-out preachers, their wives, widows, and children, are literally suffering for the want of funds given in trust for their support—funds to which the General Conference of 1844 not only declared them entitled, but solemnly stipulated to divide with them upon principles of "Christian kindness and strictest equity."

"'The division of property and funds stipulated contemplates no gratuity to the South, for it is well known that, in receiving all the Plan of Separation accords to us, we are receiving but a part of what the South has contributed to the common fund in question.

"'There is another view of this subject, which, in our judgment, should not be overlooked by the commissioners. The proposed change in the restrictive rule was regarded by all who favoured the Plan of Separation in the General Conference of 1844, merely as means to an end. The end aimed at was an equitable division of the Church property, and the more certainly and securely to effect this, within the established forms of law and order, the change in question was proposed; such change, however, or the want of it, cannot possibly affect, in any form, the question of right, or the true issue in a legal process, should it be found necessary to institute such process.

"'The Methodist Episcopal Church, South, intends a most sacred appropriation of the funds they may receive exclusively to the purposes specified in the sixth restrictive article; and not intending to divert them in any way to any other object or purpose, the change recommended by the General Conference can only be regarded as a matter of form, subordinate, in every high moral and legal sense, to the end had in view by the body in the adoption of the Plan of Separation. The object in calling attention to this view of the subject is not in any way to supersede the Plan of Separation, but to insist, as we shall always continue to do, that unless the letter of the Plan shall interpose insuperable difficulties, its spirit and intention plainly and imperatively demand, at the hands of the commissioners, that they carry it into effect, and that they cannot fail to do so without a grave abuse of the trust reposed in them. Hence, again, we urge that a meeting of the commissioners at an early day, is necessary to settle this preliminary question, which it appears to us can be conclusively settled in no other way.

"'It certainly cannot be necessary that we remind the commissioners and book agents of the Methodist Episcopal Church, that the peace and quiet, not less than the character and hopes of the Church, North and South, urgently require that this great property question be settled as soon as practicable; and we are most anxious that it should be done amicably and with good feeling, and especially that it may be done without an appeal to the civil tribunals of the country; and the General Conference of the Methodist Episcopal Church, South, have accordingly instructed their commissioners to look to such an issue as the last resort, in view of the adjustment aimed at.

"'In conclusion, the commissioners of the Methodist Episcopal Church, South, in view of the facts and considerations to which they have adverted in this communication, would respectfully and urgently call upon Dr. Bangs, as chairman of the commissioners of the Methodist Episcopal Church, to call a meeting of the joint board of commissioners, as hereinbefore indicated, and we cheerfully concede to him the right, so far as we are concerned, of fixing *the time* and *place* at any period between the last of October and the first of March next. Very respectfully,

"'H. B. Bascom,
A. L. P. Green,
S. A. Latta.

"'*Cincinnati, Ohio, August* 25, 1846.

"'P. S.—We would respectfully ask and claim, upon the ground of justice and right, that the commissioners and book agents of the Methodist Episcopal Church, make a direct call, by authority of the General Conference of 1844, upon the secretaries of all the annual conferences of the Methodist Episcopal Church, for an authentic, attested statement of the vote or action of each conference, in relation to the change of the sixth restrictive rule; and the commissioners of the Methodist Episcopal Church, South, will do the same within the limits of the Southern organization.

"'H. B. Bascom,
A. L. P. Green,
S. A. Latta.'"

"'*To H. B. Bascom, A. L. P. Green, and S. A. Latta, Commissioners of the Methodist Episcopal Church, South.*

"'Dear Brethren,—We have received your communication dated the 25th of August, 1846, requesting us to call a joint meeting of the commissioners appointed by the General Conference of 1844 of the Methodist Episcopal Church, and the commissioners appointed by the General Conference of 1846 of the Methodist Episcopal Church, South, in order to adjust the property question, as provided for in the provisional Plan of Separation adopted by the General Conference of 1844.

"'In reply to this we have to say that, in our judgment, we have no authority to act in the premises, as we have never been officially notified that the requisite number of votes in the several annual conferences has been given in favour of the alteration in the sixth restrictive rule in the constitution of the Church, nor have we any authority to call on the secretaries of the several annual conferences to give us the requisite information as you have suggested.

"'On these accounts we must respectfully decline to act in the premises, as our action would, in our opinion, be null and void.

N. Bangs,
Geo. Peck,
J. B. Finley.'"

"'*New-York, October* 14, 1846.

The communication of H. B. Bascom, and others, commissioners, to the bishops and members of the Methodist Episcopal Church, in General Conference assembled, dated Pittsburgh, May 11th, 1848 :—

"*Pittsburgh, May* 11, 1848.

"*To the Bishops and Members of the General Conference of the Methodist Episcopal Church in General Conference assembled.*

"Rev. and Dear Brethren,—The undersigned, commissioners and appointee of the Methodist Episcopal Church, South, respectfully represent to your body, that pursuant to our appointment, and in obedience to specific instructions, we notified the commissioners and agents of the Methodist Episcopal Church, of our readiness to proceed to the adjustment of the property question, according to the Plan of Separation adopted by the General Conference of 1844 ; and we furthermore state, that the chairman of the board of commissioners of the Methodist Episcopal Church informed us they would not act in the case, and referred us to your body for the settlement of the question as to the division of the property and funds of the Church ; and, being furthermore instructed by the General Conference of the Methodist Episcopal Church, South, in case of a failure to settle with your commissioners, to attend the session of your body in 1848, for the 'settlement and adjustment of all questions involving property and funds, which may be pending between the Methodist Episcopal Church, and the Methodist Episcopal Church, South,' take this method of informing you of our presence, and of our readiness to attend to the matters committed to our trust and agency by the Methodist Episcopal Church, South ; and we desire to be informed as to the time and manner in which it may suit your views and convenience to consummate with us the division of the property and the funds of the Church, as provided for in the Plan of Separation, adopted with so much unanimity by the General Conference of 1844. And for our authority in the premises we respectfully refer you to the accompanying document, marked A.

"A. L. P. Green,
C. B. Parsons,
L. Pierce. } *Commissioners.*
Jno. Early, *Appointee.*"

To this communication no reply was received.

THIRD DAY.—Wednesday, May 21, 1851.

Mr. Choate,—May it please your Honours, I shall have occasion, on behalf of the defendants, to make a few additional references ; and I have arranged with Mr. Lord, if it may be sanctioned by the Court, that those references may be made, and those passages read, after he shall have concluded his argument.

Judge Nelson,—The Court have no objections.

Mr. Lord,—Give me the pages.

Mr. Choate,—I will refer to the "First of the Proofs," p. 136 ; the Journals of the General Conference of 1848, p. 177, to prove that the number of votes required by the Discipline, to change the sixth restrictive rule, had not been given.

At the request of Mr. Lord, I will read a passage on the subject of the vote of the conferences :—

"The Committee on the State of the Church beg leave further to report in part, That they have received of the Commissioners of the Church, South, an account of the vote in the Southern conferences in relation to the change of the sixth restrictive rule, and from a count of the votes from all the annual conferences, find the following result :—

"The votes from the conferences at the South stand thus :—For the alteration 971, and against it 3. From the conferences now embraced within the Methodist

Episcopal Church, for the alteration, 1,164; against it, 1,067. Whole number for the alteration, 2,135; against it, 1,070. The whole number necessary to authorize the alteration, 2,404. Subtract from this number, 2,135, the number of votes actually cast for the alteration, leaves 269, which is the number of votes wanting to authorize the change of the rule. GEORGE PECK, Chairman."

MR. LORD,—The page containing that report was pasted in after the book seems to have been published. Will you inform me when it was put there?

MR. CHOATE,—I am unable to state.

MR. LORD,—My learned friends on the other side published that report of the "Committee on the State of the Church," from the Journals of the General Conference of 1848. The Court may see that a part of the Journal of 1848 is printed in book No. 1, but it does not contain this report of the vote on the change of the sixth restrictive article.

MR. CHOATE,—Mr. Lord will find that it refers to it. I will read it from page 136 of the Book of Proofs, No. 1:—

"May 18th.—The Committee on the State of the Church presented a report on the state of the vote to alter the sixth restrictive rule, to the effect that the number of votes required by the Discipline to change said rule had not been given."

I shall refer to p. 47 of the same book, for the purpose of bringing to the notice of the Court which conferences voted against making a grant to the Canada conference of a portion of the funds; to the same book, pp. 131–134, containing the address of the bishops to the General Conference of 1844; to the same book, pp. 154–165, on what are called infractions by the South of the Plan of Separation.

MR. LORD,—Does Mr. Choate understand, on the subject of these minutes of 1848, that they are not evidence that the things there stated took place?

MR. CHOATE,—Certainly; they are all read under stipulations. The same observation will apply to what Mr. Lord read.

MR. LORD,—The transactions of the General Conferences, up to 1844, are introduced as the joint acts of both parties. After 1844, the minutes and journals of each party are introduced, to show what the bodies did and said, but not to have the effect of establishing as facts the recitals which they say other people said or did. They are merely admitted as authentic papers, to show the action of the bodies.

MR. CHOATE,—I shall refer many times to the "History of the Discipline," but I will indicate such passages as I have on my brief, for the information of Mr. Lord. They are p. 47, p. 10, p. 251, and pp. 254, and the following. And I am sure Mr. Lord will be glad to have me correct one mistake into which he inadvertently fell, and which I will enable him to correct for himself. It was said that Bishop Andrew was not allowed to take part in the inauguration of bishops in 1844. I shall refer to the journals of that conference of 1844, p. 83, to show that the vote upon the bishop's case was on the 1st of June. That is an admitted date. I shall then refer to the same journals, p. 139, to show that the inauguration of the bishops took place upon the 10th of June; and again to the second of the Proofs, p. 105, to show from a letter of Bishop Andrew that he left New-York on the 2d day of June.

MR. REVERDY JOHNSON,—The vote, I believe, was on the 1st.

MR. LORD,—Bishop Andrew, in his letter, says:—

"Immediately after the passing of the memorable resolution in my case in the late General Conference, I left the city of New-York, and spent the next day, which was the Sabbath, at Newark, N. J."

Mr. Choate,—I am informed that he did not return. I believe that is quite certain.

I shall refer also to pp. 43, 46, and 47 of the first of the Proofs, for the purpose of showing that it has been the usage of the General Conference to canvass votes given by the annual conferences upon the subject of the restrictive rules—the usage of the General Conference holden next subsequently.

Before commencing his argument, Mr. Lord presented to the court the *Points of Complainants*, as follows:—

I. The capital arising from the profits of the Book Concern was the result of the common labours and services of all the members of all the conferences.—It was not a charitable fund merely from donations.—It was a fund of earnings, to make up the deficiency of compensation for services rendered, and to provide for those who earned it, when they became incapable of labour, and for those who were dependent upon them.

II. It was distributed by the annual conferences, but belonged in actual right to the beneficiaries, and as such was, and is, protected by the sixth restrictive rule.

III. The title of the beneficiaries, at the time immediately before the separation of the Church into two parts, was perfect; and it cannot be defeated or forfeited without a clear proof of breach of condition by the beneficiaries.

IV. Even if a breach of condition by the annual conferences, by whom the fund was to be distributed, could forfeit, there has been no forfeiture, because the General Conference of 1844 had the power to consent to an amicable division of the conferences on grave causes, touching the general efficiency of the Church.

V. The General Conference of 1844 did, in fact, and on a proper ground, consent to such division, to take effect immediately, in the choice of the Southern conferences, and without any condition.

VI. The General Conference of the Church, South, was duly and properly organized, according to the Plan of Separation, and is in every respect as properly a General Conference within its limits, as the General Conference of the Churches North.

VII. The beneficiaries of the fund in question, therefore, who belonged to the Southern conferences, did not, by the new organization, lose any rights, nor were they disqualified in any manner from claiming their share of the funds. And such claim is appropriately made through the General Conference, South, which succeeds to the place of the prior General Conference of the whole Church.

VIII. An account should therefore be ordered of the proportions of the profits of the Book Concern, according to the numbers in the minutes of 1844, and at the same ratio of the profits since.—Also the capital of the fund should be decreed to be divided in the same way, and paid over to the commissioners, South, as new trustees, or to proper trustees to be appointed by the Court.

The profits of the past are to be subject to distribution, according to the directions of the General Conference, South, whether the fund remain with the present trustees, or be paid over to new trustees.

D. D. Lord, *Solicitor of Complainants.*

D. Lord,
Reverdy Johnson, } *Of Counsel.*

Mr. Lord,—May it please your Honours; there is a starting-point in this controversy, as to which we are all agreed—about which there is no manner of doubt. That is this: that immediately prior to the separation, whether it took place in 1844 or 1845, all the supernumerary, superannuated, and distressed travelling preachers belonging to the Southern conferences, whom we now represent, and their wives, widows, and children, in that Connexion, were entitled to an interest in this fund, as well as the persons in similar relations, belonging to the Northern conferences. What the character of that title was, it is scarcely necessary to inquire. I suppose it was a charity—one of those uses which attach themselves to transitory objects, so to say, rather than one of those specific trusts which are held by titles analogous to those of legal estates. But it seems to me, that, for the purpose of starting our reasoning on this subject, it may be averred as agreed upon, that as a matter of right, not as a matter of mere gift or charity, the supernumerary and superannuated preachers, their wives, widows, and children, were entitled to participate in the profits of this Book Concern. It may be that this fund was to be distributed by the judgment of the annual conferences, and not by any act of the General Conference. As to the General Conference, on that subject its action was purely ministerial. It merely took the account, and enforced the obligation of having the profits of that fund properly placed in the hands of the annual conferences for distribution. It had no real discretion on that subject. Without an utter and entire abandonment of its primary duty in relation to the subject, it had nothing to do but to enforce all the accountability of the book-steward to them for the appropriation of the profit of this fund properly; and it superintended the management of it, or at least supervised that superintendence, and the fund was obliged to be distributed through the annual conferences.

Now, as to the duty of the annual conferences, as to their right on that subject. They had no interest in this matter. All that they had, was the obligation incumbent upon them, as Christian and faithful men, to see that the profits assigned to each annual conference should be distributed according to the intent and purpose of this fund. That is, it should be applied to those whom they should ascertain within their limits to be supernumerary and superannuated preachers, and travelling preachers having their salaries deficient, and to the wives, widows, children, and orphans of preachers. Now, you will see that until we get to the actual beneficiaries, we find no person having anything but a mere administrative right, a mere agency, and as to selection, no discretion. They had not a right to select a meritorious or an unmeritorious man, woman, or child. They were bound to ascertain simply certain facts. Is this a supernumerary preacher? Is this a superannuated preacher? Is this the wife or child of a preacher? Are these the orphans of preachers? Is this a travelling preacher unpaid his small salary? There was no discretion in the conferences on this subject at all. Their duty was the simple ascertaining of a plain fact—a fact, I suppose, always ascertained by the simple declaration of the parties entitled to receive; because in this Connexion of religious men, of the character of preachers, and families of preachers, it is not only a proper assumption in point of law, but a proper presumption in point of fact, that the mere statement by these various beneficiaries would be taken as decisive on the subject.

Now, then, we come ultimately to this proposition—and I think it will scarcely be denied—that these beneficiaries had directly an interest in this fund, through the medium of the administration of a charity. I do not go into the question, whether they had a legal right or an equitable title. In this Court it is enough to say, that they had that sort of right which cannot be violated without a breach of trust on the part of those who administer this fund. If they have no legal estate—no legal, equitable estate, so to say; that is, no such permanent estate in equity as has an analogy to legal estates—it only operates to make the obligation on the consciences of the trustees more binding and powerful; and these persons, unprotected by legal securities, and by those things which are equitable protections, are more entirely protected in their absolute right by the uncovered character of this fund. In other words, it has become a right—a valid, perfect, and established debt of conscience and of honour; such a debt of conscience and of honour as comes within the administration of relief by courts of equity under this doctrine of charities. On that subject I propose to define my view of a charity, and then to inquire into the character of this fund, to show that, except in the mode of its administration, in law it is in no sense a charity, but a right.

I suppose that the distinction between a specific trust, and one of those trusts which are administrative as charities, is this: a specific trust has individual beneficiaries who are marked out, who take, either for periods of time, or for life, or in succession, by way of perpetuity—that is, such a perpetuity as the law allows under definite limitations—limitations as to the person, when the right is once vested in that person through some legal mode of succession. A charity, I suppose, is a trust where the beneficiaries come in by a casual conformity to the descriptions of the charity. I mean a casual conformity: that is to say, a man may this year come within the description of the poor living in Water-street, for whom a foundation of charity is established, and next year he may not. It is that transitory character of the beneficiary which I suppose in law defines a charity, and distinguishes it from a trust. We are not to suppose that this right of a charity is imperfect because it is transitory. I presently intend to go into the character of this, treating it as a charity, to show that it is not one of what moralists call "imperfect obligations," but morally, and in conscience, of the highest and most perfect obligation; and that the only imperfection of the obligation is that which turns you over from the specific administration of the law of trust, to the more liberal administration of the law of charity.

Now, supposing, for a moment, that I am right in this character of the title of these beneficiaries, and that the women, the children, the supernumeraries, and worn-out preachers of the Southern conferences had rights which the Court would regard prior to that separation, the question comes up, and that is the great question we are discussing, Have they those rights still? Why have they not? Are they not Methodists? Have they departed one scruple in doctrine or in discipline? I mean the beneficiaries whom I represent; they are not the bishops. Some of them are members of conferences, and some of them are not, and the right is equal to them all. But why have they not those rights still? Have they ever been tried? The gentlemen put it in their answer most distinctly and clearly on the ground that they have forfeited the right. They use the term "forfeited" in their answer. They say, they "forfeited" it by secession. Secession from what? That is the question, and the question between us is to be, whether there is, in regard to this fund, any such forfeiture as is set up by these gentlemen. And in saying "set up by these gentlemen," I ought, perhaps, to explain myself, that I may not be misunderstood. By "these gentlemen," I do not mean these defendants whom I conceive to be not volunteers in this matter; they are legal personages, representing, as I suppose I may say without giving offence, a rather tumultuous body behind them, a changeable body to whom they are accountable, and in regard to whom they must protect themselves by the most careful conduct. They, however, taking advice on the subject, say we, the beneficiaries, have "forfeited" this right. We forfeit it; by which I understand, there is some implied condition which we have broken, or some term of the grant which renders this charity no longer applicable to us.

Before going into the inquiry which I propose first to institute, I beg leave to say one word on the subject of the mode of relief. There will be no difficulty on this subject. There need be no apprehension of a difficulty in regard to the subject of the dividing of the fund. I suppose it must be divided. I suppose the reasoning which we shall adopt on this subject, will call for a division of the fund, of the capital itself; but that does not necessarily embarrass our case; for if these beneficiaries for whom I speak are entitled, then the fund may remain in the hands of the agents here, an undivided fund, and be administered by them; and relief would be afforded by ordering them to take the minutes of the conferences of the South, in regard to the preachers and persons of the South entitled, and turn over the annual dividends to them as long as there is a Book Concern yielding profits to be divided, that they may thus be distributed. There is, as I conceive, no formal or technical difficulty of that sort to be set up. I am sure, that if the relief to which I conceive beyond all question we shall be adjudged to be entitled, if these beneficiaries shall have their rights, it will be an advantageous arrangement all round, that the fund should be divided, and I presume there will be no difficulty in law in doing it. But that is not essential to the relief to which we are entitled under this bill. Nor is it essential that the proper persons who are entitled to take the capital of the fund should now be before the Court. You have the travelling preachers before you. You have the supernumerary and worn-out preachers. You have no wives and children before you. But these three descriptions of persons come before this Court, so that this Court is bound, in acting, to declare that these persons are prosecuting in behalf of themselves and of those who possess the same right with them; so that the question is not embarrassed by any formal difficulty of that sort. It comes up clearly, distinctly, and fairly, for the judgment and decision of this Court.

In the consideration of this subject, I propose to inquire into the character of this fund. That is the inquiry in the first point which I have laid before your Honours. In all these cases of charities, you are aware that there has been a vagueness in the character of the trust which is designated for a charitable use. That vagueness seems to be almost essential. It has almost always existed in regard to them. Sometimes they exist only by implication; for instance, the case of Lady Hewley's charity, a leading case in modern days, in which the law has probably been finally summed up. It was held that her gift of a piece of land, as a foundation for Protestant Dissenters, in a very vague and general way, should be administered by a Court of Equity, and they should inquire into the character of Lady Hewley's religious opinions, in order to ascertain whom she meant by "Protestant Dissenters." That inquiry into the character of the fund, as growing out of the character of those who contributed, of those who formed it, and, if a gift, of those who gave it, has always been a material, necessary, and legitimate subject of inquiry in the administration of these charities.

I will give your Honours all the references to cases which bear on the subject. It is not a controverted subject, as I believe; but it may be convenient for the Court to have the references, and I will give them all together. The first one to which I refer, is that of Field *vs.* Field, 9 Wendell, p. 400, decided in October, 1832. That decided the question at law. It went upon a mere question of actual organization. It was not a question of equity as to the proper administration according to the intent of the donor, but a question of the mere actual succession of one organization to another. This subject was very fully canvassed in this State, in the case of the Lutheran Church, (Miller *vs.* Gable, 2 Denio's Reports, 518, in the Court of Appeals,) decided finally in December, 1845. It had been previously discussed by the Chancellor, (10 Paige, 646,) and prior to that by Vice Chancellor Hoffman in his reports, to which I have no reference; his opinion, however, went so much on the theological parts of the question, that it does not enlighten us as much as the other. There the whole subject was canvassed. That was a religious charity, and the question arose in a double shape. One was the question of a departure from religious doctrines ; the other, a question of departure from adherence to the religious governing body. In all these cases it was held that the adherence should be in point of doctrine, or a Court of Equity would reform or correct the abuse of the property ; and when it was plain, and evident, and clear, that the charity was founded in connexion with a religious government, they would always establish it in a Court of Equity; but they held that in that case it must be very clear. They also held, that if in the origin of the charity, it was not so subject, but that those who administered the charity afterwards by agreement and voluntary connexion did subject it, that it was not misapplied, although the body afterwards withdrew from that ecclesiastical connexion, and it then stood only on the question of conformity of doctrines. However, your Honours will no doubt find great instruction upon this subject from that case.

The other cases bearing on the subject I will give without comment. In 1814, the case of Davis *vs.* Jenkins, 3d Vesey and Beame's, 152. You will find in this case a very minute and careful inquiry, free from all collateral inquiries, into the character and understanding of the founders of the charity. I cite it to show that this inquiry into the character of the original foundation of the charity, the nature of the contributions, and the character of the men who contributed to it, goes to enlighten the Court in ascertaining the character of the charity in order to execute it. The case of the Attorney General *vs.* Pearson, 3 Merivale, 352. It also appears in 7 Simon's Reports, 290, republished in 10 English Chancery Reports, 61. That merely upholds the principle that the doctrines of the founder of the charity, it being a religious one, should be enforced, and that a majority of the trustees, a temporal body, should not be permitted to use the property in deviation from those doctrines. Again : in the case of Leslie *vs.* Burney, 2 Russell, 114, also reported in 3 English Chancery Reports, 46, which was the case of a meeting-house in London of the Scotch Presbyterian Church. There was an election by the elders and communicants, excluding the seat-holders. That was contested, on the ground that these seat-holders had all contributed; but it was held that as that Church was founded by Scotch Presbyterians this was right, and such a mode should be upheld. This shows that in going into this inquiry, the character of the fund, the character of the donors constituting it, and all that contribute to a fund which grows out of its origin, should be looked at and regarded in the decision upon it. The case of the Attorney General *vs.* Shore, 7 Simon's, 290, note, was a similar case to that of the Attorney General and Pierson. Another case, not however bearing very directly on the question, but to which I will give a reference, is Milligan *vs.* Mitchell, 3 Milne and Craige, 77.

We contend, in regard to the character of this fund, that the capital arising from the profits of the Book Concern was the result of the common labours and services, of all the members of all the conferences. It was not a charitable fund merely from donations. It was not a charity of that sort in which the beneficiary comes, without any previous right, to beg alms. It was not a gift. It was a charity which grew, as we shall attempt to show, out of actual, laborious, self-denying, beneficial services, just as much as any Savings' Bank or Life Insurance. At the same time, from the transitory character of the beneficiaries of the fund, it became in law one of those things which must be administered as a charity. We say it was a fund of earnings to make up the deficiency of compensation for services rendered, and to provide for those who earned it, when they became incapable of labour, and for those who were dependent on them.

Now let us look to the character of this fund ; and this, in my humble judgment, is a very material inquiry in this case; for the question of "forfeiting," as it is put in the answer, is a very different thing from entitling yourself to alms. It is a question here distinctly put as a question of forfeiture. A man comes to me for alms; it is a matter between me and my conscience whether I will give him alms—he has no right. But if a servant, who has rendered me services during the prime of his days, upon the understanding that I should take care of him in his old age, and I gave him no bond for it, and he has become old and decrepid, the Court will see how different is the application he makes to me, from a man with whom I have had no connexion at all. You cannot but see that in this case there is in the outset a natural equity—there is an appeal to the very foundation out of which the charity itself springs. There is in the very nature of the subject, a light to guide us in the consideration of this matter.

How did this fund arise? Your Honours, in examining Emory's History, will find that it had its origin with the preachers of the Methodist Church. They undertook to see to the supplying of books, and they were to see to payment for the books. Upon our book, No. 1, page 17, we find this extract from the "History:"—

"Ezekiel Cooper is appointed the superintendent of the Book Concern," (Ezekiel Cooper was in fact the founder of the profitable Book Concern,) "who shall have authority to regulate the publications, and all other parts of the business, according to the state of the finances from time to time. It shall be his duty to inform the annual conferences if any of the preachers or private members of the society neglect to make due payment."

There you perceive the preachers and private members subject to ecclesiastical jurisdiction. They are to see that these books realize money.

"He may publish any books or tracts which, at any time, may be approved of, or recommended by, the majority of an annual conference, provided such books or tracts be also approved of by the book committee, which shall be appointed by the Philadelphia Annual Conference."

It was therefore the taste of the annual conferences which was to determine what books were to be printed. Ezekiel Cooper had not the right of a common bookseller to print what he pleased; that was a right of the preachers, meeting in annual conferences, which were composed of all the preachers, and were not delegated bodies. In 1800, the General Conference was composed of all the members of all the annual conferences. Their taste in the selection, their reading, their examination of subjects, was that which led to the adoption of the books which should receive the *imprimatur* which gave them a currency, and made their publication profitable.

"Let his accounts and books be examined by the Philadelphia Conference at the time of the sitting of the said conference.

"It shall be the duty of every presiding elder, where no book-steward is appointed, to see that his district be fully supplied with books."

So your Honours will see that it did not merely mean that this community, which perhaps lacked intelligence and information more at that day than at the present, should be left without having the benefits which the press distributes over every community where it is known. There you have one of the elders determining that matter; but they did not leave it there.

"He is to order such books as are wanted, and to give directions to whose care the same are to be sent; and he is to take the oversight of all our books sent into his district, and to account with the superintendent for the same."

"Our books." Whose books? Why, the books of these preachers; their books as a denomination; those which they sanctioned, which they selected and caused to be distributed, and in fact persuaded to be purchased. Again:—

"He is to have the books distributed among the several circuits in his district, and is to keep an account with each preacher who receives or sells the books; and is to receive the money, and to forward it to the superintendent."

Every preacher, therefore, was an agent in the diffusion of the literature of the Church; a wise, very wise plan—wise for the people, and wise for the government of the Church: but it was the act of the preachers; it was the labour of the preachers that made this the great Book Concern, which it ever came to be. The preachers, we have already seen, selected the books; the presiding elders had it in charge to see that they were supplied to the preachers in their several circuits; and they were to sell them. Again:

"When a presiding elder is removed, he is to make a full settlement for all the books sold or remaining in his district; and is also to make a transfer to his successor of all the books and accounts left with the preachers in the district, the amount of which shall go to his credit, and pass to the debit of his successor."

Thus it will be seen, that this was a business most strictly and directly connected with the ministry of this Church, calling not only for activity and labour on their part, but pecuniary accountability on the part of every preacher in every Methodist circuit.

"It shall be the duty of every preacher, who has the charge of a circuit, to see that his circuit be duly supplied with books, and to take charge of all the books which are sent to him, from time to time, or which may be in his circuit; and he is to account with the presiding elder for the same."

That does not mean that he is merely to bring the books, that his people may purchase them, although that would be a meritorious participancy in this fund; but it meant, "Sir, in your preaching press upon your people the necessity of learning, as well by the press as by the living voice, the doctrines, practices, morals, and virtues of this religious faith which you preach to them." Again:—

"When a preacher leaves his circuit, he must settle with the presiding elder for all the books he has disposed of; he is also to make out an inventory of all that are remaining unsold, which shall be collected at one place; the amount of which shall go to his credit, and be transferred to his successor, who is to take charge of the same. If the preacher who has charge of the circuit be negligent in dispersing the books, the presiding elder shall commit the charge of the books to another."

What more distinct agency could be established? What more distinct services called for? What stronger and more conscientious accountability upon a mortal man than is by this system established upon all the preachers?

"The superintendent of the book business may, from time to time, supply the preachers with books in those circuits which are adjacent or convenient to Philadelphia, and settle for them with the same; in such cases the regulations respecting the presiding elders are not to apply."

That is, in the districts adjacent to Philadelphia, you need not go through the formality of receiving the books from the presiding elder, but the superintendent may supply you directly. Then again:—

"Every annual conference shall appoint a committee or committees, to examine the accounts of the presiding elders, preachers, and book-stewards, in their respective districts or circuits. Every presiding elder, minister, and preacher, shall do everything in their power to recover all debts due to the Concern, and also all the books belonging to the Concern, which may remain in the hands of any person within their districts or circuits. If any preacher or member be indebted to the Book Concern, and refuse to make payment, or to come to a just settlement, let him be dealt with for a breach of trust, and such effectual measures be adopted for the recovery of such debts, as shall be agreeable to the direction of the annual conferences respectively.

"There shall be no drafts made upon the Book Concern till its debts are discharged, and a sufficient capital provided for carrying on the business; after which, the profits arising from the books shall be regularly paid to the Chartered Fund, and be applied, with the annual income of the funded stock, to the support of the distressed travelling preachers and their families, the widows and orphans of preachers," &c.

There was the foundation of this fund. And I ask if ever a fund exhibited, under the name of a charity, so much of the aspect of the accumulations of a partnership; and if there ever was a fund which provided so equitably and justly a retiring pension for these men, who, for a trifling yearly salary, not enough to pay for a fashionable dinner, served year after year in the wilderness, and spent their best days in toil? Have they not a right, above the ordinary beggar of alms, to a fund growing out of their own exertions? We are to look at this matter in all its aspects. When we look at the administration of this fund, to see how it is to be dealt with, your Honours must not lose sight of the character and the services of the persons by whom it was established. You see that the character of this fund is thus impressed upon it by its establishment; and nothing, it seems to me, can be clearer than that it was intended to create a fund, so far as was practicable, for the first great object of enlightening this Methodist community as to religious truth, as to their morals, and as to their habits of life; and that the second great object was, that when this institution should be carried out, the preachers themselves might have some little stimulus for activity, and that they should be entitled to look for an absolute support from this fund for the wants of old age, and the wants of their dependents, and the wants of their poor and suffering brethren. This was first given to the "Chartered Fund." That "Chartered Fund" it is not necessary to notice further than to say, that it was an incorporation for the mere purpose that is expressed—the support of distressed travelling preachers and their families.

The next thing in the history of this fund is in the Conference of 1804—the last General Conference before they became delegated bodies. There was then this variation, that instead of being paid to the Chartered Fund, it was to be administered through the annual conferences. The Conference of 1804 provided that,

"The profits arising from the Book Concern, after a sufficient capital to carry on the business is retained, shall be regularly applied to the support of the distressed travelling preachers and their families, the widows and orphans of preachers, &c. The general book-steward shall every year send forward to each annual conference an account of the dividend which the several annual conferences may draw that year; and each conference may draw for their proportionate part, on any person who has book-money in hand, and the drafts, with the receipt of the conference thereon, shall be sent to the general book-steward, and be placed to the credit of the person who paid the same. But each annual conference is authorized, at all events, to draw on the general book-steward for $100."

This continues to be the establishment of this fund up to the present time. There has been no change as to this. It is yet paid to the annual conferences, and by them distributed.

Before I make any further remarks on this, I beg to call your Honours' attention to the allowance made to the preachers of this communion during all this period. I say, "during all this period;" for though I quote the amount from the Discipline of 1840, you will see that it never could have been much less. On page 29 of Book No. 1, I read,—

"*Of the allowances to the ministers and preachers, and to their wives, widows, and children.*

"The annual allowance of the married travelling, supernumerary and superannuated preachers, and the bishops, shall be $200, and their travelling expenses."

Two hundred dollars is the entire allowance to travelling preachers, if they are married; it was the entire amount allowed these gentlemen who were travelling in this wilderness, and disseminating Christianity. And if they were bishops, they had the same allowance. Then we have another class of persons,—

"The annual allowance of the unmarried travelling, supernumerary, and superannuated preachers, and bishops, shall be $100, and their travelling expenses.

"Each child of a travelling preacher or bishop shall be allowed $16 annually, to the age of seven years, and $24 annually from the age of seven to fourteen years; and those preachers whose wives are dead shall be allowed for each child annually a sum sufficient to pay the board of such child or children during the above term of years: *Nevertheless*, this rule shall not apply to the children of preachers whose families are provided for by other means in their circuits respectively.

"The annual allowance of the widows of travelling, superannuated, worn-out, and supernumerary preachers, and the bishops, shall be $100.

"The orphans of travelling, supernumerary, superannuated, and worn-out preachers, and the bishops, shall be allowed by the annual conferences the same sums respectively which are allowed to the children of living preachers. And on the death of a preacher leaving a child or children without so much of worldly goods as should be necessary to his, her, or their support, the annual conference of which he was a member shall raise, in such manner as may be deemed best, a yearly sum for the subsistence and education of such orphan child or children, until he, she, or they, shall have arrived at fourteen years of age. The amount of which yearly sum shall be fixed by a committee of the conference at each session in advance."

We should have printed in Book No. [illegible]; an extract from the Discipline of 1840, to show how the fund of the preachers is made up. I find on pp. 170 and 171 of the Discipline of 1840,—

"The more effectually to raise the amount necessary to meet the abovementioned allowance, let there be made weekly class collections in all our societies, where it is practicable."

Now this was a very peculiar charitable fund, and the question about all these funds of charity is, how far is the intention of the founders established by their language, or by their circumstances taken in illustration of the language and the character of the fund, at its original establishment, in connexion with the uses to which it is designed to be applied. I, therefore, remark, concluding upon the point of the peculiarities of this fund, it was a profit from the services of the travelling preachers, as an earned profit of common labour. This book fund was nothing but a profit from this bookselling, and this bookselling was conducted by the preachers. The books were selected and supplied by the preachers. The preachers were accountable for the debts in the first instance. If they were not careful, if they were guilty of any neglect of duty, they stood responsible to their community for a breach of trust.

During the time that they were rendering this service what were they getting? Two hundred dollars a year, if married, to support themselves and their wives. Besides this they were allowed "travelling expenses," not for the expenses when the travelling was terminated, but for the actual *travelling* expenses. If they had to go from New-York to Boston the expenses on the journey were paid, but those were all that were included under "travelling expenses." Upon this system this community lived, and flourished, and prospered. Now, was there anything for these men to depend on? To what could they look in futurity—for themselves in old age, for their wives when they became too old to labour, for their children in their infancy, and for their widows? What was that which would permit a man, with any regard to his obligations to his family, to go into this missionary service, except that he thought he might be provided for by a miracle? It was this, substantially this, fund; for excepting the Chartered Fund growing out of donations, and that not a very large one, this fund was the only hope of infancy and old age, and the only means of the discharge of all that parental duty, and that duty of economy which every man owes to himself in making some provision for the future, and not presumptuously tempting Providence to supply him by a miracle. That is the character of this fund.

When you come to dispose of it, your Honours surely are not going to take it like a fund for the propagation of certain doctrines where the slightest deviation from the doctrine will forfeit it. If it were a question of that kind, I am sure no Court could ever sit in judgment upon this subject which would not struggle in every way possible, if a struggle were necessary, which would not consider it the plainest of its duties, to see that there should be no forfeiture of such a fund without the gravest, and clearest, and most perfectly-established breach of a substantial obligation; no breach of some trifling thing, no breach of a thing merely technical in its character would be permitted to forfeit that which was the common patrimony of the old, bereaved, and fatherless. These classes of persons all stand together. There is no provision applicable to the preachers, superannuated and supernumerary, different from that which applies to the widows and orphans. And if the conference is out of the pale of this Methodist Church, so that it has no right to the fund, the orphans and widows go with them. That is the doctrine of our friends on the other side. It comes to this; and I therefore submit to your Honours, when you come to examine this subject, that upon this question of forfeiture my learned friends must make the sun shine brightly. It must be a noon-day sun which will enable you to see any forfeiture by which the rights of such beneficiaries to the fund thus established shall ever be thought of. It was in no respect a mere gratuitous and charitable fund growing out of donations to maintain a particular faith or mode of ecclesiastical government. It was a retiring pension, or savings' bank, for the supernumerary and worn-out preachers, and their widows and orphans. I do not deny that a connexion with Methodism, that good standing in a Methodist Episcopal Church, was probably an implied condition in the establishment of this fund. I say an implied condition, because it is not expressed; it is implied from the fact that the provision in the Discipline of the Methodist Church speaks of these superannuated and worn-out preachers; but it is merely implied, and the extent and degree to which it is to be implied is very much in the judgment of the Court taking into view the nature and character of the fund.

Let us ask ourselves, if any of these men, when they were at their labours, should have had it put to them: "Well, my friend, by-and-by you will become feeble and decrepit, and perhaps you may go to a Baptist or a Presbyterian Church, do you mean, now, that if you do that, you shall have no share in this fund?" perhaps, if he was a very zealous man, he would say, "Yes, I mean that." But I think men in general would say, "Well, that is a thing which I did not think of; I do not know: it would be very hard, in my old age, to visit my infirmity in that way." My learned friends have, on this subject, it seems to me, a heavy task to make out, that the most strict, and perfect, and literal conformity to everything is necessary before this fund can be partaken of by these beneficiaries. Certainly, the exact conformity could not apply to widows and children. The establishment of this fund had for its primary object, (as the most of these charitable funds have,) the spreading of religious faith and the supplying of religious instruction. But it was not established to preach Methodism after a dividend had accrued. It was retroactive. Its benefits were thrown backward; it was for past services; the benefits lay before them to be sure, but the services out of which they became entitled to them were behind, and the contribution every year was not for the services of the preacher who preached this year, but for the services last year.

Let us look a little now into the application of this question as it arises. Here are the widows, and the old and worn-out preachers of the Methodist Church of the South of the present day. This fund began to be established in 1800—fifty years ago. It seems most probable that a vast majority of all those who can now participate in this fund are the very persons who have become worn-out; that is to say, taking the whole Connexion of the North and the South, the supernumerary and superannuated preachers, who would now partake of the fund, are the men who were at work from 1800 to 1840, or 1845, and who became superannuated and worn-out. So you will see what a sacred trust it is, what a sacred charity, if it is to be called a charity; with what rights those come whom we represent, when they come on the ground that here has been a divided dominion—when the question has been put,

> "—— Under what Prince, Bezonian? Speak, or die,"

and they are charged to have made an unfortunate answer. I am sure, when you come to examine this subject, you cannot examine it as stoics. You cannot do it but as men, Christian men, men used to the instruction of the pulpit, and who cannot but admire the self-denial of those who have gone about disseminating Christianity among the poor and ignorant of this country, and for such a paltry consideration in money.

I submit that there was in it the nature of a common property of earnings, not of gifts, and it can only be called a charity by reason of the technical manner in which it is to be administered.

I come now to another feature of this plan. That which is relied upon to forfeit it from our beneficiaries, is the act of the annual conferences in the South. Those conferences, our learned friends say, have done that which made them seceders. Well, what had they to do with this fund? What right had they? The supernumerary and worn-out preachers belonged, nominally, to those conferences; they had a right to be present, but I suppose, in point of fact, that those who were too old to preach would not very extensively mingle in those warlike acts to which our friends, in the report of 1848, on the state of the Church, which I understand is to be referred to, allude. Are the wives, and the widows, and the children, to be affected by the action of the annual conferences? If the forfeiture is to be enforced according to the doctrine of our learned friends, then it attaches not to the absence of the Methodistical character, because any one of these beneficiaries may be as orthodox as can be, may be perfect as a Methodist, yet if the annual conference has gone off it is forfeited. Is an annual conference to forfeit it when it has no more right to the fund, than has the clerk of a bank to the money which passes through his hands? It is the act of that body which is relied upon as the forfeiting act. I shall be glad to hear the argument which shall establish any right of forfeiture by the action of a mere agent. At any rate, it must be established by something exceedingly clear, because it certainly is a thing the most revolting in the world, not only to every legal, but to every common idea of justice. A man can hardly begin to apprehend what justice is, and not see that such a thing as this would be most grossly unjust. It would be equal to the laws of Draco, excepting that instead of dealing in blood it dealt in starvation.

One other proposition on the subject of this fund to show how sacredly it was regarded by this Church itself. I say it was distributed by the annual conferences, but belonged in actual right to the beneficiaries, and, as such, was and is protected by the sixth restrictive rule. This is the second point which I have submitted to your Honours. A word now as to the general character of these rules, which I shall afterwards more particularly examine. They are on pp. 28 and 29 of Book No. 1. The General Conference, prior to the establishment of these restrictive rules, consisted of all the Methodist preachers, who, instead of meeting in annual conferences, met in the General Conference. Their power was unlimited. But when they came to act by delegations, the power, as we contend, remained equally unlimited, except as it was restricted by the restrictive articles. When they came to put these rules in, the Court will notice in what connexion they put in this provision for retiring preachers and their families. They provide in the sixth rule the following :—

> "They shall not appropriate the produce of the Book Concern, nor of the Chartered Fund, to any purpose other than for the benefit of the travelling, supernumerary, superannuated, and worn-out preachers, their wives, widows, and children."

This is put as a restriction, and it is the only money restriction in these articles. As to all matters of finance and of money, the General Conference can do everything except in this single particular. They put this restriction alongside of the articles of religion. They put it alongside of their episcopacy. They put it alongside of the general rules of their United Societies which form their Church. They put it alongside of the trial of preachers and members. They invested it, indeed, with the most sacred sanctions. They do not say anything about being in connexion with the society, or continuing in it. All that can be said on the subject is, that it is implied, from the rule being a rule of this Church, that it applies to persons who hold the relations of preachers to the Church. And in what relation of preachers to the Church? Preachers who are to be deprived of everything when any change or difficulty may occur in the working of so extensive a system as this, whereby a man may remain a most perfect Methodist, and yet change his allegiance? For instance, if instead of our taking Texas, Texas had taken Mississippi, and it had been a conquered country, and conferences had been forbidden, so that the Church could not be held in that country, would it be held that, in such a case as that, entirely unforeseen, and not expressly provided for, a Methodist preacher who still lived in the conquered country, with his wife and children, was cut off from a participation in this fund, because Methodism in his country had become extinct?

When your Honours come to carry out this charity, you will be glad to be guided through all its difficulties, if they are difficulties, by the consideration of the great equity, the great humanity, and the great justice which pertains to the original institution of this fund. This Church, in this most simple way, provides this fund "for the benefit of the travelling, supernumerary, superannuated, and worn-out preachers, their wives, widows, and children." That is the trust. It is not connected, except impliedly, with the ecclesiastical connexion; and the extent to which it is to be thus connected, is a matter which will be afterwards discussed. But what I mean to say, and rely upon as having established, I am sure in your hearts, and I trust in your judgments, is, that that which is to defeat this claim, and that which is, in the language of the answer, *to forfeit it*, is not to be any technical departure from one or another mode of government. It must apply to the substantial elements and quality of Methodists, as men of faith and practice, conforming to the faith and practice, to the substantial elements of the Methodist faith rather than to the mere elements of a particular shape of a hierarchy. In this aspect of the case —in the aspect in which the gentlemen on the other side claim it as a forfeiture—it is emphatically an *Indian war*. It does not spare the old man. It does not spare the wife, nor the widow, nor the orphan. It scalps every one. But it is an Indian warfare, not in their intentions. I am very sure that the gentlemen, even the most heated of the partisans in this warfare, would never carry this principle out if they had seen the extent to which the doctrine necessarily led. I absolve them, from all my heart, from any such thought. Nothing in the history of this society shows that they would ever have thought of or done such a thing; and if the necessary consequence is, that it is to be an Indian warfare, nothing more need be said to establish the fact, that it was not originally intended. For I venture to say, it is not intended by the most heated men of the present day, that that should be the operation of what they claim to be the system of forfeiture which they would apply to it.

One other word upon this part of the case. In illustrating a little, in anticipation of an argument which I shall presently lay before you, I would now explain that they do not set up any deviation of faith on our part, or any deviation of discipline. All they set up is, that we are not in harmony with their General Conference, and that they are the real, true General Conference. Now I suppose no Methodist will deny, that it is essential that the preachers should be in connexion with an annual conference as with a General Conference. I find in the Methodist Book of, Discipline that the annual conference is as necessary a body as the General Conference; nay, four times as essential. It is the primary body, and the power of the General Conference is only the powers of the annual conferences assembled together. What shall we say of all the Southern country, where, according to the learned gentlemen on the other side, there is not a single man, woman, or child, in connexion with an annual conference as they put it; because they say these annual conferences are not annual conferences. Certainly, it is a most extinguishing doctrine. Suppose we had every heart and desire to continue with the annual conferences; suppose, instead of there being an almost unanimous vote of the Southern conferences in favour of division, there had been close majorities, then the minorities of every conference overruled by the majorities, according to my learned friends, must form a seceding conference, or they would have no right to the fund. Now, can it be that that was in the contemplation of those who established this fund, or shall it be in the contemplation of those who take it up in a new and unforeseen case, and undertake to say what would have been the decision of those who established it, if they had foreseen the case? Can it be that those are to be excluded who are in connexion with the annual conferences? Here are annual conferences, adopting every principle of Methodism; the primary governing bodies of the Methodist Church. These people are in firm, and in close connexion with them, but merely differing from a certain number of those who represent the other conferences in a General Conference. Can you conceive of a slighter ground of forfeiture than that? That is what is set up in the answer. They do not say that we make ourselves unworthy recipients of this charity; it is, that admitting us to have rights, we forfeit them, and that the forfeiture is by reason of our remaining in connexion with the primary governing bodies, submitting to the Discipline, adopting the doctrines, and conforming to the practices and usages in every respect, but that our conferences think it necessary, for the harmonious action of the Methodist Church, for its action as a Christian body giving light in the Southern country, that they should act separately; and that that act of independence is a schism, a secession, and such a departure from faith and doctrine, as to strip even the widows and children of a provision made for them by their husbands and fathers in their better days. I cannot conceive that such a doctrine can be established.

This being the character of the fund, I now propose to inquire into the grounds on which the defence say it has been forfeited. The first ground they set up is, that the General Conference had no power to sanction a division. They say, that supposing the General Conference had undertaken in the most explicit way to sanction a separation, they never had any power to do it. In the second place, they say that this grant of the power of separation as actually assented to, was contingent upon the experiment being made in the Southern Churches of whether they could be ruined first and repaired afterwards, or whether they should prevent the ruin and go on without it. They say: "You should have gone on and experimented, to see whether you would have been ruined; because you should not go to this until you were nearly ruined." That is the second ground of forfeiture—not stated, to be sure, in that form, but such is the substance of it. They say: "You should have tried an experiment; and not having experimented, you have not taken the proper means of carrying out your grant, supposing that the General Conference had a right to make it." The third ground is, that we violated the borders as laid down in that Plan of Separation. And the other ground is, that it was all conditioned on the passage, by the annual conferences, by the requisite vote, of an alteration of the sixth restrictive article. In other words, it comes to one of these two propositions: First, they say the General Conference could not grant it; and secondly, if they could and did grant it, it was conditional, and the condition has not occurred or has been broken. I propose to examine these several questions in detail. I have discussed my third and fourth points—that the title of the beneficiaries at the time immediately before the separation of the Church into two parts was perfect, and it cannot be defeated or forfeited without a clear proof of breach of condition by the beneficiaries. And even if a breach of condition by the annual conferences, by whom the fund was to be distributed, could forfeit, there has been no forfeiture; because the General Conference of 1844 had the power to consent to an amicable division of the conferences on grave causes touching the general efficiency of the Church.

The question presented here is entirely uncovered, so far as my inquiries have extended, by any precedent; nor have I seen any principle laid down by any writer on the subject which covers it, except in one case in Kentucky, to which reference will hereafter be made. The question that I shall first discuss, must be disembarrassed of all those questions of whether they did it on condition or not, or whether the condition has been complied with or not. I first wish to discuss the question of whether, suppose they had in express terms enacted, "Be it resolved, by this General Conference, that the slaveholding conferences (naming them) and the Northern conferences (naming them) shall hereafter hold their sessions separate, and they shall be the General Conferences of the Methodist Church called for in the Discipline, and applying to the extent of country in which these annual conferences have jurisdiction," it would have been binding. That is the first plain proposition into which this subject is to be distributed, and which must be examined.

I remark, in the first place, that this case is unprecedented, because here is no dispute at all as to doctrines. It is not set up in the answer that we are heterodox by the shade of a hair. It is not set up that we have violated even the least rule about dress. There is no sort of pretence of any deviation in doctrine, nor anything in morals, in practice, or in Methodist usages. We have adopted their Book of Discipline, word for word, except where alterations are called for by the mere change of the meeting of the General Conference, our meeting being of thirteen annual conferences; their Discipline has nothing about that. In every other case that has occurred in this branch of the law, there has been a claim that there was a departure in doctrines, and the Courts have always said, that although at law we only look to the regularity of the organization and succession, yet in equity, let the organization be ever so regular, let the succession be ever so regular, if there be a deviation in doctrine it is a misapplication of the trust, if it be held for the diffusion of that doctrine. But here the case is disembarrassed of any such consideration. There is no deviation in morals or doctrines; in rites, ceremonies, or usages. They have classes; so have we. They have circuits; so have we. They have elders; so have we. They have travelling preachers who travel all around; so have we. They have bishops; so have we. They elect their bishops; so do we. We institute bishops by the same form of service as they do. In everything we are alike. They are governed by a General Conference; so are we. Our General Conference have the same powers as theirs,—they have no more power than they had before the separation.

You now see how peculiar this case is. It is a mere question as to the right of these two bodies, while one, to divide and govern themselves by a duality instead of a unity. If that is a thing which forfeits every right depending on this matter, it would not come up upon one side of this question merely. Both sides would forfeit; that is to say, the Northern Methodist Church would have no more right to this book fund than the Southern Methodist Church. So long as there was a Northern and Southern Methodist who stood opposed to this division, they two would form a whole Church, and all other Northern and Southern men would stand excluded; because the doctrine which I am now considering, and which my friends must either abandon, or adopt in the strongest manner, is, that the Conference had not the power to consent to a division of it into two bodies. If it had not, is the party who gave the consent any better off than the party who took it? Was it one body who gave the consent and another who took it? No, it was the same body who gave it, and the two parts of the body who took it; and the fund would stand without an owner, unless it should be some stray, worn-out preacher, who had not voice enough to give any dissent, but who had sense enough to employ counsel and claim the whole fund. If the General Conference had not the power, that would be the result.

Again: here is no dispute as to the supreme ecclesiastical body to which submission is due. In all these disputes which have heretofore arisen in this country, it has been as to adherence to this General Assembly or that General Assembly which claims to be the only one, and by its mode of succession establishes the right to be the only one. This is not a claim of that sort. It is a claim of this sort: the parties consent that the general body should act in two parts, and each part be governed by its own general body. But, according to the argument of our friends, there is no General Conference, and there could be none after the act of 1844; there could be none in the sense of the Discipline of the Methodist Church. The Conference had consented that the Southern conferences should no longer be represented in that General Conference. I am now considering the question apart from the conditions, supposing the consent to be a clear one. We are now on the question of the power. They having consented that the Southern conferences should not send their delegates to the General Conference, and the Northern conferences should send up their delegates to the Northern Conference at a particular place, I submit that, if their doctrine is true, the Methodist Church is literally cut in two and dead—there is no General Conference. If they deny the power of the General Conference to grant a separation, then there never was a General Conference after that of 1844, and there is an end of this question; because the general body, to whom the subordinate bodies are supposed to owe allegiance, being destroyed—the king being dead, there is no treason to that king—there is no government. It is another question, and it is a question which I think our learned friends will say does not arise here, because I am sure they cannot meet it.

Again: I submit that this is not the case of a hostile separation; and notwithstanding the warmth exhibited in the Convention of 1844, they took the wise part, of which Scripture gives a most eminent illustration, when Abraham and Lot separated, that, as they could not agree when together, they might agree when separated.

They adopted that principle; and although it had been preceded by heats, although the acts which were done were, to the manifest observation of every observer, such as would establish separation, not lead to it—such as to render the co-operation of the two parts of the body any longer perfectly hopeless—they parted in good-will. They shook hands when they separated; they spoke in terms of affection on both sides. I am very glad to be corrected by my learned friend, as to an error into which I had fallen, in the Conference of 1844 not having excluded Bishop Andrew from the consecration of the other bishops. If you will look at the debates and closing acts of that Conference, you will find that the idea of both parties was, that they should no longer be tied together in this struggling relation; but should be permitted to go off untramelled, each with their own particular views, to do good in their own way, and among their own people. This feeling harmonized the termination of that Conference. This, therefore, is not the case of a hostile separation; and in that respect I am happy to say, that whatever took place afterwards through mischiefs, which I think grew out of the press, the Conference when it separated, when it agreed to this division, did it harmoniously, did it kindly, and in the expectation of a kind communion afterwards.

I submit that this General Conference had the power to consent, from the very constitution of it. Originally there was only one conference, and that was annual. When that came to be divided into several annual conferences, they yet all met together; and in 1792, I think it was, for the first time they determined to meet every four years. But all the preachers who formed the annual conferences, met in General Conference. I think it will not be denied that in 1792, or in 1800, or in 1804, this body had a right to divide itself. They were all there. To say they had not a right to divide, would be to say that men whose connexion grew, in fact, out of meeting together, had no right to meet otherwise. I do not suppose it can be contended, with any force of argument, that the General Conference before they came to be a delegated body, could not have divided themselves, for grave reasons of convenience, into two. For instance: if there had not been the present great facilities for travelling, they might have established a conference on the eastern, and another on the western side of the mountains. The mere difficulty of communication would have been a sufficient reason, and would have justified it; and every Court, and every man of sense would have said that it was a proper, prudent, and reasonable thing that the power of the Church, in such a case, should be exercised in a double instead of a single form, or a divided instead of a single meeting.

In 1808 arose a new system; it was of acting by delegations, and by peculiar delegations. It was acting rather by committees than by delegations. Instead of having fourteen clergymen come to a General Conference, one of the fourteen was selected to carry the power of them all; and I submit to your Honours, as a proposition which I am sure you will not fail to adopt, that the Conference of 1808, and its successors, had all the powers of the previous General Conferences, except so far as they were limited by the restrictive articles. In vain will you look into this Methodist system prior to 1808, for any restrictions on the General Conference of that Church. If that body had chosen to become Socinian; if it had chosen to adopt the Presbyterian or Baptist forms, either of government or of doctrine, it was in its power to do it. There was no limit. They represented the Church; they were the Church. The Church dispersed its light from the preachers. The laity were not known in the governing body. Matters of doctrine, discipline, and everything were in the governing body. If that was so up to 1808, what was that body after that period? It was the same General Conference. Before, it is probable that preachers from the more distant parts could not attend as well as those who lived near the place where the sessions were held, and that those who lived nearer would be more fully present than those more distant; and yet its powers were the same. What then did this change of the system in 1808 effect? Why, it left the body with the same powers it had before, only that it prevented that inequality, and put specific limitations upon it. I submit that the Conference of 1808, and all which succeeded it, were invested with the full powers of the ecclesiastical government of the Methodist Episcopal Church; and this is unlike any other Church, because its historian tells us, as I read the other day, that every General Conference provides a Book of Discipline, which contained the articles of religion, and the form of the hierarchy of the Church; and all its rites and ceremonies, and financial and other arrangements, were superseded by the new Book of Discipline, sanctioned by the new Conference, and published by it. This is put in very plain and intelligible language by Mr. Emory in his History, on the second page of our first book of the Proofs:—

"In our civil governments, the statutes are scattered through the several volumes of laws which have been published from time to time, and therefore these are all preserved. But in the Methodist Episcopal Church, the Discipline, as revised at each General Conference, being in itself complete, supplants all that had gone before it, and the previous editions are cast aside as of no further use. Thus it has continued, until now nearly sixty years have elapsed since the organization of the Church, and the Discipline has undergone about twenty distinct revisions."

Before I go into some other considerations, growing out of these restrictive articles, which I think most fully establish the plenitude of the power, I propose to consider historically one or two events, to show that my proposition is correct.

The whole American Methodist Episcopal body was an amicable separation from that in England, and this separation never impeached the quality of any Methodist preachers. Our civil institutions began in revolution. Our civil government was a schism of the most grievous kind; one of those schisms that warranted an Indian warfare, that warranted execution, hanging, bills of attainder, everything that is known in revolutionary warfare. But the religious separation of the Methodists was the most kindly, peaceful, and regular separation, by the consent of the body of which it was a part, so that from that day to the present they have been in such harmony, that the preachers of one part of it are received, as I understand, without examination as preachers in the other. Looking at the origin of this separation, we find that those who separated were treated as being in perfectly good standing with their brethren, not only in England, but all over the world. I read from page 3 of our book:—

"The close of the year 1784 constituted a new and most important epoch in American Methodism. The independence of the United States having been confirmed by the peace of 1783, the authority of England over them, both civil and ecclesiastical, came to an end. The connexion with the Church of England being thus providentially *dissolved*, Mr. Wesley, who had always resisted a *separation* from it, took measures, on the application of the American societies, to organize them into a Church. In explanation of his views and wishes, he addressed to the brethren in America the following letter."

I will not read the whole of the letter, but a paragraph from it on page 5:—

"As our American brethren are now totally disentangled, both from the state and from the English hierarchy, we dare not entangle them again either with the one or the other. They are now at full liberty simply to follow the Scriptures and the primitive Church. And we judge it best that they should stand fast in that liberty wherewith God has so strangely made them free."

That letter was written Sept. 10, 1784. It probably reached this country in the course of the next month. I read on page 5 of our book the following:—

"To carry into effect the proposed organization, a General Conference of preachers was called, to meet in Baltimore, at Christmas, 1784. Sixty out of the eighty-three preachers then in the travelling connexion, attended at the appointed time. 'At this Conference,' say the annual minutes for 1785, 'it was unanimously agreed that the circumstances made it expedient for us to become a separate body, under the denomination of "The Methodist Episcopal Church."' And again they say: 'We formed ourselves into an independent Church; and following the counsel of Mr. John Wesley, who recommended the episcopal mode of Church government, we thought it best to become an episcopal Church, making the episcopal office elective, and the elected superintendent or bishop amenable to the body of ministers and preachers.' They adopted a form of Discipline for the government of the Church. This was substantially the same with the Large Minutes, the principal alterations being only such as were necessary to adapt it to the state of things in America."

These "Large Minutes" were Mr. Wesley's minutes. I will read from the Discipline of this Conference, (page 6:)—

"*Ques.* 2. What can be done in order to the future union of Methodists?
"*Ans.* During the life of the Rev. Mr. Wesley, we acknowledge ourselves his sons in the Gospel, ready, in matters belonging to Church government, to obey his commands. And we do engage, after his death, to do everything that we judge consistent with the cause of religion in America, and the political interests of these States, to preserve and promote our union with the Methodists in Europe."

This was after Mr. Wesley's letter, and after the dissolution of their connexion with the European Methodists. Again, (page 7:)—

"*Ques.* 3. As the ecclesiastical as well as civil affairs of these United States have passed through a very considerable change by the Revolution, what plan of Church government shall we hereafter pursue?
"*Ans.* We will form ourselves into an episcopal Church, under the direction of superintendents, elders, deacons, and helpers, according to the forms of ordination annexed to our Liturgy, and the form of Discipline set forth in these minutes."

The Discipline they adopted was the same with that of the English Methodists. It was the Large Minutes of Wesley. The organization was the same, excepting that Mr. Wesley was not here, and this body pledged themselves to conform during his lifetime to his commands, and after his death to what should be consistent with the cause of religion, and the preservation and promotion of union with the English Methodists.

Again: upon this subject I would refer to what took place in 1789, which will be found on pp. 10 and 11, which I will not read, but which, I trust, will receive from your Honours the attention it deserves. I shall read now from the Discipline of 1840. I believe it was not read in the course of the reading of the Proofs, but I think it material on this subject—page 36, chap. i., sec. 8.

On Receiving Preachers from the Wesleyan Connexion and other Denominations.

"*Ques.* 1. In what manner shall we receive those ministers who may come to us from the Wesleyan connexion in Europe or Canada?
"*Ans.* If they come to us properly accredited from either the British, Irish, or Canada Conference, they may be received according to such credentials, provided they give satisfaction to an annual conference of their willingness to conform to our Church government and usages.
"*Ques.* 2. How shall we receive those ministers who may offer to unite with us from other Christian Churches?
"*Ans.* Those ministers of other evangelical Churches, who may desire to unite with our Church, whether as local or itinerant, may be received according to our usages, on condition of their taking upon them our ordination vows, without the re-imposition of hands, giving satisfaction to an annual conference of their being in or-

ders, and of their agreement with us in doctrine, discipline, government, and usages; provided the conference is also satisfied with their gifts, grace, and usefulness."

After the separation from England, and after the separation of the Canada Methodists, when their ministers came to the Methodist body in this country they were to be received, they were not to be re-ordained, there was to be no re-imposition of hands, they were simply to declare their conformity, or their willingness to conform, to the Church government in this country. But when ministers come from any other denomination, although there is no theological re-ordination, yet there is a most complete act of re-institution into the ministry as into the ministry of a different evangelical Church, not holding the orders of other denominations theologically invalid, but holding that this was a necessary change into another Church calling for all those things which indicate a change of allegiance.

On the subject of the Methodist Church in this country separating from the Methodists of England, peacefully and without blame, and remaining unimpeachable Methodists in every sense, the address of the British Conference and the answer to it, from the minutes of 1840, (pp. 64 and 65 of Book No. 1,) are very material. The whole character of this address and the reply to it, is that of parts of the same body addressing each other. The reception of a letter so plain in the character of its reflections, and the kind spirit of the reply to it made by the Conference of 1840, show that these two bodies after the separation did not treat each other as schismatical, as being on the one side seceders and on the other the genuine body. And I cannot but call your Honours' attention to the passage with which the American Methodist Conference closes its reply to the British letter—a sort of *argumentum ad hominem*—in which they adopt the very language of the British Conference in 1833. They quote the language of the English Methodist Missionary Society in their instructions to missionaries, as follows:—

"As in the colonies in which you are called to labour, a great proportion of the inhabitants are in a state of slavery, the committee most strongly call to your remembrance what was so fully stated to you when you were accepted as a missionary to the West Indies, that your only business is to promote the moral and religious improvement of the slaves to whom you may have access, without in the least degree, in public or private, interfering with their civil condition."

I now submit that the separation of the Canada Conference from the American body was one of those separations which were not schisms nor schismatical. In the short examination which I shall give this subject, and yet which I intend to be a rather full one, the Court will please to understand that I do not pretend to say that some of the gentlemen who took part in that did not consider that, before a consequence of that separation, *viz.* a division of the money, could take place, it was necessary to change the sixth restrictive article. Some of them did certainly so consider, and they agreed to submit to the annual conferences the question, whether the money should be divided. They decided that it should not be done. Then the General Conference almost unanimously voted, that instead of dividing the money or the capital, they would reduce the price of books furnished to the Canada Methodists so that no profit should be made on them for a certain period of years. If they were thus selling the books to seceders, to strangers, they were committing a palpable breach of trust. They gave to the Canada Conference seven per cent., for sixteen years, of the profits of the Methodist books which they sold to them. According to the position of our friends on the other side, they had no more right to give this much away to them than they had to give it to establish a billiard-room.

Let us look into this case. My object in referring to it is to show that in that separation the Methodist conferences had no idea that there was a schism created, whatever else may have been their notions. I speak respectfully when I say "notions." By notions, I mean opinions very hastily formed, not very well considered, and as I believe, (after reading the documents,) not adopted by the sounder men among them. They acted upon a principle of concession, and finally leaped over a difficulty which they could not bridge. They did wisely; but what I wish to show is, that in that matter there was no idea entertained that there was any secession or schism. The history of this is to be found from page 32 to page 52 of our book of Proofs.

Your Honours will see that this began by a petition in 1828. The Canada Methodists—a portion of the Church held in the highest esteem and respect—put it plainly on the ground that it was their idea that the General Conference could consent to a separation; and in their petition they gave such reasons as I think would satisfy every one as to the power of the General Conference and the propriety of its exercise. The petition begins, (page 32 :)—

"Rev. Fathers and Brethren,—The Canada Conference having, after mature deliberation, deemed a separation expedient, most humbly pray that they may be set off a separate and independent Church in Canada."

If there had been any idea of secession and schism it was only for the Canada Methodists to avow it. They needed no petition, no consent to secede. They might on the ground of the necessity of the case, of their distance from the place of meeting, have seceded and justified themselves, standing the charge of schism. This they did not do; but they went at once, as a body of Methodists of character and respectability, and declared to the Methodist General Conference that the latter had the power to sanction a separation: and they asked for a separation. They then gave the reasons for separation: first, political relations and political feelings; next, the local circumstances of their societies; then, the religious privileges which it is probable they would obtain from their government if they were separated; then, their wanting a bishop who should act exclusively in that Province. This was presented in view of the fact, that in the war of 1812, still in fresh recollection, the people of the conferences were found in arms against each other, and it was impossible for a bishop from the United States to exercise his functions in Canada. They then refer to the general wish of the people in Canada for a separation. These are the things which made a palpable necessity for separation.

They would not certainly ask for a separation if they did not suppose the Conference had the power to grant it. Now look at the manner of the petition. They say, (pp. 33, 34 :)—

"Your petitioners, likewise, most humbly and earnestly solicit that the General Conference may also be pleased,

"1st. To maintain with the British Conference, as far as practicable, the main principles of the late arrangements with regard to Canada.

"2d. That the General Conference will appoint such an individual for a superintendent of our societies in Canada, as may be nominated by the delegates of the Canada Conference.

"3d. That the Church in Canada may be embraced in the general and friendly principle recognised by the two Connexions,—'The Wesleyan Methodists are the same in every part of the world.'"

That was the legend which was the "*E Pluribus Unum*" upon the flag of this society: "The Wesleyan Methodists are the same in every part of the world." After the original separation from the Methodists of England, it was adopted; when the Canada separation took place, they presented that as the great maxim. It is as much as to say: "Whether we are separated by distinct organization or not, it is the same body; it is no schism, no want of orthodoxy in any respect. The petition add, (p. 34,)—

"4th. That the General Conference will, together with an independent establishment, be pleased to grant your petitioners a portion of the Book Concern, of the Chartered Fund, and a portion of the fund of the Missionary Society."

They did not think there would be any difficulty in having their part of the fund granted, because, I venture to say, they considered that the least of all difficulties would be a money difficulty. And yet it proved the greatest, and one which, more than any other act of the Methodist body, exhibits it in a light somewhat equivocal in regard to the duties of its own discipline, if it is as they seem to suppose it be. Then the committee, under the chairmanship of Dr. Bangs, to which this matter was referred in their report, (pp. 34, 35,) say:—

"The committee are unanimously of the opinion, that, however peculiar may be the situation of our brethren in Canada, and however much we may sympathize with them in their present state of perplexity, this General Conference cannot consistently grant them a separate Church establishment, according to the prayer of the petitioners. The committee, therefore, recommend to the General Conference the adoption of the following resolutions:—

"1. That, inasmuch as the several annual conferences have not recommended it to the General Conference, it is unconstitutional, and also, under the circumstances, inexpedient, to grant the prayer of the petitioners for a separate Church establishment in Upper Canada.

"2. That an affectionate circular address be prepared by this General Conference, stating the reasons why their request cannot be granted, and expressing the unabated attachment of this Conference for their brethren in Canada, and their earnest desire for their continuance in the fellowship of the Church. All which is respectfully submitted. (Signed) N. BANGS, *Chairman.*

"*Pittsburgh, May* 12, 1828."

It was the language of the report that it was unconstitutional to grant the prayer of the petitioners, inasmuch as the annual conferences had not recommended it. Your Honours will see, however, that the separation was granted by the almost unanimous vote of this body, without the slightest hesitation and without the recommendation of the annual conferences. On pp. 35 and 36 I find:—

"MAY 17.—Rev. John Ryerson, one of the delegates from the Canada Conference, offered the following substitute for the report under consideration:—

"'Whereas the Canada Annual Conference, situated in the Province of Upper Canada, under a foreign government, have, in their memorial, presented to this Conference the disabilities under which they labour, in consequence of their union with a foreign ecclesiastical government, and setting forth their desire to be set off as a separate Church establishment; and whereas this General Conference disclaims all right to exercise ecclesiastical jurisdiction under such circumstances except by mutual agreement;

"'1. *Resolved*, therefore, by the delegates of the annual conferences in General Conference assembled, that the compact existing between the Canada Annual Conference and the Methodist Episcopal Church in the United States, be, and hereby is, dissolved by mutual consent.

"'2. That our superintendents or superintendent be, and hereby are, respectfully advised and requested to ordain such person as may be elected by the Canada Conference as superintendent for the Canada Connexion.

"'3. That we do hereby recommend to our brethren in Canada to adopt the form of government of the Methodist Episcopal Church in the United States with such modifications as their particular relations shall render necessary.

"'4. That we do hereby express to our Canada brethren our sincere desire that the most friendly feeling may exist between them and the Connexion of the Methodist Episcopal Church in the United States.

"'5. That the claims of the Canada Conference on our Book Concern and Chartered Fund, and any other claims that they may suppose they justly have, shall be left open for future negotiations, and adjusted between the two Connexions.

"'G. R. JONES,
MOSES CRUME.'

"'*May* 17.

"The question on the first resolution was decided in the affirmative—104 for, and 43 against it."

Thus the Court will see that the first resolution, which purported to dissolve this connexion between the conferences, had the voice of 104 for it, to 43 against it.

MR. CHOATE,—The gentleman must remember that that vote was afterwards reconsidered.

MR. LORD,—I will give the history of that. The only effect of the reconsideration was to authorize a separation without this first resolution. But what is the meaning of this first vote? It is that one hundred and four thought this was constitutional, and forty-three thought that it was not. Is that nothing? Suppose they did reconsider it. How was the question presented? There was a report from Dr. Bangs, that as this was without the recommendation of the annual conferences it was unconstitutional, and a Canada gentleman, apparently a stranger, proposes a substitute that it is constitutional, and one hundred and four vote in favour of the substitute, and forty-three doubt the constitutional power. Now, how idle is it to talk about reconsideration upon such a subject as this! There might be a reconsideration on the subject of expediency, but upon the question of constitutional right, let gentlemen explain it to me in consistency with the fairness and maturity of the men who gave that vote, how can it be that one hundred and four deliberately considered it both constitutional and expedient, and then reconsidered it, unless that reconsideration was on the question of expediency and not of constitutionality? When they gave the first vote they must have considered it both constitutional and expedient, and when they reconsided it, it might have been in view of a better and more harmonious plan, or it might have been in view of a simple question of expediency. But how can one hundred and four have voted for it, if they did not suppose it was constitutional? Then the record says: "The other four resolutions were, on motion, referred to a special committee, to consist of five members." Those four resolutions were those carrying out the Plan of Separation. That committee reported other resolutions which formed the substitute eventually adopted in place of that first resolution. The first resolution reported by this committee was:—

"If the Annual Conference in Upper Canada, at its ensuing session, or any succeeding session previously to the next General Conference, shall definitely determine on this course, and elect a general superintendent of the Methodist Episcopal Church in that Province, this General Conference do hereby authorize any one or more of the general superintendents of the Methodist Episcopal Church in the United States, with the assistance of two or more elders, to ordain such general superintendent for the said Church in Upper Canada, provided always that nothing herein contained be contrary to, or inconsistent with, the laws existing in the said Province; and provided that no such general superintendent of the Methodist Episcopal Church in Upper Canada, or any of his successors in office, shall at any time exercise any ecclesiastical jurisdiction whatever in any part of the United States, or of the Territories thereof; and provided also that this article shall be expressly ratified and agreed to by the said Canada Annual Conference, before any such ordination shall take place."

The second and third resolutions reported by that committee were consequences of this. Then we find (pp. 38, 39):—

"WEDNESDAY MORNING, MAY 21.—It was, on motion, *Resolved*, That the subject of the petition from the Canada Conference be resumed; whereupon the resolutions, as reported by the last committee appointed on that subject, were read. It was then resolved that the subject shall now be considered and acted on.

"Samuel H. Thompson moved, and it was seconded, that the resolutions, as reported by the committee, be adopted. The question being taken, it was decided in the affirmative—108 voting in favour of adoption, and 22 against it."

These resolutions, as has already been seen, provided for the manner of the organization of an independent Methodist Episcopal Church in Canada. It was providing completely for the case contemplated by the first resolution of Mr. Ryerson. Then (page 29):—

"May 23.—J. Emory moved, and it was seconded, that the resolution first adopted on the subject of the separation of the Canada Conference from the Connexion in the United States, be reconsidered, and the motion prevailed. It was then resolved, on motion, that this resolution be rescinded."

This resolution first adopted they had superseded by the passage of the resolutions reported by the committee. This second series of resolutions, which were adopted, provided for the complete establishment, at its own choice, of a Methodist Episcopal Church in Canada, with its bishop, and its bishop not to have power in the United States, but to be limited to Canada. They then repealed the first resolution, which they had previously passed, but which had become perfectly unnecessary, because it spoke of dissolving a compact, when here provision was made for the establishment of an entire and separate Church.

From the reading of these documents, in regard to the Canada case, it does seem to me very clear that the General Conference of 1828, not only by its vote of 104 to 43 asserted the power of consenting, upon such reasons as were there presented, to the establishment of separate Churches, but also absolutely carried it out by the resolutions reported by Dr. Fisk, as the chairman of this committee, which were adopted by the Conference. And when this report was adopted, the less efficient provision before adopted was rescinded as useless. This would seem to be the natural supposition, also, because on this complete plan the vote was 108 to 22, and it was adopted by a much larger majority than the other prior resolution had been.

Then came up the difficulty about the Book Concern; and it is somewhat unpleasant to see that there should be so much more difficulty about dividing funds than dividing members. There has always certainly been a bone of contention about that which did not exist in regard to theological difficulties. It is a difficulty which I confess is surprising to me, because everything about this body, and everything about its institutions, exhibits such an adoption of honourable poverty, such self-denial in regard to money and money affairs; and it is one of the strange things which this investigation has brought me to notice, that with a body so entirely honourable as this, there should be this poor business of making difficulties as to dividing funds which did not exist with regard to dividing bodies. As will be seen on pp. 40, 41, a report of a committee came in on this subject. It will be noticed that after this organization of the new Church, there remained several new things to be done in connexion with it, and one was as to the supply of books and the apportionment of the book-fund. The provision for the organization of a new Church in Canada did not settle the question in relation to the book-fund. In 1832 this subject came up, and in what manner? Not on a "petition" from the Canada Conference. In 1828 the question first arose on a "petition," but now in 1832 we find it come up in a very different style on "An Address from the Delegates of the Methodist Episcopal Church of Canada." Here you have a newly-organized Church, perfectly independent of this body, addressing it—addressing it not as schismatics, not by way of recantation, not by way of asking forgiveness, not by way of any deprecation, but claiming rights. Here was a Church which had been organized by the very consent of this body, now presenting itself in its new organization, and in its new independence, not with a petition, but with an address—not with a supplication, but with an ambassador.—Page 39.

"MAY 4, 1832.—An address from the delegates of the Methodist Episcopal Church of Canada was presented and read; and, on motion, that part of it relating to the Book Concern was referred to the committee on the Book Concern, and that part of it relating to missions, referred to the committee on missions.

"MAY 18.—On motion, the report of the committee on the Book Concern, respecting the Canada business, was called up."

A debate was then had upon it. It was again debated on the 19th, 21st, and 23d of May. This address, as has been seen, related to two subjects—the Book Concern and missionary concerns. The report here referred to, related to the Book Concern. It will be found on page 41. It was :—

"The committee to whom was referred the business of the negotiation with the delegates of the Canada Conference on the subject of our Book Concern, having had the same under their serious consideration, are of opinion that, in consideration of their former relation to us, and the friendly feeling and brotherly affection which now exist between the two Connexions, as well as in view of the liberal and efficient support they have formerly given to the Concern, an apportionment of the property of the Concern ought to be made to them."

These gentlemen, after consenting to the establishment of a new Church, declare that it is an equitable principle that an apportionment of the property ought to be made, particularly on account of the former relations which had subsisted between them. Here we have a principle of equity declared, which must govern, and ought to govern, in regard to this Book Concern, in every case. This Conference of 1832 declared as a principle of equity, that in consideration of the past—and it was a much better past in the Southern Church towards this great body, than the past of that poor Canadian Church, whose benefit to the general body was for the most part to allow them to exercise charity—an apportionment of the property ought to be made.

I ask nothing of your Honours in this case, but to incorporate that phrase into your decree; that you will only declare, with regard to us, as the Conference of 1832 declared in regard to Canada—that in consideration of our former connexion with this body, and the friendly feeling and brotherly affection which now exist between the two Connexions, as well as in view of the liberal and efficient support which we formerly gave to the Concern, it is equitable an apportionment of the property of the Concern ought to be made to us. Now, what prevented this being done in the Canada case? I will continue to read the report :—

"But as constitutional difficulties are believed to be in the way of such an appropriation by this Conference, because they have not been instructed on this subject by their constituents, according to the proviso at the end of the restrictive regulations, they beg leave to submit, for the adoption of the Conference, the following resolutions."

These resolutions were to submit the matter of apportionment to the annual conferences. But what is the meaning of this report? Why, the fair and honest view is, that "we consider in justice this thing ought to be done; this fund is not our fund, exclusive of the preachers in the Canada Conference, and ought to be divided; but we regret that we have not the power to do it,—that there are constitutional difficulties to such a thing being done; but, inasmuch as it ought to be done, we shall refer the question to the annual conferences." So far as the act of the General Conference is concerned, it is decisive of the question of equity, and not decisive of the question of power over the fund, as they left that to the annual conferences, and the latter would not agree to it. Our learned friends on the other side intend to refer to the fact that the Southern conferences at that time did not agree to this division. That does not establish the law. Undoubtedly, the view of the General Conference, the great legislative body of this Church, when it was enlightened by discussion, was, that though there was doubt as to the constitutional power, yet there was a plain equity which ought to direct a part of it to the support of the Canada preachers. That is the way in which this thing stands. So far as our friends ask to have your Honours consider the weight of the authority of the Southern conferences, they are very welcome to it. I conceive that these questions of constitutional power over funds belong more properly to a court of justice.

The manner in which the vote was taken on this subject is worthy of great consideration in this connexion. In the first place, the Conference sanctioned the formation of a separate Church in Canada, and they treated this separate Church as not schismatical. Secondly, they conceive there are difficulties in regard to the restrictive article. Whether these difficulties were such as would have precluded any particular preacher from coming and claiming, after that separation, a right to this fund, was not before them: the right to divide the fund itself they think ought to be known, and they therefore thought it was safe to submit it to the annual conferences; and the conferences voted that they would not consent to this. Then what took place? I would call attention, without reading them, to pp. 43, 44, and 45, to show the character in which the two bodies held each other after this separation. The vote came in, whereby the conferences decided not to consent to this Book Concern being divided. The Conference of 1836 then took up the subject, and they appointed a committee. That committee examined the votes, and found that the necessary number of votes had not been given by the annual conferences; and then the committee go on to say (page 49):—

"But inasmuch as the General Conference have ever claimed and exercised the right to regulate the discount at which our books may be sold to wholesale purchasers, and with a view to an amicable and final arrangement of all the difficulties which have existed on this subject, and especially with a sincere desire to go as far as justice to the Methodist Episcopal Church will authorize, to encourage and perpetuate the friendly and fraternal feelings which should ever exist between the different members of the great Methodist family, the committee submit to the consideration, and for the adoption of the General Conference, the following arrangement, mutually agreed to by the delegates from Canada and the book agents, and which we are assured will be satisfactory to our Canadian brethren, if sanctioned by this Conference.

"Whereas the Canada Conference, now in connexion with the Wesleyan Methodists of Great Britain, was formerly united to, and formed part of the Methodist Episcopal Church; and whereas the union, which by mutual consent then subsisted, was dissolved at the earnest and repeated solicitations of the ministers and members of the Church in Canada," &c.

Was this the language of a Church towards schismatics? Then comes the agreement.—Pp. 50, 51.

"The agents of the Methodist Book Concern shall furnish to the book-steward of the Canada Conference any of the books which may be issued from its press at the following rates, subject to the conditions and provisions hereinafter named:—

"The general alphabetical catalogue books, whether in sheets or bound, shall be sold at forty per cent. discount from the retail prices, as long as the present discount of one-third shall be made to wholesale purchasers; but should the discount be hereafter changed to one-fourth, then, in that case, the books sold to the book-steward of the Canada Methodists shall be charged at a discount of one-third from the retail prices, which shall, from time to time, be affixed to them respectively."

That is to say, instead of giving you a part of the fund directly, we will give you a share of the profits by a reduction of seven or eight per cent. on the prices of the books we furnish to you. Then on page 52 :—

"It is understood and agreed, that the privileges herein secured to the Canada Conference, shall be binding on the Methodist Book Concern until the first day of May, 1852, next ensuing the present date."

So that this arrangement was to continue for sixteen years. Then again, (p. 52 :)—

"Finally, it is hereby mutually understood and agreed, that the foregoing arrangement is considered as a full, and definite, and satisfactory adjustment of the question which has arisen between the Canada Conference and the Methodist Episcopal Church, on the subject of the Methodist Book Concern."

Then on the 23d of May, 1832, (p. 52, but which should be on p. 41,) after the Canada Church had presented itself as an independent, we find :—

"MAY 23, 1832.—On motion of P. Akers, which was seconded, *Resolved,* That a copy of the resolution of the last General Conference, by which the Canada Conference was allowed to dissolve connexion with the Methodist Episcopal Church in the United States, and also a copy of the acts of this General Conference on Canada affairs, accompany the resolutions about to be presented to the annual conferences."

Now, what was the result of this Canada transaction? In the first place, the Canada Conference conceived that this General Conference could divide itself without schism. Secondly, this Methodist Church did consent to the Canada Conference organizing itself as a Methodist Episcopal Church without a schism. Thirdly, it dealt and treated with it upon a claim of right, as a Church properly organized, and not schismatic. And what did it hesitate about? The General Conference hesitated only on the subject of its power to divide the funds, under the sixth restrictive article, with the Canada Connexion. In other words, they assented in the fullest manner to its being not a schismatic Church, but a separation merely. All that they hesitated about was the effect of that upon the sixth restrictive article in reference to the Book Concern, and whether they would change it. They submitted that to the annual conferences, and these decided against the change. That is to say, they decided that although these persons were still distressed travelling preachers, supernumerary, and worn-out preachers, perfectly good Methodists, yet after the separation they conceived that the sixth restrictive article prevented the Conference from turning over the funds. That was all they doubted. They doubted not that these beneficiaries remained entitled. They did not, they could not doubt that; but they had the doubts which usually belong to persons who deal in literal considerations. That was their doubt. So far as it went, it is a decision against our views. I do not blink the question; nor do I trouble my friends to prove that the Conference considered that the sixth restrictive article prevented them from dividing these funds even with the meritorious ministers in this conference. But I say, moreover, that if they had not terminated that question by a settlement, it would have been subjected to a much better determination as a question of law from the courts of law, than it received as a question of charity by the votes of the General and Annual Conferences. It would have been brought to some legal tribunal, which would have exercised legal skill and legal judgment, and exercised a wider view on the subject of charity than it was possible for gentlemen, limited as these were in knowledge on a subject of this sort, to do. So far as their action went, they acknowledged a separation of the Church as being no schism, and that the Canadian ministry was a perfectly Christian ministry, and that they remained in that Canadian Church without blame and reproach. After the separation, the judgment of three General Conferences most distinctly recognised as valid and proper this separation, and not as seceding or schismatical.

Moreover, the whole effect of this judgment, as the gentlemen may choose to claim it, is altogether weakened when you look at the manner in which they felt themselves constrained to deal with the subject and with this Church. They, in the first place, and in the most explicit manner, acknowledged this as a matter of right, and were acting in reference to what they conceived to be a very wrong idea of the subject on the part of the annual conferences. When they originally submitted it to the annual conferences, it was probably upon the belief of that General Conference of 1832 that the annual conferences would view this question as they themselves did. They were disappointed when the vote of the annual conferences came in. Being disappointed in this result, what did they do? They gave to the Canada Conference out of this fund, which, if it belonged to any one, belonged to these distressed travelling, supernumerary, and superannuated preachers, their wives, widows, and children, seven per cent. on the gross proceeds of the books with which they furnished them. If the position of our learned friends is correct, they had no right to give it. Now, they had acknowledged the principle of right, they had acknowledged the principle of law, they had themselves confessed that they did not carry it out, they had confessed it was wrong that they did not carry it out, and that they had done that which they were not justified in doing except under the imputation of a breach of charitable trust. They knew that was not right, and they meant nobly and honourably to repair the wrong they had committed. That is the Canada case.

I submit to your Honours that the necessity of the case, in a body constituted as this General Conference was, necessarily involves the power of division. This, be it remembered, is not the power to sanction deviation as to doctrine, it is not the power of sanctioning secession; it is the simple power of separating for the sake of convenience and efficiency into separate bodies with the same doctrines, and to be in every respect the same, except as to the unwieldiness of the general body which is to govern. I call attention to the twenty-third article of religion, upon p. 19 of the Discipline of 1840, and p. 26 of our book No. 1:—

"XXIII. *Of the Rulers of the United States of America.*—The president, the congress, the general assemblies, the governors, and the councils of State, *as the delegates of the people,* are the rulers of the United States of America, according to the division of power made to them by the constitution of the United States, and by the constitutions of their respective States. And the said States are a sovereign and independent nation, and ought not to be subject to any foreign jurisdiction."

Then in a note, they add:—

"As far as it respects civil affairs, we believe it the duty of Christians, and especially all Christian ministers, to be subject to the supreme authority of the country where they may reside, and to use all laudable means to enjoin obedience to the powers that be; and, therefore, it is expected that all our preachers and people, who may be under the British or any other government, will behave themselves as peaceable and orderly subjects."

Now, this article of religion evidently supposes that the Methodist Church may extend itself by having Methodist societies "under the British, or any other government." That is to be taken as a part of the constitution of Methodism. Now, suppose that, instead of the conquest by this country over the vast West, it had been merely the natural progress of emigration into Spanish or uncivilized countries, and they had declared themselves independent. Then the Methodist societies which had been established, would have been in connexion with the Methodist Episcopal Church. That extension of territory has taken place under the circumstance of the same civil dominion, instead of its being under different civil dominion. Is it possible to suppose that the legislative body of a Church, looking to such a spread over the world, should have conceived that it should have no power to separate itself into governments for different parts of it, without those governments being actually schismatic and separate?—that whatever difference of circumstance might be, it was not in the power of this general body to form itself into separate bodies, without those separate bodies being essentially schismatical, so that whatever belongs to the preachers of the general bodies shall not belong to the preachers of a separate body, except as a matter which is to be got over by some leaping over the difficulty, as was done in the Canada case? Would they say, that that which was a question of right should not be decided by the general governing body of the Church, but should be decided by an artificial and fettered judgment, which, when I come to consider it, I think I can show to the Court, has not, and cannot have any relation to this subject. I say, when you take into consideration the idea of the Methodists as being a strongly aggressive body, spreading itself over the earth, so as to embrace the lower classes of the people in a degree which no other denomination has ever pretended to do; and when you consider this provision in the very articles of religion looking to its spread beyond the limits of the United States, you cannot for an instant suppose that in that Discipline the general governing body is restricted (without their being any restriction in terms on the subject) from consenting to a separation of the Church into as many general governing bodies as the necessities of the case might require.

As to the consequence of that principle upon the fund, I prefer to suspend any argument until I come to consider it specially. I am now considering, and solely considering, whether this General Conference has not the power to consent to a division without its being schismatic, and without its disqualifying those members and clergy who adhere to the separate body. Not only does the extension of territory contemplated by the Discipline look to this, but the physical difficulties which grow out of that extension require us to contemplate it. How does this operate on the power of the Church, looking to the case of delegates to the conferences from Oregon and from California, making five or six months' voyages, or coming in the costly way in which passengers come from the gold regions. By-and-by the Methodist Church in those countries will embrace large classes of people. They are now under the government of the General Conference here. What is to become of these men when this becomes to be a very populous region on the Pacific coast? Are they to be represented in any General Conference? Are the men from California and Oregon, and all the States which will be created in that region, to meet here? Or are those here to go over the mountains? Is time and space to be so absolutely obliterated, that the Church can go on and govern the whole of this country by one single, general body of delegations. I submit, that although that is no difficulty in the eye of a statesman with the wealth of the general government at his beck, yet to this Church it is an insuperable difficulty. The very extension of territory this distance, and the great population which may be collected in these quarters, prevent the possibility of this Church not separating at some time or other amicably, properly, and faithfully, into separate governing bodies. And when that separation shall become expedient, it seems to me, that it would be strange doctrine to say, that this General Conference, which succeeded to the powers of a conference composed of all the power of the Church, and which in this act was not restricted, for there is no restriction on the power of division,—it would be against the very starting principle of the diffusiveness of this Church to hold, that it could not provide for its own government by separating the meeting of these ministers in a delegated body, in the manner to which I have alluded.

But there is the itinerancy of the bishops, according to the theory on the other side. It is not the theory which we adopt, that the itinerancy of a bishop means that he must actually visit or be capable of visiting every part, not of a diocese, but of all the conferences of all the Methodist Episcopal Church. Who are to be bishops? Are they to be young men of from seventeen to twenty years old, able to endure these fatigues? Or are they to be, for the most part, men of maturity, men of age, of ripened experience, becoming somewhat infirm from their labours? That is the material of which the bishops of this Church have always been composed. Now, let us see whether it would be possible, in relation to this, to carry on this Church without a separation. It seems to be impossible. The argument of our friends on the other side as to the itinerancy of the bishops has very little force, because it is obviously impossible that every bishop could visit every part of the jurisdiction of all the annual conferences. This itinerancy we suppose must be deemed to mean an itinerancy as opposed to a diocesan episcopacy,—that there shall not be a bishop confined to one conference, but that he shall have the duty, and shall take the office, of visiting all the conferences in a certain large Connexion.

Again: differences of climate may well call for a division or separation of the Church. The population of this Northern country, although considerable, is yet very far short of that which upon every principle we may soon expect to find it. So of the Southern country. Therefore, the labours of these bishops will very materially increase with an increase of population, and it may be very difficult to find bishops who would be able to serve in this Northern and Southern Church, under this difference of climate. That very difference of climate may make a very grievous difficulty with this Church to carry on its system without a separation into parts. And is it a fact that this constitution, which contemplates this great activity and diffusiveness, is so limited by implication—because there is no expression to limit it—that it can never adapt itself to such a pressing difficulty, which is already at hand? I suppose, in fact, this difficulty existed before the separation; the Northern and Southern bishops could not very well interchange with each other; and I am told, that one of the bishops has not been South for some ten or fifteen years, and no doubt for the best of reasons.

I propose, now, to allude to another difficulty, which is the very thing that has occurred in this case—a difference in the temper of the people. Here is a part of this great community which tolerates slavery, and a part in which slavery is unknown. How do they treat it? This Church treats slavery as an evil—the same as the existence of crime, of poverty, of disease; and the difference between the two parties is how to treat it. One says, "Extirpate it;" the other says, "We cannot extirpate it, but we shall be extirpated if we attempt it." This body has said to its private members, "You may entertain your views about this and be in good standing and connexion." These members are the ones to whom the bishop is to make his visitations, and over whom his supervision of the preachers is eventually to take effect. Now, is it possible to say, that in such a country as ours, where this difficulty has always been more or less great, this Church could prosper if they did not tolerate it? It would be like supposing a man could run when his legs were manacled. I contend that it was a necessary act of preservation, that, in the event that the temper of the people made a co-operation of all the parts inconvenient and impracticable, they had the power of division or separation, in order to reach a large body of the people of this country. Is it to be conceived of, that the constitution of this Church did not allow, but forbade by implication, that there should be an organization adapted to the different temper of the people? Why, if the doctrine which is presented here be correct, that no bishop should be a slaveholder, that he should have no sympathy with those who held slaves, the Southern country would always be visited by really foreign bishops. Is it not palpable, that such a system could not operate in the Southern country? Must not these gentlemen have seen that men never would receive religious instruction altogether from strangers, and whose being strangers would be evidence of contempt towards those whom they visited? I submit, that it would be the last thing to suppose of the wise constructors of this system, that they should have made no provision whereby this Church might adapt itself, by a division, to the great end of carrying the Gospel, without offence, to all the different parts of this extensive country.

I would advert now to another matter—political dissensions, political disruptions. Is this Church so constituted, that it shall be powerless to meet any such exigency? Look to the case of Canada. That was in the connexion of the Church in this country. There was a war between this country and Great Britain; and members of this Church were arrayed against each other. Both parties had felt the consequences of war. And was this Church so powerless that it could not lawfully consent to the Methodists in Canada organizing a separate Church, without their being schismatical and separatists? They have practically solved the question, and solved it according to good sense, and solved it against that restrictive implication which they wish to insert in this Discipline.

Again: the number of delegates which might be sent, might make a necessity for a division. There is an extent to which this evil might be limited, by lessening the ratio of representation. It was originally one for five; then one for seven; then one for fourteen; and finally one for twenty-one. It is perfectly plain, that to carry it very much further would leave no representation at all. If the ratio was one for one hundred, there would be no real representation. It might be a representation from a people to a government, but this was to be a representation of delegates from preachers. It was a delegation from one governing body to a superior governing body. What would be a ratio of one delegate to one thousand preachers? How could such a delegate feel for his constituents? How could he express their feelings? There must be a limit to this; and when this limit should be reached, the only remedy would be the organization of a separate body under similar principles.

The increase of population in this country, for the next fifty years, would of itself render this body so unwieldy, that, for that reason alone, a separation would be a necessary measure. I say that these considerations, growing out of the history of this body, and out of the necessity of the case, are entirely consistent with the substance of this Discipline.

I turn now to the rules touching the General and annual conferences; I come to the text of the constitution, so to say, (p. 27 of No. 1,)—

"Who shall compose the General Conference, and what are the regulations and powers belonging to it?

"Ans. 1. The General Conference shall be composed of one member for every twenty-one members of each annual conference, to be appointed either by seniority or choice, at the discretion of such annual conference; yet so that such representatives shall have travelled at least four full calendar years from the time that they were received on trial by an annual conference, and are in full connexion at the time of holding the Conference."

Observe the character of this body. These delegates are "to be appointed either by seniority or choice," and they are to be taken from the constituent body whom they represent:—

"3. At all times when the General Conference is met, it shall take two-thirds of the representatives of all the annual conferences to make a quorum for transacting business. * * * * * * * * * * * * *

"5. The General Conference shall have full powers to make rules and regulations for our Church, under the following limitations and restrictions."

I submit that we should construe these articles, on the supposition that the powers of the Conference were great enough to have these restrictions carved out of them. These powers would have embraced everything which the restrictions carved out, if these restrictions had not been imposed. The expression on this subject, in logic, I suppose, is, that "the exception proves the rule;" that is, if there is a necessity for the exception, it is a proof that the rule would extend to the excepted case if the exception did not exist. Now, what is the first restriction?

"The General Conference shall not revoke, alter, or change our articles of religion, nor establish any new standards or rules of doctrine contrary to our present existing and established standards of doctrine."

Does not the putting in of this restriction admit that the power of the Conference would have been extensive enough to change their doctrines, if this restriction had not been inserted? Otherwise, it would be idle to put it in. How extensive then are the powers of this Conference! It could now change the whole character of the body but for this restriction. Then the second restriction is:—

"They shall not allow of more than one representative for every fourteen members of the annual conference, nor allow of a less number than one for every thirty: provided, nevertheless, that when there shall be in any annual conference a fraction of two-thirds the number which shall be fixed for the ratio of representation, such annual conference shall be entitled to an additional delegate for such fraction; and provided also, that no conference shall be denied the privilege of two delegates."

If it had not been for this second restrictive article, the General Conference might have allowed the rate of representation to vary in any indefinite mode they pleased. They might have bridged the difficulties which are constantly occurring in the history of large bodies. They might, as is sometimes done in England, have swamped the peerage by the creation of new peers. They might, on a temporary occasion, have allowed to the Northern or the Southern conferences a double or triple representation. This restriction was introduced to prevent this being done. Does not this show a kind of omnipotence, so to say, in the power of this body, so far as this Church is concerned? Is it not the power of parliament itself, that can change the time for which it was elected to serve? It can change the subject of representation; it can change and alter the franchise; it can change everything about it. So could this body; and so can this body, except according to this restriction. Then,

"3. They shall not change or alter any part or rule of our government, so as to do away episcopacy, or destroy the plan of our itinerant general superintendency."

"Destroy" is the word. Without this restriction could they not have altered and done away with episcopacy? Could they not have destroyed the general superintendency? They were in fact the Church; they were the general council of the Church, with the primitive and original power and authority of the Church as a Church. What does the phrase, "so as to do away episcopacy," mean? Why, that they may vary episcopacy; they may limit it, but shall not "destroy" the plan of our itinerant general superintendency. They may make the itinerancy, instead of being absolutely general, general according to circumstances; they may excuse a bishop from running all over the United States; they may excuse a man disqualified by his peculiar notions, and not disturb the plan of general itinerant superintendency. I know very well the extent to which we go for these gentlemen's benefit in the case of Bishop Andrew, when we make these remarks. But we cannot read this article without seeing that whatever can be done in consistence with the language and spirit of the third restrictive article, the General Conference can do. They, therefore, can do anything with the plan of episcopacy, except doing it away. That is their power, without regard to the annual conferences. Then,

"4. They shall not revoke or change the general rules of the United Societies."

These are the rules of Church membership. They are the modes by which men attach themselves to the integral societies of this Methodist Connexion. Then again,

"5. They shall not do away the privileges of our ministers or preachers of trial by a committee, and of an appeal; neither shall they do away the privileges of our members of trial before the society, or by a committee, and of an appeal."

They are not to do away with the mode of trial, but they may regulate everything about it; they may say how the trial shall be conducted. They are not to do away these privileges of the preachers and members. Then, finally,

"6. They shall not appropriate the produce of the Book Concern, nor of the Charter Fund, to any purpose other than for the benefit of the travelling, supernumerary, superannuated, and worn-out preachers, their wives, widows, and children."

They may deal with it in any way, except that they shall not appropriate it to any other purpose; but we are not upon that now. We are now upon the question of consenting to a separation of the Church into parts. Is there any restriction which prevents that? Is there any provision which says that this Church shall not divide itself into parts? But the gentlemen will doubtless say, this constitution contains within itself an article for its own amendment. I beg their pardon. It contains an article for amendment only, in regard to these restrictive rules. If the thing proposed to be amended is not in the restrictive articles, then the vote of the conferences cannot change it, and the vote of one single conference standing out, would defeat any change in the constitution of the Church. There is no power of change as to matters not in the restrictive articles; and the very fact that there is no power of change except as to these restrictive articles, shows that there is no limitation of the authority of the Church except these restrictive articles.

On the subject of this power of the General Conference, I would ask, What restrictive article is conceived to be violated by a Plan of Separation which adopts every restrictive article, and all the terms of the constitution? Which is the article that is violated? Is it changing the articles of religion? If it does, it is restricted; if it does not, it is not restricted. I am at a loss to know what article of religion is changed, by allowing the Southern Church to organize itself as a new Church, with the very same article. Does it change the ratio of representation? Does it, in the sense of the third restriction, do away episcopacy, or destroy the plan of general itinerant superintendency? In other words, does it convert the Methodist bishop into a diocesan bishop in any sense whatever? I know that this may be a matter of degree—a bishop might be limited to one or two conferences. That would be, I admit, a violation of the spirit of the article, and indeed of the article itself; but I ask, if limiting a bishop to thirteen conferences, more conferences than existed at the time this constitution was adopted, with more persons to be governed, was doing away with the episcopacy, or destroying the plan of itinerant general superintendency? Does it revoke or change the general rules of the United Societies? Does it take away the privileges of preachers and members to trial? Does it appropriate the produce of the Book Concern, or of the Chartered Fund, to any other purpose than the benefit of travelling, supernumerary, and superannuated preachers? Does it vary the persons by whom these contributions must reach the beneficiaries? I suppose that, under the Plan of Separation, the part of this Book Concern which must go to the beneficiaries in the Southern Church is to be applied according to the Discipline of 1840.

Suppose, now, that the Plan of Separation is absolutely void, and that, by reason of the mistake into which we have been led, we are not schismatical, but merely contumacious, and have not come up to the General Conference. The fund is to be distributed. Who are to distribute it? The very annual conferences at the South, as they are now constituted. They are the very original bodies of Methodism. They would take this fund, and they would distribute it to the very same beneficiaries. This is a practical thing; and our learned friends, when they come to speak of the Plan of Separation violating the order of the Church, in allowing it to divide itself into two parts, and to give to each part the vitality of a complete organization, must show practically how it defeated this restrictive system. I submit that it did not.

I come now to the judgment of this body on this very subject. I have said what I need to say on the subject of the judgment of the Canada Conference. The General Conference never left it to the annual conferences to determine whether they had the power of assenting to the Canada Methodists forming a separate body. They never hesitated about that; they never doubted that that formed a true Methodist Episcopal Church, not separatist nor schismatic. That was the Conference of 1832; it was followed up by the action of the Conference of 1836. That of 1840 had no connexion with this subject. The judgment of the Conference of 1844 was in favour of this view of the power of division. I shall examine the Plan of Separation more particularly hereafter; but I would now remark that it was never submitted to the annual conferences to say whether there should be a separate organization or not. The question submitted was a very different one, whether they should alter the sixth restrictive article, so as to put this fund at the command of two-thirds of the General Conference; so that, instead of having the profits of this Book Concern applied to the relief of beneficiaries, they might, if that proposition had passed, have voted it to the establishment of a colony in Liberia, or to any other purpose than this. They did not submit to the annual conferences the question whether they should separate the Church into two parts, so that each should be a genuine, a true Church; and I may be permitted to say, in relation to that Conference, that it was composed of exceedingly able men, as the documents show.

One other remark on this subject, and I leave this particular question—this power to divide itself into two bodies,—that is, the opinion of the bishops, p. 101, book No. 2. I think our reference to this, in our bill of complaint, has not been understood by the other side. I do not believe that the bishops have power to alter the constitution of this Church, nor give any declaratory opinions which can bind the Church. We do not present it in that way, no more than we would present the judgment from Lord Lyndhurst to bind this Court; but what we do present it for, is, to show that in the judgment of the coolest, best, and the wisest men in that Church, there was no hesitation as to the existence of this power, and that it was properly and well exercised in 1844. It is, as I might say, the opinion of highly-respectable persons conversant with that which we are now discussing. I will read it.

"This council met in the city of New-York, July 2, 1845, and was attended by Bishops Hedding, Waugh, Morris, and Janes. Bishop Hamline sent his opinion in writing on the points to be acted on by the council; Bishop Soule did not attend; and Bishop Andrew, being suspended, was not invited. Besides agreeing on a new plan of visitation, the bishops adopted the following resolutions, intended for the government of their own administration:—

"'1. Resolved, That the Plan reported by the select committee of nine at the last General Conference, and adopted by that body, in regard to a distinct ecclesiastical connexion, should such a course be found necessary by the annual conferences in the slaveholding States, is regarded by us as of binding obligation in the premises, so far as our administration is concerned.' "

That is to say, we regard it as binding on us, and shall obey it; the Conference of 1848 said they considered it null and void, and that the Conference of 1844 had no power to pass it.

"2. Resolved, That in order to ascertain fairly the desire and purpose of those societies bordering on the line of division, in regard to their adherence to the Church, North or South, due notice should be given of the time, place, and object of the meeting for the above purpose, at which a chairman and secretary should be appointed, and the sense of all the members present should be ascertained, and the same be forwarded to the bishop who may preside at the ensuing annual conferences; or forward to said presiding bishop a written request to be recognised, and have a preacher sent them, with the names of the majority appended thereto."

They not only declare it is binding so far as their administration is concerned, but they institute a mode to carry out successfully that which their successors call a separatist and schismatic body. I do not propose this as binding your judgments; perhaps the judgment of these bishops is of the least value in this matter. But so far as this religious body is concerned, I must submit, and certainly out of respect to the character of these bishops, that when they adopted these resolutions, and signed this paper, and undertook to carry out this plan of organization of the Southern Church, by having a vote taken as to which Church the societies should adhere, their judgment was in favour of the validity of the separation; that it was competent for the General Conference, for grave reasons, to separate itself into two bodies, each of which should be a true, genuine, and authentic hierarchy in this Church, and calculated to carry out its excellent purpose. This minute was passed July 2, 1845; the Southern Church had organized and issued its manifesto May 17. It was therefore a declaration in the very sight of the difficulties. Let us look a little at these acts.

The Conference of 1844, without any hesitation, passed a plan for an amicable division. Here is nothing said against it; they felt themselves at liberty to vote to organize a new Church. The bishops take the act up when the Church was organized, and when it was still in the power of individuals to withdraw, and say, "We act in obedience to this administration; we, the Northern bishops, acting together, some of us being present, and another giving his opinion in writing, tell you, Go on, form that Southern body; choose your adherence,"—and they do it. What then? Says the Conference of 1848, "By that act you become separatists, and all this great fund, the produce of common labour, toil, economy, activity, and suffering, you, by adopting this plan, and acting as your bishops have acted, in conformity and obedience to it, have forfeited for yourselves, for your wives, for your children, for the orphans of your brethren; and as a matter of conscience we cannot let you touch a dollar of it; but our beneficiaries shall have three parts where before they had but two." That is the way in which this controversy presents itself, I am sure unwittingly and unexpectedly to those who brought themselves to make it. But there it is; we have become schismatics. We have forfeited not for ourselves, we who are the belligerents; we, who engage in the revolution, may afford to be hanged if we do not succeed; these are the terms on which we enter. But after this act, into which we enter by their invitation, sanctioned by a General Conference composed of men of greater ability, perhaps, than ever met in the same Church, and sanctioned by their bishops who co-operated with us in the formation of this Church, we are told, in 1848, "when you did that, you put yourselves out of the pale of this Church; you forfeited, not your right to take alms, but your retiring pensions, your savings'-bank deposits, your life insurances; your wives, your widows, and your children, all suffer in this common calamity." It is the visitation of the sin of Adam in a very different way upon all this connexion of this Church, for doing an act which everybody, in 1845 and 1846, thought lawful. That is the way in which the controversy now stands; and I propose now to take up the subject of whether there was any doubt on the effect of that Plan of Separation. I have finished what I have to say on the power of the Conferences.

Upon this point I say that the General Conference of 1844 did, in fact and on a proper ground, consent to such division, to take effect immediately, in the choice of the Southern conferences, and without any condition. This Plan is found on p. 128 of our book. I will first read it, and make some remarks upon its text; and then consider the circumstances under which it was passed, to see whether it was considered transitory, or whether it was adopted as a final thing which everybody supposed would be acted upon and become permanent.

"The select committee of nine, to consider and report on the Declaration of the delegates from the conferences of the slaveholding States, beg leave to submit the following report:—"

It has been made a question, whether this Plan of Separation was adopted upon the existence of the difficulties to which we have been led in the reading of the Proofs. Our friends on the other side say it did not.

"Whereas a Declaration has been presented to this General Conference, with the signatures of fifty-one delegates of the body, from thirteen annual conferences in the slaveholding States, representing that, for various reasons enumerated, the objects and purposes of the Christian ministry and Church organization cannot be successfully accomplished by them under the jurisdiction of this General Conference as now constituted."

That is the declaration of an existing fact in the opinion of those delegates.

"And whereas, in the event of a separation, a contingency to which the Declaration asks attention as not improbable, we esteem it the duty of this General Conference to meet the emergency with Christian kindness and the strictest equity."

This bears on what I have said as to its being an amicable separation. They thought it their duty to meet it with Christian kindness and the strictest equity; to which I would introduce as a note what they declared when the Canada Conference spoke on the subject of the Book Concern, that it was just in regard to their former relations and their liberality that they should have their share.

"Therefore, Resolved, by the delegates of the several annual conferences in General Conference assembled,

"1. That, should the annual conferences in the slaveholding States find it necessary to unite in a distinct ecclesiastical connexion, the following rule shall be observed with regard to the Northern boundary of such connexion."

Permit me to call your attention to an alteration here; it stood as originally presented by the committee, "That should *the delegates* from the conferences in the slaveholding States find it necessary;" thus leaving it to the delegates then present. These delegates shrunk from that responsibility, and on motion of Mr. Paine, the words "delegates from the," were stricken out. But it was intended as a Plan to be made and acted upon as much, whether it was the delegates who decided for it, or the conferences from which they came. The object of those delegates was to change the responsibility of the mode of action from themselves to the conferences which they represented.

"All the societies, stations, and conferences, adhering to the Church in the South, by a vote of a majority of the members of said societies, stations, and conferences, shall remain under the unmolested pastoral care of the Southern Church, and the ministers of the Methodist Episcopal Church shall in no wise attempt to organize Churches or societies within the limits of the Church, South, nor shall they attempt to exercise any pastoral oversight therein; it being understood that the ministry of the South reciprocally observe the same rule in relation to stations, societies, and conferences adhering, by a vote of a majority, to the Methodist Episcopal Church; provided, also, that this rule shall apply only to societies, stations, and conferences bordering on the line of division, and not to interior charges, which shall in all cases be left to the care of that Church within whose territory they are situated."

Here is a provision as to how the boundary shall be ascertained. It does not define it exactly, but says: "Here are Southern delegates; we are satisfied where the boundary shall be, but there will be bordering societies which may be divided, and to provide for that, we adopt this article;" and this article the bishops, in 1845, attempted to carry out. I think it shows very clearly that it was to be an immediate division.

"2. That ministers, local and travelling, of every grade and office in the Methodist Episcopal Church may, as they prefer, remain in that Church, or, without blame, attach themselves to the Church, South."

Could that consist with the idea of a separating and schismatic Church? If my learned friends take up the doctrines of their answer and the Conference of 1848, and make this Church schismatic, they have to give some beautiful reason for the introduction of this provision. They could not, certainly, but be blamed for uniting with a schismatic Church. They would have committed an absurdity in sanctioning a schism which they had no right to sanction in any way. It meant to say to all the parties attached to the Church, South, that there should be no blame about it—that they should be just as good Methodist ministers as before. That is what we mean by an amicable separation, and treating with the "strictest equity."

"3. *Resolved*, by the delegates of all the annual conferences in General Conference assembled, That we recommend to all the annual conferences, at their first approaching sessions, to authorize a change of the sixth restrictive article, so that the first clause shall read thus: 'They shall not appropriate the produce of the Book Concern, nor of the Chartered Fund, to any other purpose other than for the benefit of the travelling, supernumerary, superannuated, and worn-out preachers, their wives, widows, and children, and to such other purposes as may be determined upon by the votes of two-thirds of the members of the General Conference.'"

That was a recommendation in no respect conditional to the two previous. It involves something so very different from what was called for by the idea of separation, that it is evident that its being found here was simply because an occasion was thus presented of having a question of this kind made and disposed of. The effect of it was, that while it preserved the same right in these original beneficiaries, it would allow the General Conference to apply that fund to any other purpose that two-thirds of the Conference should choose. That goes widely beyond anything connected with the separation of the Church into two parts. There had been difficulties in the Canada case, a compromise had then been made, and the body had been put in a very awkward position as the administrators of the charity. They wished to avoid that here. But they did not make this as a condition upon which the Church should be separated; if it had been adopted, it would have had an effect beyond this separation.

"4. That whenever the annual conferences, by a vote of three-fourths of all their members voting on the third resolution, shall have concurred in the recommendation to alter the sixth restrictive article, the agents at New-York and Cincinnati shall, and they are hereby authorized and directed to deliver over to any authorized agent or appointee of the Church, South, should one be organized, all notes and book accounts against the ministers, Church members, or citizens within its boundaries, with authority to collect the same for the sole use of the Southern Church, and that said agents also convey to the aforesaid agent or appointee of the South, all the real estate, and assign to him all the property, including presses, stock, and all right and interest connected with the printing establishments at Charleston, Richmond, and Nashville, which now belong to the Methodist Episcopal Church."

It was in ease of the agents that this was done. If this should be done, then it was a case in which the agents needed no legal protection. They were trustees; it might be that the trustees could be changed, and the fund dealt with upon intrinsic right by representatives of beneficiaries in the Southern conferences without this, but it would undoubtedly be a case calling for judicial construction. The object was to make it easy to the agents. They did not pretend to say anything about the matter of right. That was already adjudged.

"5. That when the annual conferences shall have approved the aforesaid change in the sixth restrictive article, there shall be transferred to the above agent of the Southern Church so much of the capital and produce of the Methodist Book Concern as will, with the notes, book accounts, presses, &c., mentioned in the last resolution, bear the same proportion to the whole property of said Concern that the travelling preachers in the Southern Church shall bear to all the travelling ministers of the Methodist Episcopal Church; the division to be made on the basis of the number of travelling preachers in the forthcoming minutes."

As I remarked, that was done in ease of the agents. The only thing to which a condition was applied was the turning over by the agents. It was not left to three-fourths of the conferences to determine whether the new Church should be formed. That was upon the Plan, showing that it would be absurd to base it upon this restrictive article. In the minutes of 1848, it is set up that the whole of this Plan was conditional upon the passing of that restrictive article. I submit upon that subject, here and finally, that by the first resolution the decision of the separation was left to the slaveholding conferences, whereas the restrictive article was to be acted upon by three-fourths of all the conferences; and I submit that it is an end to the question of what the Plan of Separation meant. It may be avoided; but as to saying that a Plan of Separation, which was to depend upon the election of the Southern conferences, was to be avoided or not, according to the election of three-fourths of all the conferences, I submit is a plain, palpable contradiction and absurdity.

Now upon the mode of operation of this Plan. It was for a division of the funds. The produce of this fund was always divided according to the numbers returned in the minutes of the annual conferences every year to the book-steward, the principal of the Book Concern. The number of preachers would change exceedingly every year, and if we can ascertain *when* the proportion was to be taken by which this division was to take place, we ascertain the *time when* the division was to take place. This gives the most positive determination of time. It adds: "the division (of the capital) is to be made on the basis of the number of travelling preachers in the forthcoming minutes,"—minutes that were then prepared. If the Plan of Division had not taken place then, immediately, it never could have taken place under this Plan, except with great inconvenience. I suppose, therefore, in reading this paper there can be no doubt that it contemplated an immediate division.

"6. That the above transfer shall be in the form of annual payments of $25,000 per annum, and specifically in stock of the Book Concern, and in Southern notes and accounts due the establishment, and accruing after the first transfer mentioned above; and until the payments are made, the Southern Church shall share in all the net profits of the Book Concern, in the proportion that the amount due them, or in arrears, bears to all the property of the Concern."

I submit that there is a precision about that which looks to something already provided. They had no doubt of the judgment of the Southern conferences; they had no doubt that that judgment would be passed. One cannot read those reports of 1844, without seeing the most settled principles in hostility, which show that no change was to be expected until men shall change their most settled, permanent convictions. They had no doubt that the separation was to take place.

What next do they do? Taking that doubt of the continuance of life which fills every preacher's discourses—that uncertainty of life-estates which visits every lawyer when dealing with life, what do they do?

"7. That Nathan Bangs, George Peck, and James B. Finley be, and they are hereby appointed commissioners to act in concert with the same number of commissioners appointed by the Southern organization, (should one be formed,) to estimate the amount which will fall due to the South by the preceding rule, and to have full powers to carry into effect the whole arrangement proposed with regard to the division of property, should the separation take place. And if by any means a vacancy occurs in this board of commissioners, the book committee at New-York shall fill said vacancy."

Were these the gentlemen who were to live until the experiment was tried of Virginia, Georgia, and South Carolina submitting to have bishops chosen who might live not in that State, and who should be acceptable to the Northern people? Was it that these commissioners were to remain a sort of immortals until this thing could be tested? Is it meant that they named these gentlemen, men of age, not looking to very great endurance of life, but looking rather to its uncertainty, and did not expect the Plan to be acted upon without delay? They were to estimate the amount which fell due to the South, and have full powers to carry into effect the whole arrangement. They were not to wait for another General Conference to supply a vacancy, but to have men on the ground for it.

"8. That whenever any agents of the Southern Church are clothed with legal authority or corporate power to act in the premises, the agents at New-York are hereby authorized and directed to act in conference with said Southern agents, so as to give the provisions of these resolutions a legally-binding force."

"A legally-binding force," without the action of three-fourths of all the annual conferences. As soon as the Southern Conference organized and appointed commissioners with legal authority, that is, according to the law of the Church, to act upon the matter, they were to act, and their acting was to be legally binding.

"9. That all the property of the Methodist Episcopal Church in meeting-houses, parsonages, colleges, schools, conference funds, cemeteries, and of everything within the limits of the Southern organization, shall be forever free from any claim set up on the part of the Methodist Episcopal Church, so far as this resolution can be of force in the premises."

Granting the most suspensive fact of that resolution, as to the doubt of the power to convey property, yet no one can doubt it was intended to operate immediately as a present relinquishment and abandonment to this Southern Church of all that belonged to it. This brings me to the notice of another question—and it is a vast question involved indirectly in this case—that if we are a schismatic Church, every meeting-house can legally be taken away from us by any one from the Northern Conference. If it recognises the Southern Church as a true Methodist Church, then this resolution was of no force, except merely to show that this possession of that property by the Southern Church was with the entire assent of the Northern brethren; and with that sort of assent they say, We have no title to it, and therefore this resolution does not give us a title.

"10. That the Church so formed in the South shall have a common right to use all the copyrights in possession of the Book Concerns at New-York and Cincinnati at the time of the settlement by the commissioners.

"11. That the book agents at New-York be directed to make such compensation to the conferences South, for their dividend from the Chartered Fund, as the commissioners above provided for shall agree upon."

That Chartered Fund was located in Philadelphia, and held under charter there. It could not be specifically turned over.

"12. That the bishops be respectfully requested to lay that part of this report requiring the action of the annual conferences before them as soon as possible, beginning with the New-York Conference."

It has been asserted in the Answer, and minutes, and journals of 1848, and in the report on the state of the Church, that all this document was conditional upon being acted upon by three-fourths of the conferences. What does the Plan ask the bishops to submit to the conferences? The whole of it? No; but that part requiring the action of the annual conferences. What part? The third resolution. So that the idea that the Plan is conditional all through, is contradicted by this last article, whereby nothing is to be submitted to the annual conferences by the bishops, but that part which relates to the alteration of the sixth restrictive rule. The third resolution is all which the bishops ever did submit to the conferences.

Having drawn your attention to the terms of the Plan, I propose to go into the circumstances under which it was adopted, to show that it was, and must be, permanent in its nature.

The Court then adjourned.

FOURTH DAY—Thursday, May 22, 1851.

Mr. Lord,—If your Honours please—I yesterday had reached that part of the discussion of this case which led me to the language of the Plan of Separation. I had read that Plan, and made some comments upon its language, to show that it was a clear assent of the Methodist Episcopal Church of 1844 to this separation; that it was not conditional upon the assent of three-fourths of all the conferences to the change in the sixth restrictive article. My object at present is to consider that Plan of Separation under the circumstances in which it was adopted, so that we may take them into view as determining the exigency to which the Plan applied, and to see from that whether the idea of its being a contingent thing is properly admissible; and also to see whether some other allegations of the Answer, which allege that the separation which took place was not in pursuance or in consequence of pre-existing difficulties, but was a sort of fraudulent abuse of the authority conferred upon the Southern conferences by that Plan of 1844, are in any degree founded upon the evidence or upon truth. The parts of the Answer which draw these matters into consideration, will be found in the references which I shall give. At the 10th folio of the Answer they deny

"That it was thereupon," (that is, upon the idea of the separation being necessary,) "as erroneously alleged by the plaintiffs, that the resolutions which they denominate the 'Plan of Separation,' and which are set forth in their bill, were passed at the General Conference of 1844, held in the city of New-York; and these defendants say, that then, and always hitherto, the greater portion of the Church have not thought there was any sufficient cause for a separation or division of the Church."

Then again, upon folios 16 and 18 of the Answer, the defendants say:—

"That the adoption of this resolution" (that is, what I call the sentence of degradation of Bishop Andrew) "gave offence to a minority of the members of that General Conference, and who were delegates from annual conferences in the slaveholding States, and principally, if not wholly, induced those delegates to present a formal Protest against such action of the General Conference, which was admitted to record on its journal."

They seem to make a distinction in the Answer between the serious difficulties on the subject of slavery, and the particular and single action of that Conference in the case of Bishop Andrew.

"And which resolution, in the case of Bishop Andrew, further induced such delegates, (although without the authority of the General Conference, and in no manner sanctioned by any action of that body,) immediately after the adjournment of such General Conference of 1844,—before the happening of the contingencies mentioned in the so-called 'Plan of Separation,' necessary to give the same effect, and before such delegates had departed from the city of New-York,—to address a circular to their constituents and the ministers and members of the Church in the slaveholding States, therein expressing their own opinion in favour of a separation from the jurisdiction of the General Conference, and advising the annual conferences within those States to elect from their own bodies, severally, delegates to a convention, proposed by them to be held at Louisville, Kentucky, in May following, to consider and determine the matter; all which finally led those annual conferences, or portions of them, at that convention, to withdraw and separate from the Methodist Episcopal Church; to renounce and declare themselves wholly absolved from its jurisdiction, government, and authority; and to institute a new and distinct ecclesiastical organization, separate from, and independent of, the General Conference of the Methodist Episcopal Church, under the denomination of 'The Methodist Episcopal Church, South,'—which is the same organization mentioned in said bill of complaint; and the plaintiffs, and all those whom they professedly represent, are adherents thereof, and are no longer attached to the Methodist Episcopal Church; and these defendants believe and submit, that these proceedings were, in no part, authorized by the rules of government, or the constitutional law of the Methodist Episcopal Church, as contained in its Book of Discipline, but were in palpable hostility thereto."

Then it follows with a declaration, (folios 21 and 22,) that the resolution

"In the case of Bishop Andrew, instead of moving to a secession, called for due submission and respect from all the delegates of that Conference, and all the ministers and members of the Church; and the defendants upon their belief, say, that the same, and all the proceedings of that body leading thereto, were regular, constitutional, and valid; that the voluntary connexion of Bishop Andrew with slavery was justly considered by a majority of said General Conference, and by most of the ministers and members of the Church, as 'improper conduct;' and that every bishop is, by a law of the Book of Discipline, amenable to the General Conference, who are thereby declared to 'have power to expel him for improper conduct, if they see it necessary;' and that such resolution and proceedings, in the case of Bishop Andrew, were in due accordance with the good government of the Church."

Then, upon folio 23, they say, after referring to the Plan of Separation, that it was passed

"By a majority of over three-fourths of the entire body, although, as these defendants state, such resolutions were, in respect of their operation or effect, provisional and contingent, were occasioned by, and based upon, the said Declaration of the Southern delegates, and were intended only to meet the future emergency predicted therein, should the same arise; and that such resolutions were connected with, and preceded by, the statement and preamble embodied in the report of the said committee of nine, appointed by the General Conference to consider and report on such Declaration—which report was adopted by the Conference, as will appear by its printed journal (pp. 130, 137)—and which statement and preamble are to be taken, in connexion with said resolutions, as a part of said report thus adopted, and to which the defendants crave leave to refer as a part of this answer. But these defendants are advised by counsel, that the said resolutions, embodied in such report of the committee of nine, called the 'Plan of Separation,' were not duly or legally passed, and that the General Conference of 1844 had no competent, nor any valid power or authority to pass or adopt the said resolutions, called the 'Plan of Separation,' or any or either of them, except that portion thereof comprising the recommendation to the annual conferences to change the sixth restrictive rule; and these defendants are also advised by counsel, that the last-named resolutions, when adopted, were null and void, and without any binding force or validity, except in the matter of such recommendation merely."

Then they go on and give a history of the Church. Again, upon folio 34:—

"And these defendants, further answering, submit, as further advised by counsel, that even had the so-called 'Plan of Separation' been constitutional or valid, it merely provided a prospective plan, which, without the happening of certain future conditions, or, on the failure of which conditions, or either of them, could never have, by its express terms, and, as defendants say, was never intended to have, any force or validity. And these defendants expressly aver, that these conditions have not happened; and they, therefore, further insist and submit, that the said so-called 'Plan of Separation,' has always been inoperative; has never had any force or validity; and is absolutely null and void."

Then, upon folio 42, after stating that we had made this organization at the South, under this very nugatory, unconstitutional, conditional plan, they say,—

"Wherefore, these defendants insist and submit, that the 'Methodist Episcopal Church, South,' exists as a separate ecclesiastical communion, solely by the result, and in virtue of the acts and doings of the individual bishops, ministers, and members attached to such Church, South, proceeding in the premises upon their own responsibility; and that such bishops, ministers, and members, have voluntarily withdrawn themselves from the Methodist Episcopal Church, and have renounced all their rights and privileges in her communion and under her government."

They then set up what they consider violations of the Plan, in some interference by preachers from the South, with societies lying north of the border; their idea being that this Plan was in all its parts absolutely conditional, so that if any single grain failed to be delivered rightly, according to the condition, it forfeited the whole. And then, as a climax to the force of this argument, they declare, in the Answer, that the General Conference, which met in May, 1848, consisting solely of members of the Northern annual conferences, declared, that this Conference of 1844 had no power to grant the division; that is to say, these twenty Northern conferences, in the absence of the thirteen, fourteen, or fifteen Southern, passed a solemn resolution, that the act of the Conference of 1844 was nugatory, was null and void, with no effect; and in consequence of all this, we are seceders. I read now from folio 58:—

"They have voluntarily withdrawn from the Methodist Episcopal Church, and separated themselves from its principles and government; and have thereby renounced and *forfeited* all right and claim, at law or in equity, to any portion of the funds and property in this cause."

Your Honours might have supposed, in using the word "forfeiture" so often as I did yesterday, that I was rather stigmatizing the argument on the other side, and presenting it in a light they did not adopt. Now you see they put it upon the distinct ground of forfeiture, by which we understand a penal infliction in its character, though it be a stipulation; for the very idea of forfeiture, as distinguished from specific execution or compensation in damages for the want of it, is, that you impose something of much higher consequence than a mere result of a breach of condition which insures the performance of it, and which also supposes you have some existing right in that which you forfeit. They, therefore, go, in that case distinctly, on the ground that by our acting under this Plan of Separation, we, having previously a right, did by some matter not co-equal, not co-extensive with the character of the damage or injury to them, draw upon us the serious consequences of forfeiting a right—such a right as I had the honour to discuss before you yesterday.

Now I am not only to consider the language,—supposing that there may be anything in that which would admit either of its being unconditional or conditional,—but I propose now to look at the exigency of the case, the existing state of things at the time these resolutions were passed, to see whether it was a contingent, a future, an unlikely thing, and one regarded merely as possible; or whether, in fact, it was really and truly certain, that is, so certain as to scarcely leave the expectation of anything contrary, so that the not happening would be the matter which would surprise us; and to see, also, whether, under these circumstances, this was a matter done hastily, or in any manner as an abuse of the authority granted to organize as a separate Church.

The first question was this subject of slavery, which I certainly do not mean to discuss here in any extensive way, my object being to show, that upon this subject, whichever party in this Church may be right upon its discipline or doctrine, there was such a disagreement as to the discipline, as to the manner in which the Church was to deal with it, that without imputing blame to the one or the other party, it had then become so ripe that the body could not act together—a body acting not merely as a body to resist external violence on it, and held together by a sense of self-preservation in the nature of political union or league, but as a body whose object was to act by voluntary co-operation upon the minds of people who were to receive truth from peace-speaking men. I propose to show whether that state of things did not come to pass, in which, by reason of what had existed prior to 1844, and which was then simply developed,—whether that state of irreconcilable disagreement, not hostility in the breaking of friendly relations of gentlemen, but a hostility as to principles, and the mode of carrying out what may be considered the policy of this Church,—did not exist which made it suicidal to go in this state to attempt the achieving of anything upon ignorance, vice, or irreligion in any part of the world.

On this subject of slavery, the position of this Church was ever conflicting. It began upon the first organization of the Church. Mr. Wesley wrote his letter in 1784, and it was received at the Christmas conference in that year. Then, under the influence of Dr. Coke, a gentleman of education from Oxford, the widest principle of emancipation was adopted, taking it from the rule of discipline of the United Societies, that no one should be engaged in buying or selling men for the purpose of enslaving them. He attempted to bring in that speculative truth, which was clear in his own mind, and to make it practical in a country with which it was perfectly evident he had but a slight acquaintance, and in regard to which it very soon appeared that his ministrations could not be successful. He enacted rules exceedingly strong and exclusive on the subject of slavery, but even in them there came in, of necessity, a proviso, which definitely fixed the policy of this Church upon this subject. Those rules are prefaced by an acknowledgment that it was introducing a new term of communion into the Church, showing how great the power of this Conference was. It says:—

"We are deeply conscious of the impropriety of making new terms of communion for a religious society already established, excepting on the most pressing occasion; and such we esteem the practice of holding our fellow-creatures in slavery. We view it as contrary to the golden law of God, on which hang all the law and the prophets," &c.

They provide that every member of the society who has slaves in his possession, shall execute and record an instrument of manumission.

The third of these rules is:—

"In consideration that these rules form a new term of communion, every person concerned, who will not comply with them, shall have liberty quietly to withdraw himself from our society within the twelve months succeeding the notice given as aforesaid; otherwise the assistant shall exclude him in the society."

The fifth rule is:—

"No person holding slaves shall in future be admitted into society, or to the Lord's supper, till he previously complies with these rules concerning slavery."

And in what follows, the whole system showed itself to be lame and imperfect, and that it never could be carried out:—

"N. B. These rules are to affect the members of our society no farther than as they are consistent with the laws of the States in which they reside."

This clause never could have been introduced by the man who introduced the rest of the resolutions. It was yielding to the necessity of the government, and the condition of the people in which this society was expected to have, and where it has had great operation. You will see that this society in all its dealings on this subject, in the midst of its fluctuations as to rules, has always maintained the same principle. We hold slavery to be a great evil; and I am free to say, that that declaration is held as well by gentlemen of the South, as by those of the North; but the difficulty was how to deal with it. Some of the gentlemen said then, and say now, and have always said, this is a thing which, in the nature of the government under which we live, and the character of the institution, you cannot destroy by extirpation, that is, by any immediate measures directly addressed to it; you must destroy it by enlightening both master and slave, inducing the master to love the liberty of the slave, and the slave to be fit for the enjoyment of liberty. The others took the ground that this is a distinct moral offence, like any other crime—like stealing—and shall not be tolerated at all.

Here, at the outset, in the strongest declaration on the subject ever contained in a Methodist Discipline, you have a deference to the law of the country incorporated. Even with this qualification it was modified and abandoned next year. This system was found so utterly Utopian, so much like the constitution of Mr. Locke for South Carolina, that I venture to say it was never practised upon; and it was one other example of the folly of a speculative man in one country, undertaking to regulate the practical operations of civil and domestic, as well as of political life, in another country with which he had but a very slight acquaintance. I do not mean to go through with any detail on this subject; suffice it to say, that in 1785, experience—and behold how short an experience it was—less than one year!—convinced this society that those rules, even with the modification made by somebody who understood the subject better than Dr. Coke, were utterly impracticable; it would have been the end of Methodism in that part of the country to which it had the greatest reference. In 1796, the matter was referred to the yearly conference. In 1800 a more distinct reference to the subject of the local law was made. In 1804, the rules were still further modified, and the very striking provision introduced, that the preachers were to instruct the masters to allow their slaves instruction, and teach the slaves obedience to their masters. By the Conference of 1808, the subject was left to the management of the annual conferences, and that seems also to have been the state of it under the Conference of 1812. In 1816 we have the following introduced :—

"No slaveholder shall be eligible to any official station in our Church hereafter, where the laws of the State in which he lives will admit of emancipation and permit the liberated slave to enjoy freedom."

There you see a distinct provision for the case of any official station, not excepting a bishop, preacher, or elder; no one possessing slaves should hold office where the laws permitted emancipation; and the qualification is as extensive as the rule. This was the only objection on the subject. If you are a slaveholder you shall not be admitted to any official station, if the law allows of emancipation. If the law does not sanction it, the article does not apply; in other words, it directly sanctions it. In 1824 the following was added :—

"All our preachers shall prudently enforce upon our members the necessity of teaching their slaves to read the word of God; and to allow them time to attend upon the public worship of God on our regular days of Divine service."

In 1840, you will see that the agitation had become extreme. So far from slavery not being the subject of agitation, it was a subject of the most serious agitation, as you will see by the minutes; and upon this subject, the Reply to the Protest, which the gentlemen on the other side put in, gives us something instructive. If I wished to show the irreconcilable state of opinion in this Church upon this subject—I do not mean hostility between party and party, but the irreconcilable state of opinion—which would prevent this Church from acting in a body, I would call for this Answer to the Protest as the most decisive proof on the subject.—P. 113 of the first of the Proofs.

"It is known and acknowledged by all Southern brethren, that Bishop Andrew was nominated by the delegates from the South Carolina and Georgia Conferences, as a Southern candidate for whom Northern men might vote, without doing violence to their principles, as he was no slaveholder."

Here you have a most distinct avowal that it was a violence to their principles to elect as a bishop a man with those principles which the Church most distinctly in its Discipline tolerated. Let us see whether in the history of that principle it showed any diminution of growth. The "Reply" continues :—

"Bishop Andrew himself perfectly understood the ground of his election, and often said he was indebted to his poverty for his promotion. Since the year 1832, the anti-slavery sentiment in the Church, as well as in the whole civilized world, has constantly and rapidly gained ground; and within the last year or two it has been roused to a special and most earnest opposition to the introduction of a slaveholder into the episcopal office."

What do the gentlemen mean when they say there was no difficulty on this subject prior to 1844? What was it in 1832? "The anti-slavery sentiment in the Church," that is, in their Church, "and in the whole civilized world has been constantly and rapidly gaining ground, and within the last year or two," that is prior to 1844, "it has been roused to a special and most earnest opposition." "Roused;" that is to say, men have gone about taunting and stimulating each other upon the subject, and, as a matter of conscience, to rouse this feeling, and they tell us that their principles were settled against this institution, which had been provided for in their constitution, so that the anti-slavery sentiment became roused and more decided. And pray, let me know when it has become more quiet or more peaceable since 1832, or more likely to be assimilated by living in close juxtaposition with the opposite sentiment. Yet they tell us that in 1844 there was no real difficulty, and that it was all made by these gentlemen declaring that there was a difficulty, thus stimulating their constituents to make it one. This, they say, was the case in 1844. We see what it was in 1832 :—

"The subject was discussed everywhere, and the dreaded event (that is, Bishop Andrew being a slaveholder in any form) universally deprecated as the most fearful calamity that ever threatened the Church."

What a state of feeling was this in which the two bodies of this Church were to go on together!—two bodies whose particular notions had been provided for in the Book of Discipline,—in the North, where emancipation was practicable, the rule was absolute that it should be performed; in the South, where it was not practicable, the rule was that it need not be complied with. Here you find parties writing a Reply to a Protest in 1844, which was to be the manifesto of the majority of that Conference, and they tell us that they deprecated this thing as the most fearful calamity which ever threatened a Church, and yet they tell us in the Answer that they consider all the difficulty arose from the Declaration of these delegates, and they went and stimulated the opposition out of which grew the organization of this Church, and it was not owing to any preceding difficulties.

Now turn to the proceedings of the Conference of 1840, on page 56 of the first of the Proofs. "May 2d;" these Conferences all began the first of May. They had hardly got seated, before

"May 2.—O. Scott, of the New-England Conference, presented a petition from persons residing in New-York, on the subject of slavery. On the presenting of this petition, J. Early moved the appointment of a standing committee on slavery, to whom all papers, petitions, and memorials upon that subject shall be referred. Adopted. Ordered that the committee consist of twenty-eight members, one from each annual conference, and appointed by the respective delegations."

Look at that, and see if this Church did not then find that that was a vast and terrible difficulty for them to deal with, and that they needed to deal with it not by a committee of a few prudent, discreet men, but by a committee which should embrace one member from every one of the conferences of their Church. Then, again :—

"May 8.—E. Dorsey presented the memorial of the stewards and others of Westmoreland circuit, Baltimore Conference, complaining of the action of the Baltimore Annual Conference, in refusing to elect to ordination local preachers, on the single ground of their being slaveholders."

Surely, that was not a fancy; that was a substantial difficulty. Here, in Westmoreland county, in Virginia, local preachers were refused to be ordained on the ground that they were connected with slavery, when the very provision of the Discipline on that subject left every one free to be elected to any official station in the Church, in the Southern country, if emancipation was impracticable, although he was a slaveholder. To whom were these preachers to address themselves? To vast audiences of slaves and masters—and were they to be addressed by a foreign ministry; a ministry who held the very institution in the midst of which they were walking, as a thing so offensive that it would defile a man and unfit him for the sacred garb? That is the state of the thing here indicated; and if that was the state of the thing in a conference so far South as Baltimore, calling itself, I believe, "The

Breakwater Conference," what was to be supposed to be the general state of things in that Church? The minutes continue :—

"The memorial was read, and ineffectual efforts made to procure other reference. After discussion it was, on motion, referred to a select committee of nine, to consider and report thereon.

"May 13.—On motion of J. A. Collins, the report of the committee on the judiciary, of 1836, in relation to a memorial from Westmoreland and Lancaster circuits, Baltimore Conference, was referred to a committee raised on the memorial from Westmoreland circuit to this Conference.

He takes up an old memorial on that subject, left in 1836, and not disturbed from that time. They tell us in the Reply, that this anti-slavery feeling in 1832 became strong, and it was increasing, not only in the Church, but in the civilized world. In 1840 you have applications upon the subject, treating it as an existing evil; and you find members of the body, when that subject comes to be dealt with, digging up a memorial presented in 1836 on the same subject, and referring it to the same committee. May 21st, Mr. Bangs, chairman of the Committee on Slavery, presented a report, which was read. O. Scott stated the minority of the committee had a report to present; the report of the majority, and also that of the minority, were laid on the table. On motion, the report of the Committee on Slavery was taken up. Then we have a very slight circumstance to be sure, but indicating the character of this difficulty :—

"O. Scott, rising to speak, and intimating that he would probably extend his remarks beyond fifteen minutes, it was, on motion, resolved to suspend the rule restricting a speaker to fifteen minutes, so as to permit brother Scott to proceed at his own discretion."

This, then, was no trifling subject. Brother Scott, I suppose, in ordinary cases, dealt with the usual brevity, and fifteen minutes were enough to pour him out; but upon this subject his depth and fulness were entirely inconsistent with the fifteen minutes' rule.

"After brother Scott had proceeded some time with his remarks, he gave way for a motion to adjourn, which prevailed; and Conference adjourned, to meet to-morrow morning at half-past eight o'clock.

"*Friday morning, May 22.*—Conference proceeded to the consideration of the unfinished business of yesterday, it being the first resolution accompanying the report of the Committee on Slavery. The discussion was renewed.

"On motion, Conference resolved, that when it adjourn, it adjourn to meet this afternoon at three o'clock."

On ordinary occasions, I suppose, these gentlemen took the afternoon for social intercourse; probably dined together; but brother Scott and slavery had now taken a degree of interest, which threw these mundane considerations quite into the shade, and on they went in the afternoon :—

"During the debate, brother Crowder being on the floor, and having spoken fifteen minutes, a motion was made that he have liberty to proceed with and conclude his remarks. For this, a substitute was moved in these words, That the rule restricting speaking to fifteen minutes be suspended during the discussion of the subject before the Conference. Lost."

They had the experiment of two absolutions of the rule, and that seemed to satisfy them. Then a report was made, which took a course, which is to my mind more distinctly indicative of the gravity and difficulty of the subject, than any other thing which the report could have contained. Here were two parties, which, it was evident, never could be satisfied by a report of the committee which should adopt the sentiments of one or the other; and what did they do? Your Honours will find in this Methodist body no small degree of talent, and also some adroitness. They adopted a report which effectually declared the principle, that this Baltimore Conference was altogether wrong in the Westmoreland matter—that connexion with slavery was no objection to official standing in the Methodist Church, in States where emancipation was impossible. "But how do we know," said they, "that it was done on that ground?" Nobody doubted it; nobody denied it. It was perfectly palpable; but it was not on the minutes. They avoided the difficulty, and satisfied both parties. They refused to disturb the action of the Baltimore Conference, because it would infringe on the freedom of this conference, in passing upon the character of the ministers proposed for ordination, if they compelled them to put down their reasons; and as they could not tell by the record that that was their reason, they would not disturb the report. That was to satisfy the Baltimore Conference and the North; and then to the South they say, if that was the reason, then it was wrong. Exactly telling how the man would have swapped, if he had had a horse.

It was exactly a report indicating a state of things in that Church in 1840, which called from their wisest men, their most peaceful men, measures the most careful, adroit, and temporizing, so far as should be consistent with truth, and without a violation of distinct and clear duty. These gentlemen found it was a subject they could not manage. They had to temporize; they had to satisfy both parties, by saying to one, we cannot reverse your judgment, and to the other, if the judgment was on the ground you say it was, it was all wrong. Can anything more clearly indicate the character of the irreconcilable difficulty; that showed it was vain to hope or expect submission to a decree on that subject in that Conference? I submit that it was a most palpable exhibition of the difficulty; and when this Answer says, that in 1844 there had been no difficulty before that time which rendered a separation likely, or a subject of consideration, it seems to me many things have been overlooked, and that it has been a thing said in the way of argument in presenting the case, rather than as an averment of the truth. Indeed, it is not averred in the Answer upon the knowledge of the gentlemen, but I think there is a qualifying declaration, informed or advised by counsel, or something of that sort. I submit it stands proved that the difficulty then was great and irreconcilable.

Upon p. 58 of our first book of Proofs, is the bishops' address, with which that Conference commenced. It appeared that in 1840 this subject had already led to a partial dismemberment of the Church. I will read a part of the address:—

"It is justly due to a number of the annual conferences, in which a majority, or a very respectable minority of the members are professedly abolitionists, to say that they occupy a very different ground, and pursue a very different course, from those of their brethren who have adopted ultra principles and measures in this unfortunate, and, we think, unprofitable controversy. The result of the action had in such conferences, on the resolution of the New-England Conference, recommending a very important change in our general rule on slavery, is satisfactory proof of this fact, and affords us strong and increasing confidence that the unity and peace of the Church are not to be materially affected by this exciting subject. Many of the preachers, who were favourably disposed to the cause of abolition, when they saw the extent to which it was designed to carry these measures, and the inevitable consequences of their prosecution, came to a pause, reflected, and declined their co-operation. They clearly perceived that the success of the measures would result in the division of the Church; and for such an event they were not prepared."

I beg leave to comment upon this. These gentlemen saw the result of the abolition measures would be the division of the Church, and for that they were not prepared. And what do the bishops say these gentlemen did? They exercised forbearance. If they did not forbear, they saw it would lead to a dissolution of this Church. Here is a plain intimation of the danger directly before them, and the means of avoiding it, which means peace-loving people had adopted with the view of avoiding the danger. These bishops hoped, and spoke from hope, that they would be continued, and then the danger of separation might be avoided. But every one must see in this address, that if this subject continued to be agitated, the inevitable consequence would be a division of the Church. This is an official document, declaring what has since occurred, in terms almost prophetic. If the difficulty existed, where is their "answer," in which they say there never was a difficulty justifying a contingent separation growing out of it. The bishops, speaking from the hopes of good men, go on to say :—

"They have no disposition to criminate their brethren in the South, who are unavoidably connected with the institution of slavery, or to separate from them, on that account. It is believed that men of ardent temperament, whose zeal may have been somewhat in advance of their knowledge and discretion, have made such advances in the abolition enterprise as to produce a re-action. A few preachers and members, disappointed in their expectations, and despairing of the success of their cause in the Methodist Church, have withdrawn from our fellowship, and connected themselves with associations more congenial with their views and feelings; and others, in similar circumstances, may probably follow their example. But we rejoice in believing that these secessions will be very limited, and that the great body of Methodists in these States will continue as they have been, one and inseparable."

In other words, it is now evident these two principles cannot coexist in this Church. Either this business of abolition must cease to be agitated and talked of, or there must be secession. There has already been the secession of ultra gentlemen from the Northern conferences, because they will not go far enough, and everybody sees, if this thing continues, separation is inevitable ; and the bishops hoped, with this thing laid before the Church, with the pastoral admonition and communication, that quiet would ensue. Again they say :—

"Rules have been made from time to time, regulating the sale, and purchase, and holding of slaves, with reference to the different laws of the States where slavery is tolerated; which, upon the experience of the great difficulty of administering them, and the unhappy consequence both to masters and servants, have been as often changed or repealed. These important facts, which form prominent features of our past history as a Church, may properly lead us to inquire for that course of action in the future, which may be best calculated to preserve the peace and unity of the whole body, promote the greatest happiness of the slave-population, and advance generally, in the slaveholding community of our country, the humane and hallowing influence of our holy religion. We cannot withhold from you at this eventful period, the solemn conviction of our minds, that no new ecclesiastical legislation on the subject of slavery, at this time, will have a tendency to accomplish these most desirable objects. And we are fully persuaded, that, as a body of Christian ministers, we shall accomplish the greatest good by directing our individual and united efforts, in the spirit of the first teachers of Christianity, to bring both master and servant under the sanctifying influence of the principles of that Gospel which teaches the duties of every relation, and enforces the faithful discharge of them by the strongest conceivable motives. Do we aim at the amelioration of the condition of the slave? How can we so effectually accomplish this, in our calling as ministers of the Gospel of Christ, as by employing our influence to bring both him and his master to a saving knowledge of the grace of God, and to a practical observance of those relative duties so clearly prescribed in the writings of the inspired apostles?"

Now, I submit to the good sense and fair judgment of every reader of that address, if it was not the action of the nurse stepping about softly in the sick chamber, where the patient lay in that state in which noise might destroy him; and whether the whole aspect of it does not import that here was a dangerous crisis in the malady of the

Church, when agitation would lead to a separation and division, which, say the bishops, Northern gentlemen are not now prepared for. Does it show that there was no evil on this subject, no danger, no aspect of separation, no difficulties, no differences, (in the language of this Answer;) so that when these gentlemen, in 1844, after an agitation unparalleled in its character, and acts of the most wounding style committed against the feelings of the Southern delegates, made a declaration that a continuance in that state was no longer possible, did they declare some new thing, a thing then originating, and which required them to be active in bringing their prophecy to pass? or were they speaking historically as to matters they had observed for a long time, and which then flashed upon them with a light no one could resist. I think your Honours will read with advantage the Address to the British Conference, and the answer to it.

These conciliatory measures were adopted in 1844, and yet it will be said that this shows there was no danger. What does it show? It shows there is no danger if you keep still; your patient may recover if you keep quiet; but if you fire a cannon about him, you may kill him? What was done? What was the history of things from 1840 to 1844? I speak quite within a moderate form of expression, when I say that in 1844 the agitation was fiercely renewed, and that agitation had grown from the state of things between 1840 and 1844. You will see the beginning of the Conference of 1844 flooded with petitions on the subject of slavery from Northern conferences. You will see the "Breakwater Conference" anew standing up to make the waves break. The Conference took up the case of Mr. Harding as early as May 4. This Mr. Harding, of the Baltimore Conference, had been suspended from his ministerial standing for refusing to manumit certain slaves who came into his possession by his marriage. On the 8th May this business was taken up and debated, and on the 10th also. On the 11th it was again taken up, and decided; and they then sustained the degradation of a man living in a State where it was shown he could not manumit the slave, except by submitting him to be transported out of the State by the sheriff, and if the slave had connexions, wife, children, all would have to be abandoned. Was this the quiet of the tender friend to a sick patient? Was this behaving according to the recommendation of the Conference of 1840? Or was it not breaking with thunder upon this wished-to-be peaceful body? It seems to me that no gentleman of discretion in that Conference, could have looked at that thing, and at the historical and prophetic declaration of the bishops in 1840, without seeing proof of the now-existing state of things. It seems to me that the knell of this peace was then sounded—the division was then declared; and look at the consequences. Immediately, under the impulse which a large majority gives—for men acting in bodies are acted upon by their sympathies, and, as Lord Chesterfield expressed it of the House of Lords, every great assembly is a mob; that is to say, they go more by sympathies than by individual wisdom—it produces action in the case of Bishop Andrew. I need only refer to that: I do conceive it is a touching history; no one, I think, who ever read the account of the proceedings can ever let it be obliterated. In the first place a resolution is offered asking him to resign. That would have been, to be sure, advisory, but pretty strong advice, like inviting a man to leave your room; you invite him peaceably first, and if he does not go, your servant takes him by the coat, and says, "That is the way, sir." But this at first was an invitation. Either it was rude, or offensive in some way, or it was insufficient,—I am unable to say which,—and then a resolution was presented by Mr. Finley, that he desist from his episcopal functions. I wish to read this now, in reference to what is disputed between the two parties in 1844, as to whether this is advisory merely, or covertly a sentence of degradation.

"Whereas the Discipline of our Church forbids the doing anything calculated to destroy our itinerant general superintendency, and whereas Bishop Andrew has become connected with slavery by marriage and otherwise, and this act having drawn after it circumstances which, in the estimation of the General Conference, will greatly embarrass the exercise of his office as an itinerant general superintendent, if not in some places entirely prevent it; therefore,

"Resolved, That it is the sense of this General Conference that he desist from the exercise of this office so long as this impediment remains."

It seems to me that any one skilled in ecclesiastical sentences would find here every element of a sentence of degradation. It refers first to the Discipline—it forbids so and so. What is the use of the recital, if the gentleman has not done something forbidden? Why recite the law to say that it has been kept? It is cited to show that it was broken, and that these gentlemen acted under warrant of the law. I am at a loss to know what a judicial sentence is, if that was not. It recites what the Discipline forbids, and then that Bishop Andrew had become connected with slavery, which drew after it certain consequences. Here is the only thing which is different from a judicial sentence: it is a sentence of a bill of attainder; in other words, instead of saying this violation has drawn after it consequences which the law imputes to crime, it says it draws after it consequences which are adjudged to be inconsistent with the social state. You may search the history of bills of attainder in England and analyze them, and you will always find some grave misdemeanor which has never been precisely defined by the law, but which has satisfied those who sat in judgment and passed the bill, that it was a grievous offence, not by reason of violating some known law, but some great principle which those who sat on it thought needed protection, and for that they pass the attainder, forfeit the estate, take the life, bring the subject to the block.

But what did they do here? Did they advise Bishop Andrew to manumit his slaves? That would have been absurd. They knew he could not do it. When you advise a man, you suppose it is something which he can do. Why did they not advise him to manumit his slaves? It would have struck every one as an absurdity. Manumit them in Georgia! Every one would have said, it is like asking him to run when manacled. They passed a judicial degradation. They said, "It is the sense of this General Conference that he desist from the exercise of this office." "That he desist!"—that is not a term of advice. He is not invited to do anything, but it is "the sense," the judgment, of the Conference "that he desist." Is not that a judicial degradation of this gentleman? What is the office of a bishop? Let us see whether this is a degradation or not. "He that desireth the office of a bishop, desireth a good thing." What is the good thing? Is it to be called a bishop? Is it to be printed in the Hymn book and Book of Discipline with no functions? Is it to receive $200 a year? Surely not; and last of all in this Connexion, among whom we are now walking, self-denying men, living in contented poverty, and in their contentment being richer than any of the bishops who wear mitres. What is desirable in the office of a bishop? It is the duty and functions of the bishop; the opportunity of glorious labour; the noble duty of supervising the religious instruction and conduct of the ministers among whom he walks. These are the things which make the office of a bishop desirable. That is the "good thing" to be desired. It is the carrying out of the great principle, that it is the glory of the labour which is the glory of the office; it is not the glory of the title, of wealth, of ease,—it is the glory of the functions of the episcopacy which he is exercising, which induce him to accept it, and make him honoured. "From all these things, Bishop Andrew, you must abstain." "Violated any law?" "Yes, you have violated a law,—not exactly that we can try you for; but you have done that which satisfies us of a violation of our principles of policy, as the high, supreme, sovereign, judicial, and legislative body, for which we attaint you." There it lies. That is the sentence; and when afterwards in the Conference somebody, certainly with more kindness of heart than judgment, moved a resolution that it should be considered advisory, the good sense of the members rejected it, because it would have been absurd to call it advice. The sense of this Conference is that you desist; the judgment of the Conference is, that in consequence of a violation of the principle of Discipline, you must desist. Here was an action of the most permanent character, bearing upon this question in such a way as most effectually to bring into view the prophecy of the bishops in 1840, that a further agitation of this subject would render a separation of that Church unavoidable. I cannot forbear calling your attention to the deliberation with which this was done. If it had been a transient ebullition, which it might be expected cooler moments would have quieted, our learned friends might say there was nothing to be apprehended; but this thing was debated from May 23d to some day in June. In the meantime the bishops all came out with some advice. They say, Postpone this subject until 1848—let time come and heal the agitation and heat upon this subject—let it come with its healing, its cooling influence; and so would have been the advice of every man who did not believe the evil incurable. After that was presented, one of the bishops, Bishop Hedding, thought, "well I am sure this will do no good," and revoked his signature. The other bishops, for different reasons, stood by that recommendation. Now see how deliberate this was. Would it not be a libel upon this body to suppose that this indicated a transient feeling, or anything likely to pass away between 1844 and 1848? Can anybody say that the Conference was so reckless of the safety of the Church that they preferred acting immediately, although it would lead to such consequences, rather than to wait till 1848?

I say that by this act the bishop's itinerancy and episcopacy were plainly destroyed, and he was disqualified without conviction of anything. It was a legislative declaration as to slavery disqualifying every preacher, in Harding's case, and every bishop, in Andrew's case; so that thereafter in that Southern country no man connected with slavery, however involuntarily, could ever be a preacher or a bishop, and for the same reason he could hold no official station in that Church. I ask whether that did not indicate a foregone state of opinion, which had been previously produced? because it is in vain to say that it was all got up by the Northern men at the meeting of that Conference. It was the result of previous deliberation, then only ripened and discovered. It is in vain to say, with such a disqualifying sentence upon all the preachers of this body belonging to the Southern conferences connected with slavery, that it was possible for them to go on as co-operating members of a ministry.

Was there any change to be hoped for on this subject? In 1832, as the Reply to the Protest tells us, the anti-slavery feeling had got a great headway and was constantly increasing. We have seen what it was in 1840. We now see what it was in 1844, after an experience of twelve years, resulting in acts of a very extreme character. Certainly I speak in moderation when I say these two acts were of an extreme character. Was there any hope that gentlemen who were adverse to slavery would give up their opinions? It would be contrary to experience to expect that that which had gone on increasing would not continue to increase, but would, because it had increased, diminish. How was it with the South? Was this the way to conciliate them? The bishops, in 1840, had told the Conference "Keep quiet," and in the very face of that they go on with the most serious acts, wounding to everything the Southern people considered distinctive of themselves. Is that a thing which would conduce to peace on their part? Is that a measure likely to result in a better state of the Church?

This Declaration was handed in on the 5th of June. It says, (p. 97,)—

"The delegates of the conferences in the slaveholding States take leave to *declare* to the General Conference of the Methodist Episcopal Church, that the continued agitation of the subject of slavery and abolition in a portion of the Church; the frequent action on that subject in the General Conference; and especially the extra-judicial proceedings against Bishop Andrew, which resulted, on Saturday last, in the virtual suspension of him from his office as superintendent, must produce a state of things in the South which renders a continuance of the jurisdiction of this General Conference over these conferences inconsistent with the success of the ministry in the slaveholding States."

I beg your attention to the last four lines of this. They speak of causes which are past, and the effect that they must produce. They speak of effects which are certain. They do not say "we suppose they will;" they speak with certainty of the fact, and of consequences within their own knowledge; and then they declare what those consequences are "which render," not "which will render," or "are likely to render," but which render the separation necessary. This was a declaration of sensible men,—a declaration, I think, in the very spirit of peace to that Church,—because at every Conference there would have been trials, degradations, and elections of bishops more and more free from any connexion with slavery, and therefore more and more foreign from the people among whom they were to minister. That Declaration was signed by all the delegates from the Southern conferences. It was referred to a committee. Then,

"J. B. McFerrin offered the following resolution:—

"'*Resolved*, That the committee appointed to take into consideration the communication of the delegates from the Southern conferences be instructed, provided they cannot in their judgment devise a plan for an amicable adjustment of the difficulties now existing in the Church, on the subject of slavery, to devise, if possible, a constitutional plan for a mutual and friendly division of the Church.'

"T. Crowder's motion to strike out the word 'constitutional,' did not prevail, and the resolution was adopted."

This shows how distinctly the question of constitutionality was brought in. The committee of nine was composed of five of those who voted for the sentence, and four who voted against the sentence of Bishop Andrew. Then came the Protest and the Reply to it, both of which I ask your Honours to read, not as detailing facts, because these gentlemen, no doubt, took different views of facts and especially of inferences, but with a view of looking at the character of the principles detailed in both these papers, and to ask yourselves whether, supposing them both to be sincere, they did not declare principles on each side, under the same Discipline, which prevented this Church from ever being anything but nominally in unity. The moment those papers came in,—one the manifesto on the one side, and the other on the other,—there was as entire a separation in fact as afterwards was accomplished in form. I do not intend to read either of these papers, but I beg very briefly to say what principles they avowed.

On the part of the Southern gentlemen, the Protest avowed that the Conference adopted this sentence as degrading Bishop Andrew without a trial. On the other side they declared such things might be done, and it was not degrading the bishop; that they had a right to do it without trying him. There was a principle of Church government involved, vital to the episcopacy of that Church. One side say, "You do, in effect, punish this bishop by bill of attainder." The other side say, "We have a right to do that with the bishop, for this cause or a similar one." Here was a division on the subject of episcopacy in the Church government, which would seem to make it perfectly idle for them to expect to go on together as a Church, each maintaining their sentiments. Was there any hope of these gentlemen changing? I am at a loss to see in anything that afterwards took place the slightest indication that anything would have produced an amelioration.

The Protest avers that this sentence rested on a mere aversion to slavery, and that it thus announced a purpose destructive to the unity of the Church, and adopted the anti-slavery principle, and that so a division was already made. Now, my learned friends set up in their Answer, that the division was not made until after this Protest; and the gentlemen who made it, endeavoured to make good their prediction.

What do they say in the Reply? They set up that no slaveholder ever had been a bishop. The allegation of the Protest is, You adopt the anti-slavery principle, and the degradation of the bishop, on the mere ground of aversion to slavery. They set up that no slaveholder ever was a bishop intentionally in this Church. Here is a principle broadly declared and united in on both sides,—both uniting in the fact, the only difference being one saying that it was, and the other, that it was not right.

The Reply declares that his acting as bishop would be injurious to the North, and they say he could have no itinerancy at the North; in that way averring that the Northern sentiment should control in this Church. Does any one suppose that was a thing to enable this Church to stand as an undivided Church? They then aver another thing, in which it seems to me they had the letter though not the spirit of their Discipline with them, that the General Conference was not limited in its powers as to slavery. The Protest had averred that there had been a compromise on the subject of slavery, and their Discipline showed it. On the other side, they averred there was no compromise upon the subject which bound the General Conference. It seems to me that though it did not bind them in letter, yet it was one of those things upon which both parties had so acted that it was in honour as valid and complete a compromise as anything ever done. It was very much like those things which have taken place in this country called "compromises." You cannot limit Congress; but when large sections of country are agitated, and measures adopted which are on both sides considered as concessions for peace' sake and compromises, they are binding in honour and conscience, although not binding in law and by legal technicality. That was exactly the state of things here; but the gentlemen who had the majority in the Conference of 1844, very clearly declared "We will listen to no considerations in that spirit; we will consider ourselves entirely free on that subject, to go to the utmost limits of the sovereign power of the General Conference."

Again: this reply clearly alleges that the Southern Churches and conferences were bound to receive bishops who held anti-slavery sentiments. So they were; but how was it to conduce to the peace of the Church that all the bishops who were sent to the South should go without the slighest sympathy which the relation of master and slaves in any of its forms could ever give rise to? Was that an episcopacy? Was that a ministry which in a Protestant country ever would be received and listened to, or permitted to exercise its functions? After this Protest and Reply, could this body continue together? and is it not evident that unless the Methodist Church could extinguish slavery, it must leave the South? On that subject, it seems to me, it is too much to say, that after what had taken place during this series of years, and had thus ripened and discovered itself in 1840, and more especially in 1844, the Declaration was the cause of the disruption. You might as well say that the doctor who tells you that you have a fever, gave you the fever. I will simply refer your Honours to the result on the queries of the bishops as to how they were to treat Bishop Andrew. Their inquiry was made on the sixth of June; it will be found on p. 124 of book No. 1. As I have abbreviated it, it comes to this. He is to do nothing; but his name is to be published in the Hymn Books and all the publications of the Society. If I wanted to make degradation most complete, that is the course I should have taken, only adding to it, if I could, the publication of a Methodist Spelling Book, and having his name printed in connexion with the names of the other bishops, whom they were in the habit of seeing.

I have by anticipation spoken of the report of the committee of nine, on the 8th of June, 1844. This committee of nine were originally to consider whether they could devise a plan for amicable adjustment, and if they could not, then they were to devise a plan for separation. The committee reported a plan for separation, turning it upon this Declaration, which had been made, being verified by the delegates from the Southern conferences. The delegates from the Southern conferences, under the lead of Mr. Paine, who was afterwards a bishop in the Southern Church, moved to transfer that burden from themselves to the Southern conferences. That was agreed to. What was meant by leaving it to the Southern conferences if they should find a separation necessary? When were they to make the search? What experiment were they to try in the South? The gentlemen who made the Declaration knew the sentiments of their constituents. What was meant by this finding? It meant what a jury does when it finds. They were to sit down and consider the subject, and if in their conclusions they found that this was so, then they were authorized to make a separate organization. That is all I have to say upon that part of the subject.

This was a plain and distinct authority to these Southern conferences to organize themselves into a new Church. This was in no sense conditional. In the first place, it was not conditional upon any future event which was to determine the conferences. It was to be left to their sober judgment to pass upon this question, of whether a division was necessary to the peace of the Church; and there is not a word of condition in regard to the separation, except "if they should find it necessary." In the next place, no new event was expected to occur. Who was to tell what was to satisfy these gentlemen? Suppose we adopt the conclusion that they were to look for something else to happen. The Southern conferences met in September, 1844. What were they to do? Why, it was to be talked about among the people, and the general sense of the people was to be ascertained on that subject. But did the General Conference of 1844 appoint any judge to determine whether these gentlemen had exercised the power? That was left to these conferences themselves. If their judgments were satisfied, either by what they knew had happened or would happen, that it was necessary, they were to organize a separate Church. What was done? This thing was committed to the conferences by the delegates; they were invited to judge of it. It is complained of, that they advised a separation. Why, they had a perfect right to do so. If in conscience they believed it necessary to the peace of the Church, it was their duty to have done so. The resolutions adopted by the conferences show that it was a matter of discussion; they passed upon this subject, and their judgment was the judgment intended to be conclusive on the Church. Their judgment was to be the concluding judgment on the subject, because there is no pretence that this was to be left to another General Conference, and because they had appointed commissioners to carry this division into effect; showing that they had not anticipated an act of another Conference. If they did not suppose that this was to have been done under that act of the Conference, then they authorized these gentlemen to pass judgment and organize a Church, and when it was done, unless it should suit the General Conference, which was to meet in 1848, that organization made them seceders. Why, by the very nature of the power, by the very invitation to judge on this subject, their judgment was made the concluding and final judgment which was to protect those who acted under it

Again: it is alleged, and perhaps it will be argued—it is set up in the Answer—that it was all conditional upon the vote on the change of the restrictive rule. Now, that cannot be so, for one very plain reason. The change of the restrictive rule was to authorize the turning over of the property to commissioners from the "Church, South." It imported that there should be a "Church, South," before any necessity could arise of voting upon a restrictive rule. Unless the Church, South, was organized, or unless it was certain that it would be organized, the proposition to change the restrictive rule was a mere hypothetical sort of thing. It seems to me that the changing of the restrictive rule was made a condition to only one thing, and that thing was the agents turning over a part of the funds without the decree of a court of justice, or an act of the General Conference, to the commissioners of the Church, South.

Moreover, it has been suggested, in some papers which have gone forth on this subject from our friends on the other side, that all this was a plan to stand and be adopted together. There is nothing of that kind in the Plan. What had taken place with regard to Canada shows that it was perfectly competent, and according to the usage of this Church, to allow of a separation, and to leave the question of property to be afterwards adjusted according to equity. There is nothing in that Plan which makes any part of it conditional, one upon the other, except only that which relates to a change of the restrictive article; and that is a condition only to the action of the agents, and the action of the agents as to turning over the capital.

It is also said that it was conditional upon our conforming to the limits; and they assert, in some of their papers, two violations, as they say, where Southern preachers went into bordering Northern conferences and established preaching houses. That cannot be a condition, because the effect of it would be to make the rights of every one of the Southern conferences depend upon the acts of that conference which happened to be delinquent. That was the provision of a treaty, and not a condition. This was a covenant, and the violators of it stood as the violators of a covenant between two contracting parties. It might be said it was a shame, if the fact were such; and I do not intend to discuss that, because I consider it utterly immaterial. Who gave that border conference that did this, the right to jeopardize the interests of thirteen or fourteen other conferences growing out of this Plan of Separation? Never can this be considered a condition. How long was such a condition to continue? If it was a condition at all, it must be of perpetual obligation. Is it a perpetual condition, so that at any distance of time, after the organization and establishment of the Southern Church, if a conference of that Church should violate it, everything would be annulled which preceded that, and things would be precisely in the same condition as they were before the adoption of the Plan of Separation? That is the effect of holding it to be a condition. It cannot be so. I speak this, I am sure, with the concurrence of the enlightened judgment of the Court.

Then, on the subject of the votes on the change of the restrictive article, it seems that the necessary number of votes were not given to authorize the change. I chiefly notice this, because your Honours will see that it shows no lack of strength in our cause. On the journals of the Conference of the Northern Church of 1848, page 177, I find this report:—The votes were, for altering the sixth rule, from the South 971, and from the North 1,164, in all 2,135; and against it, from the South 3, from the North 1,067, in all 1,070. The three-fourths required was 2,404; so that even at the North there was a majority of about 100 for it. But inasmuch as it required three-fourths, the whole number should have been 2,404; there were 269 votes lacking, out of over 3,000 cast. We have, however, this fact evinced by this, as to the equity of the claim, that the Northern gentlemen themselves, by a very decisive majority, certainly a working majority under any other circumstances, were in favour of acknowledging this right in the South to part of the funds.

Now, I submit that after what took place, there was no secession; that those who organized and belonged to the Southern Church did it without blame; that they are in every sense preachers of the Methodist Episcopal Church, in good standing, belonging to yearly conferences, adopting Methodist doctrines and Methodist discipline. Then, I ask, suppose there be no alteration in the sixth restrictive article, what is the effect of it upon the rights of the superannuated and worn-out preachers of the Southern conferences? To determine this, we must look to the article. And here I wish to say, that if we are not seceders, if we are as truly the Methodist Episcopal Church in our part, as they are in their part of the country, then I wish to know upon what principle it can be held that it would be a violation of trust in the Book Concern, or its agents, to pay over to our preachers their share of the produce? The article reads (page 28):—

"They shall not appropriate the produce of the Book Concern, nor of the Chartered Fund, to any purpose other than for the benefit of the travelling, supernumerary, superannuated, and worn-out preachers, their wives, widows, and children."

I submit that even if we were a secession, even if we have ceased to be in the Methodist Connexion in the sense of the Methodist Discipline, whether, after all that has taken place, a change of the restrictive article was required to entitle our beneficiaries to this fund. I ask now whether, supposing the book agents had paid out this fund to the Southern beneficiaries, to the widows and children (taking them first as the non-combatants in this matter) their share, would any court in the world say that was a breach of trust in these book agents? Upon what principle could they say so? Are these widows and children not in good standing in that Church? The Northern delegates had said to our people, "You may join this Southern organization without blame." Then are we not in good standing? We have done an act which you say we might do, and do without blame. If we have done it without blame in the sense of the Discipline, without blame in the very view of an alteration of the restrictive article, how are we to be excluded from our share? Although there may be a difficulty, rendering it necessary for these agents, when they are asked to part with the capital of the fund itself, to require the sanction of a court, I can see, I confess, no difficulty as to their being bound to make a distribution among the beneficiaries belonging to the Southern conferences under this article, just as well without as with an alteration of it.

Moreover, if it was intended that the whole of our rights should depend upon the alteration of the restrictive article in this respect, then, beyond all doubt, it would have been arranged, so that the alteration should have covered this case and no other. Then, beyond all doubt, the change in the restrictive article would have proposed so as to have made the article read, "They shall not apply the produce of the Book Concern to any other purpose, than the benefit of travelling, &c., preachers in our Connexion or in any Connexion authorized by us;" but the alteration recommended is to add, "and to such other purposes as may be determined upon by the votes of two-thirds of the members of the General Conference." I submit, and on this subject I need not enlarge, for the considerations are very plain, that if we are not seceders, then all these beneficiaries are entitled, even though these book agents should retain possession of the fund, and they must distribute it through these annual conferences.

This being a subject of equitable administration, I have one other consideration to submit on this part of it. Here is in equity an estoppel to the claim, that we are seceders. There is in equity an estoppel to the claim, that we, who formed this organization under the invitation of the Plan of Separation, by the co-operation of the bishops, and without an intimation from any authorized body of this Church that we were doing wrong, are seceders. We organized ourselves into a separate Church, on the invitation of the General Conference ; and it seems to me against all equity, that they should be permitted to set up that act as the forfeiting act. But forfeiture may be waved ; and it may be waved by acts before as well as after. If I grant permission to a man to do that which would otherwise be a forfeiture, it ceases to be a forfeiture. And after a forfeiture I might do that which sanctions it, and it waves the forfeiture. The law lays hold of everything to defeat a forfeiture. What our learned friends claim in this, is simply a forfeiture, acknowledging our prior right, and acknowledging that it is a penalty beyond the damage, claiming much punishment for little transgression. Now I submit, that the Conference of 1844, has given such a consent as prevents this being a forfeiture, unless your Honours shall say it was one of those plain and direct breaches of trust which come under a very different category. I therefore say, according to my seventh point, that the beneficiaries of the fund in question, who belonged to the Southern conferences, did not by the new organization lose any rights, nor were they disqualified in any manner from claiming their share of the fund ; and such claim is appropriately made through the General Conference, South, which succeeds to the place of the prior General Conference of the whole Church. Our claim to a share of the profits stands on the fact of our not being seceders. Even if the organization of the South should be considered defective, it would not make us seceders in the sense of forfeiting. Upon an idea which I have presented to your Honours, that this General Conference had the power to consent, and did consent, to the organization of a new body, a new General Conference, then, without going to the powers of another General Conference, we have a right to administer that part of the fund which properly belongs to our beneficiaries, in the same sense, and with the same right, that the General Conference of the whole Church had over the general fund when the Church remained undivided. We succeed to our share of the sovereignty —to the sovereignty in our district. This fund is to be administered through the annual conferences, and they are subordinate to the General Conference of the Church, South ; and the General Conference of that Church has the same right to appoint a book agent to carry out their administration, that the General Conference of the whole Church had when the Church was undivided ; or, as the General Conference of the Northern Church has to the fund in their hands. I submit, that if my reasoning has been correct on the subject of a division of the Church, that necessarily follows.

There is no difficulty of form in any part of this case. If there is any difficulty it is upon the substance ; and the substance is, Have our beneficiaries forfeited? If not, they are entitled, either through their conferences or an individual, to be paid their share of the profits ; and if the Southern Church has been organized according to the doctrine and discipline of the Methodist Church, then we have a right to have that fund appropriated by new trustees. Therefore, in conclusion, I say, that an account should be ordered of the proportions of the profits of the Book Concern, according to the numbers on the minutes of 1844, and at the same ratio of the profits since. That is, according to the "Plan of Separation." Also, the capital of the fund should be decreed to be divided in the same way, and paid over to the commissioners, South, as new trustees, or to proper trustees to be appointed by the Court. The profits of the past are to be subject to distribution, according to the directions of the General Conference, South, whether the fund remain with the present trustees or be paid over to the new trustees.

I have not thought it necessary, and it certainly is not necessary that I should go over the steps that led to the organization of the new Church. I believe there can be no objection to them as a matter of form. I therefore leave this matter in the judgment of the Court.

If your Honours please, the attention with which we have been favoured by the Court in this cause, leaves us nothing to fear as to the calmness and care with which its judgment will be formed. We have argued it at great length, and we thank your Honours for the indulgence extended to us. But we have felt, and no doubt it has been a common feeling among us, that no cause, probably, with which any of us have ever been concerned is fraught with greater consequences, or the subject of more intense solicitude than the present. It involves the feelings and the interests of millions. It touches a question of the gravest consequence to the well-being of this religious community. No political question, nothing that has ever presented itself on this subject, touches in any degree interests so great, or men so influential. We know that it will be disposed of according to its merits. We, on our part, have studiously intended to avoid, however earnest we may have been in advocating our views on this subject, anything that should be offensive to our friends on the other side, or which should tend, in any degree, to irritate the wound in this body. On the part of the gentlemen here, I believe, they are our friends, for the Northern majority, although not amounting to sufficient to warrant this distribution of the funds by the agents themselves, is a majority of our friends. What we have spoken in earnestness, we trust we have guarded so as to give no personal offence, and not tend to aggravate any breach. We trust that the full discussion which this matter will receive on the part of our friends on the other side, as well as ourselves, may so enlighten this Methodist community, that it is to be hoped, whatever judgment your Honours may form on the subject, the principles of equity and of right which seem to us, and, I think, seem to every one, to be those principles of equity and right which lie on the surface, will be most willingly adopted; and that this great controversy, under the enlightened judgment of the Court, may have its final end.

Judge Nleson,—Mr. Ewing, you had, perhaps, better put in your proofs now.

Mr. Ewing,—Mr. Fancher will read our evidence in a few minutes.

Mr. Lord,—If your Honours please, there is one authority which, in the absence of Mr. Johnson, I had forgot to quote. I intended to refer the Court to the reasoning of the Court of Appeals of Kentucky, which passed upon this very subject, when a controversy arose in relation to some of the preaching-houses. It was the case of Armstrong *vs.* Gibson. It has been published in pamphlet form.

Mr. Ewing,—I think it has also been published in 9th Ben. Monroe.

Mr. Lord,—The Court in that case decided.

Judge Nelson,—When was that?

Mr. Johnson,—Since the separation.

Judge Nelson,—Since 1845?

Mr. Johnson,—Yes, sir.

Mr. Lord then read the following note of the case referred to, from a pamphlet published by Mr. Bascom and others, on the subject of this controversy:—

"Extracts from the decision of the Court of Appeals of Kentucky, in the celebrated Maysville case, in which opinion the whole ground of controversy between the North and the South of the Methodist Episcopal Church, affecting the most important rights of the parties, is subjected to elaborate and careful examination by the distinguished jurists composing the Court:—

"The General Conference of 1844 having adopted measures which, by many Southern delegates, were deemed injurious to the rights, and character, and usefulness of the Southern ministry of the Methodist Episcopal Church, a Declaration, signed by the Southern delegates, and stating their apprehension of the necessity of a separation, was presented to the General Conference, which thereupon passed a set of resolutions providing for the manner and consequences of the anticipated separation, should it be found necessary, and authorizing, in that event, a distinct Southern organization.

"Under the sanction of these resolutions, a convention of delegates from fifteen Southern conferences assembled in 1845, renounced by solemn act their connexion with the pre-existing organization and the jurisdiction of the General Conference as then constituted, and, retaining the same faith and doctrine, the same rules and discipline, and the same form of constitution and government, established for themselves a new and independent organization, under the name of 'the Methodist Episcopal Church, South.'

"We are called on to apply to the consequences of a catastrophe which, if it had not occurred when and as it did, must at some time have happened, the provisions of a deed which, having been made when the Church was united and division not contemplated, refers, as might be expected, to the existing name, and organs, and action of a united Church. The one united Methodist Episcopal Church, referred to in the deed, and extending its name and authority to the utmost limits of the United States, having ceased to exist, by division into two Churches of distinct territorial jurisdiction, there is, in fact, no such Church as is contemplated in the deed; and, therefore, no General Conference of such a Church, no ministers and preachers of such a Church, no members of such a Church.

"Does the fact that there still remains a portion, whether small or large, of the original body, under the original name of the whole, invalidate the separation, or the rights of the separating portion? Could the remaining portion of the original body re-assert, in the name of the whole, the jurisdiction which had been renounced by the whole, or revoke the assent which the whole body had once given to the independence of the separating portion? Certainly, if the whole body had power, by assent and co-operation, to legalize the separation and its independence of a part of itself, the remaining portion of the original body, though retaining the original name of the whole, would have no power, after such assent had been given and acted on, to undo, by its own mere will, what the entire body had authorized. Whatever else may be implied from the identity of name, it cannot give to the present Methodist Episcopal Church a jurisdiction which the original Church had alienated.

"But it seems to us too evident to require illustration, that the rights and jurisdiction of the Southern Church, and the rights of its members, are precisely the same within its own organization, as if the present Methodist Episcopal Church were called the Methodist Episcopal Church, North; that if the Southern organization has the sanction of the original Church, it can suffer no disparagement from having been the separating portion, but its independence and jurisdiction are complete; and that, to the extent of its jurisdiction, it stands in the place of the Methodist Episcopal Church, and is to be so regarded, as well in giving construction and application to these deeds, as in determining the rights and duties of its members.

"That a Church organization, a self-created body, subject, so far as its own constitution and organization are concerned, to no superior will, cannot, by its own assent, authorize and legalize its own dismemberment, is a proposition contradicted by reason and analogy. That such a measure is inconsistent with the motives and ends of its institution, is no more true with regard to such a body, than with regard to other associations, private or national. Even in the case of states and empires, the unauthorized separation of a part, though originally illegal, and subjecting the separatists to reclamation and punishment by the remaining government, is legalized by its subsequent assent, with the effect of establishing, in the separating portion, all the rights of independence and self-government.

"It does not admit of question that such a power belonged to the Methodist Episcopal Church, and that *prima facie* the General Conference, the supreme active organ of its government, clothed with powers of legislation almost unlimited, and having alone, in case of unlawful secession, the right of recognition or reclamation, might effectually exercise the power in advance. Indeed, the history of the Church shows that many years since, the General Conference, without reference to its constituents, assented to the separation and independence of the Canada Conference, then forming an integral portion of the general organization, and having, or entitled to have, its delegates in the General Conference itself. And although there seems to have been some doubt on the question of power, we do not perceive that the grounds of that doubt bring in question the power of the General Conference, any more than that of the Church at large, which is unquestionable. The measure, however, was adopted, and no doubt has been since entertained of the lawful independence of the Canada Conference.

"We think it must be conceded that, in the absence of express provision to the contrary, the General Conference has the right, on its own judgment of the necessity of the case, to assent to, and thus to legalize the separation of a part of the Church.

"The evidences in favour of the validity of the act of the General Conference now in question are so strong, as almost to preclude the possibility of a conclusive demonstration against it, and certainly too strong to be overthrown by any doubtful construction.

"If the question of power were doubtful, we should be bound to regard the act of the General Conference as the act of the Church, and therefore as effectual.

"The resolutions, constituting the Plan of Separation, do not expel any individual from the society of which he was a member, nor deprive him of any privilege of property or worship pertaining to that society. But as they propose and provide for a complete separation, according to the organic or territorial divisions of the Church, they necessarily involve a partition of the governing power between two jurisdictions, each possessing, within its territorial limits, the same authority and power as had previously belonged to the whole Church.

"To say that the Church could not be legally or rightfully divided, according to its organic or territorial parts, without the unanimous consent of all the members of the entire Church, or even of all the members of the part proposed to be separated, would be to deny the power of division by any mode of action, since it would subject it to an impossible condition.

"And although one or more annual conferences might be incompetent, by their separate action, against the consent of the General Conference, to bind to an independent organization the local societies connected with them, we are satisfied that the joint and co-operative action of the General Conference and the several annual conferences concerned, was fully competent to determine the question, and fix the limits, of separation, and to establish, over the several societies within whose limits, the jurisdiction of the new organization.

"In determining upon the legality of the actual state of things consequent upon a great movement of this character, every part of the proceeding should be liberally construed, to effectuate the apparent and reasonable intention of the parties; and there is no room for technicality. Then it is apparent upon the face of the resolutions, that there is but one condition upon which the separation and the sanction of the General Conference are to depend, which is, that the annual conferences in the slaveholding States should find it necessary to erect an independent ecclesiastical Connexion, &c. The distribution of the Book Concern and Chartered Fund is obviously intended to be a consequence of the separation, and not a condition on which it is to depend. And the reference to the several annual conferences for a modification of the restrictive rule, was evidently for the purpose of authorizing the intended distribution, and not of authorizing the separation. The slaveholding conferences, referred to in the first resolution, are such as were situated wholly in the slaveholding States. And the delegates from all these conferences assembled in convention, having declared the necessity of separation, and erected an independent ecclesiastical Connexion, the prescribed condition has been complied with

"As to the actual necessity for separation, that is, the existence of such a state of things as justified it, or rendered it proper, this, if it could ever have been a judicial question, is no longer so. It has been decided by the concurring judgment of the General Conference and the Southern or slaveholding conferences, to which it was referred, and by the fact itself of an actual separation by agreement between the whole and the separating part, which is presumptively the strongest evidence of a high expediency, amounting to necessity.

"But the separation having, as we have seen, been effected by competent powers in the Church, and under the condition and in pursuance of the Plan prescribed by the General Conference, its legality, in view of the civil tribunal, can be in no degree dependent upon the sufficiency in point of discretion or policy of the causes which led to it. It is sufficient that the Church, through its competent agents, has authorized the separate organization and independent self-government of the Southern conferences, and that they have so acted under the authority, as to clothe their movement with the sanction of the Church. This being so, the Southern Church stands not as a seceding or schismatic body, breaking off violently or illegally from the original Church, and carrying with it such members and such rights only as it may succeed in abstracting from the other, but as a lawful ecclesiastical body, erected by the authority of the entire Church, with plenary jurisdiction over a designated portion of the original association, recognised by that Church as its proper successor and representative within its limits, commended as such to the confidence and obedience of all the members within those limits, and declared to be worthy of occupying towards them the place of the original Methodist Episcopal Church, and of taking its name. Such, though not the express language, is the plain and necessary import of the resolutions, in authorizing the formation of a Southern ecclesiastical Connexion or Church, and prescribing a rule for ascertaining its limits; in leaving to the unmolested care of the anticipated Southern Church all the societies, &c., within its limits, and stipulating that within those limits no new ones shall be organized under the authority of the Methodist Episcopal Church; in declaring that ministers may take their place in the Southern Connexion without blame; and in denominating the Southern Church 'the Church, South.' The provision made for a ratable distribution of the funds of the Church, and the relinquishment of all claim to the preaching-houses, &c., within the limits of the Southern Connexion, are of a similar character with the other features of the resolutions, and attest the equity and magnanimity of the late General Conference. That body had, however, no proprietary interest in the preaching-houses, and could only transfer its jurisdiction over them, which is done by the resolutions and the proceedings under them.

"The result is, that the original Methodist Episcopal Church has been authoritatively divided into two Methodist Episcopal Churches, the one North and the other South of a common boundary line, which, according to the Plan of Separation, limits the extent and jurisdiction of each; that each, within its own limits, is the lawful successor and representative of the original Church, possessing all its jurisdiction, and entitled to its name; that neither has any more right to exceed those limits than the other; that the Southern Church, retaining the same faith, doctrine, and discipline, and assuming the same organization and name as the original Church, is not only a Methodist Episcopal Church, but is in fact, to the South, the Methodist Episcopal Church as truly as the other Church is so to the North, and is not the less so by the addition of the word South, to designate its locality. The other Church being, by the plan of division, as certainly confined to the North as this Church is to the South of the dividing line, is as truly the Church, North, as the Southern Church is the Church, South. The difference in name makes no difference in character or authority.

"That the resolutions constituting the law of the case, intended that the minority should acquiesce in the determination of the majority, is manifest, not only from their general tenor and objects, but more especially from the failure to make any provision for a seceding minority, and from the express stipulation that the Church to which such minority might desire to adhere, shall organize no societies within the limits of the other.

"It is sufficient for the purposes of this case to have ascertained, that the Methodist Episcopal Church, South, has within the limits of its organization, as fixed under the rule prescribed by the General Conference of the original Church, all the rights and jurisdiction of that Church, to the exclusion of the present Methodist Episcopal Church.

"It has already been sufficiently shown, that the addition of the word 'South' to the name of the Southern Methodist Episcopal Church, cannot affect the rights either of that Church or of its members; and that the members of a local society, entitled to the use of local property under this or other similar deed, before the division, do not lose their right by adhering to the Methodist Episcopal Church, South, under the resolutions of the General Conference of 1844."

Mr. Reverdy Johnson,—May it please your Honours, before the counsel for the respondents proceed with the reading of their proofs, I rise for the purpose of stating, that upon the main question of the case—the question of the power of the General Conference to authorize a separation under the authority of the Constitution of that Conference—I shall rely upon the case of the American Insurance Company *vs.* Canter, in 1 Peter's, beginning at page 511. That part of the opinion on which I shall more particularly rely, will be found as given by Mr. Chief Justice Marshall, on page 542. The language of the Constitution of the Church, as relates to the powers of the Conference, is to be found on page 27 of Proofs, No. 1, and is in these words:—

"The General Conference shall have full powers to make rules and regulations for our Church, under the following limitations and restrictions."

The power thus subject to restrictions is a power to make rules and regulations for the Church, or, in the language of the clause, "for our Church." The language in the third section of the fourth article of the Constitution of the United States, upon which the case in 1 Peter's turns, is, "Congress shall have power to dispose of, and make all needful rules and regulations respecting the territory or other property belonging to the United States." This clause, so far as it is applicable to the power of Congress over the territories of the United States, gives Congress power to make all needful rules and regulations respecting the territory belonging to the United States. The power of the General Conference is to make rules and regulations for the Church. The counsel upon the other side will at once see the purpose for which I cite the case. The question in that case was, whence did the government of the United States derive the authority, from time to time, to govern the territories by involving them all under one form of government, by dividing them from time to time, as in the judgment of Congress a division might be thought expedient, or by admitting them afterwards into the Union as States, under the authority of another clause of the Constitution? The Chief Justice, in giving the opinion, says, that as they had authority to declare war under another clause, and under another clause they had the authority to acquire by treaty, the acquisition whether acquired by force or by treaty, would necessarily carry with it the authority to govern, and it was unnecessary to dispute as to the extent of the authority to govern, because it was to be found in the very words of the third section of the fourth article of the Constitution, which conveyed to Congress the authority to make needful rules and regulations for the territory of the United States. If, therefore, under that power Congress may to-day establish one territorial government, and may to-morrow divide it, if they may keep that territorial government in existence until such time as they think proper to admit its inhabitants into the Union as a State, I contend that the General Conference, as a government for the Church, has the power to make any form of government for the Church, subject to the restrictions imposed, and under the clause which gives to the Conference the authority to make needful rules and regulations for the Church.

Mr. E. L. Fancher,—May it please your Honours, I refer, in the first place, as to the powers of the General Conference with respect to the bishops as to the system and polity of the Church, which requires that the bishops travel through the Connexion at large, to book of Proofs No. 1, pp. 131–134,—"Extracts from the Address of the Bishops to the General Conference of 1844," which is dated New-York, May 2d, 1844, signed by all the bishops, including Bishops Soulé and Andrew, who are now bishops in the Southern Church.

"It should never be forgotten that those fundamental principles which define and limit the powers of the General Conference, and secure the privileges of every minister and member, were settled by the body of ministers assembled in conventional form, with great unanimity, after long, deliberate, and careful investigation. And it is equally worthy of regard, that the Church, with almost unanimous consent, and with heart-felt satisfaction, looked to the system as a haven of safety, and a dwelling-place of 'quietness and assurance.'

"In this happy state of things, embracing all the essential elements of the voluntary principle, the ministers dependant upon the people whom they served in the Gospel word and ordinances, and the people united to their ministers by the bonds of affection and esteem, the work of the Lord steadily advanced; new and extensive fields of labour were constantly opening before us; the borders of our Zion were greatly enlarged; and thousands and tens of thousands were brought under Divine influence, and joined in the communion of the Church. The events of each succeeding year have afforded additional proofs of the soundness of the system, and of its adaptation to the ends for which it was designed.

"The general itinerant superintendency, vitally connected, as it is believed to be, with the effective operation, if not with the very existence, of the whole itinerant system, cannot be too carefully examined or too safely guarded. And we have no doubt but you will direct your inquiries into such channels as to ascertain whether there has been any departure from its essential principles, or delinquency in the administration in carrying it into execution; and in case of the detection of error, to apply such correction as the matter may require.

"There are several points in this system which are of primary importance, and on that account should be clearly understood. The office of a bishop or superintendent, according to our ecclesiastical system, is almost exclusively executive; wisely limited in its powers, and guarded by such checks and responsibilities as can scarcely fail to secure the ministry and membership against any oppressive measures, even should these officers so far forget the sacred duties and obligations of their holy vocation as to aspire to be lords over God's heritage.

"So far from being irresponsible in their office, they are amenable to the General Conference, not only for their moral conduct, and for the doctrines they teach, but also for the faithful administration of the government of the Church, according to the provisions of the Discipline, and for all decisions which they make on questions of ecclesiastical law. In all these cases this body has original jurisdiction, and may prosecute to final issue in expulsion, from which decision there is no appeal.

"With these safeguards thrown around them, we trust the Church has nothing to fear from the exercise of that authority which has been committed to them in trust, to be used for the conservation of the whole body, and for the extension of the Redeemer's kingdom, and not to oppress or afflict any. Without entering minutely into the details of what is involved in the superintendency, as it is constituted in our Church, it is sufficient for our present design to notice its several departments.

"1st. *Confirming orders, by ordaining deacons and elders.*

"2d. *Presiding in the General and Annual Conferences.* But there is a marked difference in the relations the president sustains to these two bodies. The General Conference, being the highest judicatory of the Church, is not subject to the official direction and control of the president any further than the *order* of business and the preservation of decorum are concerned; and even this is subject to *rules* originating in the body. The *right* to transact business, with respect to matter, mode, and order of time, is vested in the Conference, and limited only by constitutional provisions; and of these provisions, so far as their official acts are concerned, the Conference, and not the president, must be the judge.

"II. Having noticed in what the superintendency chiefly consists, it is proper to observe that the plan of its operation is *general, embracing the whole work in connexional order, and not diocesan, or sectional.* Consequently any division of the work into districts, or otherwise, so as to create a particular charge, with any other view, or in any order, than as a prudential measure to secure to all the conferences the annual visits of the superintendents, would be an innovation on the system.

"III. If we have taken a correct view of this subject, *our superintendency must be itinerant, and not local.* It was wisely provided in the system of Methodism, from its very foundation, that it should be the duty of the superintendent '*to travel through the Connexion at large.*' And although the extension of geographical boundaries, and the great increase of the annual conferences, have made it necessary to increase the number of the bishops, still the duty required, and the obligation to perform it, remain the same.

"That such a system as our itinerant ministry could not be preserved in harmonious and efficient operation under the direction of local bishops, is too obvious to require proof. If we preserve a travelling ministry, we must have travelling superintendents. They must add to their official authority the power of their example. Remove the latter, and the former will be divested of the chief element of its strength.

"It is, indeed, a work which requires a measure of the zeal, and self-sacrificing spirit of the apostles, and first ministers of Christ, who followed them. And we devoutly pray that the ministry may never so far relax in the spirit and power of the great commission, '*Go ye into all the world, and preach the Gospel to every creature,*' as to lack men well qualified for this vocation—men whose minds, grasping the work of God in all its length and breadth, will count nothing dear to themselves as appertaining to the present life; but giving themselves wholly to God and his Church, will live, and labour, and suffer for the promotion of Christ's kingdom and the salvation of souls.

"With the foregoing remarks on the duties and responsibilities of the superintendents, we submit to your consideration the importance of having this department supplied with such a number of effective men as will enable them, in consecutive order, to travel through the whole Connexion without subjecting any one to such a continued weight of care and labour as is sufficient to prostrate the mental and physical energies of the strongest constitution, and thereby indirectly defeat the ends designed to be accomplished; and, on the other hand, to guard against the increase of the number beyond the actual demands of the work. In whatever light we view it, but especially in the light of example, the existence of a sinecure in the episcopacy should be regarded as no ordinary evil.

"JOSHUA SOULE,
ELIJAH HEDDING,
JAMES O. ANDREW,
B. WAUGH,
THOS. A. MORRIS."

"*New-York, May* 2, 1844.

I refer next, as to the usage of the General Conference in canvassing the votes of the annual conferences on a proposed change of the restrictive articles, to Proofs No. 1, pp. 43, 46, and 47. I also refer to p. 47, to show that all the annual conferences, including the Southern annual conferences, in the Canada case, admitted the necessity of a change in the sixth restrictive rule before any part of the profits of the Book Concern could be apportioned to the Canada Conference. On p. 43 is this minute from the journals of the General Conference:—

"*Resolved, &c.*, That until the will of the annual conferences shall be ascertained, and a final settlement be made, the Canada Conference shall receive the same equal annual dividend of the profits of the Book Concern as heretofore.

"5th. A motion for the adoption of this resolution was made, voted, and carried.

"On motion, The secretary is hereby directed to furnish the delegates from Canada with a copy of the decision of this Conference on that business.

"The resolution was presented to the annual conferences, and the following was the result, (according to the minutes of the secretary of the committee to whom the business was referred, at the General Conference of 1836:)—"

Then follows an address which is out of its place. On p. 46 commences the report of this committee:—

"CINCINNATI, OHIO, May 6, 1836.

"Committee on Canada Claims met on Friday evening, May 6th, at the Preachers' Office, Cincinnati. Committee consists of R. Paine, T. A. Morris, A. Griffith, M. Richardson, and C. Sherman. The whole committee present. C. Sherman chosen secretary. Rev. Mr. Lord presented to the committee a copy of the resolutions of the General Conference of 1828 and of 1832, on the subject of an appropriation from the Book Concern of the Methodist Episcopal Church to the Canada Conference, which was read. (See Doc. Nos. 1 and 2.) Copies of the resolutions of the annual conferences, concurring or non-concurring with the General Conference resolution, were then handed to the committee by Rev. B. Waugh, and read. (See Doc. No. 3.) The conferences concurring were as follow:—

New-England Conference, held June, 1832	Ayes 73	Noes 1
Maine Conference, held July 24, 1832	" 71	" 0
New-Hampshire Conference, held August 8, 1832	" 71	" 0
Oneida Conference, held 1833	" 77	" 2
Genesee Conference, held July, 1832	" 69	" 1
New-York Conference, held June 9, 1833	" 142	" 13
Six conferences.	For concurrence, 503	Against, 17

"The conferences non-concurring were as follow:—

Kentucky Conference, held Oct. 22, 1832	Non-concurring, 66	Concurring, 0
Indiana Conference, held October 17, 1832	" 36	" 0
Pittsburgh Conference, held August 23, 1832	" 61	" 6
South Carolina Conference, held April 22, 1833	" 26	" 24
Mississippi Conference, held May 15, 1833	" 15	" 7
Ohio Conference	" 62	" 28
Holstein Conference, held March 29, 1833	" 34	" 8
Virginia Conference, held March 6, 1833	" 84	" 0
Baltimore Conference, held April 5, 1833	" 90	" 0
Philadelphia Conference, held April 24, 1833	" 89	" 1
Missouri Conference	" 24	" 2
Georgia Conference	" 41	" 13
Alabama Conference	" 22	" 3
Illinois Conference	" 19	" 2
Tennessee Conference	" 72	" 2
Fifteen conferences non-concurring.	Number for, 741	Against, 96
	17	503
Whole number in the several conferences against,	758	For, 599
" " " " for,	599	
Majority against granting Canada claims,	159	

"Brother Case then addressed the committee, making several remarks and statements in favour of the claims being answered. Committee was then addressed by brother Lord. After some information, obtained by brother Waugh, committee adjourned, to meet again next Tuesday evening.

"(Signed,) C. SHERMAN, *Sec'y.*"

To show that the annual conferences of the South voted upon the proposition to change the sixth restrictive rule in 1844, I refer to the report on the Journal of the General Conference of 1848, p. 177. That report has already been read.

MR. LORD,—Mr. Fancher, do you consider that report as evidence on the subject?

MR. FANCHER,—It is in evidence.

MR. LORD,—The report is evidence that somebody said such was the fact; but it is not evidence of the fact.

MR. FANCHER,—I understood that it might be read.

Mr. Wood,—It may be read subject to the decision of the Court.

Mr. Lord,—If my friend will read any one of the certificates from the annual conferences as to the result, I will admit that the numbers stated in the report are correct. I wish the Court to see how the question was submitted to the annual conferences.

Mr. Fancher,—I will read the certificate from the Troy Conference.

"Troy Annual Conference, Friday Afternoon, June 28, 1844.—" The president brought before the conference the third resolution in the series adopted by the General Conference, relative to the alteration of the sixth restrictive article of the Discipline, and other matters; so that the first clause shall read as follows:—' They shall not appropriate the produce of the Book Concern, nor of the Chartered Fund, to any purpose other than for the benefit of the travelling, supernumerary, superannuated, and worn-out preachers, their wives, widows, and children, and to such other purposes as may be determined on by the votes of two-thirds of the members of the General Conference.'

"The question being taken on the motion to adopt the resolution, it prevailed—one hundred and twenty-three voting in the affirmative, and six in the negative."

"I hereby certify that the above is a true extract from the Journals of the Troy Annual Conference.

"J. B. Houghtaling, *Secretary of the Troy Annual Conference.*

"West Troy, *March 7th*, 1851."

Mr. Lord,—I am now ready to admit the number stated in the report; and I will sign a consent to that effect with you.

Mr. Fancher,—That is not material; the report states the numbers, and the report is before the Court.

Mr. Lord,—The report is before the Court, to show that such a report was made; but it does not, of itself, prove the facts there stated. We will sign a consent, however.

Judge Nelson,—If the counsel insists, the facts stated in the report cannot be considered proper and legal evidence of those facts; the report is only evidence that such a report was made.

Mr. Lord,—I will sign a consent to the admission as evidence of the numbers stated in the report.

Mr. Ewing,—The consent can be signed in the recess.

Judge Nelson,—I understood the counsel in his argument to concede that the necessary number of votes was not given to authorize a change of the restrictive article.

Mr. Lord,—They have not proved that the requisite number was not given.

Mr Fancher,—It is not necessary for us to prove it. In the complaint they assert that the necessary number of votes was obtained. We denied it in our answer. Therefore the proof was for them to furnish.

Judge Betts,—Let me suggest that it would be, perhaps, advisable for Mr. Fancher to yield to Mr. Lord's suggestion, in order to give perfectness to the evidence. The case should not be put to the peril, if it should go further, of being sent back on account of informality in the admission of evidence.

Mr. Fancher,—Very well. We have acted on the principle that what was the truth should be submitted.

Mr. Lord,—My friend has acted on that principle throughout.

Mr. Fancher,—I refer, in the next place, to show that thousands of ministers and members in the territory of the Church, South, were adverse to the proceedings of their Southern brethren, and preferred to remain in the Church of their early choice, to the Journal of the General Conference of 1848, pp. 19 and 37, where petitions were presented from the South on the subject; to the journal of 1848, pp. 116 and 117, where reports were made on the subject; and p. 175, where the General Conference mention it in their Pastoral Address.

Mr. Lord,—That, you will understand, is not admitted. It is admitted that it was reported to your Conference that such was the fact.

Mr. Fancher,—I do not understand it as evidence of anything, except that such a report was made to us.

Mr. Johnson,—How did the subject come before the Conference of 1848?

Mr. Fancher,—On petitions to the General Conference of 1848.

Mr. Johnson,—Have you got the petitions before you?

Mr. Fancher,—No, sir.

Judge Nelson,—If you deem this material, Mr. Fancher, it must be proved by some other evidence, or be admitted by consent of the counsel on the other side.

Mr. Johnson,—We do not admit the facts there stated.

Mr. Fancher,—The journal of the Conference of 1848 is, I believe, admitted under the same consent as Book No. 2. We refer, therefore, to the facts there stated in the same light, and expect the same effect to be attributed to them, as they refer to their Book No. 2.

Mr. Ewing,—That is the true exposition of the matter.

Mr. Lord,—I will sign a consent.

Judge Betts,—The stipulation admits these journals to be "considered as duly authenticated and verified by proof."

Mr. Fancher,—The journal of the Conference of 1848 is admitted under the same stipulation as Book No. 2. I shall ask no more on this point than that the Court take a note of these references, and give them what effect they may be entitled to.

I refer also to the journal of the General Conference of 1848, pp. 164–171, as to alleged infractions of the Plan of Separation. This is also in Proofs No. 1, pp. 154–164:—

"*Infractions of the Plan.*

"The attention of the committee has been directed, by sundry memorials submitted to their consideration by the General Conference, to numerous infractions of the provisions of the so-called Plan of Separation, upon the part of the Methodist Episcopal Church, South; and upon this subject present to the Conference the following statement and facts:—

"I. *The Methodist Episcopal Church, South, has officially and authoritatively taught the infraction of the Plan by her Convention, her General Conference, her Bishops, her Annual Conferences, her Elders, and leading Ministers.*

"1. *The Louisville Convention taught the violation of the Plan.*

"In the report on organization, passed Saturday, the 17th of May, 1845, the new Church is declared to be formed out of the conferences represented in the convention. (See History of the Methodist Episcopal Church, South, p. 186.) But while the convention in their formal acts of organization, on Saturday, the 17th of May, make this declaration, we find them on the Monday following passing these resolutions, (See Western Christian Advocate, vol. xiii, page 42, col. 7,)—

"'*Resolved*, That should any portion of an annual conference, on the line of separation, not represented in this convention, adhere to the Methodist Episcopal Church, South, according to the Plan of Separation adopted at the late General Conference, and elect delegates to the General Conference of the Church in 1846, upon the basis of representation adopted by the convention, they shall be accredited as members of the General Conference.

"'*Resolved*, That, in the judgment of this convention, those societies and stations on the border, within the limits of conferences represented in this convention, be constructively understood as adhering to the South, unless they see proper to take action on the subject; and in all such cases, we consider the pastor of the station or society the proper person to preside in the meeting.'

"Thus, although the convention, in their formal organization, confine themselves to the original limits; yet two days after, when the way was prepared for further inroads, they enlarge the provisions of the Plan, and extend it into the boundaries of the Philadelphia, Baltimore, and other conferences. And in all societies within the border where no votes would be taken, these societies must be *constructively* understood as adhering to the South. Hence their preachers have generally prevented any voting wherever they could by any means hinder it; although the Plan of the General Conference required the societies to vote. The conclusion is, that the convention taught the infraction of the Plan in two very important respects.

"First. They exceed the provisions of the Plan by extending it into the territory of the Baltimore, Philadelphia, Pittsburgh, and other conferences. Thus they teach to cross the line.

"Secondly. And in all societies where no vote would be taken, they claim them constructively as belonging to their Church.

"2. *The bishops of the Methodist Episcopal Church, South, have taught the infraction of the Plan.*

"Bishop Soule, in his letter dated Lebanon, Ohio, August 4th, 1845, and published in the Western Christian Advocate of August 22d, 1845, vol. xiii, p. 75, col. 2, teaches the breach of the Plan. It is addressed 'to the preachers and border societies of the Kentucky and Missouri Conferences, and of other conferences bordering upon them.' The bishop here calls on the societies on the Southern verge of the Ohio, Indiana, Illinois, and Iowa Conferences, to vote whether they will, or will not, remain in the Methodist Episcopal Church. Bishop Soule, however, makes these regulatious in reference to his own administration. But this same course was sanctioned by Bishop Andrew immediately, and afterward by their General Conference, and by all their bishops. And indeed Bishop Soule, in his letter to the Rev. Wesley G. Montgomery, dated Nashville, April 30th, 1847, and published in the Western Christian Advocate of May 21st, 1847, hints broadly enough that minorities had best be accommodated. He says: 'Minorities on either side of the line of division are entitled to a kind and respectful consideration, and should be treated accordingly. And I should think it far better for such minorities, being on the borders, to receive preachers from the Church to which they desire to adhere, provided they believe themselves able to support them, than for majorities to be interdicted the exercise of a right plainly secured to them by the provisions of the law, or rule, in the case.' Now with this instruction about minorities, as well as the maintenance that the line is a sliding one, and no limits of time are given in which its sliding operation ceases, Southern preachers will find little difficulty in passing over any limits which may be in the way.

"But Bishop Capers' letter to Rev. Mr. Moorman, and published in the Christian

Advocate and Journal of April 21st, 1847, claims all the territory in the slaveholding States, and this too according to the Plan, or, as he calls it, the 'Deed of Separation.' Now as Bishop Capers claims all slaveholding territory and Bishop Soule as much of the territories of the free States as the accommodation of minorities and the sliding line will transfer, it would be difficult indeed to fix any line at all.

"It were useless to insist, in a matter so clear, that the bishops of the Methodist Episcopal Church, South, have taught officially the violation of the Plan.

"3. *The General Conference of the Methodist Episcopal Church, South, has taught the infraction of the Plan.*

"For proof of this we need go no further than the famous report on the episcopacy, in which the Conference sanctions the breaches of the Plan as taught by the convention, and as was taught and practised by Bishops Soule and Andrew, from the session of the convention in May, 1845, to the session of the Conference in May, 1846. This document will be found in the Western Christian Advocate of June 26th, 1846, and in the Richmond Advocate of May 21st, 1846. The report fully clears Bishops Soule and Andrew of any blame for occupying Cincinnati, the Kanawha district, &c., and gives such full latitude of interpretation, that the limitations of the Plan became a perfect nullity. Our limits will not allow us to quote the report, but it can be perused in the papers, as cited above, as well as in all the Southern papers.

"4. *The annual conferences, editors, and leading members of the new Church, maintain the infraction of the Plan in perfect accordance with the acts of their convention, their General Conference, and their bishops.*

"It were useless to make quotations on this point. Their press teems with approving acts of annual conferences, and the laboured essays and constant admissions of editors and correspondents, upholding fully their conventional, episcopal, and General Conference decisions and acts. And from all this there is no dissent in any quarter.

"II. *The bishops of the Methodist Episcopal Church, South, in their official administration, have actually broken the Plan.*

"As undoubted and official testimony on this point, we need only quote the report on this subject, by our excellent and devoted bishops, which, at the request of the General Conference, they furnished the committee. This official document is as follows:—

"'*To the Committee on the State of the Church.*

"'In compliance with a request of the General Conference, made on the 6th instant, the superintendents present to you such information as they possess in regard to alleged infractions of the "Plan of Separation," on the part of the constituted authorities of the Methodist Episcopal Church, South, by which the Methodist Episcopal Church has been injuriously deprived of portions of its territory and members. They must be understood as giving the most authentic statements which have come to their ears, without vouching their own personal knowledge for the correctness of every item thus presented. They are, nevertheless, impressed with a conviction of the truth of the statements generally, as hereinafter made.

"'They commence first with *Baltimore Conference.* Within its bounds there is a portion of the State of Virginia, situated between the Potomac and Rappahannock Rivers, commonly called the "Northern Neck," embracing the counties of King George, Westmoreland, Richmond, Northumberland, and Lancaster. These counties contained the following circuits, (having a membership of eight hundred to a thousand,) namely, King George, Westmoreland, and Lancaster, each having preachers annually appointed to it from the Baltimore Conference. At different times each of those circuits determined to attach themselves to the Methodist Episcopal Church, not as border *societies,* but as *circuits.* To all of them preachers have been sent from the Virginia Conference, who are there at present, to the exclusion of the ministers of the Methodist Episcopal Church. From the conference of 1847 preachers were sent to this portion of the Baltimore Conference, who found on their arrival the circuits under the pastoral care of ministers of the Virginia Conference. The ministers sent from the Baltimore Conference, not being able to have access to the preaching-places or societies, were withdrawn after suitable time, and sent to places where they were needed, except one, who was left in charge of the whole field of labour. At present this place appears on the minutes, "to be supplied."

No minister of the Methodist Episcopal Church is now in this ancient portion of the Baltimore Conference.

" 'Warrenton circuit has been occupied between one and two years with preachers from the Virginia Conference; but as the circuit did not go to the Church, South, in whole, a portion thereof continuing in the Methodist Episcopal Church, a preacher from the Baltimore Conference has been continued there. Some of the societies which voted to go to the Church, South, were strictly border societies, but others also went which were as strictly interior societies. One of the churches, (Wesley Chapel,) where a majority adhered to the Methodist Episcopal Church, was forcibly entered and new locks were attached to the doors; and the Church, South, has it in possession at the present time, unless the civil court has recently decided a suit, which was instituted for the property, in favour of the Methodist Episcopal Church.

" 'Harrisonburg, in Rockingham county, Virginia, unquestionably an interior society, having by a majority of votes determined to connect themselves with the Methodist Episcopal Church, South, a preacher from the Virginia Conference has been appointed to labour there. A minority adhering to the Methodist Episcopal Church, are under the pastoral care of one of its ministers. The church was in a course of litigation a few months since, and probably the case has not been decided by the court. An attempt was made to get possession of the parsonage in Harrisonburg for the Church, South, but with what success there is no information.

" 'Leesburg, a station belonging to the Baltimore Conference, clearly an interior society, has been visited by a preacher from the Methodist Episcopal Church, South, much agitation produced in the society and in the community, and a suit at law commenced for the church edifice. Whether the effort is still persisted in to occupy this place is not certainly known. That which makes this case even a glaring one, is the fact, that the majority of the society voted to adhere to the Methodist Episcopal Church. There are other instances of the violation of the Plan of Separation, in the opinion of some equally apparent with the instances given in this paper, of which more certain information may be obtained from Rev. Messrs. William Hamilton, N. J. B. Morgan, S. A. Roszel, John Bear, and J. A. Collins, members of this General Conference.

" '*Kanawha District*, in the North-West part of Virginia, is a part of Ohio Conference. In 1845 that work was supplied from the Ohio Conference, as usual. The preachers were received, with one exception, as far as we know, namely Parkersburg station. A part of the members there refused to receive any preacher from Ohio Conference. They rejected the preacher sent to them, not for any objection to him personally, but because he came from Ohio; and by threats of violence, and preparation to execute those threats on a given day, compelled him to leave the place, and took possession of the chapel. He, however, returned after some weeks, and in connexion with the preacher of the adjoining circuit, to which they were transferred, served the remaining members of the scattered flock in another house. These outcast members have since erected a chapel for themselves, in which they worship undisturbed; while the old chapel is supplied from Kentucky Conference, of the Methodist Episcopal Church, South. Parkersburg is not a border station. It is the county-seat of Wood county, situated at the junction of Little Kanawha and Ohio Rivers, and is about seventy-five miles from the nearest point of the Kentucky State line; so that the Kentucky preachers had to travel that distance through our work to reach it, though they now occupy other places through our work between that and Kentucky. No preachers were appointed from the Kentucky Conference of 1845 to the Kanawha district; but some were sent there, as we learn, during that conference year, by a presiding elder, that made breaches in some of our circuits. In 1846 the Kanawha district was all supplied from the Ohio Conference, as usual, though the societies in some places were divided by Southern influence. A few weeks afterward a second supply was sent from Kentucky Conference, as we learned from the newspapers. Since that time there have been two presiding elders, and two sets of preachers there; one from Ohio Conference, and the other from Kentucky Conference. Indeed it is alleged that, at the last session of the Kentucky Conference, they divided the district; so that the old Kanawha district is now occupied by three presiding elders—one from Ohio, and two from Kentucky.

" 'These are the most material facts which have been reported to us, bearing on the point of inquiry submitted to us, so far as Kanawha district is concerned.

" ' " *Soule Chapel*," *Cincinnati*.—In 1834 Cincinnati, which had previously been one charge, was divided into two, " Wesley Chapel" and " Fourth-street." Each had definite bounds, within which the stationed minister had exclusive pastoral functions. Private members were *advised* to observe these limits in fixing and holding their membership, but were not considered *bound* to do so, and did not in all cases practise it. But class-meetings, &c., were held in strict regard to this provision.

" ' New preaching places have been opened in these charges, under the direction and countenance of the presiding elder and preachers in charge, have matured societies, and have been finally formed into stations by the presiding bishops, and received preachers.

" ' In 1844 the first city missionary was appointed, and was supported by a City Missionary Society, whose object was *to carry the Gospel to the destitute*. The first year, with the approbation of those having authority to direct him, he formed three societies, namely, the Bethel, Ebenezer, and Maley Chapel, and succeeded in erecting two small chapels for " Ebenezer" and " Maley," in the North-West part of the city and suburbs. By permission, he exercised pastoral authority in some or all of these societies.

" ' In 1845 the same brother, Rev. G. W. Maley, was reappointed to the same mission. At the same time two of the aforesaid societies, Bethel and Ebenezer, were made stations, and Rev. J. W. White and Rev. Joseph Bruner were appointed to serve them. These two stations were marked out by metes and bounds, as had been invariably done when new stations were formed in Cincinnati. This was done in council with the presiding elder of Cincinnati district, two or three days after conference closed, it having been forgotten in the pressure of conference business. Letters were written by the presiding bishop to brothers White and Bruner, defining by streets, &c., the bounds of the new charges; and the city missionary had Maley Chapel, and the region around it, set apart from all the stations as his special field of labour, within which, *and nowhere else*, he was to exercise pastoral functions. As the superintendent, however, was in haste, he did not write to the missionary, but requested the presiding elder, brother Morley, to give him the information.

" ' Three objects were sought in this arrangement:—

" ' *First*. As the city mission had lost two principal appointments, it seemed proper to encourage the missionary by assigning him the pastoral charge of this precinct territory, which was fast filling up, and which must, of course, receive most of his labours.

" ' *Second*. Ebenezer station bordered on Maley Chapel, and the population and territory were enough to be under the pastoral care of one man, after Maley Chapel and its territory were taken off.

" ' *Third*. It seemed to the presiding bishop proper that each city preacher should have exclusive pastoral authority within his own charge; and, though no rupture was then dreamed of, it was thought the exercise of pastoral functions by the missionary within the different charges would derange and disorder the work.

" ' Within three or four weeks after these arrangements were made, the city missionary obtained leave from the City Missionary Board to *preach* in "Vine-street church," an old, deserted building within the bounds of Morris Chapel charge, from one-half to three-fourths of a mile from Maley Chapel charge, and in the heart of the city. If we understand correctly, both the presiding elder and the board deny that the missionary received any authority to form a society there, or do any other act which belonged to the pastoral oversight. He received no such authority from the bishop.

" ' A number of brethren, however, obtained certificates, and presented them to the city missionary, not in his own charge, but at " Vine-street," and in the very heart of the city he proceeded to take possession of his brother's territory, and form a society. Having increased it to a company of several scores, it voted to go South, was created " a charge" by the authority of Bishop Andrew, and Revs. E. W. Sehon, G. W. Maley, (the missionary,) and S. A. Latta, were appointed to serve it as ministers of the Methodist Episcopal Church, South. Bishop Andrew named it " VINE-STREET CHARGE, a border society," &c. In a short time this society purchased a church, in the heart of " Wesley Chapel charge," so that between it and the border, or the Ohio River, interposes one whole charge, the Bethel, which makes Soule Chapel as truly an interior station as though it were in Columbus or Cleaveland.

" ' " *Andrew Chapel*," *Cincinnati*.—" Andrew Chapel" was purchased a few months since by the "Soule Chapel" society, and stands within the bounds of Ninth-street charge, having, like "Soule Chapel," one whole charge—"Morris Chapel"—between it and the border or river. It is understood to have regular preaching, but whether placed on the minutes of the Methodist Episcopal Church, South, as a distinct charge, we know not, but understand that pastoral authority is exercised there in the formation of classes, receiving members, and exercising discipline.

"'*Statement of encroachment on the territory of the Philadelphia Conference by the Methodist Episcopal Church, South.*—Accomac and Northampton counties, Va., are separated from the Virginia Conference by a broad bay, (the Chesapeake,) in every place from fifteen to thirty miles wide. The first place that voted to unite with the Church, South, was Capeville in Northampton, about seven miles north of Cape Charles. The next place at which the vote was taken was Salem, eight miles north of Capeville, which, by a strong majority, had previously determined to stay with us. The next place was Johnson's Chapel, about ten miles north of Salem, which, by a small majority, preferred the Church, South. The next place reported to have chosen the Church, South, was Bethel, in Occahannock Neck. Here no vote was taken, but some friends of the Church, South, went around to the houses of the members, and reported that they had obtained a majority for the new organization. These were all that had declared for the South before Mr. Moorman was sent over. Some time after his arrival, Franktown, five or six miles north of Johnson's, gave a majority of one vote for the South, by getting together members who had not attended class for years. Pungotraque, in Accomac county, about ten miles further north, after giving a majority to remain in the old Church several times, at length chose the new Church by a small majority. And, finally, Craddockville, a few miles south-east of Pungotraque, in a neck, gave a majority for the Church, South. There is no appointment between any of the above and the Chesapeake Bay.

"'Signed,
E. Hedding,
B. Waugh,
Thomas A. Morris,
L. L. Hamline,
Edmund S. Janes.'"

Mr. Lord,—That is subject to the same difficulty.

Mr. Fancher,—I suppose it is.

As to the action of the General Conference of 1848, upon the so-called Plan of Separation, I refer to the final report on the State of the Church,—Proofs No. 1, pp. 138–154:—

"*Final Report on the State of the Church.*

"The committee on the state of the Church, after a full and careful examination of all the sources of information within their reach, including, as they believe, all that are essential to a just understanding of the subjects hereinafter named, do recommend to this body the adoption of the following as their final report:—

"1. We claim that the Methodist Episcopal Church, South, exists as a distinct and separate ecclesiastical communion, solely by the act and deed of the individual ministers and members constituting said Church.

"In support of this position we set forth the following facts:—On the fifth day of June, one thousand eight hundred and forty-four, John Early, W. A. Smith, Thomas Crowder, and Leroy M. Lee, of the Virginia Conference; H. B. Bascom, William Gunn, H. H. Kavanaugh, Edward Stevenson, B. T. Crouch, and G. W. Brush, of the Kentucky Conference; W. W. Redman, W. Patton, J. C. Berryman, and J. M. Jameson, of the Missouri Conference; E. F. Sevier, S. Patton, and Thomas Stringfield, of the Holston Conference; G. F. Pierce, William J. Parks, L. Pierce, J. W. Glenn, J. L. Evans, and A. B. Longstreet, of the Georgia Conference; James Jamieson, Peter Doub, and B. T. Blake, of the North Carolina Conference; J. Stamper, of the Illinois Conference; G. W. D. Harris, Wm. M'Mahan, Thomas Joyner, and S. S. Moody, of the Memphis Conference; John C. Parker, William P. Radcliffe, and Andrew Hunter, of the Arkansas Conference; William Winans,

B. M. Drake, John Lane, and G. M. Rogers, of the Mississippi Conference; Littleton Fowler, of the Texas Conference; Jesse Boring, Jefferson Hamilton, W. Murrah, and G. Garrett, of the Alabama Conference; Robert Paine, John B. M'Ferrin, A. L. P. Green, and T. Maddin, of the Tennessee Conference; and W. Capers, Wm. M. Wightman, Charles Betts, S. Dunwody, and H. A. C. Walker, of the South Carolina Conference, did present to the General Conference, then in session in the city of New-York, the following Declaration, to wit:—'That the continued agitation of the subject of slavery and abolition in a portion of the Church, the frequent action on that subject in the General Conference, and especially the extra-judicial proceedings against Bishop Andrew, which resulted, on Saturday last, in the virtual suspension of him from his office as superintendent, must produce a state of things in the South, which renders a continuance of the jurisdiction of that General Conference over these conferences, inconsistent with the success of the ministry in the slaveholding States;' from which it is evident that they sought their remedies for alleged grievances, not in any constitutional acts, but in a violation of the integrity of the Methodist Episcopal Church.

"And further, on the sixth day of June, in the year above-written, the above-named gentlemen, and N. C. Berryman, of the Illinois Conference; I. T. Cooper, W. Cooper, T. J. Thompson and Henry White, of the Philadelphia Conference; E. W. Sehon, of the Ohio Conference, and T. Neal and T. Sovereign, of the New-Jersey Conference, in addition, presented a Protest to the above-named General Conference against its action in the case of Bishop Andrew, in which they assert, 'If the compromise law be either repealed, or allowed to remain a dead letter, *the South cannot submit, and the absolute necessity of a division is already dated.'* Now, while we wholly deny the existence of any 'compromise law,' in the sense here claimed, the indication in this extract, and, indeed, in the whole document, of a purpose upon the part of those protesting brethren to secure a division of the Church is too plain to be mistaken.

"And further, at the close of the General Conference, on the eleventh day of June and year above-mentioned, fifty-one of the above-named brethren assembled in the city of New-York, and by formal resolution recommended to the Southern conferences the appointment of delegates to a convention, to commence in Louisville, Kentucky, on the first day of May, one thousand eight hundred and forty-five, said delegates to be instructed on the points on which action is contemplated, conforming their instructions, as far as possible, to the opinions and wishes of the membership within their several conference bounds. And the said brethren issued from this unauthorized meeting an address, in which they call the attention of the Southern Methodists 'to the *proscription and disability* under which the Southern portion of the Church must, of necessity, labour in view of the action alluded to, unless some measures are adopted to free the minority of the South from the oppressive jurisdiction of the majority in the North in this respect;' and they declare, 'that they regard a separation at no distant day as inevitable.' There is, therefore, no room to doubt that the appointed Louisville Convention was one of those leading 'measures' adopted by these fifty-one brethren for the express purpose of freeing the minority of the South from what they are pleased to term 'the oppressive jurisdiction of the majority in the North,' and that the contemplated separation, if it actually occurred, must be the legitimate result of these premature preliminary arrangements.

"And further, the several annual conferences now included in the Church, South, did, at their meetings, successively, of their own will and accord, vote to approve the holding of the Louisville Convention, for the purposes proposed by the members of the aforesaid meeting at New-York, appointed delegates to said convention, and in various forms of expression, directly assumed, as far as they were able, the responsibility of the dismemberment of the Church evidently contemplated in the appointment of said Louisville Convention.

"In the meantime Bishop Soule wrote to Bishop Andrew, requesting him to resume episcopal functions, and, in the character and office of a bishop, to attend the sessions of annual conferences, which he did, though said act was clearly in contravention of' the expressed will of the General Conference, 'that he desist from the exercise of the' episcopal 'office so long as the impediment' of slaveholding 're-mained.' By which acts both Bishop Soule and Bishop Andrew openly repudiated the authority of the General Conference of the Methodist Episcopal Church.

"And further, in the convention assembled at Louisville, May, one thousand eight hundred and forty-five, delegates from the following conferences, namely, Kentucky, Missouri, Holston, Tennessee, North Carolina, Memphis, Arkansas, Virginia, Mississippi, Texas, Alabama, Georgia, South Carolina, Florida, and Indian Mission, Bishops Soule and Andrew presiding, did formally resolve, 'That it is right, expedient, and necessary, to erect the annual conferences represented in this convention into a distinct ecclesiastical Connexion, separate from the jurisdiction of the General Conference of the Methodist Episcopal Church, as at present constituted,' and they did 'solemnly *declare* the jurisdiction hitherto exercised over said annual conferences by the General Conference of the Methodist Episcopal Church *entirely dissolved*; and that said annual conferences shall be, and they hereby *are, constituted* a separate ecclesiastical Connexion.' Accordingly a delegated General Conference from the annual conferences above-named, held at Petersburgh, Virginia, May, one thousand eight hundred and forty-six, did assume the powers and privileges of authorized representatives of a separate ecclesiastical Connexion, under the style and denomination of 'the Methodist Episcopal Church, South,' to which Church many of the former ministers and members of the Methodist Episcopal Church, some evidently from choice, and others from the force of circumstances which they felt themselves unable to resist, did, formally or informally, attach themselves, thereby withdrawing themselves from the Methodist Episcopal Church.

"Finally, while a clearly-marked line of history, extending from the first-named Declaration to the final action of the General Conference of the Methodist Episcopal Church, South, shows the independent action of the ministers and members of said Church, in its organization, we affirm it to be impossible to point to any act of the General Conference of the Methodist Episcopal Church erecting or authorizing said Church, nor has the said General Conference, or any individual or any number of individuals, any right, constitutional or otherwise, to extend official sanction to any act tending directly or indirectly to the dismemberment of the Church.

"2. In view of the formal Declaration of the brethren herein first named, that certain acts of the General Conference, especially the act in the case of Bishop Andrew, 'must produce a state of things in the South which renders a continuance of the jurisdiction of that General Conference over these conferences inconsistent with the success of the ministry in the slaveholding States;' fearing that ministers and members of the Methodist Episcopal Church would, according to the opinion expressed in the Declaration above quoted, deem it necessary to erect themselves into a separate and independent Church, in the intervals of General Conference sessions, when no remedies for so great an evil could be provided in time, and desiring, as far as practicable, in accordance with suggestions made by brethren from the South, to adopt measures calculated to pacify our members and ministers in the South; the General Conference, at its session in New-York, A. D. one thousand eight hundred and forty-four, did *propose* a Plan for the adjustment of relations between the Methodist Episcopal Church and her separating members and ministers, when such separation should, by their own act and deed, if at all, occur. Such Plan, based entirely upon the first-named Declaration of the delegates from thirteen specified and above-written conferences in the slaveholding States, having relation to those conferences, and to no others, *proposed* an amicable division of territory between them and the Methodist Episcopal Church as follows:—'The Northern boundary' of the prospective new Church to be fixed at the Northern extremities of those 'societies, stations, and conferences,' a majority of whose members should, of their own free will and accord, vote to adhere to the said Southern Church; and ministers, travelling and local, to be allowed to remain in the Methodist Episcopal Church, or attach themselves to the 'Methodist Episcopal Church, South,' at discretion. And said Plan further *proposed* to make over and give to the prospective 'Southern Church so much of the capital and produce of the Methodist Book Concern as will, with the notes, books, accounts, presses,' &c., in the South, due and belonging to the Book Concern of the Methodist Episcopal Church, (the transfer of which is provided for in the fourth article of said Plan,) 'bear the same proportion to the whole property of said Concern that the travelling preachers in the Southern Church shall bear to all the travelling preachers of the Methodist Episcopal Church.' And said Plan further *proposed*, that 'the book agents at New-York be directed to make such compensation to the conferences South for their dividend from the Chartered Fund as the commissioners to be provided for shall agree upon.'

"But the whole of this plan was expressly or otherwise conditional, as follows, namely:—

"(1.) That the asserted 'state of things in the South, which renders a continuance of the jurisdiction of that General Conference over these conferences inconsistent with the success of the ministry in the slaveholding States,' should be '*produced*' by the action of the General Conference in the cases referred to.

"(2.) That three-fourths of the members of all the annual conferences should, 'at their first approaching sessions,' concur in the vote of, at least, two-thirds of the General Conference so to alter 'the sixth restrictive article' of the Discipline, as to add to it the following words, to wit:—'and to such other purposes as may be determined upon by the votes of two-thirds of the members of the General Conference;' it being certain, that should such vote be refused by the annual conferences, the financial part of the Plan could not go into effect, which financial part was deemed by both parties essential to the Plan; and it being probable that those who were opposed to the Plan as a whole, would vote against the change in the sixth restrictive article.

"(3.) It was clearly and necessarily implied, that the friendship and fidelity of the parties should be evinced by voluntarily keeping inviolate the principles and ordinances of the Plan, pending the settlement of the important conditions upon which its validity and binding force depended.

"In support of the above statement of facts, we refer expressly to the aforementioned declaration of the fifty-one Southern brethren, and to the report of the committee of nine, presented to the General Conference of the Methodist Episcopal Church on the seventh day of June, 1844.

"And further, it will be observed that the *declaring* brethren of the South did not claim that a state of things *already existed*, that required any separation of the South from the jurisdiction of the Methodist Episcopal Church; or that required the positive enactment of any unconditional plan of such separation. They only asserted that (in their opinion, of course) certain acts of the General Conference '*must produce*' this state of things. And hence they did not proceed upon the supposition that they were the official judges of the facts, which might require the separation of the Southern ministers and members of the Methodist Episcopal Church from her jurisdiction. It is true that the report of the committee of nine, as it was first presented, made these delegates from the thirteen conferences South the judges of that necessity; but it was so changed as to leave the question to the annual conferences from which they came, thus showing that the General Conference would by no means allow this question of necessity to be decided by these men. From all of which it appears, that the Plan proposed rested, not upon the present or future *existence* of any state of excitement in the South, which might be produced by causes entirely apart from the General Conference; but upon *the production of such a state of things* as was predicted *by the acts of the General Conference* alone. Certainly if, upon returning to their charges, our Southern brethren had found that no such 'state of things' as they had supposed existed, and hence no separation had occurred, *they* would not assert the validity of the proposed Plan; and if it would have been of no binding force, in the absence of the predicted necessity, produced solely by the action of the General Conference, it follows inevitably that such necessity so produced was an indispensable condition of the Plan. And, though this necessity had actually been so produced, and the Southern ministers and members had actually separated on this ground alone, in this case one of the conditions of the Plan would have been met, we nevertheless affirm that in failure of this condition, the Plan became invalid, though *every other condition* of it had been literally fulfilled.

"And further, in proof that the proposed alteration of the sixth restrictive article of the Discipline was a fundamental condition of this Plan *as a whole*, we refer to the third resolution of the report of the committee of nine, in which it is expressly asserted. Also to the published speech of Rev. Dr. (now Bishop) Paine, from which the following language was reported:—'This separation would not be effected by the passage of those resolutions through the General Conference. They must pass the annual conferences, beginning at New-York, and when they came round to the South, the preachers there would think, and deliberate, and feel the pulse of public sentiment, and of the members of the Church, and act in the fear of God, and with a single desire for his glory.' Every word of which, in its connexion, would be entirely incompatible with the idea that he referred merely to an extension of the power of the General Conference in relation to the appropriation of funds; but it is perfectly consistent with the doctrine here asserted, that a vote on the change of that restrictive article was understood to be a vote on the merits of the Plan *as a whole*. So, we believe, many of the members of the annual conferences regarded it, and hence so many of them voted against it as to defeat the measure. Indeed, so essential to the Plan did our Southern brethren consider this change of the sixth restrictive article, that they never have, in any way, signified their willingness to accept of the Plan without it. With this agrees perfectly the Address of the above-named fifty-one brethren, from their meeting in New-York, held the 11th day of June, 1844, in which they hold the following language:—'It affords us pleasure to state that there were those found among the majority who met this proposition (the Plan, not 'of formal and specific separations,' but to provide for the results of separation, should it occur under the necessity above explained) with every manifestation of justice and liberality. And should a similar spirit be exhibited by the annual conferences in the North, when submitted to them, as provided for in the Plan itself, there will remain no legal impediment to its peaceful consummation.'

"But 'if a similar spirit should' not 'be exhibited by the annual conferences in the North, when submitted to them, as provided for in the Plan itself;' then, of course, by the showing of these fifty-one Southern brethren, 'there will remain a legal impediment to its peaceful consummation' as a Plan. It is true that the question of a ratification of the Plan was not *directly*, and in so many words, submitted to the annual conferences; but it is evident, that in the honest opinion of these Southern brethren, it was *in effect* so submitted. Nor could it by possibility have been otherwise, from the language of the Plan, which submits an amendment of the Discipline absolutely essential to the Plan as a whole, the preachers being obliged to vote upon said amendment in view of its bearing upon the whole Plan; and the failure of said amendment rendering the Plan as a whole entirely unsatisfactory to the South: therefore, in the event of a failure of three-fourths of the members of all the annual conferences—the Southern conferences included—'at their first approaching sessions,' to vote for the change proposed in the sixth restrictive article, said Plan would be, *as a whole*, and hence of necessity in its details, rendered null and void.

"And further, we claim that the position, that a sacred, though voluntary observance of the requirements of the proposed Plan by the Methodist Episcopal Church, and the brethren South, who should separate from her, was a fundamental condition of the Plan, is a clear and undeniable inference from the whole design and scope of said Plan. It was, as its friends openly claimed, *a peace measure*. It was designed to prevent aggressions from either party, and thus to prevent unchristian feelings and angry collisions between those who claim to be brethren. If, therefore, this great object, lying at the very foundation of the scheme, and in the light of which alone any part of it has the least significancy, were disregarded or trampled under foot by either party, the other, as a whole, and every individual of them, would be entirely absolved from all obligations to it whatsoever. If, therefore, this shall be found to have been done, then, though all other conditions of the Plan were certainly fulfilled, it will be to all intents and purposes null and void.

"Finally, it has fully appeared, that to meet, in what was then supposed to be the best manner possible, the disastrous results of a violent dismemberment of the Methodist Episcopal Church, should it occur, and provide for an amicable adjustment of all relations between the two parties, this provisional Plan was adopted by the General Conference at its session, in the year 1844—that to provide for, or sanction a division of said Church was therefore no part of the intentions of said General Conference. And that it rested upon three distinct and fundamental conditions, the failure of *either of which* must be fatal to its validity and binding force. And though, in the light of four years' history, we are fully convinced that the act implied a degree of faith in men not justified by the facts, and under all the circumstances of the case it was not adapted to secure its intended results, we cannot for a moment question the Christian liberality in which it had its origin.

"3. It is evident to us, that the acts of the General Conference complained of, did not produce a state of things in the South, which rendered a continuance of the jurisdiction of said Conference 'inconsistent with the success of the ministry in the slaveholding States;' three-fourths of the members of all the annual conferences did not concur in the vote to alter the sixth restrictive rule, and thus sanction the Plan, for the accommodation of which said alteration was asked; and the conditions and requirements of said Plan have been violated: and hence said Plan *is* [*and*, from the first failure of the conditions of said Plan, or either of them, *has been*] null and void.

"In support of which we offer the following facts:—

"After the adoption of the proposition for a peace measure, and providing for its final ratification and use, in case the predicted separation should occur, it would, as we humbly conceive, have been in perfect conformity to said peaceful arrangement for the Southern delegates to have used their utmost endeavours, as some of them assured us they would do, to quiet the public mind in the South; and entering instantly upon the regular work, to have met every act of resentment, and every appearance of insubordination to the authorities of the Church, with a calm, dignified, and determined resistance—to have defended the General Conference, so far as they could conscientiously do so, and themselves to the utmost; for doing which their motions, speeches, votes, Declaration, and Protest, furnished ample materials. To have adopted this course would, we believe, have been doing no more than to meet the just expectations excited by their peaceful protestations upon the Conference floor, and elsewhere, both before and after the vote upon the proposed pacific Plan, and their avowed attachment to the Church of their choice, in its uninterrupted integrity. But if *active* peace measures had been either incompatible with their private opinions of self-respect, or inconvenient under their peculiar circumstances, they, as we verily believe, might have avoided all acts preparatory to the excitement of the public mind, and leading directly or indirectly to the division of the Church; by doing which, they would have given to the world an example of moderation under circumstances confessedly difficult and trying, worthy of all commendation, and afforded an opportunity for a free, spontaneous, and, in due time, decisive verdict of Southern Methodists, upon the question whether the action of the General Conference had, and 'must necessarily' have 'produced a state of things in the South, which rendered a continuance of the jurisdiction of that General Conference over these conferences inconsistent with the success of the ministry in the slaveholding States.' This, we claim and assert, the Methodist Episcopal Church had a right to exact of them, in order to *a just estimate* of the circumstances under which the conscientious and legitimate action of her highest judicatory had placed her in relation to the Southern ministers and membership. But, instead of this, these fifty-one brethren, by character and position highest in rank and influence among Southern Methodists, did, at a meeting called and had before leaving the seat of the General Conference, only ten days after the principal action, and five days after the final action, in the case of Bishop Andrew, virtually appoint a convention, to be held in Louisville, Kentucky, to commence on the first of May, one thousand eight hundred and forty-five, to take into consideration the question of a division of the Church; and thus superinduce the very excitement which they should have deprecated, and attempted by every laudable means in their power to allay. Indeed, it is evident, as it should have been foreseen, that the appointment of that convention alone was, under the circumstances, decisive of the very question which should have been left to the decision of time under the action of all the conservative elements available in the case.

"Moreover, from the said meeting in New-York, which, if it occurred at all, should have given utterance only to counsels peaceful in their nature and tendency, and strictly loyal to the Methodist Episcopal Church, an address was issued, 'To the Ministers and Members of the Methodist Episcopal Church in the slaveholding States and Territories,' in which these *fifty-one* brethren say, that the 'various action of the *majority* of the General Conference, at its recent session, on the subject of *slavery and abolition*, has been such as to render it necessary, in the judgment of those addressing you, to call attention to the *proscription and disability* under which the Southern portion of the Church must of necessity labour in view of the action alluded to, unless some measures are adopted to free the minority of the South from the oppressive jurisdiction of the majority in the North in this respect. The proceedings of the majority, in several cases involving the question of slavery, have been such as indicate most conclusively that the legislative, judicial, and administrative action, of the General Conference, as now organized, will always be extremely hurtful, if not finally ruinous, to the interests of the Southern portion of the Church, and must necessarily produce a state of conviction and feeling in the slaveholding States entirely inconsistent with either the peace or prosperity of the Church. The opinions and purposes of the Church in the North on the subject of slavery are in direct conflict with those of the South; and unless the South will submit to the dictation and interference of the North, greatly beyond what the existing law of the Church on slavery and abolition authorizes, there is no hope of anything like union or harmony.'

"Further similar quotations might be made from this Address, but we deem it unnecessary. We submit it to a candid world, whether language less respectful to the Church of which they were members, or more inflammatory to Southern minds in the midst of slavery, could well be used. Surely there is no room for surprise, that the most excited meetings soon occurred in all parts of the South, and the most indignant resolutions were passed, leading to a degree of public agitation, alarming to the peace of the Church and the nation.

"But one more quotation shall be made, to show that these *fifty-one* brethren did not hesitate, formally, to take the initiative in the work of deciding the question which they had raised, and thus *actually*, as they had already done *virtually*, give the full weight of their influence to counteract the pacific measures which they had asked at our hands, and for which they had just voted: 'As the undersigned have had opportunity and advantages, which those at a distance could not possess, to form a correct judgment in the premises, and it may be expected of them that they express their views fully on the subject, they do not hesitate to say, that they regard a separation at no distant day as inevitable.' After this declaration, of what avail was it to 'beseech their brethren of the ministry and membership in the slaveholding States to examine this matter carefully, and try to reach the conclusion most proper under the circumstances?' or 'disposed, however, to defer to the judgment of the Church, we leave this subject with you?' The result was what must have been expected. The voice of remonstrance, though sincere and beseeching, against the revolutionary measures urged on by such powerful talents and influence, was too feeble to be heard till the confusion was over, and *it was too late*. The act of separation was consummated, as we have already seen, and many thousands hurried out of the Methodist Episcopal Church into the new organization, with scarcely an opportunity to know what it was for.

"We thus see clearly that the way for separation was prepared, not by a state of things in the South '*produced*' by the action of the General Conference, but by revolutionary measures adopted by the Southern delegates at the very seat, and nearly at the time, of our General Conference session. The success of the ministry could not have been hindered by our action; for not only was there no instance of the kind alleged, but there was a want of time to produce any such result, before these fifty-one brethren, by taking the lead of the Southern mind, anticipated their decision. In view of the whole of which we claim and affirm, that the Southern organization was consummated in direct contravention of the Plan proposed to meet the results of separation, thus reducing it to a nullity, by the violation of its first great and fundamental condition. And we moreover claim and affirm, that the very acts of calling the convention and issuing the said Address, by which Southern opinion was forestalled, was an abandonment of the Plan proposed by the General Conference, and hence, for the reason above alleged, the Plan has been of no real force since the date of said call and Address—to wit, the 11th day of June, 1844.

"And further, it appears from official returns made from all the annual conferences voting thereon, including those now embraced in the Church, South, obtained since this session commenced, that the required three-fourths' majority of the members of the said annual conferences has not been given, and hence, and for this reason, as shown above, the Plan is null and void.

"And further, from information officially given by the bishops of the Methodist Episcopal Church, in answer to a call upon them by the General Conference for a statement of the facts in the premises, it appears that in numerous instances the Plan proposed in the event of a separation has been openly violated by the Southern Church, and hence that the peace upon the border and elsewhere, which it was designed to promote, has not been secured. The bishops of the Methodist Episcopal Church, South, have claimed a movable line, thus transferring, from one place to another, the scenes of strife and confusion as fast as society majorities could be obtained, which we regard and affirm to be in direct contravention of the most obvious principles of the said provisional Plan. And it is in evidence before us, that in numerous instances the sense of members on the proposed border has been taken by Southern preachers, privately, and in various other illegal and inconvenient ways, and hence that societies have been reported and claimed for the South, which, by suitable tests, would have given large majorities in favour of adhering to the Methodist Episcopal Church. And in numerous instances influence has been applied, and often varied, and obstinately persevered in, to secure a decision in favour of the Methodist Episcopal Church, South, and contrary to the wishes of many of our people. And also, in some instances, houses of worship, built at the expense, in whole or in part, of members adhering to the Methodist Episcopal Church, have been taken from them without their consent, and without compensation, and they have been discommoded by vexatious lawsuits, costs, and in various other ways, by preachers and members attached to the Church, South, all of which we claim and affirm is in direct violation of the most sacred objects and conditions of the said proposed Plan, showing that it has long since, in this way also, been rendered a nullity by our brethren of the South, and this, notwithstanding the bishops of the Methodist Episcopal Church, waving all conclusions which this General Conference were entitled to draw from the numerous ascertained infractions of the proposed Plan, resolved, 'as far as their administration was concerned,' to adhere to it strictly, which, for the sake of the magnanimous Christian example it exhibits, and in view of the right of the General Conference alone to assert the facts of the infraction and consequent destruction of the Plan, we are happy to find they have scrupulously done.

"Finally, having thus found, upon clear and incontestable evidence, that the three fundamental conditions of said proposed Plan have severally failed, and the failure of either of them separately being sufficient to render it null and void, and having found the practical workings of said Plan incompatible with certain great constitutional principles elsewhere asserted, we have found and declared *the whole and every part of said provisional Plan to be null and void.*

"4. In view of the above-named principles and facts, [as well as the constitutional rights already referred to,] we regard those who have, by their own act and deed, become members of the Methodist Episcopal Church, South, as having withdrawn from the Methodist Episcopal Church. And whereas those who are members of the Methodist Episcopal Church in good and regular standing, cannot be deprived of such membership without due form of trial, all those members who have not attached themselves to the Methodist Episcopal Church, South, are and have been members of the Methodist Episcopal Church, and as such they are entitled to its care and privileges, as provided for in another report of this committee. Respectfully submitted.

George Peck, *Chairman.*"

I wish to refer to the manuscript journal of the General Conference of 1808, to read a letter from Ezekiel Cooper, in relation to the Book Concern. I refer to it for the purpose of showing how this fund has accumulated.

Mr. Lord,—That ought to have been read before the argument commenced. You reserved no right to read it, and permitted me to sum up without its being read.

Judge Nelson,—It can be read now if it is within the stipulation.

Mr. Lord,—It is within the stipulation; but it ought to have been read before my argument, unless it was agreed to reserve it.

Judge Nelson,—I understood the counsel to allow the postponement of the reading of everything on the part of the defence.

Mr. Lord,—No matter.

Mr. Fancher,—This is a letter from Ezekiel Cooper, book agent, to the General Conference of 1808; and is entered on the journals of that Conference, under date May 24th, 1808:—

"Moved by Thomas Ware, and seconded by Wm. Mills, that our present book agents be requested to inform the Conference, if they will continue to conduct the Concern, and on what terms.

"Brother Ezekiel Cooper gave in his resignation as book agent, viz. :—

"I, Ezekiel Cooper, editor and general book-steward, with affectionate and grateful emotions of heart, do hereby respectfully acknowledge to my brethren composing the General Conference, that the trust and confidence which they have reposed in me, as their editor and general book-steward, in the superintendence of their Book Concern, has and does most seriously and deeply affect my sensibility, so as to excite thankfulness to my brethren, and a grateful reverence and humiliation before God, that I have been accounted capable and qualified to fill the station, and have been considered as worthy of trust and confidence in so important and interesting a department; and it is a matter of inexpressible delight, that I can ingenuously declare to you, that I have, with conscious rectitude, served the interests of the Connexion with persevering integrity and fidelity, to the best of my ability; and as our report to you will show, from a view of the stock account now rendered, I have served your interests successfully. And may I flatter myself that I have served you with acceptance, so far as to meet the testimony of your approbation; than which, I do not know any temporary consideration that is capable of giving me a greater satisfaction and gratification.

"When I engaged in the Concern, in the spring of 1799, the whole amount of the clear capital stock, including debts and all manner of property, was not worth more than about $4,000; and I had not a single dollar of cash in hand, belonging to the Connexion, to carry on the work, or to procure materials, or to pay a single demand against the Concern, which at that time was near $3,000 in debt. Under these circumstances, and thus situated, I engaged in the business with reluctance, fear, and trembling. I maintained and established the Concern by my own personal responsibility for contracts made, and the credit that I had in the confidence of those for whom I did business. Thus, with cautious steps, and prudent forethought, and calculations in business, I had to struggle and go on by night and day; and I had in certain cases to advance my own cash to meet some of the demands against the Concern. In the course of the first year, I got the business tolerably under way, and by intense application and great fatigue got released from some embarrassments and perplexities, and the business appeared in a state of liberal prosperity. At the General Conference in 1804, the Concern had so far prospered that I could show a a capital of about $27,000, which was clearing for the Connexion about $23,000 in five years, from a capital of about $4,000, which was when I received it in a precarious and scattered situation. During which time of five years I had no help allowed me by the Connexion, further than a small consideration of $330 and my board per year. Four years ago, in 1804, the General Conference appointed Brother John Wilson to assist in the business, since which time we have progressed upon the capital of about $45,000, according to the report on your table. So that since the time I first engaged in the business, in 1799, till this time, being nine years, the capital stock has increased about eleven-fold, which is more than one hundred per cent. per annum, or about eleven hundred per cent. in nine years upon the original capital stock of about $4,000, besides the various appropriations to the conferences and other purposes, as our ledger and day-book will show for.

"And now, dear brethren, wishing all success to the Connexion, and to the Book Concern, I hereby give you notice, that it is my wish and purpose to be released from the agency in the Book Concern, and to retire from the responsibility and perplexities of the business. Therefore, I decline being considered as a candidate for the editor or stewardship, wishing you may never have an agent to do you less service, nor to serve you with less acceptance than I have done.

"With great consideration, I am, dear brethren, in sentiments of good-will, and ministerial affection, and Christian love, yours respectfully,

"BALTIMORE, *May 24th*, 1808. EZEKIEL COOPER.

"To the General Conference now sitting."

MR. JOHNSON,—Does the gentleman read that to show that the capital swelled from $1,000 to $45,000?

Mr. Fancher,—The object is to show how the capital accrued.

Mr. Johnson,—To show that there were no donations, but that the accumulation was the result of the proceeds of the books?

Mr. Fancher,—Yes, sir; I wish to make references in this connexion, to show that from the first the travelling preachers, who acted as agents, were compensated by a discount to them as wholesale purchasers,—generally, I believe, of one-third. I refer to the report finally adopted in the Canada case, (Proofs, No. 1, page 49,) to show that the General Conference exercised a right to vary the discount.

Mr. Johnson,—What was the discount then?

Mr. Fancher,—I do not know what it was then; but it was generally about 33⅓ per cent. That report, on p. 49, says, that

"The General Conference have ever claimed and exercised the right to regulate the discount at which our books may be sold to wholesale purchasers."

I refer also to the journals of the Conference of 1840, (pp. 116, 117,) when the following resolution was adopted:—

"5. *Resolved,* That we allow on all credit sales a discount of twenty-five per cent., the credit to extend to the conference ensuing, when, if not paid, to bear interest from that date; and a discount of thirty-three and one-third per cent. when the cash accompanies the order; provided, that whenever the books are longer than one month in arriving at the place of destination, after the reception of the cash by the agents, then the purchaser shall be entitled to receive interest on the amount paid, for the whole time from the reception of the money until the books are received, at the same rate of interest as is charged by the agents; provided, also, such payments are made in funds which are at par at the agency."

That rule existed until 1848; then, as will be seen on reference to the journal of that Conference, (pp. 113, 114,) this resolution was adopted:—

"*Resolved,* That a deduction of fifteen per cent. on an average, be made on the retail prices of the books of the General Catalogue; and that the discount to preachers on the books (with the exception of Bibles and Testaments) be, for cash purchases, thirty per cent.; on credit, twenty per cent."

I next refer, in relation to a point made by the counsel in opening, to the Discipline of 1840, (page 67,) to show that a travelling preacher may be located without his consent.

"Quest. 4. What shall be done with a member of an annual conference who conducts himself in a manner which renders him unacceptable to the people as a travelling preacher?

"Ans. When any member of an annual conference shall be charged with having so conducted himself as to render him unacceptable to the people as a travelling preacher, it shall be the duty of the conference to which he belongs to investigate the case; and if it appear that the complaint is well-founded, and he do not give the conference satisfaction that he will amend, or voluntarily retire, they may locate him without his consent."

I wish now to refer to the fact, which is not in evidence, that the Southern conferences, the Southern preachers, receive books from the Book Concern, and have received them since 1844, under precisely the same arrangement that was made with the Canada Conference.

Mr. Lord,—Do you mean the Southern organization, or individual Southern preachers?

Mr. Fancher,—Individual preachers.

Mr. Lord,—If you will draw up a statement of the fact as you wish it admitted, I will sign it with you; though I think it ought to have been notified to us before.

Mr. Fancher,—I wish to refer to another fact not in evidence—this suit was commenced on the 15th of June, 1849.

In connexion with the reference I have already made to the votes of the annual conferences on the change of the sixth restrictive rule, I ask the Court to refer to Proofs, No. 1, page 136, the proceedings of May 18, 1848, being a statement of the report of the committee on the state of the Church, as to the votes on this question.

Mr. Lord,—That was read by Mr. Choate.

Mr. Fancher,—Very well.

I beg to state to the Court that, not having had an opportunity of conferring with Mr. Choate, and not having seen his brief, I cannot say that these are all the references we shall make; but these are all of which I have a note. I reserve the right to make other references whenever Mr. Choate may be able to attend.

The Court then adjourned.

FIFTH DAY.—Friday, May 23, 1851.

Mr. Ewing,—If the Court please—Mr. Choate, who, by our arrangement, was to proceed this morning with the argument, I am sorry to say, is ill. His physician says he will be able to proceed on Monday. We would ask, as a favour of your Honours, that the case be postponed until then.

Mr. Wood,—Mr. Choate has prepared to open this case upon the evidence; and, as your Honours are aware, it is a very different preparation for the one who is to open and the one who is to follow, and it would derange our whole proceedings if we were to change the order of speaking.

Mr. Johnson,—The complainants have no objection to the postponement. The clients whom I represent, and I myself, will suffer some inconvenience from it, but that is nothing compared to the absolute necessity of granting this indulgence to Mr. Choate. I am satisfied that the counsel associated with him are not prepared to take his place in the argument. It will be perfectly satisfactory to us if your Honours yield to the application.

Mr. Wood,—If the Court will allow this privilege, we shall arrange to go on with the case on Monday, whether Mr. Choate be able to attend or not.

Judge Nelson,—That must be understood; the case must go on on Monday. In consequence of the illness of Mr. Choate, who is the counsel selected to open the argument on the part of the defendants, we shall be obliged to postpone the argument until Monday morning. I was informed yesterday afternoon that Mr. Choate was quite unwell, was under the charge of a physician, and it was doubtful whether he would be able to come to Court this morning. It seems this morning that he is not as well as he was yesterday. He is not able at present to come to Court to open the argument on the part of the defendants. Of course, from the necessity of the case, we shall be obliged to postpone the argument, however inconvenient it may be to the business of the Court, or to the counsel concerned. The argument of the case therefore will be postponed until Monday morning at ten o'clock. Then it must go on, without regard to the condition of the counsel.

The Court was then adjourned to Monday.

SIXTH DAY.—Monday, May 26, 1851.

Mr. Fancher handed to the Court the *Points of the Defendants*, as follows :—

I. The Methodist Episcopal Church is a religious society, established for the promotion and spread of Christianity, organized in 1784 as an episcopal Church, independent of the English episcopacy ; and prior to the secession hereinafter mentioned, extended through every part of the United States.

II. Said religious society or institution existed under and subject to the law of public or charitable uses.

III. The government and discipline of the society prior to 1808 was under the jurisdiction and control of district or annual conferences, held in each of the several districts into which the territories within their limits were divided—composed of the clergymen within their respective districts : and from the proceedings of those bodies generally an appeal lay to a general convention, consisting of the ministers comprising the annual conferences; and which convention exercised original as well as appellate powers.

IV. Property consisting of real and personal estate, commonly known and distinguished as the Book Concern, has been, and still is, held by trustees, subject to the management of said ecclesiastical jurisdictions of the Methodist Episcopal Church, which is subject to the use following, viz. : to be appropriated "for the benefit of the travelling, supernumerary, and superannuated, and worn-out preachers, their wives, widows, and children."

V. The said Book Concern was originally commenced by the travelling preachers, and it has been held, more especially since 1808, in connexion with, and in subordination to, the judicatories of the Methodist Episcopal Church, who are the managers of the charity.

VI. The Methodist Episcopal Church, through its annual conferences, as such managers, cannot be deprived of their power and control over said funds, unless guilty of a breach of duty, established by the decree of a court of equity.

VII. The trustees are accountable for these funds and proceeds thereof to the Methodist Episcopal Church and its judicatories, and are bound to pay over said income, in fulfilment of the trust under their management and direction, to the beneficiaries.

VIII. The beneficiaries—to wit, the travelling, supernumerary, and superannuated preachers belonging to the Methodist Episcopal Church, and their families—have no estate in, or right to, the said funds, or the income thereof, otherwise than as the same are given out to them from time to time in the administration of the charity.

IX. Said trustees are not under the control or direction of the persons who may have contributed to the charity, and who thereby irrevocably parted with the same.

X. The members in the Southern annual conferences or districts, who left the General Conference in 1844, and subsequently formed a new General Conference, and a separate ecclesiastical jurisdiction, under the name of the Methodist Episcopal Church, South, seceded and separated from the Methodist Episcopal Church, and are no longer in connexion with the Methodist Episcopal Church, which is now composed of that portion of the former members who remained in it, and are identified with it.

1. The General Conference who adopted the Report of the Committee of Nine—a Plan of Separation so called—had no power to act in the premises.

2. Said report did not authorize such separation, but was prospective, and was accompanied with conditions and terms that have not been complied with.

3. There was no cause of complaint against the action of the General Conference to render a separation necessary or expedient; their general action (and more especially in the case of Bishop Andrew) being warranted by the rules and usages of the Church.

4. There was a special agreement about the property in question, which should govern, (if the action of the General Conference is available,) in virtue of which agreement the plaintiffs, under the facts of the case, can have no right thereto.

XI. The secession of the members newly organized as a separate Church, if it had been legitimate and fully authorized, and with the entire consent of the Church, would not entitle them to any portion of said funds, without an express agreement to that effect, sanctioned by a court of competent jurisdiction.

XII. The plaintiffs are not entitled to any relief prayed for in their bill.

HON. RUFUS CHOATE,—I feel extreme regret, may it please your Honours, that I have been obliged to avail myself so largely of the unfailing kindness of the Court; and I hope I shall be able to requite it by reasonable brevity at last. I regret nearly as much that I could not hear the close of Mr. Lord's argument, although, apart from the instruction and delight which I am sure I should have derived from it, it is of less importance since I do not intend to attempt a reply to his address, but rather to confine myself to opening at large and independently somewhat the general answer to the plaintiffs' case.

The question presented upon this record, and upon these proofs, arises, doubtless, out of a transaction of singular and sad interest, and one suggestive of many admonitions, and thoughts, and fears—I mean the dismemberment, partial and *pro tempore*, of the Methodist Episcopal Church. But it is after all a question of mere property, to be decided according to a strict rule of law. In the decision of that question, I have not supposed the Court would be greatly assisted—I have feared they might be embarrassed rather—by any attempt on my part to trace in any considerable detail the causes which have conducted to this dismemberment, or to appreciate the relative measures of blame or responsibleness which may seem to attach to the actors or antagonisms that have produced it, and still less by hearing us at the bar, if we were inclined to do so, criminate and recriminate upon the motives that have led to the institution or defence of this particular suit. All that office, if it is to be done, will be done better, perhaps, elsewhere. History, which, it is said, keeps a durable record of all characters and all actions, and before whose tribunal and judgment of the dead, Church, and priest, and people must answer one day, will perform that office far better, *sine ira et sine studio*,—if not now, when some generations shall have passed away. I could desire, therefore, to confine myself exactly and closely to the merits of the question as a question of property. Some observations, however, which have fallen necessarily from my learned and able friend in the course of his very skilful and powerful address, some things that have been very emphatically read from the proofs in the case, and the peculiarities of the extraordinary controversy itself, make it necessary, perhaps, that I should spend a few minutes in the outset upon topics which, I must own, seem to me only quite remotely bearing upon these merits. And we naturally feel a little anxiety, in the first place, to address ourselves to an observation—not perhaps in terms made by my learned brother, yet obviously presenting itself to any one adverting to the aspects of the controversy and these parties—that our attitude is not a very graceful one to begin with, inasmuch as we seem to stand here assenting to a division of the Church, and dissenting from a partition of its funds.

I hope it may be thought enough, in the first place, before advancing further, on behalf of the defendants on the record to say—I mean the defendants who have charge of the property which is the very subject of the bill, the Book Concern—that they received it some time since, upon trust, to apply it to certain definite, inflexible, and peremptory charitable uses, for the benefit of a certain limited and particular description of members of the Methodist Church, their wives, families, and their widows, *remaining mem-*

bers—remaining members, may it please your Honours, for that is the qualification on which this title in every beneficiary begins, and is to be held to the last—to be applied to those beneficiaries under the direction of the General Conference of this Church; and that they have never been directed nor authorized, so far as they can understand it, to withdraw a farthing from these uses, or to pay one farthing of money in any other direction, and therefore they must suppose that they hold it under the original trust unaltered in the slightest particular. Still it would be enough, I humbly submit, for me to say, on behalf of these defendants on narrower grounds, and for the other two defendants on this record,—I mean the commissioners appointed under the Plan of Separation, to act in the division of this fund,—it would be enough to say for them, that according to that very Plan on which these parties bring their bill to-day, they are directed to pay nothing to the plaintiffs, but upon the happening of a certain definite contingency, the rescision of the restrictive rule by the annual conferences, and that contingency has never happened. *Prima facie*, I am quite sure this is a sufficient excuse for those defendants refusing the demand out of Court, and defending a suit in. *Prima facie*, I am sure this requires them to do both one and the other. Whether these annual conferences ought or ought not *in foro conscientiæ* to have acceded to the recommendation of the General Conference is not for these defendants to consider. Whether, if they had done so, it would have answered the purposes at large, I shall, perhaps, have occasion to consider in the progress of this discussion. But until they have done it, surely, surely we hold the fund still under the old trust of half a century ago, according to which this property has been administered as a sacred thing, without the interruption of a moment to this hour, on the faith of a religious and consistent interpretation and administration of which scores, hundreds, thousands have lived, and laboured, and died, or live and labour still, within the vineyard and bosom of the Methodist Episcopal Church, and which we do not admit, as I understand, to be modified or displaced in the slightest degree.

Of the nature of that fund, and of the character of the rights of the beneficiaries in it, I shall have occasion to speak very much at length in the progress of this debate. Enough now, and for the defendants of record, that it exists, and that, according to that very Plan, but for which these plaintiffs upon their own concession are only a mass of disconnected seceders, it is our bounden duty to everybody so to keep, and guard, and administer it, until the annual conferences, or the supreme authority of this tribunal, shall ordain a different disposition of it.

So much for the defendants of record. But what shall I say of the beneficial and larger part of the Methodist Episcopal Church behind? Is their attitude a graceful one, assenting to the division of the Church, and yet not assenting to a division of the funds? In the first place, the Court will perceive when we have advanced a little further in this argument, that we do not admit that the Methodist Episcopal Church—that old, grand, well-compacted, and once beautiful community, designed by its Creator, by Wesley, and by the generation of Wesley, for a duration on earth without end—is dismembered legally and totally. We do not even admit that it has been dismembered *de facto* and by secession permanently. We know very well, what we will call for convenience in the progress of this discussion, secession *de facto*, has taken place—a secession, improvident, needless, and never sufficiently to be deplored; and creating I know not what extraordinary and anomalous relations between the seceder and the Church. But we have not yet renounced the hope,—I, personally and professionally, at any rate, however it may be with my clients and associates, have not yet renounced the hope, and spare me if you may to cherish the grateful error still, that when your Honours shall have pronounced this secession unauthorized in matter of law, as well as unjustifiable, perhaps, upon the circumstances in point of fact in which it occurred,—I have not renounced the hope that the sober second thought may supervene, that the old instincts of the Methodist community may come again into activity, that in the language of the Louisville Convention, for whose parting words of kindness I, for one, stand here to thank them, some plan of reunion may yet be proposed by the wisdom and Christianity that still enrich this Church, whereby it may to a considerable extent be reunited, whereby it may to a considerable extent become the same old Church again, and shine with something like the brightness of its rising. That hope, for one, I have not yet relinquished. Peradventure, if this step which the plaintiffs have taken shall turn out to be unprofitable as well as devious, it may be the easier to retrace it. Many times, I remember the historian tells us, many times the alienating states of Greece had all but made up their minds to discontinue the common consultation of the Oracle of Delphi, and seek for the will of Jove in divers local temples, had not the impracticability of partitioning the treasures which the piety of so many generations had gathered on the charmed neutral ground, necessitated a salutary delay. So, possibly, may it be here.

Allow me to make another observation or two entirely preliminary to the consideration of the merits of this case. The complaint here at last must be, before this forum and before the outer forum, that the annual conferences have not adopted the recommendation of the General Conference, and have not concurred in the rescision of the restrictive article. Will our friends of the South take a little time when they go home, and inquire whether the South has not it to answer for itself? I do not know that if I should pause I could establish it by these proofs in every particular as I shall assert it, but I do aver, that when the annual conferences, in 1844 and 1845, began first to vote on this recommendation, the first votes that were thrown were such as led every man to believe that it would have been adopted; and it was only because the temper of the South began to be so warm, and so high, and so exasperating, that these hopes were, I believe, to the regret of a great majority who were either observers or concerned, wholly overcast. One thing I know, and that is, that the first conferences that voted—I mean the New England and the Northern conferences generally, from which the greatest opposition had been anticipated—voted favourably; and when the time came for conferences from whom less opposition had been anticipated, there was an unexpected and scarcely intelligible turn and change of opinion. It will be for your Honours to infer what may be the explanation of the indisputable fact. I apprehend if the South would take time and revise those publications with which her secular and her religious press were teeming through the summer, and autumn, and winter following, the explanation might there be found. To show that the suggestion is not wholly imaginary, I think I am able to find some proofs in the very evidence which the plaintiffs have introduced, in the proceedings of the annual conferences of the South, which resulted in the calling of the Louisville Convention, where I find the temper of the Southern press recorded, exposed, and proved. Here, for example, on page 13 of the 2d of the Proofs, in the Missouri Conference, it was

"Resolved, That we have read with deep regret the violent proceedings of some of our Southern brethren in the primary meetings, against some of our bishops and others."

They "have read with deep regret." Again, in the proceedings of the Arkansas Conference I find the following:—

"Resolved, That, though we feel ourselves aggrieved, and have been wounded, *without cause*, in the house of our friends, we have no disposition to impute wrong motives to the majority in the late General Conference, and no inclination to endorse those vindictive proceedings had in some portions of the South, believing it to be the duty of Christians, under all circumstances, to exercise that *charity* which *beareth all things*."

I could read more; but I have read enough, I think, to convey my meaning, and read enough to establish my suggestion. Your Honours will judge what the temper must have been that induced such observations, and will easily appreciate its probable or its inevitable influence upon the North.

Let me say one thing more, and I come nearer the merits of the case. Was there not, at the time of the General Conference of 1848, a still subsisting Methodist Episcopal Church, although that Conference deemed itself obliged to pronounce the proceedings of the Conference of 1844, as to the Plan of Separation, a nullity from beginning to end; partly because the annual conferences had not adopted its recommendations, but also on larger and broader grounds, to which I shall make allusion in a moment? Your Honours will find that nevertheless, on page 95 of the journals of that Conference, (and the reference has been made to the Court,) they proceeded to provide for an amicable adjustment of this great controversy by arbitration. The Court will find there, in much detail and particularity, directions given to their agents to prefer an arbitration of the cause to the gentlemen representing the South, if, by the advice of counsel, they should ascertain that it could be legally and properly done; and if it could not be legally done, they were to proceed to submit the matter to the annual conferences in succession, to obtain their consent. That matter was submitted to the annual conferences, their assent was in the course of being rapidly and warmly given, when they were interrupted by the institution of this suit. I submit, then, that it is no fault of ours that this cause comes on to be heard and determined here to-day under the strict principles of law and equity, instead of being committed to a tribunal where the strict principles of law and equity might be tempered by the delicacies of the extraordinary crisis. I have hesitated much in determining whether or not I ought to say anything, and in what connexion and how much I should say upon the question, whether either of these parties here before the Court, and which of them, may be thought to be in any degree of fault *in foro conscientiæ*, or otherwise, for the dismemberment of the Church. I am bound in candour to say in advance, that it seems to me to be too remotely connected, under any respect, if at all, with the real merits of the case; and yet it is so far connected with those merits under certain views, that I do not know that it can be altogether dispensed with as a consideration to be adverted to. This consideration is very remotely, if at all, connected with the merits of the case; for whether the proceedings of the General Conference of 1844, touching Bishop Andrew, were competent or expedient or not, and even if they were neither competent nor expedient, yet, beyond all manner of controversy, unless this Church was divided in twain by a body constitutionally competent to so transcendent an act, unless every condition of the Plan of Separation has been performed, unless the annual conferences have in point of fact acceded to the recommendation of the General Conference, and rescinded the restrictive rule, I do not see how the plaintiffs can by possibility maintain themselves on this bill. On the other hand, if that Church has been divided by an authority constitutionally competent to so great an act, if the conditions of the Plan of Separation have been severally complied with by the annual conferences, then I agree that the plaintiffs are entitled to recover, however causeless, and however deeply and forever to be deplored, however severely to be condemned by morality and by patriotism, was the act of secession itself. Therefore, I think the Court is not called upon directly to discharge the very delicate office of inquiring on which rests, mainly or at all, the blame in this business. Yet I hope your Honours will indulge me when I proceed to say that I cannot tacitly admit that the party I represent here has been in the least degree in fault for this transaction.

I cannot, either as a citizen in the most private capacity, or as a professional party in this cause, admit that this has been the result of an inevitable moral necessity. I do not believe in the suggestion which we find so liberally scattered through the defence, and of which so much has been said by my learned friend, that the dismemberment of this Church has been the result of an invincible or an inevitable moral necessity. Why, excellent good reasons have been given why the Church should be dissolved, if not now, hereafter; excellent reasons have been given why, on account of the great extent of country, and the difficulty of traversing it by the itinerant superintendent organism, it should be dissolved; reasons why it should be dissolved on account of antagonisms on the subject of slavery. Reasons have been given for this dissolution. So reasons may be given, and good reasons may be given, why everyting should be dissolved; why the Union, the larger secular Union that embosoms them all, should be dissolved; why the solemn temples and gorgeous palaces of the globe itself should be dissolved. To what catastrophe the progress of events might have, some time or another, carried this Church, or may carry anything; to what sea, shoreless and bottomless, and lighted by no sun, the stream of progress might have borne the Church, or may bear the nation, nobody of course can be certain that he knows. But I do submit that the dismemberment of this Church, as it actually happened, in the time, under the circumstances, and for the reasons, on that day when it happened, was causeless and needless, as well as deplorable in the highest degree. Is it not *pessimi exempli* that we should allow persons standing in a public capacity to trace the consequences of their own acts, and the work of their own hands, to the finger of Providence?

May it please your Honours, the will, and reason, and Christianity of one generation made this Church; the will, and reason, and Christianity of another generation might have kept it together. One ten-thousandth part of the ability of speech and pen, and one ten-thousandth part of the piety, and patriotism, and morality, by which in both its sections it has been enriched, could have held it together; and I say should have been required to hold it together, until the kingdoms of this world should become the kingdoms of the Ruler of kings. I do not admit then, in the first place, that there is no fault anywhere in the division of this Church; and I do not admit that that fault, any appreciable portion of it, rests with us.

I know the prodigious ability by which I am to be followed. I am a unionist, as my learned friend is a unionist, to the very last beat of my heart. I deplore this as few can deplore it; but it is before your Honours; I am called upon to examine it in the course of my professional duty. I meet it, and mean to meet it, directly in the face. I therefore respectfully submit:—1st. That the separation has not irrevocably happened; 2d. What has happened has not been the result of a blind and over-ruling necessity; 3d. If there have been moral faults, they have not been ours.

We cannot of course take one single step in this discussion without pausing to see on what ground it was that the minority in the Convention of 1844 declared their judgment of a necessity of a separation. We cannot advance one step, as I apprehend, in the attempt to appreciate the true origin of the controversy, or the responsible authors of it,—or the responsible participators in it,—until we ascertain the precise ground on which the minority, looking the majority in the face, apprized them why they initiated here in New-York the proceedings of separation which were consummated by the Convention at Louisville.

It is perfectly clear that the main ground on which they took this step and announced their purpose of accomplishing it, was the proceedings of the Conference of 1844, in the matter of Bishop Andrew. That was the main, and substantial, and prominent ground on which they then and there declared their purpose to effect a separation. I know very well that now all manner of reasons are given, and may well be given, and have forcibly been given. But it is now we hear it said that the country has grown a great deal too large. We hear it said now that irreconcilable antagonisms were being developed in regard to freedom and slavery. We hear it said that moral necessity has intervened and has done this work. The question which I put to the Court however, is, what reason the minority gave in that Convention that day before the act was irrevocably done, whilst it was still within the control of the majority, while they might have tempered it, receded from it, abandoned it, while both sides still held it under their own control a great trust for the nation? The question is, I contend, What is the reason the minority then, looking the majority in the face, assigned for the act of separation on which they were about to enter? And I respectfully submit, that when your Honours come to sift that, and sift it carefully upon these proofs, you will find that it rested on the action of this Conference, whose whole action, as I shall only have too much pleasure in showing the Court, down to that time, had been marked uniformly by conciliation, by conservatism, by a parental and equal regard to the feelings and interests and sentiments of every section of the country, touching the case of Bishop Andrew. That was the main cause assigned by the minority; and that I may leave no doubt about that, let me call the attention of the Court to No. 1 of the proofs, p. 97, where we find in their own declaration, under their own hand, the reasons assigned. One or two others are assigned, but I submit most respectfully, as I shall attempt to prove, that these are reasons of no importance at all, and that it comes at last to the proceedings against Bishop Andrew. But I will read it exactly as it stands :—

"The delegates of the conferences in the slaveholding States take leave to *declare* to the General Conference of the Methodist Episcopal Church, that the continued agitation of the subject of slavery and abolition in a portion of the Church," (that is one reason,) "the frequent action on the subject in the General Conference," (that is two,) and *especially* the extra-judicial proceedings against Bishop Andrew, which resulted, on Saturday last, in the virtual suspension of him from his office as superintendent, must produce a state of things in the South which renders a continuance of the jurisdiction of this General Conference inconsistent with the success of the ministry in the slaveholding States."

Laying that aside for a moment and turning to the Discipline of this newly-organized Southern Methodist Episcopal Church, constructed, as it seems, much more deliberately a year or two afterwards, I find them there reciting, *totidem verbis*, the same three reasons, the leading one of which is the proceedings against Bishop Andrew.

If the Court choose to pursue that inquiry a little further, I refer to the proceedings of the annual conferences of the South, which have been put in evidence as among those proceedings which led to the call of the Louisville Convention, and ultimately to the separation. Your Honours will be struck with the fact, that, with the precision of stereotype, they repeat one another right over again, almost from New-York to the Gulf of Mexico. By reading in our Proofs No. 2, we find that they abandon every cause of separation but the proceedings against Bishop Andrew and Mr. Harding; that of fourteen annual conferences, five forgot the case of Mr. Harding altogether, and confined themselves to the case of Bishop Andrew; so that, in point of fact, it is nothing in the world but just this: That these conferences take up the declaration published by the minority, drop the first two causes therein alleged for the separation, and lay hold upon the proceedings against Bishop Andrew, some of them adding to it the proceedings against Mr. Harding, and then away it goes, the mere echo from this city of the cry beginning here—an echo running without the *vires acquirendum*, for it loses rather than gains as it goes, until it dies in the Gulf of

Mexico. There, before the majority, and here before this Court, stand the reasons on which the Methodist Episcopal Church was severed by its guardians.

I have now to ask your attention back again with a little particularity, I hope not too much detail, to the reasons in the declaration of the minority themselves; and I proceed, in the first place, with great brevity to eliminate, to throw out, the first two, in order that I may, if I can, conduct the judgment of the Court to discern that it is Bishop Andrew, and nothing but Bishop Andrew, upon which this Church was at last dissolved. Your Honours will observe they give three reasons. I turn back to page 97. In the first place, they declare as one of the causes "the continued agitation of the subject of slavery and abolition in a portion of the Church." "The continued agitation of the subject of slavery" in some of the Northern conferences—that is a reason for which a minority propose to dissolve the Church. The agitation in a portion of the Northern conferences, I shall show to the Court, created no more difficulty for the South, carried no more menace to the South, endangered the rights of the South no more than the idea that Lake Winnipiseogee up in New-Hampshire at the next change of the moon will overflow its banks and lay the cotton lands of South Carolina under the water; not a particle, not a particle in the slightest degree. To be sure there had been local agitation in the Northern conferences; there is local agitation everywhere, and the sky is not at all the clearer or the purer for it. How stands the fact here? I do not go beyond the proofs before the Court. How stands the matter of local agitation in the Northern conferences? Of course nobody supposes that I am here to defend it; but I am not here to see it overstated, and such consequences as the taking down of a structure built for immortality on earth deduced from it, without giving our commentary. How stood that matter? Here began an agitation in our conferences. After having aired the local vocabulary and breathed through the local lungs as long as it could before it came here in 1836, it met with a dignified rebuke by the General Conference, and went home for a time. That was in 1836. It came here again in 1840, upon a petition of O. Scott and others, and was met in a very admirable manner, and with the same decisive result, and back it rolled again; and those very petitioners, to whom Mr. Lord has referred, O. Scott and others, went back and seceded from the Northern annual conferences, because although they found them, in a certain sense, anti-slavery conferences, they found them Methodists, they found them Unionists, they found them true to the discipline, and order, and the preservation of the peace of the Church, and, through the Church, of the larger interests which surround the Church, if there are larger interests than those of the Church. They seceded, and the local conferences had rest.

I now propose to submit to your Honours that, upon a view of these facts, we have in 1840, and again in 1844, under the hands of the bishops themselves, reporting the condition of Methodism to the General Conference, proof of everything I have said, and conclusive proof, that although there had been some local agitation, though there were some exceptions to the general fact, the general condition even of New-England Methodism was calm, and quiet, and steady. I call your attention, in the first place, to an "extract from an Address of the Bishops to the General Conference of the Methodist Episcopal Church.":—

"It has been the constant aim and united endeavour of your general superintendents to preserve uniformity and harmony in these respects; and, as far as practicable, prevent conflicting action in all the official bodies in the Church. But although we record with unfeigned gratitude to the God of all grace and consolation, the general peace, and harmony, and prosperity of the body since your last session," (what more can you say of the general human condition anywhere than this?) "it becomes our painful duty to lay before you some exceptions to this happy and prosperous condition."

So then the general prosperous, peaceful, and harmonious condition of the body is the great fact for which they thank God, and it is only the exceptions to that on which they proceed to observe. And our secular Union would not last long if general contentment, general peace, general harmony, would not testify it. If because there is a "Shay's insurrection" in one State, and a ripple here and there floats over the surface, the Union is to be taken down by the patriotism of this land, surely, surely it is not the creation forever which we had the dream it was.

Let me pursue now the course of this address throughout the address, and I will verify from it exactly what I state. There had been some exceptions, some of what we may colloquially call "flare-ups," here and there, and had met, not the breakwater of the Baltimore Conference, but the breakwater of the General Conference, which had rolled them back. The bishops say there were some exceptions to this prosperous condition. Then they go on:—

"At the last session of the General Conference the subject of slavery and its abolition was extensively discussed, and vigorous exertions made to effect new legislation upon it. But after a careful examination of the whole ground, *aided by the light of past experience*, it was the *solemn conviction* of the Conference that the interests of religion would not be advanced by any additional enactments in regard to it.

"In your Pastoral Address to the ministers and people at your last session, with great unanimity, and, as we believe, in the true spirit of the ministers of the peaceful Gospel of Christ, you solemnly advised the whole body to abstain from all abolition movements, and from agitating the exciting subject in the Church. This advice was in perfect agreement with the individual as well as associated views of your superintendents. But, had we differed from you in opinion, in consideration of the age, wisdom, experience, and official authority of the General Conference, we should have felt ourselves under a solemn obligation to be governed by your counsel. We have endeavoured, both in our official administration, and in our private intercourse with the preachers and members, to inculcate the sound policy and Christian spirit of your Pastoral Address. And it affords us great pleasure to be able to assure you, that our efforts in this respect have been very generally approved, and your advice cordially received and practically observed in a very large majority of the annual conferences, as will more fully appear to you on the careful examination of the journals of those bodies for the last four years. But we regret that we are compelled to say that in some" (exceptional, it will be perceived) "of the Northern and Eastern conferences, in contravention of your Christian and pastoral counsel, and of your best efforts to carry it into effect, the subject has been agitated in such forms, and in such a spirit, as to disturb the peace of the Church. This unhappy agitation has not been confined to the annual conferences, but has been introduced into quarterly conferences, and made the absorbing business of self-created bodies in the bosom of our beloved Zion."

The bishops then go on to indicate the garb under which this presents itself, and then express the opinions of wise men as to its character and tendency. On page 60 they come to the great result in point of fact:—

"It is justly due to a number of the annual conferences, in which a majority, or a very respectable minority, of the members are professedly abolitionists, to say, that they occupy a very different ground, and pursue a very different course, from those of their brethren who have adopted ultra principles and measures in this unfortunate, and, we think, unprofitable controversy. The result of action had in such conferences on the resolution of the New-England Conference, recommending a very important change in our general rule on slavery, is satisfactory proof of this fact, and affords us strong and increasing confidence that the unity and peace of the Church are not to be materially affected by this exciting subject."

So, then, without advancing a step further, it is all narrowed down to this: a single conference, the New-England Conference, proposes an important change in the general rule on slavery; that is submitted to conferences, a majority of whose members are actually abolitionists; and even these conferences, a number of them—so many that their example is cited as satisfactory proof of the fact, that the peace and unity were not to be seriously affected—so many even of the abolition conferences disapproved the change proposed, that the bishops are relieved, as they declare, from all possible apprehension of difficulty from that source. The bishops go on to say:—

"It is believed that men of ardent temperament, whose zeal may have been somewhat in advance of their knowledge and discretion, have made such advances in the abolition enterprise as to produce a reaction. A few preachers and members, disappointed in their expectations, and despairing of the success of their cause in the Methodist Church," (surely they were the best judges of what success the Church promised to their enterprises,) "have withdrawn from our fellowship, and connected themselves with associations more congenial with their views and feelings; and others, in similar circumstances, may probably follow their example. But we rejoice in believing that these secessions will be very limited, and that the great body of Methodists in these States will continue as they have been—one and inseparable."

If that continued to be the state of the Church down to 1844, I ask whether it is possible to attach any weight to the reason which stands first in the declaration of the minority in this case, that is, the continued agitation in the local Church? Now, there is not a solitary particle of proof in this case, that from 1840 to 1844 the local agitation increased in the slightest degree. In 1840 the bishops say they had substantially encountered and suppressed it. In 1840 they had so far suppressed it that they believed the peace and unity of the Methodist Church was quite sure not to be seriously endangered by it; and that state of things, so far as there is a scintilla of evidence in this case to control it, remained, by the mercy and blessing of God, down to 1844. Yet then, when a foregone conclusion was to be adopted and vindicated by a manifesto, our brethren of the South suffered themselves by habit to take up and repeat again the cry of local agitation on the subject of slavery in the Methodist Church. To show that this does not rest altogether on the mere absence of proof, on the part of the plaintiffs, to show that this agitation went on increasing in the meantime, I have the pleasure to call attention in this immediate connexion to a portion of the address of the very same bishops, including Bishops Andrew and Soule, and every Methodist bishop of 1844, to the General Conference of 1844. It is to be found on page 131 of the 1st of the Proofs. They are dealing with another subject, speaking *diversa in toto*, and sum up in the fulness of grateful hearts and intelligent official superintendents, the condition of this Church. They say:—

"In this happy state of things, embracing all the essential elements of the voluntary principle, the ministers dependant upon the people whom they served in the Gospel word and ordinances, and the people united to their ministers by the bonds of affection and esteem, the work of the Lord steadily advanced; new and extensive fields of labour were constantly opening before us; the borders of our Zion were greatly enlarged; and thousands and tens of thousands were brought under Divine influence, and joined in the communion of the Church. The events of each succeeding year have afforded additional proofs of the soundness of the system, and of its adaptation to the ends for which it was designed."

I submit that we show that the first reason assigned by the minority in their Declaration of reasons why a state of things would be produced which would render a separation necessary, is totally unsupported in matter of fact, and that I shall have no difficulty, as I believe I shall have none, in satisfying the Court that the single reason at last was the action upon the case of Bishop Andrew.

The second reason which they assign is, on the facts of the case, stranger still—

"the frequent action on that subject in the General Conference." Why was it so much a question whether there had been frequent action on this subject in the General Conference, as what that action had been? And will it not almost astonish the Court when they come to see, upon a review of the evidence to which I will ask their attention, that although the action of the General Conference had been somewhat frequent, yet it had been eminently—I may say admirably—all the while the most calm, conservative, parental, and discreet that ever marked the action of any administrative body under any system, ecclesiastical or political, on the face of the earth; that it had been from beginning to end, I mean over the period to which the remarks of the declarant minority apply, nothing less and nothing more than an anxious desire to stand on the old path, to administer the old discipline, to respect every local sensibility, and to preserve the spirit of unity in the bonds of a universal peace. Let us see if it be not so; and for the proofs of it I need not go beyond fifty or one hundred pages of the evidence which both parties have united in laying before this Court. There had been frequent occasions for the action of the General Conference upon this subject, for which they were not responsible. I have already stated, in addressing myself to the subject of local agitation, the fact that as early as 1836 local agitators sent their petitions to the General Conference, asking for new legislation on the subject of slavery. I have once read, but it is so much to my present purpose that I hope your Honours will indulge me in reading it again, how that effort in 1836 was met by the General Conference. At the opening of the Conference in 1840, the bishops in their address say (page 58):—

"At the last session of the General Conference the subject of slavery and its abolition was extensively discussed, and vigorous exertions made to effect new legislation upon it. But after a careful examination of the whole ground, *aided by the light of past experience*, it was the *solemn conviction* of the Conference that the interests of religion would not be advanced by any additional enactments in regard to it."

This General Conference, whose "frequent action" on the subject of slavery was to lead to a dissolution of this Church, opens the series of its action, on which it is this day to answer before this tribunal, by resolving, as far back as 1836, that, aided by the light of past experience, it was their solemn conviction that the interests of religion would not be advanced by any additional enactments on the subject of slavery. They had occasion to act again. In 1840, O. Scott presented it on behalf of an annual conference whom he represented. About that same time, or rather in the interval between 1836 and 1840, our admirable Wesleyan brethren in England, for the purpose of showing how indissoluble the tie of Methodism always remains, came here, in the true spirit of an uninstructed and mischievous foreign philanthropy, with their suggestions upon the subject of our slavery. And again, during that same interval, from 1836 to 1840, some difficulty arose in one of the annual conferences as to some proceedings in Westmoreland, Virginia. On all these occasions, as well as on the particular occasion to which I have made reference from the bishops' address of 1840, the General Conference was called upon to act. I shall not go particularly into that subject, although it would give me great pleasure to do so, and I should find from it a refutation, the most brilliant and perfect, of the suggestion, that the frequent action on this subject by the General Conference afforded any ground for uneasiness or separation on the part of the South. Yet I can only leave it to the Court, with an earnest entreaty that in judging of these last days of the session of a General Conference of a united Church, they would read—I am sure as evidence it is important that it should be read, and as instruction on the general case, I am sure it is not undeserving the attention of the Court—the address of the bishops in 1840, the reply to the British Wesleyan Conference in 1840, the report upon the proceedings on the Westmoreland petition, also in 1840; all bound in this book, a series entire, and making up the record of the last days of that body. I submit that the result is beyond a solitary particle of doubt, as I have before said that it was, eminently calm, and conservative, and just. I am constrained to say, but I say it with regret, that when the minority put into their Declaration the frequent action of the General Conference on this subject, as a reason why they should quit us, it is a reason against a parental hand, that down to that instant had done nothing in the world but distribute the paternal goods, and the paternal heart, with an equal and just impartiality, upon all the objects of a common love. I strike that reason, then, out of the Declaration.

The case of Mr. Harding, as your Honours will observe, is not mentioned by the declarants. It is not mentioned in the Discipline of the Church, South, as a case on which the separation was effected. I believe, in matter of fact, that it was not even a subject of protest in the Conference of 1844. In that very powerful paper, which was read so emphatically and so well the other day, which is called "the Protest," there is not a word in relation to the proceedings against Mr. Harding. Therefore, perhaps, I need hardly pause here for a moment, even to throw that element out of this general controversy. Yet it would hardly do to leave it unnoticed in these general reasons. I do not intend to say one word upon the point of law; that I refer to my eminent associate. But morally, what is this Harding case? Exactly and merely this: There is, and has stood on the Discipline of this Church for I know not how many years, but nearly coeval with its origin, that if a person hold office in the Church in a State in which emancipation is legally practicable, he shall be suspended from his office until he emancipates his slaves. It seems that under that rule Mr. Harding's was a case of having become the holder of slaves and of living in a State where emancipation was practicable. He belonged to the Baltimore Conference. The Court knows that it is a settled rule of discipline of this Church that every preacher, under the degree of bishop, is tried by the annual conference to which he belongs. This gentleman was tried by his own conference, convicted by his own conference, and suspended *durante impedimento.* He appealed to the General Conference of 1844, and they approved the decision of the Baltimore Annual Conference. That is the Harding case. Without entering into an inquiry whether here was or was not a mistake in a matter of law—and I am assured that emancipation is legally practicable in the conference in which he lived, that it is achieved there without scandal or difficulty, although that may be a subject upon which there is divided professional opinion—I ask your Honours if it be competent to the minority to stand before the majority, and before the Church, and before this higher tribunal, and allege such a trial and such a conviction as that gravely as a reason for the dissolution of such a union as this. Suppose it a mistake in point of fact and law. Suppose, if I may take an illustration which my learned friend employed the other day not exactly in the same way, that a Judge of a Circuit Court pronounces a decision, it is carried to his brethren of the Supreme Judicial Bench, and affirmed, and thereupon a local community becomes exasperated, and declares itself aggrieved, and is to dissolve the Union. Is it a case for the dissolution of the Union, admitting a mistake in fact, and a mistake in law? Is an exasperated local constituency an admirable judge of law and fact? Is that one case of a conscientious error in the judgment of conscientious men to shake down pillars that ought to reach the centre, and support capitals that should sparkle in the skies? Is that a reason which is to stand here or anywhere? Would the historian of this more than Council of Trent, when he comes to write its history, recognise its title to be so considered? What harm did the decision in Mr.

Harding's case do anybody? Did it menace the safety of any preacher in the whole South? Certainly not at all. The position of the Baltimore Conference is somewhat anomalous. My friend says, they call themselves the Breakwater Conference. They are on the frontier. Part of them are in free States and part in slave States. Their position is anomalous, their feelings intense, and their action sharply marked and characteristic. But every preacher in the Southern country, who stands from off the frontier line, reposes in safety, as a child in arms, within the circle of his own annual conference. Therefore, to get up an alarm and pretend that any man's safety was endangered, from here to the Gulf of Mexico or the Pacific ocean, in the least degree, by the decision of a local conference on the case of Mr. Harding, is simply an extravagance of falsehood. For the practical judgment of this Court, the only view of it would be to treat it as evidence that a body of men in a General Conference—a Conference of which I have had the honour to say that for the last six, ten, or twelve years it had been building a monument of fairness, and justice, and impartiality in its administration at every step, and whose monument the plaintiffs have united with the defendants in asserting on these proofs—for the very first time in its administrative life, made a mistake of law and fact, and the union is to be dissolved on that account. God have mercy on and take care of all unions, the larger and the less, if such reasons as these can be assigned for their dissolution. Nothing human can stand, no ordinance of man can stand if anything can be made out on such ground as this.

Did this declaration of the majority, when they came to look their brethren in the face, observe and present a moral and absolute silence upon the case of Mr. Harding? Very well, indeed, was it when the Southern Church came to construct their Discipline, and prefix this manifesto of the causes of separation to the articles of their common and substantially sound faith,—very well: was not everyone of them totally silent on the case of Mr. Harding?

I lay that aside, and submit to the Court, with entire and perfect confidence, that we stand this day to be judged alone for our proceedings in the matter of Bishop Andrew; and if we are guilty in any degree of having contributed to the dissolution of this union, all that we have done—" the head and front of our offending hath this extent, no more"—is the proceedings in the case of Bishop Andrew. That is all. I now have to call the attention of the Court with great confidence, in some little detail, under a conscientious conviction that I have a duty not very interesting, and yet important to perform, to the proceedings of the General Conference in the matter of Bishop Andrew, and the grounds upon which they stand.

The first question is, what those proceedings were? For the first time in the trial of this case, I am going to bring these proceedings altogether under one view. I have not yet heard them read altogether by anybody. The first branch of them is to be found on p. 92, of the 1st of the Proofs, and the residue of them—quite as important—on p. 124. I believe I have satisfactorily evinced to the Court, that the action of the General Conference on the case of Bishop Andrew, was the sole ground on which this secession was declared and achieved. I wish to know, whether such a proceeding affords the least particle of justification in any aspect for secession. On p. 92 of the 1st of the Proofs, the Conference resolved,—

"Whereas the Discipline of our Church forbids the doing anything calculated to destroy our itinerant general superintendency, and whereas Bishop Andrew has become connected with slavery by marriage and otherwise, and this act having drawn after it circumstances which, in the estimation of the General Conference, will greatly embarrass the exercise of his office as an itinerant general superintendent, if not in some places entirely prevent it; therefore,

"*Resolved*, That it is the sense of this General Conference, that he desist from the exercise of his office, so long as this impediment remains."

16*

I proceed to p. 124, and find,—

"*Resolved*, As the sense of this Conference, that Bishop Andrew's name stand in the Minutes, Hymn book, and Discipline, as formerly.

"*Resolved*, That the rule in relation to the support of a bishop, and his family, applies to Bishop Andrew.

"*Resolved*, That whether in any, and if any, in what work, Bishop Andrew be employed, is to be determined by his own decision and action, in relation to the previous action of this Conference in his case."

There it is at last a whole. There at last is the deliberate and reconciled judgment of an embarrassed body acting doubtless in a case of great perplexity. The first question upon this proceeding would naturally be, whether or not the General Conference had the constitutional power to pass any such votes as these. To decide that, the first thing to be done is, I think, to ascertain what this vote is. This case of the separation and dissolution of this Church, opens with the extraordinary fact, about which there is no controversy at all, that this entire South has gone off in a body, and the hopes of the men that created this structure, so far as they have been disappointed, were disappointed and frustrated upon a vote as to the meaning of which the South cannot agree, as to the meaning of which the North cannot agree among themselves, as to the meaning of which the South and the North are irreconcilably divided among themselves to this day, and as to which no two persons that I ever had an opportunity of conversing with in my life, were agreed. That is the first great fact in this case. They have gone off on a vote perfectly unintelligible to any two persons to whose judgment I have ever submitted it. As well as I remember it, the old doctrine of nullification was to require that there should be no nullification unless, among other things, the unconstitutionality of an act should be palpable, as well as very violent. It must be a palpable unconstitutionality; and the first great difficulty here is, that instead of the act being a palpable unconstitutionality, it is an act unintelligible, and upon which there remains to this hour an irreconcilable diversity of opinion among all men. My learned friend, who preceded me, called it evasive and queer. If it is evasive and queer, it would hardly seem to be reason enough for dividing the Methodist Church. I think I can see many reasons why this might be termed ambiguous or perplex, but not why it should be designated evasive and queer, without any objectionable motive upon which to base the charge of evasiveness and queerness.

The Conference was embarrassed how to act on the case. A great diversity of opinions had to be brought together, and to be reconciled. The case was perfectly old in point of principle, although novel in its circumstances. A great deal of feeling came to be developed. There was a conscientious conviction that something should be done. Every man prayed to God to be guided. There was a general conviction, that something should be done, which, while it should spare the feelings of an aged bishop, should be effectual, and should satisfy men in every region; so that they might be able, under the embarrassment of the crisis, and the embarrassment of the moment, to put some record on the files of this Church, and yet to do no act of unkindness and harshness. Therefore, their action was not marked by the sharp and well-defined lines of tyranny. Tyranny and headlong fanaticism make deeper marks than these. They write their lines sharp and keen, and there is no mistake as to their meaning. It is because they were neither fanatics, nor abolitionists, nor tyrants, but Christian men, members of a Christian Church, solicitous mainly to keep the Church of their love together, yet called upon to keep that Church together in circumstances of great and extreme character,—it was in consequence of these embarrassments, that they reconciled themselves to this proceeding. These considerations may not have their full influence on those who do not have to act on such a crisis. Yet, how any man, how any minority of men, should have found in it a *casus belli* of such transcendent magnitude, I am sure, on these proofs, I have never been able to explain.

What is the meaning of the vote? Upon that question there are two schools, consisting of a million of people. All agree, in the first place, that this vote did not design to remove, nor attempt to remove, nor suspend, nor attempt to suspend Bishop Andrew from the office of bishop. I pray the attention of the Court to that to begin with. This vote does not pretend to suspend him from the office of bishop; it does not ask him to suspend himself; it does not advise him to do so. It leaves him a bishop as before. The resolutions to which I last called attention leave his name standing affectionately, not derisively as my learned brother seemed to suppose, on the record of the Minutes, the Hymn book, and Book of Discipline, as formerly. They resolve that the rule for the support of a bishop and his family still applies to Bishop Andrew, and that in any, if in any, work he be employed should be determined by his own decision, having reference to the previous action of the Conference.

So then it is not true that they remove him from the office of bishop, or suspend him from the office of bishop, or advise him to suspend himself from the office of bishop for half a minute. When my learned brother supposes that they left him in such a position, that the little children in the Methodist Church, every time they sung their hymns, would look inquiringly for Bishop Andrew, and thus subject him to a good deal of pain and distress, I think he misconceives the matter altogether, and does not allow his own heart to judge for him in regard to it. They left his name in the Hymn book for this reason: that Hymn-book is one of the muniments and records of the history of this Church; and they leave his name in it, so that whoever gathers the history of the Methodist Episcopal Church from this record of its biography, shall find that he was a bishop. The result is, if I may so express myself, that this light temporary cloud which came over his reputation shall be interred with his bones, but his fame and the name he bore should live after him. That is what is to be understood by this vote of the Conference; not that he should be laughed at by little children, but that he should be honoured by generations of men and women yet to come.

What are the two schools as to the meaning of the proceedings against Bishop Andrew? One class holds, that these proceedings amount to a mere opinion and wish that he would, *durante impedimento*, suspend the exercise of the duties of the office of a bishop, taking into consideration local excitement, having regard to the recorded doctrines of this Church on this matter, having regard to the ancient and general course and practice of the Church touching the connexion of the episcopacy with slaveholding. This class, both at the North and South, to this day, hold these proceedings to be nothing more than an opinion, that *durante impedimento* he should retire from the duties of his office, but nevertheless referring it, in the most explicit terms, to his own judgment and conscience, whether he would do so or not. That opinion is now held by many at the South; and perhaps the Court will be astonished when I bring it to their knowledge, that this very bishop himself, together with his associate and compeer, Bishop Soule, construed these resolutions as referring it entirely to his own judgment and discretion, whether he would perform the duties of the office of bishop or not, leaving him as much a bishop as ever. Under that view of the meaning of that proceeding, his associates in the episcopacy actually did proceed to assign him the ordinary episcopal duty in the summer or autumn of that year.

Your Honours will find the proof of that in Book No. 1, p. 141, and Book No. 2, p. 86,—both documents, I believe, written by the very able and energetic Dr. Bascom, to whom reference has been made, and certainly written with great ability, and embodying in all its strength the *gravamen* of the complaints of the South. Thus we find that it is the opinion of prominent Southern gentlemen, that the entire action of the General Conference on this subject amounted to no more than a mere wish, founded upon an opinion, that he would abstain on account of a temporary impediment, from a discharge of the duties of the office of bishop—and not from the office of bishop—and that was referred so absolutely to his own judgment and discretion, that, upon their own responsibility, they persuaded him to go to work. If your Honours will be kind enough to look at Proofs No. 1, p. 104, you will find that a portion of the North always held the same construction. There you find the same writer of the same pretty powerful protest against this proceeding, which was read the other day by one of the clients of my learned friend, dealing with this explanation of the matter by the North. He controverts it; but recognises that this interpretation exists.

On the other hand, some regard this as a command. What sort of a command that may be regarded, when he who commands notifies to him, *uno et eodem flatu*, that he is expected to do exactly as he pleases, that no penalty is to be attached, in any form or shape, to his disregarding the command, I have not the organs to comprehend. I therefore respectfully submit it was nothing, at last, but a mere dispute about words between the two schools; and that it is nothing but a strong opinion, and an ardent, urgent wish, under the circumstances, by the Conference to the bishop, that he would yield to the necessities of the case temporarily, and suspend the exercise of the duties of his office, with the distinct notice, that in what work he should be employed was to be determined by his own decision and action, in relation to the previous action of this Conference in his case. That is to say: "Bishop Andrew, we have elected you to the office of bishop, and we maintain and reverence you there; we appreciate a certain temporary and local state of feeling in this country, which, in our judgment, makes it expedient that you should yield to it, and, for the present, retire from the duties of your office; nevertheless, you are bishop still; you can survey a wider plain than we, and therefore to your judgment and conscience we commit it at last, and if you think your duty requires it, go on without delay and without pause, in the performance of every one of your duties; we have not another word to add." For that vote they dissolve this union! One might very well exclaim, "*Tantæne animis cælestibus iræ!*"

I was upon the inquiry as to whether the General Conference had the power to pass such a vote as this. I do not intend to stand here and consume time in discussing that point, because if it is nothing more than the mere expression of a wish, of an opinion, and yet referring the matter entirely to the judgment and discussion of the incumbent, nobody will deny the constitutional competence of the General Conference to pass it. I made some preparation earlier in this case, when I was stronger and had anticipated a different line of argument, to show that the constitutional power existed; but I shall have so much to say on the constitutional powers of the Conference on the subject of dividing the Church, that for the present I would spare your Honours and spare myself. Enough for the present to say, that if this be interpreted, as I think the Court will interpret it, to be only an expression of a wish, of an opinion, no one can stand here to deny to the General Conference the right to pass such a vote. They have power generally to make rules and regulations for the government of the Church. The bishops are directly amenable to the General Conference, and is it such an impoverished body that it has not power to ask anybody to do something, telling him at the same time that he may or he may not do it, just as he pleases? It is not worth while to pursue the subject. I shall take that for granted, and not lose time on it, because the time of the Court is important, and my time, as I had proposed it to myself, presses me to other considerations. I take it that the constitutional power is undoubted.

The next question, then, is whether, although the constitutional power to pass such a vote as this is undoubted, there is here, under the forms of law, such an outrage upon the rights of the South, such a social injustice to the Methodists of that section, as to warrant the action which the South proceeded to take upon it. That is the result of the inquiry—the only one upon which I will further trouble the Court on this point. Heavily, very heavily, I submit the burden is upon the plaintiffs, to show that under the forms of law a real outrage has been practised upon the rights of the members of the Church, warranting *in foro conscientiæ* so transcendent and irrevocable a step as this. The burden of proof is upon the plaintiffs. I respectfully submit that they have entirely failed to meet it.

In considering that question, which I intend to do somewhat rapidly, and yet under two or three different aspects, I am willing to take the matter here, somewhat as it was taken by the very powerful Protest of the minority in that Conference at the time the Conference did the act. I am going now to raise and meet the question, whether, in the proceedings of the General Conference touching this case of Bishop Andrew, my clients were attempting to introduce any substantial innovation upon the course and practice of the Methodist Episcopal Church, touching the connexion of slaveholders with the episcopacy. That is the question I mean to put—and the question of blame or want of blame in relation to this extremely important part of this great transaction, I am willing, taking the thesis propounded by that Protest, to meet exactly under that aspect, which party was it that was attempting in that Conference to introduce a substantial innovation into the settled, ancient, and general course of the Methodist Episcopal Church, touching the matter of a bishop being the holder of slaves? I do not mean to admit, however, that even if the North should be declared to be innovators, it would afford a justification for the action of the plaintiffs on which I am here to observe. Still, I respectfully submit to your Honours, that if you should think these proceedings hasty, passionate, and irregular, the moral sentiments of men and the intrinsic justice in the case make it proper enough in inquiring for the first fault to ask for the innovator. I call for the innovator in the General Conference. Who was it, North or South, that day that was attempting to introduce any substantial innovation into the settled, recognised, and existing practice of that Church upon the subject of a bishop being the holder of slaves? I respectfully submit that the North were not the innovators. I mean that in expressing an opinion or a wish that a slaveholder should not be a bishop, that a bishop should not be the holder of slaves, they were doing nothing before God but simply applying to novel facts the recorded Discipline, and the ancient, recognised, and immemorial practice of that Church since it was a Church upon the subject of electing slaveholders to the office of bishop. I submit that what they did, they did timorously, delicately, under every embarrassment, and under every desire to consult every description of feeling. All they did, in its whole length and breadth, was to apply to novel facts the recorded Discipline and ancient practice of that Church upon the subject of the connexion of the episcopacy with slaveholding. Let us see if that be not so.

What was the subject of contention in the Conference of 1844 on that occasion? It was contended on the part of the South that a slaveholder might just as well be a bishop as any other man; and that there was nothing in the recorded Discipline of the Church, nothing in local opinion, nothing in the ancient course and practice of that body, that should operate even in point of expediency to prevent a slaveholder being a bishop, just as well as another man. On the part of the North, on the other hand, it was contended that having regard to a certain local opinion, to a great and overruling question of expediency, having regard to the established Discipline and settled practice of the Church, slaveholding should be considered a great practical difficulty. That was the contention between the parties at that time. I know it did not arise in that general and abstract form. I know the question raised there was, what should be done with a person elected to the office of bishop not holding slaves and afterwards becoming a slaveholder? This is the reason why the contention assumed such an embarrassing character. That is the true reason why such a passionate feeling was aroused. The South could not bear that it should be said a slaveholder should not be a bishop; and the North thought that under the circumstances of the case it ought to be said a slaveholder should not be a bishop. Who were the innovators on that contention on that day in that Church? As I said before, this is not a question of right or wrong, it is not a question of wise or unwise, it is not a question of freedom or slavery; but who innovated on the jural society as between the parties in that Church? Who stood on the old code? Who innovated on that code? That is the question to examine. I would therefore like to extricate and take it out of the scope of mere incidental and collateral considerations, take it away from the case of freedom or slavery, take it away from the case of fanaticism, and call it concomitancies; and to take it and try it as the jural rights of these parties in consolidating the Church, and through the Church evangelizing the nation, and keep it together.

The question was on their jural rights and jural duties, according to the law of this society, *lex societatis*. Who innovated that day? and who stood on the old practice of the society? By that let the defendants be tried. I apprehend—I do not know what causes there may be underneath, I do not know how to explain the state of feeling on the part of the South—if I read correctly the nature of the ties, the *fœdera* into which the parties relative entered, that there never was a plainer question presented to a Court.

The first great fact is this: from the organization of this Church to that hour no slaveholder had been a bishop. During a period of sixty years, when there had been nine bishops chosen, no slaveholder had ever been chosen bishop. Bishop Andrew was nominated by the South, and elected because he was not a slaveholder. No slaveholder had ever been elected a bishop in the Methodist Church. And why not? The question is whether we are innovators because we object to a slaveholder wearing the mitre. Why had not a slaveholder ever been elected a bishop? Clearly because it was the sense of the Conferences, it was the recorded practice and sense of the Church; it had been notified to the North, notified to the South, constitutionally promulgated; it was the fundamental law of the Church, that a bishop was to be free from connexion with slavery. Was it because of a narrow emulation with the South? We gave them six out of nine, as we always do. It was not the honours that we sought. We gave them six bishops out of nine, and all we stipulated was that they should be a particular kind of bishops. And what complaint can there be to the vote of 1844, declaring the sense of the Conference, that the Church forbade them doing anything calculated to destroy the itinerant superintendency, and that a bishop could not hold slaves, and that a slaveholder could not be a bishop, when the sense of that document had been published and republished, through the unequivocal intimations of nine elections and sixty years? Are we then innovators? Did we innovate on that day?

There are three answers to this, and I proceed now very briefly to examine the three answers that can be made to it. The first is, that this very refusal theretofore to elect a slaveholder to the office of bishop was a social injustice, and therefore was more honoured in the breach than in the observance. The Protest and the proceedings at Louisville say it is a social injustice. The second answer is, that the case of a bishop elected because he did not hold slaves, and afterwards becoming the holder of slaves, is not within the principle of originally electing nobody not free from slavery. The third and principal answer is, that in point of fact this very question of a bishop elected because he did not hold slaves, was a question that had been settled by a compromise of the parties as early as 1804. I will notice these arguments briefly, and in their order.

In the first place, was there anything like a social injustice in the practice of the Church to which I have adverted—their never having elected a slaveholder, during such a long period, to the office of bishop, and having adopted and carried into effect the rule that a slaveholder should not be elected to the office of bishop? I was pausing to turn to a passage in the Protest of the Southern delegates, and in the proceedings of the Louisville Convention, in which I find that while this practice of never electing a slaveholder to the office of bishop is recognised as a matter-of-fact, it is still regarded as being in itself a social injustice. I have, however, no occasion to turn to these passages. The Court may remember hearing them read. The question whether this has properly been termed a social injustice, I submit that nothing is so unfounded. By a social injustice, I mean an injustice *ad societatem*, any injustice which is a violation of the jural right of the society, of the Church member. So far from its having been a long social injustice never to have elected for sixty years a slaveholder to the office of bishop, it was nothing in the world but the carrying out by the General Conference, into its own acts, that which it had laid down in the Discipline to be the general rule for the whole Church, in the election of every one of the subordinate officers.

The general rule of the Methodist Church, from the time it was instituted to that hour, was, that slaveholders ought not to hold office in the Church. Therefore, I say, this is not a social injustice, because it is nothing in the world but carrying into effect, in this case, by the Conference itself, that which it had prescribed in its Discipline, and promulgated to the world, from its institution as a Church, as a general rule of election to every Methodist office. This general rule was always enforced, with a single exception of a limited local character, upon which I shall have something to say in a few moments. Still the general rule was, that a slaveholder ought not to bear office in the Church. Such had been the general rule since 1784. This general rule had been re-enacted in 1796, in 1800, in 1804, in 1812, in 1816, over, and over, and over again. The general rule of the Church, as prescribed by the general lawgiver of the Church—the General Conference—was, that slaveholders were not eligible, with a single limited and local exception. This law of the Church had been cotemporaneous with its origin. It had been promulgated over and over again. Every man and woman in the Methodist Church from the South had entered the Church with a perfect knowledge of the fact that this was its fundamental and general law of election. Therefore, for the General Conference, in any one instance, from 1784 down to this instant, to have elected a slaveholder to the office of bishop, would have been to violate in its own action what it had unweariedly and studiously propounded and reiterated as a rule of action for every Methodist elective body from the birth of the Church down to that day. If it is a social injustice for a corporation to execute its own fundamental law, then by analogy this is a social injustice. Really, however, it is just as much an abuse of terms to complain of it as a social injustice on the part of the South, as it would be for a man to buy the stock of a railroad corporation, and then complain because they would not go into the manufacture of cotton; or for a young man to pass himself through one of the colleges in the university of Cambridge, England, and at the end complain because, being a Protestant dissenter—say a Presbyterian—he could not get a scholarship. *In hæc fœdera venisti*, is the answer; you have entered the Church and have been its strength and its ornament—would to God you would again contribute to her glory—you have been in it for sixty years, knowing perfectly well that, wise or unwise, liberal or illiberal, ill-calculated or well-calculated to maintain the Church in the South, this was its rule in relation to slavery; you knew it was a rule of the Methodist Church that slaveholders ought not to hold office in the Church; and now for you to turn round and say it is a "social injustice"—I will leave it to the Court to say whether it is well warranted in point of justice between these parties.

I had intended to read to your Honours, from the Proofs, to show the legislative action of this Church on the subject of slavery. But the proofs are all before the Court, and I will not trouble the Bench with what might be very wearisome. I have this to say, however: it is the recorded consistent opinion of the Church, from 1784 to 1844, as the general law of election, that slaveholders ought not to have office in the Church, with one exception, of which I shall have a great deal to say in a moment. Your Honours will find that everywhere in the evidence. You will find it particularly in the address of the bishops to the Conference of 1840, and in the report drawn up by Mr. Bascom on the Westmoreland petition. It is there recognised as the general law of the Church upon the subject of slaveholders' eligibility to office in the Church. I therefore feel that I am well warranted in putting that as the general rule, recognising particularly the exception of which they speak, and pledging myself to discuss that at even greater length than even the learned counsel on the other side would wish me to discuss it.

I submit, then, so far as the substance of the contention in 1844 goes; so far as the contention on the part of the North, that there were grave, practical objections to the connexion of slaveholding with the episcopacy, is concerned, the North were no innovators at all. I submit they were standing on the old practice of the Church, and only executing a recorded act, communicated to the South, and under which everybody from the South had joined the Church. So then there was no social injustice in our having declined and refused to elect a slaveholder to the office of bishop from the birth of the Church.

The next question, and it is briefly disposed of, is whether in expressing the opinion in the case of Bishop Andrew, which is the subject of consideration—that is to say, the opinion that a person who was elected because he did not hold slaves, becoming a slaveholder afterwards ought not any longer *durante impedimento* to exercise the duties of the office of bishop—they were guilty of any innovation. Undoubtedly this was the case of the application of old principles to new facts. That, certainly, made a slight degree of embarrassment. I agree that the case had never arisen before of a person elected as not being a slaveholder, becoming afterwards the holder of slaves. That case had never arisen before, and I might even introduce it as the first count in my indictment of innovation against the South, that on this occasion they would not allow Bishop Andrew to resign, and thus relieve the embarrassment of the Conference. Before I have done, I shall point to the proof of it on the record. I put this as a proof of innovation on the part of the South, that they thus bring before the Conference, and press upon the Conference, and stood before the Conference upon the perilous innovation of the connexion of the episcopacy with the holding of slaves. The question is, whether on that occasion the North met these new facts with old principles or new principles. I submit that the Church could not, with any consistency whatever, with its settled practice of more than half a century, and with the principles on which that practice had been established, have done anything but what it did, touching this new phase of the connexion of the mitre with the holding of slaves. What were the great principles which lay at the bottom of that practice, at the bottom of the recorded discipline of the Church? I understand them to be: first, that by refusing the bishopric to a slaveholder, the evil of slavery is the more likely to be extirpated, which all the way down in the Discipline is one of the great moral efforts which this Church proposes to itself. The other reason was, that in consequence of excited local opinions the office of a bishop was rendered less universally useful than it would otherwise be. It is, as I understand, on these two general principles that the practice was adopted of never electing a slaveholder to the episcopal office. This never was made much of a point in the Conference; and I will therefore only say in general, that it is perfectly plain if, under such principles as these, it had become the judicial law of the society, promulgated and known as such, that the candidate could not hold slaves, it was senseless and absurd to suppose the incumbent could hold slaves. If under this practice ordinary or less brilliant abilities were sometimes elected to the office of bishop, because they were adorned by this great qualification, could it be understood by anybody that the successful candidate, the moment he got the office, could divest himself of the very qualification on account of which he was chosen? I submit, therefore, without taking further time on the point, that this was only an application of settled principles to novel facts; and, indeed, as I have said, that was not much the subject of contention in the Conference.

I come now, however, and I have to solicit the attention of the Court to it for a very few moments, to the main ground upon which the South in the Conference did, and here do contend that the proceedings in the case of Bishop Andrew were an injustice to them as members of the Church; and I submit that if they make out in point of legal interpretation one of the rules in the Discipline—a point upon which I am now about to comment—as inoperative, then they fix on the North the charge of innovation to that extent. If they fail to make that out, then they fail on that charge in its full length and breadth. That ground is this: the Court must have noticed the other day, when the Protest was read in its hearing, that the whole burden of it, from beginning to end, was exactly and merely this—that it was too late for the North, in 1844, to contend that a person elected to the office of bishop because he did not hold slaves, afterwards becoming the holder of slaves, should not hold office, because, by a vote passed in 1800, and qualified or interpreted in 1804 or 1812, the Church had, by a compromise, provided for that very case. That is the ground taken in the Protest. It is not argued with the ability which I am sure such a pen as that of the writers of the Protest could have argued it, if they had appreciated as I appreciate the difficulties attending that proposition on the part of the South. But this is taken for granted and made the foundation of a powerful, nay, upon its principles, an irresistible appeal to the conscience and reason of the Northren members of that Conference; and the ground there taken was, that a certain rule in this Discipline, which says every travelling preacher who becomes a slaveholder, shall be therefore suspended from his office, provided he live in a State in which emancipation is practicable, means bishops as well as travelling preachers; and, therefore, that the *casus* is exactly provided for. If that be so, I admit that the North were innovators on that day; for though they did not turn Bishop Andrew out of the office of bishop, although they did not suspend him from the office of bishop, although they only went so far as to express a wish that he should temporarily desist, yet if that case had been provided for beforehand, if the rule to which I have referred, by any just interpretation of it, cover the bishop as well as the travelling preacher, the North were wrong and the South were right, to the extent of a formal innovation—not that it would justify these transcendent consequences. On that point I respectfully meet the able argument of the opening counsel for the plaintiff. On that point I am respectfully, in advance, to endeavour to encounter briefly the argument of the counsel, who is to close on the part of the plaintiff. I submit that if a man's life stood in it, and not merely the life of the Church, and through that, perhaps, the life of a more dear and comprehensive Union, it is perfectly clear as a proposition of interpretation that the South is totally in the wrong, and that this Protest was ill calculated, as it was read, and always must be read by whoever reads it, to make an impression as it proceeds upon a mere assumption without foundation.

Let us see now that we understand exactly what was adopted in Bishop Andrew's case. It turns on the meaning of this provision, (p. 22 of Proofs No. 1,)—

"When any travelling preacher becomes an owner of a slave or slaves, by any means, he shall forfeit his ministerial character in our Church, unless he execute, if it be practicable, a legal emancipation of such slaves, conformably to the laws of the State in which he lives."

The South contended that "any travelling preacher," in the clause, includes bishops. The North contended that it does not include bishops at all, but, on the contrary, by the force of the terms, by force of the language, and on grand reasons discriminating in the practice of that Church between the travelling preacher and the bishop, this indulgence did not extend to the case of a bishop, and was not intended to embrace it; and therefore whenever the *casus* did arise of a bishop becoming the owner of slaves *ex post facto*, in whatever State he lived, it was to be judged of only by the sense, and judgment, and conscience of the Conference itself. The question then is, whether the term "travelling preacher" in this law of 1800, upon the evidence before the Court, appears judicially to embrace the case of a bishop. I deny that there is a solitary particle of evidence for it. How is this to be tried? And by what kind of evidence is it to be established? The Court will notice, that in the Protest to which I have occasionally made references, it is stated over and over again, as in some measure a matter of fact within the knowledge of the writer, and the knowledge and belief of a portion of the protesting minority, that that law of 1800, as it stands written, had come to be, in 1808 or 1816, construed to embrace the case of a bishop. There are many passages in that document wherein this is assumed as matter of fact. The difficulty of that argument is, that it is met on the other side by the most categorical and comprehensive denial of the fact. I will now read from the Reply of the majority of the Conference, so much as to show the Court that we cannot rely for the interpretation of this article, in the least degree, upon the counter assertions as to the matter of fact. If your Honours will look at pp. 116, 117, you will see how flatly and decisively, as a matter of fact and memory, this assertion of the Protest is contradicted:—

"If additional proof of the truth of this proposition were needed, it might be adduced in the fact, that the section which the Protest represents to have been settled in 1804, was not only altered at the General Conference or Convention of 1808, but also at the delegated General Conferences of 1812, 1816, 1820, and 1824. And although the Protest speaks of it as 'usually known' by the name of 'the Compromise Act,' the greater part of this General Conference have never heard either that appellation or that character ascribed to it until the present occasion."

I will not read more; but if the Court will examine both documents, the Protest and the Reply, they will find, that while the protestants assert that this was really settled as a matter of fact, and allege it within their knowledge to have been settled as a matter of compromise, all that source of light is withdrawn by the equally solemn asseveration to the contrary. We are therefore brought back to a mere question of interpretation. That question is, whether the term "travelling preacher," in the rule of 1800, upon the lights before this Court, includes a bishop or not. Does that mean anything but travelling preachers proper?

The first difficulty in the point of interpretation is, that this rule does not say anything about bishop. It is, "when any travelling preacher," &c. It says nothing about bishops *eo nomine.* It does not say, "when any travelling preacher or bishop;" it says nothing about bishops. Proceeding to investigate the problem of interpretation, the first great fact which stares us in the face is, that by the settled *usus loquendi* of this Church, we know that, in its Discipline, "travelling preachers" is a term that does not include bishops. Bishops are not included in the rule, in terms; and by the *usus loquendi* of this Church, which construes its language, we know that "travelling preacher" does not mean a bishop. To make that clear, let me turn your Honours to page 29 of Proofs No. 1, to arrive at the meaning of the term "travelling preachers," in the written language of this Church :—

"1. The annual allowance of the married travelling, supernumerary, and superannuated preachers, *and the bishops*, shall be $200, and their travelling expenses.
"2. The annual allowance of the unmarried travelling, supernumerary, and superannuated preachers *and bishops*, shall be $100, and their travelling expenses.
"3. Each child of a travelling preacher *or bishop* shall be allowed $16 annually, &c.
"4. The annual allowance of the widows of travelling, superannuated, worn-out, and supernumerary preachers, *and the bishops*, shall be $100.
"5. The orphans of travelling, supernumerary, and worn-out preachers, *and the bishops*, shall be allowed by the annual conferences the same sums respectively which are allowed to the children of living preachers."

So then, by the *usus loquendi* of this Church, in its Discipline, there is a difference between travelling preachers and bishops—travelling preachers do not mean bishops. There it is *prima facie.* They have not a tittle of evidence that the word "bishop," not occurring in the rule, the law of speech of the Church does not exclude bishops.

Then I inquire how they can be included, and I look in vain for a scintilla of proof to support the position of these Southern gentlemen. They say this was known to "all mankind," and yet three-fourths of all mankind reply that they never heard of it. That mode of proof is excluded; dogmatism is excluded; and secession is excluded; and these parties are brought back to the determination of this great question to their jural rights, to the meaning of the record; the meaning of the record is to be settled by a settled law of interpretation, and *prima facie* that law of interpretation is entirely against them.

I present now a third difficulty on the point of the interpretation of this clause, to show that the words here are to be taken as they are elsewhere taken in the Discipline. I beg your Honours to take notice of one thing, which, I think, has escaped the notice of the reverend disputants on both sides. I am instructed, that in this clause of the Discipline, the lawgiver speaking is the General Conference, and that lawgiver is speaking to the annual conferences for their guidance and direction. He is not speaking to himself, and for himself, but to them, and for them. Of course, as the annual conferences, to whom he is laying down the law, have nothing in the world to do with bishops, he is not laying down any law as to the choice of bishops, but he is laying down the law to them for the election of the subordinate officers which the system of the Church commits to their direction. If I am right in my position, that the General Conference is here speaking in the capacity of a lawgiver to the annual conferences, and not proclaiming a mere dogma or rule for its own guidance, nothing in the world is more clear, than that they would not be guilty of the absurdity of prescribing a rule of election to the annual conferences, that should have application to an officer whom the annual conferences did not choose, and with whom they had nothing to do. I accordingly propound it and undertake to verify it, and I say the fact will turn out to be, that this whole series of legislation, from 1792 to 1844, was nothing but a series of prescripts sent out by the superintending governor for the direction of the inferior annual bodies. The superintending body would of course do this in advance. Why should the General Conference lay down a law for its own action? It met every four years. They knew when they came to meet, at the expiration of the next Olympiad, as it has been happily called, they would elect a bishop under the general law. Therefore there was no need of putting a rule for their own guidance on the record. They knew also, that whatever rule they might put on the record, could be changed the moment they came to choose. Therefore, I say, it was needless and useless for them to lay down a general rule for their own action. On the contrary, as they met every four years, and various annual conferences were to be held during these four years, and as it was needful that, during that whole period, the forecast of the General Conference should, by its law, be extended in advance over them, they made the law. And the Court will see, by looking a little at the language of one or two of these provisions, how exactly they all take the language of a prescript by the General Conferences to the annual conferences. To show this, I will read from p. 21 of Proofs No. 1:—

"Quest. What regulations shall be made for the extirpation of the crying evil of African slavery?

"Ans. 1. We declare that we are more than ever convinced of the great evil of the African slavery which still exists in these United States, and do most earnestly recommend to the yearly conferences, quarterly meetings, and to those who have the oversight of districts and circuits, to be exceedingly cautious what persons they admit to official stations in our Church; and in the case of future admission to official stations, to require such security of those who hold slaves, for the emancipation of them, immediately or gradually, as the laws of the States respectively, and the circumstances of the case will admit; and we do fully authorize all the yearly conferences to make whatever regulations they judge proper, in the present case, respecting the admission of persons to official stations in our Church."

Again, on p. 22, you find that the annual conferences were directed to draw up addresses to the legislatures of the States for the gradual emancipation of slaves; and on the next page that proper committees should be appointed by the annual conferences for conducting business, and so on. Then I submit that this is in the form of a direction to the annual conferences, which have nothing at all to do with the bishops, not to press beyond its strength anything on the learning of this Bench.

I submit in the next place that a very familiar rule of interpretation at common law, the rule as it is commonly called of denying legislation, *et ad ea quæ frequentius accidunt jura adaptantur*, applies directly to the case before the Court That rule, as stated in Dwarris, p. 730, is this: that where the words of the law imply that they may be satisfied by applying them to the common case, they shall not be extended by interpretation to the rarer case. The words "travelling preachers" may be satisfied by the ordinary and common case, and therefore they ought not to be extended to the rarer case. The common case in this instance, in the contemplation of the lawgiver, was the ordinary travelling preachers; they are elected many times by the annual conferences. The common case, then, was the election of the travelling preachers by the annual conferences. The rarest case was the election of bishops by the General Conference, which met once in four years. Could they adopt this rule to apply to them in this rare case when they might change it, or the progress of time might change, like a passing cloud, before the time of administering it came?

Leaving that point, I have to entreat the attention of the Court to another consideration of very great and decisive urgency in my mind; and that is, that there are reasons of a most palpable and weighty character why a distinction should have been made in 1800 and 1804, and ever since in the Church, between the travelling preacher proper and the bishop, as to allowing a dispensation to one or the other from the consequences of holding slaves. I mean to say that so different are the official life and official duties of a travelling preacher proper, from those of a bishop proper, that the former might very well be allowed an indulgence, which the latter could not be allowed: and therefore this legislation, so far as it is an element of dispensation or injustice, might very well apply to the travelling preacher, and by no means to the bishop proper. In order to enable you to appreciate that argument, I ought perhaps to say in advance, that this legislation, even so far as travelling preachers are concerned, is legislation in extirpation of slavery; and it therefore proceeds by the establishment of the general rule that slaveholding disqualifies. That is the general rule on the face of the written Discipline. A particular exception is allowed under special circumstances. Disqualification is the rule, dispensation the exception; disqualification the rule, indulgence the exception; disqualification is the general rule, according to the express terms of the Discipline, in the case of every officer below the grade of bishop; and disqualification was the general rule in the case of a bishop, not by the express terms of the Discipline, but by the universal action of the Church. Therefore, my rule of interpretation is, that in inquiring whether or not "travelling preachers" for the purpose of indulgence, embraces bishops, your Honours will give the utmost expansion and energy to the general rule, and compress the exception within the narrowest possible limits. That is a universal and familiar rule of interpretation.

I submit now, that there are two reasons at once obvious and recognised, and entirely decisive, why this Court may perfectly well say, that the General Conference of 1800 should have been willing and felt obliged to extend an indulgence to the travelling preacher, which it could not extend to a bishop, but at the hazard of all a bishop is created to do. In the first place, there were reasons why a travelling preacher should be indulged, which did not apply to a bishop. The home of a Methodist clergyman is his assigned field of labour. The home of every Methodist preacher under the degree of a bishop is in his assigned field of labour, and his assigned field of labour is commonly a large circuit, but narrow, compared with the imperial sweep over which the episcopal duties carry the bishop. There the travelling preacher must live, and there he must labour; and therefore, if he has slaves and cannot emancipate them there, it is safe and proper that he should labour without emancipating them, or else he cannot labour at all. But on the other hand, the field of a bishop's labour in the Methodist Church, is our universal united America. His field of labour, under the system of this Church, is the whole of America, and therefore he may live anywhere in America. I am submitting to your Honours not a harangue and declamation on the subject of the episcopacy, but I hope and trust a sound interpretative argument. Therefore, I say, the General Conferences of 1800 and 1816 might very well have supposed that a bishop would be willing to live anywhere, throughout his vast and expanding diocese, that he would be willing and only too happy to be allowed to live where he could best discharge the duties of that great office, where he could best depurate, if I may so express myself, and unclothe himself of all influence tending in the least degree to mar the whole measure of his usefulness, where he could best go and put on a virtue that should approve itself to more than a local standard, where he could best attend to the whole beauty and protection of that holiness which should best recommend him to the universal sentiments and scruples of the whole Methodist Episcopal Church. Why, then, might not the General Conference have very well drawn a line of distinction on this ground between him and the travelling preacher? Why might they not very well have deemed, that in taking upon himself the discharge of the new office he would relieve himself of all embarrassments? Why might they not have done him the honour, in advance, of supposing that in becoming a bishop he would prefer to stand on the general rule, instead of sheltering himself under a narrow dispensation? Why might they not have presumed on the part of a bishop, as discriminated from the narrower and humbler labours of the travelling preacher, that for the sake of holding such an office as that, for the sake of being a successor of the Asburys and the Wesleys; for the sake of being a successor of those older, and better, and more famous men; for the sake of the privilege under Almighty God of bearing the glad tidings, the venerable presence and admonitions, and authoritative instructions, and satisfying consolations of this Church everywhere, from North to South, and from East to West, from Britain to Gaul, from Marseilles to Rome, from Rome to Antioch, from Antioch to Jerusalem,—that for the sake of these, he would be only too glad, I will not say to forego the luxury of slaveholding, for that might involve a sarcasm, which I do not mean, but, to break away from such an impediment as slaveholding, that he would choose rather to proceed instantly to place himself where he might soonest and most effectually rid himself of all participation in what would make him objectionable to any portion of his flock; and that if he should prefer the other alternative, to continue to hold slaves, he should see no hardship in allowing the mitre to pass to another brow? Can any man, on this question of interpretation, stand here and tell me, that this Methodist Episcopal Church in 1800 and 1816 might not, on that exact discrimination, have said, "The travelling preacher needs a dispensation, and shall have it; but the bishop will never ask for it, and shall not have it." On that ground alone, I say, there might be a necessity for this distinction.

But there is one other reason connected with this office—and when I state it I shall leave this branch of the argument—and that is, that the life and duties of a bishop differ altogether, and in so great a degree from those of the travelling preacher, as really to afford a necessity for a different standard and example. I suppose that to the usefulness of a local or travelling preacher in the South, slaveholding constitutes no objection. It probably affords no drawback at all. On the other hand, this Court knows perfectly well, this whole Church and this country know perfectly well, that to the utility of a bishop, slaveholding constitutes an objection of the gravest and most practical, not to say decisive, character. This Court knows perfectly well that over large tracts and fields of his episcopal journey, such a bishop is but half a bishop. Your Honours know perfectly well that the itinerant superintendency of the bishop is fundamental in the practical polity of Methodism. Methodism may give up almost everything, but it cannot give up that. Methodism may give up this tenet or that tenet, and become more Calvinistic or less Arminian. But she would cease to have a particle of Wesleyanism upon her front, in her life, in her services, and in her name, if she did not retain a superintendent episcopacy, who can carry the presence and counsels of that Church to the most extreme locality, however remote, however sectionalized by extremity of local opinion,—who can carry them everywhere, and be everywhere unblamed and unreproved of all men. That is of the very essence of Methodism. When this is dispensed with, everything is dispensed with. Instead of stopping to prove this, as I could prove it, I will content myself by referring your Honours to the address of the bishops in 1844. You will there see that I do not exaggerate the importance of this ornament of Methodism. It is of the essence of practical Methodism that the bishop may go, and shall go—he shall go on foot if necessary, he shall go barefooted if necessary, he shall take sackcloth, he shall take the cross, he shall not go figuratively by staying home and sending another; but the theory of the system, the demands of the system, the administration of the system, what it has achieved for the world, depend upon this:—

that the bishop shall go and be required to go everywhere personally, from time to time, from one extremity of his circuit to another. What then more inevitable than that this General Conference of the whole Church, that recognised from the beginning the right of the South to its proportion, and more than its proportion, should have settled it as a rule, that he from the South who would aspire to it, must bring a virtue that would approve itself to more than one side of the line—a virtue that did not need the apology of birth-place and residence—a virtue that should come directly as it were of Divine perfection and character, that should be winged, created, clothed to be welcome everywhere, by whatsoever things are lovely, by whatsoever things are honest, by whatsoever things are of good report in the sight of all men. That became perfectly indispensable. Therefore, to tell Northern members of such a Church as this that they ought to elect, that they are required as Methodists to elect a slaveholder to the office of bishop, or that, finding him to become such, they must still continue him there, is to tell them they must cease to be Methodists, to be Wesleyan Methodists, must dismiss themselves of an itinerant episcopacy; in other words, a change of discipline, a change of faith. While they had a recorded general rule that slaveholders should not bear office in that Church, and while they yielded with the sensibilities and common-sense of men to the necessities that required a particular exception, they never dreamed of an exception for an hour in the case of a bishop. I submit that the action in the case of Bishop Andrew, shows that the sense of the Conference of 1844 was that such an exception had never been dreamed of.

Then I submit that the great North was right, and the great South was wrong, that day, on the question of mere innovation. I say we did not innovate on the South in the slightest degree. Bishop Andrew was not tried, was not sentenced, was not removed, was not suspended from his office; advice was given him, and in giving that advice we kept entirely within the practice of the Church, as settled upon the record of the Church. Suppose this were doubtful. In the name of common-sense and reason, was a structure like this, reared as this was, built for the offices for which this was built—should a structure like this have been demolished; first, on a doubt on the meaning of our act; and, secondly, on a doubt of the meaning of one of the articles in the creed? The future historian of that Conference will, I think, say that the minority were in the fault in this business. I feel bound to go as far as to say that from what I have seen in the evidence, prodigious abilities were in that minority. I have seen some proofs of it from their pens. It contained men of the highest character for patriotism, and all the qualities we love,—all that we would take back to our embrace if we might. But I feel bound to hold them responsible for that day's work to a certain and just extent. I must say, that although there may be undercurrents of which we cannot judge, for we are here in a court of law and on the proofs, I believe if that minority had not, among themselves, under the exasperation of the vote in Bishop Andrew's case, resolved on this act, and had not thereupon thrown themselves into it with a passionate energy, if they had not thereupon prepared a circular, to which I may or may not have time to call the attention of the Court, to the South, not merely predicting but initiating that result, if they had not then gone home and delivered themselves over to that easy and yet so responsible a trade—so easy to such abilities, and yet so responsible for such a use of them—the manufacture of public opinion,—that opinion under which the annual conferences of the South convened, and the Louisville Convention assembled, and did the work,—I believe, before God, the Church would have stood fair as the moon, with all her banners today as in the day of her birth. Some local excitement there might have been here and there. There always is. And it is the very use of reason to deal with such local excitement. To what purpose these endowments of mind, and this force of character, but to struggle with such agitations as these! All our American warfare is nothing but a war of sense and nonsense—nothing else, in the world. Some local excitement there probably would have been; but if fifty of these gentlemen—twenty-five, ten, five—had remembered that they were patriots as well as Methodists, and Methodists as well as patriots—if they had remembered that this Church was originally created in 1784 for the nation of America—that it was designed by its founders that through and by an original unity, not merely embracing that territory, but expanding to the universal territory of the New World, through that organism Methodism was to work out its mission and enjoy its life—that the chief among its agents is the agency of itinerancy, and prominent in its itinerancy is the office of bishop, whereby a bishop may travel from shore to shore, and be everywhere a father among his children, a presence and power equally beloved and authoritative—if they could only have remembered that, in addition to all that was demanded of it as a Church, it was one of those beautiful instrumentalities—how rare and indispensable!—by which the larger union outside, which embosoms it, was to be kept together—if they could have gone back under these influences, and spoken their fervent feelings and weighty speech to the reason of the South, that Church, *Troja nunc stares*, would have stood this day. Such is my confident belief.

I have been looking over the proceedings of the Southern annual conferences as put in evidence in the case. I was about referring to some beautiful passages from the proceedings of the conferences in Kentucky, Missouri, Arkansas, and—the farther the better—Texas, which still breathe a longing, lingering love of the union, and which manifest the most strong and reiterated expression that they will not separate if they can by possibility avoid it; thus showing that they could not tear themselves from the warm precincts of the cheerful day. They waited for the assembling of the wise men of the Convention of Louisville, and waited for nothing but to hope they would consider that there should be no necessity for separation. The journals of our Conference of 1848 show you that nearer 3,000 than 2,000 have come back, and asked permission to be taken again into the old fold of their fathers' and mothers' baptism. I say such Methodists as these might have been kept; and heavy, heavy is the responsibility which will allow such delicious and priceless affections as these to run to waste, and water but the desert. Still heavier is the responsibility of him who puts out that Promethean fire which no hand may rekindle.

Now, what was done? Did the minority of the South anywhere put on the record of that Conference of 1844 their opinion, that what we had done ought to dissolve the Church in matter of conscience and political ethics? Nothing like it; but they put on the records merely a declaration that what had been done must produce a certain state of things at the South, which would render their continuance in the Church impracticable. It is a very striking fact that they did not place on the records a deliberate declaration of their own opinion, that what the General Conference had done in matter of law and matter of conscience, made it proper and fit for them to dissolve the union of the Church. They told the General Conference that in consequence of its action a certain state of things would be produced at the South—that the laity of the South would be aroused, and that when they went home, if they found it impossible to rule the roused Methodism of the South, they would have to choose between ties to them and ties to us. Thereupon the General Conference said, that if such a *casus* as that should arise, they would do nothing to throw any impediment in the way. I have made inquiry, and I am satisfied that no member of that Conference—certainly, not a great majority of them—had any more idea that they were voting for a division of the Church, than that they were voting for a division of the State.

But they verily believed tnat their ready manifestation of a willingness to help their Southern friends—if when they got home they found such an excited state of feeling, would help to maintain the connexion—that this would operate in some measure as oil on the troubled waters, and thus anticipate, and prevent in some measure, the catastrophe which had arisen. They adopted what has been called the Plan of Separation, not as a measure of division but as a preventative. I do not think this quite relieved the minority from all responsibleness in that behalf. It was still their duty to have endeavoured to prevent a state of feeling which in the Conference they undoubtedly seemed to fear, and for their opinion we had great respect. Their counsels guided. I admire their abilities, and appreciate their patriotism, and love them well enough, with all my heart, to wish them back again in the same Church with my clients, and I do not know that I could breathe them a better wish. As to the act itself, if I may not call it, in the language of Mr. Burke, "the fond election of evil," was it not, in the language of the same great man, "the unforced choice of evil?" I escape with great pleasure from matter connected but remotely with the merits of the case, and come to those immediate merits.

The case actually stated in the bill is very simple and very clear. The learned counsel who opened, states or intimates in his argument another case totally distinct from that stated in the bill, as I understand it, which creates some confusion in my own mind. Before I raise the real question which I wish to present to the Court, I would seek for myself a clear idea of the equity on which the plaintiffs claim. Looking, then, to the bill, the case put is exactly that a body of persons and of annual conferences, heretofore members of the Methodist Episcopal Church, have, by their own act or concurrence, and volition, under a certain Plan of Separation, separated themselves from that Church, and formed themselves into another totally distinct and independent Church. The case stated in the bill, in other words, is, that the Methodist Episcopal Church has been divided in twain by a geographical line, and that they have attached themselves voluntarily to the Church on the Southern side of the line, and that this has taken place under such circumstances that they still remain entitled to their share of the original fund. This case thus stated in our general way is a perfectly intelligible one. It is a case of voluntary separation. It raises the mere question of the effect of such separation on the rights of the separatists to the original common property. But your Honours will, perhaps, have observed that, in the course of his argument, my learned brother perpetually kept introducing another case, not stated in this bill, and not before the Court, to derive from that case some aid to the one stated and argued. He said there were widows and orphans who were to lose their rights on the doctrines of this defence, without any act of their own, and thereupon he pressed us to know if we would put such a class of non-combatants as these to the scalping-knife and the tomahawk, whatever we might be inclined to do with the great body of the plaintiffs whom we have to encounter. In regard to that, I have to say, in the first place, that no case is before this Court but that of voluntary separatists, or those whom other volunteers have separated from the Church. If there are widows and orphans on the Southern side of this line, who have not voluntarily separated from the Methodist Episcopal Church, or who have not been carried away from that Church by the acts of other persons, themselves volunteers, with whom they are ecclesiastically connected, then the defence which we make to the plaintiffs' bill excepts such a case—and no such case is stated in this bill, or prepared in argument for the consideration of this Court. This bill is for voluntary separatists, not for those who have not participated in the act of separation; and therefore the defence we here make has no application to the class of people for whose title to the sympathies, not to say the justice, of this Court, my learned brother seemed desirous to borrow some kind of advantage. I hardly know that I need say anything as to that limited and anomalous description of persons further than this.

If the Court will look into the journals of the General Conference of 1848, to the action of that Conference upon petitions of thousands from the South who have sought to return to the body of the Church, they will see that the doctrine which we have there declared on record is, that everybody who has not withdrawn, or who has not been expelled, is still a member of this Church. Therefore, if it be true of these widows and orphans, or any of them, that they have not acted at all, they still remain, for aught I know, within the pale of the Church; and we should be but too happy, so far as they are concerned, to apply the fund to them. But their case is not stated on the record, it is not presented in the bill, it is not argued substantially by counsel. To their case our defence has no application whatever. I object, therefore, to my learned friend drawing to his banner, and bringing to his aid such a description of parties as these. He will give us leave to say, that it is hardly fair, although it is very skilful warfare in him to do so, to come to us at the head of some 500,000 Southern combatants, less or more; and when we turn round to fire upon them, to say, "Take care; you will kill some widow or some orphan, and these widows and orphans are no combatants, no marks for you." Our answer to that is, that with that class of parties we have no encounter, and if his clients would avail themselves of the immunities of orphans, they had better begin by clothing themselves with the innocence of orphans. It is with the voluntary separatists of the bill alone that we deal.

Turning then to the case, as it is exactly stated, and taking it under its most formidable aspect, that is to say, of an income for these beneficiaries, which is, perhaps, the most formidable and most plausible aspect in which the learned counsel presents the case,—and by preachers, I mean the limited description of preachers to whom the fund is directed,—our answer is, that they have no claim, because they have lost by their own act the one fundamental and indispensable qualification of continuing membership in the Methodist Episcopal Church. To maintain this, we shall submit, that the acts of the plaintiffs worked a simple secession from the Church, without lawful authority, terminating their own membership, and yet leaving the identity of the Church altogether unaffected. If so, we say, it can scarcely be denied that they have lost the right in losing the qualification. To open our general answer to the bill a little more broadly, if we should suppose that the plaintiffs had succeeded in establishing the position that they left the Church and terminated membership, which was the qualification under which they held the title, by lawful authority, leaving the original Church, in fact, in its associated identity, still we submit that they have not carried with them a particle of right to any portion of this fund, principal or interest; because, on such secession and termination of membership as this, it is a universal proposition of law, as we understand it, that the seceder takes nothing, unless at the time of secession, or before, or afterwards, the act is attended and qualified by a grant of property from a body competent to make such a grant. In this case we say, that even if the plaintiffs have left the Church under the sanction of competent ecclesiastical authority, they have no such grant of authority: 1st. Because the General Conference had no power to make it; 2d. Because it did not assume the power to make it, if it had it; and 3dly. Because both the General and annual conferences together, could not take it away from the uses to which it was originally devoted; the travelling supernumerary and superannuated preachers of the Methodist Episcopal Church remaining members in it.

It will be convenient for me however, instead of now adverting to the fund, to advance at once to the proposition that the plaintiffs' act in leaving the Church was a simple, bold, and unauthorized act of secession, unauthorized by any ecclesiastical authority whatever; and, therefore, according to the universal law, as we apprehend it, the right of property terminated by the act of secession.

We say, then, in the first place, that the proceedings of the plaintiffs were a simple, unauthorized secession, and that they leave the identity of the old Church entirely unaffected. I suppose it will be hardly controverted on the part of the plaintiffs, certainly it is entirely and perfectly clear, that independently of the proceedings of the General Conference of 1844, the act of the plaintiffs, and of everybody who participated in the proceedings of the Louisville Convention, would be a simple and unauthorized secession from the Methodist Church. *Prima facie*, I mean to say, that unless they shall be qualified by the action of the General Conference, called the Plan of Separation, the proceedings of the plaintiffs, and those with whom they are associated and act, work a simple and mere secession from the Church. If your Honours will glance at the resolutions of that Louisville Convention, as they are stated in the plaintiffs' bill, p. 6, fol. 20, you will find that they in terms declare, and then proceed to achieve a separation from the Methodist Episcopal Church. They in terms proceed to renounce the jurisdiction of the General Conference in all its terms, and in all its forms, and to impede the organism through which that jurisdiction could be exerted. They then proceed to constitute the portion of the Church which acts in and through them into a separate and distinct ecclesiastical association and organization, for whose government, and faith, and discipline, and indefinite existence, they go on to make complete and independent provisions. Now, of course, the effect of all this—unqualified, as I have said, by the act of the General Conference, to the influence of which I shall have occasion to proceed in a moment—is secession and nothing else. In its effect, it is exactly as if, instead of five hundred thousand persons, five persons had turned from Methodism to Presbyterianism or Congregationalism, and had gone off by themselves from the body. I take it to be altogether too clear to discuss, that the number of those who go, their continuing Methodism, their simultaneous organization of themselves into a Methodist Episcopal Church, the farewell words of kindness with which they take their leave, and the protestations which we find scattered over the proceedings of the Louisville Convention, to the effect that they do not intend to separate or secede, do not control the matter in the slightest degree. Actions, here as elsewhere, overrule words; and no protestations, and no declaration of the purity of their course can possibly extricate their case from the influence of a conclusive presumption of law, *prima facie*, unless they can qualify it and transform it by resorting to the Plan of Separation. They have deserted the Church in the boldest possible form and most intense extent. I may perhaps anticipate, though not in the immediate course of my intended discussion at this time, so far as to say, that I understand it to be perfectly clear, according to the doctrine universally accepted on this subject, that a simple secession, such as this would be but for the vote and plan of the General Conference, is perfectly futile to claim the property asserted in this bill, however that property may be holden,—whether it belonged to the society in the aggregate, or was held by certain of its members in trust as a charitable use for certain other members. I understand it to be universally holden by the jurisprudence of all civilization, that such a secession as this would be, upon that hypothesis, secession unauthorized by ecclesiastical property, and forfeits the title as a matter of course. Indeed, I suppose it is just as clear—it is one of the points which we have presented to the Court this morning on our brief—that, even if the secession were completely authorized by competent ecclesiastical authority, but leaving the old organism in its local identity, it works the very same consequences on the title. I suppose it entirely true that if a religious association, incorporated or unincorporated, holds a fund by any title belonging to the society in the aggregate, or held by a part in trust for the rest, and thereupon a secession takes place by their consent, the seceder carries no interest in the fund. I understand that to be universally true of all incorporated or unincorporated associations. This is a common case, and we have referred the Court to many cases of it. In New-England, if a portion of a city or town is set off into a separate town, it does not carry with it any portion of the funds of the old corporation without a special agreement to that effect. There was a strong illustration of it in a case reported in the 16th of Massachusetts Reports, where the old county of Berkshire was divided into three counties, and the legislature, inadvertently at the time of making the act of division, perhaps, forgot to provide for a division of the corporate property, and the very next legislature undertook to correct the mistake. In that case it was holden to be unconstitutional, as there was no provision made for a division of property in the act authorizing the division of the county. So that I understand it to be a universal proposition, that upon a secession, authorized or unauthorized, as the general rule, the seceder carries no property in the fund which before belonged to the whole association, unless his act be attended and disarmed of its consequences by an accompanying grant of a share of the property by the competent authority. Not, however, to anticipate, but to confine myself for the present merely to the act of secession, to qualify the *prima facie* influence of this secession, and the consequences of that act, the plaintiffs have, of course, the burden of proof; and to encounter it, they invoke the vote of the General Conference, called the Plan of Separation. That Plan, as well as I can, with all the attention I have been able to give it, understand it, the plaintiffs assert divided the Church in two, and by some operation or other, that I am not quite confident to this hour I distinctly understand, even without the assent of the annual conferences, it enabled them to depart, and yet to carry with them a portion of the original common fund.

Upon this a great many questions arise; but the first to which I wish to call the attention of your Honours is, whether or not this act of the General Conference is not a mere nullity in the contemplation of ecclesiastical law, in so far as it was an act assuming to divide the Church under which, of course, the plaintiffs take no right. My first proposition is, that it is an entire and perfect nullity, for want of authority in the body called the General Conference to divide the Church according to the Methodist ecclesiastical polity. This, then, raises two general questions,—1. What is the nature of the act? and 2. What are the powers of the body that did this act?

It is to be observed, in the first place, with regard to the nature of the act, that in in order to avail the plaintiffs in the slightest degree, it must be held to be an act whereby the General Conference divides the Church into two—everybody agrees it must do that,—and whereby it divides the Church in two, but wholly destroys the old association, and produces two new ones in its place. I have already indicated, and I shall by-and-by have occasion to submit more at length, that if the act does not go to this extent—if it goes no further than a mere setting off a part from the whole, leaving the identity of the original whole unaffected, and does not at the same time accompany it by a grant of any portion of the estate—then it does not avail the plaintiffs. Therefore, I submit, though in the bill they confine themselves to the mere allegation, that this act has divided the Church in two, without advancing so far as to say whether it has destroyed the original Church and made two new ones, in order to avail themselves of the act in the slightest degree, they must go that extent. Therefore, they must establish the two constituents of the Ovidian metamorphosis, not merely the *forma mutata,* but also the *novum corpus,* or their case fails. If, however, it does not go so far as the destruction of the old Church, and the production of two new ones, it is at least a division of the Church; and it is in that aspect of the act that I desire for a moment to consider it, and then to inquire whether or not this Conference had the constitutional competence to do such an act.

It is, then, a division of the Church; it is so urged in terms, and is unquestionably so in every view of the case. To avail the plaintiffs, however, it must be made out in matter of fact that it is a division of the Church; that it divided an existing Church theretofore one, established to be one, organized completely, and covering jurisdictionally and spiritually, *secundum subjectam materiam,* a certain territory, into two Churches, separated by one geographical line running directly through the original territory, and each Church totally distinct, and totally independent. That is the nature of the act. It is not a mere dismission of a single member from the Church *in malam partem,* or *in bonam partem.* It is not the excommunication of a party; not the dismissal of a party with letters of recommendation; it is not the calling in of a missionary on a lying-out frontier, ascertained to be too far distant for the prosecution of his enterprise of benevolence; nor is it, as was the case between this Church and Canada, the dissolving of a treaty, or the terminating of a compact between two Churches theretofore existing legally independent, but united by a temporary tie. On the other hand, it is a division of an existing substance into two. It is, ecclesiastically and in fact, precisely such an act as it would be politically, if the general government were to-morrow to assume to divide the United States by Mason's and Dixon's line prolonged from sea to sea, and proceed to establish two independent nations on the different sides of the line, and then to go on indicating a plan for dividing the buildings, the ships, the arsenals, and the flag equally between us. May that omen at least be averted! It is a division, and nothing less nor more than a division of the Methodist Episcopal Church.

I ask the Court, before I proceed to inquire into the powers of this body constitutionally to do such an act, to pause for a moment in the still further contemplation of the act itself. This is a division of a Church which had existed in 1844, called the Methodist Episcopal Church. It was one Church. At that time it had been one sometime longer than these States in this Union had been one under the constitution of the general government. Methodism, as I have read in these proceedings, had its birth and baptism in an upper chamber somewhere in the city of New-York, in 1766. Thence it spread and grew, embarrassed somewhat by the troubles that preceded the breaking out of the revolutionary war, and still more by the revolutionary war itself, until at last, in 1784, its hymns were sung, and its fervid oratory spoken, in the pine woods and upon the river banks, in some seven States, and in the hearing of some 14,000 or 15,000 members. That was in 1784. Still, down to that time, it recognised a certain British tie. Its founder and its ruler was Wesley, who was an Englishman to the last day of his life. Its preachers were, I believe, all of them, down to that time, of British ordination. Its sacraments were denied to it through the agency of its own service, and could be enjoyed only by leaving the Methodist meeting, and seeking for them within the walls of an Episcopal Church by the English law, to which Wesley all his life, certainly as late as that period, continued to adhere. In 1784, sympathetic with the new American national life, Methodism, the Methodism of the United States, the collective general will of American Methodism, expressed by the preachers and by the laity, assembled in an extraordinary Convention, for that was the true character of it, expressly on that subject, convened under a letter from Wesley recommending that proceeding, decided to form itself into one Church—one independent and indivisible by the terms of its creation. The Court will see that it was expected to be a Church in and for these United States, that it was expected from its origin to grow with their growth, and to expand with their area, to breathe over their gigantic frame its spiritual culture, to contribute to their amelioration, to consolidate their unity, and to attend their various fortunes through the corporate, and associate, and connected life of both. I pray your Honours' attention, in this immediate connexion, to the letter under which the Conference was called by which the Church was formed. And it is very striking to remark how the Church, in its very origin, had a national character and a national tie, and might very well expect to survive and perform a series of national service as long as there was a Church to work or a nation to serve.

On pp. 3 and 4 of Proofs No. 1, Wesley, in his letter, says—

"By a very uncommon train of providences many of the provinces of North America are totally disjoined from the British empire, and erected into independent States. The English government has no authority over them, either civil or ecclesiastical, any more than over the States of Holland. A civil authority is exercised over them, partly by the congress, partly by the State assemblies. But no one either exercises or claims any ecclesiastical authority at all. In this peculiar situation some thousands of the inhabitants of these States desire my advice, and in compliance with their desire, I have drawn up a little sketch," &c.

Your Honours will observe the exigency. In consequence of the independence of a new nation, Mr. Wesley advised the establishment of a Church for that nation. He says that thousands of its inhabitants solicited his advice, and he proceeds to recommend the creation of a new Church for the new independence. He constitutes Coke and Asbury joint superintendents over the American brethren. By turning to pp. 5, 6 and 7, your Honours will observe that it is certain citizens of the United States, who, under this letter, they having undoubtedly formed part of the thousands who solicited his advice, proceed, in contemplation of the same crisis—the erection of a new nation to independence—to found a Church for it. I beg leave to read a passage from page 5:—

"To carry into effect the proposed organization, a General Conference of preachers was called, to meet in Baltimore at Christmas, 1784. Sixty, out of the eighty-three preachers then in the travelling connexion, attended at the appointed time. 'At this conference,' say the annual minutes for 1785, 'it was unanimously agreed, that circumstances made it convenient for us to become a separate body, under the denomination of the Methodist Episcopal Church.'"

Turning from that, I ask attention to some of the questions in the Discipline of 1784, page 6:—

"*Quest.* 2. What can be done in order to the future union of the Methodists?

"*Ans.* During the life of the Rev. Mr. Wesley, we acknowledge ourselves his sons in the Gospel, ready, in matters belonging to Church government, to obey his commands. And we do engage, after his death, to do everything that we judge consistent with the cause of religion in America, and the political interests of these States, to preserve and promote our union with the Methodists in Europe.

"*Quest.* 3. As the ecclesiastical as well as civil affairs of these United States have passed through a very considerable change by the revolution, what plan of Church government shall we hereafter pursue?

"*Ans.* We will form ourselves into an episcopal Church, under the direction of superintendents, elders, deacons, and helpers, according to the forms of ordination annexed to our liturgy, and the Form of Discipline set forth in these Minutes."

So, then, contemporaneously with the emerging of a new nation to life, a new Church—the Methodist Episcopal Church—by the same general agencies, or sympathetic with the same general agencies, was brought into existence. In its first breath, it was a unit, it was one Church. The evidence that it was to be and remain a unity as long as it should exist is just as unequivocal as the evidence that it was to exist at all. There is as little dream of duality in this birthtime of the Methodist Church as there is of deism or pantheism. Duality is no less a heresy, according to the objects and original destiny of this Church, than either the one or the other. Its territorial extent, present and future, was meant to be perfectly defined, and *ab origine* it was, and was to be co-extensive with these States. By a solemn compact of all with each, and each with all, that power which created that Church in 1784, whoever that power was,—call it the whole body of preachers, the whole body of Methodist laity, that vast body of preachers and laity, preachers acting for the laity and laity for the preachers,—ordained from its birth that it should be one Church. Even then, it is striking and beautiful to observe, that they saw in it the promise of an abiding and an expanding agency, for the benefit of the nation whose members they were become.

I submit that everything in the history of Methodism, everything in its origin, everything about it, is unity. Unity is the law of its being. From the start everything implies, everything expresses it. Go back to its origin, and you find that from its birth-time till 1844, unity is everywhere. It is as frontlets between its eyes. It is written on every fold of its robe. It is garnered up in every corner of its large heart. Every one of its institutions was originally adapted to the preservation of that unity to the end. For the administration of local business it has local judicatories; for the conduct of its general affairs, proceeding on the plan of our grand secular Union, it has a general body; and then, above all, is that extraordinary distinguishing and characteristic element of a grand superintending itinerancy, whereby the universal Methodism of America may be said to be brought together from season to season, in one vast creation, homogeneous and identical, to be kindled with one flame, to be melted in one tide of emotion, to sit down to eat and drink unreproved and unblamed at the same promiscuous banquet of charity. That Church, thus created for unity, of which unity is a part and parcel, the General Conference of 1844, it is said, has divided in twain. Forgetting their own subordinate and administrative relations to the Church, and to the sovereign will behind, that created and produced it; forgetting that the grand idea of Wesley and the generation of 1784 was, that the Methodism of these United States should work out all its ends in and through and by the instrumentality of a compacted and organic unity, and that when it ceased to be one, whatever it became, it ceased to be the original Methodism of Wesley; forgetting that its essence was itinerancy, and through itinerancy a whole nation was meant to be kept within a single fold; I will not say, forgetting their duties as patriots and as men, but, as it seems to me, with great respect, misconceiving those duties, and showing themselves for the moment, a little unequal to the forbearance, and self-control, and humility which the hour demanded, and which ennobles more than it degrades any man—forgetting these, this General Conference divided this Church in two as coolly as a mathematician would draw a great circle on a wooden globe. It was divided in an instant, even as if a child were cut through the head and heart to compose the dissensions of stepmothers.

I know that a great deal of ingenuity has been employed by my learned and able friend on the other side, to prove that all the Methodism has not been divided. A great deal of pains has been taken to show that Methodists, whoever they are, and wherever they are, are one body. I believe some poetry has been printed, to the effect that although mountains rise and rivers roll between nations of Methodists, still a certain tie of Methodism unites them at last. I submit that that is nothing at all to the purpose; for after all, this forgets entirely that the Methodism of 1784 was the Methodism that was to exist, and act, and do its work, only through and by means of an organic unity; and when that organic unity is cloven down, and that structure destroyed, it is in vain to say that, though unity is gone and the Church is dead, Methodism is alive. Why, suppose the National Government to-morrow should divide these States into two independent nations, or thirty-one, or thirty-two, or five hundred independent nations, I suppose about the same absolute quantity of democratic liberty might remain and lift up its voice all over this land. I dare say, inasmuch as a certain tie is said to connect us everywhere, we should still retain a tie of connexion with one another till, through a series of affliction, and struggle, and strife, we had been fain to take refuge all of us beneath the Dead Sea of despotism, just as we are connected with patriot Hungary and patriot Poland, and other patriotic falls. I dare say the same quantity of republicanism would be left; but this national unity, through which our liberty was achieved—this constitutional unity—where would it be? Just exactly where the Methodism of 1784 went when the Church in which it was embodied, and through which it was to act, was destroyed by the act of the Conference.

The question now is, whether the General Conference had the constitutional authority, under the ecclesiastical polity of Methodism, to make such a division as this. We utterly deny it; and I feel an extreme anxiety to bespeak in advance the indulgent attention of the Court to the perhaps very tedious historical argument, to some extent, by which I am now about to endeavour to establish that proposition. I submit that they had not a particle of authority, under the ecclesiastical polity of Methodism, to divide the Church at all. The question might perhaps be avoided on the part of these defendants, for, as I have said, according to a view of the act on which we shall much insist before the argument shall be concluded, even if it had power to divide the Church, he who retires takes no fund with him, unless by a special grant. But the question lies in that. It is one of a great deal of interest, and a right determination of it, which we shall be sure to have from the learning of this Bench, will, in my humble judgment, do something to conduct these parties back again, which I personally certainly very much desire.

It is common to say, and it is said in the case cited the other day from Benj. Monroe—a case which I brought with me, as it is the one which discussed this subject—that there is a sovereign and ultimate power in all bodies competent to destroy it. There must be, it is very common to say, some power to dissolve the Union; there must be a power somewhere competent to dissolve a corporation, a firm, to dissolve the Church, to dissolve society itself. This may very well be so; and this was an argument which was very much pressed by my learned brother, in adverting to a great variety of circumstances which might occur, in the progress of events, to render a division of this Church expedient, and perhaps necessary. But then it does not follow that any specific body in a given polity is the organic depository of this transcendent and fatal power. Whether any specific body, as the General Conference, has it or not, or whether such a body itself is a mere subordinate or administrative function, depending on a higher and secret sovereign will, is a question in every case of history and of law. That is a question in this case as applicable to the General Conference.

Somewhere, I may admit, the power must exist. It must exist, if your Honours please, in the General Conference, or in the sovereign will which created the Church behind it; but whether in one or the other, is a question of law and of history—a question of ecclesiastical law to be illustrated by the history of the Church—a question of ecclesiastical law upon the polity of Methodism itself. I have drawn out with some care a proposition which I shall endeavour to maintain, in regard to the powers of the General Conference. Our proposition is, that the General Conference in the Methodist Episcopal Church, whenever, as in 1844, it is called and assembled in its ordinary course, under its ordinary and appointed designations of meeting, is a mere administrative body of the Church. It is, and always has been, the superintending legislature, judiciary, and executive of the Church, created and existing to administer its affairs from time to time, and for that purpose *durante vita* to make rules and regulations for its government, and provisions for its unity, and growth, and good; but it was a subordinate agent, a servant of the Church itself. It never was the original creator of the Church. Sitting in its ordinary capacity, and under its ordinary call, it never represented the sovereign power which created the Church; it never was made to be the destroyer of the Church; and it has never had, in any era, more power to dissolve or to destroy the Church than the General Government has to-day to divide the Union by a line of partition drawn across it from East to West. The Methodist Episcopal Church itself was created in 1784, by an extraordinary and special Conference, convened for that precise purpose, under a letter from Wesley, and in accordance with the universal wish of Methodism, lay and clerical, in the United States. That Conference created the Methodist Church for the whole United States—created it to be one, to exist forever, or while such Churches exist upon the earth. When that Conference had done its work of creating the Church, it retired, disappeared, and has never again been assembled in the history of Methodism. By virtue of that act of creation, the Methodist Church has existed ever since, and will exist until another Conference called for the purpose, representing and embodying the will of the real sovereign—that is, universal Methodism as a whole—shall decree its dissolution; and long, late, and distant may that be. After this Church was created, it had, and necessarily must have had, administrative bodies, through which in various spheres to carry on its daily business. Such are the officers of the Church, such are the annual conferences, such are the quarterly conferences, and such is, or such at least was in 1792, the General Conference. These, all of them, are subordinate, executive agencies of the principal, the constituent—the Church. When they are called together in the ordinary way, and under the ordinary call, they have none of them any more power to destroy the original sovereign creator and constituent than an attorney employed to execute a deed of land has power to shoot his principal through the head. Such is our proposition. I now have respectfully to ask the attention of the Court to the general outline of proof by which I shall endeavour to establish it. I have stated it as it applies to every one of the conferences, and to every one of the eras of the General Conference. For the discussion I must to some extent follow the example of my learned brother, and consider the General Conference as existing in the Methodist Church before 1808 and after 1808, which is the period when it became strictly a representative body, called the General Conference; and under that division I mean to submit these two propositions: in the first place, that the body called the General Conference, meeting in its ordinary course, and under no extraordinary call, instructed to do or consider no specific or extraordinary act, did never, even before 1808, have power to divide the Church, or any analogous power, but was strictly an administrative body, existing to govern a Church which another distinct body had previously created; in the second place, I mean to say that even so, its actual administrative powers were reduced to some extent in 1808. I shall first consider the earlier eras and first proposition.

To know what the General Conference prior to 1808 was, what it was created, and what it was authorized to do, I shall have to treat the subject somewhat historically. The history of the Conference before 1808 lies precisely in these few facts. I will present the facts to the Court as I suppose them to exist, and call your Honours' attention a little more in detail to the evidence. The history of the Church before 1808 stands on these facts, and these alone. First, the creator of the Methodist Episcopal Church in 1784 was not a General Conference meeting in the ordinary course, but it was a power totally distinct from, and other than, any General Conference that was ever convened. It was an extraordinary body, such as never assembled before or since, convened under the apostolical letter of Wesley, the real father and founder of Methodism in America, for the express purpose of considering on the organization of a Church for a new nation, composed of all the travelling preachers *en masse*, and not of a representation or delegation, acting in execution of a strong and general demand of the laity for a Church that could administer its own sacraments. That is my first historical proposition.

2d. After this body had created the Church, it separated to appear *de facto* no more.

3d. After that attempt there was not, and there never had been, such a thing as a General Conference, with any recognised character, and duties, and powers, known to Methodism in this country; and there never was a General Conference called by that name, and with known and recognised powers, until the year 1792. Advisory bodies, under the name of regular conferences, had been called by the general assistant before, but with no power of deciding in any instance against his voice.

4th. This convention extraordinary which made the Church, did not provide for any General Conference then to exist in it at all for any purpose, but it set it going with an administrative economy made up of various administrative agents, variously subordinate—bishops, annual conferences, quarterly conferences, and on one occasion a body called a council. So it continued to exist till 1792, without any General Conference in it, or about it, or recognised by it at all.

5th. After some years' experience of these administrative agencies, in 1792 a General Conference developed itself. The proper mode of expressing it, perhaps, would be to say that the General Conference was the last and most perfect in the series of mere administrative agencies. The General Conference from this time down to 1808 was never endowed with a particle of power to dissolve the Church, with a particle of analogous power, with a particle of power to do one act which the bishop had not done by his own regular conference. So it existed down to 1808, and at that time these administrative functions, such as they were, were actually reduced instead of being enlarged. In other words, I shall say when I come to present the proofs of it a little more fully, that it merely developed itself and took the place of the bishop and his advisers, and had exactly the same power to dissolve the Church which the bishop had, and not one solitary particle more. I beg your Honours' pardon for occupying so much time in the narration of the five great facts which compose the history of that period; and now pardon me if I trespass a little further to return and endeavour successfully to establish them.

Who, then, created the Church organization? That, I suppose, is the first question in an inquiry like this. Of course I need not say that it was no such General Conference as this that existed in 1844—that is, a body of delegated representatives, for no such Conference had before 1808 existed at all. I should say, before I proceed to adduce the proofs on which I rely for it, that the creator of the Methodist Episcopal Church was an extraordinary body, such as had never assembled before, called for a convention—under the name of "The General Conference," it is true, but composed of all the travelling preachers, not of a part of them selected by the annual or the quarterly conferences, or otherwise, of the whole body of the preachers *en masse*. This body assembled under Mr. Wesley's letter of invitation, in accordance with the general and strong demand of the laity of the country for a separate organization, and for a Church capable of administering its own sacraments. That convention, thus composed, and thus called in obedience to such a demand, created this Church. The true sovereign then, I submit, the true sovereign by which alone it was created, and by which alone it can be destroyed, may be said to be the preachers in a mass, acting in obedience to the wishes of the people, through the advice of Wesley, and upon their own judgment of expediency, utility, and duty, and convened (I must not allow to be forgotten for an instant) for the express purpose of doing that very work. So that it was, in a remarkable degree, as distinguished from any General Conference that ever sat before or ever convened afterwards, analogous to the convention that created the Federal Constitution in 1787, and the various conventions which from time to time have been assembled to create the various constitutions of the several States. That body was the true creator of the Methodist Episcopal Church. It may be variously stated, but every mode of statement is equally decisive for the use to which I would hereafter endeavour to apply it. It may be stated that the true creator of the Church was the general and collective will of American Methodism, acting through the laity and through the preachers. Or it may be said that it was the collective will of American Methodism, expressing itself and acting through an extraordinary convention, called under a letter of Mr. Wesley for that express purpose, which did its work, and then disappeared. But, however it may be denominated, I submit that I am right, in an abbreviated and general way of stating it, in saying that it was an extraordinary convention called for that express purpose, under the name of a General Conference, but not in the least degree resembling any General Conference convened before, or any General Conference that has been assembled from that hour to this. It was a great ecclesiastical convention of the Methodists of America.

This brings me to the consideration of a question of some importance, and that is this:—it may be said that, inasmuch as the body creating the Church assembled under the name of a General Conference, therefore, wherever we find in the history of the Church, a body sitting under the name of General Conference, it may be presumed to have all the powers and to be clothed with all the authority, with the same transcendent powers, with the original convention. In other words, the argument may be, that whereas this body, which I have called an extraordinary convention, really assembled under the name of General Conference, therefore, whenever you afterwards find a body in the Methodist polity assembling under the same denomination, it is fair to presume that it assembles for the same general ends, and is clothed with the same transcendent powers. Now nothing can be more erroneous than this; for the second historical fact, to the proof of which I am now about to ask the attention of the Court, is, on the contrary, exactly this, that at that time, 1784, when this body assembled, there existed no such thing as a General Conference in the Methodist Church with defined and recognised character, or with any character or any powers whatsoever; so that this body was not only new, but was exactly and merely a convention of creation and of independency, no less and no more. That is the second fact, and to prove it, I shall have, perhaps, to take a little more time than I desire.

Before 1784, then, there was nothing in the Methodist system in this country under the name of General Conference, or with any recognised powers of any description, even to make rules and regulations for the Church. I think important consequences flow from this fact, and I shall therefore take pains to see whether it is controverted on the part of the counsel for the other side, and if it be controverted, I shall proceed to establish it by the histories of Methodism, if they are admitted for the purpose; if they are not admitted, I shall content myself with stating what I understand and am satisfied the historic fact really is, and then to say that the plaintiffs have the burden of proof on this part of the cause, and they are to evince the contrary if they maintain it.

It is true then, that from 1773—that is the first period to which I go back—there were occasionally convened by the general assistant of Mr. Wesley in this country, a body under the name of regular conference, for the purpose of advising the assistant upon the administration of the affairs of the Church. That first began, as far as we can learn, in 1773, which is perhaps a date not unimportant for your Honours to bear in mind. That body, however, was simply an advisory body, and it must be perfectly clear that it had no power, on any debatable matter at all down to 1784. And, extraordinary as it may seem, the fact is indisputable that the general assistant, who convened it for his own advice, after he had heard a matter debated, decided it for himself independent of the conference. Such continued to be the state of the case from 1773 to 1784. As to the proofs of this, I should begin first by referring to the History of the Discipline, page 10, where we find some allusion to a conference of 1773; but I feel bound to say that for the complete exhibition of the evidence on this point, I shall desire to refer to Dr. Bangs's History of the Methodist Church, which I suppose to be an authoritative and satisfactory account of these proceedings, and which fully supports the statement I have had the honour to make. I would turn your Honours' attention in the first place, to 1 Bangs's History, page 342, for the general statement that no such thing as a General Conference, by that name, ever existed in this country until 1792. I refer to it merely in proof of a fact which is really very well established in the History of the Discipline itself, that, down to 1792, there had been no General Conference at all. Until 1773, there seems to have been no sort of conference at all. For the purpose of showing the Court that when after that time, between 1773 and 1784, the general assistant called regular conferences, they were advisory only, and had no powers to pass on any debatable matter at all, I refer to 1 Bangs's History, pages 131 and 132. That passage is of so much pertinence and importance, that I shall pause to read it. He is writing the History of 1779; he has not yet arrived at 1784, but this is subsequent to the calling of these conferences. What he says, therefore, throws light on their power:—

"These resolutions were adopted at the conference held at Judge White's, in the State of Delaware. It seems, therefore, that they were not in the habit at that time of determining debatable questions by a majority of votes; but, in imitation of the practice of Mr. Wesley, after hearing all that could be said *pro* and *con*, the presiding officer decided the point."

In confirmation of that fact, and for the purpose of showing how it probably had its origin, I will make two references to different parts of the History of the Discipline, and then leave the subject. In 1773, History of Discipline, page 10, it is recorded that—

"At the first conference held in Philadelphia, June 1773, the following queries were proposed to every preacher:—

"*Quest.* 1. Ought not the authority of Mr. Wesley and that conference to extend to the preachers and people in America, as well as in Great Britain and Ireland?

"*Ans.* Yes."

So that the real truth of the matter is, that by an ordinance of the first conference of 1773, the proceedings of subsequent conferences and Methodist denomination in this country were subject to the determination of Mr. Wesley's conferences in Europe. Therefore it came to pass exactly as the historian had recorded it, that down to 1784, these bodies were nothing but advisory bodies, without any power to decide a matter which was debatable. I will not trouble your Honours with any further references or citations to establish that proposition. I think it will not be controverted.

Now it follows from this that the body which in 1784 created the Church was, as I have denominated it, a new and extraordinary body, called for a new and extraordinary purpose, and under a new name in that Church; because, as I have shown, down to that time a General Conference had never existed, and the regular conferences that existed had been advisory bodies, without the slightest power of determination.

The next important fact is, that this body, which thus created the new Church, then retired, and did not create or provide for any General Conference at all, even to administer its affairs. This is a fact of very great importance, and when I come by-and-by to apply it to an important problem, *i.e.*, with what powers the General Conference of 1792 came into existence, I think it will be found to throw very great light on that inquiry. The fact is, that this General Conference of 1784 did not create or provide any General Conference even to administer its affairs; but on the contrary it seems to have assumed that the administration would be carried along very well by the annual conferences, and quarterly conferences, and the officers of the Church. In point of fact, therefore, there was no General Conference in the Church to do anything under any name. The amount of the matter is, that this extraordinary convention made it at first, set it in operation, with a bishop, and with annual conferences and quarterly conferences to advise him as to its administrative economy. Therefore your Honours will see that the General Conference of 1792, which is relied upon as starting all at once into existence with power to destroy the Church, did not originally even come into the contemplation of the plan for creating the Church and providing for its administration, for it started, and began, and proceeded eight years unattended and unaided by a solitary particle of administrative agency, except its bishop and its annual and quarterly conferences, and for a very brief period a body called a council, to which I shall call attention in a moment. This fact is not controverted by anybody. Everybody agrees that no General Conference existed until 1792. What was the administrative economy of the Church during this time? A bishop at its head, quarterly conferences and annual conferences, that is to say, local assemblages called from time to time by the bishop to give him advice, composed the entire administrative economy of this Church, from 1784 to 1792, and in the contemplation of its creators seems to have been thought likely to be enough for the Church in all periods. The bishop from time to time in these annual conferences, and in these quarterly conferences, and in his regular conferences, if he chose to call them, conversed with them on changes of Discipline which he proposed to introduce; and if he found by that consultation that his changes would be likely to be acceptable to the body of the Church, of his own authority he changed the Discipline. That was so for eight years; and those were what we should usually call the first and purest years of the Church, inasmuch as they were those which immediately succeeded its creation. Nay, so little was a General Conference thought of by the generation of 1784, that in 1789—I will show it from the historian to whom reference has been made—it was mutually taken for granted that a General Conference was entirely impracticable, and therefore, by way of adding a new administrative agency to the Church, and for the purpose of collecting the general will of the Church more easily and more completely, the bishop actually projected the measure of a council, *i. e.*, a small body that should act and confer with him. That proposition was adopted, and for some time that body and the conferences, annual and quarterly, and the bishop made up the whole administrative polity of Methodism. Let me call your Honours' attention to this administrative economy as I find it in 1 Bangs, page 302—a very instructive chapter, as I regard it, for more purposes than one, as I hope to have strength enough and voice enough to make the Court understand before I am through. He says, speaking of 1789 :—

" Having thus noticed the progress of the work of religion in different parts of the country, let us return to the doings of the conference. In consequence of the extension of the work on every hand, spreading over such a large territory, there were two difficulties which arose in the way of proceeding in the manner they had done heretofore.

" 1. It was very inconvenient for all the members of the conference to assemble together in one place to transact their business. Hence, as we have already seen, the bishops had appointed several separate conferences for the despatch of their ordinary affairs.

" 2. But anything which was done in these separate conferences was not binding, except simply the ordinations and stationing the preachers, unless sanctioned by them all. And as this could rarely be expected, constituted as human nature is, it was plainly seen that there was danger of their falling to pieces, or of their having divers administrations.

" To provide against this evil, and to remedy the inconvenience above mentioned, it was determined this year, as the best thing which could be devised, to have a *council*, for the reasons and purposes, and with the powers set forth in the following questions and answers :—

" ' *Questions*. Whereas the holding of General Conferences on this extensive continent would be attended with a variety of difficulties, and many inconveniences to the work of God ; and whereas we judge it expedient that a council should be formed of chosen men out of the several districts, as representatives of the whole connexion, to meet at stated times ; in what manner is this council to be formed, what shall be its powers, and what further regulations shall be made concerning it ?' "

The Court will have been struck, I am sure, by the recital of the impracticability of holding General Conferences to collect the general will for the administration of ordinary affairs. Therefore the idea of a council develops itself. The answer to the question then is :—

" *Answer*. 1st. Our bishops and presiding elders shall be the members of this council ; provided, that the members who form the council be never fewer than nine. And if any unavoidable circumstance prevent the attendance of a presiding elder at the council, he shall have authority to send another elder out of his own district to represent him ; but the elder so sent by the absenting presiding elder shall have no seat in the council without the approbation of the bishop, or bishops, and presiding elders present. And if, after the above-mentioned provisions are complied with, any unavoidable circumstance, or any contingencies, reduce the number to less than nine, the bishop shall immediately summon such elders as do not preside, to complete the number.

" 2dly. These shall have authority to mature everything they shall judge expedient. 1. To preserve the general union. 2. To render and preserve the external form of worship similar in all our societies through the continent. 3. To preserve the essentials of the Methodist doctrines and discipline pure and uncorrupted. 4. To correct all abuses and disorders ; and, lastly, they are authorized to mature everything they may see necessary for the good of the Church, and for the promoting and improving our colleges and plan of education.

" 3dly. Provided nevertheless, that nothing shall be received as the resolution of the council, unless it be assented to unanimously by the council ; and nothing so assented to by the council shall be binding in any district, till it has been agreed upon by a majority of the conference which is held for that district."

This council, thus and then and upon that policy created, existed but a little while ; but as it was really the prodecessor of the General Conference proper, and was the first large or general administrative body ever collected under the new Church, I believe your Honours will be inclined to say the child was the father of the man in this instance. And when you come by-and-by, when we arrive at 1792, to inquire with what scope of power the General Conference then met, you will regard as a fact of extraordinary importance, not to say decisive interest, that it was immediately preceded in this very line of development of administrative agency by a bishop's council intended to collect the general will. There will not be a particle of doubt left on the mind of any fair historical inquirer, that there never was the least intention, from 1792 to 1808, to clothe the General Conference with a scintilla of authority more than was given to the bishop's council. It is for that reason, that I have somewhat solicitously called the attention of the Court to the powers and objects of the council, as they are stated in Dr. Bangs's History. The first is, to promote the general union. They were not creating a body to provide means for facilitating the destruction and disruption of the Church, but simply and solely, when, after having provided a series of administrative agency that had worked well, outgrowing its infancy, the Church demanded something more, this further administrative agency was provided, to collect the general will more easily, and do greater service. Then and for that purpose, to meet that exact want, this council was devised and introduced. It was tried for a brief space of time, and then abandoned, and in its stead was substituted the General Conference. But I submit that there cannot be a particle of doubt that it was intended to have, and did have, through its brief period of somewhat unpopular existence, the very same work to do, and did the very same work, nothing less and nothing more, which the General Conference which assembled in 1792 did. Therefore I hope I shall be excused for reading again the powers of the bishop's council, that you may see whether the Methodists at this time were carving, and whether they were anything more than carving out, a mere series of devices for a more perfect Christian and associated life, which the old convention of 1784 organized, and organized to exist. The powers of the council are :—

"1. To preserve the general union."

Not to destroy the Methodist Episcopal Church, but to preserve the general union of the Church, simply and solely by enabling this wide-spread community to concentrate their wills upon the administration of its affairs from day to day.

"2. To render and preserve the external form of worship similar in all our societies through the continent. 3. To preserve the essentials of the Methodist doctrines and discipline pure and uncorrupted. 4. To correct all abuses and disorders ; and, lastly, they are authorized to mature everything they may see necessary for the good of the Church, and for the promoting and improving our colleges and plan of education."

This council I have said was unpopular. The next fact we find is, that in 1792 the first General Conference ever convened in America under the Methodist Episcopal Church, assembled. We find all at once, in 1792, that it had been ordained by the constituent body, by the Methodism of the country, that from that time forward such a body should assemble once in four years, for the same purpose and clothed with the same powers. Now the problem is, with what powers, and for what purposes, the constituent creator and sovereign of 1792 all at once wakes up and ordains that there shall be in the Methodist ecclesiastical polity, from that time forth, a General Conference, assembled, and sitting, and doing its work every four years. I submit that *prima facie* we have established, that the only purpose for which the constituent body could have all at once called a General Conference into existence, was for the purpose of enabling it to act as a body of mere administrative power, and with no power at all beyond it. The sovereign will in 1784 had made the Church, and set it in operation, and left it to carry on its practical life by officers and annual and quarterly conferences. For some time these answered that purpose very well. In the progress of events it was found that a council would be a convenient addition to the existing, appointed series of administrative devise, and thereupon a council was created; but nobody will pretend, that in creating a council they meant to go beyond the creation of a mere administrative body, with no more power to dissolve the Church than the bishop had. That body was unpopular, and did its work but for a little time. Then comes the General Conference. *Prima facie*, I submit that the very date of its birth, the very order in which it comes into existence in the series of administrative agencies, the very fact that the great want of the Church at that time was not a power to destroy, but a power to administer, the very fact that the Church was already created, and set going forever, shows that the General Conference came into existence as an administrative body, and an administrative body alone. This is the inference the historian would make, if he were to inquire into the matter independent from this controversy. This is the inference, I think, which this Court will make. It actually was created to be, and became to be, just what we should infer from the historic facts—the time when it came into existence, the order in which it stood, and was probably designed. I have a right to stop here, and call on the counsel on the other side for a particle of proof, that the *prima facie* inference is not the true inference in regard to the character of the General Conference. I call upon them now to exhibit to the Court one solitary scrap of proof, that the General Conference of to-day possesses a particle more power than the bishop's council of yesterday. I press them on the historical question. If it were a question on the history of Rome, to be illustrated by a Niebuhr, or by a Neander on the history of the Church, I respectfully submit that it is perfectly manifest as a solution of the historical problem, having regard to the dates and series of events and the demands of the Church, that at the time the General Conference came into existence, it was just exactly what the bishop's council had been, what the bishop had been, what the annual and quarterly conferences had been—administrative functionaries, but neither creators, nor destroyers, nor participators in a particle of that transcendent power. I call then on the other side for a historical deduction; and I have only to submit, and I demand judgment for the defendants in this case on it, for it puts an end to this controversy, that the plaintiffs have not furnished your Honours with a solitary particle of proof, to show that the powers taken by the General Conference exceeded those which I have been attempting to present.

Then where is the proof to come from? There are only two sources of evidence. They may, in the first place, call attention to the Discipline of 1792, to find there written a code defining the powers of the General Conference. It is silent on the matter. There is not one word in the history of the Church, not one word in the written constitution, showing with what powers the constituents, in 1792, intended to invest this body at the time it was called into existence.

Then we are driven to the other source of inquiry. How are we to ascertain the powers possessed? By looking only at the powers which it put in exercise. The Court are, therefore, simply on these proofs, which the parties on both sides lay before them, to see if the General Conference, from 1792 to 1808, ever dreamed, so far as its powers and intentions can by possibility be conjectured, that they were clothed with a solitary particle of power beyond the authority possessed by the bishop's council, which preceded it. On the contrary, the General Conference went on in the path of the bishop's council and the annual and quarterly conferences. We find it going on, in the same useful, but well-defined and comparatively humble path of mere administrative service. We find it here and there making changes in the Discipline of the Church, and those not considerable changes. I submit that not one act of a higher degree of power was done in this period, and that nothing was done by the General Conference, from 1792 to 1808, which had not been done over again in the period which preceded it. Therefore, unless the learned counsel are prepared to say, that the bishop's council, before 1792, could have dissolved the Church, the plaintiffs have not presented a scrap of evidence that the General Conference, after 1792, could dissolve the Church.

The only answer I heard suggested to this by my learned brother was, that this Conference must have had all power to dissolve the Church, because it was composed of all the preachers. Because it was composed of all the preachers, did it necessarily have power to destroy the Church? On the contrary, I suppose the question is exactly this: With what powers, and for what purposes, do the preachers appear to have decided, all at once, to introduce and establish a General Conference? That is the question. The question is not, whether all the preachers, assembled under a special call for that purpose, might or might not, at any period before 1808, pull down the Methodist Episcopal Church. That is not the question. The question is, for what purposes, and with what powers, they decided, in point of fact, that they would at once introduce, and make part of their regular polity, a General Conference? We do not advance one solitary step to the solution of that, by being told that all the preachers were members of that Conference. Suppose they were. The very last thing they might have dreamed of on earth would be all at once to set going a body that should have power to destroy the Church. They might have introduced such a General Conference beyond all doubt; but the question is, whether they did so in point of fact. For the proof of that we have to go back again to the language of the constitution of the Church, in which there is not a word about it from beginning to end.

I therefore submit, with very great confidence, at least so much as this, that the plaintiffs have entirely failed to show that even before 1808 this General Conference could ecclesiastically work a division of the Church. There is an utter failure to show it in point of fact. We deny it by our answer. The fair result of the historical investigation seems to be that they did not possess it; and unless it be held that because the preachers might have clothed it with all powers, they necessarily decided so to clothe it, there is a total failure, as far as I can see, of this part of the plaintiffs' case.

The hour of adjournment having arrived, the Court adjourned until to-morrow morning.

SEVENTH DAY.—Tuesday, May 27th, 1851.

Mr. Choate resumed,—May it please your Honours, if, on this review, or any review of the history of the Church, and of the Conference of 1792, the Court should be of the opinion that it is a probable inference that that Conference came into existence as a mere body of administration—the last and ripest of the series of administrative agencies—then the case on this point is ended. If your Honours should only doubt on that question, the case on this point is also ended. If, however, you are of opinion that it has been clearly and certainly established as a proposition of historical fact, by the proper species of evidence, and the requisite degree of it, that this Conference, *ab origine*, was clothed with these extraordinary powers, then we have arrived at the question, whether or not the same extraordinary power was bestowed upon the representative General Conference created in 1808? This is a mere matter of intent. It all turns on the single inquiry, and that, I think, is not extended and not difficult, whether the constituency of 1808 intended, as a matter of intent, to clothe the General representative Conference, which it then, for the first time, brought into existence, with a power to dissolve and destroy, by dividing the Church. For, I take it that it is a universal and elementary proposition, that the powers of a representative and delegated body are exactly what the constituent creator meant to give it—no less and no more. I take this as a universal and elementary proposition, running throughout all agency, as between parties of substitution, of representation, of delegation, from the broadest to the narrowest, that the intention of the constituent defines and measures the power of the delegate. While this is true, undoubtedly, throughout the law of agency, in a general way this is recognised to be true by every school of politics in its application to the highest departments of government under the constitution. Even they who hold that the representative is not to be palsied by the will of his constituents, place themselves on the broad, general, original ground, that the constituent, by the act of creating the representative function, at first intended to clothe the representative, as a matter of intent, with the power and to devolve on him the duty of acting from time to time, of acting upon his own independent judgment, unaffected by the occasional interposition of the irregular and uninstructed will of the constituent. So that I believe I may submit it as a doctrine universally accepted, and everywhere applied, that the will of the constituent is the limit and the measure of the power of the representative.

Turning, then, to this transaction of 1808, in search of the intention of the constituent, I do not know that it is not enough for me to say that I can discern no trace of an intention to confer such power. Your Honours will find the history of that transaction on p. 13 of Proofs No. 1. You will there find that the constituent body began, in the first place, by composing the new representative General Conference, and then, in article 5, on the same page, it proceeds to define the power which it intends to confer. The language is simply and exactly—"The General Conference shall have full power to make rules and regulations for our Church."

Now, resting there, and not advancing to the subject of the restrictions by which this grant of power is presently to be limited in a very important degree, I must say, that I discern no evidence that this bestows the capacity of destroying or dividing the Church at all. On the contrary, what it seems to me I find the constituent body doing is exactly this: The Methodism of the United States had long before decided to become, and to be one Church; had, by a paramount and fundamental law, ordained unity as the form of its organic being; and here, in furtherance and execution of that ordination, it goes on to create a body which, under certain restrictions and limitations, shall make rules for the guidance of the affairs of that unity thus previously created, existing and intending to exist indefinitely. I deduce this as all that the constituent body intends to do in the first place, from the nature of the act that he is doing, and from the character of the actor that is doing it. What is the act being done? And who is the actor that does it? An existing Church, already a quarter of a century old, created by the general Methodism, for a life all but perpetual on earth, having an existing government, is found simply amending a single feature of that government. It is found to be doing nothing less, and nothing more, than altering the third article in the Discipline of the Conference which preceded it. I now respectfully submit that from the act which is being done and the actor who is doing it, from the nature of the act and the actor, the indefinite future existence of the association is properly assumed as a thing beyond controversy, and *aliunde* established and settled; and therefore the implication is simply this—that whereas here is a Church, to exist long, if not forever, and to its administration and government a General Conference is needful, they proceeded to constitute such a General Conference, with power to make rules and regulations for it during its whole life. That, I submit, is the implication which inevitably results from the nature of the act and the character of the actor. However broad are the terms in which the power is bestowed upon the General Conference, it is all at last to be considered *secundum subjectam materiam*—it is all to be taken back, and rendered *ad hoc* and *ad rem.* It is to be considered at last, however broad the terms in which it is conveyed, as an auxiliary and administrative power alone. Why, is it not so throughout the whole range of analogous law? A power of attorney may be conveyed in language the broadest, putting the agent, apparently in all things, in the condition of the constituent—but it only means at last that he shall have power within the specific agency, and for that particular constituent. A partnership makes an agent with the amplest authority, but he is not to dissolve the partnership; his powers are to be taken to be for the partnership, and under the partnership, and in aid of the partnership; he is not to alter the identity of his constituent, or put an end to his civil life. A corporation, to pursue the same analogy, creates a board of directors, with power to make rules and regulations, and by-laws, for the corporation. Would any body suppose they had power to dissolve the corporation and surrender its charter? Why, of course, the constituent was not dreaming of a dissolution. He reserved all that power and all that subject-matter to his own control; he expects to live a corporate immortality, and on that idea he hires a servant to enable him to live while he lives.

I deduce the same conclusion in the next place from the language in which this power is bestowed upon the General Conference. They are "to have full powers to make rules and regulations." For what? For Methodism? Certainly not. For Wesleyanism? Certainly not. Rules and regulations for the promulgation and spread of Methodism by the destruction of the Methodist Church? Not at all. But "rules and regulations for our Church"—affectionately and specifically—rules and regulations for Methodism through our Church, through and by that specific instrumentality. They are to have power not to make rules and regulations for the destruction of the Church, but for the Church. That is to say, they shall rule it, it being all the while an existing thing. Who could possibly mistake such language as this, if it were found in any other connexion, or on a question anything less than the momentous one which now engages this Court? If we found the phrase "rules and regulations for our firm," "rules and regulations for our corporation," would not everybody understand, as a matter of course, that it meant rules and regulations whereby "our firm," undissolved, "our corporation," undismembered, should go on, and order its existing and identical life?

I had not the honour to be present and hear the commentary made the other day, by one of the learned counsel on the other side, upon a case from 1st Peters, which, I believe, is to be cited and commented upon. It is founded on language in the Constitution, supposed to be somewhat analogous to the grant of power to the General Conference, but which, I think, the learned and eminent counsel must admit to be substantially unlike. I will not pause to comment on the language of the Constitution, but my learned friend knows that the subject-matter of the "rules and regulations" referred to in the Constitution, makes all the difference in the world. Congress is to have power to make rules and regulations for the territories. What is to be done with territories? Instead of being preserved in an existing and inflexible identity, the territory is to undergo a thousand changes. It must undergo a thousand transformations before it can reach and achieve the grand uses for which it has been spread out westward. It must be cut in two; it must be made into lots; it must be built up by the hand of man; it must be broken up into plantations and into States, and then, at last, it reaches its ultimate destination. Rules and regulations for the territory of the United States, I submit, imply necessarily that they are to be rules and regulations that are to attend it through a thousand metamorphoses, enlarging, diminishing, changing, until it reaches its ultimate destiny. The Church, on the other hand, is a perfect identity at the beginning; to translate into English a familiar expression, it is "a fact accomplished;" it is intended to exist until the end of time, enlarging and beautifying itself, if you please, but its identity forever unaffected, and all for an ulterior and specific end. Before I leave the argument, which I do not intend to extend, and on which I have only entered and generally indicated, of the intention of the constituent body in 1792 and 1808, to bestow a power of destruction, I should like to ask my learned friends on the other side, if, in the course of their researches, they have found any breaking out of a *dira cupido* for destruction in the history of the Methodist Episcopal Church, and whether or not, beginning in 1784, and coming down to 1792 and 1808, they find men's thoughts began to be directed to the importance of facilitating the means of breaking the charmed unity, and converting the Church into two, or two thousand; because, I admit, that if they can find historical evidence that the Methodist mind was taking such a direction as that, we should be led the more readily to anticipate that this intention was carried out by lodging such a power of destruction in the bishop's council, or in the Conference of 1808. So far from that being the case, however, is it not most striking and beautiful, that the very preamble by which the Constitution of 1808 was ushered into existence—I have it here in 2 Bangs's Hist., p. 229—solves this problem, and answers the question which I have referred to my learned friends? Before I read that preamble, let me remind the Court that the very problem which we are now investigating is, whether that constituent body was then about lodging in the General Conference a power to destroy the Church. The preamble is:—

"Whereas, it is of the greatest importance that the doctrine, form of government, and general rules of the United Societies in America, be preserved sacred and inviolable; and whereas, every prudent measure should be taken to preserve, strengthen, and perpetuate the union of the Connexion."

Therefore do they on that policy proceed to clothe a body with power to destroy the Church? Certainly not. Before I leave this matter, I wish to notice another topic, and the subject of the restrictions on the power of the General Conference. I have thus far been considering it, independent of the restrictions, upon the general ground of power. I respectfully submit, as I take my leave of this part of the argument, that if any doubt existed, it is removed by the language of these restrictions. My learned brother was pleased to say, that there was no prohibition in these restrictions against dissolving and destroying the Church. I respectfully submit, that that is because no grant of power had been previously given or dreamed to be given, which could be supposed capable of being tormented into a power to divide the Church. But I meet my learned friend beyond that suggestion, by inquiring how we shall possibly account for it, that an assembly of intelligent men, not to say men fit to be out of Bedlam, should have set themselves to work, more like the philosophers of Lilliput, than the intelligence and character of a great denomination like this, to restrain, as they have done here in half a dozen articles of restriction, the exercise of powers comparatively subordinate, and leave so tremendous a power as this unrestrained? how they should sedulously and laboriously prohibit by all manner of man-traps and springs, the cutting off of this leaf or that twig, and yet leave the party entirely at liberty to pluck up the noble tree by the roots? In the humour of restraining, would they not restrain the larger and more formidable power? If, as the historian tells us, to preserve the unity of the Church, they thought it needful so anxiously to guard its Discipline from change, the rules of its societies from change, the plan of its episcopacy from change, would they leave power to make a direct attack on unity itself? I submit, that the inconsistency of such a proceeding refutes the argument. Look at it. The General Conference shall not have power to alter the articles of religion, but they may alter the Church; they shall not change the creed, but they may kill the believer; they shall not alter the Discipline, but they may create two Churches or two thousand Churches, every one of whom may go off; as I read in the newspapers the other day,—I hope it was not true,—that they had already in South Carolina altered that very Discipline in face of the Discipline which was produced before this Court; they shall not deprive an individual member of his right of trial and appeal in this Church, but they may send them off by thousands and thousands without trial; they shall not so alter the plan of episcopacy, as to say to a Northern bishop, "You shall only go to Mason's and Dixon's line on your way South," and to the Southern bishop, "You shall only go to Mason's and Dixon's line on your way North," but they may with great constitutional propriety say to the Northern bishop, "When you go to Mason's and Dixon's line you shall find no Church beyond it," and to the Southern bishop travelling this way with scrip and sandal, "You shall find no Church north of it." I respectfully submit, that such inconsistencies as these could not possibly have been entertained and embodied by men fit to represent the grand constructive intellect of Wesley, and perpetuate a system, giving him a fame among the builders of mitres.

So much for the law of 1808. Is any light thrown on this interesting inquiry by what has happened since 1808? Now there are only three occasions on which anything has been done which anybody supposes throws any light on the subject of the inquiry. They are,—1st, the Canada case; 2d, the action of this very body in 1844; and 3d, the action of our own body in 1848. I begin for a moment or two with a few words on the Canada case.

I respectfully submit, that the Canada case affords evidence perfectly conclusive to show that they had not this power in point of fact. What was this Canada case? It was this exactly. The Methodist Episcopal Church from its origin was created by the Methodism of the United States, in consequence of the independence of the United States, in and for the United States alone. Expansive as they have been, the Methodist Church, from the nature of its constitution, and in point of fact, although the very day it came into existence it spread itself to the limits of the territory of the United States, yet it has never exceeded, and it could not exceed the limits of that territory for a hair's breadth. It may go up to the line; it may meet on the other side of the line a separate and independent Methodist Church, and they may shake hands across the line; they may organize by agreement or compact a connexion, but there it ends. There it is, and there it will remain, nothing in the world but an American Methodist Church in league or in treaty with a foreign and equally independent Methodist Church on the other side of our frontier line. That is the condition of the Methodist polity. I deduce it from the letter of Wesley, who says, that in consequence of the unexpected independence of this nation, he gives it a separate Church. Wesley, as everybody knows, through important periods of his life, clung fast to the old Church of England, and left it with reluctance. He bestowed the boon of a new Church upon American Methodism with reluctance, and he limited the precious grant by the necessity of the case, and that necessity, blessed be God! was a pretty ample and energetic necessity in American independence. He gave it no further than the limits of the United States.

The same thing is proved by the fact that the Church was created by American citizens. The Conference of 1784, which I denominated an extraordinary convention, that created it, was a conference of American preachers alone, and no work created by their hands could *proprio vigore*, or by its probable destination, have existence without the United States. Your Honours cannot, I think, fail to remember that significant recognition of the political interests of these new United States, which they bring forward into the very constitution of the creation of the Church, their measure and their end, ultimately subordinate to the greater ends they had in view. The Methodist Church then was a Church for this land, it was a Church for all of it : but let that pass.

While this is true, Methodism from the beginning recognised the beautiful enterprise of missions, and therefore it had always been in the habit of sending its missionaries, by their own consent, into Canada. There they met a germ of North American Methodism growing up in Upper and Lower Canada. An acquaintance was matured, and at last it came to pass, that the Canadian Methodist Church conceived a desire to be connected, by such ties as they thought appropriate to such jurisdictions, with the larger and more prosperous Methodism of the United States. Thereupon, as your Honours will find recited on every page of these proofs which contains the history of the Canada case, a compact was made, an agreement was entered into, a league was concluded; and the result was, not that the Church extended itself to the North pole, or to the line of perpetual congelation, not that it extended beyond its territory, but that it filled up to the territory of the Canadian Church, and that Church occupied the region beyond, and the two then and there meeting, formed this league and brought themselves under that well-known rule of law recognised, I believe, in 2d Denio, that two Churches entirely independent of each other may voluntarily conclude a treaty of union, which shall leave their identity perfectly distinct, as the sweet and bitter fountains that flow together without mingling, and which union either may terminate without schism, with or without the consent of the other. That was exactly in ecclesiastical law, as I understand it, the condition of these Churches. As it seems not, as a statement of fact, to be entirely appreciated or admitted to be correct on the other side, I shall presently call the attention of the Court to the proofs from which I gather it. I shall find them on the recitals of the gravest and most deliberate action of the General Conference, and I apprehend the Court will receive them as the very highest historical evidence upon a historical inquiry of fact. Such was the transaction.

In that state of things time passed on, and the nationality of the Canadas came to be a little more developed. The political interests of the two countries, which Methodism always recognises, and which I commend to her special care to-day, led to a necessity for separation; and thereupon Canada applied for a separation of the connexion. Now we come to the constructions of that case. Notwithstanding such had been their relations, although this had not been an identical and homogeneous Church extended by fusion over a common territory, but two Churches identically distinct, connected simply by a conventional tie, yet when the Canada Conference came here to apply for a dissolution of the connexion, the first judgment of the General Conference was, that it exceeded their constitutional powers to grant it, and they thereupon proceeded to announce a set of doctrines, after great deliberation, which give to the winds the assumptions of the hasty and ill-considered proceeding of 1844. In the first place, it was reported by a committee to which the subject was referred, that it was beyond the constitutional power of the General Conference to grant the request in the form in which it was presented. On pp. 34, 35 of Proofs No. 1, your Honours will find, that the committee on Canada affairs, to whom the subject was referred, reported :—

"The committee are unanimously of the opinion, that, however peculiar may be the situation of our brethren in Canada, and however much we may sympathize with them in their present state of perplexity, this General Conference cannot consistently grant them a separate Church establishment, according to the prayer of the petitioners. The committee, therefore, recommend the adoption of the following resolution :—

"1. That, inasmuch as the several annual conferences have not recommended it to the General Conference, it is unconstitutional, and also, under the circumstances, inexpedient, to grant the prayer of the petitioners for a separate Church establishment in Upper Canada."

The extreme anxiety felt in relation to the matter, and the very kind acquaintance that seems to have been entertained, led the Conference to hold the matter under consideration; and there is very satisfactory evidence to show that it was thereupon subjected to the best lights in that Conference, and after several days of deliberation, it was discovered that the peculiar relations between the two Churches, the fact that they did not constitute one single homogeneous and identical Church, but a league between two independent Churches, afforded a source of power, and indicated a means of escaping from the difficulty. Therefore we find, on page 35, that the following resolve was adopted, on the motion of Mr. Ryerson. This is the second stage to which the deliberations of the Conference conducted them :—

"Whereas the Canada Annual Conference, situated in the Province of Upper Canada, under a foreign government, have, in their memorial, presented to this Conference the disabilities under which they labour in consequence of their union with a foreign ecclesiastical government, and setting forth their desire to be set off as a separate Church establishment; and whereas, this General Conference disclaim all right to exercise ecclesiastical jurisdiction under such circumstances, except by mutual agreement :—

"*Resolved*, therefore, by the delegates of the annual conferences in General Conference assembled, that the compact existing between the Canada Annual Conference and the Methodist Episcopal Church in the United States, be, and hereby is, dissolved by mutual consent."

I need not say this would be most extraordinary language as applicable to the Methodist Episcopal Church dealing with one of its outlying conferences. I need not say it would not be competent, because it would not be historically true, in such a case, to talk of a "union with a foreign ecclesiastical government," or of a union existing by means of a "compact" voluntarily entered into. Why, the union which binds the Methodist Episcopal Church, its identity and organism, is a union derived from the original act of creation, not something done first, and then that which was first created forming a succession of leagues with various annual conferences; but *uno et eodem flatu*, by one and the same creative act, by the ordinance of the extraordinary Convention assembled under the letter of Wesley, the Church instantly existed co-extensively with the land, and thenceforward every annual conference, then existing or ever afterwards to exist, came into being, not by virtue of successive compacts, but under and in obedience to the original plan of growth,—they were nothing less and nothing more than successive developments according to the original organic law.

I should not care, for the purposes of this discussion, whether the Conference of 1828 had or had not left the Canada case with the passage of the resolution which I have read. What do they say by that resolution? That they have power to dissolve the existing Methodist Episcopal Church? Nothing like it; but they say, on the contrary, "Whereas we have not the constitutional power to do what we first thought was something resembling it, after a week's study, and a week's prayer to

God, we have found out a legal method by which we can grant the prayer of the petition, and yet abstain from doing anything resembling, in the least degree, a division of the Church; for we have discovered that it is not one Church which is to be cut in two, but only a union between two that is to be divided, and we therefore do it." How different that is from the power of dividing an existing identical Church let one illustration suffice to show. I suppose to-day the general government, with all its power, cannot divide the Union that is committed to its care; but I suppose it very competent, indeed, for the general government, by its appropriate organ, the treaty-making power, or the legislative power, acting under its commercial authority, to put an end to a treaty with England, or with Austria. Therefore, it is not competent for my learned friend to argue that because this Conference have put an end to a treaty with another Church, they have the power to divide their own Church. But the sober second thought of the Conference of 1828 did not dare to leave the matter rest exactly there, and after some more reflection it was discovered that even to go so far would perhaps be to go too far; and, therefore, you find its ultimate opinions on this question, the result of a great deal of thought, of a great deal of conscientious and charitable desire to grant the request, at last embodied on page 37 of Proofs No. 1. The resolution on which I have been remarking was rescinded, and the ultimate determination of the Conference embodied in these words:—

"*Resolved*, by the delegates of the annual conferences in General Conference assembled, that, whereas the jurisdiction of the Methodist Episcopal Church in the United States of America, has heretofore been extended over the ministers and members in connexion with said Church in the Province of Upper Canada, by mutual agreement, and by the consent and desire of our brethren in that Province; and whereas this General Conference is satisfactorily assured that our brethren in the said Province, under peculiar and pressing circumstances, do now desire to organize themselves into a distinct Methodist Episcopal Church, in friendly relations with the Methodist Episcopal Church in the United States; therefore, be it resolved,"

That if Canada will dissolve the treaty, we will send her a bishop, and assist her in organizing for the new ecclesiastical life on which she will thus have resolved to enter.

There it is exactly. I think no historical and legal inquirer can doubt that the fair construction to be gathered from the Canada case is, that it denies the power to dissolve or divide an identical Church, and the first impression of the Conference was that they could not sever a treaty between them and an independent Church, and afterwards they thought that could be done, but ultimately they receded from even that proposition. That is the whole of the Canada case. I shall refer to it for a moment hereafter, when I come to its bearing on the property question, but I have addressed myself to it now, only as it might be thought to throw light on the judgment of the Conference as to the existence of a power to divide the Church.

Then, the only other occasions on which it may be supposed that any light can be thrown by the action of the General Conference on the question which is now the subject of inquiry, are the proceedings of 1844 and 1848. I did not understand the eminent counsel for the plaintiffs to place great reliance on the proceedings of 1844, as evidence of the law. I do not intend to say anything disrespectful to that body, but it is my duty to remind the Court, that under the circumstances in which it met and did its work, its proceedings, as evidence of the law, will be considered, I think, by no fair inquirer as entitled to any considerable degree of weight, when compared with the more deliberate, and prolonged, and instructive discussions and investigations of the Conference of 1828, on the Canada case. In the first place, this Conference of 1844 was a body assembled in the ordinary way, so that, so far as we can learn, no constituent to any member elected had the slightest intimation that such a transcendent question as this was coming into consideration at all. Then, the transactions of that body unfitted them for the deep and calm inquiry. The greater part of the time they were together was occupied in debate touching the proceedings in Bishop Andrew's case, and when they arrived at the close of that discussion, somewhat exhausted, a little dispirited and peevish, needing the air of the mountain tops and the firesides of their own families to restore them to their habitual temper, not to say free action of the Methodist brain, they left themselves no time to deliberate on this matter, for the vote was taken on Bishop Andrew's case on Saturday, and on the next Saturday they cut the Church in two, as a man would serve a cucumber, and the intervening time was occupied in writing the Protest and the Reply to it. There is not a particle of evidence that a single member of that Conference ever in his life, before he came or after he came, reflected for half an hour on the constitutional question which is to be decided by this Bench. If I am wrong my learned friend will correct the statement; but I repeat, there is not a particle of evidence that in their preparatory studies, in the annual conferences, they thought of it; there is not a particle of evidence that there were three lines in a newspaper preparing the Church and the country for this thunderbolt out of an unclouded sky. They came in the ordinary course of business to do ordinary business, and were not called for any extraordinary purpose. Being there, under the circumstances to which I have referred, the work is done. Hence, I respectfully submit that it is not high and satisfactory evidence of the law on such a question as this.

I ought to take in this review, and in answer to that in some measure, the proceedings of the General Conference of 1848, which declare a rule of law directly the other way, to the end that the Court may have in a single view all the considerations which may be deemed important on the point. My learned brother does not go further than I do when he says, that he who bereaves me of our South bereaves me of most precious and valued jewels; but he goes a little too far, when he says that the Conference of 1848 met bereaved and shorn of all its strength. Not quite so. On the contrary, the annual conferences in 1848 were most ably represented—public opinion had developed itself; men had cooled. That Conference stood on higher ground. I agree that it then had a somewhat sectional character, but I shall pray your Honours by-and-by to look with some attention on reports in that body on which we rely, to see whether ability enough did not remain, circumstances in other respects being the same, to investigate and elucidate such a question as this. I would state here that the decision in the case cited from Benjamin Monroe, which was read from a pamphlet the other day, was made before 1848, and there was nothing before that decision to show that there was the conflicting judgment of another General Conference on the subject. The mention of that case reminds me of a singular suggestion on the subject of power, which I remember is advanced in the opinion of the Court in that case. I do not know that the learned counsel for the plaintiffs adopted that argument, which certainly would have given a great deal of respectability to it, but it is an argument advanced by the Court in that case, and will therefore come under the observation of your Honours. It is said that if, without any facilities being afforded by the General Conference, the South had gone forward and done this very act, the General Conference would be the body, according to ecclesiastical polity, to go on and arrange and adjust between the separated and mutilated fragments; it would be the constitutional body to draw the new line of boundary and to adjust the terms of future union with the new Church, which convulsion and violence had thus unexpectedly erected by its side; and that, therefore, by analogy, the General Conference should have a power to do in advance that same thing. I beg to say, that that is the old logical sophism of *ignotum per ignotius*, because there is no manner of certainty that, in such a crisis as that, there would be devolved on the General Conference the absolute power of arranging for a crisis so extraordinary. Nobody knows whether it would be or not. What is the value of the argument in the supposed case? Nobody knows whether it would be devolved on the General Conference by a great moral, civil, or ecclesiastical convulsion, tearing away half the Church. Nobody can show me anything in the history or polity of the Church to prove that the General Conference would be the only body charged with the adjustment of such a crisis as that. On the contrary, I say it is ten thousand times more probable that thereupon the united remaining sovereign will would be assembled *en masse*; for the great question would be, What should then be done with this mutilated fragment? Shall it be deemed that the Methodist Episcopal Church still exists? Or shall it be deemed disintegrated? And hence, until you see that the General Conference would, in such a case, certainly do this, to argue in this way is, in the first place, *ignotum per ignotius*.

There is, however, a deeper difficulty. It does not follow that because the General Conference may act constitutionally on a crisis produced by the action of another, it may therefore proceed and initiate and facilitate that business in advance. I apprehend that before the least weight can be given to such an argument as this, your Honours must see that the power, which it is said they possess in that case, is so exactly like the power they would exert in the supposed case, that you can see no reason why the original constituent body could not have given one as well as the other. Therefore, if you were judicially to discern that the constituent body might perfectly well have clothed them with the constitutional competency to deal with such a case as that, and yet have withheld it from them, then this power does not follow from that power, and there is the fallacy of the argument. Let me take a case—*Quod omen avertat Jupiter!* If a convulsion in one State spread into another and carry off a range of States, that same general government, when that crisis shall have arrived, would be the constitutional body to recognise the foreign existence and to arrange the terms of frontier connexion, to define the line of boundary, and to act on the crisis. Could we infer from that that they could divide the States? So here exactly. I put this argument with very great confidence of its general soundness. Cannot this Court say judicially, perfectly well, that the constituent body of 1808 might have said exactly this to the General Conference: "Consider yourselves charged with the great mission of preserving the unity of the Church; let that unity be first and last in all your thoughts, and counsels, and prayers; if an excited locality hereafter shall come to you and solicit to be let off, discourage them, hang over their heads every terror of the Church, hang over their heads all the undefined terrors of excommunication, and thus, if you can, restrain the dire desire, and bring them back again; but if, unmindful of this your action, they go out, remember you have unity to preserve; what you have, keep and adorn; for unity, take care of what is left, and for unity do not throw out facilities in advance for its dissolution." To tell me, then, that because this body would find itself charged with the great duty of saving all they could, and arranging a frontier of peace with this separated secession, in the case I have been putting, they may therefore divide, is to say that extreme medicine may be made into daily bread, and a shield into a sword of death.

I therefore respectfully submit that that analogy does not, in the slightest degree, apply to the case before the Court, and that unless your Honours do clearly discern that, in arguing from one thing to another in this case, and especially to *ignotius* from *ignotum*, and the reverse, the powers are so identical that one being given the other follows necessarily, neither of the powers is given.

I have said all that I intended to say on the subject of power. I am ready to leave it with a single suggestion. Your Honours are aware that we take another ground, and that is, that if this power existed, it was exerted only on a contingency by the General Conference, *i. e.*, upon a representation made to them by the minority from the South that a necessity would certainly develop itself for such a change, and thereupon, in anticipation of such necessity to be afterwards developed, the General Conference proceeded to do what they have done in the way of a division, and that that contingency never has happened in matter of fact. That is the substance of the point. The minority feared a local excitement. Their brethren of the North said to them, "If you find you must desert them or us, we will let you go." We say they did not find it, but made it so. We say that whether it existed or not, the General Conference next to sit was to decide, or this Court was to decide. If it was the General Conference next to sit which was to decide, they have decided against them. If it was this Court, we respectfully submit that your Honours will decide against them. I propose to submit all that part of the case to the official report on the state of the Church, to be found on page 138 of Proofs No. 1. It is an argument of great ability, embodying all I could wish, and more than I should be able myself, on the same point, to say to the Court. I have done, then, with the question of power and the exertion of the power.

It remains for me very briefly to open, not to attempt to enforce, in the first place, that the legal consequences of this proposition, if maintained, are fatal to the plaintiffs' claim ; and, in the next place, that even if this proposition of the want of power or the exertion of it is not maintained, still the plaintiffs cannot sustain their bill. In the first place, and in a general way, if the plaintiffs have voluntarily seceded and separated themselves from membership, without competent ecclesiastical authority terminating their membership, I am not able to understand how it can be seriously contested that their rights of property have also terminated. To avoid that consequence, the plaintiffs must show that the beneficiaries of this fund have such a right that a voluntary unauthorized abandonment of membership does not lose it. This conducts us to the very important question of the nature and limitations of the right of the beneficiaries in this fund. I do not know that we have very much to observe on in the statement made by the eminent counsel for the plaintiffs in regard to the origin and nature of this fund, the Book Concern, except, perhaps, if he will give me leave to say it, a certain degree of indistinctness in the exhibition of the capital qualification, on which all the rights of the beneficiaries in it are limited—that of continued membership. In his interesting outline of its history in a general way, we concur. We may pause to refresh ourselves for a moment. That history goes back to the year 1787. It was very early discerned, as my learned brother has said, that a sacred written literature would be among the most important instrumentalities by which the great ends of this Church could be accomplished. Some books of devotion and worship, at any rate, there must be provided for the humblest and least literate of its numerous and growing congregations. Therefore, as early as 1787 individual preachers appear to have conceived the idea of publishing and circulating such books and creating such a literature as this. To this end, as we gather from history, they began, as we are very apt to begin in America, on borrowed capital. A contribution may have been occasionally made, but the main source of growth undoubtedly was from the profits of the business. It has grown, under the administration of the Church, from 1787, when it was started with $4,000 capital and $3,000 debt, to the very large amount of $750,000—from $1,000 to $750,000. These relative sums are not important to the determination of the legal point, though a very large perennial contribution of spiritual, and, I am glad to be able to add, intellectual as well as moral food.

It was very early discerned that this business could be made, not only to support and enlarge itself, but also to yield a surplus of profits ; and it is very interesting to observe, that from its origin it was determined to dedicate that sort of profits to, what we call at the bar, a charitable use,—that is to say, technically and legally, a charitable use, but not at all excluding meritorious service, and giving a great deal more prominence to meritorious service in the beneficiary's title than our friends on the other side contend. From its very origin this fund was devoted to a charitable use. The designation of the beneficiaries and the mode of administering it have varied a little ; but from 1796 to this day, by a law passed in 1796, standing on the record of its Discipline, re-enacted in 1800, re-enacted in 1804, re-enacted in 1808, and continued, that surplus fund has stood explicitly, and irrevocably, and unequivocally devoted to a perfect and well-defined description of beneficiaries—to travelling, supernumerary, superannuated, and exhausted preachers and their families, being, as we say, all the time in membership in the Methodist Episcopal Church. That appropriation of these funds was made by law in 1796 ; to that appropriation of them this Church has adhered, without the interruption of a moment. Under that dedication it has grown up from $1,000 to $750,000 ; under that dedication, many laborious men, of the living and the dead, came into the Church, lived there, laboured there, died there, and live there and labour there yet, on the faith of a sound interpretation and an exact form of administration of that trust. And I am here to-day for nothing but the true interpretation of that trust. Find me the beneficiary according to the law, and that beneficiary shall have his share of the funds in the hands of my clients. The Court knows how the matter stands. The trustees are my clients, the book agents on record ; the beneficiaries are the persons indicated ; those who manage the fund are the annual conferences and the General Conference ; and the mode of doing it is this :—these book agents designate the amount to which each annual conference is entitled, and each thereupon draws its amount, calls the beneficiaries, and proceeds to measure to each party according to his claim.

So much for the history. Passing from this to the legal questions, I will not stop to say anything on the first two points which are contained on the plaintiffs' brief, although perhaps they would warrant the criticism that they are somewhat inadequately conceived, a little overstated ; but I pass them without particular remark. It is on arriving at the third point that we find the beginning of the controversy. We think, with very great submission, that the learned and eminent counsel, in this point and in his argument, overstates the right of any beneficiary when he calls it a perfect right, and that they misdescribe it when they call it a right in a fund of earnings in the nature of a partnership derived from work and labour about books. We must submit on this that they fail, as it seems to us, to appreciate that the capital qualification under which every beneficiary is to acquire and hold it, is the qualification of original and continued membership in the Methodist Episcopal Church. That qualification we think they fail, in all its importance, to appreciate. I will not pause at this moment to indicate with what propriety it is said that the right of any beneficiary is a perfect right. In regard to the qualities that are properly attributable to it in a legal point of view, it is a right which began to be acquired by coming within the *designatio personarum*, but it is a right to be maintained and perfected only by the continued performance of certain conditions. He who becomes a travelling preacher initiates a right ; but if he is expelled, as he sometimes is, or if he is located, as he may be, he loses that right. So also of a supernumerary and even of a superannuated. So then I submit that it is a right, beginning by one coming within a certain *designatio personarum*, but which is lost for want of a continuance in official well-doing afterwards.

Nor will I pause at this moment to inquire, because I attach no sort of consequence to it, although there is some diversity of judgment as to that point, if this right of the beneficiary is in the least degree better or worse from the circumstance on which my learned friend places some stress, that the fund has grown from profits on books which the travelling preachers of the society sold. I suppose it altogether immaterial. The right of the beneficiary on this dedication to charitable uses does not depend in the least on the kind of work which, as a travelling preacher, he does, or, as a supernumerary or superannuated, he has done; but the right depends on this—that he became a preacher and continued to be a preacher under the Discipline, under the dedication which gives a preacher a certain allowance and a certain claim on this fund. That I submit in point of law is exactly the origin of the preacher's right. There is no natural right under any circumstances, no right raised by implication for work and labour done. The only requisite is—becoming a travelling preacher, continuing a travelling preacher, continuing a supernumerary or superannuated preacher, under the same dedication, in whatever field of Methodist labour he may have been employed. Whether this preacher was, what they call in some societies, a colporteur of books, is of no importance. He who never carried a book for sale in his life is as clearly within the grant as he who has carried libraries of books. Some preachers carried books and some did not carry them. If he carried them, it adds nothing to his title; if he did not, it detracts nothing from his title. My learned brother will give me leave to say that the most conservative and best instructed on the other side really can find nothing better to put their case on than absolute socialism at last. "He has laboured about the books, and therefore has a natural right to the fund," they say. Is not that socialism? To be sure he has laboured about the books, but the books were not his. Did he write them? No. Did he own them? Certainly not. Did he own their profits? Certainly not. On the contrary, they were the property of another party, to wit, the trustee, for charitable uses, and that party hired him to work for him, and told him, "If you work and be a travelling preacher, supernumerary or superannuated, you will have an interest in this fund." But in the meantime books and profits belonged to his employer, and his right at last cannot be placed or maintained for a minute on any ground but that he is a servant and labourer, and therefore, according to the highest authority, "worthy of his hire," according to the terms of that hire. I shall therefore take it for granted, without stopping to develop it, that while the right is no doubt perfect, in a certain sense, if he continues in well-doing officially to the end, it is not accurately described, it is not described according to law, it is not described according to the jurisprudence of conservation, by the plaintiffs. There is not a labourer in the service of New-York that might not allege an interest in the fund on the same grounds exactly. Does he not carry out the milk? Does he not take care of the chyme? Is it not immediately and directly attributable to his skill that the fund was gathered? Why has he not a right to it? Because he did not work in a state of nature, but under a convention *quae vincit legem*, under a contract with the owner that he should do his work and receive certain wages. I have not therefore attached a great deal of importance to this view, although much has been said about it.

We come directly at last to the great decisive qualification which is overlooked on the other side, whether membership is not an indispensable qualification to initiating a right, and continuing membership indispensable to the continuance of the right. I submit that is perfectly plain—too plain for me to argue for a moment. I do not believe either of the eminent counsel mean to say that there can be any pretence that this description of persons, at the time when their right inchoates and attaches to them at first, are not to be members of the Methodist Episcopal Church. My learned brother surely does not mean to say that a travelling preacher in Bermuda has a right to this fund. Nobody contends for that. Beyond all doubt, when they first come within the *designatio personarum* on which the right takes its inchoation, they are to be members. The question is, whether they can go away and still be members. I submit that they cannot, for this general reason, that the right is not perfect at the start, but it is a right to be kept alive and matured by a series of service—because the Church may exact duties from him, in the administration of which he may lose the right. The travelling preacher, if he is expelled, loses the right; if he is turned into a local preacher, he loses his right. Now, can it be pretended that while a travelling preacher remains and works in the Methodist Church, and holds his interest on condition that he does not get expelled and does not get located, another preacher, who came into the Church on the same day, can retire from its service, and thus relieve himself from the conditions and inconveniences and qualifications under which the other holds his right, and retain his right? Can he retire, and thus avoid the *onus*, and retain the *commodum?* I respectfully submit that he cannot. The meaning, therefore, of the system is, if he becomes a travelling preacher, if he remains a travelling preacher, he earns a right; but if he lives so that the Church cannot follow him by the conditions, so that it cannot follow him by the qualifications, cannot hold him to any responsibility, his right is gone; or else it is to be conceded that by departing from the Church he may, by his own act, change the tenure of title granted to all alike by the original law. That is just as true of the supernumerary as it is of the travelling preacher. A supernumerary (if my ecclesiastical friends will permit me to say it) is nothing but an officer on shore waiting orders. He is subject to the call of the Church, and is liable to be put in active service, liable to be expelled, liable to be located, as well as another. This seems to be just as true of the superannuated. One would think that if anybody could retire from the Church and retain title, it would be the superannuated, the exhausted preacher. Yet there can be no doubt that he also is required by the discipline of the Church to stay and serve. It is true that his day of active, manly exercise is done, but it is also true that there remains a service of loyalty and love. His silvery cord may be about to be loosened and the bowl to be broken at the fountain, yet he may testify of the Church by the beauty of a declining and ripe age; his lips may continue to speak for her, his hands may continue to be lifted up. Therefore it is that the Church that maintains him, follows him with a duty gentler and gentler, and more and more kindly executed, but a duty to his grave. There is never an hour when the longest official life entitles the most meritorious superannuated preacher to throw off the weight of age, to retire from duty, and yet enjoy support. This is what makes this Church what it is—small pay, hard work, constant superintendence, justice to all men according to the contract. I do not know that it is necessary to add anything to this general argument.

My learned brother cannot conceive how a Methodist going occasionally to a Presbyterian meeting should lose his share of the fund. I think that perhaps it might do him good occasionally to go to a Presbyterian meeting. He may go anywhere until he gets expelled, and do anything that does not terminate membership. That is all. This Church is not strict, this Church is not narrow; and strict, or narrow, or otherwise, while the membership remains undissolved by expulsion, the right remains. My learned friend did not seem to consider that remaining a Methodist was necessary to continue the right. Why, says he, he was to be a preacher, and nothing is said about his being a Methodist. He deduced it, however, that the object was to promote Methodism, and he was a little shocked that a person should lose his right because he was promoting another religion. Does my friend mean to say that in the first instance a man can take a right to the fund because he preaches Methodism? I suppose he preaches it in Bermuda under the pine trees, or in Canada among the regions of perpetual snow—does he take title? It is perfectly clear that he does not. I submit that it is not accurate to say this fund was created to promote Methodism. It was created by the Methodist Episcopal Church to promote its own efficiency and strength for good, and thus enable it to spread Methodism. That is the object of the Methodist Episcopal Church and of this fund. Then it is not to promote Methodism generally, but to strengthen the Church, to enrich it, to make eloquent tongues, and touch lips as with fire, to the end that by the Church Methodism shall be spread.

Why should I argue the matter at large when we have two such memorable constructions before us as the Canada case and the case of 1844? What was the Canada case, as a property case? I have touched on it at considerable length as it bears on the ecclesiastical question. I submit that it was settled on that occasion with great deliberation, against every wish of every man's heart, that this fund was to be used within these uses for travelling, supernumerary, and superannuated preachers; and that in departing, not merely in peace, but with every benediction of the Church, the Canada Church could take nothing. That is the Canada case. Canada left this Church in peace. Did not the members of the Canadian Church remain Methodists still? Did they not continue to give, in Methodistical spirit, the advice of foreign philanthropy about slavery, to show how affectionately they remembered us? They went in peace, they remained Methodists, and yet you find this Church, by a unanimous and deliberate judgment, declaring that they were not entitled to a farthing. That is the very question now before the Court. I am now departing from the case of unauthorized secession, and speaking of the case of secession authorized, and attended by the greetings of those who gave the leave. In that case it is settled. Your Honours, by referring to the case, will find that there was a strong desire to indulge the Canadians; it was a struggle between conviction and inclination. Your Honours, as men as well as learned judges, will appreciate the value of such a decision as that. It was a decision wrung from the Conference by a perfectly understood sense of duty. We are on that very identical question, Who is within these uses? It is to be devoted to travelling preachers, supernumerary and superannuated. Where and who? Members of what? Members of this Church; and that decision is that if they cease to be such, although by consent of everybody, and affectionate dismissal of everybody, the right was gone.

Have we not a still stronger case in this very proceeding of 1844? Have we not here all but the unanimous judgment of this body, that persons no longer members, even if they depart in peace and by consent, cannot take a dollar? Does not the action of that body record the unanimous judgment of the body, that these uses fail on failure of membership, and that this retirement, although peaceable, is a failure of membership, and that therefore, unless the uses could be enlarged, the retiring member was no longer within them? Was not that the very reason why they recommended to the annual conferences a change in the restrictive article? I suppose then we have here the highest evidence of law; we have the contemporaneous exposition of its makers, under extraordinary circumstances, and they certainly relieve me from the trouble of pursuing the argument further. I had intended to trace the connexion between such an association as this and a partnership; but I remember by whom I am to be followed, on the part of these defendants, and I gladly relieve the Court from the further consideration of this part of the case.

Then, if this be so, the case is ended in every view. Authorized or unauthorized, membership has gone, and with membership right is gone. The only answer to this, which we have been able to appreciate, is, that the old Church is destroyed, and two new ones created upon its site, and upon that destruction everybody was remitted to his natural rights—the ship had gone ashore, and every man was to get a nail or a plank as he could—everybody upon that dissolution is remitted to his natural right, as in a joint-stock company or in a partnership. That is the only case, as I understand, which is left for the plaintiffs. To this there are four answers, each of which is, I think, equally decisive. In the first place, I have already argued that the General Conference has no power ecclesiastically to destroy the Church. I am not now speaking of a division leaving the old identity untouched. I have argued that they cannot destroy the Church, and raise two or two thousand Churches from its ashes. In the next place, the General Conference in this great transaction did not assume to destroy the Church, but on the contrary, the Plan of Separation, from beginning to end, shows that what they intended to do was to authorize a departure, leaving the old identity untouched. If your Honours will do me the favour to look into the Plan as it is stated in the bill you will find :—1st. That the General Conference never assumed, in terms, to destroy the Church. 2d. That they never assumed, in terms, to divide the Church. On the other hand, it is quite striking to remark, that while it speaks of a division of property, it never speaks of a division of the Church, but simply and merely of a separation of parties from the Church; it deals throughout with a contemplated act of other persons, and calls that act a separation by them, and all it authorizes is a separation by others leaving itself to exist. It calls itself by the old name of Methodist Episcopal Church, and designates the new one, thus to be erected, by the name of the Methodist Episcopal Church, South; and I submit that to retain the name is to retain the identity. I would call the attention of the Court to a single section in the bill on page 4. It embodies the entire theory of the Plan of Separation. Article 2 of the Plan of Separation says :—

"That ministers, local and travelling, of every grade and office in the Methodist Episcopal Church, may, as they prefer, remain in that Church, or, without blame, attach themselves to the Church, South."

Your Honours will find the proof of my argument on pp. 4, 5, and 6 of the bill. In that connexion, I may be permitted to say, that such is the view of this transaction taken in 7 Ben. Monroe, p. 507, in the case which has been cited. (For extract, see p. 368.)

Let me add two auxiliary suggestions. The first is, That the Louisville Convention throughout all their resolutions say nothing at all of a division of the Church, but characterize their own act as a separation from an identity already existing, and which it leaves exactly as it was before, only abridged. 2d. The frame of the plaintiffs' bill so treats the affair. They do not call us, or anybody representing us, a new Church, nor these defendants the agents of a new Church; but it is assumed throughout that the old Methodist Episcopal Church exists *ab eo nomine*. If your Honours will turn to pp. 10 and 11 of the bill, you will find this remark abundantly verified.

In the third place, not only does the General Conference not assume to destroy, and thus to allow the plaintiffs to interpose their theory of the natural right of all the stockholders, but it goes further. It does not content itself with authorizing a separation and stopping there, but it goes further, and takes care to ordain solicitously that the party seceding shall have nothing at all on the ground of natural right, nothing at all on the ground of natural equity, attaching to dissolution and growing out of an old *quantum meruit* for work and labour about books, but that he shall have nothing except according to the existing law of the society—except the annual conferences would give it. I think we find here evidence of the proposition. Then in the bill to which I have been making reference, we find evidence of it also. The work was consummated by the Conference, and I submit that no man is to take anything on the ground of natural right—no man is to take anything except under the *lex societatis*, *i. e.*, if the annual conferences will give it, and they recommend them to do so. Instead of a dissolution, there was a withdrawal of parties; and it was ordained that everybody not withdrawing, should be subject to the still existing law of the society. Therefore, I submit that it is impossible, against this reiterated question of intent, that the plaintiffs can imply a constructive equity on which they can come in and insist upon remission to natural right.

Is it not perfectly plain, as a matter of meaning, that the General Conference intends that nobody shall take a dollar by secession or natural right, unless the annual conferences give it? Is it not absurd to suppose they would go on providing, that if the annual conference do so and so, something shall follow, if they meant to ordain, whether the annual conferences do so or not, that every man should have part of the fund? Is it not perfectly obvious that they meant to recognise the law of the society as in force, to interpret it as giving the property only to members, and thereupon to confine their action to the advisory alteration of the use without which no right was to arise at all? Is it not then perfectly plain, that against this ordinance of the General Conference on this express agreement no possible implication can be raised? How can the plaintiffs take a part of this bill and reject the rest? Can they take so much of it as suits them, and go for natural equity for the rest of it? Would the Conference of 1844 have divided the Church, if the effect would be to let in natural right, on which the seceder should take as much as he that remained, when they were sitting under a constitution expressly prohibiting them from committing any such act?

Finally and fourthly, there is another answer to the suggestion that the division lets the plaintiffs in on natural equity against the meaning of the Conference; and it is, that if such must be the effect, whether the General Conference can by express declaration help it or not, we know they had no power to make a dissolution. Your Honours will observe that it adds another element to the argument I had the honour to submit yesterday, whether ecclesiastically they can divide or not. If it be so that a division, in spite of the General Conference and everything they can ordain to qualify it, must necessarily carry the property out of its use, by carrying it to one not a member, we know they cannot make it, because they are a representative body, with no power but what the constituent gives; and we know by the terms of the constitution under which they exist, that they are forbidden to do that act directly, and they cannot do indirectly what they cannot do directly. Therefore, I say that if the General Conference is so situated, that it cannot divide this Church without the additional consequence that the property goes to one not entitled, it follows that they cannot divide the Church, and that is no great harm in my humble judgment. They cannot divide, if to divide is to break the constitution. They cannot grasp doubtful ecclesiastical power with the effect of violating plain civil right.

I need not, then, in conclusion, suggest the other point which, however, I believe, stands on proof that the annual conferences and General Conference together could not set this use at large. The general grant may be thus stated. The right is in cestique and his continuing a member. Therefore, if the annual conferences had acted on this recommendation, they could not have given the fund to the retiring members. Such was the original grant. The use was created in 1792 or 1800, and renewed in 1804, and it became the law of the Church, and thenceforward I suppose remained the law of the Church. The authorities for the proposition are on the brief. It is, however, a moot-point, and of no sort of consequence, as the annual conferences did not unite in agreeing to the recommendation.

I have been too much indulged by the kindness of the Court to trespass for another moment on your Honours' attention. I have certainly supposed that the plaintiffs have no legal and no equitable right to the relief for which they ask, in any of the forms in which they ask for it. I cannot admit that they have been misled into their present position by any act of the defendants. The General Conference did for them all it could; it recommended to the annual conferences to rescind. They did not rescind. The plaintiffs will give me leave to say that they knew perfectly well from the beginning, and at every step they took, that they took it under the hazards of the action of the annual conferences, and that they ran the risk of an unfavourable judgment, even if they themselves did not procure that unfavourable judgment. One consolation and one certainty we have. We know that the law of the case will be discerned and applied. We know perfectly well that whatever may be the result of the case, or the result of the general controversy, it will vindicate and exemplify, what needs neither to be vindicated nor exemplified—the administration of justice according to a settled rule. With the consequences of their judgments, this Court is not in the habit of troubling itself in advance to inquire. But I may be permitted to say for myself at the bar, looking a little beyond the immediate professional inquiry here involved, that I do not know that there is anything this day which a wise man and a lover of his country should as much desire as the re-establishment, in some good measure, of the Methodist Episcopal Church, one Church again for the North and the South. Whether and to what extent one may surely entertain such a hope as that, I am sure I have not a satisfactory means of determining. For myself, let me tell the Court, however, before I take my leave of them, that my clients this day are a Methodist Episcopal Church for North and South, shorn of some beams, bereaved of some auxiliary talent, and impaired to some extent of their strength and means of utility. These defendants are this day still a Church for the North and the South. This Methodist Episcopal Church, the old organization, exists this day in many a slave State. In Delaware, in Maryland, in Eastern Virginia, in Western Virginia, in Kentucky, in Missouri, in Arkansas, in Texas, it has thousands of attached affectionate adherents. I rejoice to be able to believe that it is enlarging. I will not deny that, and in addition to the reasons of gratification with which I believe the law of the case is with the defendants, I feel also that a decision in their favour will do something to enable this Church to enlarge itself in that direction, will add something to its means of winning back, by its ample provisions and its ever open arms, the whole ancient household of its faith.

Mr. Wood,—May it please your Honours, so much time has already been occupied in the investigation of this case, and the evidence has been so fully and so ably sifted and detailed by the opening counsel on both sides, that I think it would be a waste of time for the closing counsel to occupy much of your attention in going over the evidence. I shall therefore condense the remarks which I propose to make on that branch of the case in as narrow a space as possible, and confine myself principally to the argument of the law of the case, considering the facts in a great measure as already fully developed before the Court.

It is important that we should understand, at the very threshold of this argument, the precise issue between these parties. The plaintiffs in this case, claim a portion of this fund, corresponding in amount with the relative proportion of the members who have gone off from the Methodist Episcopal Church, and formed the new Church, South. They have brought this suit for the purpose of recovering this property. There has been an actual separation of the ecclesiastical body. That is not disputed; and the question now is, whether that separation entitles them to recover and receive a ratable proportion of the property, the income of which belongs to certain beneficiaries for the time being, who are attached to the Methodist Episcopal Church. That is the important issue between the parties in this cause. It certainly is a most unfortunate controversy—for if there are any subjects which ought to be kept out of dispute, which ought to be marked emphatically with the spirit of peace, they are religious subjects. Every controversy of the kind has a most deleterious effect upon the morals of the community. The rising generation lose, in a great measure, their respect for religion, when they see the heads of the Church quarrelling and dividing. We have seen the baneful influence of these controversies in divisions of other Churches which have heretofore taken place; and I will venture to say that the Methodist Episcopal Church and the Church, South, will soon discover it, by sad experience. But there is another point of view in which it is unfortunate. This Methodist Episcopal Church, in its territorial jurisdiction, is commensurate with the entire Union. It is one of the largest Churches in this country. It has been the pioneer of religion. It has gone on with the advance of civilization and improvement in this country. It has carried religion along with settlement and civilization, and has ameliorated the condition of the different classes of the community upon our gradually extending borders. A division of this kind, therefore, may be said, in some measure, to be a national concern; and when we find in the present condition of our country, that there has been, as is admitted on all hands, and as many believe still to exist, serious danger threatening the unity of this federal government, it is of importance that a controversy of this kind should, if possible, be adjusted, and it is to be seriously regretted that such a controversy has arisen. It is seriously to be regretted that the Southern members of this Church have thought proper to bring their claim into a court of justice, more especially while it was in a course of amicable adjustment, and when, with a little more patience and forbearance, there was every probability that it would be finally adjusted. But, unfortunately, they have commenced this controversy, and it is our duty now to defend ourselves.

The counsel on the other side have mainly rested their claim upon grounds which appear to me to be entirely fallacious. They seem to look upon themselves, or rather upon the beneficiaries whom they say they represent, in what is called the Southern branch of this Church, as having a sort of vested right to this property. They draw a distinction between property which has been given to a Church, and property which has been acquired by the labour of individuals belonging to a Church. They treat this as property of the latter kind, and they claim they have a right to it, a vested right; and upon the division of this Church they are entitled, as in the case of a partnership or tenancy in common, to have a division of the property and receive a ratable proportion. It appears to me that this is an entirely erroneous view of this subject. I am aware they are somewhat warranted in this course of remark by the decision which was made in the Maysville case, whch they refer to, and on which they mainly rely. But I trust I shall be able to satisfy this Court that the principles upon which that decision rests, and the principles upon which they now base their claim, are entirely fallacious and unfounded.

I consider, and they admit, I believe, in their claim, that their rights in this case depend upon the law of charitable uses. It is important, therefore, that we should understand precisely the nature of that kind of property, and of the claim which they make. A charitable use is a *public* use. It is called charitable mainly because the largest portion of that kind of public property in every Christian country is based upon a charitable foundation. There are four elements in every class of charitable use. There are, in the first place, the founders of, and contributors to, the charity, those who have created and bestowed the property or the funds to the charitable purposes. There are, in the second place, the trustees of the charity, those who hold the legal estate in trust. In the third place, there are the managers of the charity, those who take charge of it, who conduct it, and who distribute it. Managers are essentially necessary, because there are no certain persons taking a temporal interest in the property. And, lastly, there are the beneficiaries among whom the property is distributed, according to the purpose of the charity, the use which was originally impressed upon it. The management of the charity is according to the scheme or plan which was originally impressed upon it by the founders, or where it is of a general nature, and a charity at large as it is called, a court of equity which protects all kinds of uses, takes charge of it and establishes a scheme. Such a scheme will be found in the case of Mogridge *vs.* Thackwell, in 7 Vesey's Reports.

These beneficiaries in this case have no vested estate, no fixed right, and hence they have no power of alienation. They cannot dispose of this property. Suppose, before any division of this Church took place, all the superannuated and supernumerary ministers of the Church for the time being, all who come within the description of the beneficiaries of this charity, had undertaken to alienate, what would the alienation have been good for? The attempt would have been perfectly visionary. They would have had no right to do it. They have no right, except as they answer the description of the beneficiaries, to receive from time to time the income or profits of the fund, as it is dealt out by the managers in the administration of the charity. Their right, therefore, is enforced and managed by the managers of the charity according to the scheme, and their right too in a court of equity, wherever it comes into dispute or difficulty, as between them and the trustees, managers or founders, is protected by the attorney-general. Your Honours will find in the case of Duke *vs.* Fuller, 9 New-Hampshire Reports, 536, a case which will fully illustrate this subject. That was the case of a charitable use, in which the beneficiaries of the charity undertook to dissolve the institution altogether, and to divide the funds among themselves individually. A bill was filed by the attorney-general in order to deprive them of the property which they had thus taken and appropriated among themselves, to establish the charity, and to have a plan devised and adopted for the administration of it. The claim in that case was enforced by the Court. Well, if in the case cited, as the counsel on the other side seem to think is the case here, the property really belonged to these beneficiaries; if they had acquired it, and they were to be considered as tenants in common of the fund, they would have had a right to divide it, to dispose of it as they pleased, each individual to alienate his share. But if it is under a charitable use, and if they are entitled to nothing more than a portion of the funds as administered under the charity, then they take them whenever they are doled out in that way; and they have no other right, except what is derived in that manner under the management of the charity.

This law of charitable use is enforced in this State and in this country. It has been involved, I admit, in a good deal of doubt and difficulty heretofore But I believe it has come now to be thoroughly understood. You will find it adopted in this State in the case of the Garden-street church, 7 Paige, 78; and you will find that the chancellor, too, in that case, takes back some positions which he had advanced in another case at an earlier period. You will find it further devolved in the case of Shotwell *vs.* Mott, 2 Sandford's Chancery Reports, page 46, and in Vulcan *vs.* Yates, 3 Barbour's Chancery Reports, 242. I will not detain the Court with reading these authorities—you will have an opportunity of referring to them at your leisure. This doctrine has now been adopted and fully settled in the United States Courts. This was done in the case of Vidall *vs.* Girard's Executors, 2 Howard's Reports, 195. The subject had been enveloped in some doubt by a decision made by that Court in the Baptist Association *vs.* Hart's Executors, 4 Wheaton's Reports. In this case a doubt had been raised, whether these charitable uses were recognised at all by the law of England, except as they were protected and enforced under the statute of Elizabeth. In the case of Burr's Executors *vs.* Smith, 7 Vermont Reports, where the subject was investigated, that decision of the Supreme Court in the 4th of Wheaton was not followed, and a vast variety of authorities were cited, showing conclusively that this law of charitable use existed in England long prior to the statute of Elizabeth; and there was as much evidence, I think I may venture to say more evidence, in support of that head of equity existing anterior to the reign of Elizabeth, than of any other equity doctrine whatever that can be adduced. That case of the Baptist Association, however, was regarded in various State courts as authority for some time, but it was finally abandoned in the case in 2 Howard. I will refer the Court to a case in Georgia, Beale *vs.* Fox, 4 Georgia Reports, 404, where you will find that subject ably treated and fully investigated; and I think it may now be put down as settled, that this law of charitable uses exists at common law, independently of the statute of Elizabeth, and that it is enforced wherever the common law prevails, and wherever charities exist of this public kind, although the statute of Elizabeth may not have been introduced.

A question, however, arises here which I shall briefly consider, because it is of some importance to the case, and that is, whether this law has been repealed in this State by the Revised Statutes. This charity was created, of course, long prior to the introduction of these Revised Statutes. But it may be said, if it has been repealed by the Revised Statutes, all the property of this Book Concern acquired since such repeal, and which is now held by subsequent acquisitions, is not protected by the law of charitable use. I must admit in candour that there has been one decision in one of our Supreme Courts—I mean one of those various Supreme Courts which have been lately created in this State—which goes the length of declaring that they have been repealed. But I apprehend it has not yet gained such a footing in this State as to be considered as settled law; and I think your Honours will come to the conclusion that it is entirely fallacious. There are two grounds upon which this doctrine rests. One is, that the chapter in the Revised Statutes which treats of trusts begins by stating that all trusts are abolished, except those contained in that chapter. Your Honours are perfectly aware that general words are always construed in reference to the particular subject-matter; and you will find that that whole chapter treats of *private* trusts, not of public trusts and public uses, which are entirely different; and it is confined, too, to private trusts of *real* property. It does not touch personal estate; it does not touch charitable uses. Every man, who is at all familiar with the doctrine of charitable uses, knows perfectly well that it is as different from the law of private trusts as public crimes are different from private trespasses. And you might just as well contend that a statute which made especial provision in regard to private trespasses, covered and applied to public crimes, as to say that a statute which makes provision in regard to private trusts of real property, has any bearing upon public charitable uses. They are entirely different in their nature and in their character. They are always treated differently, and they are generally treated in authors separately and distinctly. I took occasion the other day to look over the law of trust as it is explained in "Tickling on Equitable Estates," the object of which is to show the analogy between equitable interests created by trusts, and legal estates. There is not one word in that book upon the subject of charitable uses. And on the contrary, in works which treat of charitable uses, such as Duke and Shelford, you find nothing on the subject of private trusts, unless it is in some particular case where an analogy exists, and where it is followed out.

There is another ground relied upon for the purpose of showing that all these cases of charitable uses are repealed by the Revised Statutes, and that is the provision which is contained in those statutes in regard to perpetuities. They are brought within narrower limits. The alienation of property shall not be prevented now beyond two lives in being at the creation of the estate, and inasmuch as in the case of charitable uses the equitable interest is in perpetuity, it has been held that that repeals the whole doctrine of charitable uses. May it please your Honours, the law of perpetuity itself as it has always been understood in England and in this country, was in perfect harmony with the existence of these charitable uses. It was never considered as extending to these public uses beyond the legal estate, and yet the law of perpetuity has always been enforced. Before the creation of this provision in the Revised Statutes, the restriction in alienation extended only to lives in being at the creation of the estate; but the Revised Statutes confined it to two lives, and that is the difference between them. Well, now, will it be pretended that a mere alteration in the law of perpetuity, as to the time of its continuance, has the effect of extending it to a subject which was never embraced in that law at all—to a public use? Your Honours are aware that after the decision upon Thellison's will, the Thellison act was passed, which made an alteration, and imposed some new restrictions upon the law of perpetuity, but what lawyer in Westminster Hall ever dreamed that that altered and destroyed the law of charitable uses? Now, why should an alteration in the mere time of continuance of the perpetuity in our statutes have the effect of abolishing the law of charitable uses? Real estate could always be alienated under the law of charitable uses, but it is done under the sanction of a court of chancery. If the alienation of the legal estate in real property, therefore, was protected, under the law of perpetuity, it could not be bound up beyond the limits which the law of perpetuity allowed. The equitable use was always an exception to that law, so far forth as the equitable use continued attached to the property in which the proceeds of the alienation was invested, and I apprehend that there is nothing in the Revised Statutes which has, in any particular whatever, altered that exception; and that you will, therefore, consider in this case, that the law of charitable use applies to all this property, as well that which has been acquired since as that which was acquired before the Revised Statutes went into effect.

It is true, in some few cases, since the adoption of that code, the legislature have authorized and regulated the holding of this kind of property, but it has been done at the instance of applicants, out of abundant caution. In the same way special provisions have been inserted in manufacturing charters, like those in the general act, applicable to all such companies. It would be a poor compliment to the revisers who assisted in framing that code, to suppose that they would recommend the entire abolition of this law, and throw all the property invested—and which, from the nature of things, will continue to be invested in that way while Christianity lasts—completely afloat.

Having considered the general elements of a charitable use, with a view to this claim for a division of the property, I shall next consider them in reference to this particular case. You will find here all the elements which I have already considered as existing ordinarily in the creation of a charitable use. You have the founders of this charity. Who are the founders? Those who originally advanced the funds; and you have those, too, who have subsequently taken up those funds, and by industry, exertion, and cultivation, have improved and enlarged them from some 3,000 or 4,000 dollars, to some 700,000 or 800,000. All these persons are the contributors to this charity. Some, perhaps, originally contributed money; others have contributed their services and labours; but they all constitute contributions to this charitable fund; and all who have participated in the original creation or in the accumulation of this fund, are to be considered as the contributors of this charity. You have, in the next place, the trustees to hold the legal estate subject to this trust. They are now brought before this Court as defendants to this suit. It sometimes happens that more than one of these different offices or functions are vested in the same persons. Sometimes the trustees are also the managers of the charity. Sometimes they are distinct. In this case the functions are distinct. The managers of this charity are the Methodist Episcopal Church in the United States of America—the Methodist Episcopal Church as an organized, ecclesiastical institution, acting in an organized form. There is one additional peculiarity about this charity, to which I will call the attention of the Court, and that is, that the managers of the charity themselves exist under the law of charitable uses. The Methodist Episcopal Church, as an ecclesiastical body, entitled to hold property, entitled to temporalities, entitled to legal privileges, holds them all under the law of charitable or pious uses, and the institution itself exists under that law. In this case, however, we are to look upon them principally as the managers of this charity. And how are they to manage it? They manage it through their General Conference and their annual conferences, all participating, in their respective spheres, in the management of this concern, and in the distribution of the profits among the beneficaries. The General Conference performs its functions. It takes the general direction and superintendency over the whole concern; it appoints the trustees and changes the trustees. The annual conferences perform their functions. They seek out the beneficiaries who are entitled to relief, and in their respective local jurisdictions, after receiving from the trustees their respective shares of the income, distribute those shares among the various beneficiaries within their respective local jurisdictions. Here you have the managers of this fund. In the last place, you have the beneficiaries. Who are they? They are the superannuated and supernumerary travelling preachers of the Church, their wives and children, and, in the case of death, their widows and children. They are the beneficiaries of this charity. They take this income as it is thus doled out in charity, and they take it as answering the description of beneficiaries. They must be *designatio personarum* of the charity, to entitle them to take anything; and if they do not answer that description, they are entitled to nothing. What is that description? Is it all poor persons, paupers, who happen to be within the territorial jurisdiction of the Methodist Episcopal Church? Not at all. Is it all ministers who are superannuated, and who are entitled to relief on a claim of relief? Not at all. Is it all Methodist ministers? By no means. It is the superannuated and supernumerary ministers of the Methodist Episcopal Church, of that body thus organized—that body under whose auspices this fund was originally created, and under whose management and direction this fund has subsequently accumulated. They are the beneficiaries. They must answer that description to entitle them to take. If they do not answer it, they cannot take. In order to answer to that description, what must they be? They must be of the Methodist Episcopal Church. And what is this Methodist Episcopal Church? It is a unity. It is a body, not exactly incorporated under the law, but it is a body possessing, to a certain extent—so far as respects its charitable purposes, and in a court of equity, and in reference to property—a corporate capacity. It has precisely in equity that sort of a capacity, which an association of individuals, who are not a mere partnership or a tenancy in common, at law have, when they are at liberty to act in a certain collective capacity, if not actually clothed with all the powers and attributes of a corporation. Your Honours are aware of the existence of that class of bodies generally called *quasi* corporations, and that is the character in a court of equity of the Methodist Episcopal Church.

And in all charitable uses, the bodies and individuals when they take under the charity, in succession, take in that *quasi* corporate capacity.

I will refer the Court, upon this subject, to a passage or two, in the opinion of the Court, in the case of Decow *vs.* Hendrickson. It is fully reported, but not in any regular Book of Reports. It is a leading case in this country upon this subject; and the opinion is collected in a book, as it was delivered in the Court below, by Chief Justice Ewing, who, as every one acquainted with him knows, was a very profound lawyer. He bestowed upon this subject a vast deal of attention. I will read from pp. 21 and 39 of the opinion. He is describing the yearly meeting of the Society of Friends, which is held in Philadelphia, which was never incorporated. It was an ecclesiastical institution. The property in question, in this case, was under that religious institution, the yearly meeting being at its head. The question which arose in that case was, which of the subordinate meetings, which had become divided, and claimed this property, was entitled to it. In order to settle that question, as there had been a division in the head of the Church, the yearly meeting—which, in this particular, answers to this General Conference in the Methodist Episcopal Church—it became important to inquire into the character of that body, and which of those two separate institutions was the legitimate yearly meeting. What I now read is the description he gives of that body, as a charitable use protected under its law, and according to which law that case was to be decided. He says, at page 21,—

"This body was not a mere incidental, casual, disconnected assemblage, convening without previous arrangement, ceasing to exist when its members separated, and formed anew when individuals came together again at some subsequent time. It was a regularly organized and established body, holding stated sessions, corresponding with other bodies of the same religious denomination, consulting together for the welfare of a portion of their Church and its members, the ultimate arbiter of all differences, and the common head and governor of all belonging to the Society of Friends within its jurisdiction, which extended over the territories just mentioned, while they were called Provinces, and since they assumed the name and rank of States. The meetings of this body were annually held, as its name imports, and as long and steady usage has wrought into a part of its structure. The time and place of convention are subject to its control, and have accordingly, in several instances, been fixed and altered by it. The time and place, however, when and where only the body can constitutionally assemble and act, must, when fixed, so remain, until the voice of the body, in a yearly meeting capacity, which alone has the power and right to govern its own proceedings, shall resolve on and enact a change."

I will read another passage from p. 39. Speaking of a resolution of this body, he says:—

"The resolve was an act, not of private or individual benevolence, but of this meeting in its collective capacity."

If this meeting is to be considered an organized body, having existence in an organized form, and as such performing functions and having a "collective capacity," the consequence is that it is of a corporate character so far. You will find this same doctrine laid down in Shelford on Montmaine, p. 712. The case of M'Gurr *vs.* Aaron, in 2d Pennsylvania Reports, was one where this same doctrine came up. In that case the property was limited to the support of a minister of a certain Church and his successors. Why, your Honours are aware that no property can be limited in that way, under any legal title, or in any creation of any private trust, and in such cases the property cannot go to successors. Yet, under this law of charitable use, it can be limited to the successors. In these cases of charitable uses, the majority, as a general rule, dispose of the property, and that doctrine is laid down in Shelford on Charitable Uses, p. 712. But in the case of private property held by a private association of individuals, a majority cannot control it. Each one has a right, as a tenant in common, to his respective share, and he can alienate that right. But the majority of the individuals have no control over it. But that is not so in the case of a charitable use. An attempt was made, in a private association, to transfer the property, by a majority, without all joining, and it was decided to be unavailable, in the case of Livingston *vs.* Lynch, 4 Johnson's Reports, 573.

If I am right in this view of the subject, then we have a case where these beneficiaries take no vested title; nothing that they can dispose of; nothing that they can claim in any other way than simply under the management of this charity, and they must necessarily answer the description of the objects of the charity. How do they overcome this doctrine on the other side? On what does that decision in the Maysville case rest? The gentleman tells us that this property is not *given*—that it is no donation—that it was acquired by these travelling preachers? Suppose it was; does that alter the case? Who were to claim it? Can the travelling ministers claim it? Have they in fact devoted the fund to their own private use, as an association of individuals? Nothing like it. On the contrary, they have devoted it to a certain purpose, and that is, such that the income is to be bestowed upon the superannuated, supernumerary travelling ministers, their wives, widows, and children. These are the individuals upon whom it is bestowed. These are the persons who are entitled to the income. The travelling ministers, therefore, cannot claim it. It is, so far as they are concerned, a donation by them to the Church, and they, the trustees, hold it in trust, not for them as donors and founders, but for the individuals who are the objects of charity. It is, therefore, just as much a case of donation, as if one individual should bestow a capital of one hundred thousand dollars, for the purpose of applying the income to the support of these supernumerary and superannuated ministers. It is no answer to this to tell us, that some of these persons who become supernumerary and superannuated ministers, may originally have contributed a portion of this fund. That does not alter the case. That gives them no greater right, nor does it deprive them of any benefit.

Let me illustrate my view of the case upon this branch of the subject, because it is a main point on the other side. Let us suppose a class of mechanics in New-York—for instance, masons—should create a fund; that each should contribute a certain sum, say five dollars a year; that it should be put into the hands of trustees to be managed; that a certain religious society should be appointed managers of that fund; and that the profits should, from time to time, be distributed among the superannuated mechanics of that description, their wives, widows, and children: would not that be a charitable use? Unquestionably it would. Here would be a donation. It would not be a donation of one individual, or of a few individuals; it would be a donation by a body of men. It would be a donation devoted to a charity. It would be a donation devoted to persons answering a certain description. They would be, of course, a portion of those who had originally contributed, some more, some less, some perhaps lately come in, and become superannuated, before they contributed anything at all: it would be a charitable use. It would have all the elements of a charity; it would have the donors, the trustees, the managers, and the beneficiaries.

Let me suppose another case. Suppose that some fifty of these mechanics should contribute certain funds, that should be put into the hands of trustees to be managed for the purposes of speculation, and the profits to be divided, not among certain beneficiaries, objects of charity, who answer a certain description, from time to time, but among the donors themselves, in proportion to their respective shares. Here they would be entitled to it as tenants in common. They would have private rights. They would have the power of alienating their respective portions of the fund, and bringing in others as their alienees, as tenants in common, and be entitled, at any time, to make a division of that property, and on a division, each would take a ratable proportion of the original funds and property of the concern, with the accumulations. That illustrates the distinction between these tenancies in common in a private trust, and a case of charitable use. In the latter case, all would have to join in a suit; all could bring a suit; all might alienate the entire property; any one individual could alienate his portion of the property at any time; and it would be perfectly immaterial whether they held it at law or in equity, because there is a complete analogy between private trusts in equity and a legal estate as protected by the common law. But in the case of a charitable use it is entirely different; and I will take the liberty, in order to explain this doctrine further, and show the distinction, to refer your Honours to the existence of this doctrine as it stood before it was introduced into the common law. I will read from 7 Vermont Reports, 246:—

"The doctrine of charitable uses had its origin in the civil law. Hence it spread through the different countries of modern Europe.

"In Domat's Civil Law, vol. 2, pp. 168, 169, 170, (book iv, § vii,) are the following passages: 'Legacies to pious uses are those legacies that are destined to some work of charity, whether they relate to spiritual or temporal concerns. Thus a legacy of ornaments for a church, a legacy for the maintenance of a clergyman, to instruct poor children, and a legacy for their sustenance, are legacies to pious uses.

"'We may make this a just difference between legacies to pious uses and the other sorts of legacies, that the name of legacies to pious uses is properly given only to those legacies which are destined to some work of piety and charity, and which have their motives independent of the consideration which the merit of the legatees might procure them; whereas the other legacies have their motives confined to the consideration of some particular person, or are destined to some other use than to a work of piety and charity.

"'All legacies which have not for their motive the particular consideration of some person, are not for all that of the number of legacies to pious uses, although they be destined for a public good, if that good be any other than a work of piety or charity. Thus a legacy destined for some public ornament, such as the gate of a city, for the embellishment or conveniency of some public place, and others of the like nature, or a legacy of a prize to be given to some person who should excel others in some art or science, would be legacies of another nature than those to pious uses.

"'If a pious legacy were destined to some use which could not have its effect—as if a testator had left a legacy for building a church for a parish, or an apartment in a hospital, and it happened either that before his death the said church or said apartment had been built out of some other fund, or that it was no ways necessary or useful—the legacy would not, for all that, remain without any use, but it would be laid out on other works of piety for that parish or for that hospital, according to the directions that should be given in this matter by the persons to whom this function should belong.

"'Since legacies for works of piety and charity have a double favour, both that of their motive for holy and pious uses and that of their utility for the public good, they are considered as being privileged in the intention of the law.'"

Your Honours see all the elements of a charitable use as it exists in our courts of equity, and as it exists independent entirely of the statute of Elizabeth. It was derived from the civil law, into which it was introduced by the emperors after Christianity became the law of the empire. It exists in the nature of things wherever Christianity exists, because wherever Christianity does exist there will be charity, there will be the founders of these public charities for the benefit of individuals who may come into being long after the founder is laid in his grave. Therefore, to abolish this law, to undertake to destroy it, would be nothing more nor less than placing this kind of property beyond the pale of the law. That would be the effect and the only effect.

You find that when the court in Kentucky is freed from the influence of this particular subject, and is called upon to decide on these cases, it applies this doctrine very fully and very forcibly. I will refer the Court to a case in 7 Ben. Monroe's Reports, 611, 618, and 621, where you will find the doctrine fully developed. That was a case of a devise of property for the dissemination of the Gospel. Well, now every lawyer knows that such a devise, such a disposition of property, according to any other law, would be invalid, for want of the requisite certainty as to persons. But it was protected there under the law of charitable uses, and devoted to those public and religious purposes, and a court of equity would see that it was administered according to some scheme devised to carry the charity into effect.

I therefore submit to your Honours that the view taken of this subject on the other side, that here is property which has been acquired by these beneficiaries, that they have a vested right to it, and that they can divide it among themselves, as so many tenants in common, is without any foundation, and that they must, in order to claim this property, take it as beneficiaries answering the description contained in the foundation of this charity. Some of these may, perhaps, have contributed a little, many of them have contributed nothing at all. Many of these ministers who have contributed may never receive any of the bounty. In order to entitle these plaintiffs, as representing the beneficiaries of this Church, to recover any portion of this fund, they must make out, to your satisfaction, that they answer the description of that charity; that they are the representatives of travelling, supernumerary, superannuated ministers, their wives, widows, and children, belonging to the Methodist Episcopal Church, the institution which originally created this charity, under which it is protected, and according to the original principles upon which the charity was founded. It will not do for them to say they are Methodists. It will not do for them to say that they have adopted all the laws, and regulations, and discipline, and government, and all the faith and doctrines that were acknowledged in the Methodist Episcopal Church, which was in existence when this charity was formed, and under whose auspices it has been accumulated to the immense amount it has. It will not do for them to advance any doctrine of that kind. But they must make out that at the time they filed the bill they were members of this Methodist Episcopal Church, and that they are entitled, as members of this Church, to a portion of this fund, or that they, as agents, represent them, and that in the administration of that charity they stand in that position.

Now, they tell us that they do stand in that position. There is no difficulty here about the fundamental doctrines of the Church. The question arises upon topics relating to the discipline and government. There has been no split in this Church upon any fundamental rule of faith, or Christian belief. There is nothing of that kind. But they claim that they are a portion of that same Methodist Episcopal Church divided, and that although they are divided, yet they are sufficiently identified to entitle them to a portion of the *corpus* of this estate, and to entitle the persons answering the description of being supernumerary or superannuated ministers, their wives, widows, and children, as beneficiaries, to take it. According to the argument, so far as I have been able to gather it, they claim on two grounds: First, on the ground of an agreement between the members of this Church, thus constitutionally representing the whole Church, and composing its head—the General Conference—to divide the Church, to form two separate institutions, and yet identical with the Church, each party representing it in succession and continuance, and each party entitled to its ecclesiastical privileges and private rights of property. In the next place, they contend, that if the agreement does not amount to this, and independent of the agreement there has been a division in this Church, that that division and separation of this body from the other, the majority, was rendered necessary and indispensable by the misconduct of the defendants, and therefore they are entitled to a portion of this fund in equity. These I take to be the two grounds upon one or the other of which they must rest their claim.

Now, in the first place, I assume there was an absolute agreement to divide this Church. That agreement, they tell us, is contained in the report of the committee of nine, which was made in the General Conference of 1844, and adopted by that body. Under that agreement they say they are entitled to set up the Southern branch, which they call a division of the same Church, and under which they are entitled, in equity, to claim a relative proportion of the *corpus*, and of course a relative proportion of the profits of this fund. I may here remark, that your Honours have nothing to do with the ecclesiastical privileges any further than as they are connected with the subject of property; but wherever a trust is created, which trust is in some measure identified with or dependant upon the ecclesiastical institutions, you will inquire into the subject of these institutions, in order to settle the question properly. It is in that way and in that point of view that you get jurisdiction over that branch of the subject. You are aware that in all cases where the Court has a jurisdiction over a particular subject, if it becomes necessary, in order to settle the right of property, to inquire into some collateral matter over which the Court has no direct jurisdiction at all, they will investigate it in order to settle that right of property; and in that point of view a court of common law will inquire into a maritime subject when it becomes necessary to do it, as a collateral matter, to settle some question of property over which the common law court has direct jurisdiction. Mere ecclesiastical questions you have nothing to do with directly, and in themselves, and there are no tribunals in this country connected with the government of the country which have any control over them. There is in this country a complete separation of Church and State. But you will inquire into ecclesiastical matters wherever a trust is created which is dependant in any measure upon the existence and character of the ecclesiastical institutions. Here there is this complete connexion. This property is placed under the control and direction of this Methodist Episcopal Church. They are to be the managers of this fund. Well, in order to settle the question, when two parties claim the property, or claim the control over any portion of it, you must inquire into that Methodist Episcopal Church, where it is, who compose it, and who are the persons entitled to the direction of it. In no other way can you settle this question of property. You are therefore led, necessarily, to investigate it collaterally, with the view to settle the question of jurisdiction over the property. You must find out who compose the Methodist Episcopal Church now, and at the timo this suit was brought. Who are they? Are they the plaintiffs or the defendants? Has it been legitimately and legally divided in reference to the matter of property, so that both can claim it? Or is the Methodist Episcopal Church still connected and identified with the defendants in this case? If it is, the plaintiffs are entitled to nothing. They can claim nothing.

Hence, you inquire into this matter, and you will observe in this case that there is something more than a connexion arising from the management of the property, because you find out that these beneficiaries must be members of this very Church to entitle them to take. It often happens that the management of a charity is in the hands of persons who are in no way connected with the beneficiaries, otherwise than merely as individuals to conduct it, and to distribute the profits among the beneficiaries. But here you see a complete connexion. The Methodist Episcopal Church is entitled to the management of this charity, and not only so, but it is to be distributed among beneficiaries, which beneficaries are to be, and continue to be from time to time, members of that very Methodist Episcopal Church. They are, therefore, completely identified with it; and there is another important consideration, whenever a a charity is given to pious purposes to be distributed among the officers of the Church, it is considered as given in ease of the Church. You will find that doctrine very fully illustrated in the case of McGurr *vs.* Aaron, in 2 Pennsylvania Reports, to which I have already referred. If property is given to a charity to be distributed in support of the ministers of a Church and their successors, it is intended and is considered as being given by the founders for the benefit of the entire Church, and in ease of it. There is, therefore, that connexion between the Church in this case and the beneficiaries, and it is indispensable, to come to a right decision of this case, that you should find out who are this Methodist Episcopal Church which was in existence at the foundation of this charity, which has been in existence during its accumulation and continuance, and which was in existence at the time this suit was brought.

Now, as to the agreement to divide the Church, I may say, in the first place, that I might take this objection which has already been laid before the Court, that this agreement is prospective and contingent, and has never been consummated; and the further objection, that the General Conference, as a delegated body, has no power, without the concurrence of the annual conferences, to make such a division. When I say they have no power to divide the Church, I speak in reference to this property, because the annual conferences are managers of this charity as well as the General Conference. But waving for the present the further consideration of this branch of the case, and assuming that there had been a present agreement instead of one that was executory, and that it has been consummated, then an inquiry arises, Has there been a *division* of the Church? has there been any agreement to that effect? This split in the Church may have been effected by an agreement in two ways:—it may have been an agreement to divide the Church into two separate branches, creating two new Churches in the place of the one which before existed; or it may have been an agreement that the Methodist Episcopal Church should remain, and that this other portion should be detached from it, and should form a separate independent Church. Your Honours will see at once that there is a vast difference between these two modes of proceeding. The first would necessarily destroy that Methodist Episcopal Church which was previously in existence, and would form two new Churches in the place of it. The last would leave that Church in existence already formed and operating, and there would be a mere division or separation from it, to form a new and separate Church, leaving the old body to stand, and leaving the new to be formed and created into a separate, distinct, and new body. There is just the difference in this case that there would be between cutting off a man's leg, leaving the person remaining, and dividing the body, and thus destroying it; the difference between maiming a man and killing him.

If this matter of agreement is allowed to speak for itself, there is no difficulty in discovering what was intended. I will refer your Honours to the first volume of these Proofs, p. 129, where we have the so-called "Plan of Separation." It is upon this that the plaintiffs stand, and must stand, if they can stand at all, and if I comprehend it, they leave the old Church remaining, and they separate from it, and form a new Church. I read the 2d resolution:—

"That ministers, local and travelling, of every grade and office in the Methodist Episcopal Church, may, as they prefer, *remain* in that Church, or, without blame, attach themselves to the Church, South."

"*They may remain in that Church*, or, without blame, attach themselves to the *Church, South.*" Can anybody misunderstand this? Did they not intend that that

Methodist Episcopal Church should still continue in existence, that it should remain, and that they, in case their Southern conferences found it necessary, should form a new and separate Church, to be the Church, South? Read the 4th resolution :—

"That whenever the annual conferences, by a vote of three-fourths of all their members voting on the third resolution, shall have concurred in the recommendation to alter the sixth restrictive article, the agents at New-York and Cincinnati shall, and they are hereby authorized and directed to deliver over to any authorized agent or appointee of the Church, South, should one be organized, all notes and book accounts against the ministers, Church-members, or citizens within its boundaries, with authority to collect the same for the sole use of the Southern Church, and that said agents also convey to the aforesaid agent or appointee of the South all the real estate, and assign to him all the property, including presses, stock, and all right and interest connected with the printing establishments at Charleston, Richmond, and Nashville, which now belong to the Methodist Episcopal Church."

And you will find that throughout this whole agreement they speak of the Methodist Episcopal Church as intended to remain, and treat themselves as separated from it, and as forming a new Church, South. Well they go on. At Louisville they form this Church, and how do they consider it? Let us look at the 2d volume of Proofs, p. 59. They resolve,—

"That it is right, expedient, and necessary, to erect the annual conferences represented in this Convention, into a distinct ecclesiastical Connexion, separate from the jurisdiction of the *General Conference of the Methodist Episcopal Church, as at present constituted*; and accordingly, we, the delegates of said annual conferences, acting under the provisional Plan of Separation adopted by the General Conference of 1844, do solemnly *declare* the jurisdiction exercised over said annual conferences, by the General Conference of the Methodist Episcopal Church, *entirely dissolved*; and that said annual conferences shall be and they hereby *are constituted*, a separate ecclesiastical Connexion, under the provisional Plan of Separation aforesaid, and based upon the Discipline of the Methodist Episcopal Church, comprehending the doctrines and entire moral, ecclesiastical, and economical rules and regulations of said Discipline, except only in so far as verbal alterations may be necessary to a distinct organization, and to be known by the style and title of the METHODIST EPISCOPAL CHURCH, SOUTH."

Can anybody read this without seeing what the design is?—that they mean to leave the old Methodist Episcopal Church to stand, and that they mean they will separate from it and form a new Connexion, speaking of themselves as separatists, and taking the new name of The Methodist Episcopal Church, *South*.

Well, now, we have their agreement. The purpose is too plain to be mistaken. It speaks for itself. I am aware it has been stated in that Maysville case, that a Church may change its name, and that, therefore, the name is a matter of very little importance. But I apprehend, that when a Church does not change its name; where the name remains, and where a portion goes off, separates, and takes a new organization and a new name, leaving the old name and old organization to remain, that is a circumstance of very considerable importance, and ought to be attended to in all cases of this kind. And I think the Court will have no hesitation in coming to the conclusion, that the intention here of the parties in this agreement, and as carried out by the Southern conferences, at the Louisville Convention, was that the Church should remain the Methodist Episcopal Church, and that a new Church should be formed, and that they should be looked upon as separatists, and take a new name. Well, what is the effect of such a separation by agreement between the parties? If any subject can be considered as settled, I apprehend this is settled by the law of the land, that they leave behind them, under such an agreement, the property of the Church, which belongs to the body that remains. I will take the liberty of reading a passage from a case which was referred to by the counsel concerned with me, the case of Baker *vs.* Fales, 16 Massachusetts Reports, p. 503 :—

"If a Church may subsist unconnected with any congregation or religious society, as has been urged in argument, it is certain that it has no legal qualities, and more especially that it cannot exercise any control over property which it may have held in trust for the society with which it had been formerly connected. That any number of the members of a Church, who disagree with their brethren, or with the minister, or with the parish, may withdraw from fellowship with them, and act as a Church in a religious point of view, having the ordinances administered and other religious offices performed, it is not necessary to deny; indeed this would be a question proper for an ecclesiastical council to settle, if any should dispute their claim. But as to all civil purposes, the secession of a whole Church from the parish would be an extinction of the Church; and it is competent to the members of the parish to institute a new Church, or to engraft one upon the old stock, if any of it should remain, and this new Church would succeed to all the rights of the old, in relation to the parish. This is not only reasonable, but it is conformable to the usages of the country; for although many instances may have occurred of the removal of Church members from one Church, or one place of worship to another, and no doubt a removal of a majority of the members has sometimes occurred, we do not hear of any Church ceasing to exist, while there were members enough left to do Church service. No particular number is necessary to constitute a Church, nor is there any established quorum, which would have a right to manage the concerns of the body. According to the *Cambridge* platform, chap. 3, § 4, the number is to be no larger than can conveniently meet together in one place, nor ordinarily fewer than may conveniently carry on Church work. It would seem to follow from the very structure of such a body as this, which is a mere voluntary association, that a diminution of its numbers will not affect its identity. A Church may exist, in an ecclesiastical sense, without any officers, as will be seen in the platform; and without doubt, in the same sense, a Church may be composed only of *femmes-covert* and minors, who have no civil capacity. The only circumstance, therefore, which gives a Church any legal character, is its connexion with some regularly constituted society; and those who withdraw from the society cease to be members of that particular Church, and the remaining members continue to be the identical Church. This is analogous to the separation of towns and parishes—the effect of which, by law, is to leave the original body politic entire, with its powers and privileges undiminished, however large may be the proportion which secedes. And so it is of all voluntary societies, having funds to be disposed of to charitable uses, in any particular place. A refusal of a majority of the members to act, would devolve all power over the subject upon those who might choose to persevere."

This shows that in all these cases where there is a separation, if the old Church remains, even if the majority go away, it still continues the old Church, and, as you find it decided in that case, retain all the rights and all the property of the Church. A number of other cases might be cited from the Massachusetts Reports, but I apprehend it would be unnecessary, and that the doctrine is firmly settled without dispute. In the case in 9 Barr's Pennsylvania Reports, part 321, you will find the same doctrine laid down, that the Church property belongs to those who adhere to the ecclesiastical government, though they are in the minority. Those who depart from the government of the Church are not to take the funds along with them. It is perfectly immaterial whether it is done by agreement or without agreement. If they leave the Church by consent they leave the property behind. It is very common in the case of corporations, to pass acts to separate a portion of a town, or a portion of a corporation. This is all done legitimately, just as strong as if there was a formal agreement; but the new town, the new parish, the new Church, does not take any portion of the property with them. They leave that behind, and in all cases where there is a separation from the government, or departure from the doctrine of the Church, they also leave the property behind with the Church that remains, and they cannot call for a division of property. I will call the attention of the Court to the case of the Attorney-General *vs.* Pearson, in 3 Merivale, beginning at p. 367. It is a very long case, and runs through a considerable portion of the book.

"In this case the defendants set up a plea that they were a majority of the congregation, and that they had united in the choice of another parson who was a Unitarian. They had for many years been Trinitarians. In 1813, they made choice of a Unitarian clergyman, Steward, who afterwards, in 1816, became a Trinitarian clergyman. In consequence of this change an information was filed by the attorney-general. The chancellor decided that it being a trust for religious purposes, a court in equity would take complete jurisdiction—that in the formation and endowment of a chapel for religious worship, in which the kind was not mentioned, the Court would for explanation resort to usage—that it was not in the power of individuals to change the purposes of such an institution, if only established for Trinitarian purposes it could not be converted to purposes anti-Trinitarian—and that the Court had nothing to do with religious doctrines, except to ascertain the purposes of the trust, and the Court is bound to determine that question."

Here the original purposes of the trust were inquired into, if it were necessary to inquire into religious doctrines in order to ascertain them, and that party who seceded from the doctrines of the Church had no right to claim any portion of the funds. You will find the same doctrine in 2 Bligh's Reports, 529, further in 2 Jacobs and Walker, 427, and in the case of Field *vs.* Field, 9 Wendell, 394, in the Supreme Court of this State, where there was a separation. That portion, though a minority, who adhered to the course of discipline and mode of proceeding marked out by the discipline and government of the Church, were entitled to the property. I will refer to the case of Den *vs.* Bolston, 7 Halstead's Reports, 206. This was the case of a Dutch Reformed Church. Some persons set up a new classis—they have, in that Church, an ecclesiastical jurisdiction called the classis—and called themselves the True Dutch Reformed Church. In this particular case the congregation divided, and the question arose as to which party was entitled to the property. It was decided that those who had set up the new classis had ceased to be members of the Dutch Reformed Church, and could not carry the property away with them or call for a division of it. That is a case precisely in point. There was a case in which a portion of the Church, and I think it was a majority, undertook to form a new classis, and they took a new name, and called themselves "The *True* Dutch Reformed Church," as in this case under consideration they here call themselves The Methodist Episcopal Church, *South*. They claimed they had a right to a division of the funds, but the Court decided that, if they chose to leave the Church, to leave that ecclesiastical jurisdiction which was there formed and in existence, to form a new institution and take a new name, they could not claim any portion of the property The old Church exists under a certain organism. It exists as a unit, and the body cannot be thus divided, so as to carry the property with them. And you will find the same doctrine in the case of the State *vs.* Crowell, 4 Halstead's Reports, 390. This was the case of a Presbyterian Church at Perth Amboy. They had a clergyman who was silenced in their Church by the Church judicatories; but a large majority of the congregation, as many as three-fourths, remained attached to him. The Presbytery sent supplies. The majority refused to pay up the old subscription list, and set up a new subscription for the support of another minister, the one who had been silenced by the Church judicatories. Their language to the minority was, "If you want supplies you must pay for them." Here was a case, where, if this doctrine of separating and dividing would entitle the separatists to a portion of the property, they would have been entitled. They were a large majority. They insisted upon adhering to the minister settled there. He had been silenced by the higher Church judicatories, and the minority, who were disposed to adhere to the Church judicatories, elected a new pastor. The others refused to join with them, and claimed the property. The question was, which was entitled to it, or whether they were entitled to make a division of the property, as well as to secede from the Church. The Court decided that it belonged to that party which was identified with the Presbyterian Church, and adhered to its judicatories.

I will not trouble the Court with the citation of any further authorities upon this point. There was one case, however, which was cited by the counsel on the other side, to which I will refer the Court—the case in 2 Russell's Reports, 114,—where the pew-holders claimed the right to vote on the ground of their having a property, and interest, and consideration in the Church ; but according to the established discipline and government of the Church they were not entitled to vote, and it was decided, according to the discipline and government, that they had no right, and that they could claim no right to the property consequent upon a division grounded upon the refusal to allow them to vote.

I submit then to your Honours, that there are two radical errors in the claim upon the other side, and two radical errors committed by the Court, in relation to two facts, when it undertook to carry out the claim in the Maysville case. They are—First, that in this case there was no agreement to *divide* the Church into two distinct parts fairly made ; that, on the contrary, the agreement was that the Church should remain, and this particular body, constituting the minority of the Church, should be at liberty to withdraw and separate. That was the agreement. And in the next place, there was no agreement to divide the fund, and no right to have the fund divided. In this case the agreement required, so far as it goes to divide the fund, the concurrence of the annual conferences, which has never been obtained. If they rest on the agreement, they must take it as it is. Unless there has been that concurrence they have no right to set up the claim.

I now come to consider the next ground of the claim on the other side, and that is, that in the absence of any agreement, and upon the supposition that there was no agreement, there has been such misconduct on the part of the defendants and those connected with them, constituting, as we say, the Methodist Episcopal Church, as warranted them in separating, and that they are entitled in consequence of that misconduct to recover a proportion of this property. As I have before observed, it is not pretended in this case that there has been any departure on the part of the defendants from the true doctrines of the Church. That cannot be pretended. The complaint is, misconduct in the administration of the affairs of the Church, in its government or in its discipline ; and the misconduct all has reference to that most unfortunate subject in this country, which seems to create trouble wherever it appears, in State and in Church—the subject of slavery. I apprehend upon this subject, the defendants, and their adherents, and the Methodist Episcopal Church, have carried out to the very letter the entire doctrines and regulations of the Church upon that important point, and that there is really no ground of complaint, on the part of the plaintiffs, against them for the manner in which they have deported themselves upon that delicate subject. There can be no pretence for alleging that this Methodist Society are abolitionists—I do not use that term in any disparaging sense ; I advert to it simply to designate a certain class of doctrines and positions which have been maintained. It cannot be pretended that this Church, as a Church, have adopted any of these doctrines. They have not undertaken to interfere with slavery, to abolish it. They have simply carried out those principles and views which have always existed in the Church, in which the brethren of the South have always concurred—views of a practical character, and which were designed to subserve the interests of the Church, both North and South. They have not gone one jot or tittle further than the ancient, well settled, and established principles and usages of the Church would warrant. I do not mean to trouble the Court with going over the evidence upon this subject, as to what are the opinions and doctrines of this Church; that has been pretty fully developed already. I will barely make one or two remarks on that subject.

In the early history of this Church, in this country, there certainly was, under the auspices of the foreign members who took the control of the government of it, a disposition at once to abolish slavery, and they introduced such a provision as, if carried out, would lead to that result. But your Honours are aware that it was at once abandoned, and a rule of practical convenience was substituted in its place. They gave up all such pretensions. They adopted what ought to have been, and what was properly the true rule upon that subject—to let it alone, to leave the domestic institutions of the different States to the States themselves, and not to interfere with it any further than was necessary and convenient for the wholesome and conservative administration of the affairs of this Church. I might refer you to the address which was delivered to the British Conference upon this subject, which has already been read to the Court, which shows what their principles are. Their doctrines in 1804, settled down to this principle: individuals were at liberty to hold slaves or not, as they thought proper. Officers of the Church were required to free their slaves when it was practicable—when it was allowed in the States in which they lived. But as to the bishops, the doctrine never extended to them. It has always been maintained and held, that bishops should not be the holders of slaves, and we have this most important fact in the history of this Church, that until the time of Bishop Andrew, there never had been a slaveholding bishop in it. Prior to this time, at least two-thirds of the bishops had been taken from the Southern conferences, and all of them, without any apparent difficulty or dispute among them, had been men who neither owned nor held slaves. Bishop Andrew did not own or hold a slave at the time he was created a bishop. This is a most important circumstance upon this point. Usage, in the absence of any express provision, goes far. In the absence of express provision, I may say, it is conclusive upon what are the true principles of the Church. Ancient usage is the common law of the Church, and must govern it. In one of those cases to which I have called your attention, you will observe that ancient usage was resorted to, to ascertain what were the doctrines of the Church, and in order to ascertain the doctrines, with a view to settle the question of property. Now, when you find that in this Church one portion, and a very large portion of this territory, is slaveholding; when you find, at the time of the creation of this Church, and for a long period, every State held slaves, the fact that no one of the bishops has ever been a slaveholder until the case of Bishop Andrew, and that he was not a slaveholder at the time of his appointment, I think it may be stated as conclusive evidence, that there has been a doctrine in this Church, well settled and constantly acted upon, to elect to that important office no person who was a holder of slaves. Now, you observe that there is nothing in all this proceeding on the part of these Methodists, in their government and discipline, which is at all hostile to the existence of this domestic institution in the South. They, of course, believe it would be better not to have slaves if it could be avoided, but they adopt this belief upon the same principle that they would decide upon any abstract question; for instance, that it would be better that the serfs of Russia should not exist, or that the labouring, the manufacturing population of England should be in a much better condition than they are, which is really a great deal worse than the condition of our Southern slaves. They would hold all this in the abstract, and they consider the condition of the Russian serfs, and of the manufacturing and labouring population of England, as an evil in the abstract, as they consider slavery an evil, and they would endeavour, as far as practicable, to improve both; but they would not be so Quixotic as to undertake to abolish the institutions of Russia, or the institutions of England, when doubtless such an abolition would cause more evil than good, though it might be better if these portions of the human race were in a better condition. And for the same reason they would not undertake to abolish slavery in the United States. In that particular they leave each State to work out for itself. But in consequence of the opinions of many persons who are members of the Church, who are opposed to slavery, and in order to make the officers of their Church useful, and dispense the benefits of religion through the whole territory of the Church, they have gone thus far. They have said that the travelling preachers and ministers of the Church shall emancipate their slaves where it is practicable, and that bishops shall not be elected when they are holders of slaves.

MR. REVERDY JOHNSON,—There is no positive rule on the subject.

MR. WOOD,—I stated, as to the bishops, there was no express rule about it; but I have referred to the ancient and established usage as settling the common law in the Church, precisely as in the case already referred to, where the common and established usage in regard to the doctrines of the Church, settled, in the absence of any express provision, that that was a Trinitarian Church.

Now, in this case, on what principle did they act? Why, it is no objection to a man in the slaveholding States that he does not own slaves. If a person not owning slaves, living in the slaveholding States, should be made a bishop, he is not the less acceptionable to the community because he does not own slaves; but when he comes to the free States, where many persons believe that slavery ought not to exist, and that he ought to manumit his slaves, it would destroy his usefulness, or greatly mar it, if he held slaves. They have simply adopted it as a conservative rule of action. I must call the attention of the Court to some passages in the Address which they made to the foreign conferences. In the address of the British Conference to the General Conference, page 64 of the First of the Proofs, is the following:—

"But while we freely indulge in sentiments such as these, we cannot forget that on one subject especially—the subject of American slavery—you, our beloved brethren, are placed in circumstances of painful trial and perplexity. We enter, with brotherly sympathy, into the peculiar situation which you are now called to occupy. But on this question, we beg to refer you to what occurs in our address to you from the Conference in 1836, a proper copy of which will be handed to you by our representative; as also to the contents of the preceding letter of 1835. To the principles which we have affectionately but honestly declared in these two documents we still adhere, with a full conviction of their Christian truth and justice.

"The time which has elapsed, and the events which have taken place, since the preparation of the above-mentioned papers, serve only to confirm us yet more in our views of the moral evil of slavery. Far be it from us to advocate violent and ill-considered measures. We are, however, strongly and unequivocally of the opinion that it is, at this time, the paramount Christian duty of the ministers of our most merciful Lord in your country, to maintain the *principle* of opposition to slavery with earnest zeal, and unflinching firmness. May we not also be allowed, with the heart-felt solicitude of fraternal love, to entreat that you will not omit or qualify the noble testimony which we have extracted, in a note to our address, from your Book of Discipline, but that you will continue to insert it there in its primitive and unimpaired integrity."

I will read one or two passages from the answer to this:—

"Of these United States, (to the government and laws of which, 'according to the division of power made to them by the Constitution of the Union, and the constitutions of the several States,' we owe, and delight to render, a sincere and patriotic loyalty,)" [no "higher law" here set up,] "there are several which do not allow of slavery. There are others in which it is allowed, and there are slaves; but the tendency of the laws, and the minds of a majority of the people, are in favour of emancipation. But there are others in which slavery exists so universally, and is so closely interwoven with their civil institutions, that both do the laws disallow of emancipation, and the great body of the people (the source of laws with us) hold it to be treasonable to set forth anything, by word or deed, tending that way. Each one of all these States is independent of the rest, and sovereign with respect to its internal government, (as much so as if there existed no confederation among them for ends of common interest,) and therefore it is impossible to frame a rule on slavery proper for our people in all the States alike. But our Church is extended through all the States, and as it would be wrong and unscriptural to enact a rule of discipline in opposition to the constitution and laws of the State on this subject, so also would it not be equitable or Scriptural to confound the positions of our ministers and people (so different as they are in different States) with respect to the moral question which slavery involves.

"Under the administration of the venerated Dr. Coke, this plain distinction was once overlooked, and it was attempted to urge emancipation in *all* the States; but this attempt proved almost ruinous, and was soon abandoned by the doctor himself. While, therefore, the Church has encouraged emancipation in those States where the laws permit it, and allowed the freed man to enjoy freedom, we have refrained, for conscience' sake, from all intermeddling with the subject in those other States where the laws make it criminal. And such a course we think agreeable to the Scriptures, and indicated by St. Paul's inspired instruction to servants, in his First Epistle to the Corinthians, chap. vii, ver. 20, 21. For if servants were not to care for their servitude when they *might not* be free, though if they might be free they should use it *rather*, so neither should masters be condemned for not setting them free when they *might not* do so, though *if* they *might*, they should do so *rather*. The question of the evil of slavery, abstractedly considered, you will readily perceive, brethren, is a very different matter from a principle or rule of Church discipline to be executed contrary to, and in defiance of, the law of the land. Methodism has always been (except perhaps in the single instance above) eminently loyal and promotive of good order; and so we desire it may ever continue to be, both in Europe and America. With this sentiment we conclude the subject, adding only the corroborating language of your noble Missionary Society, by the revered and lamented Watson, in their instructions to missionaries," &c.

Now, I apprehend that no man, however sensitive he may be upon this subject of slavery, can see anything in the conduct of this Church with which to find fault. They are disposed to be eminently loyal, to submit to the laws and government of the country, to leave this domestic institution to those who are concerned with it, to let them act in their own way. If there is any evil in slavery, they must bear it; if there is any danger in any sudden abolition of it, they must be subjected to that danger; and therefore they ought to be allowed to judge for themselves. That is the doctrine of Methodism. Some of these early bishops, it is true, who were not familiar with our institutions, coming from abroad, undertook to go further, and meddle with this subject, and turn Quixotes in philanthropy, as there were formerly Quixotes in knight-errantry. But they abandoned that very soon, and took a broad and practical ground. They allowed slavery to exist; they carried out the old primitive doctrine of the apostle, who, when he converted a runaway slave, advised him to go back to his master, and advised the master to treat him well. They are aware, and they have been aware, that if they promote a sound body of Christian morality, and leave that to work itself, it will more effectually modify and ameliorate anything that may be harsh or severe in political or domestic institutions, than by attempting directly to meddle with them; and therefore they give to Cæsar what belongs to Cæsar. I take that to be the old sound doctrine of the Methodist Church, and that it has always been carried out. And the Southern branch of this Church always acted with them, until they had become (and I do not blame them; it is not for me to blame any of the parties in this case) extremely sensitive upon that subject from the conduct of certain individuals in other portions of the United States, who have undertaken to go beyond this sound doctrine, and interfere with their domestic institutions, beyond what reason, good sense,or Christianity would call for or admit.

Now, what is the reason why the officers of their Church, their travelling ministers for instance, are required to emancipate their slaves where it can be done? and what is the reason why a bishop in no case is allowed to hold slaves? Not that they want to interfere with the domestic institutions of the South. All they want is to render their officers acceptable, and acceptable to all men; to be all things to all men, in the sense in which St. Paul used that phrase; to be acceptable, in order to do good. That was their object; and they believed, and they now believe, that to carry out the great purposes of their Church, it is all-important that those rules should be observed, without attempting to meddle with the domestic institutions of the South. They were willing to appoint Southern ministers to the bishopric, as they always have done, but just select those who do not own slaves. Among these Christians of primitive habits, where there are ministers in abundance who do not own property of that kind, and who own very little property of any kind, where the land they cultivate is Immanuel's land, there is no difficulty in selecting proper persons for that office, who are free from this objection.

One great principle—it is a radical principle, and was set forth in the Address of the bishops, which was signed by the two Southern bishops, Soule and Andrew—is the doctrine of the itinerancy of the bishops. It is looked upon as one of the essential doctrines of that Chureh. It will not do to establish local bishops. It will not do, they say, to make any exceptions. They have adopted in this case the primitive rule of the apostles—to travel, not to abide in one place; to go abroad, to scatter the seeds of the Gospel through every land. Their bishops are to travel, each and all of them, over every portion of the dominions and jurisdiction of their Church. But when they go into that part of the country where slavery happens to be in bad odour, and where they are to make their efforts not only to confirm those already in the faith, but convert others to it, any one must see that they become inefficient if they are the owners of slaves; and therefore it becomes necessary to do one of two things: either require that the bishops elected shall not be slaveholders, or dispense with the rule that they shall be itinerant, and make them local. The latter they could not do without abandoning Methodism, because the great founder of Methodism laid that down as an essential rule. He adopted the episcopacy of the English Church, but it was not a mere local, lazy episcopacy, such as he found there. He wanted an active travelling episcopacy, and to keep them active and efficient he determined to introduce this as an indispensable rule of the Church, that they should be itinerant; and they have continued to be so. Here is the great origin of all their doctrines in regard to slavery—doctrines in which the Southern branch, as well as the Northern, until a comparatively recent period, all concurred, and about which there appears to have been before this not the slightest difficulty. And what is this recent difficulty? How did it arise? We first hear of it in the General Conferences of 1840 and 1844. It appears that among individual members of this Church in the Northern and Middle States, there were some abolitionists. And when we consider the state of society in this section of the country for a number of years past, the vast influence which the foreign abolitionists have had upon our country, and the attempts which were made by the foreign bishops to introduce these doctrines here, meddling with institutions with which they had no concern; meddling with our servants who are in a state of slavery, but in a much better condition than their own at home, many of whom are in a condition at present which a British minister lately described as formerly applicable to a certain portion of their society in early periods of their history—without pantaloons,—when, I say, we look at this, and the constant efforts which they had made, is it surprising that there should be individual members of this Church who should adopt these doctrines, and who should undertake to flood the conferences with their petitions and memorials, as the same class of people undertook to flood the congress of the United States? And they actually did for a number of years overwhelm it with these worse than useless petitions, backed by an old gentleman in congress of great distinction, but whom I have always considered as acting very erroneously on that subject. If, when these petitions came in, the conferences had adopted and acted upon them, there would have been some ground of complaint. But how was it? Did they adopt them? We have a resolution passed by the Church in 1840 upon this subject, which, I apprehend, ought, with all prudent men who are disposed to be guided by their reason instead of their passions, to have calmed and quieted this Church. I read from the First of the Proofs, page 74, a resolution which was passed upon a report of the committee upon these petitions:—

"*Resolved*, by the delegates of the several annual conferences in General Conference assembled, That under the provisional exception of the general rule of the Church on the subject of slavery, the simple holding of slaves, or mere ownership of slave property, in States or territories where the laws do not admit of emancipation and permit the liberated slave to enjoy freedom, constitutes no legal barrier to the election or ordination of ministers to the various grades of office known in the ministry of the Methodist Episcopal Church, and cannot therefore be considered as operating any forfeiture of right in view of such election and ordination."

This was nothing more than the adoption of the ancient and established usages of this Church, in defiance of all these petitions which were thus sent in, carrying them out, and showing, on the part of this Church, a determination to carry out their ancient and established doctrine and rules. Now, I submit, that that is no foundation for a secession from this Church. The Southern brethren cannot complain of any misconduct on the part of this Church as a Church. On the contrary, their conduct was exemplary, and was in perfect harmony with the established usages and practices of the Church.

As to the case of Mr. Harding, who was one of the travelling ministers in the Baltimore Conference, which the counsel on the other side, in the indulgence of a little imagination, calls the "Breakwater Conference," it seems that in that conference there is slaveholding territory and free territory. Mr. Harding had not purchased slaves, but had acquired them by marriage. Well, two questions arose in that case: one was, whether slaves could be emancipated in that State; and the other was, whether he was to be considered as voluntarily acquiring this kind of property when he obtained it by marriage? I admit that was a pretty nice question, because, although the Methodists adopt the American doctrine of free will, yet in the case of matrimony, perhaps, there is not always perfect free will. However, it was a very delicate and nice question to determine whether it came within the rule of voluntary acquisition. Another question arose, and that was, whether in that State manumission was allowable? It seems that some gentlemen gave opinions that it was, and others thought differently. The conference had to pass on these delicate subjects. It was a question which could not often arise. It was a mere isolated case, and one which they had to pass upon with the best lights they could get, and the annual conference decided that he ought to be suspended from the ministry until he emancipated the slaves, or showed cause for not doing it. If you will read the argument, you will see that he had not made any effort to do it; perhaps his wife would have joined him in emancipating them. He appeared to be active in retaining the property. Therefore, under all the circumstances, as in this conference there was jurisdiction over free territory and slave territory, and ministers who held slaves would not be acceptable in the free part of it, and as travelling ministers are to travel over the entire territory in the conference, they thought best, until that difficulty should be removed, that he should be suspended from the ministry. The General Conference, on an appeal, seeing no foundation for reversing, confirmed the decision.

Let us take the next case in connexion with it, that of Bishop Andrew. He, it seems, also married a wife, and that wife had slaves. He had acquired by will a slave who refused to be free, who refused to go to Liberia. So far from making any effort to emancipate, or showing any disposition to do it, he had executed an assignment in trust to secure the slaves thus acquired to the joint benefit of himself and his wife. That case came up before the Conference. What were they to do? Here was a bishop, against whom there was no objection originally, but who had become unacceptable to a considerable portion of Methodists in some parts of the territory; and according to a radical and fundamental doctrine of that Church, he was to travel through all that territory. That must be admitted to be a very nice question. Suppose they were wrong in their decision upon the case—let us suppose, upon the whole case, which would bring even a judicial mind, who happened to be a member of that Church, to a pause, that they had come to an erroneous decision, and had committed an error in this one particular case, is that to break up the Church? Does that warrant a secession? Is that a *misconduct* which would entitle them to be treated in the light of seceders? I apprehend not.

I will refer the Court, on this subject, to the case of Miller *vs.* Gable, 2 Denio's Reports, 492. Judge Gardiner observes, in going over this subject, in regard to doctrines—and it will throw light on the subject of the government and discipline—that in order to constitute a departure from the trust, with regard to doctrines, there must be a settled deviation from some substantial doctrine of the Church. You will find the same position in 2 Bligh's Reports, 529. This was the case of an Associate Congregation of Perth.

It establishes two important principles:—

Firstly. "Where a difference of doctrines prevails, the Court will decide in favour of the party which adheres to the ancient doctrines of the Church.

Secondly. "That when there is a difference in regard to government, the Court will decide in favour of those who adhere to the old government. But the question of doctrine furnishes the primary rule—an adherence to the ancient established doctrines of the Church is indispensable to constitute Church membership."

This case was carried up to the Court of Appeals—the Parliament of Great Britain—and it was there decided that there had been a deviation in some respects from their doctrines, but in no very essential point. It was on the subject of the administration of an oath.

But it must be in some substantial, essential point, where there is a departure, in order to warrant a court in treating them as seceders from the Church. If there had been in this case a determination to depart from some important radical portion of the Discipline, which is considered essential, there would have been ground for a secession; but to say that in this Church, because, in two particular instances, in very nice cases, they had given a construction which the gentlemen on the other side say was not correct, but where it is manifest they decided according to their best judgments —to say that in this Church a decision in such cases, standing out of any direct rule, and where a rule was to be applied without any precedents to guide them, was a misconduct which would warrant a dissolution of the union of the Church, break it up, and entitle those who did thus dissolve it, and break it up, to be considered as the true Church, and to carry property along with them, is, I apprehend, going too far. I will call the attention of the Court to the view which this Church takes of this subject of union in their Discipline, chap. 1, sec. 18 :—

"Let us be deeply sensible (from what we have known) of the evil of a division in principle, spirit, or practice, and the dreadful consequences to ourselves and others. If we are united, what can stand before us? If we divide, we shall destroy ourselves, the work of God, and the souls of our people."

They here inculcate with great stress the importance of union and the necessity of enforcing and preserving it. The principles they advance are important and highly conservative. It would be well for all good citizens to adopt those principles, to guide them in their allegiance and their duty towards the government of the country under which they live, and from which they have received all that they are and all that they ought to be. Deeply imbued with those principles, while anxious to assert their rights, they would be equally mindful of their duties. Then follows a variety of regulations to preserve the union of the Church.

Well, when we find a rule of law upon this subject, that in order to constitute a right to separate or secede lawfully, there must be in the opposite party a settled violation of or departure from some essential and important rule of action in the government or discipline, of course the same law will apply more strongly to a similar departure in a matter of faith and doctrine, because it is more important in an ecclesiastical body that its faith should be observed than its government or discipline. The religious faith of the Church is the great object in view in establishing the Church. You will always look and inquire in considering who are the adherents to any institution, what is the object of that body? for what is it created?—the rules, government, and discipline, are merely subordinate. They are merely instrumental in carrying out the great purpose which is here—the promotion and propagation of religious faith. But a departure from the religious faith in a matter of very little importance, as we have seen, is no foundation for a separation. Can, then, a mistake in a decision in a doubtful, difficult case, a new case, one which does not come directly under any fixed, settled principle, but to which principles are brought to apply inferentially and impliedly, warrant the members in breaking up and destroying the society? I submit that it cannot, and more especially, too, when you see that this Church is considered as a unit; that it is a regularly organized body, and its union in all its branches, in all its entirety, is considered essential for the promotion of morality, and the preservation of the souls of its members. Yet, such are the grounds which are now relied upon on the other side to legalize the separation of this Church.

I now proceed to consider the objections which are taken to the manner in which this trial of the bishop was had. We are told that Bishop Andrew did not receive a regular trial, that he was not regularly summoned, and that he was not condemned according to any fixed and settled rule of law. Well, upon the subject of the trial and notice, I apprehend he has had all the trial which could be required in an institution of this kind. They have no regular formal proceedings by summons, no pleading, and no jury trial. It is sufficient if the man was heard, and had an opportunity for defending himself, and presenting his case fully. Bishop Andrew had this. He wrote a letter in which he stated the whole case; and no further trial, or notice, or evidence could be required, because they took the case precisely as he had stated it in that letter, and thus adopted and acted upon it. He had every opportunity of presenting every reason and every consideration that could occur to him, as proper to be heard in his case, either to justify, excuse, or mitigate. What more trial would you have? It will be borne in mind, too, that in this Church the bishop is amenable to this Conference. He may be dismissed or suspended for "improper conduct." That is the language of the Discipline. What is meant by "improper conduct?" Does it mean a crime, according to the law of the land? Does it mean any positive and express violation of some positive rule of the Methodist Discipline? I apprehend not. On p. 16 of the first volume of Proofs, is the following extract from the Discipline :—

"To whom is the bishop amenable for his conduct?

"To the General Conference, who have power to expel him for improper conduct, if they see it necessary."

"Improper conduct," I apprehend, is not confined to some violation of law or some settled rule of Discipline. A bishop may commit acts of impropriety which cannot be brought under any fixed rule of law. I might refer your Honours to the injunction upon bishops to be found in Timothy, with which, no doubt, you are perfectly familiar, and which you will find, goes much further than any requirement of law, in reference to his behaviour and deportment. Suppose any bishop, where it is allowable, should set up a hotel, or allow gaming in a country where it is not condemned by law. Perhaps you would find nothing specified in the rules of the Discipline, and nothing in the law of the land about it, but every one would say it was improper for a bishop to act in that way, and clearly under the rule of Discipline the Conference might condemn and expel him for such improper conduct. There are a hundred, a thousand things, which, according to the usages of the Churches, it would be improper for a minister to do, and yet which would violate no law, and be done with perfect propriety by persons who were not in that venerable position in the Church and society at large, a position calling for a most guarded circumspection of conduct. Now I presume that this rule was intended to meet that class of cases, to confer full power upon the Church to reach all such cases which could not be reduced to any fixed, settled rule of law.

Now, if a bishop acquires slaves after he becomes a bishop, when, by the ancient usages of the Church, he would not have been elected to that office if he had then held them, for reasons which I have already assigned, and which rules have been in that Church always deemed imperative, and he omits to manumit them, or if he should persist to act as bishop while he holds them, and is yet in a condition to manumit them, his conduct would be "improper" according to the rules of the Discipline of that Church. It would be improper, because it would tend to destroy his efficiency as an itinerant bishop; and in that point of view, this Conference would have a perfect right to inflict the censure prescribed in the Discipline upon him. But they did not do it. They avoided it. They took the mildest measure that could be taken in the case. They were determined to support their Discipline as far as they could; to have an acceptable bishopric, and an itinerant bishopric, and at the same time relieve Bishop Andrew from any imputation, except so far as it was indispensably necessary to carry out these points. Instead, therefore, of expelling or suspending him, instead of passing an act of a punitive character, they simply advised (for it is clearly an advisory proceeding) that he should "desist" from acting. At the same time, on account of the delicacy of his situation, they left him all the privileges and advantages of a bishop. Well, say the gentlemen on the other side, it is placing him in a very awkward predicament to act after such an advisory letter or request as this. Well, that could not be helped. It was placing him in that position unquestionably, but at the same time it was treating him with as much delicacy as the case could admit of. In a case like this, under all these circumstances, when they all felt, deeply felt, the necessity of preserving their ancient landmarks, of preserving the episcopacy, and at the same time preserving its itinerancy, and of connecting the two with the usefulness and efficiency of their bishops, they took that course which in their opinion was most advisable; and the question for you now to determine is, (for the other side mainly rest on that ground—there they plant themselves,) Was that a sufficient foundation for this Southern branch of the Church to secede—to leave them? and are they entitled as seceders to carry with them the property of the Church, on the ground of a radical, substantial departure from the discipline of the Church by the body they leave behind? I submit to the Court that no such charge can be legitimately brought against us. They cannot rest on that foundation for a claim to this property. I admit in all these ecclesiastical institutions, and it must be admitted on all hands, and I have no doubt the Southern Church will admit, the importance of preserving the discipline. Faith and doctrines are paramount, but at the same time, discipline is important, because it is enjoined upon them (to be Scriptural) to do all things in order, and so to do them, they must have rules of action, and they must comply with them.

We are not left here to draw legal inferences from the doctrines or government of the Church as to the consequences of this separation upon the property. I have considered this subject so far, in its bearings upon the property, upon the supposition there was not any agreement about it. Has there been in this case, such a separation by agreement to separate as would entitle them to a part of the property? and if not, has there been such misconduct, on the part of the old Church, as to warrant them in separating, and still entitle them to hold the property? That is the view I have taken of it; and in so treating it, I have laid out of view any agreement about the *property*. But if there is an agreement between the parties respecting the property itself, it must govern, supposing they have any right to agree about it one way or the other. They say the General Conference had a right to make an agreement with them, by which they should separate from the Church. Carry that out; assume they had the right. We say, that even if there was an agreement about the property, that agreement was, that they should detach themselves from the main body of the Church, and leave that behind; and, therefore, they could not carry the property with them upon principles of law. In the next place, we contend that there is, in the absence of an agreement, no such misconduct on the part of this Church as would entitle them to claim any portion of the property. But I come now to this important point, that there was in this case an express agreement about the property; and that must settle the question. You can deduce no inferences, you can draw no conclusions, you can raise no implications, when you have an express agreement. That must stand by itself, and they must either stand or fall by it. Let us see what that agreement was. It is to be found in the First Proofs, p. 129:—

"4. That whenever the annual conferences, by a vote of three-fourths of all their members voting on the third resolution, shall have concurred in the recommendation to alter the sixth restrictive article, the agents at New-York and Cincinnati shall, and they are hereby authorized and directed to deliver over to any authorized agent or appointee of the Church, South, should one be organized, all notes and book accounts against the ministers, Church members, or citizens within its boundaries, with authority to collect the same for the sole use of the Southern Church, and that said agents also convey to the aforesaid agent or appointee of the South all the real estate, and assign to him all the property, including presses, stock, and all right and interest connected with the printing establishments at Charleston, Richmond, and Nashville, which now belong to the Methodist Episcopal Church.

"5. That when the annual conferences shall have approved the aforesaid change in the sixth restrictive article, there shall be transferred to the above agent of the Southern Church so much of the capital and product of the Methodist Book Concern as will, with the notes, book accounts, presses, &c., mentioned in the last resolution, bear the same proportion to the whole property of said Concern that the travelling preachers in the Southern Church shall bear to all the travelling ministers of the Methodist Episcopal Church; the division to be made on the basis of the number of travelling preachers in the forthcoming minutes.

"6. That the above transfer shall be in the form of annual payments of $25,000 per annum, and specifically in stock of the Book Concern, and in Southern notes and accounts due the establishment, and accruing after the first transfer mentioned above; and until the payments are made, the Southern Church shall share in all the net profits of the Book Concern, in the proportion that the amount due them or in arrears bears to all the property of the Concern."

I think no man who will read this case over candidly and impartially, can hesitate to say, that this General Conference acted upon the idea, that before this branch, who were thus to separate and form a new organization in the South, could take any portion of this property, which was devoted to this charitable use in the Methodist Episcopal Church, the annual conferences should concur. The counsel on the other side, tell us, that that is not the true construction; that it was intended that they should have the right absolutely; and that all that was required by this agreement—all that was rendered contingent was, that it should not be *transferred* until the annual conferences thus concurred. It appears to me, that that would be perfectly peurile. What! Give them the right without this concurrence of the annual conferences, and yet tell them it should not be transferred until the annual conferences did concur! Give them the right, but not let them take the property? If they intended they should have the right absolutely, clearly they would allow the property to be transferred at once. If they intended, before any transfer of this property should be made, that the annual conferences should concur, they clearly intended no right until that concurrence should be obtained. I think that it is too clear to dispute about. A distinction like that, if it was carried out, would be perfectly refined and peurile, and totally devoid of that common-sense which guides this Methodist Episcopal Church in their conduct. They manifestly meant, that the annual conferences should concur before any portion of this property should be divided. They said to the delegates from the South: "If you find it necessary, when you come to meet in your annual conferences, that you should separate, we will agree that you shall; but we cannot agree—and you must take this as connected with your action upon this subject in your annual conferences—we cannot agree that any portion of this property shall pass from us as composing the Methodist Episcopal Church, until the annual conferences concur." And I think there was some reason and sound sense in this. Suppose that this institution, as the managers of this charity, were so connected and identified with it and with the beneficiaries as to entitle them to dispose of this property in this way in an emergency of that kind, ought it to be done until the concurrence of all the managers is obtained? Were the General Conference the exclusive managers? Certainly not; the annual conferences participated in the management of it as much, and perhaps more efficiently than the General Conference; and for that reason, when they undertook to adjust this matter of property in their capacity of managers, without the sanction of a court of equity, with great propriety they required that their concurrence should be obtained before any portion of this property should be taken.

Well, now, who is to lay this matter before the annual conferences? It is not required by the General Conference that it be done by any person concerned. The other party could see and undertake to bring it before them, as well as ourselves. If they, the annual conferences, act upon it and concur, when the subject is brought before them, there is an end of the question. Have they concurred? That is not pretended. They do not set that up on the other side. The counsel on the other side says that the annual conferences have not *refused;* that there was a mistake in the voting; that the proposition presented to them was so general and broad, as not to reach the case properly; that the question was put to them, whether there should be an absolute and unqualified repeal of the sixth restrictive article; and that it should have been put, whether it should be altered so far as to allow the Church, South, to take this ratable proportion of the property. I admit this is a fair and reasonable interpretation of that agreement. The proposition as presented is drawn in general terms, but it is fair to restrict and modify it according to the subject matter, and it would have been proper to have put it in that shape; and it is very probable that some of these conferences did not concur in it, on account of the generality of the proposition. What then ought to be done in a case like that? Why, wait until the subject shall be laid before the annual conferences anew, until they shall have passed upon it in its new shape; and when they have passed upon it fairly and fully—when it is presented in a modified form, which will bring up the entire question, fairly and distinctly, for their consideration—then it will be time to pass on the final subject, in the disposition of this property. And all they had to do at the South was to wait a reasonable time until this matter could be fairly disposed of. They have not thought proper, however, to do this. What is the consequence? The consent of the annual conferences, necessary to enable them to take any portion of this property according to the agreement between the parties, has not been obtained. This agreement, stating the terms on which they shall take this property, necessarily involves the interpretation, that without the consent of the annual conferences they should not take it, and were not entitled to it. There has not been that consent. Then how are they entitled to it? Are they entitled to it independently of this agreement? Then they can violate the agreement; they are not bound by it; they can set up something in opposition to it, when it is made the plain rule of action for the parties in this particular case. All must abide by the agreement in all its parts. It does appear to me that this view is decisive upon this question. Why, suppose that in the case of a township incorporated, having property, the legislature should pass an act authorizing a portion of the town to be set apart to form a new one, and they should make provision, that in case certain bodies in that township should concur, a portion of the property should be given to the new town, could they take it without such concurrence? I think not. In the absence of such a provision, as separatists, though with the concurrence of all concerned, they would not be entitled to it at all. With such a provision, there must be a compliance with it. That is the case here. I have shown that this Southern Church are separatists; that they leave the Methodist Episcopal Church in all its identity and entirety behind them; that they set up a new Church, and in that capacity are not entitled to the property in question. They set up that agreement in their favour. But it has not been performed; its terms have not been fulfilled. They did not wait until the fulfilment of it could be obtained. They thought proper to go and carry out their new organization and establish a new Church, and then claim this property. The consequence is, they are not entitled to it. In the absence of any agreement they would not be entitled to it. The terms of the agreement have not been fulfilled, and they are not entitled under the agreement. In any point of view, they are not legally entitled to any portion of this property.

The Court adjourned until Wednesday.

EIGHTH DAY.—Wednesday, May 28, 1851.

Mr, Wood,—I shall not detain your Honours a long while with this case, this morning. In fact, if I had not been so much exhausted yesterday, I should have claimed the indulgence of the Court for a short time, and then have finished. This case, however, is too important to be slightly passed over; important in its interests, in the character of its interests and parties, and in its connexion with national concerns; for, I think, in the present crisis of our country, it has a most intimate connexion with public affairs.

The proposition to which I now wish to call the attention of the Court is, that the Church (in reference to its property I now speak) had no power to make such a division as is contended for on the other side, and part with the property. I do not put this now mainly upon the idea that this General Conference is a delegated body. I am aware of the distinction between a delegated sovereignty and a delegated agency, in a matter of business. In the latter case, the agent continues subject to the control of the principal; but in the case of a delegated sovereign power, the sovereignty controls the constituency. That is a distinction, and is one which is too often lost sight of even in our halls of legislation. I shall proceed to state, however, the grounds of objection, on which I rely, to any attempt on the part of this General Conference, or the General Conference in connexion with the annual conferences, in themselves, to undertake to divide this Church, and divide the property along with it; for it is particularly in connexion with the property we are now to consider the case.

I must here draw the attention of the Court to a distinction which does not appear to have been adverted to; and that is, that these funds are not beneficially, and even in the point of view in which an interest is taken in a public charity, the funds of the Methodist Episcopal Church. That Church has a beneficial equitable *control* over them as managers of the charity; but that beneficial equitable control is for the benefit of the classes of persons who are designated as the objects of the charitable use. They are, as has often been repeated, the superannuated and supernumerary ministers, their wives, widows, and children. Now the Methodist Episcopal Church, if they owned the property, or had the equitable beneficial interest in it in themselves, might exercise an influence over that property, which would be more extensive than they could over property of which they had the mere management. But it would not be such a vested interest in them if they held it in that sort of politic capacity, if I may call it so, in which charitable uses are generally held, and in reference to which ministers of the Church, for the time being, take simply the mere usufruct; even then they could not alienate it. But the books draw a distinction as to the powers of beneficiaries in a charitable use even of that description, and the case of a religious corporation or a religious institution which has simply a management of a charity. I will refer the Court to a case upon this subject—that of the Attorney-General *vs.* Wilson, 18 Vesey, 519; also to be found in Shelford on Mortmain, 701, 702.

The Attorney-General, *vs.* Wilson.
[Rolls.—1812. April 20.]

Leases of charity estates for twenty-one years, the lessors being not mere trustees, but having also a beneficial interest, set aside as breaches of trust by undervalue.

"The information, stating the foundation of the free school of Pocklington in the fifth year of King Edward VI., and indentures in the first year of Queen Mary, giving lands to the master and usher, and their successors forever, to hold in trust for the maintenance of the school, complained of several leases of the charity estates, for twenty-one years, at very low rents, viz.:—The 13th of August, 1800, at the annual rent of £3, the value to be let being £92 per annum; the 3d of December, 1800, rent

£2 13*s*. 4*d*., annual value £141; 12th December, 1800, rent £1 2*s*. 6*d*., value £35; 26th November, 1804, rent £1 13*s*. 4*d*., value £26; and 23d November, 1805, rent £5, value £132. On the death of the late master, in 1807, the relator was appointed.

"The information, charging that the whole of the rents, amounting to no more than £63 12*s*. 6*d*., is very inadequate to the support of the school, and that the granting such leases was a breach of trust, prayed that the defendants may be decreed to deliver them up to be cancelled, and to account for the full value since the death of the late master; and a reference for a scheme for letting the estate agreeably to the intention of the founder.

Sir Samuel Romely and *Mr. Bell*, in support of the information: *Mr. Hart* and *Mr. Shadwell* for the defendants.

"The MASTER OF THE ROLLS, [SIR WILLIAM GRANT,] (preventing the reply,) made the decree setting aside the leases, referring to his judgment in the *Attorney-General vs. Magwood*, and observing that having then had much occasion to consider this subject, he found several cases in Duke, Vernon, and modern reports, particularly the *Attorney-General vs. Gower*; that the short duration of the term was immaterial, and the only distinction of this from the late case was, that in those the lessors were mere trustees, and in this instance they had also a beneficial interest; but such leases are not to be encouraged on account of the inconvenience both ways, the trustees not doing their duty, and the lessees getting the land at a low rent."

In that case, although they had a beneficial interest, yet the grant, or rather the lease, was so unreasonable that the court of equity set it aside; but at the same time they recognised a distinction between cases where the managers of the charity have a beneficial interest, and where they have merely the management for the benefit of others who are the beneficiaries. Now, in this case, the Methodist Episcopal Church are not the beneficiaries, they are the managers of this charity for the sake of others, who are, it is true, in some sort connected with the Church, and who take the usufruct in some measure in ease of the Church, but they are nevertheless distinct in point of interest. I have already stated that there is a connexion between the officers of the Church, when the property is given for their benefit, and the Church itself; and I showed you a case from the first Pennsylvania Reports, where the disposition was considered in ease of the Church. But still there is a distinction. This Church, although this property is given in ease of it, would have no right to divert it to any other portion of the Church, or apply it to any other interest in the Church, or at least so much of it as may be required to fulfil the end designed to supply the beneficiaries. It must to that extent go according to the designation of the charity, for the benefit of those who are marked out as the objects of the charity. I believe I have already pointed out the distinction between the identity of the Church and the beneficiaries of this charity, as connected with the Church and the Methodist Episcopal faith. I have shown you that you could not apply this charity to objects which were not connected with this Church itself, in its organization, in its discipline, in its identity. That connexion must be observed; and it will not do to say that the parties, or any persons who have the management of it, have a right to apply it to other individuals who may be ministers of some Methodist Episcopal Church, or who may answer the description of wives, widows, or children of some ministers of some other Methodist Church, happening to be of the same faith. They must, therefore, be entirely connected, and, as I before observed, in addition, that organism must be preserved, and it must be carried out by the Court.

Now, the annual conferences in this case must concur with the General Conference in reference to the management and disposition of this charity, when any disposition can be made, because, as I before remarked, they are concerned just as much, in their respective spheres, in the general disposition of the proceeds of this charity as the General Conference itself. But if all of them concurred, the power is not complete to undertake to divide these funds; and before I proceed to point out my objections, I will meet the cases advanced on the other side for the purpose of overturning the principle I state. We are referred to the Canada Conference. You will recollect, however, the Canada Conference was no part of the Methodist Episcopal Church. It was simply an appendage, and it has been so treated throughout, and a connexion of a temporary character. I will call the attention of the Court to one or two items upon this subject. In 1824 an attempt was made to divide this from the Church, and in their memorial they point out the nature of this connexion:—

"Sensible as we are of the advantages derived from the connexion with which you have kindly favoured us, we are nevertheless constrained by the circumstances in which we find ourselves placed to request a separation."

You there find that the Canada Conference is treated as being no integral part of the Methodist Episcopal Church, but connected with it simply by a temporary union, or a temporary alliance, if I may so call it. Well, now, in respect to all that class of cases a distinction has been drawn. If your Honours will advert to the case of Miller *vs.* Gable, 2 Denio's Reports, you will find great stress was laid upon the fact that that particular Church formed no part, no integral part, of the German Reformed Church, but that it was connected with it in the nature of a temporary alliance. That was precisely the case in the Presbyterian Church controversy, in regard to the Churches in the Western Reserve. It was there held and finally carried out in the decisions in Pennsylvania, that it was not a constituent branch of the Church, but a temporary alliance.

I apprehend, therefore, that that Canada case has no bearing upon the subject. Besides, no part of the property, finally, was given to the Canada Conference. And when you come to look at the votes upon that subject, you will find that the Southern conferences, almost to a man, voted against their taking any portion of this property. You will find that fact stated in page 47, First of the Proofs. It is certainly true that the Church finally did make some allowance, and perhaps the remark made by the counsel on the other side was correct, that if they were not entitled to anything the General Conference was wrong in giving them such privileges as they did. The answer to all that is, that it does not alter the principle. They can draw nothing from that case to support them in regard to the power of this Methodist Episcopal Church to cut itself in twain, and then, as managers of this charity, to undertake to divide the funds in this way.

The counsel who is to close the argument on the other side, has referred to a case in 1 Peters, 542, as having some analogy to this subject. He refers to the Constitution of the United States, which gives to the federal government the power of regulating their territories, and then he says, it is claimed by the Supreme Court of the United States, in this case in 1 Peters, that they were authorized to establish over the territory acquired by treaty a territorial government, in virtue of that power which is contained in the Constitution. That is all certainly true. Such a decision was made, and I believe no sound jurist will ever attempt to impeach its correctness. They had the power. It is in the very nature of the power granted. When you look at the subject of the grant, which had relation to the exercise of a sovereign power, it was in the very nature of things that that power should be exercised by creating a subordinate delegated sovereignty. But what bearing has it upon the present case? If this Methodist Episcopal Church, in the extension of her territory, had created and set up a new annual conference under their control and jurisdiction, there would have been some analogy. Then it would have been simply the creation of a subordinate government under their control, and it would have preserved the unity and identity of the entire Church. But that is a very different affair from a division of the Methodist Episcopal Church, creating a new jurisdiction altogether and entirely independent of the Methodist Episcopal Church. Now, suppose, in order to illustrate this case, that under this power to regulate territories, the government of the United States should undertake to separate this territory, to declare it independent, and to set up an entirely new and independent government free from their control; if they were to do that, there would be some analogy. But, I apprehend, Chief Justice Marshall never would have undertaken to sanction such a proceeding, on the ground that the Constitution in that passage referred to authorized such a course to be taken. That would present a case somewhat analogous to this, and I will venture to say, such a case never will occur. If ever this country should be divided, if ever a portion of it should be separated from the rest, and it should finally, in the course of events, come to be fully established, it must rest on some power, some mode of proceeding, out of the Constitution and not there provided for; and if ever this Methodist Episcopal Church is divided, as it has been in fact divided, and if ever they take the property in consequence of that division, without a positive agreement between the parties on the subject, it must be by force of some principle which you cannot find in any provision in the government and discipline of the Church. It does not provide for any such case.

Now, I submit that there can be no such power; and the only way that I can see in which an agreement to divide this property, after dividing the Church, can be carried out by this Court, would be upon the principle of compromise; and if these parties had fairly and without precipitation gone on and carried out that compromise—if the opposite party had gone regularly on under the agreement, and waited until the concurrence of the annual conferences had been obtained, pursuant to the terms of that compromise, and had made the arrangement—then I can see that this Court could have carried it out; but even then it would have required the sanction of this Court to give it effect. Upon this subject I refer to Shelford on Mortmain, 608, referring to the case of the Attorney-General *vs.* The Merchant Tailors' School, 7 Vesey, 233, and Andrew *vs.* Trinity Hall, 9 Vesey, 535.

"*Trinity Hall* in *Cambridge*, devisee in remainder after estates for lives, in trust, for founding four new scholarships, for making additional buildings to that college, and for founding four new fellowships, were held not to have accepted the devise, by acts done merely for the preservation of the fund; and upon their refusal to accept it, after the death of the tenant for life, the Court directed the master to receive a proposal in order to have it considered whether it could be executed *cy-près;* and the testator having expressed in his will, that no person should be qualified for the scholarships and fellowships he intended to found, unless they should have been educated in *Merchant Tailors' School*, the master was particularly directed to receive a proposal on the part of that school, for the establishment of a charity within the terms of the testator's will. A compromise afterwards taking place to apply part of the fund to an establishment at *St. John's College*, in Oxford, with which college the *Merchant Tailors' Company* are connected, and to give the rest to the next of kin, it was, with the consent of the attorney-general, established by decree. And the next of kin, after this compromise, having filed a bill against *Trinity Hall*, for an account, the bill was dismissed, the Court holding the next of kin bound by the compromise."

And you will find also in the case of Black *vs.* Ligan, Harper's South Carolina Reports, 215, a case of this character and description, in which Chancellor De Saussure advised and recommended a compromise, and even went the length of delaying the decision of the Court to give the parties an opportunity of carrying it out. But in all these cases it must be done under the sanction of the Court. In the case of an ordinary alienation of property held for charitable uses, the sanction of the Court was required, and for this plain reason: that parties beneficially interested have not such an interest as will enable them to alienate it, and in all cases if a man purchases and takes a lease from the trustees of the charity which is improvident and unreasonable, the Court of Equity will set it aside, holding that a party taking a lease of such property or land, takes it *sub modo*, and it ought to be set aside if the chancellor, who represents the interests of the beneficiaries of the charity, should think that the lease is improvident and unreasonable. I refer the Court upon this subject to Shelford, 658 and 698.

The Court will find a striking case in the Attorney-General *vs.* Warren, which is to be found in 2 Swanson, 291; a case of a charity lease which required the sanction of the Court. I will refer you also to Shelford on Mortmain, 698. If in the case of an ordinary alienation of property which is held for charitable purposes, the trustees and parties having the management are bound to a provident alienation, if that alienation is considered under the control and direction of the Court, and if an alienation without any fraud, without any mistake, can be set aside merely because it is unreasonable or improvident, it shows how completely the disposition of property which is set apart for charity and other public uses, is placed under the direction and control of a court of equity; and the reason to which I have adverted shows the propriety of it. There are no beneficiaries to look after this charity—none that have a *vested* interest in it even in equity. If this is the case in ordinary alienations of property held for such uses, how much more strongly must it be the case when you come to a subject like this, which stands out of all ordinary rules of proceedings, which is not provided for by the government and discipline. I mean the case of a division of the Church, and a division taking place on account of disputes and difficulties arising in the Church. In order to sanction such a division,—I mean when you carry it into the property, and more especially when you carry it to the case of property appertaining to a charity where that Church have simply the management of the charity,—how much more important is it that every disposition of that kind should be made under the sanction and under the control of a court of equity, whose office peculiarly is required to protect this kind of charity.

Now I will venture to say, that if a little more time, and a little more patience, had been exercised in this case, that compromise would have been fully carried out. It is strange that in these religious cases, when the parties once get a little heated, they seem to be less disposed to exercise that patience and forbearance than even in ordinary cases of controversy between private individuals. The same hot haste occurred in that division in the Society of Friends to which I have frequently alluded; and Chief Justice Ewing, in his decision, at page 58, remarks, in substance, that if either party had not fallen off from the ancient principles of the Church—patience, forbearance, brotherly kindness, and charity—the meek and mild spirit which has been believed to characterize and adorn the genuine Friend would, under the blessings of Providence, have wrought out a perfect reconciliation.

I really believe, that if the members of this Church had acted with a little more caution, a little more forbearance, a little more of that charity which Saint Paul has so beautifully described, and which, I believe, this society have generally striven to act up to—if they had carried that out in this controversy, I think I may venture to say, that although they might not have united again, if the division had been consummated, there would have been an arrangement not only as to the ecclesiastical separation, but as to this property, which would have restored at least between them brotherly kindness, and perhaps more of the unity of spirit than might be expected, considering the condition of our public affairs, if they had actually continued together. But they did not take this course. Any man who will read that Plan of Separation, must see that it contemplated a full and fair consideration of this subject in the respective annual conferences of the South, and that upon such consideration, before any division was actually to take place, they were to be brought to the conclusion that that separation was *necessary*—the strongest language which could have been used upon that subject. The deliberations and decisions of those conferences would have required time, and all great questions of this kind ought to receive time for their settlement and adjustment. That would have given the General Conference, North, and the leading men in that Church, an opportunity of going before the other annual conferences, and presenting the matter of changing the sixth article in its true light, and modifying, on sober second thought, the general nature of the proposition, so as to present it in a more definite form; and no doubt the consent would have been obtained. All the members of this Church, with whom I have had any consultation upon this subject, have been satisfied that in that way it would have been effected. But the gentlemen of the South, instead of taking that course, issued that address at the very time that the General Conference passed the resolutions—an address which was manifestly, instead of leaving the subject to the annual conferences, inviting and urging them, though in form submitting it to them, to make a division of the Church, instead of going through the process of submitting it to these conferences and getting their decision. All that was done was to advise them to appoint delegates to meet at Louisville, to form a Convention; and the delegates forming that Convention carried out the division without any consultation and decision upon the necessity of the case by the various annual conferences in the South. This led to the difficulty, and to the bringing of this suit. And they did bring this suit, and no further efforts at adjustment were made, because, from the moment they took this course, the leading members that were left behind in the Methodist Episcopal Church, knew that it was perfectly vain to attempt to effect the concurrence of the annual conferences with this suit pending over their heads. And I think I may venture to say, that if this suit was now out of the way—but I hold no gentleman's proxy in giving this opinion—and a disposition manifested on the other side to meet in the true spirit of compromise, this whole matter would be settled before eighteen months should pass over.

But while I make these remarks, I am perfectly aware, that there is some excuse for these Southern gentlemen—an excuse which ought to be considered by the Church that I represent. That unfortunate question of abolitionism—which has been, for the last fifteen or twenty years in this country, Pandora's box, to let out every evil—has wrought them up to a pitch of excitement which forms, if not a justification, at least some excuse for the precipitancy with which they have acted; and therefore allowances ought to be made on both sides of this question, and no doubt in the spirit of concord and conciliation they will be made. When I make these remarks on the subject of abolitionism, I do not mean any censure particularly of any persons who have suffered themselves to be carried away by that spirit. I know very good men, and pious men, have suffered themselves to engage in it; and this most difficult subject to deal with in the world—this spirit of wild enthusiasm which sometimes takes possession of a man's mind—is a subject which is not perfectly understood as yet. It will require a new chapter in the science of mental philosophy fully to develop it. A man sets out with the best philanthropic motives in the world to carry out some great principle of benevolence. He may not be accustomed to take very enlarged views of things; hence he suffers that one idea to take full possession of his mind. He goes on, filled with benevolence and good feeling towards all the world; but he finally comes to meet with opposition, and that opposition only stimulates him the more, excites a feeling utterly polemical, and altogether different from that benevolent motive by which he was originally actuated; and what is more extraordinary, he becomes the victim of the grossest delusion, imagines himself entirely free of all animosity, and actuated still by his original good feeling. I say that these enthusiasts act upon principles of mere individualism. They do not look upon subjects on a large scale. A man takes it into his head that a slave would be better off to be free, and therefore he makes every effort to free him. That does very well in a mere isolated, individual case. But when you take a slave population, composing the entire labouring population of a country, and undertake to free them, you are doing something more than engaging in a mere subject of individual philanthropy. You are creating a new political power, especially in a country imbued as ours is with the principle of universal suffrage, and a power which may be the source of tremendous evil. There is no case in history in which the whole labouring population of a country, being in a state of slavery, have been suddenly freed, except by our British brethren, who have urged us to that course—a course by which they have prostrated completely their West India colonies. This matter of freeing the masses in a state of slavery has been, heretofore, in the history of the world, a work of time. It has taken that course which Lord Bacon tells us is the course of nature. All great reforms require time—long time—to work them out without producing more evil than good.

I have made these remarks upon this subject, because I consider it as deeply connected with the great interests of this country. I have endeavoured to show, and I hope have successfully shown, that the body which I represent, the real abiding members of the Methodist Episcopal Church, as a body, are not to be charged with being guilty of that kind of offence, as it is considered in the Southern States, and by our Southern brethren, and that it ought not to be imputed to them. That there are individual members who adopt these abolition views, and who have even in this Church, by their petitions, excited the Southern mind, and induced them to act with the precipitancy to which I have adverted, there can be no doubt.

I have now, I believe, gone over this case, and I think I have said enough to satisfy the Court that these plaintiffs can have, upon sound principles of law and equity, as administered in cases of this kind, no right to this property; that they have not waited to abide by the agreement which was made between these parties, which I verily believe would have effected a division of the property, as well as a division of the Church, if they had waited, and which I verily believe also on sound principles might have been carried out under the sanction of a court of equity, but not without such sanction. And I do think if they were to discontinue this suit, and let it pass away, that an arrangement would be effected between these parties in a spirit of peace, and in the spirit of that religion which they all profess, and which I trust most of them, or the great body of them, feel and act upon. Why, it would be most extraordinary if compromises in these religious controversies could not take place. Nine-tenths of the disputes of the world are settled by compromise; and is a religious controversy to form the only exception? Are men who are bound together by the same religious faith, professing the same principles, worshipping the same God, seeking the same home hereafter, and by the same religious process,—are they alone to be an exception to this great principle of settling controversies by compromises? I trust not; and that I believe is the way, and the only way, in which this question ever can be settled.

If the Court will allow me, I will call their attention to another subject. I am aware that an attempt has been made to raise a prejudice against my clients, for holding on to this controversy. I will call the attention of the Court to some resolutions of the Conference of 1848 on this subject, to be found on pp. 94 and 95 of the Journal:—

"Whereas it is now ascertained that the recommendation of the General Conference at its session in 1844, to change the sixth restrictive article, so as to allow of a division of the property of the Book Concern with a distinct ecclesiastical Connexion which might be formed by the thirteen annual conferences in the slaveholding States, has not been concurred in by a vote of three-fourths of all the members of the several annual conferences present and voting on said recommendation;

"And whereas the thirteen protesting annual conferences in the slaveholding States have formed themselves into a separate and distinct ecclesiastical Connexion, under the title and name of the 'Methodist Episcopal Church, *South*,' and their General Conference in 1846 did authorize three commissioners (whose credentials have been received by this General Conference) to present and adjust their claim on the funds of the Book Concern of the Methodist Episcopal Church;

"And whereas our *common* and *holy* Christianity prescribes and enjoins the most pacific measures for the settlement of all matters in dispute between individuals, as well as associations of professing Christians, and the whole Christian world will expect ministers of the Lord Jesus Christ to adopt the most peaceful and conciliatory measures for the settlement of any claim that may be urged against them;

"And whereas this Conference desires to advance, as far as its constitutional powers will authorize, toward an amicable adjustment of this difficulty; therefore,

"*Resolved*, By the delegates of the several annual conferences of the Methodist Episcopal Church in General Conference assembled, that we hereby authorize the book agents at New-York and at Cincinnati to offer to submit said claims to the decision of disinterested arbiters; provided that if said agents, on the advice of eminent legal counsel, shall be satisfied that when clothed with all the authority which the General Conference can confer, their corporate powers will not warrant them to submit said claim to arbitration, this resolution shall not be binding upon them.

"2. *Resolved*, That should the agents find, upon taking such legal counsel, that they have not the power to submit the case to voluntary arbitration, and should a suit at law be commenced by the commissioners of the Methodist Episcopal Church, *South*, said agents are hereby authorized, then and in that case, to tender to said commissioners an adjustment of their preferred claims by a legal arbitration under the authority of the Court.

"3. *Resolved*, That should the agents find that they are not authorized to tender a voluntary arbitration, and should no suit be commenced by the commissioners aforesaid, then and in that case the General Conference, being exceedingly desirous of effecting an amicable settlement of said claim, recommend to the annual conferences so far to suspend the 'sixth restrictive article' of the Discipline, as to authorize our book agents at New-York and Cincinnati to submit said claim to arbitration."

It thus goes on with a number of resolutions to the same effect, inviting an amicable adjustment of this case. My clients then cannot be blamed for having brought on this controversy, or for its continuance.

Hon. Reverdy Johnson,—May it please your Honours, I propose to consider the question in this case under four general heads:—

The first is, the power of the General Conference of 1844 to adopt the Plan of Division of the 8th of June of that year.

2d. The construction of that Plan; which, as I shall maintain, is that the division of the Church was made to depend exclusively upon the decision of the conferences in the States in which slavery exists, and upon no other contingency, and that the change in the sixth restrictive article in the constitution of the General Conference was made to depend, and solely to depend, upon the decision of all the annual conferences of the entire Church as at that time constituted.

3d. That by force of the division of the Church, produced under the Plan, by the decision of the annual conferences in the States in which slavery exists, the property of the Church is to be divided, upon equitable principles, between the two Churches, North and South, without regard at all to any change of what is termed the sixth restrictive article.

4th and lastly. That admitting that the Conference of 1844 had no authority to adopt the Plan of Division which they undertook then to adopt, or that that Plan was conditional, and the condition not carried out, the state of things which still exists entitles the plaintiffs to relief upon the present bill.

These inquiries are, all of them, plain and simple. To be fully comprehended they require no extent of legal learning—no depth of particular research. To be properly enforced they demand no particular ability; and I should therefore approach the argument, if the controversy turned upon them alone, with no other solicitude—great as the pecuniary amount which depends upon this decision may be, and important as it is to those whom I represent—than that which ordinarily and properly belongs to the relation of counsel. But I confess a deeper and more absorbing anxiety; and that I rise oppressed by the responsibility which I feel is upon me. When I remember the origin of this dispute, I lose sight of the dollars and cents which it involves, and for a moment forget the direct and peculiar interest of my clients. There are reflections connected with that origin of such general and pervading interest,—so directly and vitally important to the usefulness of this very estimable denomination of Christians heretofore so harmonious and prosperous,—so material to the quiet of the public mind, and possibly so important to the very existence of the form of government under which we live, that I feel a trembling and nervous apprehension lest the proper adjudication of it by this Court, instead of being assisted, may be, in a measure, impeded by the manner in which I shall discharge my duty. The heart of the entire nation has been feverishly palpitating for the last few years, and yet so palpitates, in fear that, unless the very cause from which this dispute springs, is speedily and forever terminated by the good sense, virtue, and patriotism of the people and of all the authorities, state as well as national, the peace and happiness, the power and the glory which have heretofore illustrated our career, and made us the admiration if not the envy of the world, will be substituted by discord and wretchedness, debility and degradation, civil war and bloodshed. And is it too much to say that this alarmed state of the public mind is, in a great measure, to be attributed to the very controversy which your Honours are now called upon to settle? I have an abiding hope, and it is a consolation which will go with me through the argument, that the principles of law which the Court will have occasion to inculcate, and the rights which your duty will call upon you, as it will be your pleasure, to maintain as existing in the various sections of these United States, are such, and so firmly established, that, with the claims to the respect and confidence of all, which station, attainment, and patriotism give to this tribunal, the settlement of this case will tend much to quiet the public apprehension as well as to settle the particular dispute. It will be my part, as far as I am able, to assist the Court in the deliberations, which I trust will lead to this happy result.

First. Had the Conference of 1844 the power to adopt the Plan of Division of the 8th of June in that year?

My learned brothers upon the other side deny the power, and deny it with an earnestness and an ability which demonstrates a foregone conclusion in their own minds, that if the power can be maintained the rights of the complainants will be established. Where then in 1844 was the Methodist Episcopal Church in these United States? An associated body of men, tracing their origin, as far as their particular and exclusive organization was concerned, to the proceedings of what has been denominated the General Conference of December, 1784. In the exercise of their rights as citizens of the United States, inspired by the spirit of the holy calling to which the men of that day had devoted themselves, with the assent of Wesley, the founder of Methodism, they resolved upon establishing a particular and exclusive ecclesiastical jurisdiction for themselves within the limits of the United States, if not co-extensive with the continent of America. I understand my brother, who spoke first upon the other side, as conceding, what indeed could not be denied, that in the very nature of such an association, whether looking to its original and inherent rights at the moment of the adoption of its constitution, or at the objects to be accomplished through the instrumentality of that constitution, there must exist somewhere a power to change;—and indeed it cannot be true that such power does not continue to exist, unless it be true that as a matter of law the exercise of such a power, by reason of that exercise, exterminates then and forever the power itself. Now if I can show to the Court—standing upon the authority of that concession, if I had not even higher ground to stand upon—that the Conference of 1808, which delegated its powers to the Conference by whom the Plan was adopted of June 8, 1844, had all the powers of the original Conference of 1784, the controversy in this branch of it is at an end.

Methodism, as you know, honours, and may well and proudly honour, as its author and founder, John Wesley, of England, an Elder in the Church of England, whose holy life and extent of foresight and of wisdom, well challenge admiration. Upon prudential and patriotic reasons, which I commend to those who differ with my clients in this particular exigency, he resolved that it was his duty as a man, and a subject, and a Christian, to take no step which could endanger the political institutions of his country. He established, therefore, no peculiar Church ecclesiastically with reference to the government. He rendered a ready and willing obedience, from the moment he was converted to the lights of Methodism, to the established Church of the land, believing, as he did, that that Church was inseparably connected with the political institutions of his country. His power over Methodists was absolute and despotic. The only government, so far as it was a government, that Methodists recognised, rested in his will, and reposed, and confidently and safely reposed, upon his virtue and piety. He appointed the preachers. In him was vested the property of the Church. He controlled it in everything; and the members who devotedly followed him were too happy to live under the government of such a man.

The tide of conversion rolled on. From the few who originally met in the private room of Wesley, thousands were seen coming under his banner, until at last, for convenience' sake, and for convenience' sake alone, without stripping himself of any power which by the original form of government was his, he asked from time to time the advice of his followers, following it or not, just as he thought advisable for the interests of the Church. In anticipation of his death, he intrusted the whole property of the Church, which stood in his own name, and was to stand until his death, and the entire government of the Church, to one hundred of his followers—preachers of his own selection. From that time until a comparatively recent period in the history of the sect, the whole government was centred in these one hundred men. At last, Wesley's spirit being called to the Author from whom it came, and the progress of enlightened civilization having yet more illuminated the public mind, and broken down many remains of former religious persecution, the Methodist Church within the last fifteen or twenty years in England has become a separate ecclesiastical establishment, governed by a president and governors invested with all ecclesiastical power. But from first to last the entire power of the Church, whatever that may have been, was vested, first in Wesley, then in the one hundred men, and now is in the particular organization which prevails in England, without a remnant of power to be found elsewhere in any of the followers of this faith.

My learned brother who concluded to-day, stated in perfect fairness, and by his statement answers, if he will permit me to say so, a great part of the argument of his colleague, that there was a leading and important distinction between the delegation of mere power from a principal to an agent, and a delegation of sovereign power by a sovereign body to those to whom the sovereign body thinks proper to intrust such sovereign power. Now such was the condition of things in 1784, as far as concerns the power of John Wesley, when he wrote his letter of the 10th of September in that year. The preachers in this country, during the revolution and before it, had vainly solicited from him authority to establish a religious government for themselves. This he steadfastly refused. He was restrained, as he says in that letter, by the patriotic considerations to which I have adverted, that such an establishment might endanger the institutions of the country to which he owed allegiance. A train of events sundered the American provinces from the political government of England, and a new state of things existed which rendered Wesley's scruples inapplicable, and made it his duty to agree that there should be such a peculiar and distinctive establishment. Where did the predecessors of the Northern preachers, from whom all authority is derived, look for the power to call the Conference of 1784, for the purpose for which it was called? To John Wesley, as the person in whom, at that time, was vested *the entire and exclusive sovereign power of the Church.* It is unnecessary to inquire whether by virtue of some inherent and inalienable right, the power might not have been found in these gentlemen in 1784 irrespective of the will of Wesley. It is sufficient for me to show that in 1784 they claimed, and claimed alone, the power they exerted in the Conference of that year, under the authority of Wesley, *as the author, sovereign, and founder of the Church.* Who constituted the Conference of 1784? My learned brother, who spoke first upon the other side, would have had your Honours to believe, what of course he satisfied himself was the fact, that that Conference was called together not only by the preachers of the Church, but by all the lay members. There is not a word of truth in the statement, although, of course, the learned counsel believed it to be true. It was a general assembly of the preachers connected with the Methodist denomination of Christians, convoked only as preachers, without reference to any lay authority express or implied. Not being as familiar with the history of the Church as my colleague, who was kind enough to undertake to lay before the Court the evidence which is found spread upon the records in the case, I inquired, as soon as the statement was made, whether there was any foundation for the assertion that the Conference of 1784 had any other authority for its convocation than the authority of Wesley, and the authority in themselves as preachers alone connected with the Methodist Association. I found that there was not. If your Honours will turn to page 5 of the Proofs, No. 1, you will find, that immediately succeeding the letter of Wesley, which authorized the separate organization, it is stated: "To carry into effect the proposed organization," (Wesley's proposed organization,) "a General Conference of preachers was called, to meet at Baltimore, at Christmas, 1784. Sixty out of the eighty-three preachers then in the travelling connexion attended at the appointed time. At this conference, say the annual minutes of 1785, it was unanimously agreed that circumstances made it expedient for us" (that is the preachers) "to become a separate body," &c. They admit no constituency. The time is perhaps coming when, in all probability, they will be obliged to admit one for the good of the Church. They resolve for themselves, and for themselves alone, as the possessors of all the ecclesiastical power known to the Methodist Church, to carry out the particular organization authorized by John Wesley, without reference to any other authority than his, and their own conviction that the good of the Church demanded such a special and particular organization.

It is true, the Church being organized in 1784 through the instrumentality of this

Conference, the travelling preachers who constituted the Church—supposing the Church and the governors of the Church, for the sake of argument, to be identical—that from the period of that Conference until 1792 there was no other General Conference of the Church. But why? Because of the difficulty, in the then condition of the country, the wide and almost exhaustless spread of territory over which these pioneers in the cause of Christ were obliged to travel, of getting to any particular location for the purpose of consulting as a body upon the true interests of the Church. But in 1792, as will be found upon page 12 of Proofs No. 1, it was deemed advisable by these governors—it being always understood that the governors mean the travelling preachers and nobody else—to bring together another general assembly of themselves. That was called in the same way, consisted of the same parties, was clothed with the same power, and bound to discharge the same duties, limited only by a rational and proper consideration of these duties—and the first thing that they did was to say of whom the General Conference thereafter should consist. The inconvenience of convoking the whole was still found to be pressing. The government in the abstract was a good one; in the particular it was objectionable, for the whole could not be brought together. Then they determined in 1792 who should constitute the General Conferences thereafter to be convened; and it was done in the form of question and answer. The question propounded was,—

"Who shall compose the General Conference?
"*Ans.* All the travelling preachers who shall be in full connexion at the time of holding the Conference.
"*Quest.* When and where shall the next General Conference be held?
"*Ans.* On the first day of November, in the year 1796, in the town of Baltimore."

Now you look in vain for any decision of that Conference of 1792 limiting the powers of a General Conference called under the authority of the Conference of 1792. You look in vain for anything to be found in that part of the record, or anywhere else in the Proofs, indicating a design upon the part of these travelling preachers, who originally constituted the entire government, to cabin and confine the jurisdiction of the General Conferences which were thereafter to be convened under the authority of that Conference. In the language of my brother who spoke last, the Conference convened, under the authority of that of 1792, in Baltimore in 1796 had, by the very terms of the constitution under which they were convened, *all the sovereign authority of the sovereign body by whom it was delegated.* No *modicum* of power was left elsewhere. The Church was not to look elsewhere for any portion of authority. The entire Church—meaning by the Church the government—the entire sovereignty within the Church and over the Church, possessed first by Wesley as its founder, then, under Wesley's authority, by the General Conference of 1784, and then by the Conference of 1792, assembled under the authority which convened the Conference of 1785, was devolved upon the Conference of 1796, and descended, in an unbroken line of succession, to that of 1808, in which consequently was vested the entire sovereignty and authority of the Church.

It is unnecessary, for the purpose I have in view, to trace the action of the Conferences, in particular, from 1796 to 1808. Let us come to that of 1808. I beg your Honours' attention while, with some additional particularity, I discuss the question of the power devolved upon the Conference of 1808. For that purpose I refer to p. 27 of Proofs No. 1. 1796 has passed; 1800 has passed; 1804 has passed; 1808 has arrived; and from 1796 down to 1808, not a suggestion is to be found, not an indication is given, in any part of the history of this Church, which authorizes, by the most forced and distant implication, the inference that the Conference of 1808 and the antecedent Conferences were not clothed with the entire sovereign powers of the

Church. I beg your Honours, throughout the argument, to remember this. What is the state of things in 1808 ? The Church, by the blessing of God, had proceeded in a career of prosperity which the world had never before, in the history of the Christian religion, witnessed. The lights of Christian civilization had been carried by these servants of God into the remotest parts of the continent. The densest wildernesses had been penetrated—Christian faith, and charity, and hope, had been conveyed everywhere by these humble, zealous, devoted ministers of the Saviour. The comparatively limited population of the United States in 1796, and the still more comparatively limited one of 1784, had swelled to the extent of millions. The entire territorial territory of the United States was beginning to be populated, and the prospect was certain and absolute that that population would increase even in a still greater ratio. Preachers must be left at home. The work of God, in the hands of these good and pious men, is not to be postponed for a moment. There must be such men always left in the vineyard. The flock must be ever sedulously and anxiously watched. Some of the shepherds must at all times remain at home. A delegated Conference then becomes absolutely necessary to the object which the original government of the Church had in view—the spread of the Gospel everywhere,—and for that delegation, the Conference of 1808 decided it was their duty then to provide.

Before I take up the terms in which that provision was made, let me ask *a priori*, looking to the necessity which forced the conviction upon the Church, whether it could have been then the purpose of the Church to strip that General Conference of the powers with which those from 1784 down to 1808 were clothed, so as to render them incapable of accomplishing that which all other Conferences were capable of, and had been authorized in terms to accomplish—the salvation of the Church, the prosperity of the Church, the tendency, by means of the doctrines and practices of the Church, of wedding a man still more efficiently to the interests and safety of his country, the preservation of that fraternal affection and love which had so beautifully and nobly illustrated the character of the governors of this Church, the preachers, up to the moment of this unhappy controversy—a spirit which I trust in God is not dead, but only sleepeth. What, then, was the condition of things in 1844 ? I propose by-and-by to call your attention to the authority on which I speak on that subject, to show that the existence of Methodism in thirteen States of the United States was then so hazarded, that its destruction was considered as absolutely inevitable, if things were permitted to remain as they were.

Now is it to be imagined that such a body of men as composed the Conference of 1808 was so short-sighted, so blinded, that they would necessarily provide in advance against the exercise of an authority which it might be absolutely necessary thereafter to exercise in order to save the Church itself ?—meaning by the Church, Methodism, as contradistinguished from its mere government; meaning by the Church, the Methodistical sense of the term—the connexion of good and pious men, who make the Bible their creed, and hold fast only to that which is there expressly disclosed, or may be thereby, by clear reasoning, maintained and established. Here is the argument, in terms, of my learned brother, by whom the case of the defendants was opened. The power existed in 1784, because it was a peculiarly convened Conference; the power existed in 1792, because it was a peculiarly convened Conference; the power existed in the two Conferences, because they were called together for special purposes, which these preachers had in view at the time the calls were made; but that the Conference convoked in 1808, being convened for no special purpose, was deprived of the authority to accomplish this vital and special purpose of preserving the Church. I asked my brother, and I think the Court heard me, "Do you mean to deny that there existed in 1808, somewhere in the Church, the authority to devolve the power, which was exercised in 1844, upon the General Conference?" The answer was, "That is a moot-point;" and by a species of argument which I could not understand, he did not argue it, because it was mooted. He had admitted it away, as I stated, at the commencement of his argument. Then I have a right to assume that the power was somewhere in 1808. Where was it, if not in the Conference of 1808? I crave your Honours to ask yourselves that question, when you come to deliberate on the case in your chambers. This Church, be it remembered, even unto the present time, and I speak it in no offensive sense, as regards its government, has been absolutely, since the days of Wesley, an aristocracy. Laymen have had, and now have no voice in it. If there is a layman within the sound of my voice, he knows he has no voice now. Heretofore they have been satisfied with the government. They have acted upon the saying of Pope,—

> "For forms of government let fools contest,
> That which is best administered, is best."

They perhaps will be found changing their opinion, when they find it is not always best administered.

Now I want to know, if the entire sovereign power of the Church was in the ministers, the preachers, what other body on the face of God's earth was there in 1808 upon which to devolve the power of dividing the Church, which must have been in the ministers, than the Conference of 1808. The ministers made the Church. The ministers, in the governmental sense, are the Church. The sovereigns are the ministers, and if it be a part of the sovereign power, in a body of this description, to divide itself, then that power existed in the Conference of ministers of 1808, or it is gone. The admission is that it cannot be extinguished. It is absolute, inherent, and inalienable, as my brother, Mr. Choate, admitted. A body unlimited in the authority to create, is equally unlimited in the authority to destroy, responsible only to their consciences for the manner in which either authority is exercised.

That being the case, and I could not make it plainer by dwelling upon it, and the Conference of 1808 having for the first time authorized a delegated General Conference to manage the concerns of the Church, the question is, Have they not delegated all their power? How are you to ascertain this? Whether they can resume it is another question. But as far as the delegation of power could be made by those who in 1808 possessed all the power, the inquiry is, whether the Conference of 1808 did not invest the General Conferences, to be called under the authority of the constitution they then adopted, with all their own authority. Now, what doubt can there be about that? I will not deny, it would be unjust to myself, and what is worse, disrespectful to the Court, to contend, that the aristocrats, in the ecclesiastical sense, in whom the authority of this Church was vested in 1808, might not have said, that they would reserve to themselves a part of their aristocratic power; and I am not here to contend that, to the extent in which they have reserved a part of such power, the Conference called under the authority of the constitution established in 1808, possesses all the powers of the antecedent Conferences. I admit it does not; but that only shows that all is granted which is not excepted from the grant of power. If there are general terms, devolving the power upon the delegated body, sufficiently comprehensive of themselves to transfer all the power of the body delegating, then it is for him who alleges that any particular power was excepted out of the operation of the general terms, to make it good. What, then, is excepted? Is the power which I shall assume existed in the Conference of 1808—that is, the power to adopt the Plan of 1844—communicated by the terms of their delegation, as these are found in the constitution they then created, to the body provided for by that constitution?

I said that *a priori* such a power is to be assumed. If you will turn to the minutes of the Conference of 1784, you will find the first governors of this Church, saying :—

"And we do engage, &c., to do everything that we judge consistent with the cause of religion in America, and the political interests of these States, to preserve and promote our union with Methodists in Europe."

"The political interests," therefore, of the States of the United States, are to control them in the union which they desire to keep up with their brethren across the waters. The exigencies of the cause of our religion here, as those exigencies should address themselves to the Church here from time to time, were to control them in keeping the union between themselves and England. What is the design of the Church? We are told by themselves, in 1784 :—

"What may we reasonably believe to be God's design in raising up the preachers called Methodists?

"Not to form any new sect; but to reform the continent, particularly the Church, and to spread scriptural holiness over these lands."

Almost a world is to be saved. The American continent is to be the theatre of their labours. The safety of man throughout the American continent is to be the object of their efforts; and how, according to their own notions, was that to be accomplished? I ask you to look at p. 26 of the Proofs, No. 1 :—

"It is not necessary that rites and ceremonies should in all places be the same, or exactly alike; for they have always been different, and may be changed to the diversity of countries, times, and men's manners."

You are not to confound "rites and ceremonies" here spoken of with the sacraments of the Church. They, the sacraments, are unchangeable. They are ordained of God, and no authority is communicated to his Church to alter them; no power is given to the Church to neglect them. At all times, in all places, under all circumstances, God's ordinances are to be observed. The "rites and ceremonies" mean, therefore, a peculiar mode of government of the Church. And the Church, speaking for itself, says: "Show me the country which requires a different form of organization in order to accomplish the holy object in view—the safety of sinners—and you not only show me the right to change such organization, but you establish it as a duty to make the change, a Christian duty to make it. Show me the existence of a state of things, at any time, amongst any people, that requires an alteration of the form of Church government, and you make not only a case of authority, but you establish the obligation to make the change." And this for the very obvious reason, that otherwise, according to the doctrine of this Church—whether right or wrong is immaterial—the spread of Christian faith, as that faith is found to be disclosed by the Bible; the spread of Christian doctrine, as that doctrine is believed to be found in the Bible; the spread of Christian truth and Christian tenets, as such truths and tenets have been revealed by the Gospel, is to be made, under all circumstances, at all times, in all places, the paramount object. Once show the field in which the Church is to operate, in the Methodistical sense of what the Church is, then the mere form of government is but as leather and prunella.

Well, that was the condition of things, and the obligation upon these pious men when they were about to adopt the constitution for the General Conference which was to meet thereafter. Now, suppose I was to read that constitution, with the addition of some restrictions, which by way of argument it is supposed to contain, let us see how it would present and exhibit the authors of that constitution to the approval of the Church or of posterity. "The General Conference shall have power to make rules and regulations for our Church, under the following restrictions and limitations, to wit:" that they shall not admit into communion with the Church any slaveholder as a member! That they shall not admit into any official station in the Church any slaveholder! That they shall not admit into the high and important station of bishop, the superintendent of the Church, any slaveholder! although they, as governors of the Church may be satisfied, that without the addition of slaveholders as members, officers, or bishops, the Church is extinguished in the South. I am assuming the fact for the sake of argument, would they not be obnoxious to the objection, "Why, gentlemen, you are a halted and crippled body. You are not only not invested with the power of your Creator, God, and in a condition to carry out the great and vital objects which he has in view, by bringing upon the earth his Church; but you deprive an entire land of the benefit of this, your Church, which you profess to believe, and no doubt sincerely believe, is as good, if not the very best of sects into which Christians are divided. If you have done that, have you not gone directly counter to one of the articles of your religion? (for what I read from p. 26, is the 22d Article of Religion.) Have you not said, that the mere form of government is to give way to the exigency which arises from the diversity of country, peculiarity of times, and peculiarity of manners? Do you not know that the South, in relation to this particular institution of slavery, is diverse from the North? Do you not know that the times in the South are not your times in the North? Do you not know that there is, in relation to the particular domestic institution in the South, a peculiarity of manners, and a conviction consequent upon it, which is not to be found in the North? What do you mean, therefore? Do you, can you mean, that the Church which you are about establishing, is not to be established with authority to accommodate itself to the change of country, change of manners, and peculiarity of times? Are you Christians? Do you not wish the South to be enlightened? Do you not wish your brother-man, master and slave, there to be saved? Do you not see that if in the spirit of fanaticism you keep the Church from the master and rob him of the blessings it is calculated to confer upon him, you deprive the slave of the blessings it is calculated to confer upon the slave? Do you not discover, if you are sincere, and are right, that there is in the existence of Christianity a soft and mellowing influence, which lessens for the time the thraldom of the slave, and may eventually lead entirely to disenthral him; and are you about to deprive master and slave of the happy results which must sooner or later flow from the preaching of your tenets? Do you not see that you leave the South blinded, wallowing in the very mire of their own sin? If you are sincere, and believe it to be a sin, do you not see that you rivet over and over again the chains of the slave by depriving him of the blessings of the Christian hope, and of the expectation of that happiness which your religion teaches, is in the next world, if not in this, to be his? Do you mean to abandon such a field?" Why, they would say, No. One of my friends whom I have in my eye, a Northern preacher, almost looks no. The heart says, No. It instinctively goes in advance of the judgment. (Addressing the defendants.) The South, gentlemen, is the theatre for your labours as well as the North; then it is your high Christian duty to accommodate yourselves to the South, to the times in the South, to the peculiarity of manners in the South. Be kind, and affectionate, and fraternal, and Christian to your Southern fellow-men.

Throwing all national considerations out of view,—high and lofty as they are, they are nothing compared with those that spring from the higher obligations of Christian duty; and great and important as are the blessings which those institutions confer, they are nothing when compared with the blessings which Christian hope, charity, and faith teach us we may possess,—as Christians, is it possible that the Conference of 1808, on whom the entire power was devolved, could have designed to start upon a miserable, sickly existence, by adopting an ecclesiastical government, utterly impotent to accomplish the leading object of its existence—the dissemination of religion over these lands, and the enlightening, through the instrumentality of this Church, of this continent? Well, then, if you could not read it in the proceedings of the Conference so as to strip it of the authority to carry this Church throughout the South, without convicting the authors of the constitution of worse than folly and absurdity, but of clear, palpable, and manifest violation of Christian obligation,—I demand of your Honours, and I know what the answer will be, whether, if such would be the character which they would have earned, if such had been the limitations of the constitution they adopted, you will not bring to the consideration of that constitution every intendment, that the powers necessary to extend and enlarge the Church by all means in the power of the Church were intended to be vested in the General Conference, provided for in 1808. My associate and brother, from the existence of particular limitations in this constitution, to be found in the six restrictive articles, has proved, as I think, to demonstration, that unless some one of these articles prohibits the Conference from adopting the particular Plan of 1844, it had the power. I do not go over that argument. I could not make it stronger. I could not state it as well. There are, however, two other considerations connected with the subject, to which I beg leave to call the attention of the Court.

The General Conference, (on page 27, 1st Proofs,) after providing for the manner in which the Conference shall be composed, which had been done before, go on for the first time to define, to limit that which was before undefined and unlimited—the power of the General Conference of the Church. Nothing is plainer than that. As I have already had occasion to say more than once, the Conference of 1784 had the authority to establish two organizations, for the same reason that they had the authority to establish one. They had, consequently, the power to refuse to establish one. Now the General Conference, under the constitution of 1808, are to have "full powers to make rules and regulations for our Church under the following limitations and restrictions." Let me stop here and read it as it must be read, because I shall only add, in my reading, words which are clearly to be implied: "The General Conference shall have powers to make *all* rules and regulations for our Church under the following limitations and restrictions, *and no other*." Now mark that. It is not a delegated authority at all, in the sense in which the Constitution of the United States is a delegated authority. The whole power is given to manage the Church. The whole power is given to rule and regulate the Church in any and everything in which it may be advisable that a Church should be ruled and regulated. Nothing can be more clear than this—until we come to the restrictions, the entire power to rule and regulate the Church is in the Conference, and is to be considered only as restricted in the single particulars in which it was meant not to delegate the power. All the rest you have. You are not to imply any other limitations and restrictions than are to be found in the assigned limitations and restrictions. We stand in this our construction of this constitution upon the general terms of the grant. Let our opponents show that these general terms are to be taken *secundum subjectam materiam*, and because to be so taken are to be subject to specific restrictions. What is the *subjecta materia?* It is not restriction. Why, said one of my learned brothers on the other side, the authority to rule and regulate the Church is not the authority to destroy it. That begs the question—in fact, was the Church destroyed? Would it not have been the Methodist Episcopal Church, precisely as it is now here at the

North, if the original Conference of 1784 had provided for two distinct organizations as to government? Nobody can deny it. The proposition confounds the Church with the government of the Church. They are as distinct as day from night. The Church, according to the Methodistical sense of the term, is necessarily unchangeable, because it consists of a body of men who preach that only which appears in the Bible, or can be made out by the true and fair interpretation of what is in the Bible. The government of the Church, or, according to the language of Methodists, "the rites and ceremonies" of the Church, which are synonymous with the government of the Church, unlike the Church, which rests upon the truths of the Bible, may be modified, must be modified, to accommodate themselves to times, places, and manners. These *subjectæ materiæ*, therefore, which my learned brother, to whom I am now particularly replying, seems to suppose throw a limitation upon this power, so far from doing so, operate demonstrably to prove the existence of the power. Recollect, it is a body of Methodist preachers who are speaking in 1808, not the priests or the local authorities of the Church of Rome, nor the bishops nor the other authorities of the Church of England. It is, then, these preachers, these Methodist gentlemen, who start their existence in the world by proclaiming that their Church is one thing, their government of the Church another. Their Church is indivisible and indestructible. It stands upon the Rock of Ages. The government of the Church is to be founded in the prudence, and wisdom, and foresight of men, and is to be changed from time to time, as circumstances render it necessary for the well-being of the Church.

There is a limitation, however, upon the power of the Conference, which, for the very reason I have adverted to, is placed beyond their power: that is the limitation to be found in the first restrictive article. I ask your Honours to come with me for a moment, to see the effect of that particular restriction upon the question which you have to decide. They have given all powers to make all rules and regulations, subject to certain restrictions, and among them is :—

"First. The General Conference shall not revoke, alter, or change our articles of religion, nor establish any new standards or rules of doctrine contrary to our present existing and established standards of doctrine."

Articles of religion, of course, are not mere governmental provisions. Now if you will turn to the proviso in the sixth restrictive article, which authorizes contingently a change of the restrictive articles, you will find that this first article is specially excepted. Upon the recommendation of two-thirds of the General Conference, and the subsequent sanction of three-fourths of the annual conferences, the second, third, fourth, fifth, and sixth restrictive articles may be changed, but not the first. The language is :—

"Provided, nevertheless, that upon the concurrent recommendation of three-fourths of all the members of the several annual conferences, who shall be present and vote upon such recommendation, then a majority of two-thirds of the General Conference succeeding shall suffice to alter any of the above restrictions, *except the first article:* and also, whenever such alteration or alterations shall have been first recommended by two-thirds of the General Conference, so soon as three-fourths of the members of all the annual conferences shall have concurred as aforesaid, such alteration or alterations shall take effect."

The first article, therefore, is beyond change. It stands as the Rock upon which the Church is built. Everything else connected with it may be beat upon by the storms, and finally washed away and destroyed, but that is there now and forever, until the great judgment-day itself shall arrive, when the hearts of all shall be disclosed, and the consequences of that religion, in blessing or in woe, shall fall upon saved or sinning men. What are the articles of religion of this Church? What are its existing and established standards of doctrine? Go to page 25 of the Proofs No. 1—Extracts from the Discipline of 1840. You have been told that this Discipline is published by each General Conference, as one entire Gospel, so to speak, of the Church. If errors have been discovered, they are corrected. If omissions are to be found in antecedent Disciplines, they are supplied, and each revolving four years gives to this Church the entire evidence of its articles of religion and its doctrine. Now in 1840, as from the first, there is no change. This comes, as it were, from the mouth of Wesley; he is speaking to you, almost as it were, from the dead, through his successors; and you are told by this Church in 1840, and of course in 1844—for there was no change in this particular—that

"The Holy Scriptures contain all things necessary to salvation: so that whatsoever is not read therein, nor may be proved thereby, is not to be required of any man, that it should be believed as an article of faith, or be thought requisite or necessary to salvation."

Do as you please, brothers, in everything else. If you keep within the truths expressly inculcated by the Bible, or which may be established by a reasonable and fair interpretation of the Bible, you are blameless in the sight of the Church, in the sight of man and of God. What is your doctrine? Turn to the succeeding passage. What is your doctrine in relation to the peculiar mode of governing the Church? First, I should have asked the Court to look to article 13, in order to see what is the Church in the contemplation of these Methodist gentlemen and their predecessors:—

"The visible Church of Christ is a congregation of faithful men, in which the pure word of God is preached, and the sacraments duly administered, according to Christ's ordinance in all those things that of necessity are requisite to the same."

Here, then, we have the Methodistical opinion of what the Church is. We have the Methodist declaration of what the articles of belief of the Church are; and going to the succeeding article, upon the succeeding page, we have the doctrine of the Church comprehending the mode of government, and it tells us that the mode of government may be altered from time to time as occasion demands. I have not time, nor is it necessary, to go through everything that has been referred to. I refer in the general to the debates in the Conference of 1840 in Baltimore; to the debates in the Conference in New-York, in this very celebrated year of 1844; to the answer of the American bishops to the letter of the English Church in 1836 and 1840; to the speech of Bishop Soule in the Conference of 1844; and to the speech of now Bishop Hamline, in what is called the Methodist Episcopal Church, in 1844, to show that this very subject of slavery, if continued to be pressed, and suffered to become a doctrine in the government of the Church, would necessarily lead to the ruin of the Church, South. I speak it not in terms so strong as they addressed to the Conference. In that kind and affectionate appeal to the Conference of 1844, which, trampling, as I think, on all law, pronounced a severe judgment of condemnation upon one of its bishops, when addressing the Conference with all the authority of that wisdom which belonged to the bishops, and all the persuasiveness to be found in the long lives they had spent in devotion to the Church, and in the fact of their intimate and entire association with the Church, South and North, the bishops said: "For God's sake," (I do not profess to give the words,) "for the sake of our common Father, our common God, for the sake of the Church to which we have devoted our lives, stay your proceedings for another four years, or the Church will be ruined!" The British Conference are told by the bishops, North as well as South, in the kind and Christian response which they gave to their application, which I forbear to speak of, lest I should go beyond the limit which charity would prescribe, "You do not know the condition of things in this our America. This very subject of slavery was sought to be made a fundamental doctrine in our Church in 1784. It was obliged to be suspended in 1785. It was renewed from time to time until, in order to save the Church from disruption, to keep together this body of preachers constituting the Church, to keep in existence the body of men who believe and preach the doctrines which we pronounce to be the doctrines of the Bible, it was absolutely necessary that we should consult, even if they are so to be considered, the prejudices of the South."

Now if this state of things existed in fact,—and the evidence is all one way until we come to the proceedings of the Conference of 1848, of which I shall have occasion hereafter to speak, North and South in the main proclaiming the same truth, that the fate of the Church was sealed, if the doctrines and government of the Church upon the subject of slavery were made more stringent than they were made in 1808 and 1816,—is it conceivable that the Conference to whom was delegated all power to pass all rules and regulations, except so far as specially restricted, for the Church, was not clothed with power to preserve the Church? The state of things which existed presented the question, Is the Church to be destroyed or to survive? Are the doctrines of this our Church to be carried throughout these United States, and spread over the continent of America by and through us, or not? That is the question. The argument of my learned brothers on the other side is, that because under the power to rule and regulate, given to a governmental corporation, political or associated, there is not delegated the power to destroy, it is a legitimate inference that in the particular case under the delegation of power to rule and regulate the Church there is not delegated the power to preserve the Church. It is perfectly immaterial, as far as the existence of the power is concerned, (I am sure your Honours will not think you have a right to decide as to the mere exercise of the power,) whether this state of things, believed to exist in 1844, existed or not. If it did exist, the authority to rule and regulate the Church gave authority so to rule and regulate as to save the Church; and whether it existed or not was a question upon which the judgment of the governing power was to be passed, and exclusively passed. From that judgment there was no appeal. Once devolve upon the Conference the power, the jurisdiction, to do the deed challenged, under any state of things which will justify the doing of the deed, then the exercise of the power is conclusive. Without making any particular reference to the case, your Honours will remember the opinion of Chief Justice Marshall, in the case of McCullough and the State of Maryland, reported in 3 Wheaton, in which he maintained the constitutionality of the Bank of the United States upon the ground of necessity, or its being one of the means of contributing to the wholesome exercise of the delegated powers to Congress. The Court said, upon the existence of the necessity, the judgment of Congress is conclusive; and nothing can be more true as a question of law. So we say here, that the Conference of 1844 had the authority by rules and regulations—and the Plan of June 8th is but a rule or regulation to preserve the Church—to govern the Church, which implies the authority to preserve and keep it from destruction. A state of things existed which they adjudged rendered that rule necessary—whether wisely or unwisely, correctly or incorrectly, is, in this connexion, perfectly immaterial; it was their judgment, and the thing judged was within their jurisdiction, just like the case to which I have adverted. The Bank of the United States, as a fiscal instrument by which to enable the Congress to carry into beneficial operation some of the powers expressly devolved upon them, was for Congress alone and exclusively to decide.

A word or two more and I leave this point. This Church was not, as is supposed by the other side, designed to be confined to the United States. It is a great error to suppose it. It does great injustice to the Church; and if our brethren of the North had had the privilege of getting up and denying such a proposition, I am almost inclined to think that all of them would with one accord have said, "It is not so. We stop not at the limits of the United States, great as those limits are. The world is before us. The world is to be the theatre of our labours." Have they not sent far and wide their missionaries to preach their doctrines of faith to the benighted the world over? What part of the habitable globe is not, as far as they have had the power, the scene of their labours? Wherever man is to be found, there are these soldiers of the cross to be found, fighting for man's salvation. Upon the great ocean of human sin, they might with almost literal truth exclaim,

"Far as the breeze can bear the billows' foam,
Survey our empire, and behold our home."

An empire not protected by the pirate's blood-stained flag, but blessed and heralded by that pure and holy banner which, bathed in the blood of a Saviour God, is the proud and hallowed emblem of a God's love and of man's redemption. To say that such a body of men, with such holy objects in view, fighting under a Leader who knows neither colour nor clime in the disposition of his providence under the laws which he thinks proper to impose, should have no field of labour but the limited field embraced within the territorial compass of any mere human government, is, I speak it with all deference to my learned brother, to libel the Church, to disparage the Almighty.

The Court adjourned.

NINTH DAY.—Thursday, May 29, 1851.

Mr. Johnson,—May it please your Honours, I continue the argument of the first point a while longer, as to the authority of the Conference to adopt the Plan of Division of 1844. My learned brothers on the other side have supposed that in the constitution of this Conference, as it existed in 1844, there is to be found an analogy, as far as concerns its powers, in the Constitution of the United States. A word upon that subject. The well settled doctrine in relation to the Constitution of the United States is, that no powers are conferred by it upon any of the departments of the government, except such as are expressly delegated, or are fairly to be implied from those that are so delegated. It is a government of enumerated powers; it came into existence by force of that enumeration. The body that created it, or the bodies that created it,—for although in one sense it was created by the people, yet in another sense it was adopted by the States—and the States had themselves the inherent sovereign power which belonged to separate and organized communities. Except, therefore, so far as they communicated portions of such powers to the government of the United States, the powers themselves still remained in the communities by whom the delegation was made. If I was successful yesterday, I must have satisfied the Court that the parties creating the constitution of this Conference which assembled in 1844—that is to say, the parties constituting the Conference of 1808, under the authority of which the particular Conference of 1844 was assembled—were themselves the entire, perfect, absolute sovereigns over the whole sphere of the power belonging to the Church. It is, therefore, a matter of construction whether, by the terms in which the constitution of that Conference was created, it was the purpose of its authors to communicate to the government which was to be brought into existence under that constitution all of the powers with which the constituents creating it were clothed. But I am not left without authority, which must be persuasive on such a point, if it were important to refer to authority at all. I rely upon the authority of the Conference of 1844 itself, and of that portion of the Conference of 1844 which thought it their duty in 1848 to deny the authority of the Conference of 1844 to adopt the Plan of Division which was adopted in that year.

The Court will remember that amongst other things, which were, as I think, outrages, although of course not so intended, perpetrated by the Conference of 1844, was the *quasi* trial, the *quasi* judgment, as it is admitted to be, the *quasi* suspension of Bishop Andrew from his station as bishop in that Church, upon the ground of some alleged misconduct on his part prior to the sentence. The friends of Bishop Andrew, and Bishop Andrew himself, maintained, and, in my humble judgment, triumphantly maintained as a proposition of law, that under the Discipline of the Church, as it stood in 1844, in regard to the holding of slaves by the bishops or other officers of the Church, Bishop Andrew's asserted offence, which it was admitted consisted only in holding slaves after he had been made bishop, was not an offence provided for by any law of the Church. Now, the members of that Conference, who thought differently in 1844, and who degraded Bishop Andrew, in justifying themselves in that sentence of degradation, pronounced under some general sweeping pervading authority which they supposed to be vested in the Conference, over the entire official and private conduct of its ministers, state the true doctrine of the powers of this Conference upon which we rely. Your Honours will find it on page 116 of 1st Proofs. It was the law of the Church, said the ministers from the South, that slaves might be held by the bishops as well as the preachers living in the South; that slavery was not only tolerated where emancipation was prohibited, but it was a law of such binding and general operation as to be equivalent to a constitutional injunction. In the answer to that ground assumed by the South, these gentlemen from the North, in the Reply, which was prepared by a committee of themselves, to the Protest made on the part of the Southern members against the conduct of the Conference in the case of Bishop Andrew, and which Reply was sanctioned by a vote of the Conference, tell us (p. 116) that the condition of the Church with reference to its powers is this :—

"It is, indeed, true, that the question of slavery had been long and anxiously agitated in the Church, and the various General Conferences had endeavoured to adjust the matter so as to promote the greatest good of all parties: but this very fact goes to disprove the position assumed in the Protest; for as the attention of the Church had been thus strongly called to the subject, if it had been the intention to guard the question of slavery by constitutional provisions, it would have been done when the Church actually did meet to frame a constitution. But nothing of the kind appears. For when, in 1808, it was resolved that the General Conference, instead of consisting, as before, of all the travelling elders, should be a delegated body, and when it was determined that that body (*unlike the general government, which has no powers but such as are expressly conferred*) should have all powers *but such as are expressly taken away*—when this vast authority was about to be given to the General Conference, among the limitations and restrictions imposed, *there is not one word on the subject of slavery; nor was any attempt made to introduce any such restriction.*"

The clients, then, as if by anticipation, meet the argument of the clients' counsel. There is, they say in advance, no similitude between the two governments—the Church and the national. The one is a government of delegated powers, the other is a government of vast, and sweeping, and universal powers, over any and every subject connected with the Church, except in the particulars in which these vast powers are pared down by express qualifications or exceptions, so as to place them in these particulars beyond the reach of the Conference. It is true that the writers of this Reply were looking only to the authority to pronounce the sentence against Bishop Andrew; but it is perfectly immaterial what may have been the object with which a reference to the elementary principles of the constitution was made. If those elementary principles are such that all power exists, except in the particulars in which it is expressly taken away, then, if there existed in the preachers, in the constituency of 1808, a power to divide this Church, there existed in the Conference created by them in 1808, and under the constitution defining the powers of the Conference created in 1808, a power to divide as one of the inherent powers of the original body, unless there is to be found in the constitution so created in 1808, in some one of the six restrictive articles, a prohibition upon the exercise of that particular power then originally vested in the constituency of preachers. There is no room for doubt on the subject. It is demonstration. He who runs may read.

They now deny that the Conference of 1844 had a right, acting under the constitution established in 1808, to divide this Church, upon the ground that all power was not communicated, although the counsel were unable to deny, and have not denied, that that power existed in the constituency. They maintain that in the particular instance the power does not exist; but when they are called upon to pass upon the question whether a Southern preacher has offended by becoming the holder of slaves before or subsequent to his becoming a preacher, they assert, for the Conference, in opposition to the law of the Church, an authority to pronounce a sentence of degradation, by virtue of the authority of the vast, general, sweeping, and unqualified powers communicated in 1808.

What else have this Conference of 1844 done? I ask your Honours to turn to the resolution creating the committee of nine, p. 98, to which was referred the Declaration of the Southern members of the Conference, to be found on p. 97. That Declaration was signed by fifty-one or fifty-two delegates from Southern conferences, and a Mr. McFerrin offered this resolution:—

"*Resolved*, That the committee appointed to take into consideration the communication of the delegates from the Southern conferences, be instructed, provided they cannot, in their judgment, devise a plan for an amicable adjustment of the difficulties now existing in the Church, on the subject of slavery, to devise, if possible, a *constitutional* plan for a mutual and friendly division of the Church."

They were not to devise a plan by which the South might secede, and take the consequence of being secessionists; but some mode which that Conference had a constitutional right to adopt to effect a division of the Church into two Churches, each vested with all the rights within its territorial limits that belonged to the entire Church, as it then existed within the limits of the entire Church.

A member from the South, immediately on the offering of this resolution, Mr. Crowder, from the Virginia Conference, seeming to suppose that it was possible that no constitutional mode might be found within the power of the Conference in the opinion of the committee, and impressed with the absolute necessity of a division—or, what is more likely, in order to fix upon the Conference the expression of an opinion that the Church, if divided at all, was to be divided *constitutionally*—proposed to strike out the word "constitutional," so as to leave it read, "devise, if possible, a plan for a mutual and friendly division of the Church." The Northern gentlemen voted against the amendment. They wanted no secession; they could not satisfy their own consciences with the state of things which might be brought about, of having their brethren of the South organize a Church which would not be entitled to all the rights within its own limits, that their portion of the Church would be entitled to within its own limits.

The result of the deliberations of that committee was the recommendation of the Plan of the 8th of June, 1844, under which the Church, South, has organized itself as an independent Church. I know that I am right when I say that there was not a leading man—and there were many leaders of eminent ability on both sides—in this Conference of 1844, who whispered a doubt, after this very plan was reported, of the want of constitutional power in the Conference to adopt it. I beg your Honours to bear that in mind. Not one of the fathers of the Church—justly entitled to as well as enjoying the confidence of the Church upon every ground, personal, moral, religious and intellectual—to whom the constitution of the Conference of 1844 was as familiar as the Bible of their God, even suggested, as a doubt possible to be entertained, that there did not exist in the Conference of 1844 a power to divide the Church as proposed by that Plan. There may have been expressions of opinion in the annual conferences afterwards, and there may have been, in advance of the meeting of the Conference of 1848, in some of the religious newspapers of this denomination, the suggestion of a question, or the expression of a positive opinion of the absence of any authority to adopt the Plan of 1844; but before 1844, during 1844, and pending the proceedings which led to the Plan of Separation in 1844, in all the debates on that Plan, *pro* and *con.*, the existence of a rational doubt to divide according to that Plan was not pretended. That is not all. It was a part of that Plan that the third resolution incorporated into it, which looks to a change of the sixth restrictive article in the constitution of the Church, should be submitted to the annual conferences of the Church generally; and the last resolution makes it the duty of the bishops to submit that particular part of the Plan to the annual conferences, in order to get their sanction of the Plan, so far and so far only.

Where, then, were these brethren of the North? Behind no men in the Church, or out of the Church, in worth and intelligence—where were they? I say it with no purpose of flattery; for that, I trust, I am incapable of, and they do not require it, if I were capable. The proposition is—I speak with reference to both my learned brothers on the other side—that although there exists somewhere in the Church necessarily an authority to divide itself into two organizations, yet that such authority was not vested in the particular Conference of 1844. Where were these gentlemen of the North, then, if they entertained such an opinion, when they voted upon the twelfth resolution in the Plan, which will be found on p. 131, and the twelfth resolution alone, which provides—

"That the bishops be respectfully requested to lay *that part* of this report requiring the action of the annual conferences before them as soon as possible, beginning with the New-York Conference."

What part of it? If the Conference had not the power of itself to adopt the Plan in that part of it which looked to a division of the Church without the consent of all the annual conferences, then that part of the Plan demanded the sanction of all the annual conferences. Therefore, these brethren virtually said: "We wish not the annual conferences to be consulted at all upon the subject, except with reference to that part of the Plan which by its terms is made to depend upon their sanction"—that part which is to be found in the third resolution, and which looks to a change in the sixth restrictive article. They affirm, then, that the rest of the Plan can stand on the inherent, and then unchallenged power to adopt it, vested in the General Conference. What did the bishops do in pursuance of that twelfth resolution? They issued their address to the annual conferences, to which my colleague referred, asking them to consider the propriety of changing the sixth restrictive article, and in doing so they state their opinion that the *entire Plan is obligatory.* I am speaking now of the question of power. These five gentlemen, clothed with every claim to regard, as to the law of this Church, having presided at the very deliberations which led to the adoption of the Plan, announced to the entire Church as their opinion, that the Plan was constitutionally binding in every particular, as well in the particulars in which its binding operation was made to depend on the subsequent assent of the annual conferences, as in the other particular, the division of the Church, as to which its binding operation is merely to depend upon the ascertainment of the fact that in the judgment of the annual conferences in the slaveholding States a division was necessary. Where was then the idea which we have heard commented on by the other side, of that unity of government existing in 1844 which put it out of the power of the Conference of 1844 to divide itself? Did not that Conference know—was it not engraved on the mind of each of the members constituting that Conference—that the Discipline of the Church inculcated union? Did they not know that the authority communicated to the Conference created in 1808, was an authority to make "rules and regulations for our Church?" Did they not know what had been the blessings of an itinerant superintendency and a travelling ministry? Why, certainly. They knew, therefore, of the existence of this supposed unity, and it never entered into their brains to conceive that there was to be found in such unity of the Church a constitutional prohibition upon the authorities of the Church to create two Churches, with reference to government, where one only before existed. But what is there in this idea of the unity of the Church? It is confounded in the minds of my brothers on the other side with the government of the Church. The unity of one does not depend upon the existence of unity in the other. Wesleyan Methodists are to be found wherever Christianity is to be found—Methodists who now owe allegiance to this body are to be found the world over. They all constitute one Church, one Methodist Episcopal Christian Church; but they are governed differently, and they inculcate the necessity, in order that there may be this one Church, of different forms of government, that this one Methodist Church may accommodate itself, as a Church, to the country, and the times, and the circumstances in which it may find itself.

If I satisfied the Court yesterday that the Conference of 1784 (indeed there was no necessity for it on my part, for the learned counsel admitted it) had the authority to have then organized two Churches, does it not necessarily follow that there is not to be found in the idea of Church unity any negative upon the power to divide itself into two forms of government? That must be very clear. Then would not the Conference called together in 1784 have provided that there should be two territorial organizations of Methodists with reference to government, within the limits of the United States, one South and the other North, if they had anticipated the state of things which existed in 1844; if, looking to the existence of this peculiar domestic institution to which the South adheres, and which is so obnoxious to some in the North, they had supposed either section of the United States would be liable to be put under the control of the prejudices of the other upon moral political administrative questions? Why, certainly; and yet there would then have been but *one* Methodist Episcopal Church, not two denominations preaching different doctrines and inculcating a different faith, but one indivisible united denomination of Christians, constituting, in the Methodist opinion, the one Church, clothed with all the sanctity of unity. If that could have been done in 1784, according to the same train of reasoning by which I tried to conduct the Court to the conclusion to which I invited them yesterday, it could equally have been done by the Conference of 1792, or either of the succeeding conferences, including the Conference of 1808, which created the Conference which, in 1844, adopted the Plan of Division of June, 1844.

Our brothers, and their clients, discovered only about 1848—they had, as is obvious, acted upon a different notion altogether before—that although what had been done in the case of the Canada division established the existence of the power to divide, there was to be found in the circumstances of the Canadian connexion with the American Church something which distinguished the American and Canadian Churches in their connexion from the connexion which subsisted between the Southern and Northern Methodists as members of the Methodist Episcopal Church in the United States. My friends find in that case a stumbling-block in the way of their argument against the existence of the power in question. They have told your Honours that the connexion between the American and the Canadian Churches was a mere league, existing by force of a mere treaty, not bringing about, as between the Canada Conference and the American Church, one united and indivisible Church, but one which existed not by force of any governmental existence, not by virtue of any constitutional existence, but by virtue of some supposed, undefined, unintelligible agreement, resulting in a peculiar and undefinable relationship between the two. May it please the Court, we have had, as we all know, various theories about the Constitution of the United States, in the different schools of our statesmen. The one have considered it as flowing immediately from the people, and not as constituting a compact between the States, and existing only by force of that compact, and remaining only in existence as long as each one of the contracting parties thought proper to permit. The difference between the two schools is now threatened to be put in practical operation. South Carolina now announces the rule of constitutional law to be, very many in the South out of South Carolina announce the rule of constitutional law to be, that there is no government, in the sense in which I am sure this Court believe there is a government, created by force of the Constitution of the United States, but that the States are bound solely together by virtue of a league, a treaty, to be found in the assent upon the part of each one of the States, that as between itself and all the other States it agrees to constitute a portion of the Union, and that it has a right therefore to march out of that Union, to put an end to the agreement; and this is threatened to be done. In the days of nullification, when the right to secede was claimed upon a different ground from that which now occasions its assertion, the exercise by congress of its authority to lay imposts and duties, the same doctrine was, in substance, announced. Your Honours, I am sure, are familiar with the paper, but if you desire to refresh your recollections turn, before you decide upon this question, to the memorable proclamation of President Jackson, draughted, as is well known, by the then secretary of state, Mr. Livingston, in which he meets the question as to the consequences to result from the binding operation of the Constitution of the United States, whether that constitution be considered as emanating from the people directly, or as having been the creature of a compact between each State and her sister States. The argument is this: that it made no possible difference whether it came into existence by virtue of the act of the people individually, or by virtue of a compact between the States. The question still was, What were the powers of the government which was brought into existence? Were they such powers as demanded for their execution, for their preservation, for the maintenance of the government so created, that each State of the Union should be held to be, during all time, a portion of the government of the Union, controlled by the Constitution of the United States? There was no unprejudiced man in the United States who doubted then upon the question.

Now, let us apply to the supposed distinction between the Canadian case and the case which existed in 1844 the doctrine of that proclamation. The Canadian Conference existed before they were introduced into the American Church. Suppose it did. What was its condition after it was introduced? How was it introduced?

What was the consequence of its introduction? It was introduced as an annual conference, sent its delegates to the General Conference; it became, analogically speaking, one of the States of this political hierarchy, and bound by all the obligations, and responsible to all the duties which the rest of the Church were bound by or responsible to. My brother who spoke first on the other side, said, that in the nature of things there must have been a territorial limit to the American Church, because it had no authority to go beyond the limits of the United States. Why not? Does the Gospel of Christ know any territorial limits? Is the religion of our Saviour bound by any geographical lines? I beg pardon for putting any such inquiries. There may be, in the particular, local, political governments of some countries, impediments which prevent it from getting within the limits of such territories; but when there are no such territorial obstacles in peculiar territorial governments, the world is before it, not where to choose, but where, from its high and holy calling, it is obliged to go. What says the Discipline? In the History of the Discipline, page 110, we find the following note to the 23d article of religion:—

"As far as it respects civil affairs, we believe it the duty of Christians, and especially all Christian ministers, to be subject to the supreme authority of the country where they may reside, and to use all laudable means to enjoin obedience to the *powers that be*; and therefore it is expected that all our preachers and people, who may be under the British or any other government, will behave themselves as peaceable and orderly subjects."

It would have been well for the preachers of the North, who were parties to the proceedings which resulted in the separation of 1844, to remember that it was expected of them that they should behave themselves as peaceable and orderly citizens.

"This note was added especially to meet the peculiar case of the brethren in Canada, against whom unfounded suspicions had been created, because the Methodist Episcopal Church, of which they were then a part, was regarded as a foreign ecclesiastical authority."

The Canadian Church was separated in 1828. The question is, What were its obligations, and duties, and rights when it was in? Did they claim, as South Carolina now does, to secede by virtue of any independent authority of their own, or by virtue of any reserved right, or inherent right growing out of the particular character of the constitution which brought them into the American Church?

Turning to pp. 32 and 33 Proofs No. 1, I find a petition "to the bishops and members of the General Conference of the Methodist Episcopal Church," from the "Canada Annual Conference," one of the conferences constituting the Church, and sending delegates to the General Conference:—

"The Canada Conference having, after mature deliberation, deemed a separation expedient, most humbly pray that they may be set off a separate and independent Church in Canada."

"Set off," by whom? According to the learned counsel on the other side, it was only for them to say that they willed it, and they could go off; it was only for them to say they would establish for themselves a separate Church organization, and it was done. That is not the view they took of it. They then go on to give the reasons why they ask the General Conference to set them off a separate and independent Church. They are:—

"1st. Our political relations, and the political feelings of a great part of the community, are such that we labour under many very serious embarrassments on account of our union with the United States, from which embarrassments we would, in all probability, be relieved by a separation.

"2d. The local circumstances of our societies in this Province; the rapid increase and extension of the work, both among the white inhabitants and the Indians; the prospects of division among ourselves, if our present relation be continued, render it necessary for us to be under ecclesiastical regulations somewhat of a peculiar character, so as to suit our local circumstances.

"3d. It is highly probable that we shall obtain some important religious privileges by becoming a separate body.

"4th. In the event of a war between the two nations, it would be altogether impracticable for a superintendent to discharge the duties of his office unless he be resident in this Province.

"5th. It is the general wish of our people in this Province to become separate; nor will they, according to present appearances, be satisfied without such separation."

Now let us see what was proposed to be done, and then what was done. On page 34 I find that the committee to whom this matter was referred, report:—

"The committee are unanimously of the opinion, that, however peculiar may be the situation of our brethren in Canada, and however much we may sympathize with them in their present state of perplexity, this General Conference cannot consistently grant them a separate Church establishment, according to the prayer of the petitioners."

Why not? If the theory now relied upon be correct, the relationship had existed by means of a treaty; the contracting parties were the American Church on the one side and the Canadian Church upon the other; they existed as one, simply because of the operation and authority of that treaty. If, as my learned brother, who spoke first on the other side, and to whom I am particularly replying, supposed, the connexion between the Canada Church and the American Church was only by treaty, and was like a treaty between the United States and any foreign power, that it could be divided by a treaty to which each of the original contracting parties agreed—if this be so, I ask how it is possible that a unanimous opinion could be entertained that there was no authority to grant the prayer of this petition? What doubt could there have been on the subject, if Canada was a contracting party to a treaty and desired to go, and the American Church, the only other party, was willing to let her go? Why, it would be a singular sort of treaty which the parties themselves could not get rid of. If the theory of our friends is well founded, it is a species of domestic economy that would prove very beneficial to a certain class of citizens, even perhaps members of the bar, not to speak of others, which brings into possession property which they could not get rid of. This committee were unanimously of the opinion, that as things then were there was no authority to organize a separate organization of the Canadian Church. Let us see if they believed in the theory now taken, that the connexion was the result of a treaty between these two original parties which either would be at liberty to dissolve. The committee says:—

"The committee, therefore, recommend to the General Conference."

What?

"That *inasmuch as* the several annual conferences have not recommended it to the General Conference, it is *unconstitutional*."

Then if they had recommended it, it would have been constitutional. They want a change of government, not the authority to dissolve a league. Considering that the power existed in the constituents of the General Conference, the annual conferences, they wish first to have a vote of the annual conferences consenting to the separation, and then they say the General Conference could authorize the establishment of a separate Church in Canada; then, instead of being unconstitutional, it would be plainly constitutional. This is somewhat inconsistent with the idea, relied on by my friends on the other side with so much ability, that there was something peculiar in the relationship between the Canadian Church and the American Church.

Now what did they do? Their sympathies ran so high, and they regretted so much the perplexity of their Canadian brethren, that they suffered the Canadian brethren to establish a separate Church, and that by an almost unanimous vote. How do they do it? On p. 37, we find it resolved—

"That, whereas the jurisdiction of the Methodist Episcopal Church in the United States of America, has heretofore been extended over the ministers and members in connexion with said Church in the Province of Upper Canada, by mutual agreement, and by the consent and desire of our brethren in that Province; and whereas this General Conference is satisfactorily assured that our brethren in the said Province, under peculiar and pressing circumstances, do now desire to organize themselves into a distinct Methodist Episcopal Church, in friendly relations with the Methodist Episcopal Church in the United States, therefore be it resolved, and it is hereby resolved, by the delegates of the annual conferences in General Conference assembled:—

"That if the annual conferences in Upper Canada, at its ensuing session, or any succeeding session previously to the next General Conference, shall definitely determine on this course, and elect a general superintendent of the Methodist Episcopal Church in that Province, this General Conference do hereby authorize any one or more of the general superintendents of the Methodist Episcopal Church in the United States, with the assistance of any two or more elders, to ordain such general superintendent for the said Church in Upper Canada," &c.

That was done. It is not worth while to be hypercritical in the consideration of the terms on which it was done. There was a jurisdiction existing, whether by agreement or not is not material. It all exists by agreement. These annual conferences come under the General Conference by agreement; there is no political power, no ecclesiastical power by which they can be brought in against their own consent, or kept in against their own will. The Church lives in every member of it by agreement, but still it lives as a Church, governed by its peculiar form of government as long as it does live. The Canada case is exactly a case in point. The power exerted was the same. The necessity in one sense for the exercise of the power was the same. The manner in which it was exercised was substantially the same. And from 1828, when that power was exercised, up to the time when your Honours have been called upon to hear this cause, or up to a period comparatively recent, nobody whispered the existence of a rational doubt of the power of the General Conference to divide itself into as many separate and distinct Churches as in their judgment the good of the Church demanded; as far as I am advised, no one of the annual conferences which was called upon to decide under the third resolution of the Plan of Division, whether they would change the sixth restrictive article of the constitution of the Church, ever, by vote or declaration, denied the constitutionality of the division. I beg your Honours to bear that in mind. Whether there were expressions of individual opinion was another matter; but no vote was taken, no proposition was suggested, looking to any distant and definitive action upon the part of any one of the annual conferences, North or South, against the constitutional power of the Conference of 1844 to adopt the Plan of Division of 1844.

That is not all. These gentlemen, now members of the Methodist Episcopal Church, North, have fallen very far short of their duty, if the theory upon which they are now acting be a sound one. They are responsible to the Church, and, what is still more, to their God, for a very lame and imperfect performance of their duties. They say that the division authorized and organized under the Plan of 1844 was unconstitutional. In the Conference of 1848, at Pittsburgh, they said it was brought about by the act of the Southern members without cause. They say, through their counsel now, in the presence of your Honours, that these Southern members are all secessionists. Gentlemen, do you believe it? Gentlemen defendants, do you conscientiously believe it? Of course, they must say "Yes." Then march up to the duty which is upon you. It was a part of that Plan, as the Court will see on pp. 130 and 131, not dependant in any way on the assent of any annual conferences, except the assent of the annual conferences in the slaveholding States to the first resolution,

"That all the property of the Methodist Episcopal Church, in meeting-houses, parsonages, colleges, schools, conference funds, cemeteries, and of every kind within the limits of the Southern organization, shall be forever free from any claim set up on the part of the Methodist Episcopal Church, so far as this resolution can be of force in the premises."

Now if the Plan is unconstitutional, go and take this property. Do not tell me that there is to be found in the prejudices of the Southern tribunals an obstacle to success. The tribunals of the United States are open; they are raised above the level of any possible supposed local prejudices—standing upon a more elevated platform, looking over the whole country, and bound to free themselves from the existence of anything like sectional or other prejudice or partiality. Go into the courts of the United States. The property here referred to is worth millions. Get back the meeting-houses, the parsonages, the colleges, the schools, the conference funds, the cemeteries, within the limits of the Southern Church. The men who hold them are no part of the Methodist Episcopal Church. They are mere wrong doers. Do not content yourselves with keeping merely the money which happens to be located at the North; do not satisfy yourselves with refusing to dole out the miserable pittance which has heretofore supported the wants of the aged, and infirm, and supernumerary preachers, and their families, in the South; do not keep that for your own preachers, your own wives, and your own children; but if you are right, get back this vast amount of property, devote it to the cause of your Church to which these Southern separatists have no title to belong. These Southern schismatics, with, as you pretend to believe, the branding degradation of slavery upon their brow, have no right to it;—put it in the hands of pure Christian men—men who are sufficiently pure and Christian to carry God's tidings of salvation everywhere, and administer the sacraments of his love to all; do not leave it in the hands of these lost Southern men. But they have not done this. Why not? Can any reason be given, except a conviction that the property belongs to the South? Can any reason be given consistent with their duty, except a conviction that it was made the property of the South by force of this very separate organization of the Southern Church, under the authority of the Plan of Separation of 1844? There have, it is true, been some adventurous spirits who have screwed themselves up to the sticking point of maintaining that the Plan being unconstitutional and void, fell in all its particulars to the ground, and that the Church and its property, everywhere, stands as it stood before the Plan of 1844 was adopted.

Your Honours have been referred to one case, where a gentleman named Armstrong, claiming to have been a large contributor to a meeting-house in Maysville, Kentucky, with some followers, conscientious, I have no doubt—God forbid that I should doubt that they were influenced by proper motives—contested the right of the

Southern Church to that meeting-house, upon the very ground of the absolute nullity of the Plan of Separation, and the absolute nullity consequently of the title to the meeting-house which was dependant upon that plan.

The case was first taken before a single judge vested with chancery jurisdiction, and he came to the conclusion, that, under the circumstances of the particular case, and by force of the provisions of a Kentucky statute of general operation, applying, as he considered, to the case, the equitable mode of disposing of the property would be to give the use of the house one week, or one Sunday, to one branch, and the next week, or the next Sunday, to the other branch. The case was carried up to the Court of Appeals of Kentucky. I commend your Honours to that decision, as delivered by Mr. Chief Justice Marshall, in which throughout he deems it to be too clear for doubt, (speaking not only for himself, but for the Court,) that the Conference of 1844 had the constitutional right to adopt the Plan of division of that year, and that by force of that division the entire title to this property was vested in the Southerly organized Church. They, the North, tried the question once, through Mr. Armstrong, and they tried it in vain. Now, all is acquiesced in. The South stands upon the title to all the property of which it is now in the actual enjoyment, by virtue of the constitutionality of the division authorized by the Plan of 1844—in virtue of that constitutional title, and none other. I beg your Honours to remember that. They stand, too, upon the authority of the Conference, which established a like separate organization for what was before an integral portion of the Church, in the Canada case. They stand upon the recorded opinions of almost every member of the Conference of 1844, that that Conference had the authority to sanction the division. They stand upon the unanimous opinion of the bishops, the executive heads of the Church, that the Conference had the authority to adopt it. They stand upon the opinions of the entire Conference of 1844, as far as we can find their opinions from their votes, that the Conference had the constitutional authority to adopt it. They are, therefore, covered all over with the sanctions which title can derive from precedent, from the judicial, legislative, and executive authority of this Church, and from the express adjudication of a court of last resort, not surpassed by any court in the Union, in all the qualities which give a tribunal claims to respect. They stand, above all and higher than all, upon the character, the holy character of that Power above from which the entire authority of the Church is derived; upon the charter which he gives to his Church to go throughout the world, and, accommodating itself to the wants, and the peculiarities, and the times in which his ministers may find themselves, to carry his word and to proclaim the glad tidings of salvation to all. Lest I might forget the very words in which this mighty power is communicated—which, I need not tell this Court, should never be done with any language which flows from so sacred and so revered a source—let me read to your Honours the constitution of the Church, the higher, holier constitution of the Church, as given by God himself to the apostles, the first travelling preachers in his service. He tells them, Matthew xxviii, 18–20 :—

"All power is given unto me in heaven and in earth. Go ye, therefore, and teach *all nations*, baptizing them in the name of the Father, and of the Son, and of the Holy Ghost; teaching them to observe all things whatsoever I have commanded you; and lo, I am with you always, even unto the end of the world."

"All nations." There are no territorial restrictions upon your authority, gentlemen travelling preachers of this Church. Your constituent is the Maker of the universe, under whom and for whom you act. He knows no local distinctions which we poor frail beings know; and knowing, because we are frail often do the greatest injustice in consequence of the knowledge. He wishes all brought to salvation: the master to be enlightened, the slave to be enlightened; the master to be saved, the slave to be saved. You libel the memory of the Author of your Church, you trample upon the constitution of that Church as derived from God, whom you are bound to adore, if you bring into the administration of the duties which he imposes upon you, any test which deprives you of the authority to preach to the master and to the slave. I have done with the first point.

The duty which is before me in the consideration of the next three points, is comparatively an unimportant one. But before I proceed to the consideration of the second point of my argument, although I feel that it is not necessary to the decision of this case, it is due to those that I represent, that I should say a few words upon what they believe to have been the necessity of asking for a separate organization of this Church. I shall be comparatively short, the whole subject having been so clearly and perspicuously presented by my colleague.

The agitation of slavery in the quarterly conferences, in the annual conferences, in the General Conference, the judgment against preacher Harding, the judgment in the case of Bishop Andrew, both of them in the Conference of 1844, brought about, in the opinion of the delegates from the Southern conferences in the first place, and afterwards in the opinion of the Southern conferences, a conviction that the Church itself, in order to be saved, must exist under separate and distinct organizations at the South and at the North. My learned brother who spoke first on the other side, ingeniously endeavoured to maintain that, of the three reasons which were assigned, in what is termed the Declaration of the members from the South in this Conference, for desiring a separate Church organization, two of them were afterwards abandoned, and the other, to make the most of it, was a mere erroneous judgment of the Conference upon a question over which they had clear jurisdiction. Let me, in this connexion, refer to what is the fact in relation to this matter. In 1844, not only was a division authorized by the General Conference, if the power existed, as in this branch of the argument I assume, but it was demanded for the safety of the Church. In the Canada case, whatever else may be said of it, your Honours will find, on p. 44 of Proofs No. 1, that it is asserted that a division was to be made, when division was necessary to save the Church; that is, to save the Church there—there in the particular locality—not to save it elsewhere where the exigency does not exist. When a state of things exists which endangers the usefulness of the Church, the doctrine of the Church is, divide, in order to save. Now, in the first place, the Declaration of the Southern delegates, in 1844, on p. 97, states the necessity of a division to save the Church. In the second place, the universal opinion of the Southern delegates was, that a division was necessary to save the Church. 3d. The conduct of the Conference in Harding's and in Andrew's cases proved the necessity of a division in order to save the Church. 4th. The doctrines avowed by the Northern members of the Church in the Conference of 1844, in the Answer to the Protest of Southern members against the judgment in the case of Andrew, proved, beyond all doubt, the necessity of a division to save the Church—it being always understood that I mean to save the Church in the South. 5th. The opinion of each one of the annual conferences of the South was, that a division was required in order to save the Church. 6th. The certain consequences, not relying on opinions as the only evidence, of the tendency of the acts of the members of the General Conference from the North, must have been, in the judgment of all sane men, the production of a state of things in the South, that would render a division of the Church absolutely imperative, in order to save the Church in the South. This was the opinion of the bishops of this Church as to the consequence of this slavery agitation, to be found in their address, upon

p. 58, and in their answer to the British Conference, pp. 64–66 ; and the opinion of the individual bishops, given in their collective capacity, in advance of the judgment on the case of Andrew, in their address to the Conference, by whom, almost immediately afterwards, that judgment was pronounced, as well as in the debate before the judgment, which your Honours will find on pages 88–91.

Finally : the opinion of the General Conference of 1844, as set forth in their preamble to the Plan of Separation, established the existence of the necessity to divide this Church, in order to save it in the South.

I have not time, nor would it be right, to trespass upon the kindness of the Court, already so indulgently extended to me, to read the particular evidence on either of these points ; but the Court will pardon me, for reading a sentence or two from the address of the bishops, pp. 58–60—cool, unimpassioned men, not acting under the influence of the local agitation to which this Church was subject, but whose very functions of general superintendency, freed them from the prejudices which sometimes arise from mere local opinions. The address to which I refer is the address to the General Conference of 1840. They say in that address :—

"At the last session of the General Conference the subject of slavery and its abolition was extensively discussed, and vigorous exertions made to effect new legislation upon it. But after a careful examination of the whole ground, *aided by the light of past experience*, it was the *solemn conviction* of the Conference that the interests of religion would not be advanced by any additional enactments in regard to it."

They had gone far enough ; a step further might be ruinous. They then say that they advised the subject to be dropped everywhere. On page 59, after stating that the opinion of the Conference was generally acquiesced in, they go on :—

"But we regret that we are compelled to say, that in some of the northern and eastern conferences, in contravention of your Christian and pastoral counsel, and of your best efforts to carry it into effect, the subject has been agitated in such forms, and in such a spirit, as to disturb the peace of the Church. This unhappy agitation has not been confined to the annual conferences, but has been introduced into quarterly conferences, and made the absorbing business of self-created bodies in the bosom of our beloved Zion. The professed object of all these operations"—

Of course it was the professed object, and I hope the sincere object. Fanatical error is always sincere. When it ceases to be sincere it becomes corruption, and no man can imagine that in the Church.

"The professed object of all these operations is to free the Methodist Episcopal Church from the 'great moral evil of slavery,' and to secure to the enslaved the rights and privileges of free citizens of these United States. How far the measures adopted, and the manner of applying those measures, are calculated to accomplish such an issue, even if it could be effected by any action of ecclesiastical bodies, your united wisdom will enable you to judge."

If these gentlemen could only wake up to the condition of things which they have brought about in the Southern States, they would find that, for every rivet they have loosened, they have added tens and hundreds and thousands of rivets to this very condition of slavery. One of the members who figured in the Conference of 1840 and 1844, and was one of the leaders in the proceedings against preacher Harding, and also took a conspicuous part against Bishop Andrew, has for the last six or seven months been serving as chaplain to a convention in Maryland, whose very first step—a step which never would have been taken but for the agitation in the Church and out of the Church on this question of slavery—and the only measure I think upon which they were unanimous, was to provide as part of the organic constitutional law of Maryland, that manumission should not be brought about by any legislative provision. Maryland, in the advance of the philanthropic movement, which I would have it understood did not begin at the North, but at the South, for putting an end to human bondage as far back as 1790, opened wide the doors to emancipation. But by the agitation in this Church and out of it, in other Churches, in the Presbyterian and Baptist Churches, a condition of things was brought about as far back as 1836, which caused the legislature of Maryland, then invested with the right of providing, with the assent of the next subsequent legislature, a change of the constitution, to change the constitution of the State, so as to take from the legislature the authority to authorize general manumission by an act of the legislature, unless such act was unanimously passed at one session, and unanimously sanctioned at the succeeding session—practically an impossible condition. Now this very Mr. Griffith, who in the Conference of 1844 sneered at the Maryland law which secured to a woman her slave property belonging to her at the time of marriage, on the ground that it was contrary to the law of God, which, according to him, gives everything belonging to the woman to her husband, as by Divine right, is found acting as chaplain in a convention of slaveholders who have been driven to the conviction of the necessity, brought about by the very excitement in which he and others have been engaged, to make it a part of the constitutional law of Maryland that slavery shall always exist within her limits. I speak under the conviction of a sincerity as great as I ever felt, when I say that, but for this very agitation and the making it a political matter, Maryland ere this would not have had a slave footprint within her limits. You have doomed us, those of us who have no love for that particular condition of things, and I confess myself to be one of them—but not upon the ground that there are any injunctions in the Gospel which prohibit it, for there are none. The Author of our religion came not into the world to raise the arm of one man against his fellow-man, to bring about servile war, to carry bloodshed and desolation into the homes and hearths of men; He came to save through the instrumentality of doctrines sure, when properly understood and inculcated, to save. He came not to destroy masters.

What say the bishops of this Church in that Christian but cutting rebuke to their brethren across the waters? It is due to the bishops of this Church to say that they have not only never taken part in this agitation, but they have done all they could do as Christian men to arrest it. They say, page 66:—

"Under the administration of the venerated Dr. Coke, this plain distinction was once overlooked, and it was attempted to urge emancipation in *all* the States; but this attempt proved almost ruinous, and was soon abandoned by the doctor himself. While, therefore, the Church has encouraged emancipation in those States where the laws permit it and allow the freed-man to enjoy freedom, we have refrained, for conscience' sake, from all intermeddling with the subject in those other States where the laws make it criminal. And such a course we think agreeable to the Scriptures, and indicated by St. Paul's inspired instruction to servants, in his First Epistle to the Corinthians, chap. vii, ver. 20, 21. For if servants were not to care for their servitude when they *might not* be free, though if they might be free they should use it *rather*, so neither should masters be condemned for not setting them free when they *might not* do so, though *if* they *might* they should do so *rather*."

But in these modern days, as compared with some who are to be found amongst us, in a pure and elevated morality St. Paul was a Hottentot, and in a far-seeing and far-searching wisdom Christ himself an imbecile! They seek to improve upon the morality of St. Paul. They attempt and claim authority to exercise the function of supplying the omissions of the Deity. God, speaking through Paul, tells masters to take care of their servants, and servants to obey their masters. These modern apostles, tracing their authority to some law higher even than the law of God, proclaim substantially, "Slaves, exterminate your masters; they are your oppressors, and you stand entitled to freedom upon some high, more elevated, purer law than is to be found in the Gospel of your God." I am glad to know that the extent to which this fanaticism has gone in this Church is, in the particulars to which I have alluded, comparatively limited but these gentlemen stand still within narrow and perilous limits on that question. I pray them, as servants of God, to remember that the progress of fanatacism is never backward, unless it be driven backward by the dread of force and bloodshed. The stake has often witnessed the dying sincerity of the fanatic as well as of the martyr.

Pardon me for a moment in reading to you, to show the extent to which this feeling had gone, from the address of Bishop Andrew himself to this very Conference, who were about to pass judgment on his moral and religious life, and to proclaim him to the world as unfitted to minister at the altar of God in this the Northern section of the land, however competent he might be at the South. This address, which is a long speech, and challenges commendation, your Honours will find on page 148 of the Debates of the Conference of 1844. He states how he became a slaveholder; and he then says :—

"It has been said I did this thing voluntarily, and with my eyes open. I did so deliberately and in the fear of God, and God has blessed our union."

What do you suppose he is speaking of? Why, he married a Southern lady, and it was said in the Conference that he ought not to have married any Southern woman who had slaves, that it was a sin against God to marry a female if she was the owner of slaves. He goes on :—

"I might have avoided this difficulty by a trick—by making over those slaves to my wife before marriage; or, by doing as a friend, who has taken ground for the resolution before you, suggested."

What do you suppose was the remedy recommended by this conscientious friend, who would not permit Bishop Andrew to remain in the Church because he was the owner of slaves by marriage? It was :—

"'Why,' said he, 'did you not let your wife make over these negroes to her children, securing to herself an annuity from them?'"

That would have been honest—that would have emancipated the negroes. That is it not all. He says he could not get rid of them :—

"They love their mistress, and could not be induced, under any circumstances, to leave her. Sir, an aged and respectable minister said to me several years ago, when I stated just such a case to him, and asked him what he would do,—'I would set them free,' said he, 'I'd wash my hands of them, and *if they went to the devil*, I'D BE CLEAR OF THEM.'"

There is the philanthropy of fanaticism. To free them; if we cannot do it in any other way, send them to the devil—that is our mission. I am not to be understood as intimating for a moment that the Church as a Church, or that the members generally entertain such opinions. I refer to this as an instance, to show the alarming, unchristian results to which fanaticism leads. It would be but another, and comparatively a humane step to have said: "You masters of the South, get clear of your slaves by cutting their throats;" or, "You slaves of the South, get clear of your masters and become freemen by cutting their throats." In either case the dead might go to heaven, which would be infinitely better than sending either master or slave to the devil, as one means to get rid of slavery.

I have not time to turn your Honours' attention to the grounds taken in relation to the Maryland law as to the power of Mr. Harding to emancipate his negroes. He could not emancipate them, for the very important reason that they did not belong to him, but belonged to his wife. I will, however, refer to what was said by Mr. Collins and Mr. Griffith in the Conference of 1844 on the Harding case. One of them, Mr. Collins, governed I trust by conscientious considerations of duty, takes occasion to declare, page 42 of the Debates :—

"But he would say boldly, that if the law had been ten-fold what it is, if it had actually, outright and downright, without any possibility of avoiding it, taken these slaves from Harding's control, the conference would still have acted just as they did; because *they did not intend to change their ground, and could not pretend to alter their views with every shifting of the legislature.*"

Your Discipline says : observe the laws of the country in which you are; wherever you may be, enter not into the political turmoils of the day; place yourselves not in opposition to the laws of the place in which, as the servant of God, you are ministering, for it is one of the duties of the ministry to obey the civil laws. "I will do no such thing," says Mr. Travelling Preacher Collins; "I will not accommodate myself to the shifting caprices of the legislature of the State in which I live." Hear next what brother Griffith says, page 41 of the Debates :—

"He could disentangle himself in an hour if he liked, *the laws of Maryland notwithstanding*. In point of fact the law against manumission was inoperative. It would be indeed strange if a freeman had not the right to make that disposal of his property which he might choose to make. Maryland never had said that a slave might be taken up and sold—she never had declared that slaves were property, and then in the same breath, that men should not do what they thought fit with their own property, and that she assumed the right to do that which she forbade the owner doing. No, sir; they know that a *man has a right to set his slaves free, they know the illegality and imperfection of any act to the contrary*, and yet they try to control it, and ward off the consequences by this kind of—he hardly knew how to designate such kind of legislation."

That is, if sincere, were fanaticism; that would be treason, if carried out by overt act; that, as sure as there is a God above us, would, if so carried out in opposition to those laws, have landed Messrs. Collins and Griffith, Christian ministers as they are, within the limits of the Maryland penitentiary. God forbid they should ever be there,—because in many respects they are good men, and they have declared these sentiments, it is to be in charity hoped, for conscience' sake,—but there they would have gone, and in vain would they have invoked the authority of their Gospel mission to save them, for they would find in that authority an injunction running all through it to preachers to observe the local municipal laws.

A word more, and I leave the question of necessity for the division. We have been told that it might have been avoided, that there was not the slightest occasion in the world for the division of this Church. To be sure the agitation had been kept up, and there was no promise to stop it; to be sure a preacher had been unfrocked because he came to be the owner of slaves, and there was no promise that the same thing would not be repeated in other cases; to be sure a bishop had been degraded, and there was not only no promise not thereafter to degrade in such cases, but there was an express avowal of an authority, and almost of a duty to impeach and punish; still, says my brother Choate, there was no necessity for a division. Why, says he, the South might have submitted. Submission is the remedy. "Go home, you Southern preachers, carry with you the evidences of your individual degradation. Go into your meeting-houses, and say to your brethren that, in the opinion of your Church, every one is unworthy in the sight of man and of God who happens to be a slaveholder. Tell them that the blessing of God has illuminated the minds of the Northern members of the Church, and made them at last find out the truth that such is your miserable degradation. We invoke you to submit. Admit self-degradation, admit the existence in your own persons of a moral leprosy, admit that you are steeped all over with sin, and submit." The bishops said that Dr. Coke in 1784 attempted to announce and execute the same doctrine, and the single year in which he attempted to carry it into effect almost ruined the Church. The bishops had announced that it was the opinion of this very Conference in 1836 and 1840 that the continued agitation of the subject of slavery, and the considering it as a matter of moral or religious sin, was bringing this Church into a condition of the most absolute ruin at the South. The bishops had announced in their answer to the address of the British Conference, that the whole Church was necessarily to observe the laws of the States in which slavery existed. The bishops had announced that so far from there being anything in the Gospel denouncing slavery, as of itself, and under all circumstances a sin, it was a relation to be prayed for, to be watched over, to have invoked on it the blessings of God himself.

There, then, in submission was one mode in which the necessity might have been avoided, but there was not the intimation of an opinion that it was probable that submission would, then or at any time, be adopted. There is a method left still by which a reunion may be brought about, but it is not by submission on the part of the South. If every minister in the Connexion was willing to submit, as submission would be self-degradation, he could not bring about a reunion of the Church, South, with their brethren of the Church, North. There is, however, one mode in which it may be brought about. I have no doubt God will bless the effort, looking to his past care of this Church. Abandon, preachers of the North, the ground upon which you acted in the case of Harding and of Andrew; go back to the doctrine of the Church in 1836; stand upon the platform declared to be the proper and religious platform upon which alone you had a right to stand in 1840; cease to assail your brethren of the South; and you and they, to the delight of the Christian world, will again be one: and as long as you continue to exercise your power in that spirit of fraternal and religious love, you will be indivisible.

In the Reply to the Protest, announcing the absolute necessity of a division, pag 114, the Northern gentlemen say they had no doubt that Bishop Andrew was a "very benevolent and *Christian* master." If their doctrines be right, I cannot imagine how a master can be a Christian at all. They say God proclaims freedom as the right of all, and you war against the law of God in holding a man in a state of bondage. Still, from courtesy, I suppose, they call Bishop Andrew a Christian master. They then go on to say:—

> "It was the almost unanimous opinion of the delegates from the non-slaveholding conferences that Bishop Andrew could not continue to exercise his episcopal functions under existing circumstances, without producing results extremely disastrous to the Church in the North; and from this opinion the brethren of the South did not dissent."

Then something was to be done. What had Bishop Andrew done? Why, in the State of Georgia, where manumission is not tolerated, he agreed to take a negro girl, and if possible manumit her, and send her to Liberia. He could not do it; but, as far as the laws would permit, he suffered the poor girl to act as if she were free. Then he married a woman who had slaves. Well, but they acted leniently with Bishop Andrew, because he was a "Christian master!" They did not expel him, to be sure; but what do they say they had a right to do? What is the doctrine upon which they then stood, and stand now? Let them speak for themselves. On page 115, Proofs No. 1, they say:—

"A diversity of sentiment existed as to the proper mode of treating the case.
"Some at least believed—perhaps few doubted—that sufficient ground existed for impeachment on a charge of 'improper conduct,' under the express provisions of the Discipline. The opinion was certainly entertained in several quarters, that it was 'improper' for the shepherd or bishop of eleven hundred thousand souls, either deliberately or heedlessly, to place himself in direct and irreconcilable conflict with the known and cherished moral sentiments of a *large majority of his vast flock*."

The minority might take care of themselves—these gentlemen are looking to the North alone. Are there no souls to be saved on the other side of Mason's and Dixon's line? Are you not willing to content yourselves with having bishops who are not the holders of slaves, who may by an arrangement, as between themselves and the other bishops, pursue the functions of bishops this side of Mason's and Dixon's line, in accordance with all the prejudices of the members of the Church this side of the line? Are you not content to leave, under that arrangement, to the bishops themselves to make such a provision, that the religious wants of the South may be supplied through the ministry of bishops who are not obnoxious to, or in irreconcilable conflict with, any of the moral sentiments of the South? See what the fathers of the Church told them. They had witnessed the angry contention, and wept over and prayed through the debates which characterized it. They asked that the subject might be postponed, to give them an opportunity of recommending some plan by which the Church might be saved. O! how much is it to be deplored that these gentlemen did not follow the advice of these their fathers! As I believe in my own existence, do I believe that, if their advice had been followed, the exigency in which the Church now finds herself, a state of comparatively hostile and angry feeling in which the members are arrayed against each other, would have been avoided. I will read a few sentences from the address of these bishops to the General Conference of 1844, during the pendency of Andrew's case, but in advance of the judgment pronounced on it. On page 88 they say:—

"As they have pored over this subject with anxious thought, by day and by night, they have been more and more impressed with the difficulties connected therewith, and the disastrous results which, in their apprehension, are the almost inevitable consequences of present action on the question pending before you. To the undersigned it is fully apparent that a decision thereon, whether affirmatively or negatively, will most extensively disturb the peace and harmony of that widely-extended brotherhood which has so effectively operated for good, in the United States of America and elsewhere, during the last sixty years."

Again, on page 89, they say:—

"At this painful crisis, they have unanimously concurred in the propriety of recommending the postponement of further action in the case of Bishop Andrew until the ensuing General Conference."

That would be until 1848.

"It does not enter into the design of the undersigned to argue the propriety of their recommendation, otherwise strong and valid reasons might be adduced in its support. They cannot but think that if the embarrassment of Bishop Andrew should not cease before that time, the next General Conference, representing the pastors, ministers, and people of the several annual conferences, after all the facts in the case shall have passed in review before them, will be better qualified than the present General Conference can be to adjudicate the case wisely and discreetly. Until the cessation of the embarrassment, or the expiration of the interval between the present and the ensuing General Conference, the undersigned believe that such a division of the work of the general superintendency might be made, without any infraction of a constitutional principle, as would fully employ Bishop Andrew in those sections of the Church in which his presence and services would be welcome and cordial."

No, says the Conference, the sacrifice must be made now; now must the sentence be pronounced; he has sinned past salvation, and our sense of duty will not permit us to wait till 1848; now we will pronounce our judgment; now must Bishop Andrew be deposed; and now he is deposed.

In relation to the character of the sentence passed on Bishop Andrew by the Conference of 1844, I will refer to what these Northern gentlemen say in the Conference of 1848, in their address upon the state of the Church. Our learned friends on the other side contend that this was merely an advisory measure; that Bishop Andrew was still a bishop, the mitre was still upon his brow, he might exercise still the functions of a bishop, that there was nothing in what the Conference of 1844 had done to repudiate his authority as a bishop, and his case, therefore, constituted no reason whatever for the step taken by the Church, South, in 1844. The Conference of 1848, on page 141, says:—

"In the mean time Bishop Soule wrote to Bishop Andrew, requesting him to resume episcopal functions, and, in the character and office of a bishop, to attend the sessions of annual conferences, which he did, *though said act was clearly in contravention of the expressed will of the General Conference*, that he desist from the exercise of the episcopal office so long as the impediment of slaveholding 'remained.' By which acts both Bishop Soule and Bishop Andrew *openly repudiated the authority of the General Conference of the Methodist Episcopal Church.*"

Why, how do the counsel represent this matter? Is he still a bishop? Yes. Did they not in charity leave him a bishop? Yes. Did not they, although avowing their authority and almost their duty to disrobe him and depose and punish him as a bishop under the provision of the Discipline, which made him amenable to the Conference for improper conduct, kindly, humanely, and charitably refrain, and only advise him to desist from his functions? Yes. But, inasmuch as he has thought proper to exercise the functions which we left and intended to leave to him, he, they say, openly repudiated their authority. Why, it is absurd. He did repudiate their authority in one sense, he went counter to the opinion of the General Conference, and if the General Conference had authority to pronounce that opinion, and pronounced it authoritatively, then superintending the annual conferences, after the pronunciation of the opinion and during the existence of the impediment on account of which it was pronounced, was an open and absolute defiance of the authority of the Conference. But the learned counsel give a different character to the judgment from these gentlemen of the Conference of 1848.

A word now as to the conduct of the Conference in both these cases—of Harding and Andrew. Under the laws of the Church as they were at that time, there never was, to my mind, a more palpable violation of them than was committed in the judgments in these cases. We have been told that the general rule of the Church prohibited any officer of the Church from holding slaves when elected, or during the existence of his official life; and that the general rule thereof embraced the case of a bishop as well as all other officers; and that it is incumbent upon us who vindicate the bishop to bring the case of the bishop within the limits of some exception to the general rule; and that we have failed to do this because the exception embraced only "travelling preachers," who then, in the nomenclature of this Church, are such preachers as contradistinguished from bishops.

I was a little surprised, though not much struck, with the ingenuity of the argument. The counsel using it ought to have known that the Court was to look to the evidence in this case; but my learned brother contented himself with referring to the rule upon the subject of slavery, adopted in 1808 or 1812, but did not refer to the law upon the subject adopted in 1816, nor to the declaratory law, to be found in a resolution adopted by the Conference of 1840 upon what was called the Westmoreland petition, to which, however, I shall now particularly advert. My learned brother talked about the resolution of the Church in relation to the allowances to ministers, on page 29, of Proofs No. 1; but if he had turned to page 24, to which I ask your Honours' attention, he would have found an answer, and a conclusive answer, to his entire argument on this point. That argument was, that a bishop falling within the operation of the general rule which prohibited the holding of slaves by all officers in the Church, was not excepted from the operation of that rule by the particular exception in relation to travelling preachers. I will not stop to argue whether in this he is right or wrong. The particular exception, page 31, is,—

"When any travelling preacher becomes an owner of a slave or slaves, by any means, he shall forfeit his ministerial character in our Church, unless he execute, if it be practicable, a legal emancipation of such slaves, conformably to the laws of the State in which he lives."

The learned counsel says "travelling preacher" does not include "bishop," and, as the general rule prohibits all, the bishop remained prohibited by force of it. But in 1816, as the Court will see by turning to page 24, the Conference then adopted a rule, which forms the first of the rules on the subject in the Discipline of 1840. To that the counsel has not referred. It is,—

"We declare that we are as much as ever convinced of the great evil of slavery; therefore no slaveholder shall be eligible to *any official station in our Church hereafter*, where the laws of the State in which he lives will admit of emancipation and permit the liberated slave to enjoy freedom."

I presume "any official station" covers the case of a bishop. It is not necessary to argue that. What does this show? The Church makes a general rule in 1784 or 1785 declaring war against slavery as a moral evil; they cannot execute it, the very life of the Church is about to be sacrificed by the attempt to execute it; it then becomes the settled policy of the Church in 1808 or 1812 to recognise the laws of the State in which slavery exists and where emancipation is prohibited; and it becomes consequently the duty of the Church to provide for the case of the travelling preacher in order to carry on the Church in those States in which slavery exists where emancipation is prohibited. They first except the case of the travelling preacher; but in 1816, alive to a more important necessity, they find that the usefulness of the Church depends upon the recognition, *as regards every official station in the Church*, of the laws of the States in which slavery exists and in which emancipation is prohibited, and they authorize any and every man to be elected *to any and every official station in the Church*, notwithstanding he is the holder of slaves, if *he lives in a State where slavery exists and where emancipation is prohibited*. Is not this clear? The words admit of but one interpretation. Now see what this Conference of 1840 itself said, by adopting the resolution on pages 74 and 75. He who was then of the Church, and one of its brightest luminaries, as your Honours sufficiently know from the papers in evidence, of which he was the author, now elsewhere enjoying the reward of a well-spent and a religious life—Mr. Bascom—was chairman of a committee to whom the petition of some lay members of the Westmoreland circuit, in the Baltimore Conference, was referred. Time after time that conference refused to ordain preachers upon no other ground, as it was alleged in the petition, except that the persons recommended were the owners of slaves. Mr. Bascom, whose opinions are perfectly well known on the subject, writes a report which concludes with a resolution I am about to read, in which he says they can do nothing to grant relief in the particular cases, because, on turning to the proceedings of the conference which had refused to elect these several ministers, no such reason was assigned, and it was not, therefore, to be assumed that that was the ground; but with a view to the ascertainment of what the law was in a case of that description, and in order to have again declared what the law was in the case made by the memorial, the committee *unanimously* recommended the adoption of a declaratory resolution, and these very gentlemen who constituted the Conference of 1840, and many of whom were in the Conference of 1844, adopted it. I am now, remember, endeavouring to show that the bishop's case came within the operation of the law of this Church, which said that the holding of slaves, where slavery by law existed, and where by law manumission was prohibited, should be no objection to a man's eligibility in the first instance, or to his continuing thereafter to discharge the functions of any station in the Church. That resolution of 1840 was in these words:—

"*Resolved*, by the delegates of the several annual conferences in General Conference assembled, That under the provisional exception of the general rule of the Church on the subject of slavery, the simple holding of slaves, or mere ownership of slave property, in States or territories where the laws do not admit of emancipation and permit the liberated slave to enjoy freedom, *constitutes no legal barrier to the election or ordination of ministers to the various grades of office known in the ministry of the Methodist Episcopal Church*, and cannot therefore be considered as operating any forfeiture of right in view of such election and ordination."

Is not the office of bishop a grade of ministry in the Methodist Episcopal Church? The law of this Church then, solemnly reiterated as its law by a vote of the Conference of 1840, was, that where slavery did not exist no slaveholder could be elected to any office; but that where slavery did exist, and emancipation was prohibited within the State in which the master resided, the being a slaveholder was to be no test of eligibility in the first instance, and no ground of forfeiture after election. Now, the Conference of 1844, with that law before them, depose, as we say, or censure, according to their own admission, Bishop Andrew, upon the ground of some general law in the Discipline which speaks of improper conduct, which, by a species of construction I cannot comprehend, they construe to mean the doing that which the very law of the Church authorizes to be done. "Improper conduct" is the word in the portion of the Discipline under which they act and under which they punish him. Improper conduct in the doing of what? Improper conduct in holding slaves when the law says he might hold them? Is he to forfeit his right as bishop for being the owner of slaves when you have said over and over again that it constitutes no objection to eligibility, and no ground of forfeiture? Why, that is an absolute, undefined, illimitable tyranny. Keeping within the law is no protection; observing the law is no defence. "We, in the possession of that mighty transcendental power to be found under the general authority to examine into the conduct of the ministry, can convict you of any and every act which, according to our judgment, is improper conduct, although according to our laws it is proper conduct." I say, therefore, with great respect, that in the whole history of jurisprudence, in its actual administration throughout the civilized world, where duty is inculcated by law and rights are protected by law, this is as clear and palpable an infraction of law as is to be found disgracing any of the pages of the books which illustrate the utter regardlessness of law in the early and dark and tyrannous ages of English jurisprudence. The English martyrs suffered their sentences, and without a groan or the movement of a muscle carried with them and supported through the flames the spirit by which they were animated; and these revolting sentences were perhaps, at times, pronounced by tribunals who professed, and perhaps thought, they were thereby carrying out some law of God, as these gentlemen preachers in the case of Bishop Andrew. But under such a government as that, who is safe? Bring a provision like that into the criminal code of the United States, and what would be the consequence? Your Honours have your duties defined by statute; you may, under the law and according to the express terms of the law, do this, that, or the other, without objection, without forfeiture; you may, under the Constitution of the United States, be slaveholders without forfeiting any political or private right that you may have. But bring upon the statute book of the United States a sweeping power to remove from the bench the lights that adorn it, and under a general authority to inquire into the conduct of public functionaries, to remove them, if, in the opinion of the trying body, that conduct is improper; would not the blood of every citizen boil with indignation at an attempt to bring either of your Honours within the operation of such a power, for the holding of slaves which by law you are authorized to hold? And yet these gentlemen preachers have done precisely that very thing. Bishop Andrew was a slaveholder, under the law and by virtue of the law; his rights as a bishop were protected by the very law which authorized him to hold slaves; and yet under this general sweeping authority of inquiring into the conduct of the bishops, they assumed the power of being wiser than the law, and of saying that, although the law authorized it, the thing authorized was improper, and to be punished. They go to a higher source, to that "higher law" which we have heard in modern times is an authority to disobey or not carry out a constitutional law of the United States. It cannot be so.

I was not advised until this moment that these gentlemen waked up to the consequences of having adopted the resolution on the Westmoreland petition. We find them in their own Conference of 1848, as will be seen by reference to the journals of that Conference, p. 125, rescinding that resolution:—

"Whereas the following resolution is found appended to the report on the Westmoreland petition, and was adopted by the General Conference of 1840, to wit:—"

The resolution is then recited:—

"And whereas said resolution is liable to misconstruction, and has been misconstrued greatly to the prejudice of our beloved Methodism. Therefore,

"*Resolved*, 1*st*. That said resolution be, and is hereby, *rescinded*.

"*Resolved*, 2*d*. That in rescinding said resolution, we contemplate no interference with that section of the Discipline on slavery; but wish simply to leave it without note or comment."

They do not even then, in 1848, pretend to interfere with the law of 1816. The Conference in passing that law was then speaking to itself. My friend, Mr. Choate, told the Court, that in all the rules on slavery, from 1784 to 1840, it was the General Conference speaking to the annual conferences; but you will see, that the resolution of 1816 is a resolution of the General Conference announcing for itself, as a rule for its own government, the law of the Church upon the question of slavery, and that is precisely what the Westmoreland resolution says; but these gentlemen, without giving any reason, except that it might be misunderstood, repeal the resolution, and leave the law of 1816 to stand as when it was passed. They might very well have repealed that resolution, for it was a direct censure on themselves in their votes upon Harding's case, and Andrew's case; but it was no further a censure than the law of 1816. It was a censure, because under it the act was censurable.

Now I have a word to say upon my second point, the construction of the Plan of Separation, for it is really too plain for argument, although the case is made, by the answer to our bill, to turn very materially upon it. In the answer,—in the argument it was not much pressed by our friends on the other side, for they did not seem to think they could maintain such an extravagant proposition,—as well as in the review of the state of the Church made by the Conference of 1848, at Pittsburgh, the broad ground is taken, that the Plan of Separation under which the Southern Church was established, was conditional, and that the condition was the agreement of the conferences, by a vote of three-fourths voting, to change the sixth restrictive rule. There is not a word of truth in it. It is so plain that I am saved from the necessity of detaining your Honours with discussion on the subject. The first resolution of the Plan of Separation is,—

"That, should the annual conferences in the slaveholding States find it necessary to unite in a distinct ecclesiastical Connexion,"

then, a division is to be made. The only thing upon which a division is there made to turn is the action of the conferences in the slaveholding States. The second resolution depends exclusively upon the same thing—the action of the conferences in the slaveholding States. It says, contemplating the division as already made,

"That ministers, local and travelling, of every grade and office in the Methodist Episcopal Church, may, as they prefer, remain in that Church, or, without blame, attach themselves to the Church, South."

There was something else to be done. They had said that,—

"In the event of a separation, a contingency to which the Declaration asks attention as not improbable, we esteem it the duty of this General Conference to meet the emergency with Christian kindness and the strictest equity."

Under the first resolution they divided; under the second they permitted ministers to unite themselves with either branch of the Church: now they want to carry out what they believe to be right and equitable, in the event of the division for which they have thus prospectively provided on the single contingency of the action of the Southern conferences. They say, then, according to the third resolution, that if, by a vote of three-fourths of the members of the annual conferences, such an alteration be made in the sixth restrictive rule as will give power to the General Conference to appropriate the fund in question to other purposes than those indicated by the rule, then a certain portion of that fund is to be distributed between the Methodist Church north of the line of division, and the Methodist Church south of the line of division. Then, when you come to the 9th resolution,—because the 4th, 5th, 6th, 7th, and 8th, are only provisions as to the manner in which this equitable distribution is to be made,—you find it provided, that all the property of the Church in the Southern section of the Church—in meeting-houses, parsonages, colleges, schools, &c.,—shall belong absolutely to the Church, South, organized under the authority of the first resolution. When you come to the 12th resolution you find that the action of the annual conferences is only to be demanded on the 3d resolution—the changing the sixth restrictive article in the constitution of the Church, and on no other part of the Plan.

I come now to the third point, and in arguing it I have a right to assume, as proved, these propositions:—1st. That the Conference of 1844 had a right to divide the Church, as they did divide it, prospectively, according to the first resolution in the Plan of Separation; 2d. That that division was to depend alone upon the action of the Southern conferences; 3d. That under that authority the Southern conferences did act and the Church was divided. Now, the question is, What is to be done with the property? There were different kinds of property belonging to the Church. There was a local property, such as meeting-houses, colleges, and schools; and its locality, the division being made, was to give title to it to the Church within whose limits it was located. There was another kind of property—the property in this Book Concern, amounting to about $750,000, and the chartered fund. Unlike the meeting-houses, parsonages, and schools, which were local property for local Church use, this was a general property in which all had a usufructuary interest, and it came into existence by the joint efforts of the North and South. It had, during its existence, from first to last, been administered by all for the benefit of all. That is to be borne in mind. It was, by express stipulation in the law of the Church, property held for all alike, South and North. What is the effect *per se* upon such a fund of a constitutional division of the Church, to whom, as an entire body, the funds belonged antecedent to the division? Why, one who is not astute would be at a loss to imagine any possible ground upon which it can be denied, that in the case of common property, belonging at first to the whole, to which each had the same title, and in which each had the same interest, that property must go to each ratably in the event of a legal, constitutional division of the whole into parts. Why, it would not be honest if it were otherwise. I do not mean to say, that these gentlemen admit they are dishonestly keeping the fund,—God forbid that I should say so,—but they say substantially, there is an inherent equity attaching itself to the funds and belonging to each of the two divisions into which the association is thus constitutionally and properly divided, that such fund shall belong ratably to each division. They think that in order to carry out the perfectly equitable distribution of the fund, with a view to the protection of the trustees, who are the holders of the fund, a change of the sixth restrictive article was necessary. But why did they hold that it was advisable to change the sixth restrictive article, in order to be clothed with the authority to authorize or to direct the trustees to appropriate the fund ratably to the two divisions of the Church? I am not left to say that the reason is obvious, because honour, and honesty, and justice demanded it; this very Conference say so; the very men who are now holding the funds say so, if they were members of the Conference. In the Plan of Separation they say,—

"In the event of a separation, a contingency to which the Declaration asks attention as not improbable, we esteem it the duty of this General Conference to meet the emergency with Christian kindness and *the strictest equity*."

Therefore, annual conferences, change the sixth of the restrictive rules, so as to allow us to do it, and we will pay to the South what we say in equity the South is entitled to.

Having demonstrated, as I hope, the constitutional authority to divide, exercised by the passage of the first resolution in the Plan of Division; I say, that looking to the character of the fund, the only conceivable ground, and the only ground that has been presented against a division of the fund is, that the Plan itself agrees to a division only in the contingency of an agreement upon the part of the annual conferences to change the sixth restrictive rule, which applies to the administration of the fund. Let us see, as lawyers and as honest men, where that would lead us, and lead these gentlemen, who are undeniably as honest as others. A division of the Church has been brought about constitutionally; that division, as we contend, independently of the particular mode provided in the Plan of Separation for the division of the fund, would have given to each of the branches of the Church, organized under the division, a right, upon general principles of equity, which a court of equity will administer, to participate ratably in the fund. That is the Southern argument. The other side say, that as there was provided in the Plan of Division a mode of distributing the fund, that mode cannot be now adopted, because the contingency upon which it was to be operative has not happened—that is, because the annual conferences did not assent to the change of the restrictive rule, the law of the land is to be overruled, the powers of the Court are to be limited, the principles of equity by which the Court is governed are not to be enforced and do not apply. Does it not lead us to these conclusions? You gentlemen of the Conference have tried to be honest, but the annual conferences will not permit you to be honest; you have endeavoured to do equity, but the annual conferences will not permit you to do equity; you have brought about a condition of things which, but for your trying to be honest and endeavouring to do equity, would have made it the duty of this Court to make you honest and equitable, but now the powers of the Court are gone. Why, is not this absurd?

Title to a share of this fund, under the terms of the 3d, 4th, 5th, 6th, 7th, and 8th resolutions of the Plan of Division, we have not made out, because that particular appropriation depended upon a change of the sixth restrictive article; but if, without a change of that article, a division of the fund on principles of equity entitles each party to a ratable proportion of the fund, then we make out title because of the division. If we are right, let us inquire how that division was brought about. Our friends on the other side say it exists in the nature of an agreement. That is a great mistake. In the sense of the term "agreement" which would be applied to the particular Plan of Separation, it was no agreement at all which was to be enforced, *qua*-agreement, through the instrumentality of any tribunal vested by the laws with power to enforce *inter partes* agreements. That division was brought about by a law pronounced by a constitutional body vested with authority to legislate on the subject. It operated of itself, and by itself became of the constitution of these two Churches, without the aid of any judicial tribunal, or any general law upon the subject. The division authorized by the first resolution of the Plan was a legislative act made to depend only upon the terms of that act. If we have succeeded in satisfying your Honours that the body passing the resolution had a legislative right to adopt it, then it was a legislative act made to depend, by the authority of that adequate legislative power, for its effective operation upon the single contingency of the action of the conferences in the slaveholding States, that being a condition, and it was *eo instanti* law, not agreement. Now to say that a legislative body owning, in its legislative capacity, for the benefit of its entire constituency, property, and authorized by its legislative power to divide that constituency into two bodies, do not give, by the act of division, to each of the two bodies an equal right, according to numbers, to participate in the property, is to say that the power of dividing into two is a power which must necessarily work wrong and injustice to one. That cannot be so.

May it please your Honours, there rests here, in the laws which you are bound to administer, under the chancery jurisdiction with which you are clothed, coextensive with the entire English chancery jurisdiction, an authority to see in every exigency in which man may be placed towards each other that justice is done. If the case can be brought before you in the form of a case, within the meaning of the term "case," as you find it in that part of the Constitution of the United States which devolves the judicial power upon the courts of the United States, and if the present case between the complainants and the defendants entitles the complainants to relief, upon principles of equity, they must have it. Is not that our condition? It was our fund before 1844 as much as the defendants'; it was the proceeds of our exertions as well as of theirs; it was our right to participate in it to the same extent that it was their right. We have now, by the body of our mutual choice, in whom was rested our entire, original, and inherent power, agreed to divide ourselves. Then, the fund goes—but where? Suppose we had possession of the fund, the North would not be entitled to it, if they are right in holding it now against us. I could prove, and by argument just as strong as that which has been presented on the other side, that the Southern Church is *the* Methodist Church, within the meaning of the term as we have had it from the counsel on the other side. The division has sprung out of no innovation on our part. We stood upon the law of the Church on the particular point, slavery, which led to that division—that law as was declared in 1808, 1812, and 1816, and re-affirmed in 1840. You, the defendants, have violated that law; you have stepped off the platform; you are the seceders, we are the Church. If the fund was in our hands, precisely upon the same process of reasoning upon which our learned friends rely, for the purpose of showing that the exclusive right is in the Northern branch of the Church, I could, unless I mistake myself, demonstrate that the entire right was in the Southern branch of the Church. But there is a fallacy in such an argument. It does not depend on the agreement to divide, if the effect of division, constitutionally brought about, gives a right to divide the fund. Can anything be plainer?

If the constitution of this Church as formed in 1808—and I have endeavoured to show the Court that it substantially and almost in terms said it—had given in so many terms to the Conference which might assemble in 1844, in the contingency of a state of things existing in 1844, such as did exist, authority to divide the Church; and it was a part of the same constitution that with reference to this fund it was to be administered as a fund belonging to one Church, could anybody doubt that each branch would have been entitled to a share of the fund in the event of division. A contrary doctrine would make the constitution effect a high moral wrong.

I know the tribunal I am addressing. I know that it is not necessary to caution such a tribunal against falling into the error into which the counsel on the other side have fallen, of confounding the right to participate in this fund on the part of the complainants consequent on the division, as a legal result growing out of the fact of division, with the right to participate in the particular mode pointed out by the Conference beforehand, for the purpose of enabling it to divide the fund in the event of division. If I had not the declaration of these gentlemen themselves in the Conference of 1844, that equity demanded an equal participation of the fund between the two branches, the words which instinctively dropped from the counsel would have demonstrated it. My learned brother who spoke first on the other side, devoted some fifteen or twenty minutes to the purpose of vindicating his clients against what was, he said, apparently a graceless position, in which they appeared to be agreeing to divide the Church and holding on to the funds. My brother who followed him yesterday told your Honours, and I have no doubt told you what he supposed to be true, because he seemed to be fully impressed with the equity on which our complaint rests, that if time had been allowed all would have been right. Time can do a great many things; but if it was able to accomplish the end which we are now seeking, through the instrumentality of a court of justice, it was too slow for the wants of the age. They divided in 1844; we are now in 1851. Seven years have passed away, and they still hold on to the fund with a grasp which threatens, as far as depends on them, to be perpetual. Time seems to be no remedy. After the division was effected, were our superannuated preachers, their wives, widows, and children to wait until these gentlemen could be enlightened as to the existence of their obligation of distributing the fund? How long were they to wait? They might hope on and die while they hoped. Such, too, was the instinctive sense of the justice of such a division of the fund here at the North, that, although the public mind was to a great extent poisoned upon this subject, we came within 242 votes of having such an alteration of the sixth restrictive rule as would have made it the duty of the trustees to administer the fund; and that was an alteration which was to be sanctioned by three-fourths of all those voting. We came to the Conference of 1848 at Pittsburgh, in the person of our commissioners, appointed under one of the provisions of the Plan of Separation, to bring about an equitable division of this fund. These commissioners wrote them a letter, dated Pittsburgh, May 11, 1848:—

"*To the bishops and members of the General Conference of the Methodist Episcopal Church in General Conference assembled.*

"Rev. and dear Brethren,—The undersigned commissioners and appointee of the Methodist Episcopal Church, South, respectfully represent to your body, that pursuant to our appointment, and in obedience to specific instructions, we notified the commissioners and agents of the Methodist Episcopal Church, of our readiness to proceed to the adjustment of the property question, according to the Plan of Separation, adopted by the General Conference of 1844. And we furthermore state that the chairman of the Board of Commissioners of the Methodist Episcopal Church informed us they would not act in the case, and referred us to your body for the settlement of the question, as to the division of the property and funds of the Church. And, being furthermore instructed by the General Conference of the Methodist Episcopal Church, South, in case of a failure to settle with your Commissioners, to attend the session of your body in 1848, for the 'settlement and adjustment of all questions involving property and funds, which may be pending between the Methodist Episcopal Church, and the Methodist Episcopal Church, South,' we take this method of informing you of our presence, and of our readiness to attend to the matters committed to our trust and agency by the Methodist Episcopal Church, South, and we desire to be informed as to the time and manner in which it may suit your views and convenience, to consummate with us the division of the property and funds of the Church, as provided for in the Plan of Separation, adopted with so much unanimity by the General Conference of 1844."

What do you suppose was the answer received from that Conference then in session? No answer at all. To this communication no reply was received. But, says my friend who closed on the other side, why do you not wait? There are two modes in which, in the opinion of the eminent counsel who represent the defendants in this controversy, this controversy might have been avoided. One says, submission; the other, time—wait. When did we file this bill? The letter which I have just read, was in 1848. We went almost *in formâ pauperis*, certainly in the form of Christian poverty and Christian meekness, to ask the Conference to pay over the fund. That was May 11, 1848. To that letter, which was signed by "A. L. P. Green, C. B. Parsons, L. Pierce, Commissioners, John Early, Appointee," as stated already, no reply was received. Here was almost the last resort; it has failed. These Southern Christians—if they can be Christians, being from the sunny South, where some seem to suppose there is something in the heat of the atmosphere that burns out Christianity—had failed to get what these very Northern gentlemen said it was right, and just, and proper, and equitable they should have; had failed to get that which almost three-fourths of all the annual conferences said they ought to have; had failed to get that which I venture to say nine-tenths of the laymen of this Church feel, and know, and say they ought to have. Then, as that resort, which, thank God never fails, they come to a tribunal which is clothed with the sacred office of doing justice between man and man. Upon the 15th of June, 1849, they filed this bill. What indications were there between the adjournment of the Conference of 1848, and the filing of this bill, which gave to those whom I represent the slightest reason to imagine that there was to be any justice done them—that waiting would do any good? Why, look to Proofs No. 2, at the report made by the committee on the state of the Church in the Conference of 1848, at Pittsburgh; see if in every line of it the South are not denounced as seceders and schismatics. They adjourned with the words of censure upon their lips. No subsequent General Conference could be assembled until 1852. The counsel who preceded me intimated that, possibly, if we had delayed until the assembling of the Conference of 1852, such a light would have been shed upon the members of the Conference who would then be convened—the sense of justice which animated them in 1844, the instincts of equity which came from their hearts in 1844, would be so awakened again—that they would, either cheerfully or by compulsion, carry it out, by giving to us that which they themselves admitted to be our right. Let those believe that who can.

I pass to the consideration of the fourth and last point, and upon which I have but a very few words to say. Suppose there was no authority to divide constitutionally, so as to be binding of itself, as a mere act of constitutional legislation—or that the division was made upon a condition in relation to this property which has not been fulfilled—are we not still entitled to the fund? What is the attitude of the defendants? How does the Conference of 1844 stand? These gentlemen are but the successors of that Conference, in one sense. In 1844 they told the South, "Gentlemen, a state of things now exists in the Church which, you say, if we remain together, will render the Church in the South useless. If our doctrines are acted upon in the administration of the Church, we believe, as you say, the Church in the South will be annihilated; we know that if the doctrines which you claim to be the true doctrines upon which the Church should be administered are right, and be carried out, the Church in the North will be annihilated. Now, we have got power to divide—we will divide. We cannot live together under the same form of government which has heretofore blessed us, but our objects are the same; the spread of the holy Gospel is the aim of each of us; the bringing of salvation to fallen man is the pursuit of each of us; the carrying out of the injunction of God to preach unto all nations, under the delegation of his authority, in whom all power in heaven and on earth was vested, is upon each of us; and as we have got a right to divide, it is, as we think, under the circumstances, our duty to divide, to exist as separate organized bodies—we will divide." We of the South, confiding, plain, simple, and unenlightened men—it is only for the sake of the argument I am willing to admit it—thought here was all sincerity and fair-dealing, honour and honesty, the promptings of a high religious obligation. They divided. They go home and organize themselves into a separate Church; and the moment they do that, their former Christian brethren say, "Now we have gotten you off, we will hold on to the property." Is that honest? They have got rid of us because they said and made us believe that they concurred with us in thinking there was an authority to divide the Church, and to share equally in the property of the Church.

A word or two fell from my learned brother who opened this case on the part of the defendants, which sounded strangely on my ear. He said that after some personal inquiry out of the case, as well as in the case, as it is disclosed on the record, he thought there were persons who voted for that division under the belief that by the authority over the fund, given by the power to refuse to change the sixth restrictive article, there was to be found a power to keep the South in the Church. I am sure I do not wish to do that gentleman, or his clients, injustice; I hope that I am incapable of it. He said that no member who voted for the Plan of Separation had any idea of voting a division of the Church; that the agreement to divide was intended to prevent a division. In connexion with the same argument, he suggested that one of the means to be used for the purpose of preventing it was to refuse to change the sixth article. The power of money was to be brought to bear upon the South. Now they have got rid of us. Whether they know it or not, they ought to have known it; we had told them division was inevitable; the bishops had said the same thing; the Church, almost with one voice, had said the same thing. The question now is, whether by going off with their consent, having been seduced by their asserted power to authorize it, it is honest, in the consideration of a court of equity, to refuse to us any participation in the fund? I dare not trust myself to argue it. The question answers itself.

Again, I want to know, which is the Church to whom this fund belongs? Are we not as much the Church as they are? "You are not the Church," say our friends, "because you have no ecclesiastical dominion North of a certain line; the Church, in the sense of the term Church, covers the United States." Well, if the Methodist Episcopal Church is the Methodist Episcopal Church which covers the United States by territorial jurisdiction, where is it to be found? Neither have they any jurisdiction in the South more than we have in the North. The two sections have destroyed each other. There is no Methodist Episcopal Church, if the position of our friends be correct. The Church existing in 1844 had annual conferences in the Southern States? The Church which existed in 1848 had no annual conferences in the South. If it be a part of your faith that the bishops of the Methodist Episcopal Church shall have a superintendency over the United States, and preside at the annual conferences of Methodists in the United States, then there is no Methodist Episcopal Church, because your bishops cannot go to the South; nobody there admits their authority. What is to be done in this state of things? The Church, according to your interpretation of the term Church, no longer exists; but the fund exists; who is to hold it? The trustees? They do not pretend to have any right to it. For whom, then, are they to hold it? For those to whom it originally belonged. Who are they? Who are they? Travelling, supernumerary, and superannuated preachers and bishops, and their wives, widows, and children. You bring them within the class of persons who, according to the terms of the original trust, are entitled to participate in it. If I am right in assuming that, if their doctrine be correct, the Methodist Church is extinguished, and no longer exists, then there are no travelling, supernumerary, or superannuated preachers or bishops to whom the fund can be applied. The trustees, however, are to give the benefit of the fund to somebody; keeping it for themselves is out of the question. To whom, then, in such a case, is it to go? Suppose it was a trust fund, created by certain original founders. Then it goes back to the founders, if they are living. The charity, to use the language of the law, has lapsed; the interest in the enjoyment of the fund by the original founder is reinstated and revived; he is to have the fund from the trustee; the trustee is not to have the fund upon the failure of the existence of the *cestique* trust to whom the interest of the fund was alone to be appropriated. Now the donors, or rather the founders, of this fund were the preachers of the original Methodist Episcopal Church. It is theirs or their successors'. Equity, as I suppose, as there is to be a division of the fund, distributes it equally among the donors in the relative proportion that each has contributed, as compared with all. Then, if each of these donors living in the South agrees that the Southern Church shall be the trustee of their part of the fund, and the donors in the North agree that the Northern Church shall be the custodiary of their proportion of the fund, the Court can divide the fund between the Church North and the Church South, under this bill.

My learned friends cited some books for the purpose of showing that the particular relief which we ask for, under this fourth proposition, could not be given. Your

Honours are not to be told that it is perfectly immaterial what is the special prayer of the bill. The bill looks to such a division of the fund as the Plan of Separation of the Church contemplated. Where there is a general prayer in a bill, and a case made by the bill entitling to particular relief, but not to the particular relief prayed for, the Court can grant, under the prayer for general relief, the particular relief to which the party shows he is entitled. It has been so decided over and over again. The last decision on the subject was in the case, before the United States' Supreme Court, of Taylor and The Merchants' Insurance Company *vs.* Baltimore Insurance, where the doctrine which I have laid down was asserted as a familiar doctrine of equity pleading,—9 Han. Sup. Court Rep., 390.

May it please your Honours, I am about to leave the case, and I shall do so with a word or two, by way of expressing a hope, in which I am but cordially uniting with my brothers on the other side, and which I as earnestly entertain, that this controversy may be settled. To say the least of it, it does no good, it has done no good, it can do no good. The members of this Church at the North cannot desire as men, as honest Christian men, to hold on to this fund. The very defence which their counsel make for them shows there would be something in such an act revolting to each man's sense of justice. Is it, then, too much to hope that the government of the Church, North, as well as of the Church, South, may be enlightened by the discussion this case has undergone, and by the decision which your Honours are to pronounce upon it? Is it too much to hope that each will be forced to see in the state of opinion in the Church and out of the Church, of all patriotic and Christian men of every denomination, the necessity of being roused to the consequences to result to the cause of religion itself from a continuance of this unhappy discussion, and be awakened to the very imminent hazard,—I am no alarmist, and, God knows, no disunionist,—to the very imminent hazard to which they subject the institutions which we have all so much reason to prize? Is it too much to hope that, when they see the certain consequences to their "beloved Zion," and the possible consequences to their country, which must result from a continuance of the strife, fatal to their position as men, and distressing to their hearts as Christians, that they will be brought, even in advance of your Honours' decision, or as speedily thereafter as can be, to terminate this angry and profitless contest, and to restore, in a spirit of fraternal love, to the Church the Christian principles and spiritual blessings which have heretofore made it the idol of its own worshippers, and the wonder and the pride of the Christian world?

His Honour, Judge Nelson, after consultation with Judge Betts, said:—

Some time will probably elapse before the Court will be able to take up this case and give it the examination which it will deserve and require at our hands, preparatory to a decision in the case. Our term business is pressing upon us, and, so far as I myself am concerned, I shall be compelled very soon after I leave this Court to go into another, where I shall be engaged until mid-summer. My associate, I have no doubt, will be equally pressed in his particular department. Some time will necessarily elapse before we shall be in a condition to go into a consultation and examination of the case, preparatory to a final decision. In the meantime, we cannot resist the desire to express our concurrence in the suggestions that have been made by the learned counsel on both sides, that it would be much better for the interests of this Church, for the interests of all concerned, if, after a full and fair investigation, both of the facts and the law of the case, the parties could amicably take it up, and, by the aid of friends and counsel, come to an amicable decision of the controversy. In the meantime, before the case is finally taken up and disposed of by the Court, we cannot entertain any doubt, that after the full and fair investigation that has taken place of the controversy before us, whatever may be our final decision in the case, whether upon the one side or the other, an amicable, friendly adjustment of the controversy will be, and must necessarily be, more satisfactory to all parties concerned; and that the good feeling and Christian fellowship of the different sections of the Church will be much better by an amicable and friendly adjustment of this controversy than by any legal disposition of it by the Court.

We may also add, perhaps, that whatever may be, or may have been, the doubts entertained by the parties, or by their learned counsel, as it respects the power of the agents who have charge of the subject-matter of the controversy to make a final and legal disposition of this unfortunate controversy, there can probably be no reasonable doubt but that an amicable, and equitable, and honest adjustment made by the representatives of the different branches of the Church, with the aid of their counsel, sanctioned by the Court, would be a binding, and valid, and final disposition of the whole controversy.

We have deemed it our duty to make these observations at the close of the argument, not only from the fact that there will be necessarily some delay in the decision of the case, but in response to, and in sympathy with, the suggestions made by the learned counsel on both sides.

Extract from 7 Ben. Monroe's Reports, p. 507.—(See p. 289.)

"We come then to the case actually existing, in which, according to the assumptions under which we are now considering the subject, the Church, instead of dividing itself into 'the Methodist Episcopal Church, North,' and 'the Methodist Episcopal Church, South,' leaving no residuum under the name simply of 'the Methodist Episcopal Church,' has sanctioned the independent organization of the Southern conferences, and, under that sanction, the Maysville society or congregation has been placed under the jurisdiction of the Methodist Episcopal Church, South. But is there any difference, so far as the rights and jurisdiction of the Southern Church are concerned, between the case as it actually occurred and the supposed case of a division of the original Church into the Methodist Episcopal Church, North, and the Methodist Episcopal Church, South? Does the fact, that there still remains a portion, whether small or large, of the original body under the original name of the whole, invalidate the separation or the rights of the separating portion? Could the remaining portion of the original body re-assert, in the name of the whole, the jurisdiction which had been renounced by the whole, or revoke the assent which the whole body had once given to the independence of the separating portion? Certainly if the whole body had power, by its assent and co-operation, to legalize the separation and independence of a part of itself, the remaining portion of the original body, though retaining the original name of the whole, would have no power, after such assent had been given and acted on, to undo, by its own mere will, what the entire body had authorized. Whatever else may be implied from the identity of name, it cannot give to the present Methodist Episcopal Church a jurisdiction which the original Church had alienated."

INDEX.

Page

Abolition, its origin among the Methodists, (*Mr. Lord.*) 4
Abolition, the question of, considered, (*Mr. Wood.*) 323
Address of the Southern Delegates to members of the M. E. Church in slaveholding States and Territories, 1844, (*Mr. Lord.*) 90
Adjustment of differences, a friendly, recommended, (*Mr. Wood.*) 324
Alabama Conference, preamble and resolutions adopted by, (*Mr. Lord.*) 119
Andrew, Bishop, discretionary position of, as exhibited in Minutes of Conference, [Proofs, p. 124,] (*Mr. Choate.*) 243
Andrew, Bishop, from his connexion with slavery, is requested to desist from action as a Bishop, (*Mr. Lord.*) 5, 63
Andrew, Bishop, his case reviewed, (*Wood.*) 313
——————— (*Johnson.*) 352, 354
———, his connexion with slavery, (*Wood.*) 312
Andrew, Bishop, his direct violation of the M. E. Church Discipline, (*Wood.*) 314
Andrew, Bishop, his letter to the Louisville Convention, May, 1845, (*Lord.*) 120
Andrew, Bishop, his name not omitted in the M. E. Hymn Book, (*Lord.*) 5
Andrew, Bishop, his "Pastoral Address" to the M. E. Church, 1845, (*Lord.*) 121
Andrew, Bishop, his reply to Bishop Soule's letter of invitation "to perform episcopal functions," (*Lord.*) 138
Andrew, Bishop, not a slaveholder at the period of his inauguration to the episcopate, (*Wood.*) 307
Andrew, Bishop, the case of, before the General Conference and Committee on Episcopacy, (*Lord.*) 61, 62, 63
Annual Conferences—(See *Conferences.*)
Arguments by Defendants' Counsel adverse to claims of the M. E. Church, South, (*Choate.*) 231
Arguments by Plaintiff's Counsel in support of claims of Dr. Bascom and others in slaveholding States, &c., (*Lord.*) 149
Arkansas Conference, report and resolutions of, (*Lord.*) 109
Asbury, Bishop, ordination of, by Dr. Coke, (*Lord.*) 32

Bangs, Dr., and associate Commissioners, M. E. Church, North, reply to communication of Dr. Bascom, &c., 1846, (*Lord.*) 145
Bangs, Dr., and Northern Commissioners, their reply to Dr. Bascom and others, May, 1848, (*Lord.*) 104
Bascom, Dr., his letter to Bishop Soule, &c., on the Minority Protest, 1844, (*Lord.*) .. 77
Bascom, Dr., and others of M. E. Church, South, communication to Northern Commissioners on division of funds, &c., 1846, (*Lord.*) 143
Bascom, Dr., his report in the matter of the Westmoreland Circuit, 1840, (*Johnson.*) 357
Bascom, Dr., and Southern Commissioners, letter to Messrs. Bangs, Peck, and Finley, 1848, (*Lord.*) 104
Beneficiaries of M. E. Church, their rights considered, (*Lord.*) 150
Bascom, Dr. (*Wood.*) 298
Bishop, office of a, considered, (*Johnson.*) 358
Bishops, address of the, to Baltimore Conference on subject of slavery—Extract, (*Lord.*) 50
Bishops, duties, regulations for, 1792, 1804, (*Lord.*) 34
Bishops of M. E. Church, conduct of, subject to consistorial investigation, (*Lord.*) 5
Bishops of M. E. Church never slaveholders till the instance of Bp. Andrew, (*Wood.*) 307
Bishops, letter of the, to General Conference, 1844, on case of Bishop Andrew, (*Lord.*) 64
Bishops should not be slaveholders, special objections why, (*Wood.*) 310
Bishops and Presbyters, Mr. Wesley's opinion of their qualities and powers, (*Lord.*) 30
Book Concern, 1800, duties and regulations for government of Superintendent and Book-Stewards, (*Lord.*) 26
Book Concern, distribution of profits arising from, 1804, (*Lord.*) 27
Book Concern, capital and profits emanating from, (*Lord.*) 2, 152, 155
Book Concern, funds of the, not to be diverted from their original purposes, (*Wood.*) 298, 302
Book Concern held in trust only, and for special purposes and designs, (*Choate.*). 231
Book Concern, origin and history of the, (*Lord.*) 1
Book Concern, portion of profits of the, rendered to Canada Conference on their separation from the United States Conference, (*Lord.*) 166
Book Concern, distribution of profits accruing from, (*Lord.*) 155, 203
Book Concern (*Choate.*) 285
British Conference, address of the, to the General Conference, United States, on subject of slavery—Extract, (*Wood.*) ... 308

Canada claims, Minutes of Committee on, 1836, (*Lord.*) 39
Canada Conference, letter of the, to their American brethren, 1833, (*Lord.*) 42
Canadian Methodists, their prayer for separation from the United States' General Conference, considered, (*Lord.*) 36
——————— (*Choate.*) 280
——————— (*Wood.*) ... 320, 343
Canadian Methodists, their separation from the government of the United States M. E. Church, (*Lord.*) 166-168, 170

Page

Capers, Dr., his motion and plan of special jurisdiction for a Northern and Southern General Conference, (*Lord.*) 67
Carolina, North, Conference, report and resolutions of, (*Lord.*) 112
Carolina, South, Conference, preamble, &c., adopted by, (*Lord.*) 113
Change of organization in M. E. Church, under what circumstances permissible, (*Johnson.*) 332
"Charitable Uses," law of, defined, (*Wood.*) 292
Church, M. E., doctrines of, cases cited in support of adherence to, (*Wood.*) 312
Church, M. E., final report of state of the, (*Fancher.*) 219
Church, M. E., North, their answer to the judicial citation by their Southern brethren, (*Lord.*) 13
Church, M. E. not empowered to authorize separation or division of funds, (*Choate.*) 290
———— (*Wood.*) 302
Church, M. E., organization of the, South, decided as unconstitutional by the Northern Commissioners, (*Lord.*) 7
Church, M. E., origin of, extract from Bp. Emory's History of, (*Lord.*) 32
Church, M. E., plan of separation of the Northern and Southern, presented, discussed, and adopted, 1844, (*Lord.*) 6
Church, M. E., regulations of the, for reception of Preachers from Wesleyan and other Connexions, 1840, (*Lord.*) 165
Church, M. E., amicable separation of the American from that of Great Britain, 1784, (*Lord.*) 164, 165
Church, M. E., South, bill of the, against the Northern M. E. Church, (*Lord.*) 8
Church, M. E., Unity, the great law of the, (*Choate.*) 264
Church and government of the Church distinguished, (*Johnson.*) 335
Church union, importance and necessity of enforcing and preserving, (*Wood.*) 313
Claim, relative and proportionate, of the Plaintiffs, (*Wood.*) 291, 292, 300
Climatic difference, a ground for division or separation from Parent Church, (*Lord.*) 176
Coke, Dr. T., appointed first Bishop of American M. E. Church, by Mr. Wesley, (*Lord.*) 32
Coke, Dr. T., resolutions in the matter of slavery, by the Church, under the administration of, (*Johnson.*) 351
Commissioners, Northern, for treating with the Southern M. E. Church, (*Lord.*) 185
Commissioners, Southern, report of Finance Committee, Petersburg Conference, 1846, in reference to appointment of, for settlement of their claims on the Northern Church, (*Lord.*) 103
Committee on Separation, resolutions of, adopted by Tennessee Conf., (*Lord.*) ... 105
Conference, the, 1784 to 1808, powers, &c., of, examined, (*Johnson.*) 328, 334
Conference, the, 1784, its special creation, (*Choate.*) 267
Conference, the Breakwater, case of F. A. Harding, 1844, (*Lord.*) 57
Conference, the first General, convened in United States, 1792, (*Choate.*) 272
Conference, the General, powers of the, (*Johnson.*) 209
———— (*Fancher.*) 209
Conference, the General, Limitations of the, (*Johnson.*) 335
Conference, General, power of the, to consent to a division of M. E. Church into two bodies, (*Lord.*) 162, 163
Conference, (*Choate.*) 265

Page

Conference, General, of 1824, its power to adopt plan of division examined and maintained, (*Lord.*) 326, 360
Conference, General, 1848, proceedings of the, reviewed, (*Choate.*) 282
Conference, General, 1848, resolutions of, cited, (*Wood.*) 324
Conference, General, vote of, in matter of Bp. Andrew, (*Choate.*) 243
Conference, the Holston, resolutions of, in support of Bishops Andrew and Soule, 1845, (*Lord.*) 96
Conferences, Annual, of M. E. Church, their nature and functions, (*Lord.*) 2
Conference, change of organization in, 1808, (*Lord.*) 3
Conference, division of, proposed, and power of, by select Committee of General Conference, (*Lord.*) 87, 88
Conference, General, their origin and functions, (*Lord.*) 3
Conference, General and Annual, powers, &c., of, 1792 to 1836, (*Lord.*) 33, 177
Conference, General, journals of the, 1840, 1844, and 1848, mutually admitted as evidence, (*Lord.*) 25
Conferences of Kentucky, Missouri, Holston, and Tennessee, action of the, 1845, (*Lord.*) 140
Conferences, Southern, 1844, action of the, in the case of Bp. Andrew, (*Lord.*) ... 92–94
Conferences, Southern, action of various, 1845, in favour of separation from General Conference, (*Lord.*) 97
Controversial differences, evil tendencies of, (*Wood.*) 292
Cooper, Ezekiel, his letter to General Conference, 1818, showing how the capital funds accrued, (*Fancher.*) 227

Degradation from Episcopal functions considered, (*Lord.*) 197
Difference in the M. E. Church, not on fundamental doctrines, but on the question of right of property, (*Wood.*) 301
Discipline, Book of the, for 1840, to be considered as evidence by mutual agreement, (*Lord.*) 25
Discipline of M. E. Church, change of form in the, 1787, (*Lord.*) 32
Discipline of M. E. Church, customary republication of, after every General Conference, (*Lord.*) 5
Discipline of M. E. Church, important character of the—quoted, (*Lord.*) 164
Discipline, Bishop Emory's History of the, passages quoted by, (*Lord.*) 30
Discipline, 1840, extracts from, cited by Plaintiffs' Counsel, (*Lord.*) 28
Discipline, the publication of a Book of, by the Southern Conference, regarded as a distinct and separate organization, (*Lord.*) 7
Discount compensation, always regulated by General Conference, (*Fancher.*) 228
Division of the Methodist Episcopal Church, even by consent of Conference, would be unauthorized by ecclesiastical law, (*Choate.*) 261
Division of the M. E. Church, how to have been avoided, (*Johnson.*) 3, 53
Division of the M. E. Church, want of general agreement to, a bar to all claims on funds and property of such Church, (*Wood.*) 306
Division of the M. E. Church impracticable, unless authorized by the Annual Conferences, (*Wood.*) 316, 318, 321, 322
Division of the M. E. Church not the result of moral necessity, (*Choate.*) 235

Page

Division of the M. E. Church occasioned by the proceedings in Conference of 1844, in the matter of Bp. Andrew, (*Choate.*) 235, 236
Division, plan of, 1844—analyzed, (*Johnson.*) ... 338
Division of profits of M. E. Book Concern, examined, (*Johnson.*) ... 361

Early, Rev. Jno., appointed General Agent of M. E. Church, South, by their Conference, Virginia, 1846, (*Lord.*) ... 103
Emory, Dr., passages quoted from his History of Discipline, (*Lord.*) ... 30
Emory, Dr., particulars of the Book Concern, from, (*Lord.*) ... 153
Equity of the Plaintiffs' case examined, (*Choate.*) ... 258

Florida Conference, report adopted by the, (*Lord.*) ... 118
Forfeiture, the implication and bearing of this term considered, (*Lord.*) ... 188
Fund, beneficiary, of M. E. Church, its character, &c., examined, (*Lord.*) .. 151, 159
Fund, beneficiary, of M. E. Church, intention of founders of, (*Lord.*) ... 156, 157
Fund, beneficiary, incapacity of the M. E. Church to make a division of same (*Wood.*) ... 318
Fund, beneficiary, method of augmentation of, (*Lord.*) ... 156
Fund, beneficiary, regarded as a sacred trust by the M. E. Church, (*Lord.*) ... 158
Fund, beneficiary, division of, whether contemplated by the General Conference, 1844, (*Lord.*) ... 184
Fund chartered, its origin and intentions, (*Lord.*) ... 155

General grounds of the Plaintiffs' claims to separation, division of profits, &c., (*Johnson.*) ... 348
Georgia Conference, preamble and resolutions adopted by, (*Lord.*) ... 115
Green, Rev. A. L. P., and associate Commissioners, M. E. Church, South, letter to General Conference, 1848, (*Lord.*) ... 146
Griffith, Rev. Mr., his position before and after the Conferences of 1840 and 1844, (*Johnson.*) ... 350

Harding, Rev. F. A., his case examined, (*Choate.*) ... 241
(*Wood.*) ... 311
Harding, Rev. F. A., and Bp. Andrew, the judgments on, considered, (*Johnson.*) .. 356
Hymn Book and Discipline, customary republication of, after every General Conference, (*Lord.*) ... 5

Indian Mission Conference, resolutions adopted by the, (*Lord.*) ... 115
Institution of M. E. Church, its objects and intents inquired into, (*Wood.*) ... 313
Itinerant Superintendency of Bishops of M. E. Church, (*Choate.*) ... 255, 257

Judges Nelson and Betts, their recommendation of an amicable adjustment of the question at issue ... 367

Maryland, extract from Dorsey's Laws of, 1831, (*Lord.*) ... 60, 61
Maryland, slavery laws of, extract, (*Lord.*) 59
Maysville case, extracts from decision, Court of Appeals, Kentucky, (*Lord.*) ... 206
Maysville case, extracts from, (*Wood.*) ... 298
———, (*Johnson.*) 347
Memphis Conference, reference to proceedings of, (*Lord.*) ... 106

Methodism of United States, its early determination to be one Church, (*Choate.*) 275
Methodism, its wide-spread existence in United States, (*Choate.*) ... 278
Methodism, its character and position in 1844, (*Johnson.*) ... 326
M. E. Church, an enterprise of missions, (*Choate.*) ... 279
M. E. Church, its creation in 1784, (*Choate.*) 266
M. E. Church, never had a slaveholding Bishop till the instance of Bp. Andrew, (*Wood.*) ... 307
M. E. Church, unity the great law of the, (*Choate.*) ... 264
Methodists of Canada, their petition in 1827, for separation from the M. E. Church of the United States, (*Lord.*) ... 35
Mississippi Conference, preamble and resolutions of, (*Lord.*) ... 108
Morris, Bp., letter of, to Rev. W. S. M'Murray, with reasons for declining invitation to attend the Missouri Conference, 1845, (*Lord.*) ... 141

Organization of Southern separate Conferences, report of Committee on, (*Lord.*). 123

Plaintiffs' "Right" to relative proportion of funds of M. E. Church, examined, (*Wood.*) ... 292
Plaintiffs' "Right" not supported by law or equity, (*Wood.*) ... 324
Points of Claimants, as sustaining their grounds of action, (*Lord.*) ... 148
Points of Defendants, on which their resistance is established, (*Fancher.*) ... 230
Preachers, M. E., their fields of labour, (*Choate.*) ... 254
Preachers, travelling, are Bishops to be considered as, (*Choate.*) ... 251
Preachers, travelling, reasons for distinction between the official duties, &c., of, (*Choate.*) ... 254
Preachers, travelling, rights and functions of, (*Choate.*) ... 287
Private trusts and public uses distinguished, (*Wood.*) ... 294
Property, accumulated, of the M. E. Church, its founders and guardians, (*Wood.*) ... 295
Protest, ground of the, defined, (*Choate.*). 250
——— of minority of General Conference, 1844, against action in the case of Bp. Andrew, (*Lord.*) ... 69
Protest of minority, reply to the, by the Committee of Northern Church, (*Lord.*) 77
Protest and Reply, particulars of, reviewed, (*Lord.*) ... 199

Recapitulation of Plaintiffs' case, (*Johnson.*) 361
Regret, expressions of, by various Southern Churches on "the violent proceedings against Bishops," &c., (*Choate.*) ... 233
Reply of the General Conference, United States, to the British Conference on subject of slavery, cited, (*Wood.*) ... 309
Report of Committee on Division, Kentucky Conference, 1844, (*Lord.*) ... 92
Report of Committe on Westmoreland Petition, 1840, on "Ministerial restrictions," (*Lord.*) ... 54
Report of Committee on Separation, Holston Conference, 1845, (*Lord.*) ... 95
Restrictive rules, origin and effects of, (*Lord.*) ... 3
Restrictive rules, sixth article of, only to be altered by a vote of three-fourths of the Annual Conferences, (*Wood.*) ... 315
Restrictive rules, various alterations in, 1828, 1832, 1836, 1840, (*Lord.*) ... 43, 178

Page

Secession of members from a General Church disqualifies all claim on the property of such Church, (*Wood.*) 305

Secession of Southern M. E. Church self-authorized, (*Choate.*) 259, 260

Separation of American M. E. Church from that of Great Britain, (*Choate.*) 263

Separation of M. E. Church, incapacity of General Conference to sanction a, (*Choate.*) 260

Separation of M. E. Church not sustained by the number of votes required, (*Choate.*) 146

Separation of M. E. Church a nullity in ecclesiastical law, even if sanctioned by General Conference, (*Choate.*) 261

Separation of M. E. Church, plan of the, its validity and effects. (*Lord.*) 179

Separation of M. E. Church, plan of the, examination of, (*Choate.*) 289

——— (*Wood.*) 323

——— (*Johnson.*) 360

Separation of M. E. Church, plan of the, infractions of the, (*Fancher.*) 213

Separation, the, by the Southern M. E. Church, unsanctioned by General Conference, a virtual abandonment of all claim on the great body of the M. E. Church, (*Wood.*) 303

Slaveholders especially prohibited from admission to membership of M. E. Church, (*Johnson.*) 333

Slavery, early rules of Methodist Church with regard to, (*Lord.*) 4, 189

Slavery, extract from address of British Conference, 1840, on subject of, (*Lord.*) 53

Slavery, extract from Baltimore General Conference, 1840, on subject of, (*Lord.*). 53

Slavery, laws of, in Maryland, cited, (*Lord.*) 59, 60

Slavery, necessity for its extirpation as considered, 1796, 1800, 1804, 1808, 1812, 1816, 1820, 1824, 1840, 1844, (*Lord.*) 46–49

Slavery, not the subject of action on the part of Missionary Preachers, (*Lord.*) .. 166

Slavery, petitions and memorials respecting, from New-England and Baltimore Conferences, 1840, (*Lord.*) 192

Page

Slavery Question, the, as agitated in the different Conferences, General, Quarterly, and Annual, (*Johnson.*) 349

Slavery Question, as treated in Baltimore Conference, 1784, (*Lord.*) 45

Slavery Question, the, treated in "Discipline," 1840, (*Lord.*) 44

Slavery Question, the, to be treated by the general M. E. Church only on established principle and usage, (*Wood.*) 306

Slavery, regarded as to its peculiar aspects, difficulties, &c., (*Lord.*) 176

Slavery viewed as an evil by the M. E. Church, North and South, (*Lord.*) ... 4, 190

Soule, Bp., his address to the Southern Convention, 1845, (*Lord.*)............... 99

Soule, Bp., his "letter of adhesion" to the Louisville Convention, 1845, (*Lord.*) 120

Soule, Bp., his "letter of invitation" to Bp. Andrew to perform episcopal functions, (*Lord.*) 137

Southern Convention, action of the, on "Separate Organization," 1845, (*Lord.*) 100

Speech, opening, on behalf of the Defendants, (*Choate.*) 231

Supernumeraries, conditions and duties of, defined, (*Choate.*) 287

Tennessee Conference, preamble and resolutions adopted by, (*Lord.*) 142

Trusts, administrative and specific, distinctions between, (*Lord.*) 150

Texas Conference, report and resolutions adopted by, (*Lord.*) 118

Unity the great law of the M. E. Church, (*Choate.*) 264

Virginia Conference, resolutions adopted by, (*Lord.*) 110

Wesley, Rev. J., sketch of his character as the founder of the M. E. Church, (*Johnson.*) 327

www.ingramcontent.com/pod-product-compliance
Lightning Source LLC
LaVergne TN
LVHW010133110826
845151LV00002B/342
9781425539528